MW01E30199

The Palgrave Handbook of Global Perspectives on Emotional Labor in Public Service

Mary E. Guy · Sharon H. Mastracci · Seung-Bum Yang
Editors

The Palgrave Handbook of Global Perspectives on Emotional Labor in Public Service

Editors
Mary E. Guy
School of Public Affairs
University of Colorado Denver
Denver, CO, USA

Sharon H. Mastracci
Department of Political Science
University of Utah
Salt Lake City, UT, USA

Seung-Bum Yang
Department of Public Administration
Konkuk University
Seoul, Korea (Republic of)

ISBN 978-3-030-24825-3   ISBN 978-3-030-24823-9   (eBook)
https://doi.org/10.1007/978-3-030-24823-9

This Palgrave Macmillan imprint is published by the registered company Springer Nature Switzerland AG
The registered company address is: Gewerbestrasse 11, 6330 Cham, Switzerland

Foreword

When I first learned of this volume's ambitious agenda to comparatively study emotional labor, my initial concern was seasoned by years of pre- and post-Ph.D. engagement in the developing world. My thought went something like this: "Here we go, yet another American wanting to do something 'international' but who is unaware that copying and pasting favorite concepts to other countries is rarely appropriate comparative work."

Such initial wariness and cynicism are not uncommon. It also reflects other observations of insularity within American public administration (Drechsler 2013). The insular point of view does great harm when unmindful that what works in America perhaps cannot (and *should* not) work elsewhere. This is not necessary because "the other" is less developed than our imagined America but instead, there is more than one model for appropriate administrative governance. This model need not arise in the West.

So, when Professor Mary E. Guy and her team came to the March 2019 Riggs Symposium to share their work, I was wary. The group which organized the Symposium (Section on International Comparative Administration within the American Society for Public Administration) was used to Americanists entering the global space, claiming big conceptual news, and then imagining a neat copy and paste to wherever they and their passport had visited most recently.

But this is not what was delivered on that day in March 2019. Instead, the team did the unexpected: They delivered just the opposite.

As such, it is my true pleasure to write a Foreword (about Many Steps Forward) for this volume on emotional labor. This book, its editors, and its authors thoroughly relay the humanity, character, and passions uniting public servants around the world. The labor of such servants of a global public is articulated in chapters that historically and conceptually frame their research endeavor but also, and perhaps most importantly, engage the emotional labor concept across twelve countries on six continents.

This is impressive. But what will help this book stand the test of time is that they do more than simply apply a concept (emotional labor) to multiple countries. Their work highlights six lessons for scholars who desire beyond-the-surface engagements with comparative and development administration.

By suggesting that emotional labor is complementary to rational instrumentation, New Public Management, and a still-present American administrative orthodoxy, the authors rightfully desire an administrative science in which compassion and a desire for citizen engagement and trust not only shake the proverbial "iron cage" but demand that scholars value the human relationships at the intersection of government and its citizens. This request goes beyond calls for public sector accountability. Instead, it hits at the (human) heart of the matter: the encounter between a civil servant's humanity and the citizens they serve.

This effort leads to a second lesson: Typical comparative and development administration scholarship often mirrors the cognitive and rational instrumentation (and prioritizations) of US-focused administrative scholarship. This preference harms our understanding of other administrative states (Haque 2013). By moving from an exclusively cognitive and/or rationalist comparison toward the emotive dimension of public servant labor, this volume provides important (and often undervalued) insights about public service delivery across countries and cultures.

This contribution becomes even more remarkable given perceptions that the emotive labors of public servants are too specific, too contextual, and too culture-specific to be reliably compared. This leads to the third lesson: There is a false assumption that large-n quantitative analyses should engage non-emotive aspects of public service while emotive studies are best served by qualitative research designs reliant upon single case studies.

Their work starts to readdress a still-accurate (and negative) characterization of comparative and development administration studies as a "small-scale, disparate, descriptive, qualitative, and noncomparative subfield dominated by researchers from the global North" (Gulrajani and Moloney 2012, 78). Instead, what follows in this volume is not small-scale, its case studies are not disparate, and while there are descriptive and qualitative components, this choice is balanced by confirmatory factor analysis, structural equation modeling, and large-n samples. While the majority of the volume's authors do hold a terminal degree from a global North university, its case studies include global North and South countries. Their fourth lesson is that is possible to counteract this norm.

The volume editors and authors must be congratulated for a willingness to proceed carefully in their methods and to not copy and paste US-created concept questionnaires to other countries. Instead, they piloted their emotional labor concept in multiple countries, expected measurement invariance, and then undertook confirmatory factor analysis to identify final survey questions. Such steps are crucial to good academic work even if they are infrequently undertaken in our comparative and development administration scholarship.

While their final survey instrument achieved configural invariance and partial metric and scalar invariance (Yang et al. 2018), their methodological precision is the fifth lesson. This method allows the authors to stand upon their rigor to generate theoretical insights about an emotional labor concept which, prior to this volume, may have been considered too small-scale, contextual, and culture-bound to create valid and reliable comparative insights.

Their final lesson arises via their willingness to publish chapters where dimensions of emotional labor were expressed in ways closer to the American expectation (e.g., Bolivia, Taiwan, and UK) but also where results only partially met expectations (e.g., China, India, and Rwanda). Knowledge creation occurs not just where hypotheses are met but where they are not. This readiness to share cases where fits are imperfect requires an ability to restrain one's ego and to commit to the research process. That the editors and authors have achieved such objectives is admirable.

This volume helps create a new gold standard for what is achievable. It gives us more than one way to step forward. Its approach, its emotive emphasis, and its methods will help deepen our work as comparative and development administration scholars.

Perth, Australia   Kim Moloney

References

Drechsler, Wolfgang. 2013. "Three Paradigms of Governance and Administration: Chinese, Western, and Islamic." *Society and Economy* 35 (3): 319–42.

Gulrajani, N., and Kim Moloney. 2012. "Globalizing Public Administration Research: Today's Research and Tomorrow's Agenda." *Public Administration Review* 72 (1): 78–86.

Haque, M. Shamsul. 2013. "Public Administration in a Globalized Asia: Intellectual Identities, Challenges, and Prospects." *Public Administration and Development* 33: 262–74.

Yang, Seung-Bum, Mary E. Guy, Aisha Azhar, Chih-Wei Hsieh, Hyun Jung Lee, Xiaojun Lu, X., and Sharon H. Mastracci. 2018. "Comparing Apples and Manzanas: Instrument Development for Cross-National Analysis of Emotional Labour in Public Service Jobs." *International Journal of Work Organization and Emotion* 9 (3): 264–82.

Kim Moloney is a Senior Lecturer in Global Public Administration and Policy at Murdoch University, Australia. Her research has two foci: the intersection of public administration and the administrative life of international organizations, and the intersection of public administration and island-states. She is the elected Chair of the Section on International and Comparative Administration (SICA) within the American Society for Public Administration.

Preface

Trust. Relationships. Bridgebuilder. Inclusiveness. These are attributes that are highly sought after as communities, regions, states, and nations seek to improve the quality of governance. The ability to actively listen, the appreciation for the delicate balance between process and action, the awareness that people everywhere long to hear and to be heard, these are the elements in public service that have too long been obscured by a focus on the end product measured by performance outcomes.

Bridgebuilders are those whose communication skills are good, who are sensitive to the views and opinions and feelings of others. They are the intermediaries who propel collective action. Inevitably, there will be initiatives in which stakes are high, opinions vary, and emotions run strong. In these circumstances, crucial conversations must ensue in order to achieve unity and commitment. When handled poorly or overlooked entirely, the result is programs that are not aligned with the public's preferences and a communication chasm between those who serve and those who are served. Conversely, when handled well, disparate perspectives are conjoined to achieve what no individual can achieve by acting alone.

The aim of this book is to push the needle on the public service paradigm—to nudge it away from an overweening focus on measuring results to move it closer to a focus on what is most elemental in public service: the interaction between state and citizen. Collective action of all varieties depends on leadership, followership, and interdependence, all of which involve human interaction and human interaction involves emotional labor.

The chapters achieve several goals: They explain why comparative studies are valuable in this age of global interconnectedness and they set the stage for a larger appreciation for the role of emotional labor in public service around the globe. They draw attention to four dimensions of public service, first at the individual level, then the organizational level, then the cultural level, then the exigent level, where unique situations—such as hostility toward government—affect how public service professionals feel about their work. Following these introductory chapters, the methodology for the multinational study is explained. Data from each of the countries surveyed are then presented in the voice of authors who are intimately familiar with the nation surveyed. Each chapter describes the nation's cultural heritage and contextualizes contemporary public management. The sample of public service professionals who completed the surveys is described and findings are reported. Following the chapters that present the national data, results are compared across countries. The closing chapters then speak to a path forward, urging expansion of the public administration paradigm, such that it embraces the emotive content of public service work, just as it already embraces the cognitive component.

This book contains data gathered from public service professionals who work in twelve countries on six continents, producing insights into the subjective experiences of workers in a wide variety of public service contexts. Findings make it clear that understanding how public service differs around the globe requires awareness of how political dynamics, historical traditions, and national culture combine to form a unique blend of characteristics.

Sensitivity to the differences in how public services are delivered in various nations is required for scholars who travel, consult, and conduct research internationally and who engage in comparative studies. To this end, we trust that this handbook will expand readers' awareness of the emotive content in public service work and how it is tempered and sculpted by the context in which it is performed. The objective of this handbook is not to claim expertise as scholars of comparative public administration, but rather to carefully tell a story using voices from multiple countries and to systematically conduct research across multiple contexts. The information gleaned from these chapters invites further research, in fact, begs for further research.

We are grateful for the collaboration of all the contributors to this volume and to the public service professionals who made this work possible by completing the surveys and adding to our library of knowledge about their daily work lives. And, we appreciate the constructive feedback that has been offered by our colleagues in response to early analyses of the data and drafts of this manuscript.

Denver, USA   Mary E. Guy
Salt Lake City, USA   Sharon H. Mastracci
Seoul, Korea (Republic of)   Seung-Bum Yang

Contents

Notes on Contributors

Ian Tyler Adams is a Ph.D. student in the Department of Political Science at the University of Utah, USA. He was a 2018 Founders' Fellow for the American Society of Public Administration. His research interests are centered on emotional labor and policing, and he is particularly interested in the unintended work-life consequences of police body-worn cameras. Outside of his academic work, he is a busy father of four children and two dogs and enjoys taking the family on bird-watching trips. His current CV along with links to his published and ongoing research can be found at www.iantyleradams.com.

Pallavi Awasthi is Doctoral Candidate in Public Affairs in the Department of Public Policy and Administration at Florida International University (FIU), USA. She also holds a Master's in Public Administration from FIU. Her research centers around examining leadership behavior of local government administrators. Her other research interests are the study of ethical behavior and emotional labor among public servants. Pallavi is particularly interested in developing new tools and methods suitable for leadership development of local government administrators. Prior to joining the Ph.D. program in public affairs at FIU, Pallavi worked with UNDP, India, and the Center for Leadership at Indian School of Business, Hyderabad, India.

Aisha Azhar is Assistant Professor in the School of Governance and Society at the University of Management and Technology, Lahore, Pakistan. Her areas of research include disaster management, non-profit management, social network analysis, public service motivation, and public management. Dr. Azhar has served as principal investigator for projects on women's empowerment (PUAN-USAID), public administration education in Pakistan (Aga Khan), and coordinating relief distribution activities in flood-prone areas of Punjab, Pakistan (HI^2 Brown University). A Fulbright Scholar, she received her Ph.D. and master's degrees in public administration and policy from Florida State University. She is an affiliated researcher with Brown University's Humanitarian Innovation Initiative at the Watson Institute of International and Public Affairs (http://watson.brown.edu/HI2/people/international-fellows/azhar).

Sebawit G. Bishu is Assistant Professor in the School of Public Affairs at the University of Colorado Denver, USA. She applies theories of social justice and organizational behavior to uncover organizational practices that shape unequal access to opportunities for women and minorities. She also conducts research on social justice and equity issues in urban governance. Her work aims at understanding and improving the circumstances under which government provides equitable opportunity to all its workforce and equitable services to citizens. Dr. Bishu has published in a number of peer-reviewed journals, including *The American Review of Public Administration, Review of Public Personnel Administration, Administration and Society*, and *Journal of Public Affairs Education*.

N. Emel Ganapati is an Associate Professor in Public Policy and Administration and the Director of the Laboratory for Social Science Research, International Hurricane Research Center, at Florida International University (FIU), USA. She holds a master's degree in planning from the University of Pennsylvania and a Ph.D. degree from the University of Southern California. Her research relates to emotional labor, social capital, and public participation and disaster recovery. She has published in top journals in public administration, planning, and disasters, including *Public Administration Review, Administration and Society, Journal of the American Planning Association, Disasters, Natural Hazards Review*, and *Natural Hazards*. Dr. Ganapati has served as the Principal Investigator (PI) or co-PI of several National Science Foundation (NSF) projects related to disaster recovery and resilience in the USA, Nepal, and Haiti. She received the 2006 Gill-Chin Lim Best Dissertation on International Planning Award from the Association of Collegiate Schools of Planning. She currently serves as a member of FIU's Institutional Review Board (IRB) for Social Sciences. She is on the Advisory Board of Culture and Disaster Action Network. Furthermore, she is a recipient of Florida Education Fund's state-wide 2018 William R. Jones Outstanding Mentor Award.

Mary E. Guy is Professor of Public Administration at the University of Colorado Denver, USA. Her research focuses on the human processes involved in public service delivery. Author of numerous books and articles, she has lectured around the globe on the subject of emotional labor and effective public service delivery. Winner of the 2018 Dwight Waldo Award, she is a Fellow of the National Academy of Public Administration, Past President of the American Society for Public Administration, and Past Editor-in-Chief of the *Review of Public Personnel Administration.*

Chih-Wei Hsieh is Assistant Professor in the Department of Public Policy at City University of Hong Kong, China. His research surrounds the management of human resources in public service as well as related equality and morality challenges. He has previously conducted extensive research on emotional labor using American and Taiwanese samples. In addition to emotional labor studies, his research interests also include public service ethos, workplace diversity, and employee well-being.

Ning Kang is Doctoral Candidate at the Global Development Institute (GDI) at University of Manchester, UK. Her research interests are at the intersection of international human resource management and development with a focus on organizational psychology and the impact of culture on human resource practices in multinational organizations. Her Ph.D. research investigates strategic HRM in Chinese multinational enterprises in Africa, particularly employee career development. She has also presented her work at conferences in the USA, China, and UK. Working as a Teaching Assistant in GDI, along with her research experiences in China and Africa, has reinforced her global perspective on both public administration and business-related management.

Hyun Jung Lee is Associate Professor in the Department of Public Administration at Myongji University, Seoul, Korea. Before Dr. Lee came to MyongJi University, she was a Visiting Scholar at University of Colorado Denver, School of Public Affairs. Dr. Lee earned her B.A. (in psychology) and M.A. (in public policy) in the USA and Ph.D. in public administration from EWHA Woman's University, Seoul, Korea. Most of her research focuses on emotional intelligence and emotional labor in public service. Dr. Lee's research appears in *Public Performance & Management Review, Review of Public Personnel Administration, International Review of Administrative Sciences,* and *International Journal of Work Organization and Emotion.*

Xiaojun Lu is Professor in the Department of Public Administration at the School of International and Public Affairs at Shanghai Jiao Tong University, China. Her research interests are in the areas of organizational behavior and human resource management, with a special focus on emotional labor, work engagement, and organizational justice.

Sharon H. Mastracci is Professor in the Department of Political Science at the University of Utah, USA. She researches emotional labor in public service and is interested in the affective turn in public administration theory and practice. She was a 2014–2015 Fulbright Scholar to the UK.

Pamela S. Medina is Assistant Professor of Public Administration at California State University, San Bernardino, USA. She studies comparative public administration, citizen engagement, and the role of technology in citizen–administrator relationships. Prior to her career in academia, Medina held positions in development and evaluation in the non-profit sector. Her work has been published in the *Journal of Health and Human Services Administration* and the *International Journal of Policy Studies.*

Geri A. Miller-Fox is currently a Ph.D. student at the University of Utah. She is interested in emotional labor and criminal justice research. Prior to her academic pursuits, Geri served in various administrative criminal justice roles. Most recently, she served as the Pretrial Enforcement Division Director with the Alaska Department of Corrections where she developed and implemented the state's new pretrial operations. Geri holds a bachelor's degree in psychology and biology, and a master's degree in public administration.

Meredith A. Newman is Vice Provost for Faculty and Global Affairs at Florida International University, USA. Her previous appointments include Washington State University, Vancouver, and University of Illinois, Springfield. Prior to her career in academia, Newman served with the Australian Foreign Service, the US Department of State, and the World Bank, including tours of duty in France, Viet Nam, Senegal, Malaysia, and Republic of Singapore. She is recognized as one of the leading experts in the field of public management and the emotive aspects of work. Newman is Past President of the American Society for Public Administration and is Vice President for Regional and International Cooperation, the International Association of Schools and Institutes of Administration; and a Fellow of the National Academy of Public Administration.

Amporn Tamronglak is Professor of Public Administration in the Department of Public Administration and Faculty of Political Science at Thammasat University, Thailand. She is President of the Public Administration Association of Thailand (PAAT) and the Asia Pacific Society for Public Affairs (APSPA). She teaches courses in Theory of Public Administration, Organization Theory and Management, Public Organizations Management, Project Management, Project Evaluation, Administrative Techniques and Technology, and Human Resource Management. She has served as a consultant to numerous government agencies, including the Constitutional Court, Bangkok Metropolitan Authority, Rice Department, Office of The Election Commission of Thailand, the Secretariat Office to the Senate, the Secretariat Office to the Parliament, and the Follow-up Committee on Local Decentralization, among others. Since 2014, she has served on many committees during the reform process for the National Reform Steering Committee on Good Governance, Efficiency, and Public Personnel Development. She earned a B.A. degree at Thammasat University, an M.A.P.A. degree from Northern Illinois University, and a doctoral degree from Virginia Tech University.

Ador R. Torneo is Director of the Jesse M. Robredo Institute of Governance and an Associate Professor in the Department of Political Science at De La Salle University, Manila, Philippines, and the Secretary of the Philippine Political Science Association. He is a development and governance researcher and practitioner with extensive experience in capacity building, monitoring and evaluation, and public policy research in the Philippines, the ASEAN region, and South Korea.

Mao Wang is a Ph.D. candidate and an Adjunct Instructor in the Department of Political Science at the National Taiwan University. His research interests include public personnel management, public service innovation, educational policy, and computational text analysis.

Seung-Bum Yang is Professor of Public Administration and Chair in the Department of Public Administration at Konkuk University, South Korea. He previously taught at California State University, Fullerton. He received his doctorate in public administration from Florida State University. He has published numerous articles in journals including *Asian Politics & Policy*, *International Journal of Work Organization and Emotion*, *International Review of Public Administration*, *Journal of Business and Psychology*, *Public Performance & Management Review*, *Public Personnel Management*, and *Team Performance Management*.

Yue Zhang is Postdoctoral Researcher in the Department of Public Policy, City University of Hong Kong, China. Her research interests include human resource management, organizational behavior, and employee training and development.

List of Figures

List of Tables

1

Introduction: Why Emotional Labor Matters in Public Service

Mary E. Guy, Sharon H. Mastracci and Seung-Bum Yang

Our understanding of public administration is in transition. At the tradition-bound end of a continuum is the top-down conceptualization of a century ago, where the state is in control and delegates authority and responsibility for the achievement of public ends. At the newest end of the continuum is a flattened hierarchy with broad outreach to the citizenry via collaborative endeavors, and conversely, broad input from all segments of society. New Public Management, the popular wave that introduced contracting, competitive bidding, and marketization of services in the latter twentieth century, is in the middle of the continuum, waning in popularity but leaving remnants in place that emphasize customer service and responsiveness.

The most popular terms being used to discuss governing processes already reveal an emphasis on human relations, but discourse stops short

M. E. Guy (✉)
School of Public Affairs, University of Colorado Denver, Denver, CO, USA
e-mail: mary.guy@ucdenver.edu

S. H. Mastracci
Department of Political Science, University of Utah,
Salt Lake City, UT, USA
e-mail: Sharon.mastracci@poli-sci.utah.edu

S.-B. Yang
Department of Public Administration, Konkuk University, Seoul, South Korea
e-mail: sbyang@konkuk.ac.kr

© The Author(s) 2019
M. E. Guy et al. (eds.), *The Palgrave Handbook of Global Perspectives on Emotional Labor in Public Service*, https://doi.org/10.1007/978-3-030-24823-9_1

of acknowledging that which should be obvious. Representativeness, governance, collaboration, coproduction, citizen engagement, relational contracting all are terms that connote the co-relating that is required for self-governing to succeed. A holistic approach to the citizen–state encounter is more useful than the partial approach that is provided by simplistic reliance on benchmarks and outcome measures.

This chapter contrasts the traditional way of understanding public service with the emerging need to focus more on the citizen–state exchange. The instrumentalist point of view is contrasted with more recent conceptualizations of co-production. Along with this comes more attention to the encounter between citizen and state and the work that goes on within that exchange. We argue that the affective dimension in public service delivery must be elevated so that it is acknowledged and appreciated as much as the cognitive dimension has always been.

Rational Instrumentalism

Traditional discourse on the subject of public administration is framed in notions of rational instrumentalism, framed as a set of levers to be pulled in order to achieve specified ends. For example, those who study the pursuit of public purposes call themselves public management experts, for their focus is on management, per se, as it is exercised in the public sphere. The singular focus on management, with less regard for constitutional context, democratic imperatives, and public policy dynamics, parallels the emphasis on management within the business sphere, where success is measured by outputs and profit margins. Policy experts parse the field by focusing on how the public will is expressed through state action or inaction. Public law scholars focus on the interpretation of constitutional principles insofar as they affect the pursuit of public purposes. Network scholars focus on linkages between policy actors. It is possible to study all these facets of public administration while paying too little attention to the persons being governed. Norms of neutrality and impartiality strip administrators of their human-ness and blind them to the human-ness of citizens and the connectedness that joins them to one another and to the collective, whether it is city or state.

Citizen Engagement

Citizen engagement is as close as contemporary thought comes to acknowlededging the role of the citizen. From this perspective, public officials are the mediating agents between state and citizen. That which is overlooked is how citizens feel about their government. This embodies a way of knowing about the state. To wit, if citizens are to invest in the system as a whole, the connections each has to the state must "feel" good. The overlooked dimension is the citizen–state *relationship*.

Representativeness

Representative bureaucracy theory attempts to overcome the shortcomings of public management procedures that deny or overlook the citizen–state relationship. It does so by prescribing that all constituencies affected by a public program should be included in the planning, organizing, staffing, directing, co-ordinating, reporting, and budgeting of it. By having their views and voices expressed in the design and maintenance of programs, the outcome is thought to be a product acceptable to all.

Coproduction, Collaboration, Co-optation

Coproduction and collaboration enter the lexicon of public administration in an effort to denote less direction from the top and more inclusion at the bottom. Coproduction refers to the generation of public goods via willful participation by citizens working together with government. Collaboration connotes various stakeholders working together to achieve common ends. Co-optation of the governed is achieved when they participate in decisions that will affect them. Equally, co-optation of those who govern is achieved when relationships are developed among constituencies such that interactions on a first-name basis are possible (Selznick 1949). These three Cs denote citizens and government working together toward ends that each desire. While useful constructs, each assumes affective connection between citizen and state without actually saying that.

From Hierarchy to Heterarchy

Hierarchy is giving way to heterarchy, with greater and greater emphasis on collaborations across agencies, levels of government, and stakeholder groups (O'Leary 2015). The transition is gradual but inexorable. And the move toward a more relational government (Edlins, in press) is gaining traction. Traditional public administration has focused on actions of those in the executive office, attending to how decisions are made and how priorities are set.

As hierarchies flatten, the focal point moves closer to the frontlines of public service delivery. Person-to-person interactions present a focal point for what public administration is or should be. Interactions between government and citizens are more immediate than the rarefied air of the executive suite and allow for the mediation of hard-to-resolve situations by face-to-face interaction.

Outcomes

There has been a transition from focusing on "things" that the state does to focusing on the effects that those things produce (Newcomer 2015). For instance, outcome measures have become increasingly important, in contrast to output measures. This transition marks a growing sophistication in regard to understanding that it is not action, itself, that matters. It is whether the action makes a difference. To carry this progression further, outcome measures that "take the temperature" of citizens who are affected by a program are an attempt to acknowledge the human impact. Such measures indicate a deeper appreciation for the emotive encounter between citizen and state.

Transparency

Transparency is an essential element of how governing is done in the USA. The requirement that public proceedings, documents, and records be available to anyone who wants them differentiates government from business in significant respects. It requires that public organizations are staffed to respond to Freedom of Information Act requests, and it requires that storage and retrieval are easily accessible to the public. Non-mission-based values such as the importance of transparency increase the workload and cost of governing but continue because an essential element of constitutional democracy is that citizens have a right to know what their government is doing. Sunshine is thought to be the most efficient means for ensuring honesty. In other words, transparency is about trust: Citizens trust in the actions of government and trust that state action will be in accord with constitutional processes and constraints. Feelings of trust are influential in shaping how citizens view government and how they feel about their safety.

Equity, Efficiency, Economy, and Effectiveness

The four imperatives of public administration are equity, efficiency, economy, and effectiveness. While equity is a relative newcomer to these characteristics, it was added in 2005 to denote the importance of justice and fairness to all constituencies, rather than to only those who hold advantaged status (Norman-Major 2011). This heralds a flattened, broader approach to public action in which the state is held accountable for addressing the needs of everyone rather than only those who are favored. Like transparency, there is not a direct emotive connection between these four attributes and citizens, but they give rise to positive feelings of fairness, security, predictability, and safety. For government action to be accepted, it must be viewed positively. The stuff of revolutions comes not from spreadsheets with columns of numbers but from feelings that one is unsafe, insecure and cannot trust authority. This leads to an appreciation for the human relationships that build and maintain communities.

Human Relations Versus Instrumentalism

As far back as the 1920s, the Hawthorne studies set forth to divine overarching principles that could be applied to any work setting in order to increase productivity (Mayo 1949). As it turned out, the primary lesson of those studies is that person-to-person interaction is the most important element when it comes to influencing productivity. Put simply, workers produced more when they believed the researchers were interested in them. Workers produced less when their co-workers prevailed upon them to protect one another by moderating their output so that the slowest among them would not be penalized by a pay-for-performance system. The upshot is that the personal matters, whether in the process of assembling telephones or in the process of delivering and receiving public services.

Even before the Hawthorne studies shone a light on the worker as a whole person, rather than a simple bundle of cognitive and physical work skills, Herman Finer (1931) called attention to the need to focus on the relationship of officials and the public. Why public administration has overlooked this lesson for generations is baffling. What is obvious is that the encounter matters and it is nigh time for the field to stop ignoring this fact. There are mutual orientations and expectations of clients and of officials. It is time to bring the interaction process into focus. We should understand more, and have a body of literature, about public encounters and how they enhance the quality of public service delivery and problem solving. Mary Parker Follett's writings (1940, 1941) drew attention to this but they have been overshadowed by fascination with an instrumentalist approach to governing that has become a standard script.

The Script's Iron Cage

The standard script transmogrified into an iron cage in two ways. First, overcome by bureaucratic mechanisms that segregate official duties from private life (Weber 1922/1978), public encounters were thought to be best performed by script, imprisoning officials in policies, structures, rules, and procedures. Stripped of emotion, their actions are recorded in the context of formal processes. This iron cage creates a straitjacket, blissfully overlooking the emotive dimension to each encounter, hiding it from view while never removing it from reality.

The exercise of discretion rides atop the emotive experience that occurs during the encounter. Studies of representative bureaucracy often examine factors that influence officials to exercise discretion and function as allies for those with whom they identify (Meier and Bothe 2001; Sowa and Selden 2003). This is done with a consistent focus on cognitive heuristics with no appreciation for the emotive dimension to the exchange. As Michael Lipsky (1980, 9) concluded after studying encounters between frontline officials and citizens, the objective of "impersonal detachment" is never attained. Instead, officials use heuristics to categorize, at least subliminally, and determine what services to provide. Harkening back to the classic Friedrich–Finer debate about the proper exercise of discretion (Finer 1941; Friedrich 1940), the uneasy resolution relies on organizational structures, managerial tools, and policy regulations that sculpt the personal in such encounters. All this ignores the emotive substrate that so often flavors and drives the cognitive.

The second way that the script becomes an iron cage occurs in the case of recently colonized countries, such as the Philippines, India, and Rwanda. The "iron cage" separated the governors (colonial overseers) from the persons native to the colonized territory, that is, the governed. After self-governance returns, the importance of creating trust between citizens and post-colonial civil servants is heightened. As research within comparative politics has shown, just because the new post-colonial leader is "one of us" does not mean he or she will be trusted by all. This is especially true in divided societies, where the population is riven by ethnic or religious differences. Thus, the "iron cage" in decolonized states takes on new meanings. Sometimes the new post-colonial government creates a "cage" with additional bars, marked by preference for a particular geographic, religious, or ethnic group. Thus, the emotional labor in the exchange may carry additional historical burdens as well as in-group and out-group burdens that fall on the shoulders of the public servants.

From Results to Relationships

The emotive component in public service is hiding in plain sight. Leadership, as Harlan Cleveland (1972) so aptly put it, requires "unwarranted optimism." The ability to express, display, and communicate optimism is an emotive function. Employee engagement and retention requires comprehending a person's needs and desires and what it takes to feel fulfilled. This involves empathy (Edlins, in press) and underneath empathy are the emotive skills that serve as its basis. Organizational development requires the cognitive ability to identify and understand well-functioning units as well as dysfunctional units. To move constructive units forward, and to convert dysfunction to function, requires the ability to engage in meaningful encounters where people "feel" understood. Again, the emotive component to the task is instrumental to achieving goals.

"Focus on results" was the mantra of New Public Management (NPM), whose call for management practices mirrored those enjoyed by business, where transparency is not required. The phrase is in contrast to a focus on process, where representativeness and inclusiveness in decision processes and service delivery have been a persistent trademark. After several decades of the NPM mantra, the pendulum is now turning not to one or the other, but to a blend that emphasizes both process and results. The transition is heralded by Denhardt and Denhardt's coining the phrase, *New Public Service* (2015), which denotes public officials working *with* citizens rather than over them.

There are personal demands in public jobs. Public service workers search for meaning, and discovery of meaning comes from making a difference in people's lives. This is at the heart of public service motivation. Many innovation initiatives fail because they lack meaningful goals. As existentialist philosopher Viktor Frankl explained, the search for meaning is an intrinsic motivation and intrinsic motivators are more potent in guiding behavior than are extrinsic motivators, such as pay-for-performance or other piece-rate mechanisms, such as bonuses and special awards. To the degree that the canon can aid in the search for meaning, the more durable and resilient it will be.

Usual lists of training offered by human resource specialists and management consultants focus on four main areas: personal development, leadership development, employee engagement and retention, and organizational development. For all of these, there is a large emotive component. Personal development requires understanding where people are in their career development versus where they want to be. With emphasis on *want*, understanding the person's desires paired with an appreciation for their knowledge, skills, and abilities requires a level of understanding that contains cognitive awareness as well as an emotive comprehension of the person as a whole human being.

The Public Encounter

The public encounter is the connective tissue in public administration. It occurs for any one of multiple reasons and it is bi-directional. For some purposes, government reaches out to the citizen. For other purposes, citizens access government at their initiative or they respond to government at its request. Table 1.1 displays these interactions.

As shown in Table 1.1, these transactions are usually thought of in two broad categories: exchange of information and control or constraint. In terms of typology, the encounters vary in duration and scope, direction of the transaction in terms of which party initiates it, and its medium and setting. This may be face-to-face, by telephone or online, or written. It may occur in a public place or in the citizen's home. Public places may range from a park ranger in a public forest to a Parks & Recreation official in a city park to a police officer on patrol. If in a public building, such as a courthouse, the ambience may be such that the encounter is infused with an aura of authority and formality. If the encounter is in a prison, the space may be sparsely and uncomfortably furnished, purposely manipulated by officials. Regardless, as noted in the third column of the table, the encounter between state and citizen is purposeful and usually suffused with emotion. To deny that is to deny the feeling of the event.

As Charles Goodsell (1981) points out, the public encounter, where government official and citizen transact matters, is a commonplace interaction that has evaded attention even after decades of study. It is a purposive, not random, meeting. The purpose of the interaction is to receive, deliver, or affect administrative actions and services. At the core of the encounters are

Table 1.1 Citizen–state encounters

From citizen to state	From state to citizen	Citizen–state encounter
To apply for or receive a service	To deliver a service	To exchange need with service
To seek control over a problem	To control or constrain	To mutually resolve problem
To deliver or seek information	To provide or seek information	To exchange information

ways of doing and being together, much as Mary Parker Follett prescribed when she wrote of the circular response that happens when two people engage one another (Follett 1919). Each person affects the other and the outcome is greater than the inputs that either brought to the encounter.

The process of communicating brings its own value as a way of doing/being together. That which emerges from the process of interacting takes its shape from the encounter. As Bartels (2013, 479) presciently states, the public encounter requires recognition of the "in-between of public professionals and citizens as a distinct phenomenon of direct influence on the ability of governments and societies to make decisions, solve problems, and coexist." This is why the emotive dimension to the encounter matters.

The encounter is different from a business encounter because it involves a power differential. It is a dyadic relationship where the official has authority vested by the state and the citizen stands alone before the sovereign. For the official, the transaction may be only a single "case" while for the citizen, a matter of personal importance is at stake. The official is constrained by display rules, standard operating procedures, and work norms in terms of his/her demeanor during the transaction. The citizen, on the other hand, is relatively unconstrained other than by social norms.

Scholars such as Maynard-Moody and Musheno (2000, 2003), Epp et al. (2014), Lipsky (1980), and Drury (2014, 2018) have investigated encounters at the street level in the context of police officers, teachers, and caseworkers and learned that there are multiple levels of work and discretion that are exercised. These transactions may be as simple as information gathering or may be serious, involving life safety, freedom, or even life itself. At the close of the encounter, citizens complain about impersonal government and inadequate service. Officials complain of harsh working conditions and disrespectful exchanges.

Government plays an ever-expanding role in citizens' lives around the globe. But as Michael Lipsky notes, public policy is better understood in the crowded offices and daily encounters of street-level workers, and less well understood in legislatures and in the ranks of top officials (Lipsky 1980). And as Maynard-Moody and Musheno (2000, 350) note, frontline workers—those who meet the public in daily encounters—define their discretion not in terms of following or bending the rules but "as pragmatic improvisations in response to these encounters." In other words, it is the nature of the encounter that drives the outcome.

A subject as essential as the public encounter has, nevertheless, received little attention despite the importance of citizen engagement and the popularity of coproduction mechanisms. Goodsell (1981), who identified this lacuna decades ago, attributes it to the fact that while public administration focuses on policy implementation, it gives little attention to the public encounter, leaving it to the work of various professions who view it not through the citizen–state lens but rather through the perspectives offered via disciplinary blinders. Thus, social psychologists focus on issues of body language and personal space while sociologists focus on the bureaucracy, roles, and functions. Social workers focus on the therapeutic exchange; educators focus on the teaching relationship; healthcare professionals focus on medical arts. Lost in this is the overarching importance of the person-to-person exchange in the state–citizen encounter.

Conceptual approaches for studying the encounter range from instrumentalist, to systemic, to critical, along with some combination of these. Instrumentalist approaches treat the encounter as a goal-seeking process. Such inquiry asks whether the goals of the citizen or of the state are achieved. Systemic inquiry focuses on the overall dynamics of the transaction, introducing issues such as symbolic interactionism, structural-functionalism, principal-agent characteristics, or communication patterns. The third type of inquiry engages critical theory and assesses the presence of exploitive dynamics, asymmetrical power relations, and selective gatekeeping.

Emotional Labor

That which is missing from this focused approach is an embrace of the personal demands of public jobs, whereby officials must sense the emotive state of the citizen, analyze what the desired state should be in order to have a successful encounter, determine what actions to take in order to achieve the desired state, and then modify their own behavior in order to achieve this. This instantaneous sensing and responding is emotional labor and significantly contributes to how the citizen "feels" during the encounter and how the citizen rates the encounter afterward. The teacher who must mollify angry parents, the caseworker who must question family members in response to a child abuse report, the emergency responder who must assure a frightened accident victim, the police officer who must arrest an agitator, the zoning regulator who must reject a waiver request, the public information officer who must address an uneasy crowd none of these encounters will go well in the absence of emotional labor. Emotive skills are essential.

Officials must balance the pressures and constraints of organizational demands and norms against the needs of the citizen and the human-ness of the situation. Thus, the official is a discretion-wielding actor who must express or suppress emotions in order to elicit the desired response from the citizen. This is necessary to get the job done. The encounter's outcome is molded by the successful performance of the official. Additional sculpting tools are the political culture and the balancing act that must be performed among efficiency, equity, effectiveness, and economy.

From Twentieth-Century Reforms to Twenty-First-Century Reforms

The ground is shifting under our feet as the European alliance is in threat of breaking apart, the role of the USA in world peacekeeping structures is in doubt, the Middle East is in continuous tumult, Africa is surging in population and development, and Asia is asserting its might. The question for public administration is less "what will tomorrow bring?" and more "what must we do today to make tomorrow?" Public leadership requires transmitting a vision of exciting possibilities and not—or in spite of—menacing threats. These challenges echo Harland Cleveland's trenchant assessment in 1972:

> … Public Executives of the future will, I think, be marked by a set of attitudes and aptitudes which seem to be necessary for the leadership of equals, which is the key to the administration of complexity. They will be 'low key' people with soft voices and high boiling points; they will show a talent for consensus and a tolerance for ambiguity; they will have a penchant for unwarranted optimism; and they will find private joy in public responsibility. (Cleveland 1972, 77)

Despite Cleveland's prescience long ago, the reforms that came about soon after his prediction stopped short, offering a customer/seller exchange instead. New Public Management encouraged officials to perform like salespeople, altering their behavior to be persuasive and "make the sale." Meanwhile, citizen-customers were expected to shop around and find the best deal. This approach denied collaborative coproduction, where interdependence between official and citizen is essential and public values drive the encounter. Ideally, encounters enhance public service by nurturing personal relationships and constructive, meaningful communication. Such exchanges, referred to as participatory governance, require a deep appreciation for emotive and communicative dynamics. They require sustained cooperation between state and citizen (Fung and Wright 2003).

If ever there were doubt about the impact of encounters, witness findings from a study that inquired into why, despite the highly structured, centrally administered Medicaid program in the State of Michigan, benefit expenditures varied significantly from one county to another (Weissert 1994). These variances were not linked to population or need and the rules governing the program were identical across the counties investigated. The researcher was left to conclude that offices that are responsive to the communities they serve and that provide outreach, in other words, encounter those who seek services, provide more assistance as compared to offices whose directors "lie low" and engage the community only when necessary.

This portends the transition to New Public Governance (NPG), which is a way of thinking about how public services reach the citizenry and how they access government (Osborne 2006, 2010). In retrospect, it is obvious that NPM was a way-station on the road from traditional top-down public administration to now. It offered a break from tradition by urging connections between government, business, and non-governmental bodies (NGOs), with the mantra that whichever entity could best deliver service should be the one to do so. As the years passed and data became available to test whether privatization of public services was cost-efficient and more effective, evidence is mixed at best (Hood and Dixon 2015). As many examples show negative results as positive. As reality overtook promise, a transition is now underway that offers a combination of the best of traditional public administration coupling with collaborative delivery of services and shared responsibility.

New Public Governance relies on coproduction, citizen engagement, and flattened hierarchies that invite more, rather than fewer, meaningful encounters between state and citizen. Recognition of these encounters is not new: Inquiry into the characteristics of effective contracting, even in the purest forms of NPM, revealed the importance of trust between principal and agent, where the relationship between parties factors into the success of the project. Spurred on by Denhardt and Denhardt's concept of New Public Service, where a flatter, more humane, approach to public service was called for, NPG adopts a blended way of thinking about authority and service delivery that borrows from each of the reforms that have attempted to improve on traditional hierarchical public administration.

At the same time that transitions in thought about how best to shape and deliver public services have been occurring, the Internet has heightened the interconnections between public actors both within and across nations. These have resulted in greater levels of interdependence and sharing among nations. All these phenomena point to the necessity of an evolving paradigm that embraces all constituencies and, at least to a large degree, flattens the hierarchy that separates one segment of society and industry from another. Thus, the segue from data dashboards to human hearts starts to take shape.

From Data Dashboards to Human Hearts

Languages create words when there is a need for them. For the purposes of a governance structure that accentuates a flattened notion of citizen–state relations, where collaboration and coproduction are paramount, the English language is already there. Words like coproduction, engagement, relational contracting, trust, and interconnectedness already dance around the focal point of the encounter between citizen and state.

In this revised paradigm, emotional labor is the "comes with" because it is the fundamental, and often nonverbal, foundational element in interpersonal interactions. Topics such as trust, rapport, representativeness, allies, democratization, empowerment, and humanization assume that the emotive component is present.

Trust

As citizens adapt to higher levels of stress while losing confidence in government, trust becomes ever more important. Decades ago, Orion White prophesied that the "search for happiness" would be found in human relationship (White 1981). He worried that the problem is not of the state and its institutions having too much power, but rather too little. Inhumane treatment results from insufficient authority for acting effectively. To overcome this, he prescribed more coproduction in the service delivery process—more exchange and encounter between state actors and citizens. Technical infrastructure cannot hold a polity together. It is the personal encounter that does that.

Trust can be defined as a state of mind in which the person opens him/herself to vulnerability based upon the positive expectation of the intention and behavior of the other. Yang (2005) found that public administrators, both at frontline levels and at upper levels, who trust citizens also encourage greater levels of citizen participation. In the absence of trust, programs are not implemented effectively. This is consistent with Weissert's (1994) findings with the Medicaid program. Findings such as these encourage more deliberative processes where the citizen–state encounter is infused with trust.

Rapport

A closely related construct is empathy. It ranges from the ability to understand and share the feelings of another, or a way of grasping another's emotive state, or the reaction of one person to the observed experiences of the other or the ability to recognize, understand, and respond to the feelings of another (Edlins, in press). Employing empathy costs not one penny but public administration's focus on efficiency causes us to overlook this vital ingredient in human encounters, an ingredient that can move us toward a more relational government.

Representativeness

For state-sponsored actions to be considered legitimate, the viewpoints of those affected by the action must be taken into account. This is why representativeness has been a hallmark of the US Constitution and of parliamentary systems around the globe. The term, itself, denotes a contrast to hierarchy in that it requires inclusion in decision-making processes.

Allies

As public officials "speak for" others, they become allies, advocating for their needs, wishes, and demands. They are also allies for the state, adhering to procedures prescribed by agencies.

The demand for greater social equity, for democratization and empowerment, and for humanization constitutes three normative drivers for revision of the canon (Wise 2002). The processes by which services are delivered are as important as the outputs and "measurable" outcomes. These drivers must be legitimated to match "accountability" if change is to happen and if the reliance on rational instrumentalism is to share a space with the emotive connective tissue that binds communities. Especially in the realm of education, social welfare, housing, elder services, and health care, healing is a reasonable metaphor that explains the role emotional labor plays in person-to-person encounters. Though therapy is not the province of the state, caring and compassion are, and these are communicated via emotive expression more than verbal expression. Straightforward "accountability" as can be captured in spreadsheets and histograms fails to tell the whole story.

Teaching the Paradigm

Training for graduate students entering careers in public service is designed to develop competencies prescribed by the Network of Schools of Public Policy, Affairs and Administration (NASPAA). In its mission to ensure excellence, it holds programs accountable for training students to achieve competency in five domains, including the ability:

- to lead and manage in public governance;
- to participate in and contribute to the policy process;
- to analyze, synthesize, think critically, solve problems, and make decisions;
- to articulate and apply a public service perspective;
- to communicate and interact productively with a diverse and changing workforce and citizenry.

These domains are broad in scope and allow for significant latitude in how students are trained and what they learn. The general interpretation is that important knowledge areas include public management, which includes human resources, budgeting, and information management; public economics, which includes tax policy and debt management; leadership and ethics; data collection, analysis, and interpretation; and understanding the policy process.

While knowledge areas focus on cognitive training, none of the five domains excludes the emotive. Leading requires unwarranted optimism, as Cleveland so aptly said. Participation in the policy process requires understanding policy actors' frames of reference and engaging them in meaningful communication. Decision-making requires not only cognitive skill but as Damasio's brain science research demonstrates, emotive skill to bring the decision task to a close (2018). Articulating a public service perspective requires putting words to public service motivation, compassion, and empathy. Embracing diversity requires adaptability, acceptance of differentness, and an ability to engage with others.

That which is needed is an infusion of the affective component to governing and the citizen–state encounter. The emphasis on the cognitive dimension should be retained but balanced with emphasis on the emotive. The current hierarchy within the paradigm is that theories and foci with the largest span have the highest status. Thus, tomes that explicate and advance theory are judged positively. Works that focus at the mid-range, at the organizational-structural level, where the exploration occurs within the constraints of bureaucracy, are rated positively but treated more as "how-to-do-it" projects. Works that focus on the person-to-person interaction are left to other fields, primarily education, psychology, and sociology. This is wrong. It abrogates the very essence of what governing is about—people joining together to set rules and processes that guide how they live. The only way that students are going to comprehend the wholeness of meaningful governance is by putting the affective alongside the cognitive in our theories and our teaching.

Leading and managing have both cognitive and affective components. Engaging citizens in the policy process is more successful when citizens *like* and *trust* government. As Damasio (2000, 2018) compellingly demonstrates, cognition is only meaningful when paired with emotion. Feelings are the catalyst for the decisions and behaviors that shape human cultures. In fact, his research into decision-making reveals that humans are incapable of making complex decisions unless their emotive function is intact. Reliance only on cognitive rules of logic ignores the holism of the human experience and the interdependence of thought, perceptions, and emotion (Mumby and Putnam 1992). It is the combination of both cognition and emotion that paves the way for meaningfully articulating and applying a public service perspective that integrates equity, efficiency, economy, and effectiveness.

Celebrating the cognitive while ignoring the emotive short-circuits the reality of humans-in-community. A more holistic embrace of means, ends, and goals would incorporate emotive skills as well as cognitive skills and would use as a criterion of success how citizens feel about their government.

Communicating and interacting with a diverse citizenry require both cognitive and affective skills, and a revised, expanded paradigm will contribute toward skill building better than the singular focus on cognitive skills that now prevails. Thus, both cognitive and emotive skills should be embraced in training for public service and in appreciating what it takes to engender citizens' positive feelings about government.

Chapters 4–7 review how emotional labor demands are manifested at the individual, organizational, and cultural levels and the nuances that affect how the citizen–state encounter unfolds. That is followed by nation-specific studies, where each chapter provides an in-depth look at a different nation's unique identity and context. Using data gathered from public service workers in each country, analyses are provided that show how emotional labor is experienced in the performance of their jobs. Building on the information provided, Chapters 21–24 compare findings across nations and draw conclusions that enrich our understanding of how emotional labor factors into the delivery of public services around the globe and the degree to which political dynamics and cultural nuances are involved.

Conclusion

The establishment of processes, procedures, rules, objectives, benchmarks, and outcome measures is important, but they represent only the civic mind. The civic heart must also be addressed. Improving life-in-community and how people feel about their government are important dimensions to public administration. They constitute a springboard for broader understanding of what public service is and does. This argument is not a new one. Pragmatist Jane Addams emphasized that we must take all elements into consideration when seeking solutions to any human problem (Perkins 1934; Shields 2017).

The explosion of interest in public service motivation and human behavior is an indicator that the field is attempting to expand its focus beyond its mechanical/cognitive heritage. Thompson and Christensen (2018), for example, probe meaningfulness and the motivators that lead to commitment. Additional evidence of the desire to understand the *human-ness* of public service is found in the work of Grimmelikhuijsen et al. (2016). Although the authors have yet to break free from framing public service as a cognitive enterprise, they nevertheless advocate greater understanding of the psychological components associated with it.

Rather than continuing to construct the field through the mechanics of scientific management and its progeny, this book urges a more forthright appreciation for the fact that the whole person goes to work each day, armed with both cognition and emotion. And at the end of the day, both sets of skills have been exercised in ways that combine to deliver public service. The confluence of scientific management and engineering norms "disappears" the affective component of work (Fletcher 1999). Reforms that adopt the rhetoric of responsiveness divert to discussions of accountability, resorting to numbers to prove that goals are being achieved. In so doing, they end up disappearing the very behavior that is responsiveness, such as acknowledging the effort required for teams to work effectively.

Shifting the paradigm from data dashboards to human hearts does not imperil rigor, theoretical clarity, or practical utility. It deepens and broadens it. Public service is primarily *service*, yet traditional job descriptions are rooted in the terminology of scientific management and they overlook the affective component of human performance and relationship. People—whether deliverers of services or recipients of services—are devalued when treated as numbered units and interchangeable parts. While tangible skills and behaviors are emphasized, all those knowledges, skills, and abilities that "grease the wheels" of teamwork and responsiveness to citizens remain overlooked, unstated, and undefined. It is time to jettison the erroneous legacy of Cartesian dualism and let the canon expand to acknowledge the emotive component to public service work. This is how a more complete tapestry of theory, research, and practice will result.

As collaborative networks, task forces, and teams replace hierarchical systems of control, interpersonal touchpoints, rather than office walls, define the boundaries of public service. As much as New Public Management promised to be the lasting change that would make government more responsive and less expensive, it did not. Rather than re-casting the nature of the field, it served as one more transitory stage in the evolution of theory and praxis. Moving from the statist and bureaucratic tradition of nineteenth-century and twentieth-century public administration, it served as the conduit from a hierarchical model to the embryonic pluralist tradition of the emergent New Public Governance, where the playing field is larger, awareness of differences is heightened, and trust and relationships matter more than ever because reliance on hierarchy is insufficient, if not missing-in-action (Osborne 2006).

A paradigm shift is underway, transitioning from hierarchical, command-and-control, processes to heterarchy, collaborations, partnerships, and working groups. Emerging in the midst of the heightened emphasis on active engagement between citizenry and state is the importance of the emotive component to each encounter. Still missing from commentary is the person-to-person experience that affects how citizens feel about their government and the dynamics that arise in the citizen–state encounter. As the shift evolves, it is essential to insert the encounter, especially in regard to those dynamics that are *sub rosa* and intangible. The emotive component— how the public official feels and responds and how the constituent feels and responds—is an important part of the exchange. As useful as data are, they tell only part of the story. They provide benchmarks for all that is external. They reveal not one iota of information about the encounter even though it is the encounter that drives everything else. It is meaningfulness that leads to engagement, and it is engagement that leads to compassionate performance. And this is where innovation will be found.

References

Bartels, Koen P. R. 2013. "Public Encounters: The History and Future of Face-to-Face Contact Between Public Professionals and Citizens." *Public Administration* 91 (2): 469–83.

Cleveland, Harlan. 1972. *The Future Executive: A Guide for Tomorrow's Managers.* New York, NY: Harper & Row.

Damasio, Antonio. 2000. *Descartes' Error: Emotion, Reason, and the Human Brain.* New York, NY: Quill.

Damasio, Antonio. 2018. *The Strange Order of Things: Life, Feeling, and the Making of Cultures.* New York, NY: Pantheon Books.

Denhardt, Janet V., and Robert B. Denhardt. 2015. *The New Public Service: Serving Not Steering.* 4th ed. New York, NY: Routledge.

Drury, Ida. 2014. "Performance Management for Wicked Problems: Reflections from Child Welfare's Front Line." *Administrative Theory and Praxis* 36 (3): 398–411.

Drury, Ida. 2018. "Exploring Emotional Labor in Child Welfare Using Frontline Stories." *Administrative Theory and Praxis* 40 (4): 342–56. https://doi.org/10.108 0/10841806.2018.1485451.

Edlins, Mariglynn. in press. "Developing a Model of Empathy for Public Administration." *Administrative Theory & Praxis.*

Epp, Charles, Steven Maynard-Moody, and Donald Haider Markel. 2014. *Pulled Over: How Police Stops Define Race and Citizenship.* Chicago, IL: University of Chicago Press.

Finer, Herman. 1931. "Officials and the Public." *Public Administration* 9 (1): 23–36.

Finer, Herman. 1941. "Administrative Responsibility and Democratic Government." *Public Administration Review* 1 (4): 335–50.

Fletcher, Joyce K. 1999. *Disappearing Acts: Gender, Power, and Relational Practice at Work.* Cambridge, MA: MIT Press.

Follett, Mary Parker. 1919. "Community Is a Process." *The Philosophical Review* 28 (6): 576–88.

Follett, Mary Parker. 1940. "The Psychology of Consent and Participation." In *Dynamic Administration,* edited by Henry C. Metcalf and L. Urwick, 210–29. New York: Harper & Brothers.

Follett, Mary Parker. 1941. "The Giving of Orders." In *Dynamic Administration: The Collected Papers of Mary Parker Follett,* edited by Henry C. Metcalf and L. Urwick, 50–70. New York, NY: Harper & Row.

Friedrich, Carl J. 1940. "Public Policy and the Nature of Administrative Responsibility." In *Public Policy,* edited by C. J. Friedrich and E. S. Mason, 3–24. Cambridge, MA: Harvard University Press.

Fung, A., and E. O. Wright, eds. 2003. *Deepening Democracy: Institutional Innovations in Empowered Participatory Governance.* London: Verso.

Goodsell, Charles T., ed. 1981. *The Public Encounter: Where State and Citizen Meet.* Bloomington, IN: Indiana University Press.

Grimmelikhuijsen, Stephan, Sebastian Jilke, Asmus Leth Olsen, and Lars Tummers. 2016. "Behavioral Public Administration: Combining Insights from Public Administration and Psychology." *Public Administration Review* 77 (1): 45–56.

Hood, Christopher, and Ruth Dixon. 2015. *A Government that Worked Better and Cost Less?* Oxford, UK: Oxford University Press.

Lipsky, Michael. 1980. *Street-Level Bureaucracy: Dilemmas of the Individual in Public Services.* New York, NY: Russell Sage Foundation.

Maynard-Moody, Steven, and Michael Musheno. 2000. "State Agent or Citizen Agent: Two Narratives of Discretion." *Journal of Public Administration Research and Theory* 10 (2): 329–58.

Maynard-Moody, Steven, and Michael Musheno. 2003. *Cops, Teachers, Counselors: Stories from the Front Lines of Public Service*. Ann Arbor, MI: University of Michigan Press.

Mayo, Elton. 1949. *The Social Problems of an Industrial Civilisation*. London, UK: Routledge.

Meier, Kenneth J., and J. Bothe. 2001. "Structure and Discretion: Missing Links in Representative Bureaucracy." *Journal of Public Administration Research and Theory* 11 (4): 455–70.

Mumby, Dennis, and Linda Putnam. 1992. "The Politics of Emotion: A Feminist Reading of Bounded Rationality." *Academy of Management Review* 17 (3): 465–86.

Newcomer, Kathryn E. 2015. "From Outputs to Outcomes." In *Public Administration Evolving: From Foundations to the Future*, edited by Mary E. Guy and Marilyn M. Rubin, 124–56. New York, NY: Routledge.

Norman-Major, Kristen. 2011. "Balancing the Four Es; or Can We Achieve Equity for Social Equity in Public Administration?" *Journal of Public Affairs Education* 17 (2): 233–52.

O'Leary, Rosemary. 2015. "From Silos to Networks." In *Public Administration Evolving: From Foundations to the Future*, edited by Mary E. Guy and Marilyn M. Rubin, 84–100. New York, NY: Routledge.

Osborne, Stephen P. 2006. "The New Public Governance." *Public Management Review* 8 (3): 377–87.

Osborne, Stephen P., ed. 2010. *The New Public Governance: Emerging Perspectives on the Theory and Practice of Public Governance*. New York, NY: Routledge.

Perkins, Frances. 1934. *People at Work*. New York, NY: The John Day Co.

Selznick, Philip. 1949. *TVA and the Grass Roots: A Study in the Sociology of Formal Organization*. Berkeley, CA: University of California Press.

Shields, Patricia, ed. 2017. *Jane Addams: Progressive Pioneer of Peace, Philosophy, Sociology, Social Work and Public Administration*. Cham, Switzerland: Springer International Publishing AG.

Sowa, Jessica, and Sally Selden. 2003. "Administrative Discretion and Active Representation: An Expansion of the Theory of Representative Bureaucracy." *Public Administration Review* 63 (6): 700–10.

Thompson, Jeffery A., and Robert K. Christensen. 2018. "Bridging the Public Service Motivation and Calling Literatures." *Public Administration Review* 78 (3): 444–56. https://doi.org/10.1111/puar.12913.

Weber, Max. 1922/1978. *Economy and Society: An Outline of Interpretative Sociology*. Translated by G. Roth and C. Wittich. Berkeley, CA: University of California Press.

Weissert, C. S. 1994. "Beyond the Organization: The Influence of Community and Personal Values on Street-Level Bureaucrats' Responsiveness." *Journal of Public Administration Research & Theory* 4 (2): 225–54.

White, Orion. 1981. "The Citizen of the 1980s." In *The Public Encounter: Where State and Citizen Meet*, edited by Charles T. Goodsell, 206–19. Bloomington, IN: Indiana University Press.

Wise, Lois. 2002. "Public Management Reform: Competing Drivers of Change." *Public Administration Review* 62 (5): 555–67.

Yang, Kaifeng. 2005. "Public Administrators' Trust in Citizens: A Missing Link in Citizen Involvement Efforts." *Public Administration Review* 65 (3): 273–85.

Part I

The Paradigmatic Shift

This part focuses on the need to adapt public administration theory to the interconnected world in which it is practiced. Chapters 2 and 3 set forth a discussion about public service paradigms around the globe. Caught somewhere between differences across countries and the interconnections that bind all nations together, discussions explore the everyday work experience of those who deliver public services. Citizens must *feel* good about their government just as public servants must *care*, so embracing emotion as well as cognition is at the vanguard for effective public service. The value of comparative analysis is discussed in the context of advancing understanding of the public service context in each country as well as preparing international civil servants whose home country differs from their work country.

2

Thinking Globally About the Public Service Work Experience

Mary E. Guy

It is time for a more comprehensive understanding of what it takes to deliver public services. As public administration professionalized over the past century, it became expert in advancing the cognitive dimension of the work. However, the field has treated the affective dimension as inconsequential. This, despite the fact that emotions and emotion regulation are inseparable parts of public service delivery.

The disavowal of the emotive component has resulted in an incomplete picture of the public service work experience both domestically and abroad. The human factor deserves attention. The field has seen a strong response to other work that focuses on the interface between state and citizen. *Cops, Teachers, Counselors* by Steven Maynard-Moody and Michael Musheno (2003), and *Pulled Over* by Charles R. Epp et al. (2014) provide examples. Emotional labor undergirds the stories told in these books and brings the exchange between citizen and state to life although it is not explicitly underlined. The passion that occurs—whether constructive or destructive—is as much a part of daily work experience as are performance measures displayed on a spreadsheet. The meaning that comes from it and its effect on job satisfaction are powerful. Scholars' attempts to explain away the affective by calling it "coping" miss the essential importance of emotion in interpersonal relationships.

M. E. Guy (✉)
School of Public Affairs, University of Colorado Denver, Denver, CO, USA
e-mail: mary.guy@ucdenver.edu

M. E. Guy et al. (eds.), *The Palgrave Handbook of Global Perspectives on Emotional Labor in Public Service*, https://doi.org/10.1007/978-3-030-24823-9_2

What we need is an encyclopedic awareness of the everyday work experience of those who work in public service around the globe. To achieve this, investigations of the daily work experience of public servants are essential, not to understand decision-making processes, performance measures, and outcomes, for which compendia already exist, but to understand the relational aspect of public service delivery and the role of the emotive component. In the tradition of Ferrel Heady (2001), Fred Riggs (1991), and more currently, Donald Klingner's (2015) recommendations, comparative work is important because it elevates our awareness by nesting emotive dynamics within national culture, revealing the influence of social and political traditions on the work of public servants. Research of this type fills three niches:

1. It expands knowledge of emotional labor in the delivery of public services;
2. adds to the comparative public administration literature; and
3. advances public administration theory.

Comparative Management Studies

To draw a parallel between the business literature and what we advocate, the work of Geert Hofstede and his colleagues at IBM provide a corollary (Hofstede et al. 2010). Their work advanced understanding of international business management from the perspective of national culture and how it affects relations between people in work settings. A similar review of how affect is exercised in public service jobs around the globe advances research and theory in public administration. With the increasing amount of international travel, expansion of public/private partnerships across national boundaries, and the growing desire to understand public service in other cultures, researchers, public managers, international public service organizations, and international aid workers benefit from a holistic examination. International aid workers, for example, encounter intense emotive demands as they deliver humanitarian aid to the starving, emergency relief in earthquake-ravaged cities, and search for ways to re-home fleeing refugees.

Scholars have called for comparative studies in public administration for a long time, but the response has been less than fulsome (Heady 2001; Riggs 1991). Today's global issues, such as climate change, terrorism, cybersecurity, pandemics, and fleeing refugees, heighten the substantial need for deeper understanding of how culture influences the citizen–state interaction (Farazmand 1999). While the need is obvious, research is sparse. One reason for this shortfall of practicable research is that foundational thought in modern public administration is based on Western notions (Klingner 2015). Paradigmatic blinders focus work on questions of formal bureaucracy (Weber 1946), the politics versus administration dichotomy (Wilson 1887), industrial production standards (Taylor 1911), rational approaches to administrative behavior (Simon 1947/1997), Western understandings of public policy (Lasswell 1951), theories of public choice (Buchanan and Tullock 1962), reliance on norms of new public administration (Frederickson 1981), and public management reforms that are rooted in reinventing government (Osborne and Gaebler 1992).

All of this work is rooted in Enlightenment era thought, which elevated the cognitive and "rational" far above the emotive. As brain research now reveals, this thought has resulted in the denial of those qualities and factors that give meaning to people's lives and workers' experiences. Antonio Damasio (2000, 2018) has updated our awareness of the harmony to which the mind and body aspire, undoing generations of scholarly misunderstanding and incorrect assumptions while confirming every practitioner's daily experience.

The Emotive Dimension in Public Service Delivery

René Descartes, a French mathematician and philosopher, was a major figure in the philosophical movement known as rationalism, a method of understanding the world based on the use of reason. Descartes' view that mind and body are separate entities—the notion that intellect and emotion are disconnected—has saturated our scholarship and management principles. Cartesian dualism insists that the mind and body work separately and are independent of each other. Brain studies reveal the naivete associated with such a dualist view and confirm the interconnectedness of reason and emotion (Damasio 2000). More recently, noted economist Herbert Simon, whose work on decision-making earned a Nobel Prize and who is renowned for his sharp-edged critique of qualitative analyses, asserted that decisions based on facts but oblivious to values are as useless as a one-bladed scissor (Simon 1947/1997). Imagine, instead, that Descartes' great contribution had been "I feel; therefore I am."

While Descartes argued for a divergence between mind and body, the reality is that to suppress the emotive while prioritizing the cognitive requires a denial of the human experience.

The separation between emotion and cognition is not a distinct line and the line fades or strengthens according to the situation. Attempting to study work behavior without considering the emotive side results in an incomplete understanding of job demands and performance. Emotions are deeply embedded in all aspects of organizational life. There are affective events throughout the day, and how they are experienced determines how the worker feels about returning to the job the next day.

Linear thinking that relies on rules of logic ignores the holism of the human experience and the interdependence of thought, perceptions, and emotion (Mumby and Putnam 1992). Damasio's (2000) work in neurology demonstrates that patients who suffer damage to centers in the brain that deal with emotion have difficulty reaching a decision. In a paralysis of analysis, these patients pursued repeated consideration of limitless options and facts, never being able to arrive at a decision.

Cultures Are Shaped by "Feeling Minds"

Based on his work, Damasio (2018) makes a persuasive argument that feelings are the catalyst for the responses that began and shaped human cultures. He argues that manual skills, coordinating visual and auditory information, learning and manipulating symbols, in other words cognition, developed in response to feelings, not vice versa. Feelings assist or undermine our best intentions: They are motivators, monitors, and negotiators of human endeavor.

> Feelings … are the unrecognized presences at the cultural conference table. Everyone in the room senses their presence, but with few exceptions no one talks to them. They are not addressed by name. (Damasio 2018, 16)

The point is that there is a cooperative partnership of body and brain, rather than a bifurcation. The human condition is tracked not by cognition alone but by the combination of feeling <u>and</u> cognition. Cultures and civilizations are shaped by "feeling minds" where emotion and cognition are joined. A mental flow only becomes meaningful when feelings are attached. The felt value of life is described in emotive terms of good or bad. Feelings are motivators to respond to a problem and they are monitors of whether the response is working. In other words, feelings are facts.

Emotions as the Language of the Face

There are eight primary emotions: interest, enjoyment, surprise, distress, fear, shame, contempt, and anger (Guy and McCarter 1978; Tomkins and McCarter 1964). Each of these exists on a continuum from moderate to high intensity, as displayed in Table 2.1.

Thoughts run with feelings by their side. Emotive responses are triggered by stimuli, ranging from tastes, smells, and visions to sounds and thoughts. Emotions power intellectual and creative processes and all have a positive or negative valence. Valence reflects the quality of an experience, which is experienced somewhere on the range of pleasant to unpleasant. Emotions are felt and we are affected by them. It is impossible to overstate their ubiquity and functional importance. Imagine a complete absence of feeling; it would be a suspension of being.

The face is an organ of communication to the self as well as to others and its language is emotive. It is the place where emotions are expressed most obviously. In a test of people's ability to interpret affect by looking at one-dimensional photographs, there was an extraordinarily high correlation of 0.86 between the emotion displayed in the photograph and the judgment of the observer (Tomkins and McCarter 1964). Researchers concluded then, as we continue to assume, that this correlation is high because everyone is familiar with their own facial expressions, as well as expressions of those who surround them. Infants learn early to read the affective responsiveness on the faces of others. Most people are capable of interpreting an extraordinary amount of information from momentary, slight facial responses. To smile in response to the smile of the other, to feel fright at the expression of fear, to

Table 2.1 Primary emotions

Moderate	Intense
Interest	Excitement
Enjoyment	Joy
Surprise	Startle
Distress	Anguish
Fear	Terror
Shame	Humiliation
Contempt	Disgust
Anger	Rage

feel sadness at the expression of grief, all demonstrate the translation from someone else's emotive display to one's own bodily feeling. The translation between muscles of the face, visual and auditory cues, and the kinesthetic language of emotion happens without verbal formulation (Bernstein et al. 2008; Krumhuber et al. 2007; Mai et al. 2011).

As Martin Buber (1958) reminds us, all real living is meeting. One becomes whole through relation with thou, the other. In everyday parlance, person-to-person interaction is the essence of civilized living. This, too, is the foundation upon which meaningful public service is conducted. Thus comes the importance of mutual engagement between citizens and those who govern.

Emotional Proletariat

It is logical to assume that the high level of uniformity in the perception and interpretation of affect is affected by culture, as if there are dialects to the language of emotion. These dialects are affected by social status and power, with those of higher status and greater power being less restrained in their emotive expressions, while those lower in status and power are expected to display deference, defined as the capacity to place oneself in a "one down" position vis-à-vis the other. Women and racial/ethnic/religious minorities occupy such subordinate status. This is especially pronounced for those whose intersecting identities place them in positions of diminished power. These workers comprise the "emotional proletariat" (Evans 2013, 4). They are more likely to hold frontline jobs while having little control over the policies and procedures that govern their work.

Performance demands of the job are heightened for those in the emotional proletariat as they attempt to achieve congruence between their emotive suppression/display and their sense of identity and dignity. For example, while men who show anger are depicted as "tough," women who show anger are depicted as "too emotional" and "shrill." In other words, feelings that are normative for those in power are not normative for those with lower status. The "proper" emotion to display is determined by those in power.

Those with lower status must do double duty: In addition to the emotional labor of the job itself, interactions based on race and gender must also be performed. Consider the example of police work, where citizen–state interactions are influenced by preconceived notions of the work itself and are framed by demographic characteristics that drive expectations of professionalism. The woman officer is expected to be more compassionate while the male officer is expected to be authoritative and "tougher than tough."

Racist and sexist ideologies infuse the workplace culture and become hegemonic, being defined as natural and normal. This carries over to the exchange between state and citizen, with those lower in status expected to behave in a manner different from those higher in status. The middle-class crime victim is treated differently than the poor, dishevelled, homeless fellow. The white-collar criminal is treated differently than the petty thief. Unequal exchanges result in implicit expectations for what emotive displays are "normal" for both state and citizen. Emotion norms exist and impel "whites only" emotive displays of anger while prohibiting it for blacks. Similarly, men's emotive displays are interpreted differently than women's. The "outsider" within workplace culture (African American airline pilot, for example) performs double duty, suppressing the emotive response that would be thought natural for the insider. The hypervisibility of the outsider requires extra work to suppress normal emotive responses, while displaying deference. As much as emotional labor is invisible work, it is even more invisible and more intense for those experiencing affronts against them due to their race, gender, or other differentiating characteristics of otherness. Thus, culture and history are reflected in the workplace and conflated with display rules. Social status drives the "normal" emotive display.

The "dialect" of emotive display is stressed even further when there are intersections of minority status. Social identity plays a significant role in the emotive display of workplace interactions. Louwanda Evans (2013) describes the emotional labor that those in the minority must exercise. Interviewing African American airline pilots and flight attendants, she learned how they must suppress anger when insulted by white passengers and how they must respond with grace when challenged about their capability. For example, the African American woman pilot is likely to be met with disbelief that she is competent to fly a plane for such a job is "out of role" for a black woman. The emotion suppression that is required of her as she displays a pleasant countenance unperturbed by the insult is an example of work-related emotional labor that stems from her job conflated with her social status.

Regardless of the work to be done, the goal in public service is for workers to be resilient and responsive to citizens, regardless of how intersections of differentness affect the exchange. The social science of what transpires when citizen meets state shapes emotional labor.

The Emotive Component of Citizen Engagement

Fluidity between facts and values, intuition and reason, and cognition and emotion remains important for public administration study because of the ultimate customer: the citizen. This is particularly important in the case of street-level bureaucrats, for they are the connectors and relationship builders between citizens and government. Emotional labor performed by operatives in public service organizations is a primary "commodity" which is bought and sold by government in pursuit of policy goals (Guy et al. 2008). Consider the example of child protective workers, who must determine whether a child is safe with its parents or whether it should be removed from the home. The interaction between parents who risk losing their child to the state and the representative of the state—the caseworker—is filled with both emotion and cognition.

Street-level bureaucrats encounter abuse, threats, violence, but also "sparkle" moments (Rayner and Lawton 2018). Surveys in Australia show that citizens want timely delivery of service, accurate information, fairness, and respect. Fairness means application of uniform standards, and respect means they want to be accorded quality care, friendliness, and answers to their questions. Interviews with workers in Australia reveal that after decades of public service reforms emphasizing "customer service," they feel pressured to be responsive and to "satisfy" the citizen even when working in "hot" policy fields, such as welfare and regulation. After analyzing interviews with Australian public servants, Rayner and Lawton conclude that emotional labor is at the center of public service and it presents a complexity to the work environment that merits far more attention than it has garnered to date.

Putting the Service in Public Service

Although sociologists have focused on emotional labor in retail settings ever since Arlie Hochschild's seminal work on airline attendants in 1983, broadbased work on jobs that are, by definition, emotionally intense, has been slow to develop. Such jobs are in public service, not retail sales. From police officers to emergency call takers to public information officers to child protective workers to public-school teachers, the work of frontline public service escalates from the mundane to the explosive in seconds. From military personnel to zoning and ordinance compliance officials, the power of the state to direct and restrict behavior brings with it job demands where emotive demands run parallel with cognitive and physical requirements.

Unlike retail exchanges, where instructions for explicit emotive display script how to deliver "service with a smile," public service delivery is marked by less acting and more authentic expression. While early work on emotional labor employs a binary dichotomy of "deep acting" and "surface acting" to describe the dramaturgy in sales exchanges, more recent work has focused on the expression of naturally felt emotion as it is experienced on a continuum (Ashkanasy et al. 2017; Guy et al. 2008).

Cognition and emotion in public service delivery are interconnected, just as Damasio explains, but one would not know it by reading traditional texts. To make chapters on human resource management, budgeting, and performance measures seem more realistic, emojis and emoticons would have to be added to the pages ☺☺☺. Their use simulates emotive expression in one-dimensional messages and presages the awareness that an essential component of relating to one another is stripped away when emotion is absent. A more holistic comprehension of the public service experience would metaphorically add emoji s to the canon.

As enamored with reason as we remain, our obsession with that which is distinctive about us as humans—the capacity to reason—forgets what is more basic and more essential to getting along. The "sympathetic fellow feeling" tempers the wholly cognitive (Zimmermann 2011). Emotive synchrony—empathy—is how persons adjust to one another. We get a warm feeling when helping someone. When humans extend help to those beyond immediate family and friends, social capital is built. Self-interest and wealth and goal achievement do not suffice to make a society successful. Happiness comes not from being wealthy, it comes from being in an environment of connection and trust.

Zimmermann (2011) argues that humans are wired for empathy and that its development requires cultivation. Empathy and hopefulness are foundational to truth and reconciliation commissions, and notions of restorative justice. As much as Enlightenment thinking prizes autonomy, in fact companionship is more important. That is why children play; it is a fundamental social activity. In children's play, they learn of the other, and themselves in relation to others, and the boundaries in between. We know because we feel, more than we know because we think. Thinking combines sensations, emotions, and abstract reasoning as a whole (Damasio 2000).

As much as freedom is equated with autonomy in American myth, it is associated with the French notion of fraternity—the companionship, trust, and sense of belonging that produce happiness. In American myth, the individual is the creative force. Thomas Jefferson's conceptualization of inalienable rights—life, liberty, and the pursuit of happiness—turns the mind to self-fulfillment. One can argue that Schopenhauer's work makes explicit that compassion, not pure reason, is the basis for morality, elevating the empathic process to a status far above that to which it is relegated by rationalists (Rifkin 2009). Information and communication technology has done nothing but exponentially expand the connections between people and heighten the degree to which everyone is enmeshed in social networks.

Anthropologists argue that social exchange precedes commercial exchange. In other words, trust must exist before markets can flourish. As the march toward social equity makes obvious, to have a fair and just society, we must treat people not equally, but differently, sizing up people's needs individually, engaging with them individually.

Most salient for public administration is the importance of empathy, for that is from which ethics arise. It is empathy that enables us to see others as we see ourselves. Street-level bureaucrats encounter this daily and also engage in intense emotive experiences because of it (Zimmerman 2011). Far beyond, and deeper set, than pure ratiocination, is the ethic of care, love, trust, and friendship (Slote 2007). It is incumbent upon public administration theory and discourse to incorporate this more fulsome approach to teaching about public service delivery if the ethos of democracy is to be achieved.

Drilling deeper into the emotive component are the requirements for workers themselves to "fit in" when they are different from others on their work teams. For example, African American women experience an intersectionality that doubles the emotive work they must do to adapt to expectations and to shape their "performance" so that it is like that of those around them. Working in a masculinist culture, organizational norms require adherence to the customs of a "white, male, citadel" (Durr and Wingfield 2011). Just as public administration practice pretends that emotion does not occur on the job, bureaucracies pretend to be gender neutral. This places an extra burden on those who are neither white nor male in terms of what emotive displays and expressions they exhibit or suppress in order to fit in (Bishu et al. 2019). Performance weariness results from the perpetual stress of being on parade and being alienated while striving to conform.

Emotional labor in the performance of public service is gaining an increasing audience and questions abound about the difference that culture makes in determining how it is perceived, executed, and appraised. It is time for a holistic approach to broadly and deeply comprehend the public service experience around the globe. For example, the question of whether collectivist cultures and individualist cultures differ in how they shape the response to emotive demands has yet to be answered. And the question of whether different collectivist countries differ from each other as much as countries that are categorized as individualist remains to be answered. Comprehensive empirical verification provides the foundation for advancing theory and research in Eastern and Western cultures, in northern and southern cultures, as well as in nation-states.

To Advance Public Administration Theory

Public administration theory reflects Western thought, balancing individualist notions of personal freedoms and inalienable rights against government power. In recent years, fascination with networks, collaborative strategies, and interconnections has propelled the language of governance, connoting connections among citizens, business interests, and formal governmental structures. But nowhere in this galaxy of thought does the emotive component to helping citizens lead better lives enter the dialogue. While the desire for collective harmony is preeminent in Eastern thought, and several Asian languages include words and phrases that capture the emotive connection between people, Western thought and languages do neither.

In contrast to the shelves of data on the cognitive component to public administration, these are the questions that need to be answered in order to produce a more comprehensive understanding of the public service work experience from a holistic perspective that embraces the heart as well as the head:

1. How does emotional labor affect the delivery of public services?
2. How does it fit within the public service paradigm?
3. How does context affect its performance at the individual level? Organizational level? Cultural level? Situational level?
4. What role does national culture play?
5. How far must the needle on the public service paradigm move to more accurately align the practice of public service with public administration theory?

Before these questions can be tackled, there first must be clarity about the relationships among individual traits, emotional intelligence, and emotional labor. For this clarity, we turn to a discussion about the relationship between emotional intelligence and emotional labor.

Emotional Intelligence Versus Emotional Labor

Two closely related terms, *emotional intelligence* and *emotional labor*, focus on the emotive component in human behavior and have entered the lexicon. The former refers to the ability to sense and regulate one's own emotions as well as to sense others' emotional state, while the latter refers to the exercise of emotive skills in order to get the job done. The terms refer to different but related aspects: The former is an individual trait while the latter is a job-related construct.

Emotional Intelligence

Emotional intelligence involves the ability to perceive, understand, appraise, and express emotion, coupled with the ability to generate and regulate feelings (Mayer et al. 1990; Mayer and Salovey 1997; Salovey and Mayer 1990). It is analogous to cognitive intelligence, which involves the ability to think analytically, exercise logic, and exercise literacy and numeracy. The construct of emotional intelligence enables acknowledgment of an essential work skill that is interpersonal in nature. Higher levels of emotional intelligence improve managerial performance and leadership ability (Berman and West 2008; Dulewicz and Higgs 2003; Newman et al. 2009; O'Leary et al. 2012; Van Wart 2010; Vigoda-Gadot and Meisler 2010).

Managing emotions requires self-awareness and the ability to access and experience emotions, to be sensitive to them, and to reflectively regulate them, especially in response to social constraints. This is demonstrated by the ability to suppress how one is actually feeling when that emotion is inappropriate for the circumstance, for example, merriment at a funeral or extreme anger when calmness is required. Below is an explanation of the three variables most often used to capture the elements of emotional intelligence: self-awareness, other-awareness, and self-regulation.

Self-Awareness

Emotional self-awareness refers to the degree to which persons are able to identify their own feelings and understand the cause. Self-awareness includes attention to one's internal state, as well as to thoughts or feelings about that state. It provides a basis for assessing one's own abilities and knowing how to respond emotively (Goleman 1995; Mayer and Salovey 1997; Mayer et al. 2008). The self-aware person is emotionally resilient, using emotions as sources of insight into the self. There are a range of intrapersonal skills that are associated with self-awareness, including adaptability, self-control, initiative, and optimism (Canfield 1990; Goleman et al. 2002).

Other-Awareness

Other-awareness is the ability to perceive and understand the emotions of others, including the ability to hear, sense, and intuit what others are feeling. This awareness derives from tone of voice, body language, facial expression, pace of speech, and comprehending how the other describes their feelings. In other words, it involves active listening, sensing the mood of an individual, and "reading between the lines."

Self-Regulation

Self-regulation relates to the ability to regulate the display of one's emotions so that the intensity is controlled to fit the circumstance. Suppressing, or quieting one's emotions, or hiding them in order to display an opposite countenance, is also a part of self-regulation. It is an aspect of emotional intelligence that involves awareness of which emotion is appropriate to exhibit and the self-regulation that is necessary to exhibit the appropriate emotional state (Erber 1996). Emotion regulation requires the use of adaptive strategies so that the emotion displayed is appropriate for the circumstances.

Emotional Labor

In contrast to emotional intelligence, *emotional labor* refers to emotive behavior that is performed for a wage. It is analogous to manual labor, which relies on physical prowess, and to cognitive labor, which relies on thinking. The performance of emotional labor is required in order to do the job and it involves emotive sensing, evaluating the emotions in play, deciding the best response, and then behaving in such a way that appropriate emotions are expressed.

As a concept, the term was first coined to capture the work requirement for publicly observable facial and bodily displays of emotion in retail sales, their purpose being to shape and enhance the customer experience. In other words, it is the management of the worker's own feelings in order to influence the emotive state of the customer. For example, when Arlie Hochschild

(1983) observed flight attendants to learn how they used affective skills in response to passengers' demands, fears, and requests, she concluded that without skill in soothing passengers' disquiet, attendants would have a plane full of disgruntled fliers. Thus, the emotive component of their jobs was an essential skill, just as was the distribution of soft drinks and pretzels and knowledge of how to prepare passengers in case of an emergency.

When applied in the public service context, studies demonstrate a positive relationship between emotional labor and job satisfaction as well as an increased probability of burnout that results when workers must suppress how they actually feel while expressing a different emotion (Hsieh and Guy 2009; Hsieh et al. 2012; Jin and Guy 2009; Sloan 2014). For example, an emergency responder may experience horror when seeing a badly injured accident victim. However, the horror must be suppressed in order to proceed with assisting the victim. This action requires the worker to wear a mask, a false-face, while performing job duties. What is the effect of emotion suppression for workers who encounter hostile citizens daily, such as with Transportation Security Administration (TSA) inspectors, or overworked clerks at the driver license station? This is an important question because it tempers public service motivation on the part of the worker and affects how the citizen perceives the state.

To summarize, *emotional intelligence* is internal to the person and is of interest in all settings: work, recreational, and personal. By contrast, *emotional labor* refers to performance solely in the work setting and is essential if the job is to be done. How it is performed is contingent on the context in which the work occurs and the feeling state of those involved. The connection between the two terms is this: When, as a part of job requirements, workers must use their emotional intelligence, then they are performing emotional labor.

Research Findings

Research that relates emotional intelligence and emotional labor has produced actionable guidance for supervisors and staff trainers. The most important finding learned from studies is that the ability to regulate one's own emotions positively correlates with the performance of emotional labor and results in reduced levels of burnout. As employees enhance their ability to regulate their own emotions, the likelihood of experiencing burnout decreases. This means that training to enhance workers' ability to regulate their own emotions will have direct payoffs in reduced turnover, absenteeism, and performance problems.

A second usable finding is that emotional self-awareness is a stand-alone ability that correlates positively with job satisfaction but not with the performance of emotional labor. This means that regardless of the presence or absence of emotional labor, employees who are self-aware are more likely to find satisfaction in their jobs. This means that whether or not a job requires a lot of emotional labor, emotional self-awareness is still an important attribute for employees if they are to gain satisfaction with their employment (Guy and Lee 2015).

Emotional other-awareness varies from what is generally assumed. Although it does not affect the likelihood of burnout, it affects the likelihood of decreased job satisfaction. We can speculate that being "on guard" or ever vigilant about what others are feeling draws workers' attention away from the work at hand. In public service, this dimension is acutely present for workers who perform unpopular work, such as regulation enforcement, tax collection, and related jobs that are resented because they constrain citizens' freedoms rather than enabling them.

In sum, emotional labor and emotional intelligence are separable but related constructs. Emotional intelligence is not a *sine qua non* for emotional labor but it affects the capacity to perform emotional labor effectively. Just as the relationship between one's IQ and academic achievement is tenuous, such that high IQ scores do not guarantee that the student will become valedictorian, there are unknown factors that affect the influence of emotional intelligence in the execution of emotional labor.

Additional research shows a tangential connection between two seemingly unrelated constructs, emotional labor and public service motivation (Hsieh et al. 2011). While the former pertains to the exercise and management of emotions, the latter refers to an intellectual state of mind that combines caring for community, empathy, compassion, and positive affect for citizen participation and public service missions (Coursey et al. 2012; Wright et al. 2012). Emotional labor is the work that is performed as a result of the motivation to serve others. In other words, emotional labor is foundational to work performance that is impelled by public service motivation.

The Emotive Dimension in Work Performance

Interest in the emotive aspects of work performance has accelerated in recent decades, as appreciation for a more holistic representation of the work experience has developed. Leaving the industrial age and its assembly line production methods in the rearview mirror, contemporary management embraces the whole person, rather than only cognitive and physical skills. Thus, appreciation for emotional intelligence emerged a few decades ago, with emotional labor close on its heels. With the global focus on citizen engagement, citizen–state interaction, and questions of effective governance, this subject sets the stage for a deeper, broader understanding of the everyday public service work experience across cultures. The more we can learn about how culture and political traditions interact with the emotive component of public service, the better will be our understanding of governance itself, as well as public service delivery, around the globe.

While the literature is filled with pages about the importance of citizen engagement, responsiveness to citizens, trust between government, contractors, and citizens, and attention to overall service quality, little attention is devoted to the mechanics of how engagement, responsiveness, and trust are nurtured. A holistic focus rounds out the conceptualization by correcting Descartes' error.

Evidence-Based Management

It is rare to have a conversation about public management that does not mention evidence-based management or performance measures. Quantitative indicators are seductive because they create the impression of certainty. Their shortcoming is that such measures ignore a significant component of the service relationship. For example, Hsieh and Guy (2009) investigated work outcomes for caseworkers who counseled troubled youth. They found that service recipients whose caseworkers were better at performing emotional labor rated their satisfaction with services higher than those who received services from caseworkers whose emotional labor proficiency was lower. Work such as this, which examines how the public "feel" about the services rendered, illuminates how impactful good emotive skills are.

The evidence is there, in stories as well as in quantitative analyses, that the emotive component of public service is important. A holistic assessment that takes it into consideration expands what we know, opens our eyes to performance that can be improved, and paves the way for a more comprehensive understanding of what it takes to deliver public services effectively. In the case of the outcomes study of troubled youth, a typical "evidence-based" study would simply report that the agency that provided the caseworkers had done superior work. The numbers would conceal why the work was superior. This is why a deeper, richer appreciation of emotional labor as a work product is important in public service delivery. Such knowledge will provide a more accurate picture of the elements in good public service.

Public Service Dynamics Versus Retail Sales

Early attention to emotional labor was in retail sales, where its immediate outcome engenders rapport between seller and buyer and increases the likelihood of making a sale. The goal of public service is different: it is to pave the way so that people can live their lives to the fullest, in an environment of safety, health, and security. These dimensions require trust, which, more than a cognitive thought, is an emotive reaction. The "what" that government does is grounded in affect, either positive or negative, approving or disapproving, happy or angry. The "how I feel about government" is a judgment based on the quality of the relationship between the public official and the citizen. In sum, quality and meaningfulness of the exchange matter.

As distrust of government grows, as governments race to figure out how best to deliver services as equitably and effectively as possible, as citizen engagement becomes a larger and larger conundrum, the relationship between citizen and state comes more clearly into focus. A positive emotive connection between citizen and state diminishes the estrangement that alienated citizens feel. A personal connection supplies a "real" person with whom the citizen can communicate.

For these reasons, the emotive component to public service moves from stage left to center stage. It is instrumental to engaging citizens and engendering trust. As citizen engagement remains an elusive goal, the emotive component becomes ever more salient.

Burnout Versus Sparkle

Emotional labor is like a two-sided coin. On one side is the sparkle—the good feeling when an exchange goes well, when citizens feel good about the sense of safety and security they have and when workers end the day knowing they made a difference in someone's life. It also risks the other side—burnout—which results from having to contain true feelings and pretend to feel differently. Wearing an emotive mask, disguising one's true feelings, is energy consuming and exhausting. When the emotive intensity is too great for too long, the risk increases. This sparkle-versus-burnout conundrum is a very human reaction to very real work.

We know from studies among public service workers in the USA (Guy et al. 2008; Mastracci et al. 2012) that several conditions hold, regardless of whether one works in the most emotionally intense jobs or in the least. Whether one works in emergency response or in consumer advocacy, the following conditions are associated with the performance of emotional labor:

1. Performing emotional labor contributes to job satisfaction, the sparkle of public service.
2. The ability to regulate one's own emotional state diminishes the risk of burnout.
3. Working in high emotive-demand jobs increases the likelihood of burnout.
4. Burnout and job satisfaction are inversely related.
5. Both women and men perform emotional labor, but cultural norms direct different forms consistent with in-role behavior: For example, women are expected to be nurturant; men are expected to be confident.
6. While expressing authentic emotions is reinforcing and contributes to job satisfaction (sparkle), having to suppress one's feelings is demoralizing, requires excess energy, and puts the worker at higher risk of burnout.

Sufficient work has already been done to show that public service workers who are better at performing emotional labor during the course of their duties cause recipients to be more satisfied with the services they received (Hsieh and Guy 2009). It is only a short leap to understanding how citizen engagement and trust in government are enhanced when workers are better at performing the emotive aspects of their job. This is consistent with, but far more meaningful than, the attention that retail sales have paid to "service with a smile" in order to enhance customer loyalty.

This subject affects organizational life. In terms of leader-member exchange, employees who work in emotionally intense jobs are more likely to remain in those jobs when the supervisor is supportive. After a certain point, however, even the most supportive supervisor cannot change an employee's decision to leave. A study of US federal workers reveals that identifying the emotive burden of a job early, acknowledging it, and providing a supportive work environment result in less turnover. Failing to appreciate the emotive burden until the worker is overloaded, however, leads to higher turnover (MSPB 2017). In other words, up to a certain point, a supportive work environment helps workers resist burnout. After a certain point, though, no amount of supportive assistance can help.

Before making global generalizations about emotional labor based on Western notions, broader knowledge is necessary. A few studies have been conducted in Asian nations and to that we now turn.

What We Know About Emotional Labor in Asian Contexts

Recent studies in Korea and China provide a peek at culture's influence on the performance of emotional labor. Although the overall patterns are consistent with findings from the USA, some aspects seem to reflect cultural nuances that result from the emphasis on collectivist harmony as compared to the Western reliance on individualism. For example, in Korea, the burden of having to pretend—to suppress how one feels while displaying a different feeling—is especially difficult for women, more so than in the USA, where gender differences fail to reach statistical significance. While pretending had no effect on men's level of job satisfaction and turnover intent, it increases job dissatisfaction for women as well as their intent to leave (Yang and Guy 2015). Does this mean that Korean women are more sensitive to pretense than are men? This is not the case among US public servants, where pretense decreases job satisfaction but there is not a significant difference between men and women. At the risk of overgeneralizing, we know that in interpersonal dynamics the person in the subordinate role is more likely to mask personal feelings. Korea's culture is in transition but remains more hierarchical and male dominated than in the USA or even its neighbor, Taiwan. Thus, women are more likely to be in a subordinate position and more often find themselves masking their true feelings in order to display socially appropriate feelings.

That which is consistent in both Korean and Western settings is the finding that emotional labor is a multidimensional construct. Pretense and authentic expression have opposite effects on job satisfaction for women, while for men pretense does not exert a significant difference in relation to their job satisfaction. Might this indicate that gender-sensitive consideration should be factored into staffing decisions to mitigate the negative effects of emotional labor and contribute toward a better job-worker fit? This question presents a conundrum because in China, the effect of emotional labor more closely approximates that which is found in Western culture, although there are subtle differences (Lu and Guy 2014, 2018, 2019). In an investigation of three work-related elements that contribute to responsiveness—emotional labor, job engagement, and ethical leadership for government workers in China—findings mirror that found in the USA:

1. Authentic emotive expression relates positively to job engagement.
2. Pretending relates negatively to job engagement.
3. While the presence of ethical leadership mitigates the negative relationship between pretending and job engagement, it does not affect the relationship between authentic expression and engagement.

In other words, authentic expression is its own reward despite the presence or absence of ethical leadership. This indicates that the satisfaction that comes with authentic emotive experiences is foundational and positive, regardless of other work culture accoutrements.

Hints from these findings in Korea and China beg for more exploration to learn whether it is correct to conclude that the emotive component of public service delivery is more foundational than other variables that ride atop it, regardless of country and culture. Are the differences at the margin or are they central? The analyses presented in the chapters of this book help to reveal the answer.

Conclusion: From Results to Relationship

The drama of public service is daily: Citizens often seek government's help in the worst moment of the worst day of their lives. Emergency medical technicians usually find themselves performing emotional labor as well as administering first aid because calming a panicked victim is as important as medical ministrations. The emotional intensity of disaster response, domestic violence, trauma care, searches and seizures, protective services for abused children, law enforcement arrests, and victim services separates public work from the more pedestrian world of production and sales. And the more pedestrian work of government—tax collection, enforcing regulations—involves restricting citizen's freedoms, something that is often met with resistance and anger. Unlike a sales relationship, where customer service means causing customers to feel that they are in control, have many choices, and can return a product if unsatisfied, public goods are different. Service with a smile goes only so far.

In an era where evidence-based management is popular, that which is easily quantifiable has more resonance than the intangible qualities of positive exchanges between citizen and state. The machinery of public administration is built to construct data dashboards that display a vast array of measures and benchmarks, all of which are facts that citizens can use to think about government. Unfortunately, there is too often a disconnect between how citizens feel and what they think. It is *feeling* that resists codification on data dashboards but it is *feeling* that citizens talk about with their neighbors and it is *feeling* that drives whether or not they care enough to vote or engage in town meetings or offer feedback.

From New Public Management with its emphasis on conducting government like a business to New Public Governance with its emphasis on collaboration, to coproduction with its emphasis on shared responsibility, to citizen engagement, there is an emotive component that affects how citizens feel about their government and how public service workers experience their jobs. In terms of contracting with vendors who can mount service delivery systems efficiently, relational contracting is increasingly talked about. This refers to the establishment of trust between purchaser and vendor. Trust is what is created by a combination of tangible reliability and the rapport that is developed through person-to-person exchanges.

Emotional labor is the "comes with" in the new paradigm of service delivery that emphasizes citizen engagement. This model focuses on collaborations across governments, nonprofits, and private sector establishments, all of which result in a panoply of programs and delivery methods. With increasing reliance on Internet-based services, the emotive component will become even more highly valued as it becomes scarcer, for it is the human part of governing. From a human resource management perspective, the emotive dimension runs the gamut of human resource functions: from job descriptions to selection and socialization processes to training and development to compensation. Emotional labor demands vary by job and requirements for its performance should be included in job descriptions. Students enrolled in public administration classes should encounter course material that reflects their everyday work experience and takes them beyond it, such that they learn how to anticipate all that will confront them, both cognitive and affective.

These pages have focused on what public service feels like and what the everyday experience is for public service workers. The preference for cognition over emotion has produced a tranche of research into tangible, measurable components, to the exclusion of those elements that contribute to job satisfaction, meaningfulness, and rapport between citizen and state—the sparkle that reinforces public service motivation. Descarte's error becomes obvious: The heart and the head are not separate; they strive to be in harmony in the public service experience. Valuing both cognition and emotion is now at the vanguard of research into effective public service and citizen engagement. Citizens must *care* just as public servants must *care*. This is the emotive component to public service. This chapter explains why it is important, why it matters in today's environment, and what remains to be learned. Our language is already there and now it is time that our scholarship arrives.

References

Ashkanasy, Neal M., Ashlea C. Troth, Sandra A. Lawrence, and Peter J. Jordan. 2017. "Emotions and Emotional Regulation in HRM: A Multi-level Perspective." In *Research in Personnel and Human Resources Management*, edited by M. Ronald Buckley, Anthony R. Wheeler, and Jonathon R. B. Halbesleben, 1–52. Bingley, UK: Emerald Publishing Limited.

Berman, Evan, and Jonathan West. 2008. "Managing Emotional Intelligence in U.S. Cities: A Study of Social Skills Among Public Managers." *Public Administration Review* 68: 742–58.

Bernstein, M. J., S. G. Young, C. M. Brown, D. F. Sacco, and H. M. Claypool. 2008. "Adaptive Responses to Social Exclusion: Social Rejection Improves Detection of Real and Fake Smiles." *Psychological Science* 19 (1): 981–83.

Bishu, Sebawit G., Mary E. Guy, and Nuriel Heckler. 2019. "Seeing Gender and Its Consequences." *Journal of Public Affairs Education*. https://doi.org/10.1080/152 36803.2018.1565039.

Buber, Martin. 1958. *I and Thou*. 2nd ed. New York, NY: Charles Scribner's Sons.

Buchanan, James M., and Gordon Tullock. 1962. *The Calculus of Consent: Logical Foundations of Constitutional Democracy*. Ann Arbor, MI: University of Michigan Press.

Canfield, J. V. 1990. *The Looking Glass Self: An Examination of Self Awareness*. New York, NY: Praeger.

Coursey, David, Kaifeng Yang, and Sanjay K. Pandey. 2012. "Public Service Motivation (PSM) and Support for Citizen Participation: A Test of Perry and Vandenabeele's Reformulation of PSM Theory." *Public Administration Review* 72: 572–82.

Damasio, Antonio. 2000. *Descartes' Error: Emotion, Reason, and the Human Brain*. New York, NY: Quill.

Damasio, Antonio. 2018. *The Strange Order of Things: Life, Feeling, and the Making of Cultures*. New York, NY: Pantheon Books.

Dulewicz, V., and M. Higgs. 2003. "Leadership at the Top: The Need for Emotional Intelligence in Organizations." *International Journal of Organizational Analysis* 11 (3): 193–210. https://doi.org/10.1108/eb02897.

Durr, Marlese, and Adia M. Harvey Wingfield. 2011. "Keep Your 'N' in Check: African American Women and the Interactive Effects of Etiquette and

Emotional Labor." *Critical Sociology* 37 (5): 557–71. https://doi.org/10.1177%2F0896920510380074.

Epp, Charles, Steven Maynard-Moody, and Donald Haider Markel. 2014. *Pulled Over: How Police Stops Define Race and Citizenship.* Chicago, IL: University of Chicago Press.

Erber, R. 1996. "The Self-Regulation of Moods." In *Striving and Feeling,* edited by L. L. Martin and A. Tesser, 251–75. Mahwah, NJ: Lawrence Erlbaum.

Evans, Louwanda. 2013. *Cabin Pressure: African American Pilots, Flight Attendants, and Emotional Labor.* Lanham, MD: Rowman & Littlefield.

Farazmand, Ali. 1999. "Globalization and Public Administration." *Public Administration Review* 59 (6): 509–22.

Frederickson, H. George. 1981. "Organization Theory and New Public Administration." In *Perspectives on Public Bureaucracy,* edited by Fred A. Kramer, 185–99. Cambridge, MA: Winthrop Publishers.

Goleman, D. 1995. *Emotional Intelligence.* New York, NY: Basic Books.

Goleman, D., R. Boyatzis, and A. McKee, A. 2002. "The Emotional Reality of Teams." *Journal of Organizational Excellence* 21 (2): 55–65. https://doi.org/10.1002/npr.10020.

Guy, Mary E., and Hyun Jung Lee. 2015. "How Emotional Intelligence Mediates Emotional Labor in Public Service Jobs." *Review of Public Personnel Administration* 35 (3): 261–77. https://doi.org/10.1177/0734371X13514095.

Guy, Mary E., and Robert E. McCarter. 1978. "A Scale to Measure Emotive Imagery." *Perceptual and Motor Skills* 46 (3_suppl): 1267–74. https://doi.org/10.2466/pms.1978.46.3c.1267.

Guy, Mary E., Meredith A. Newman, and Sharon H. Mastracci. 2008. *Emotional Labor: Putting the Service in Public Service.* Armonk, NY: M.E. Sharpe.

Heady, Ferrel. 2001. *Public Administration: A Comparative Perspective.* 6th ed. New York, NY: Marcel Dekker.

Hochschild, Arlie. 1983. *The Managed Heart: Commercialization of Human Feeling.* Berkeley, CA: University of California Press.

Hofstede, Geert, Gert Jan Hofstede, and Michael Minkov. 2010. *Cultures and Organizations: Software of the Mind.* New York, NY: McGraw Hill.

Hsieh, Chih-Wei, Kaifeng Yang, and K.-J. Fu. 2011. "Motivational Bases and Emotional Labor: Assessing the Impact of Public Service Motivation." *Public Administration Review* 72: 241–51.

Hsieh, Chih-Wei, and Mary E. Guy. 2009. "Performance Outcomes: The Relationship Between Managing the 'Heart' and Managing Client Satisfaction." *Review of Public Personnel Administration* 29 (1): 41–57.

Hsieh, Chih-Wei., Myung Jin, and Mary E. Guy. 2012. "Managing Work-Related Emotions: Analysis of a Cross Section of Public Service Workers." *The American Review of Public Administration* 42 (1): 39–53. https://doi.org/10.1177/0275074010396078.

Jin, Myung, and Mary E. Guy. 2009. "The Connection Between Performance Management and Emotional Labor: An Examination of Consumer Complaint Workers." *Public Performance & Management Review* 33 (1): 83–105.

Klingner, Donald E. 2015. "From Local to Global." In *Public Administration Evolving: From Foundations to the Future*, edited by Mary E. Guy and Marilyn M. Rubin, 64–82. New York, NY: Routledge.

Krumhuber, E., A. S. Manstead, D. Cosker, D. Marshall, P. L. Rosin, and A. Kappas. 2007. "Facial Dynamics as Indicators of Trustworthiness and Cooperative Behavior." *Emotion* 7 (4): 730–35. https://doi.org/10.1037/1528-3542.7.4.730.

Lasswell, Harold D. 1951. "The Policy Orientation." In *The Policy Sciences: Recent Developments in Scope and Method*, edited by Daniel Lerner and Harold D. Lasswell, 3–15. Stanford, CA: Stanford University Press.

Lu, Xiaojun, and Mary E. Guy. 2014. "How Emotional Labor and Ethical Leadership Affect Job Engagement for Chinese Public Servants." *Public Personnel Management* 43(1): 3–24. https://doi.org/10.1177/0091026013512278.

Lu, Xiaojun, and Mary E. Guy. 2018. "Political Skill, Organizational Justice and Career Success in Mainland China." *International Review of Administrative Sciences* 84 (2): 371–88. https://doi.org/10.1177/0020852315619025.

Lu, Xiaojun, and Mary E. Guy. 2019. "Emotional Labor, Performance Goal Orientation, and Burnout from the Perspective of Conservation of Resources: A U.S./China Comparison." *Public Performance & Management Review* 42 (3): 685–706. https://doi.org/10.1080/15309576.2018.1507916.

Mai, X., Y. Ge, L. Tao, H. Tang, C. Liu, Y.-J. Luo. 2011. "Eyes Are Windows to the Chinese Soul: Evidence from the Detection of Real and Fake Smiles. *PLoS One* 6 (5): e19903. https://doi.org/10.1371/journal.pone.0019903.

Mastracci, Sharon H., Mary E. Guy, and Meredith A. Newman. 2012. *Emotional Labor and Crisis Response: Working on the Razor's Edge.* Armonk, NY: M.E. Sharpe.

Mayer, J. D., M. T. DiPaolo, and P. Salovey. 1990. "Perceiving Affective Content in Ambiguous Visual Stimuli: A Component of Emotional Intelligence." *Journal of Personality Assessment* 54 (3–4): 772–81.

Mayer, J. D., and P. Salovey. 1997. "What Is Emotional Intelligence?" In *Emotional Development and Emotional Intelligence: Educational Implications*, edited by P. Salovey and D. Sluyter, 3–31. New York, NY: Basic Books.

Mayer, J. D., P. Salovey, and D. R. Caruso. 2008. "Emotional Intelligence: New Ability or Eclectic Traits?" *American Psychologist* 63 (6): 503–17.

Maynard-Moody, Steven, and Michael Musheno. 2003. *Cops, Teachers, Counselors: Stories from the Front Lines of Public Service.* Ann Arbor, MI: University of Michigan Press.

Merit Systems Protection Board (MSPB). 2017. "Understanding the Effect of Emotional Exhaustion on Employees' Intent to Leave." *Issues of Merit* (Spring):

4–5. Available from U.S. Merit Systems Protection Board, 1615 M Street, NW, Washington, DC 20419.

Mumby, D., and L. Putnam. 1992. "The Politics of Emotion: A Feminist Reading of Bounded Rationality." *Academy of Management Review* 17 (3): 465–86. https://doi.org/10.5465/amr.1992.4281983.

Newman, Meredith A., Mary E. Guy, and Sharon H. Mastracci. 2009. "Beyond Cognition: Affective Leadership and Emotional Labor." *Public Administration Review* 69 (1): 6–20. https://doi.org/10.1111/j.1540-6210.2008.01935.x.

O'Leary, Rosemary, Y. Choi, and C. M. Gerard. 2012. "The Skill Set of the Successful Collaborator." *Public Administration Review* 72 (51): S70–S83.

Osborne, David, and Ted Gaebler. 1992. *Reinventing Government: How the Entrepreneurial Spirit Is Transforming the Public Sector.* Reading, MA: Addison-Wesley.

Rayner, Julie, and Alan Lawton. 2018. "Are We Being Served? Emotional Labour in Local Government in Victoria, Australia." *Australian Journal of Public Administration* 77 (3): 360–74. https://doi.org/10.1111/1467-8500.12282.

Rifkin, Jeremy. 2009. *The Empathic Civilization: The Race to Global Consciousness in a World in Crisis.* New York: Tarcher.

Riggs, Fred W. 1991. "Public Administration: A Comparative Framework." *Public Administration Review* 51 (6): 473–77.

Salovey, P., and J. D. Mayer. 1990. "Emotional Intelligence." *Imagination, Cognition, and Personality* 9 (3): 185–211. https://doi.org/10.2190/dugg-p24e-52wk-6cdg.

Simon, Herbert A. 1947/1997. *Administrative Behavior: A Study of Decision-Making Processes in Administrative Organizations.* 4th ed. New York, NY: Free Press.

Sloan, M. M. 2014. "The Consequences of Emotional Labor for Public Sector Workers and the Mitigating Role of Self-Efficacy." *The American Review of Public Administration* 44 (3): 274–90. http://dx.doi.org/10.1177/0275074012462864.

Slote, Michael. 2007. *The Ethics of Care and Empathy.* London, UK: Routledge.

Taylor, Frederick W. 1911. *The Principles of Scientific Management.* New York, NY: Harper & Brothers.

Tomkins, Silvan S., and Robert McCarter. 1964. "What and Where Are the Primary Affects? Some Evidence for a Theory." *Perceptual and Motor Skills* 18 (1):119–58. https://doi.org/10.2466/pms.

Van Wart, Montgomery. 2010. "Two Approaches to Leadership Studies." *Public Administration Review* 70 (4): 650–53.

Vigoda-Gadot, E., and G. Meisler. 2010. "Emotions in Management and the Management of Emotions: The Impact of Emotional Intelligence and Organizational Politics on Public Sector Employees." *Public Administration Review* 70 (1): 72–86. https://doi.org/10.1111/j.1540-6210.2009.02112.x.

Weber, Max. 1946. *From Max Weber: Essays in Sociology.* Translated by H. H. Gerth and C. Wright Mills. New York, NY: Oxford University Press.

Wilson, Woodrow W. 1887. "Study of Administration." *Political Science Quarterly* 2 (June): 197–222.
Wright, B. E., Don P. Moynihan, and Sanjay K. Pandey. 2012. "Pulling the Levers: Transformational Leadership, Public Service Motivation, and Mission Valence." *Public Administration Review* 72 (2): 206–15. https://doi.org/10.1111/j.1540-6210.2011.02496.x.
Yang, Seung-Bum, and Mary E. Guy. 2015. "Gender Effects on Emotional Labor in Seoul Metropolitan Area." *Public Personnel Management* 44 (1): 3–24. https://doi.org/10.1177/0091026014550491.
Zimmerman, Ulf. 2011. "Empathy, Ethics, Emotional Labor, and the Ethos of Democracy." *Public Administration Review* 71 (3): 497–501. https://doi.org/10.1111/j.1540-6210.2011.02376.x.

3

Trending Interconnectedness: The Value of Comparative Analysis

Sharon H. Mastracci and Ian Tyler Adams

Global interconnectedness drives the need for richer understanding not only of different nations, but of what is required for international organizations to function well wherever they are sited. Both the home cultures of civil servants and the meta-culture of international public administration are instructive for understanding how "boundary spanning" employees must balance display rules and emotive demands. This chapter touches on several topics, ranging from International Public Administrations (IPAs) and the International Civil Servants (ICSs) they employ, to international policy issues, to ways of thinking about bureaucracy.

IPAs are organizations that implement transnational policies in a range of policy areas, such as peace and security, trade and finance, health and human rights, and poverty and the environment (Busch 2014). Eckhard and Ege note that large IPAs tend to be organized hierarchically according to Weberian organizational principles: "with a given mandate, resources, identifiable boundaries, and a set of formal rules and procedures" (2016, 964). Various terms are used to describe the implementation of policies spanning national boundaries and their agencies, including global public policy,

S. H. Mastracci (✉)
Department of Political Science, University of Utah, Salt Lake City, UT, USA
e-mail: Sharon.mastracci@poli-sci.utah.edu

I. T. Adams
Department of Political Science, University of Utah, Salt Lake City, UT, USA
e-mail: ian.adams@utah.edu

M. E. Guy et al. (eds.), *The Palgrave Handbook of Global Perspectives on Emotional Labor in Public Service*, https://doi.org/10.1007/978-3-030-24823-9_3

global governance, IPAs, and transnational administration (Ege 2017). In this chapter, we use "global administration" to refer to the implementation of policies that transcend political borders and "secretariats" to refer to the agencies engaged in implementation.

Stone and Ladi (2015) identify five types of global administration:

- Administration of policy by formal international organizations such as the World Trade Organization (WTO) or the North Atlantic Treaty Organization (NATO);
- Transnational networks administering policy via informal cooperation between states;
- Distributed administration "when domestic agencies make decisions on issues of global and transnational concern" (847);
- Hybrid intergovernmental-private administration such as the cooperation between the International Olympic Committee and the US Anti-Doping Agency; and
- Administration by private institutions, such as the International Standards Organization (ISO) and FIFA, which are private regulatory bodies.

By any name and in any of its functions, global administration is doing internationally what governments do at home (Finkelstein 1995). IPAs employ ICSs and they engage in administrative functions internationally just as domestic governments do at home. ICSs are the administrators who implement policy and manage relationships across countries. While international organizations have been studied extensively, "little systematic research has so far been done on the personnel working in international organizations" (Hensell 2016, 1487). This gap in knowledge about global administration has substantially limited comparative research into how these workers experience emotional labor.

This chapter proceeds as follows. In the first section, we discuss policy areas that span political boundaries. In the second section, we discuss the implementation of these policies, specifically those who implement global public policies—ICSs and the IPAs that employ them. Display rules in international organizations are then explored. While they are primarily determined by occupation—for example, a certain set of behaviors is expected from nurses regardless of country—culture also affects display rules (Mastracci and Adams, 2019). What can we say about culture's impact on an international organization? At minimum, we can say the display rules governing worker behavior vary by culture (Triandis 2002), and specifically, the manner in which individuals construe themselves in relation to society varies (Eid and Diener 2001). The third section focuses on comparative approaches to how public services are delivered and contrasts classical bureaucracy with market-centered reforms because these approaches differentially affect the emotion work of public servants.

A culture in which the prevailing norms comport with an independent, individual self-construal (individualist cultures) is linked to more effortful and costlier emotional labor compared to a culture in which individual self-construal is interdependent and group oriented (collectivist cultures). Because people who perceive themselves in terms of their communities are accustomed to attuning their outward expressions to coincide with the mood of the group, emotional labor appears to be less laborious to them, compared to those in cultures where people perceive themselves as autonomous, independent individuals. While other dimensions of culture may shape the effects of emotional labor, Hofstede et al.'s (2010) Individualism/Collectivism index has received the most scholarly attention (Taras et al. 2010). In relation to other areas of study, comparative public administration is among the smaller subfields but the reality of an increasingly interconnected public policy landscape has drawn attention to global issues.

The importance of comparative studies cannot be over-emphasized because there is so much yet to be learned about how political dynamics and national culture affect the delivery of public services. How compelling is the collectivism—individualism continuum? What other continua exert forces that affect the public encounter? To these questions, we devote discussion to the influence of neoclassical economic theory, which advocates market-oriented solutions, small government, and service delivery mechanisms that mirror a customer orientation. Popularized in the USA, UK, New Zealand, and South Korea, among others, as New Public Management (NPM), it demands display rules more akin to that which is required in retail sales rather than in the citizen—state encounter that is traditionally the province of government. Interestingly, the paradigm shift toward a market model has varied across countries. These reforms have proven more comprehensive in Australia, New Zealand, and the UK compared to the USA. And different still is the way in which they have manifested in Asian countries (Cheung 2012). The topic is germane to the citizen—state encounter and emotional labor because it converts citizens into consumers, modifying the dynamic between state and citizen.

The Interconnectedness of Nations

The international context is an ever-more salient one for public administration, for both its study and its practice. The rise of truly international organizations like the European Union has brought growth in the personnel who run them. This, in turn, brings the need to understand their job demands, activities, and contributions. Whether as the city manager hosting international delegates or as a civil servant of an international secretariat visiting that city manager, no longer can students or practitioners of public administration remain confident their work will not span international borders, either directly in action, or indirectly in effect. But those involved in global governance—which includes secretariats of international governmental organizations, global non-governmental organizations, global think tanks, multinational corporations, and among others—manage international relationships and implement policy without sovereign authority (Finkelstein 1995). International secretariats operate with power and resources to fulfill their missions, yet are not located in, or drawing from, the legitimacy of a single sovereign nation. Instead, they draw their legitimacy from member-states.

There are over eight hundred international organizations headquartered in 120 countries around the world (Moloney et al. 2018). This organizational form represents a relatively new phenomenon: "Most writings about public administration presuppose the ubiquity of states" (Riggs 2006, 924, emphasis supplied). States have recognized boundaries, histories, and people. International organizations borrow the legitimacy and authority to act from their member states, but themselves are not sovereign entities. The evolution from state actors to multistate actors that possess their own policy mandates is a newish development and an interesting example of states forfeiting even a small part of their own authority to another entity.

"Westphalian sovereignty" remains shorthand for describing the fundamental principles of the modern sovereign state, particularly the first principle that states retain exclusive sovereignty over their territory, which is defined by inviolable borders. Limits to the theory of Westphalian sovereignty are readily apparent. Even in the first decades of the twentieth century, states relied on systems of relationships that transcended sovereign frontiers. It was only after World War I, however, that this space was characterized as something separate: "At the 1919 Paris Peace Conference … global powers for the first time defined 'the international' as a space distinct from the sum total of member states' interests" (Eckhard and Ege 2016, 960).

Sovereignty proved difficult to maintain in a pure form, as states, and the administrations which ran them, only operated successfully to the extent they managed to not only keep their borders intact, but permeable. Permeability arose in the form of an open-systems approach among countries on the European continent with a more closed approach facing outward. The transformation from Westphalian state to international entity complicates the idea of "the public" because supranational agencies have no citizens of their own: "Globalization has erased the boundary between state and non-state actors in ways that confuse our understanding of what is 'public' administration by contrast both with private administration and politics" (Riggs 2006, 953). Roles of private, standards-setting international organizations further complicate what is public about administration and policy.

Meaning-Making Jobs

Most public service delivery does not occur during crises like multinational wars or the European refugee crisis of 2015. Even so, public service is inescapably emotion laden and inherently subjective in how it is experienced by the public. How people *feel* they have been served constitutes as much of the service they receive as their assessment of its quality. Certainly, some public services involve material transactions that can be evaluated objectively as successful or unsuccessful: One either obtains the passport, the building permit, driver's license, housing assistance benefits—or not. But a defining aspect of the process of obtaining a passport, permit, license, or benefits, involves how one feels about the process. Hochschild (1983) characterizes jobs such as these as meaning-making jobs. In public service delivery, citizens want fairness in terms of uniform standards, they want to be treated with respect, and they want help for those in legitimate need. They also expect high customer service standards to be met, in terms of quality of care, friendliness, and explanations from street-level bureaucrats (Rayner and Lawton 2018).

Rayner and Lawton's analysis of citizen expectations of public service delivery is suffused with subjectivity and emotion. Citizens want a sense of fairness, respectful treatment, friendliness, and a sense of personal service that allows the citizen to feel well informed. None of these are easy to measure and all are subject to the interpretation of the citizen and her or his emotions resulting from an encounter with government. A substantial part of the public servant's job is to convince the "citizen-cum-consumer"

(Lauer 2008, 45) that processes are fair, service is of high quality, citizens are well informed and they are treated with respect. The means by which that job is done is emotional labor, which is the effort to suppress inappropriate emotions and/or elicit appropriate emotions within oneself or in another person, where "appropriate" and "inappropriate" are dictated by the demands and expectations of the job.

New research shows that, in addition to demands of the occupation, cultural context also shapes these expectations (Mastracci and Adams, 2019). Occupational "display rules" are the (often unwritten) rules governing a worker's emotive expressions, or in many cases, suppression, of those responses that are deemed "unprofessional." For example, emergency responders must tune out the chaos, engage fully with the victim, and attend to the crisis at hand. Similarly, police officers cannot show fear to suspects or boredom to a public that needs their vigilance, else they risk public safety and their own. Social workers cannot cry or show irritation in front of their clients lest they risk being perceived as "too close" to the problem and lacking the professional distance necessary to help the client.

Different jobs and professions use different strategies of emotion management to navigate display rules. Adhering to display rules contributes substantially to the perception of professionalism and good service. This is what Hochschild (1983) emphasizes in her discussion of service-sector jobs as meaning-making jobs. One's feelings about the interaction is part of service delivery in the private sector, and the same can be said in public service. But the public-sector context is unique in that government is often the provider of last resort, or only resort, during times of crisis, and the meanings made via interactions during emergency situations are inherently different from meanings made through transactions in commercial exchanges (Mastracci et al. 2012).

The public sector is a unique context because oftentimes it is government alone that responds in times of crisis and these are fraught with emotion and immediacy. Context shapes the behavior of public servants because it affects display rules, which in turn, affect employee behaviors. John Gaus suggested as much when discussing what he referred to broadly as "the environment" and how it shapes the conduct of public servants:

> As Gaus posited, the political environment was a key variable in the determination of bureaucratic conduct … the people, place, physical and social technology, and culture determined the ebb and flow of the functions of government … environments include relationships between administrators and

political leaders, negotiations and transactions with other political units, and links with public groups. (Gaus as cited in Otenyo and Lind 2006, 2–3)

As the next section demonstrates, and as we argue throughout, the environment for public servants in any country is increasingly a global one. We base this argument, in part, on the case made by comparativist Jamil Jreisat, who observes that the environment of public administration has expanded to include contextual influences that stem from rapid globalization and the progressive universalization of administrative theory and practice (2014, 22).

Local policies attempt to address global issues. For example, cities in the USA adopt sanctuary policies and gun-control policies that contradict national-level policy. Madrid limits driving in parts of the city and at certain times of the day to improve its air quality. Migration policies are not implemented only at the national level: Nearly 100 sanctuary cities exist in the UK and the Republic of Ireland, and more than 500 states and cities in the USA have sanctuary city status. These examples demonstrate that urban sanctuary policies and practices challenge the national policies and practices that regulate migration and belonging (Bauder 2017, 175). In this way, North American and European cities implement their own migration policies. They both affect, and are affected by, immigration policies of national governments.

Understanding the unique aspects of comparative public administration is important because events that cross political borders and the policies that respond to them, such as refugee crises and climate change, lead to the growing interconnectedness of sovereign nations. Implementation of policies to address regional and global problems involves international governing organizations and the ICSs they employ. Working across national and cultural boundaries demands a different kind of training to serve diverse constituencies and the international organizations that employ public servants from many countries and cultures. We elaborate on some of the reasons why.

Global Public Policy: Issues that Cross Borders

"Kunie! Kenite [*sic*]!" the coast guard shouts to a confused face … "Kunie! Don't you speak Arabic? Aren't you supposed to be Syrian?" he asks in Greek. "Family name!" The coast guard carries on several times in English and receives no answer whatsoever. The officer gets more and more irritated and desperate …. Finally, somebody from the crowd translates the word into Arabic, and then the coast guard gets the answer he was looking for. "Hussain" he types with Latin characters in an Excel spreadsheet. In this tense atmosphere of incessant yelling, the officer requests the rest of the information needed in electronic form … most of the approximately two thousand people that the two shifts of coast guards will deal with today do not have passports and do not speak English. (Rozakou 2017, 36–37)

The above exchange took place in late 2015 on the Greek island of Lesvos, the "front line of the refugee crisis" (Papataxiarchis 2016, 5). That year, more than half a million refugees arrived on this island of fewer than 100,000 people (Rozakou 2017). During the crisis, nearly three in four refugees disembarked at Lesvos (Chatzea et al. 2018). This vignette is shared to convey the frustration encountered in cross-cultural interactions and also the sheer scale of demand for public services in times of crisis. This cross-cultural interaction took place two thousand times *each day* in a *single* reception zone in just *one* of the humanitarian crises facing governments across the world.

In this section, we discuss several areas where policy development, implementation, and evaluation can scarcely be done without regard for other countries: "The pathologies of climate change and environmental pollution, man-made disasters, economic instability, pandemics, international terrorism and organized crime, among others, show little respect for borders" (LeGrand 2015, 975). The list of topics covered in this chapter is not exhaustive and need not be to underscore the importance of public problems that transcend borders and the boundary-spanning nature of the policies crafted to address them. The opening vignette illustrates the global nature of migration. Other fundamentally global issues include climate change, poverty, regulatory policy, public health, international trade, and space exploration, all of which obviate a closed-system policy approach.

An "open systems" policy context has prevailed since the fall of mercantilism as a guiding philosophy for economic policy in industrialized nations (O'Leary 2014). Policy outputs to address supranational problems demand a different implementation approach: "Consider examples such as terrorism, natural disasters, epidemics, energy, wars, and many other big problems. They all have aspects of networks, collaboration, conflict, implementation, and international leadership. Public administration—the management of public policy—matters" (Kim et al. 2014, 205). Supranational policy problems demand public administrators who are able to span professional, organizational, and national boundaries (Bauer 2012; Broome and Seabrooke 2015; Needham et al. 2017).

The European refugee crisis was prompted by, among myriad conflicts, protracted civil wars in Libya, Iraq, Afghanistan, and Syria. "Sea arrivals of refugees and migrants peaked in 2015 when more than a million desperate people crossed the Mediterranean to Europe and almost 5000 died trying to make it … arrivals are back at pre-2014 levels and are dropping towards their long-term historic averages" (UNHCR 2018, para. 6). While the waves of Syrian refugees—the largest group—have dissipated, new crises sustain demand for public services. Of more than 68.5 million refugees in 2017, more than a third fled their countries to escape conflict and persecution. "Leading the displacement during the year was the crisis in the Democratic Republic of the Congo, the war in South Sudan and the flight into Bangladesh from Myanmar of hundreds of thousands of Rohingya refugees" (Edwards 2018, para. 4).

Just as one crisis abates, another erupts somewhere else in the world. International organizations respond and that work demands emotional labor. Rescue workers encounter seriously injured or the dead, witness the impassioned reactions of devastated survivors (distress, grief, and anger), experience disappointment when unsuccessful in saving a life, and expose themselves to potential physical harm. The emotion management required of ICSs—even if they are not among the volunteers greeting refugees at national borders—often leads to psychological distress because the stakes are so high (Mao et al. 2018). New crises force people to flee conflict across the globe, forcing nations to either collaborate on solutions or face the resulting simultaneous hyper-local and supranational effects of ignoring global problems. For example, in 2018, more than 600 migrants—about a quarter of whom were from Sudan—"had been rescued from flimsy smugglers' boats in the Mediterranean during a series of operations … [and then] were offloaded to the *Aquarius* to be taken to land" (Winfield and Parra 2018, para. 8). After being denied access to ports in Italy and Malta, the *Aquarius* was offered port in Spain. The case of the *Aquarius* refugee ship brought together civil servants from three countries and many of the refugees sought asylum in yet another country, France (Duncan 2018).

Other supranational challenges demanding supranational policy prescriptions include space exploration, climate change, poverty, and public health. The International Space Station (ISS) was an early example of an open-system, cross-border initiative that required policy frameworks that allowed program administrators to operate successfully in an international context. No longer an American pursuit alone, the ISS was successful because advocates from within and outside individual countries' space agencies were brought together to establish a flagship for human space flight. "Not to be part of this project was to be left behind" (Lambright 2014, 29). Administrators from member nations' space agencies persuaded their own governments to contribute resources to build this flagship space station.

Climate change demands an open-systems approach as well, but in contrast to the multinational efforts to build a space station, climate change thus far has lacked an organizational center or collaborative body to shape and implement policy. Kütting and Cerny (2015, 916) observe: "The lack of representation of a virtual, supra-political 'actor'—a sort of metagovernance of 'nature' or the 'planet'—is perhaps the biggest challenge." Treaties using United Nations policy frameworks have attempted to take the place of a supranational actor. For instance, the Kyoto Protocol is an international agreement that extends the UN Framework Convention on Climate Change and commits state signers to reduce greenhouse gas emissions. Many signatories—African, Asian, and South American countries—have ratified the Kyoto Protocol but have not established binding target rates of greenhouse gas emissions, and the USA has not ratified this treaty. In another example, even when the parties involved are known, effects of environmental disasters extend beyond these initial parties and continue long after the crisis ended. Deepwater Horizon was an oil-drilling platform operated by British Petroleum that exploded in US waters. The Deepwater Horizon accident spilled oil into the Gulf of Mexico for four months in 2010 (Lodge 2014). Studies showed the effects of the spill followed sea turtles across the Atlantic. Contamination is traced to dozens of countries years later, as far away as Cape Town, South Africa (Putman et al. 2015).

Poverty eradication, another global challenge, is a goal of the Organization for Economic Cooperation and Development (OECD), an international governing agency. The Framework Convention for Tobacco Control (FCTC) is part of a set of policies to address public health on a global scale. The FCTC monitors implementation of WHO policy and disseminates information on best practices to countries that have identified tobacco use as an urgent public health problem (Mamudu et al. 2015, 870). Drug trafficking has proven to be a bigger challenge than any single country can address alone. In reaction to individual nations' failed drug policies, the Global Commission on Drug Policy (GCDP) is a supranational secretariat created in reaction to a failed war on drugs by countries acting largely independently (Alimi 2015). None of these secretariats have police powers or the resources to compel countries to comply with their policy recommendations, however.

While space exploration, climate change, poverty, and public health have clear multinational implications, the decisions of individual nations in other policy areas span political borders as well, including trade, industry regulation, and tax policy. Multinational corporations offer services to clients worldwide including management consulting, legal, and accounting (Heidbreder 2015, 945). The 2008 financial crisis in the USA quickly spread to other countries because regulations in one country affected the behavior of firms doing business in other countries. Behavior changes that affected those countries' economies can be characterized this way (Lodge 2014, 99):

> The collapse of various private financial institutions highlighted how much-celebrated regulatory organizations and instruments had failed to foresee or, at least, mitigate the problems affecting financial institutions in light of over-extension in particular markets … the financial crisis highlighted the inherent interdependency of regulatory activities, with national regulatory decisions in one country having effects on economics elsewhere as internationally operating banks retreated to their national markets in order to comply with strengthened regulatory requirements.

Economic interdependency predates the global recession and economic interdependency remains today in both tax and trade policy. A benefit to being a European Union member nation is that it removes internal borders to facilitate trade and travel. However, sales tax remains a country-by-country issue. This means value added tax (VAT) collection in cross-border trade is an administrative challenge because of the abolition of border controls while leaving VAT administration under national authority (Heidbreder 2015). Tax policy constantly changes and as Internet shopping has grown exponentially, so has global interdependency. Multilateral agreements to support the free movement of goods and services include the EU—one of the three largest economies on the globe—and also NAFTA, the Greater Arab Free Trade Area (GAFTA), the African Continental Free Trade Area, and the WTO. Only a handful of all 195 countries worldwide are *not* part of a multinational trade compact. This section discussed only a few policy areas that transcend national borders. Who implements these global public policies, and where do they work? Many of these policies are implemented by ICSs working in international secretariats. It is to these organizations and civil servants that we now turn.

Emotional Labor in International Organizations

We now turn toward a discussion of ICSs, for to understand emotional labor in multinational organizations, we must understand the display rules faced by the those who work in them. "With the rise of this new 'governance architecture' and its associated bureaucracies, there is a new crop of global public professionals—largely hidden from public view—working to formulate and implement public policy in a trans-national context" (Kim et al. 2014, xiii). One example is the European Commission, which arose post-World War II, and is the civil service of the European Union (EU) (Spence 2012). Staff members come from twenty-eight countries and, as a result of their different national and cultural traditions, they have different educational backgrounds, distinct professional experiences, and diverse administrative styles (Hensell 2016). Most of the more than 40,000 EU staff work in Brussels or Luxemburg. Another supranational entity is the United Nations (UN), headquartered in New York City. The scope of international interests addressed by the UN Secretariat is vast and includes peace and security, economic and social development, environment and sustainability, refugee protection, disarmament and non-proliferation, and human rights. The United Nations Secretariat is just one of many IPAs, and the UN and EU are among the largest (Busch 2014).

Growing international interconnectedness develops through interpersonal relationships among ICSs working in these multinational organizations. In his analysis of the ISS, Lambright (2014) credits the power of individuals in multinational organizations for sustaining the agenda and keeping the organization on target. In the case of the space station, institutionalization of norms and commitment of founding members ensured the success of the project, even as new staff replaced the founders. While interconnectedness on successful projects such as this foster growth in all member nations, interpersonal relationships can also magnify the effects of failures: "One of the key reasons for the depth of the most recent international financial crisis [was] the phenomenon of 'revolving doors' between bankers, economists, and academia" (Seabrooke 2014, 337).

Display Rules in International Organizations

International civil servants embody the missions of international organizations and are their face. As such, they are subject to professional and organizational display rules. Display rules are regulations—sometimes explicit, but more often implicit and unwritten—governing a worker's observed affect, or outward expression (Grandey 2003). Different professions use different emotion management strategies to navigate display rules (Carlson et al. 2012; Steinberg and Figart 1999). Strategies of emotion management in the service of conforming to professional display rules are emotional labor.

Display rules proscribing negative emotive expression (as compared with prescribing positive emotive expression or neutrality) are positively related to burnout in civil servants, specifically law enforcement (Van Gelderen et al. 2011). As members of organizations, there is no reason to expect ICSs to be free from organizational display rules; they are part of organizational culture (Martin 1992; McLaren 1997).

If display rules are shaped by environment or culture, then what is the culture of an international organization and what might be the nature of its display rules? In David Spence's (2012) examination of a newly-formed, 5000-employee European External Action Service (EEAS), he describes the need for staffers to "accept the premises of the Euro-diplomatic mindset" (122) and establish "a streamlined corps of diplomats with new horizons, shared methods, and interests all 'singing from the same hymn sheet'" (123). The challenge was to shift EEAS staff perspectives away from the interests of their individual countries to a European point of view: "Constitutional rules and house rules create clear expectations—norms—that are expressly designed to guide Commission officials, whether as political appointees or as permanent career officials" (Hooghe 2005, 863). Spence underscores the novelty of the experiment, whose goal is to create a European mind-set that operates at the same level and shoulder-to-shoulder alongside diplomats from different nations.

Loyalty, identification with, and commitment to, a multinational European outlook rather than a nationalist outlook is crucial to cultivate and sustain among EU diplomats. Regularly monitoring for the right frame of mind is necessary because divergences in mind-sets may prove hurtful to the organization (Spence 2012). To foster development of such a mind-set, the European Union founding documents (see European Union 2015) mirror the UN Charter (Juncos and Pomorska 2013). To achieve no less than "a just and peaceful world" UN civil servants must uphold the principles of "competence, integrity, impartiality, independence and discretion … peace, respect for fundamental rights, economic and social progress, and international cooperation. It is therefore incumbent on ICSs to adhere to the highest standards of conduct; for, ultimately, it is the international civil service that will enable the United Nations system to bring about a just and peaceful world" (International Civil Service Advisory Board 2002, 2). These norms imply clear display rules for ICSs. Ziring, Riggs, and Plano underscore the complex dynamics of organizational culture in international organizations and the importance of these dynamics beyond just shaping display rules (2005, 101):

One obvious challenge is to integrate within a single administrative machine
the diverse attitudes, tongues, backgrounds, and abilities of personnel
recruited from the four corners of the earth ... With no shared global political culture, the secretariat lacks both the guidelines that would make its own
choice of actions easier and the legitimacy that would make its functions
acceptable to its clientele.

Barnett and Finnemore (1999) complicate the issue of display rules further by underscoring the important role of professions in dictating incumbents' behavior. Professional training involves norms and display rules and
the education one receives to become an attorney, accountant, nurse, and
systems analyst—even a public administration generalist—involves its own
display rules. These rules risk supplanting the organizational identity of an
international organization if, as in the early days of the EU, an organizational identity resists definition. Human resource management practices can
play an important role in overcoming this problem by developing an organizational identity. Staff training and organizational team building events reinforce display rules (Spence 2012, 133):

If support for policy positions rests upon institutional affiliation or the actors'
mind sets, there is a clear need for posts to go to officials with the 'right' mind
set. Intense training, accompanied by retreats and other devices, can reverse
the signs of regression ... The existence of various mind sets is an issue that
dare not speak its name, so it is difficult to imagine how the issue can be successfully addressed at the political level. Yet it is the key to sensible human
resource management.

Suvarierol (2008) similarly reveals a very strong identification with one's
profession among ICSs in the European Commission, which can hinder the
creation and establishment of organizational identity. Suvarierol finds that
the diverse cultural backgrounds of officials in IPA may create a barrier to
developing an organizational culture. To address this, one scholarly perspective posits that organizational culture and display rules of international
organizations are shaped in the image of Weberian bureaucracy.

McLaren argues that bureaucratic operational processes eclipse national
influences to create organizational culture. Weberian bureaucracy "has now
become a universal, a well-established means for doing the work of an international organization no matter from what country one comes" (1997, 61).
Bureaucratic processes are learned in educational institutions: "It scarcely
matters that the modern university world is a western-developed set of disci-
plines ... the modern university prepares people to follow a logical, rational

approach to operations, whatever the field may be" (McLaren 1997, 61). Whether it is Weberian notions of how bureaucracies are how to function, or alternate visions, norms are learned at university, and universities are institutions created to advance sanctioned understandings. For example, OECD uses budget support as a policy tool to mitigate global poverty. Budget support focuses on reforming a country's managerial and administrative apparatuses rather than focusing on economic development goals (Wolff 2015). It is an arbitrary approach but one thought "normal" within OECD.

Weberian principles are also found in the UN Charter, Articles 100 and 101, which defines the occupation of ICS: "The paramount consideration in the employment of the staff and in the determination of the conditions of service shall be the necessity of securing the highest standards of *efficiency, competence, and integrity*" (United Nations 1945, Article 101, para. 3, emphasis supplied). Crucially, the constitution of the European Commission also uses this language to shape and define its civil service. Behavior that conveys these standards is endorsed by these display rules, which are rooted in best practices of Weberian bureaucracy. Monitoring for this behavior becomes the business of human resource managers.

Staff Impartiality and Display Rules

Westphalian (sovereign) states give over a portion of their power and legitimacy to international organizations because those organizations position themselves as serving the whole. The power and legitimacy of international organizations derive from the perception that they are impersonal, technocratic, and neutral (Barnett and Finnemore 1999). Creating and sustaining the perception that they are in the service of a mission and not exercising power for themselves are essential to their authority. Those who work in these transnational agencies uphold and sustain the perception that their agencies are other-oriented. One means by which ICSs do this is through the separation of their professional and personal selves, as Weber prescribed: "The modern organization of the civil service separates the bureau from the private domicile of the official, and, in general, segregates official activity from the sphere of private life … the more consistently the modern type of business management has been carried through, the more are these separations the case" (Weber 1921/1968, 957). Consistent management is delivered without affect, without emotion, according to this oft-cited passage: "Bureaucracy develops the more perfectly, the more it is 'dehumanized', the more completely it succeeds in eliminating from official business love, hatred, and all purely personal, irrational, and emotional elements which escape calculation" (Weber 1921/1968, 975). Weber is very clear on these display rules: The bureaucrat is to separate his personal and professional lives and to conduct his professional affairs without observable emotional expression. And Weber clearly intends his advice to dictate individual conduct: "The rule and the rational pursuit of 'objective' purposes, as well as devotion to these, would always constitute the *norm of conduct*" (Weber 1921/1968, 979, emphasis supplied). Moreover, expertise is objectively real and separable from the individual: "The more complicated and specialized modern culture becomes, the more its external supporting apparatus demands the personally detached and strictly objective *expert*" (Weber 1921/1968, 975, emphasis original). Weberian bureaucracy is rightly credited with improving administration by emphasizing rule-based, predictable processes and proscribing capricious decision-making and favoritism. Similarly, those who work in international organizations are expected to practice and display impartiality, being loyal to the IO, not to their home-state or the state where their work is located. Impartiality and neutrality require similar emotive displays, and there are pitfalls.

While neutrality is a clear display rule for UN officials, there have been international crises in which neutrality and the desire and need to provide humanitarian assistance come into conflict (Barnett and Finnemore 1999, 724–25):

> Bosnia is the classic case in point. On the one hand, the 'all necessary means' provision of Security Council resolutions gave the UN authority to deliver humanitarian aid and protect civilians in safe havens. On the other hand, the UN abstained from 'taking sides' because of the fear that such action would compromise its neutrality and future effectiveness. The result of these conflicts was a string of contradictory policies that failed to provide adequately for the UN's expanding humanitarian charges.

Moreover, neutral, objective, Weberian bureaucracy may backfire in a culture unlike the Western tradition in which it was founded. As Chapter 12 in this book explains about India, there is a mismatch between its bureaucracy and the needs of the nation. An overview of the mismatch is provided by La Palombara (2006, 201–202):

> In a place like India, public administrators steeped in the tradition of the Indian Civil Service may be less useful as developmental entrepreneurs than those who are not so rigidly tied to notions of bureaucratic status, hierarchy,

and impartiality. The economic development of a society … requires a breed of bureaucrats different (e.g.: more free-wheeling, less adhering to administrative forms, less attached to the importance of hierarchy and seniority) from the type of man who is useful when the primary concern of the bureaucracy is the maintenance of law and order.

Whatever the bureaucratic model is, whether Weberian or market-based, or some other combination, it drives rules for appropriate workplace behavior. For example, the reification of the market under NPM as a public management strategy aligns display rules in the public sector with those of the private sector in which customer responsiveness is of prime importance. Discussion turns to this because, just as Weberian notions of bureaucracy prevail in some governments, so also does this public management strategy. And, in some countries, the public service context reflects a mix of traditional culture and bureaucratic processes overlaid with (or without) the pursuit of market principles. These are not the only models in the countries surveyed, but they provide an example of the complicated contextual frames that are useful for analyzing the data and interpreting the confluence of forces that public service professionals are called upon to balance.

Comparative Public Administration

Comparative public administration examines how and why governance differs across countries (Fitzpatrick et al. 2011; Van Wart and Cayer 1990). Organizational performance research has always followed a comparative logic by borrowing best practices and by identifying lessons learned from other contexts in order to improve performance (Jresiat 2005, 2014). However, the best comparative research accepts the fact that best practices from one setting may not work well elsewhere (Fitzpatrick et al. 2011). "Unfortunately," laments one of the earliest comparativist scholars in public administration, Fred Riggs, "most of the American literature in Political Science and Public Administration is premised on the historical experience of the United States, and the word 'comparative' is really used to refer to studies based on experience elsewhere in the world" (2006, 928). Global conflicts have reinforced the consequences of parochialism. As discussed earlier, post-World War I peace negotiations culminated in the delineation of an "international" sphere separate from any individual country, and it was World War II that catalyzed comparative research in public administration: "Comparative public administration emerged out of post-World War

II efforts to find better global development strategies. Its early practitioners worked to define the field, develop general theory, set a research agenda, and generalize 'lessons learned'" (Fitzpatrick et al. 2011, 822).

Early development administration sought to extend the traditional, Weberian bureaucratic model of public administration to other nations (Gulrajani and Moloney 2012). During the immediate postwar period at the dawn of early development administration, Robert Dahl is skeptical of extending Weberian principles to other countries. He says: "There should be no reason for supposing, then, that a principle of public administration has equal validity in every nation-state, or that successful public administration practices in one country will necessarily prove successful in a different social, economic, and political environment" (1947, 8). La Palombara (2006) is similarly skeptical of civil service reforms: "It is far from obvious that the bureaucracies of the new states should uncritically adopt American principles of scientific management. [For example] the introduction of an egalitarian system of recruitment in a highly status-conscious society would serve to reduce the status of public servants" (208). Cultural context implies particularism in public management and public service delivery. Each culture captures particularities in practice and outcomes (Fitzpatrick et al. 2011, 828):

> Ignoring cultural norms, values, and traditions leads to misinterpretation of findings. Interventions or administrative innovations may be viewed as ineffective because of the nature of the intervention itself, rather than because of cultural norms that influence the implementation or impact of the innovation.

In the developed world, traditional Weberian bureaucracy gave way to neoclassical economic theory with market-focused NPM reforms as a primary example. Regardless of the paradigm—Weberian bureaucracy or market-focused initiatives—both ignore the affective aspects of public service delivery and the latter reduce the citizen–state encounter to a buyer–seller relationship.

New Public Management reforms introduced competitive-market dynamics, emphasizing the citizen as customer alongside a customer-service ethos. This may exacerbate emotional labor demands in public services (Thomas 2013). By mimicking private sector service delivery, public sector workers experience the emotional labor of "customer service" transactions similar to their counterparts in retail sales. But this emotive burden is compounded by obligations and constraints that accompany the state–citizen relationship. When public service workers are assessed on customer satisfaction, and customer satisfaction derives from how a citizen perceives her or his interpersonal interaction with public servants (Gore 1993), marketized expectations increase the emotional labor demands upon public servants beyond what has been established already (Guy et al. 2008). Greater emphasis on running government like a business allows us to invoke theories of emotional labor generated from research on retail trade (Johnston and Sandberg 2008). But it is more accurate to move past the private sector and focus solely on the public sector context.

By the turn of the twenty-first century, the adoption of market-like principles in public management legitimized the Weberian concentration on efficiency (though defining it quite differently), while simultaneously pushing back on the lack of "customer service" that resulted from the unfeeling-née-neutral nature of public service in the Weberian model. As the lodestar, efficiency allocates according to price, just as in the private market. Because a marketized approach to public management is a reaction against Weberian bureaucracy, it emphasizes outputs instead of process. It is useful to examine the effect that such reforms have on display rules. A customer-service orientation assumes that citizen/customers express their preferences through their choices in the marketplace of services (Gray and Jenkins 2006).

Where Weberian bureaucracy attempts to rationalize processes by being neutral and formal regardless of cultural context, marketized reforms reflect local culture. The ultimate assessment of organizational performance is how the citizen/customer *feels* about the service she or he has received and how that sentiment is expressed in customer satisfaction feedback. The NPM philosophy, for example, "arose from the conviction that bureaucracy was broken and needed fixing, and that private sector solutions were the key … it promises to provide the 'Big Answer' to real and imagined shortcomings in public bureaucracy" (Savioe 2006, 593–94). Such reforms dispense with the concept of "The Public Good" by decentralizing government and empowering citizens to articulate their own individual sense of "The Good." By mimicking private sector allocation mechanisms, it is assumed that public opinion surveys and citizen satisfaction surveys are as accurate as purchasing decisions are in the private sector.

Reforms that favor buyer–seller dynamics reflect and require a commitment to the superiority of the market over government. They also reflect a belief that competition between the public and private sectors makes service delivery more efficient by making the state more responsive to the customer (Vickers and Kouzmin 2001). Lynn questions whether this calculation is too simplistic, reiterating the differences between public and private: "Americans view themselves as customers of government rather than as citizens … customers can compel responses to their wishes by insisting on receiving value for what they pay or shopping elsewhere" (Lynn 2006, 575). How feasible is it to shop for public services elsewhere? Where else? The citizen-cum-consumer operating assumption of NPM "raises issues of inequality, oversimplification, and a lack of commitment to the public interest" (Rayner and Lawton 2018, 362). Indeed, NPM also assumes a society comprised of people with individualistic self-construal and a public-choice version of The Public Good as the sum of individual choices. In addition, Savoie's (2006) critique of NPM revisits the important role of feelings to organizational success:

> The success of a business executive is much easier to assess than that of a government manager. There is also much less fuss over due process in the private sector than in government, if only because of the difference involved in managing private and public money. It is rarely simple and straightforward in governing where goals are rarely clear … *one person's red tape is another's due process.* (Savoie 2006, 597–98, emphasis supplied)

While Weberian bureaucracy prizes neutrality and objectivity as display rules, NPM prizes the importance of being responsive to the citizen/customer's needs, just as in business transactions. Under this aegis, Weberian processes and routines and codes of conduct are treated like costs and not benefits. Efficiency and responsiveness are valued over accountability and due process (Gray and Jenkins 2006). Key features of public management reforms focus on outputs and ends rather than inputs and means. Organizations are reframed as a series of exchange relationships, not interdependencies (Miller et al. 2006). Large organizations are disaggregated into functions. Competition empowers service users to vote with their feet, exercise choice, and discipline service providers through consumer demand. But in most public services, government is the provider of last resort or the only provider.

Reformers adopting a marketized public management perspective refer to their introductory microeconomics textbooks and recall that monopoly providers are inefficient because they tend to supply less than demand and charge higher than equilibrium prices. While textbook explanations apply in the case of a normal good, government traffics in services that, if they could be provided in the private market in sufficient quantities, they already would be. The discipline-of-the-market narrative falls short in the cases of providing regulatory services, humanitarian aid, or refugee legal services.

The logic for treating government as a business involves a false equivalence between the two, asserting that competition fosters efficiency in the private sector, so it will also discipline public-sector service delivery. The consequences of efficiency—the extent to which efficiency compromises equity, for instance—are not considered (Carr 1994). One significant consequence is that the emphasis on outputs over processes can produce inequitable outcomes. Another consequence is embedded in the assumption that public opinion polls provide information of similar accuracy as do revenue flows in the private sector. But government provides services where markets have failed, meaning that oftentimes, government is the sole provider or provider of last resort. Moreover, if public goods could be valued just as private-sector goods are—in other words, goods free from the problems of nonrival consumption and nonexclusive consumption—then price rationing would be the appropriate allocation method and the good would be provided by private sellers.

A third consequence relates to the motivations with which public servants choose to work in the public sector. According to his examination of the efficiency movement in schools, Carr (1994) observed that educators were asked to turn away from the principles of their profession to adopt managerialism and efficiency as the paramount objective, yet the motivations and professional display rules of educators are ignored. Public servants working with disadvantaged populations resist market-oriented, narrow, output-focused reforms that erode discretion and autonomy and prioritize the near-term bottom line over longer-term objectives (Miller et al. 2006). Vickers and Kouzmin similarly reveal detrimental impacts of such reforms on the public servants who are asked to carry them out and insist: "There must, in the first instance, be an acknowledgement that actors may be permanently damaged, traumatized, and alienated as a result of their experiences with NPM. Future research should address 'at risk' actors in organizations, those who face redundancy through downsizing, and outsourcing, violence, stress, illness, disability, substance abuse or other coercive practices" (2001, 111).

Although falling short of providing public administration's Big Answer, NPM reforms have improved service delivery in certain venues. For example, prior to NPM reforms, public sector financial management and accounting best practices were fairly rudimentary (Jones and Kettl 2006). Developed countries implemented reforms to greater and lesser degrees, but all somewhat similarly. Developing countries were encouraged to pursue reforms by international actors such as the World Bank and OECD in order to seek greater analytical clarity on how they could enhance their capabilities (Gulrajani and Moloney 2012). The nations experienced NPM reforms differently from countries in the developed world, causing La Palombara (2006) to speculate also about the degree of divergence between countries even as they relied on traditional bureaucratic government. Finally, public management reforms are credited with spurring interest in comparative research because the reform agenda was pursued by so many countries during a relatively distinct period of time. Regardless of the managerial model employed by each nation, comparative public administration fosters greater understanding of the role of emotions in public organizations, whether in the context of marketized public service delivery, traditional bureaucratic processes, or an alternate structure.

Summary and Conclusion

In this chapter, we discussed policy areas as broad ranging as climate change, migration, and Internet commerce, all of which have brought sovereign nations together to consider "the international" as a space that transcends the political boundaries of any single country. Organizations are formed to address global issues—International Public Administrations or secretariats—and people are hired to implement policies—ICSs—to govern across the borders of sovereign nations. Like employees of any organization and members of any profession, ICSs are subject to display rules (Xu and Weller 2008). Conforming to organizational and professional display rules demands emotional labor. Working across cultures requires emotional intelligence and "cultural intelligence" (Mollah et al. 2018, 480) as does working in diverse organizations. Ultimately, the capacity to perform emotional labor, which is closely related to emotional intelligence (Guy and Lee 2015; Mastracci et al. 2012), is fundamental to quality public service because public servants working in diverse organizations span cultural boundaries with both their relations with co-workers and also with the citizenry of diverse communities. Boundary spanners work in ways that cross organizational boundaries or service sectors. Most often, boundary spanning occurs between organizations, but can also be between different parts of large organizations, like states or local governments (Needham et al. 2017). ICSs working in IPAs cannot avoid spanning boundaries. The example of sanctuary cities and local-level environmental policies underscores the importance of boundary spanning at subnational levels. Observing display rules and building trust are especially important but much more complex when working across boundaries.

Boundary spanning complicates display rules and boundary spanners need to adapt and modify their presentation to accommodate different constituencies (Needham et al. 2017). We know that the experience of emotions in organizations varies by culture (Gökçen 2014; Gunkel et al. 2014; Ratner 2000). And we know that there is great variety among nations within a category, such as among collectivist states or among individualist states. Research that compares nations is required to explore the effects of culture on emotional labor.

Just as boundary spanning is important for international work, political dynamics, and geographic boundaries must be taken into account when comparing nations. This is because different governmental systems vary in the expectations that arise in the public encounter. Public management cultures that rely on traditional bureaucracy with its "neutral" delivery of services exert different emotional labor demands on public servants than cultures that rely on market principles where "the customer is always right." Another way to think about this is that citizens' attitudes about their relationship to government, and vice versa, have an effect on how public servants are treated. And how public servants are treated affects how they feel about citizens and about their work.

References

Alimi, Deborah. 2015. "'Going Global': Policy Entrepreneurship of the Global Commission on Drug Policy." *Public Administration* 93 (4): 874–89.

Barnett, Michael N., and Martha Finnemore. 1999. "The Politics, Power, and Pathologies of International Organizations." *International Organization* 53 (4): 699–732.

Bauder, Harald. 2017. "Sanctuary Cities: Policies and Practices in International Perspective." *International Migration* 55 (2): 174–87.

Bauer, Michael W. 2012. "Tolerant, If Personal Goals Remain Unharmed: Explaining Supranational Bureaucrats' Attitudes to Organizational Change." *Governance* 25 (3): 485–510.

Broome, André, and Leonard Seabrooke. 2015. "Shaping Policy Curves: Cognitive Authority in Transnational Capacity Building." *Public Administration* 93 (4): 956–72.

Busch, Per-Olof. 2014. "Independent Influence of International Public Administrations: Contours and Future Directions of an Emerging Research Strand." In *Public Administration in the Context of Global Governance*, edited by Soonhee Kim, Shena Ashley Shena, and W. Henry Lambright, 45–62. Cheltenham, UK: Edward Elgar Publishing.

Carlson, Dawn, Merideth Ferguson, Emily Hunter, and Dwayne Whitten. 2012. "Abusive Supervision and Work–Family Conflict: The Path through Emotional Labor and Burnout." *The Leadership Quarterly* 23 (5): 849–59.

Carr, Adrian N. 1994. "The 'Emotional Fallout' of the New Efficiency Movement in Public Administration in Australia: A Case Study." *Administration & Society* 26 (3): 344–58.

Chatzea, Vasiliki-Eirini, Dimitra Sifaki-Pistolla, Sofia-Aikaterini Vlachaki, Evangelos Melidoniotis, and Georgia Pistolla. 2018. "PTSD, Burnout and Well-Being Among Rescue Workers: Seeking to Understand the Impact of the European Refugee Crisis on Rescuers." *Psychiatry Research* 262: 446–51.

Cheung, Anthony B. L. 2012. "Public Administration in East Asia: Legacies, Trajectories and Lessons." *International Review of Administrative Sciences* 78 (2): 209–16.

Dahl, Robert A. 1947. "The Science of Public Administration: Three Problems." *Public Administration Review* 7 (1): 1–11.

Duncan, Magdaline. 2018. "Half of Aquarius Rescue Boat Migrants Want to Seek Asylum in France." *POLITICO*, June 18. https://www.politico.eu/article/valencia-spain-half-of-aquarius-rescue-boat-migrants-want-to-seek-asylum-in-france/.

Eckhard, Steffen, and Jörn Ege. 2016. "International Bureaucracies and Their Influence on Policy-Making: A Review of Empirical Evidence." *Journal of European Public Policy* 23 (7): 960–78.

Edwards, Adrian. 2018. "Forced Displacement at Record 68.5 Million." UN Refugee Agency, June 19. http://www.unhcr.org/en-us/news/stories/2018/6/5b222c494/forced-displacement-record-685-million.html.

Ege, Jörn. 2017. "Comparing the Autonomy of International Public Administrations: An Ideal-Type Approach." *Public Administration* 95 (3): 555–70. https://doi.org/10.1111/padm.12326.

Eid, Michael, and Ed Diener. 2001. "Norms for Experiencing Emotions in Different Cultures: Inter- and Intranational Differences." *Journal of Personality and Social Psychology* 81 (5): 869–85. https://doi.org/10.1037//0022-3514.81.5.869.

European Union. 2015. "EUR-Lex—01962R0031-20140501—EN—EUR-Lex." EUR-Lex Access to European Union Law. https://eur-lex.europa.eu/legal-content/EN/TXT/?uri=CELEX%3A01962R0031-20140501.

Finkelstein, Lawrence S. 1995. "What Is Global Governance." *Global Governance* 1: 367.

Fitzpatrick, Jody, Malcolm Goggin, Tanya Heikkila, Donald Klingner, Jason Machado, and Christine Martell. 2011. "A New Look at Comparative Public Administration: Trends in Research and an Agenda for the Future." *Public Administration Review* 71 (6): 821–30.

Gore, Albert. 1993. *Creating a Government That Works Better & Costs Less: Executive Summary*. Report of the National Performance Review. Washington, DC: Government Printing Office.

Gökçen, Elif, Adrian Furnham, Stella Mavroveli, and K. V. Petrides. 2014. "A Cross-Cultural Investigation of Trait Emotional Intelligence in Hong Kong and the UK." *Personality and Individual Differences* 65: 30–35.

Grandey, Alicia A. 2003. "When 'the Show Must Go on': Surface Acting and Deep Acting as Determinants of Emotional Exhaustion and Peer-Rated Service Delivery." *Academy of Management Journal* 46 (1): 86–96.

Gray, Andrew, and Bill Jenkins. 2006. "From Public Administration to Public Management: Reassessing a Revolution?" In *Comparative Public Administration*, edited by Eric E. Otenyo and Nancy S. Lind, 543–72. West Yorkshire, UK: Emerald Group Publishing.

Gulrajani, Nilima, and Kim Moloney. 2012. "Globalizing Public Administration: Today's Research and Tomorrow's Agenda." *Public Administration Review* 72 (1): 78–86.

Gunkel, Marjaana, Christopher Schlägel, and Robert L. Engle. 2014. "Culture's Influence on Emotional Intelligence: An Empirical Study of Nine Countries." *Journal of International Management* 20 (2): 256–74.

Guy, Mary E., and Hyun Jung Lee. 2015. "Emotional Intelligence and Emotional Labor: How Related Are They?" *Review of Public Personnel Administration* 35 (3): 261–77.

Guy, Mary E., Meredith A. Newman, and Sharon H. Mastracci. 2008. *Emotional Labor: Putting the Service in Public Service*. Armonk, NY: M. E. Sharpe.

Heidbreder, Eva G. 2015. "Multilevel Policy Enforcement: Innovations in How to Administer Liberalized Global Markets." *Public Administration* 93 (4): 940–55.

Hensell, Stephan. 2016. "Staff and Status in International Bureaucracies: A Weberian Perspective on the EU Civil Service." *Cambridge Review of International Affairs* 29 (4): 1486–501.

Hochschild, A. R. 1983. *The Managed Heart: Commercialization of Human Feeling*. Berkeley: University of California Press.

Hofstede, G, G. J. Hofstede, and M. Minkov. 2010. *Cultures and Organizations: Software of the Mind*. New York, NY: McGraw-Hill.

Hooghe, Liesbet. 2005. "Several Roads Lead to International Norms, but Few via International Socialization: A Case Study of the European Commission." *International Organization* 59 (4): 861–98.

International Civil Service Advisory Board, United Nations. 2002. *International Standards of Conduct for the International Civil Service*. Accessed February 17, 2019. http://www.un.org/en/ethics/pdf/StandConIntCivSE.pdf.

Johnston, Allanah, and Jörgen Sandberg. 2008. "Controlling Service Work: An Ambiguous Accomplishment Between Employees, Management and Customers." *Journal of Consumer Culture* 8 (3): 389–417.

Jones, Lawrence R., and Donald F. Kettl. 2006. "Assessing Public Management Reform Strategy in an International Context." In *Comparative Public Administration*, edited by Eric E. Otenyo and Nancy S. Lind, 883–904. West Yorkshire, UK: Emerald Group Publishing.

Jreisat, Jamil E. 2005. "Comparative Public Administration Is Back in, Prudently." *Public Administration Review* 65 (2): 231–42.

Jreisat, Jamil E. 2014. "Public Administration in a Changing Context." In *Public Administration in the Context of Global Governance*, edited by Soonhee Kim, Shena Ashley, and W. Henry Lambright, 22–27. Cheltenham, UK: Edward Elgar Publishing.

Juncos, Ana E., and Karolina Pomorska. 2013. "'In the Face of Adversity': Explaining the Attitudes of EEAS Officials Vis-à-Vis the New Service." *Journal of European Public Policy* 20 (9): 1332–49.

Kim, Soonhee, Shena Ashley, and W. Henry Lambright. 2014. *Public Administration in the Context of Global Governance*. Cheltenham, UK: Edward Elgar Publishing.

Kütting, Gabriela, and Philip G. Cerny. 2015. "Rethinking Global Environmental Policy: From Global Governance to Transnational Neopluralism." *Public Administration* 93 (4): 907–21.

La Palombara, Joseph. 2006. "An Overview of Bureaucracy and Political Development." In *Comparative Public Administration*, edited by Eric E. Otenyo and Nancy S. Lind, 193–220. West Yorkshire, UK: Emerald Group Publishing.

Lambright, W. Henry. 2014. "Transboundary Leadership in Science and Technology: The International Space Station." In *Public Administration in the Context of Global Governance*, edited by Soonhee Kim, Shena Ashley, and W. Henry Lambright, 28–34. Cheltenham, UK: Edward Elgar Publishing.

Lauer, Josh. 2008. "Alienation in the Information Economy: Toward a Marxist Critique of Consumer Surveillance." In *Participation and Media Production: Critical Reflections on Content Creation*, edited by Nico Carpentier and Benjamin De Cleen, 41–53. Newcastle upon Tyne: Cambridge Scholars.

LeGrand, Tim. 2015. "Transgovernmental Policy Networks in the Anglosphere." *Public Administration* 93 (4): 973–91.

Lodge, Martin. 2014. "Regulation in Crisis: Reputation, Capacity and Limitations." In *Public Administration in the Context of Global Governance*, edited by Soonhee Kim, Shena Ashley, and W. Henry Lambright, 96–115. Cheltenham, UK: Edward Elgar Publishing.

Lynn, Laurence E. 2006. "The New Public Management as an International Phenomenon: A Skeptical View." In *Comparative Public Administration*, edited by Eric E. Otenyo and Nancy S. Lind, 573–91. West Yorkshire, England: Emerald Group Publishing.

Mamudu, Hadii, Paul Cairney, and Donley Studlar. 2015. "Global Public Policy: Does the New Venue for Transnational Tobacco Control Challenge the Old Way of Doing Things?" *Public Administration* 93 (4): 856–73. https://dx.doi.org/10.1111/padm.12143.

Mao, Xiaorong, Olivia Wai Man Fung, Xiuying Hu, and Alice Yuen Loke. 2018. "Psychological Impacts of Disaster on Rescue Workers: A Review of the Literature." *International Journal of Disaster Risk Reduction* 27: 602–17. https://doi.org/10.1016/j.ijdrr.2017.10.020.

Martin, Joanne. 1992. *Cultures in Organizations: Three Perspectives*. New York: Oxford University Press.

Mastracci, Sharon H., and Ian Adams. 2019. "Is Emotional Labor Easier in Collectivist or Individualist Cultures? An East-West Comparison." *Public Personnel Management* 48 (3): 325–344. https://doi.org/10.1177/0091026018814569.

Mastracci, Sharon H., Mary E. Guy, and Meredith A. Newman. 2012. *Emotional Labor and Crisis Response: Working on the Razor's Edge: Working on the Razor's Edge*. Abingdon, UK: Routledge.

McLaren, Robert I. 1997. "Organizational Culture in a Multicultural Organization." *International Review of Administrative Sciences* 63 (1): 57–66.

Miller, Chris, Paul Hoggett, and Marjorie Mayo. 2006. "The Obsession with Outputs: Over Regulation and the Impact on the Emotional Identities of Public Service Professionals." *International Journal of Work Organisation and Emotion* 1 (4): 366–78.

Mollah, Tooba Noor, Josefine Antoniades, Fathima Ijaza Lafeer, and Bianca Brijnath. 2018. "How Do Mental Health Practitioners Operationalise Cultural Competency in Everyday Practice? A Qualitative Analysis." *BMC Health Services Research* 18 (1): 480.

Moloney, Kim, James S. Bowman, and Jonathan P. West. 2018. "Challenges Confronting Whistleblowing and the International Civil Servant." *Review of Public Personnel Administration*. https://doi.org/10.1177/0734371X18767247.

Needham, Catherine, Sharon Mastracci, and Catherine Mangan. 2017. "The Emotional Labour of Boundary Spanning." *Journal of Integrated Care* 25 (4): 288–300.

O'Leary, Rosemary. 2014. "Toward an Open Systems Perspective of Global Public Administration Citizenship." In *Public Administration in the Context of Global Governance*, edited by Soonhee Kim, Shena Ashley, and W. Henry Lambright, 9–14. Cheltenham, UK: Edward Elgar Publishing.

Otenyo, Eric E., and Nancy S. Lind. 2006. "Comparative Public Administration: Growth, Method, and Ecology." In *Comparative Public Administration*, edited by Eric E. Otenyo and Nancy S. Lind, 1–7. West Yorkshire, UK: Emerald Group Publishing.

Papataxiarchis, Evthymios. 2016. "Being 'There': At the Front Line of the 'European Refugee Crisis'." *Anthropology Today* 32 (2): 5–9.

Putman, Nathan F., F. Alberto Abreu-Grobois, Inaky Iturbe-Darkistade, Emily M. Putman, Paul M. Richards, and Philippe Verley. 2015. "Deepwater Horizon Oil Spill Impacts on Sea Turtles Could Span the Atlantic." *Biology Letters* 11 (12): 20150596. https://doi.org/10.1098/rsbl.2015.0596.

Ratner, Carl. 2000. "A Cultural-Psychological Analysis of Emotions." *Culture & Psychology* 6 (1): 5–39.

Rayner, Julie, and Alan Lawton. 2018. "Are We Being Served? Emotional Labour in Local Government in Victoria, Australia." *Australian Journal of Public Administration* 77 (3): 360–74.

Riggs, Fred W. 2006. "Conclusion: Impact of Globalization on the Study and Practice of Public Administration." In *Comparative Public Administration*, edited by Eric E. Otenyo and Nancy S. Lind, 917–967. West Yorkshire, UK: Emerald Group Publishing.

Rozakou, Katerina. 2017. "Nonrecording the 'European Refugee Crisis' in Greece: Navigating Through Irregular Bureaucracy." *Focaal* (77): 36–49.

Savoie, Donald J. 2006. "What Is Wrong with the New Public Management?" In *Comparative Public Administration*, edited by Eric E. Otenyo and Nancy S. Lind, 593–602. West Yorkshire, UK: Emerald Group Publishing.

Seabrooke, Leonard. 2014. "Identity Switching and Transnational Professionals." *International Political Sociology* 8 (3): 335–37.

Spence, David. 2012. "The Early Days of the European External Action Service: A Practitioner's View." *The Hague Journal of Diplomacy* 7 (1): 115–34.

Steinberg, Ronnie J., and Deborah M. Figart. 1999. "Emotional Demands at Work: A Job Content Analysis." *The Annals of the American Academy of Political and Social Science* 561 (1): 177–91.

Stone, Diane, and Stella Ladi. 2015. "Global Public Policy and Transnational Administration." *Public Administration* 93 (4): 839–55.

Suvarierol, Semin. 2008. "Beyond the Myth of Nationality: Analysing Networks Within the European Commission." *West European Politics* 31 (4): 701–24.

Taras, Vas, Bradley L. Kirkman, and Piers Steel. 2010. "Examining the Impact of Culture's Consequences: A Three-Decade, Multilevel, Meta-Analytic Review of Hofstede's Cultural Value Dimensions." *Journal of Applied Psychology* 95 (3): 405–39. http://dx.doi.org/10.1037/a0018938.

Thomas, John Clayton. 2013. "Citizen, Customer, Partner: Rethinking the Place of the Public in Public Management." *Public Administration Review* 73 (6): 786–96.

Triandis, Harry C. 2002. "Individualism—Collectivism and Personality." *Personality* 69 (6): 907–24.

UNHCR. 2018. "IOM, UNHCR Appeal for Region-Wide Action by EU Countries over Mediterranean Tragedies." UN Refugee Agency, June 27. http:// www.unhcr.org/en-us/news/press/2018/6/5b33d8bf4/iom-unhcr-appeal-region-wide-action-eu-countries-mediterranean-tragedies.html.

United Nations. 1945. "Charter of the United Nations." http://www.un.org/en/sections/un-charter/chapter-xv/index.html.

Van Gelderen, Benjamin R., Arnold B. Bakker, Elly A. Konijn, and Evangelia Demerouti. 2011. "Daily Suppression of Discrete Emotions During the Work of Police Service Workers and Criminal Investigation Officers." *Anxiety, Stress & Coping* 24 (5): 515–37.

Van Wart, Montgomery, and Joseph Cayer. 1990. "Comparative Public Administration: Defunct, Dispersed, or Redefined?" *Public Administration Review* 50 (2): 238–48.

Vickers, Margaret H., and Alexander Kouzmin. 2001. "'Resilience' in Organizational Actors and Rearticulating 'Voice': Towards a Humanistic Critique of New Public Management." *Public Management Review* 3 (1): 95–119.

Weber, Max. 1921/1968. *Economy and Society: An Outline of Interpretive Sociology*. Translated and Edited by G. Roth and C. Wittich. New York: Bedminster Press.

Winfield, Nicole, and Aritz Parra. 2018. "Spain Offers to Accept Migrant Ship after Italy, Malta Refuse." *Christian Science Monitor*, June 11. https://www.csmonitor.com/World/2018/0611/Spain-offers-to-accept-migrant-ship-after-Italy-Malta-refuse.

Wolff, Sarah. 2015. "EU Budget Support as a Transnational Policy Instrument: Above and Beyond the State?" *Public Administration* 93 (4): 922–39.

Xu, Yi-Chong, and Patrick Weller. 2008. "'To Be, But Not to Be Seen': Exploring the Impact of International Civil Servants." *Public Administration* 86 (1): 35–51.

Ziring, Lawrence, Robert E. Riggs, and Jack C. Plano. 2005. *The United Nations: International Organization and World Politics*. 4th ed. Boston, MA: Cengage Learning.

Part II

Individual, Organizational, and Cultural Analyses

Like turning a kaleidoscope, this part examines public service delivery from four vantages. Chapters 4–7 discuss the individual, organizational, cultural, and contextual considerations that affect human performance and organizational productivity in the delivery of public services. Chapter 4 relates emotional intelligence and the Big Five personality traits to the performance of emotional labor and concludes that the cultural context exerts influences above and beyond that which is expected from traditional theories of personality and emotional intelligence. Chapter 5 embeds emotional labor in the organizational setting, using Job Demands-Resources theory and organizational justice as frameworks for understanding the link between emotional labor and its consequences for employees. Chapter 6 elevates the focus on the cultural context and compares this study to prior multi-national comparisons. Chapter 7 bores deeply into the rough edges of the public encounter, where citizens encounter the state with hostility. Evidence is presented that reflects job outcomes for public servants who are treated abusively by citizens.

4

Understanding Emotional Labor
at the Individual Level

Seung-Bum Yang and Hyun Jung Lee

In this chapter, we explore the construct of emotional labor through the lens of individual performance. The performance of emotional labor is important because it has an impact on organizational outcomes. Sequelae that accompany emotive performance have implications for job attitudes, degree of organizational commitment, effectiveness of work performance, and citizen satisfaction. In other words, its performance leads to a variety of employment issues. On the positive end, these include altruistic behavior, personal fulfillment, enhanced job performance, and increased citizen satisfaction. On the negative end of the spectrum, these include turnover intention, absenteeism, and burnout. The magnitude of these impacts varies based on individual differences.

Organizational success depends on each employee's efforts, for, without them, there would be no organization. It is worker behavior that determines productivity and each employee's behavior is unique. This is why performance issues are hard to solve with a one-size-fits-all approach.

S.-B. Yang (✉)
Department of Public Administration,
Konkuk University, Seoul, South Korea
e-mail: sbyang@konkuk.ac.kr

H. J. Lee
Department of Public Administration,
MyongJi University, Seoul, South Korea
e-mail: Tweety06@mju.ac.kr

© The Author(s) 2019
M. E. Guy et al. (eds.), *The Palgrave Handbook of Global Perspectives on Emotional Labor in Public Service*, https://doi.org/10.1007/978-3-030-24823-9_4

To probe individual differences, scholars have developed constructs such as personality, values, attitudes, abilities, and skills, all of which combine to yield performance that varies from one person to another. Foremost among the individual characteristics that influence performance is emotional intelligence. Just as intelligence quotients (IQs) indicate the ability to perform cognitive labor, emotional intelligence indicates the ability to perform emotional labor. Personality traits also play an important role in the performance of emotional labor. Of these, the Big Five personality traits, which are composed of five major personality sets, have been well established and have proven consistent across various settings and environments.

This chapter concentrates on emotional intelligence and the Big Five personality traits to explore their role in vitalizing or devitalizing the relationships surrounding emotional labor. In addition, the chapter reviews how individual-level variables perform in the context of national culture. Discussion turns first to emotional intelligence.

Emotional Intelligence

The notion of emotional intelligence emerged from questions regarding whether workers with high IQs outperform those with lower IQs. Traditional IQ measures rely on cognitive intelligence to the exclusion of other forms of intelligence. They have been the standard-bearer for a century's worth of intellectual measurement, admission to elite schools, and competitive selection to training programs. To answer the question, researchers investigated work performance of those with high IQs and found that only twenty percent of them were top performers. The other top performers had scored within the average range on IQ tests (Goleman 1995). This finding led psychologists to conclude that cognitive intelligence is not a valid measure for predicting work performance. Instead, they determined that interpersonal skills, which require cooperative teamwork, are at the heart of success on the job.

Moving away from a singular focus on cognitive intelligence, Howard Gardner (1983, 1995) developed the theory that intelligence is a multifaceted construct, proposing as many as nine types of intelligences. Gardner's work provides a broader appreciation of individual ability, to the point that the question now is not *whether* a person is intelligent but, rather, *in what way* is a person intelligent. These multiple types of intelligences extend beyond the intrapersonal focus on cognition to an interpersonal focus, now thought of as social intelligences. Among these multiple intelligences, the focus is on what learning theorist Edward Thorndike (1920) called a discrete intelligence necessary for understanding people.

Non-cognitive intrapersonal intelligence refers to understanding one's own interests and goals (Gardner 1983). Individuals with high intrapersonal intelligence are able to tune into their inner feelings and have confidence in themselves. In contrast, interpersonal intelligence refers to understanding and interacting with others and having empathy for others. These two types of intelligences—intrapersonal and interpersonal—are, in Gardner's terminology, essential elements when interacting with others.

Rooted within this notion of intrapersonal and interpersonal intelligence is emotional intelligence (EI). Daniel Goleman (1995) popularized the concept when he focused research on the role of emotional intelligence in childhood education. The concept soon gained traction in management education and leadership studies. Goleman argued that it is emotional intelligence that enables the recognition of emotions in oneself and in others. He advocated using this knowledge to improve self-management and constructive communication with others (1998, 2005). Further, Goleman (1998) insisted that, unlike IQ which is a fixed variable and is developed by the teen years, emotional intelligence can continue to develop over the life course, such that people's EI grows as a result of experience. The existence of emotional intelligence has now been well established by research. See, for example, Cheung and Tang (2010), Dahling and Perez (2010), Day and Carroll (2004), Gross and Levenson (1997), Guy and Lee (2015), Hopfl and Linstead (1997), and Lee (2013b, 2018). These studies demonstrate that the experiences that accumulate with age and workplace exposure contribute to higher levels of emotional intelligence, especially in the form of emotion management skills.

Goleman's (1995) work is credited with popularizing the notion of emotional intelligence to the general public, but it had been recognized decades earlier. Leuner (1966) was the first theorist to describe emotional intelligence in the scientific literature, but the concept did not gain legitimacy until Salovey and Mayer's (1990) groundbreaking work decades later. Salovey and Mayer defined emotional intelligence as the ability to accurately sense one's own and others' emotions, the goal of which is to constructively regulate one's own emotive state as well as to respond to others in a manner that leads to desired behavior. Mayer et al. (2008, 2004) claim that emotional intelligence is an ability and that how much an individual is able to apply its dimensions at work or in social situations depends on individual skill. Subsequent researchers who have adopted this ability model of emotional intelligence include Guy and Lee (2015), Karim (2010), Landa et al. (2010), Lee (2013a), and Wong and Law (2002), among others.

By using the ability model, a number of researchers (e.g., Mayer et al. 2008; Law et al. 2004; Wong and Law 2002) have empirically demonstrated that emotional intelligence is different from personality traits. They have also demonstrated that all the dimensions of emotional intelligence are independent from each other. A recent study also demonstrates that each of the dimensions within emotional intelligence entails unitary ability (Guy and Lee 2015). In addition to the ability model of emotional intelligence, there are two other types of models, the trait model and the mixed model. Discussion turns now to these.

The trait model was developed by Petrides and Furnham (2000). It refers to "a constellation of emotional self-perceptions located at the lower levels of personality hierarchies" (Petrides 2011, 657). Emotional intelligence is based on emotion-related behavioral dispositions, such as adaptability, assertiveness, empathy, emotion expression, emotion management, trait empathy, trait happiness, and trait optimism (Petrides 2009). As such, the trait model integrates the intelligence elements into personality hierarchies.

A third way to understand emotional intelligence is through the mixed model, which was introduced by Goleman (1998) and Bar-On (1997a, b, 2000). From their points of view, emotional intelligence is a multi-factorial array of interrelated emotional, personal, and social abilities that influence a person's overall ability to cope effectively with daily demands and pressures (Bar-On 2000). Goleman (1995) also argues that emotional intelligence includes an individual ability that combines with personal traits. Further, he emphasizes that emotional intelligence is a learnable skill that can be refined in the form of emotive competencies. These include self-awareness, empathy, and self-regulation, along with a number of types of social awareness, such as motivation, leadership, communication, influence, and teamwork (Goleman 1998).

After constructing four dimensions of emotional intelligence—self-awareness, self-management, social awareness, and relationship management—Goleman (2005) categorized them into personal competence and social competence. Personal competence includes the dimensions of self-awareness and self-management. These determine how individuals manage themselves. Social competence includes social awareness and relationship management, and these determine how individuals manage relationships.

Some scholars criticize the trait and mixed models of emotional intelligence for three main reasons: First, some variables that are used in both the trait and mixed models overlap with those used by the ability model, such as self-awareness, motivation, empathy, and emotion management/regulation. Second, the factors that are used in the trait model are more strongly correlated with measures of personality than with emotional intelligence factors (Kulkarni et al. 2009; Lee 2013a, b). Third, there is no explanation for why certain traits and/or abilities are included in some models but not in others (Lee 2018; Mayer et al. 2004).

Although debate remains as to which of the three models of emotional intelligence do a better job of measuring it, numerous researchers have empirically proven that it is an important factor in human performance as well as in organizational performance. All three models embrace perceiving and understanding the self and others, and regulating one's own emotion for the purpose of engaging in interpersonal relationships. Simply put, the involved dimensions are *emotional self-awareness, emotional other-awareness, emotion regulation*, and *use of emotion*. Whether in education, leadership, organizational behavior, healthcare delivery, or social relationships, or in its application to emotional labor, emotional intelligence is an essential component in interpersonal relationships (see, e.g., Deepika 2016; Guy and Lee 2015; Higgs and Dulewicz 2014; Huang et al. 2010; Lee 2018; Moon and Hur 2011; Rathi et al. 2013; Vandewaa et al. 2016). Discussion turns now to these four dimensions.

First, *emotional self-awareness* refers to the degree to which people are able to identify their own feelings and understand the causes of those feelings (Guy and Lee 2015; Lee 2018; Mayer and Salovey 1997). Without accurately knowing one's own emotion, an individual is unable to perform the other three dimensions. Thus, emotional self-awareness is foundational for the other dimensions of emotional intelligence (Mayer et al. 2004).

Second, *emotional other-awareness* refers to an individual's ability to perceive and understand the emotions of those around him/her as well as the ability to interpret body language, facial expression, and tone of voice (Guy and Lee 2015; Lee 2018). People who perform emotional labor must exercise emotional other-awareness skills because interacting with others requires sensing their emotive state and altering one's own behavior to be responsive to it.

Third, *emotion regulation* refers to regulating one's own emotions by means of suppressing, expressing, or using quieting or enhancing strategies to hide how one feels or to amplify how one feels (Mayer et al. 2004). Employees who are able to regulate their emotions use the skill to govern their behavior, to control the emotion they display, and to shape the perceptions that others have of them.

The fourth dimension, *use of emotion*, is more of a cognitive than an emotive ability because it pertains to a cognitive decision to use emotion as an instrumental means to an end. Lee (2013a) argues that using emotions to achieve one's own purpose, such as facilitating problem solving or enthusing an audience, relates more to cognition; thus, it should be separated from the other emotional intelligence constructs.

In contrast to emotional intelligence, emotional labor is another emotion-related term that is receiving more attention in management circles. While emotional intelligence focuses on individual ability, emotional labor refers to work that is required in order to do one's job. The term is comparable to manual labor or cognitive labor and denotes work that must be done but is primarily emotive rather than cognitive or physical.

The way to understand the difference between emotional labor and emotional intelligence is that the concept of emotional intelligence is psychological in perspective. It is the innate ability to sense and regulate one's own feelings and to sense other people's feelings. On the other hand, the concept of emotional labor is derived from a sociological perspective on work demands. After observing the tasks that flight attendants performed in order to keep passengers happy and comfortable, researchers realized that a significant amount of the job involved managing the emotions of passengers and this work required attendants to express or suppress their own emotions (Hochschild 1983).

The two constructs, emotional intelligence and emotional labor, are related. Workers must have emotional intelligence in order to perform emotional labor (O'Boyle et al. 2011). While emotional intelligence is an attribute of the worker, emotional labor is a demand of the job. Studies demonstrate that emotional intelligence is statistically and significantly related to emotional labor and emotional labor cannot be appropriately performed in the absence of it (see, e.g., Brotheridge 2006; Guy and Lee 2015; Joseph and Newman 2010; Lee 2013a, b; Newman and Smith 2004; Opengart 2005). In other words, emotional intelligence provides the skill necessary for knowing how to perform emotional labor and how best to alter one's own emotions in order to meet work demands.

The dimensions of emotional intelligence are antecedent variables of emotional labor and they also serve to moderate and mediate its performance. Statistically speaking, a moderator is a variable that affects the magnitude or direction of the relationship between an independent variable and a dependent variable. A mediator is a variable that serves as a mechanism for the relationship between the independent variable and the dependent variable (Bar-On and Kenny 1986). Guy and Lee (2015) tested the mediating effect of emotional intelligence for the performance of emotional labor in the public service and found that emotional intelligence mediated the relationship between emotional labor and burnout. The effect is such that those who are better at regulating their own emotions are less likely to suffer burnout from emotionally intense jobs.

Based on what is known about the relationship between emotional intelligence and emotional labor, it is logical to hypothesize that emotional intelligence also moderates the performance of emotional labor. This assertion begs for these questions to be answered: To what extent do cultural differences factor into the relationship between emotional intelligence and emotional labor? And, to what extent do personality variables play a role? Meta-analytic research suggests that cultural beliefs and values impact the way of expressing and managing emotion (Taras et al. 2010).

To examine the role of culture, Gunkel et al. (2014) treated it as an antecedent variable of emotional intelligence. They tested the influence of culture on emotional intelligence with nine countries, using Hofstede et al.'s (2010) cultural dimensions (power distance, individualism versus collectivism, masculinity versus femininity, uncertainty avoidance, and long-term orientation). Gunkel et al. (2014) found that, among these dimensions, collectivism, uncertainty avoidance, and long-term orientation exert a positive influence on the different dimensions of emotional intelligence. This finding demonstrates the role of culture, but what are the effects of personality traits? It is to this that we now turn.

Big Five Personality Traits

Personality is a combination of distinctive individual characteristics that, when combined, explain a person's reactions and behavior. It has been a focus of attention for researchers for many years. Among the typologies developed, the Big Five model of personality has withstood the test of time. It is a widely accepted model and is supported by scientific research (McCrae and Costa 1997, 2003). It originated from the work of Tupes and Christal (1961), who assessed people on thirty-five personality trait variables. Using factor analysis, they identified five underlying factors that were strong, recurrent, and replicable and were judged to be fundamental to personality. The factors they identified were surgency, agreeableness, dependability, emotional stability, and culture. (Surgency is an emotive trait in which a person tends toward high levels of cheerfulness, spontaneity, and sociability.) Later, Goldberg (1981) coined this as the Big Five model and altered the names of the five factors to surgency, agreeableness, conscientiousness, emotional stability, and intellect. McCrae and John (1992) refer to the Big Five model as the five-factor model (FFM) of personality and renamed the factors to be openness to experience, conscientiousness, extraversion, agreeableness, and neuroticism. These traits are believed to transcend any differences that are based on culture because of the biological unity of humans and the belief that culture and personality act independently to shape a person's conduct.

Definitions of the factors in the Big Five personality model are as follows: Openness to experience is described as being flexible, open-minded, and creative. Conscientiousness implies such characteristics as dependable, responsible, and organized. Extraversion is on a continuum between introvert and extravert. Extraverted individuals are characterized as assertive, energetic, and outgoing. Introverts, on the other hand, are shy. Agreeableness includes such qualities as altruism, cooperativeness, and trust. Finally, neuroticism is on a continuum between being emotionally unstable and stable. Emotionally unstable people are nervous, vulnerable, and insecure. Costa and McCrae (1992) developed a personality inventory related to these five dimensions that is called NEO-PI-R (NEO Personality Inventory Revised). This personality scale contains the five personality factors and each factor has six characteristics that define the factor. Table 4.1 summarizes the NEO-PI-R scales.

With this explanation of personality as background, we return to a discussion of emotional labor and how it relates to the five factors. Because personality drives behavior, we expect that it has a significant impact on whether and how emotional labor is performed. Emotional labor is demanded in interpersonal interactions and if personality has a significant impact on social relationships, then personality also can have an impact on emotional labor. In fact, research conducted by Asendorpf and Wilpers (1998) found that conscientiousness, extraversion, and agreeableness are related to both the quantity and quality of people's social relationships but not vice versa. In other words, personality traits drive the creation and

Table 4.1 NEO-PI-R domains and scales

Big Five dimensions	Scales
Agreeableness	Altruism, Compliance, Modesty, Straightforwardness, Tender-Mindedness, Trust
Extraversion	Activity, Assertiveness, Excitement Seeking, Gregariousness, Positive Emotions, Warmth
Conscientiousness	Achievement Striving, Competence, Deliberation, Dutifulness, Order, Self-Discipline
Neuroticism	Anxiety, Depression, Hostility, Impulsiveness, Self-Consciousness, Vulnerability
Openness	Actions, Aesthetics, Fantasy, Feelings, Ideas, Values

Data Source Costa and McCrae (1992)

maintenance of interpersonal relationships but those relationships do not develop or inhibit personality traits. Subsequent to this finding, studies have found that the Big Five personality dimensions have an influence on emotional labor (Austin et al. 2008; Basim et al. 2013; Kiffin-Petersen et al. 2011; Mróz and Kaleta 2016).

The Survey

To explore the connection between personality, emotional intelligence, culture, and emotional labor, we provide empirical evidence from survey data collected from eight countries in this study: China, South Korea, Pakistan, Philippines, Rwanda, Taiwan, UK, and USA. There are 1955 individuals included in the survey, all of whom are in public service work. The sample is summarized in Table 4.2. The research model is depicted in Fig. 4.1. It provides for a comparison between countries in terms of the moderating effect of emotional intelligence and the Big Five personality factors on emotional labor outcomes. The construct of emotional labor is treated as having three dimensions: emotive capacity, pretending, and deep acting. Emotive capacity is the extent to which individuals sense emotional issues; pretending means hiding true feelings and expressing other feelings instead; deep acting is authentically experiencing the emotion being expressed (Yang et al. 2018).

Emotive capacity is measured by three items: "I am good at expressing how I feel," "I am good at getting people to calm down," and "In my job I am good at dealing with emotional issues." Pretending expression is measured by three items: "I hide my true feelings so as to appear pleasant at work," "In my job I act confident and self-assured regardless of how I actually feel," and "I wear a mask in order to deal with clients/customers in an appropriate way." Deep acting is measured by three items: "I try to

Table 4.2 Sample size for the eight countries

Countries	Sample size
China	211
Korea	208
Pakistan	386
Philippines	209
Rwanda	154
Taiwan	173
UK	360
USA	254
Total	1955

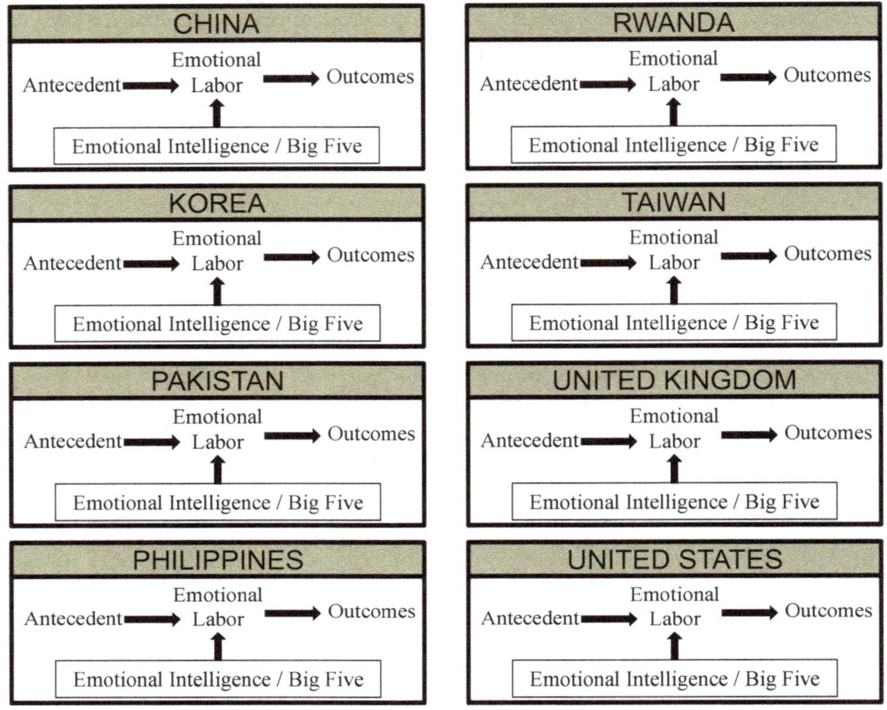

Fig. 4.1 Comparative model of the moderating effect of emotional intelligence and the big five personality factors

actually experience the emotions that I must show to clients/customers," "I work hard to actually feel the emotions that I need to show to clients/customers," and "I work at developing the feelings inside of me that I need to show to clients/customers."

Regarding the data analyses for emotional intelligence, the three dimensions of emotional self-awareness, emotional other-awareness, and emotion regulation are employed. Although we discussed the four dimensions of emotional intelligence in the previous section, one of the four dimensions, use of emotion, is removed from the statistical analyses because it is more about cognitive quality than emotive quality. Meanwhile, all of the Big Five personality dimensions are used in the statistical analyses. These are openness, conscientiousness, extraversion, agreeableness, and emotional stability. (To give a more intuitive description of the relationship, the positive term, emotional stability, is adopted instead of using neuroticism.)

Table 4.3   Correlation of emotional intelligence and emotional labor by country

Country		Capacity	Pretending	Deep acting
	Emotional intelligence dimensions			
China	Self-Awareness	0.495**	0.279**	0.579**
	Other-Awareness	0.580**	0.420**	0.572**
	Regulation	0.581**	0.302**	0.549**
Korea	Self-Awareness	0.499**	0.087	0.375**
	Other-Awareness	0.426**	0.102	0.281**
	Regulation	0.470**	0.138*	0.351**
Pakistan	Self-Awareness	0.367**	0.315**	0.215**
	Other-Awareness	0.448**	0.306**	0.265**
	Regulation	0.415**	0.334**	0.265**
Philippines	Self-Awareness	0.404**	0.245**	0.432**
	Other-Awareness	0.408**	0.239**	0.414**
	Regulation	0.403**	0.241**	0.399**
Rwanda	Self-Awareness	0.411**	0.344**	0.467**
	Other-Awareness	0.203*	0.035	0.093
	Regulation	0.485**	0.322*	0.512**
Taiwan	Self-Awareness	0.453**	0.116	0.403**
	Other-Awareness	0.353**	0.143	0.320**
	Regulation	0.473**	0.130	0.330**
UK	Self-Awareness	0.444*	−0.077	0.069
	Other-Awareness	0.484*	0.059	0.305**
	Regulation	0.276*	0.031	0.043
USA	Self-Awareness	0.387**	0.014	0.000
	Other-Awareness	0.549**	0.093	0.203**
	Regulation	0.436**	0.034	0.080

*Correlation is significant at the 0.05 level. **Correlation is significant at the 0.01 level

Table 4.3 shows correlations between the three dimensions of emotional intelligence and the three dimensions of emotional labor for each country tested. Across the board in all countries, emotional intelligence is significantly related to emotive capacity. In terms of pretending expression, there is a statistically significant relationship in China, Korea, Pakistan, Philippines, and Rwanda, but not in Taiwan, UK, and the USA. This indicates that pretending expression is culturally specific. In other words, whether one's emotional intelligence is high or low and whether one puts on a mask, or wears a false face, emotively speaking, are unrelated. Emotive pretending is likely to occur for reasons other than the level of emotional intelligence one has. For deep acting, all countries show a significant relationship between it and at least one dimension of emotional intelligence.

Table 4.4 shows correlations between the Big Five personality factors and emotional labor for each country. In terms of emotive capacity, there were statistically significant relationships in all countries across most of the

Table 4.4 Correlation of Big Five personality factors and emotional labor by country

Country	Big Five dimensions	Capacity	Pretending	Deep acting
China	Extraversion	0.198**	0.183**	0.161*
	Agreeableness	0.176*	0.178**	0.344**
	Conscientiousness	0.245**	0.183**	0.346**
	Emotional stability	0.254**	0.104	0.318**
	Openness	0.366**	0.051	0.394**
Korea	Extraversion	0.351**	0.096	0.176*
	Agreeableness	−0.117	−0.098	0.095
	Conscientiousness	0.194**	0.061	0.251**
	Emotional stability	0.022	−0.067	0.110
	Openness	0.119	0.038	0.169*
Pakistan	Extraversion	0.125*	0.167**	0.213**
	Agreeableness	0.247**	0.280**	0.230**
	Conscientiousness	0.128*	0.121*	0.237**
	Emotional stability	0.126*	0.094	0.183**
	Openness	−0.007	0.128*	0.157**
Philippines	Extraversion	0.119	0.029	−0.010
	Agreeableness	0.148*	0.026	0.085
	Conscientiousness	0.157*	0.039	0.061
	Emotional stability	0.210**	0.112	0.142*
	Openness	0.189**	0.141*	0.086
Rwanda	Extraversion	0.246**	0.130	0.277**
	Agreeableness	0.019	−0.050	−0.083
	Conscientiousness	0.264**	0.187*	0.201*
	Emotional stability	0.164**	0.210**	0.136
	Openness	0.054	−0.089	−0.005
Taiwan	Extraversion	0.309**	0.036	−0.024
	Agreeableness	0.051	−0.059	0.259**
	Conscientiousness	0.026	−0.034	0.124
	Emotional stability	0.219**	−0.034	0.146
	Openness	0.429**	−0.010	0.191*
UK	Extraversion	0.350**	0.046	0.103
	Agreeableness	0.257**	0.039	0.017
	Conscientiousness	0.128*	0.091	0.035
	Emotional stability	0.253**	−0.034	−0.083
	Openness	0.254**	0.020	0.091
USA	Extraversion	0.221**	−0.113	0.044
	Agreeableness	0.348**	−0.048	0.076
	Conscientiousness	0.102	0.016	−0.129*
	Emotional stability	0.252**	−0.133*	0.038
	Openness	0.379**	0.041	0.066

*Correlation is significant at the 0.05 level. **Correlation is significant at the 0.01 level

pairings between personality factors and the various dimensions of emotional labor. In terms of pretending expression, China, Pakistan, Philippines, Rwanda, and USA show significant relationships between some traits and emotive pretending but by no means all. And in Korea, Taiwan, and UK, there are no significant relationships between personality factors and pretending. For deep acting, there were significant relationships for at least some of the pairings in China, Korea, Pakistan, Philippines, Rwanda, Taiwan, and USA, but none in the UK. These findings lead to the conclusion that national culture influences how personality variables relate to performing different types of emotional labor.

Discussion

This chapter looked at the role of individual differences in emotional labor across the countries. We focused on two distinctive individual-level variables: emotional intelligence and the Big Five personality traits. After reviewing the theoretical background, we reported a series of statistical analyses using survey data from eight countries. The empirical analysis reveals interesting dynamics in the context of international comparative research into emotional labor. As the statistical analysis shows, the relationship between emotional intelligence and emotional labor and between the Big Five personality factors and emotional labor varies from country to country. These findings are like a windsock, hinting at the power of national culture to affect how individual behavior is modified when it comes to performing the emotional labor that is required in public service jobs. This means that, in order to have a deeper, richer understanding of public service job demands and performance, a country-by-country lens is required. This is especially important as interconnections among countries increase, as scholarly exchanges increase, as international training programs proliferate, as consultants travel the globe, giving advice on how best to deliver government services to the people, and as accreditation standards for Master of Public Administration programs are developed around the globe.

Comparative studies will be helpful for understanding the nuances of culture in this global village. As interconnected as the world already is, public administration is still resting on the fundamental assumptions of the anglophile West (Heady 1966; Riggs 1968; Klingner 2015). As Dwight Waldo (1955) pointed out, public administration is, in the end, both the art and science of management applied to public affairs. Millions of public employees perform emotional labor around the globe. Their jobs range widely from emergency responders, to police officers, to emergency call takers, to healthcare workers, to planning and zoning officials, to economic development experts, to educators, to meteorologists, and more. However, from country to country, individual-level characteristics put a different shade on the manner in which emotional labor is performed. The data here demonstrate that it is foolhardy to assume that one size fits all in terms of how personality factors and emotional intelligence and emotional labor relate across all countries.

References

Asendorpf, Jens B., and Susanne Wilpers. 1998. "Personality Effects on Social Relationships." *Journal of Personality and Social Psychology* 74 (6): 1531–44.

Austin, Elizabeth J., Timothy C. P. Dore, and Katharine M. O'Donovan. 2008. "Associations of Personality and Emotional Intelligence with Display Rule Perceptions and Emotional Labour." *Personality and Individual Differences* 44 (3): 679–88.

Bar-On, Reuben M. 1997a. *Bar-On Emotional Quotient Inventory: User's Manual.* Toronto, ON: Multi-Health Systems.

Bar-On, Reuben M. 1997b. *Bar-On Emotional Quotient Inventory: Technical Manual.* Toronto, ON: Multi-Health Systems.

Bar-On, Reuben M. 2000. "Emotional and Social Intelligence: Insights from the Emotional Quotient Inventory." In *The Handbook of Emotional Intelligence: Theory, Development, Assessment, and Application at Home, School, and in the Workplace*, edited by R. Bar-On and J. D. A. Parker, 363–388. San Francisco: Jossey-Bass.

Bar-On, Reuben M., and David. A. Kenny. 1986. "The Moderator–Mediator Variable Distinction in Social Psychological Research: Conceptual, Strategic, and Statistical Considerations. *Journal of Personality and Social Psychology* 51 (6): 1173–82.

Basim, H. Nejat, Memduh Begenirbas, and Rukiye Can Yalçin. 2013. "Effects of Teacher Personalities on Emotional Exhaustion: Mediating Role of Emotional Labor." *Educational Science: Theory & Practice* 13 (3): 1488–96.

Brotheridge, Céleste M. 2006. "The Role of Emotional Intelligence and Other Individual Difference Variables in Predicting Emotional Labor Relative to Situational Demands." *Psicothema* 18 (Suppl.): 139–44.

Cheung, F. Y., and C. S. Tang. 2010. "Effects of Age, Gender, and Emotional Labor Strategies on Job Outcomes: Moderated Mediation Analyses." *Applied Psychology Health and Well-Being* 2 (3): 323–39.

Costa, P. T., and R. McCrae. 1992. *NEO PI-R Professional Manual.* Odessa, FL: Psychological Assessment Resources.

Dahling, J. J., and L. A. Perez. 2010. "Older Worker, Different Actor? Linking Age and Emotional Labor Strategies." *Personality and Individual Differences* 48: 574–78.

Day, A., and S. Carroll. 2004. "Using an Ability-Based Measure of Emotional Intelligence to Predict Individual Performance, Group Performance, and Group Citizenship Behaviors." *Personality and Individual Differences* 36: 1443–58.

Deepika, D. 2016. "Impact of Leader's Emotional Intelligence and Transformational Behavior on Perceived Leadership Effectiveness: A Multiple Source View." *Business Perspectives & Research* 4 (1): 27–40.

Gardner, H. 1983. *Frames of Mind: The Theory of Multiple Intelligences.* New York, NY: Basic Books.

Gardner, H. 1995. *How Are Kids Smart? Multiple Intelligences (M.I.) in the Classroom.* Port Chester, NY: National Professional Resources.

Goldberg, L. 1981. "Language and Individual Differences: The Search for Universals in Personality Lexicons." In *Review of Personality and Social Psychology*, edited by L. Wheeler, 141–65. Beverly Hills, CA: Sage.

Goleman, Daniel. 1995. *Emotional Intelligence.* New York, NY: Bantam Books.

Goleman, Daniel. 1998. *Working with Emotional Intelligence.* New York, NY: Bantam Books.

Goleman, Daniel. 2005. *Emotional Intelligence.* New York, NY: Bantam Books.

Gross, J. J., and R. W. Levenson. 1997. "Hiding Feelings: The Acute Effects of Inhibiting Negative and Positive Emotion." *Journal of Abnormal Psychology* 106 (1): 95–103. https://doi.org/10.1037/0021-843X.106.1.95.

Gunkel, Marjaana, Christopher Schlägel, and Robert L. Engle. 2014. "Culture's Influence on Emotional Intelligence: An Empirical Study of Nine Countries." *Journal of International Management* 20 (2): 256–74.

Guy, Mary E., and Hyun Jung Lee. 2015. "How Emotional Intelligence Mediates Emotional Labor in Public Service Jobs." *Review of Public Personnel Administration* 35 (3): 261–77.

Heady, Ferrel. 1966. *Public Administration: A Comparative Perspective.* Englewood Cliffs, NJ: Prentice-Hall.

Higgs, M., and V. Dulewicz. 2014. "Antecedents of Well-Being: A Study to Examine the Extent to Which Personality and Emotional Intelligence Contribute to Well-Being." *International Journal of Human Resource Management* 25 (5): 718–35.

Hochschild, Arlie R. 1983. *The Managed Heart: Commercialization of Human Feeling.* Berkeley: University of California Press.

Hofstede, Geert, G. J. Hofstede, and M. Minkov. 2010. *Cultures and Organizations: Software of the Mind.* 3rd ed. New York, NY: McGraw-Hill.

Hopfl, H., and S. Linstead. 1997. "Introduction: Learning to Feel and Feeling to Learn: Emotion and Learning in Organizations." *Management Learning* 28 (1): 5–12.

Huang, X., S. C. H. Chan, W. Lam, and X. Nan. 2010. "The Joint Effect of Leader–Member Exchange and Emotional Intelligence on Burnout and Work Performance in Call Centers in China." *International Journal of Human Resource Management* 21: 1124–44.

Joseph, Dana L., and Daniel A. Newman. 2010. "Emotional Intelligence: An Integrative Meta-Analysis and Cascading Model." *Journal of Applied Psychology* 95 (1): 54–78.

Karim, J. 2010. "An Item Response Theory Analysis of Wong and Law Emotional Intelligence Scale." *Procedia—Social and Behavioral Sciences* 2 (2): 4038–47.

Kiffin-Petersen, Sandra A., Catherine L. Jordan, and Geoffrey N. Soutar. 2011. "The Big Five, Emotional Exhaustion and Citizenship Behaviors in Service Settings: The Mediating Role of Emotional Labor." *Personality and Individual Differences* 50 (1): 43–48.

Klingner, Donald E. 2015. "From Local to Global." In *Public Administration Evolving*, edited by Mary E. Guy and Marilyn M. Rubin, 65–82. New York, NY: Routledge.

Kulkarni, P. M., B. Janakiram, and D. N. S. Kumar. 2009. "Emotional Intelligence and Employee Performance as an Indicator for Promotion: A Study of Automobile Industry in the City of Belgaum, Karnataka, India." *International Journal of Business and Management* 4 (4): 161–70. https://doi.org/10.5539/ijbm.v4n4p161.

Landa, J. M. A., M. P. Martos, and E. Lopez-Zafra. 2010. "Emotional Intelligence and Personality Traits as Predictors of Psychological Well-Being in Spanish Undergraduates." *Social Behavior and Personality* 38 (6): 783–93.

Law, K. S., C. S. Wong, and L. J. Song. 2004. "The Construct and Criterion Validity of Emotional Intelligence and Its Potential Utility for Management Studies." *Journal of Applied Psychology* 89 (3): 483–96.

Lee, Hyun Jung. 2013a. "An Empirical Analysis of the Relationship Between Emotional Influence and Emotion Work: An Examination of Public Service Employees. *International Review of Public Administration* 18 (2): 85–107.

Lee, Hyun Jung. 2013b. "The Relationship Between Emotional Intelligence and Altruism Among South Korean Central Government Officials." *Social Behavior and Personality* 41 (10): 1667–80.

Lee, Hyun Jung. 2018. "How Emotional Intelligence Relates to Job Satisfaction and Burnout in Public Service Jobs." *International Review of Administrative Sciences* 84 (4): 729–45.

Leuner, B. 1966. "Emotionale Intelligenz und Emanzipation. [Emotional Intelligence and Emancipation]." *Praxis der Kinderpsychologie und Kinderpsychiatrie* 15: 183–203.

Mayer, J. D., and P. Salovey. 1997. "What Is Emotional Intelligence?" In *Emotional Development and Emotional Intelligence: Educational Implications*, edited by P. Salovey and D. J. Sluyter, 3–34. New York, NY: HarperCollins.

Mayer, J. D., P. Salovey, and D. R. Caruso. 2004. "Emotional Intelligence: Theory, Findings, and Implications." *Psychological Inquiry* 15: 197–215.

Mayer, J. D., P. Salovey, and D. R. Caruso. 2008. "Emotional Intelligence: New Ability or Eclectic Traits?" *American Psychologist* 63 (6): 503–17.

McCrae, R. R., and O. P. John. 1992. "An Introduction to the Five-Factor Model and Its Applications." *Journal of Personality* 60 (2): 175–215.

McCrae, R. R., and P. T. Costa. 1997. "Personality Trait Structure as a Human Universal." *American Psychologist* 52 (2): 509–16.

McCrae, R. R., and P. T. Costa. 2003. *Personality in Adulthood: A Five-Factor Theory Perspective*. 2nd ed. New York, NY: Guilford Press.

Moon, Tae Won, and Won-Moo Hur. 2011. "Emotional Intelligence, Emotional Exhaustion, and Job Performance." *Social Behavior and Personality: An International Journal* 39 (8): 1087–96. https://doi.org/10.2224/sbp.2011.39.8.1087.

Mróz, J., and K. Kaleta. 2016. "Relationships Between Personality, Emotional Labor, Work Engagement and Job Satisfaction in Service Professions." *International Journal of Occupational Medicine and Environmental Health* 29 (5): 767–82.

Newman, M., and S. A. Smith. 2004. "Integration of Emergency Risk Management into West Australian Indigenous Communities." *Australian Journal of Emergency Management* 19 (1): 10–15.

O'Boyle, Ernest H., Jr., Ronald H. Humphrey, Jeffrey M. Pollack, Thomas H. Hawver, and Paul A. Story. 2011. "The Relation Between Emotional Intelligence and Job Performance: Meta Analysis." *Journal of Organizational Behavior* 32 (5): 788–818. https://doi.org/10.1002/job.714.

Opengart, Rose. 2005. "Emotional Intelligence and Emotion Work: Examining Constructs from an Interdisciplinary Framework." *Human Resource Development Review* 4: 49–62.

Petrides, K. V. 2009. "Psychometric Properties of the Trait Emotional Intelligence Questionnaire (TEIQue)." In *Assessing Emotional Intelligence: Theory, Research, and Applications*, edited by C. Stough, D. H. Saklofske, and J. D. A. Parker, 85–101. New York, NY: Springer.

Petrides, K. V. 2011. "Ability and Trait Emotional Intelligence." In *The Wiley-Blackwell Handbook of Individual Differences*, edited by T. Chamorro-Premuzic, S. von Stumm, and A. Furnham, 656–78. New York, NY: Wiley.

Petrides, K. V., and A. Furnham. 2000. "On the Dimensional Structure of Emotional Intelligence." *Personality and Individual Differences* 29 (2): 313–20.

Rathi, Neerpal, Deepti Bhatnagar, and Sushanta Kumar Mishra. 2013. "Effect of Emotional Labor on Emotional Exhaustion and Work Attitudes Among Hospitality Employees in India." *Journal of Human Resources in Hospitality & Tourism* 12 (3): 273–90. https://doi.org/10.1080/15332845.2013.769142.

Riggs, Fred W. 1968. "Administration and a Changing World Environment." *Public Administration Review* 28 (4): 348–61.

Salovey, P., and J. D. Mayer. 1990. "Emotional Intelligence." *Imagination, Cognition, and Personality* 9 (3): 185–211.

Taras, V., B. L, Kirkman, and P. Steel 2010. "Examining the Impact of Culture's Consequences: A Three-Decade, Multilevel, Meta-Analytic Review of Hofstede's Cultural Value Dimensions." *Journal of Applied Psychology* 95 (3): 405–39. http://dx.doi.org/10.1037/a0018938.

Thorndike, Edward Lee. 1920. "Intelligence and Its Uses." *Harper's Magazine* 140: 227–35.

Tupes, E. C., and R. E. Cristal. 1961. *Recurrent Personality Factors Based on Trait Ratings (ASD-TR-61–97)*. Lackland Air Force Base, TX: U.S. Air Force.

Vandewaa, E. A., D. L. Turnipseed, and G. Cain. 2016. "Panacea or Placebo? An Evaluation of the Value of Emotional Intelligence in Healthcare Workers." *Journal of Health and Human Services Administration* 38 (4): 438–77.

Waldo, Dwight. 1955. *The Study of Public Administration*. Garden City, NY: Doubleday and Company.

Wong, C. S., and K. S. Law. 2002. "The Effects of Leader and Follower Emotional Intelligence on Performance and Attitude: An Exploratory Study." *The Leadership Quarterly* 13: 243–74.

Yang, Seung-Bum, Mary E. Guy, Aisha Azhar, Chih-Wei Hsieh, Hyun Jung Lee, Xiaojun Lu, and Sharon H. Mastracci. 2018. "Comparing Apples and Manzanas: Instrument Development and Measurement Invariance in a Cross-National Analysis of Emotional Labor in Public Service Jobs." *International Journal of Work Organization and Emotion*. 9(3): 264–82. https://doi.org/10.1504/IJWOE.2018.10015953.

5

Understanding Emotional Labor at the Organizational Level

Xiaojun Lu

In public service, organizations are the instruments through which public purposes are pursued. Whether collectively called "the bureaucracy" or thought of as discrete organizations with their own unique characteristics, the dynamics are similar. Strangers are brought together to achieve a mission that no one could achieve by acting alone. For all the strengths of organizations, they also bring stressors for those who work in them. This chapter first applies the Job Demands-Resources (JD-R) model as a theoretical frame for understanding the worker's experience and the outcomes of that experience. Then it discusses how organizational justice affects the emotive load for workers.

Formal organizations consist of architectural elements that structure the way people relate to one another, determine who has more or less power than others, and set boundaries around the reach of each person's job duties. The larger the organization, the more ranks there will be in the hierarchy, the more subunits there will be, the more employees there will be, and the more different kinds of tasks will be performed. Emotional labor is required in most of the jobs, and the emotive demands will vary from minor to intense. The JD-R model provides a useful framework for understanding how the emotive load factors into employees' work experience, ranging from the extremes of job satisfaction and feelings of self-fulfillment to the opposite: burnout.

X. Lu (✉)
Department of Public Administration, School of International
and Public Affairs, Shanghai Jiao Tong University, Shanghai, China
e-mail: xjlv@sjtu.edu.cn

M. E. Guy et al. (eds.), *The Palgrave Handbook of Global Perspectives on Emotional Labor in Public Service*, https://doi.org/10.1007/978-3-030-24823-9_5

Job Demands-Resources Model

The JD-R model is a useful approach to understanding worker behavior—both constructive and destructive—as it relates to the performance of emotional labor. The model suggests that strain is a response to imbalance between demands on workers and the resources they have to deal with those demands. It is a relatively new theory in the field of human resource management, developed to understand occupational burnout due to job stress (Demerouti et al. 2001). The theory posits that employees may experience burnout in various organizational settings and each occupation has its own specific risk factors that may lead to burnout. While these risk factors vary, they can generally be classified into two broad categories: job demands and job resources.

Factors that are considered to be job demands include all those elements of work that draw upon one's physical, cognitive, and emotive skills, as well as work expectations that place a burden on, or conflict with, the worker's personal life. Demands become physical or emotional stressors. Although they differ according to the job, they may include any of the following: time pressures, a heavy workload, complex or boring projects, an uncomfortable or stressful work environment, unclear goals, role ambiguity, little autonomy, excessively bureaucratic rules and procedures, heavy emotive demands such as occurs in emotionally intense work or emotionally draining work, poor relationships with peers, and few opportunities for career advancement or personal development. It has been well-established that emotional exhaustion may be triggered by excessive job demands that exceed the worker's resources to deal with them. The deleterious effect of demands magnifies as they compound.

On the other side of the coin are job resources. These are factors that include both organizational and personal resources and are thought of as positives. They are the physical, social, or organizational factors that help workers achieve their goals with little stress. They include autonomy, strong work relationships, opportunities for advancement, coaching and mentoring, a comfortable working environment, supportive peers, training and development opportunities, work autonomy, and regular constructive feedback. These resources combine to generate what is thought of as organizational support.

According to JD-R theory, stress and burnout are common when demands and resources are out of balance, such that demands are too high and resources are too low. Alternatively, plentiful resources offset the effects of job demands. It is important to note that each person responds to demands differently, so a demand that may be experienced as excessive and causing stress to one employee might not be perceived similarly by another. This is especially the case in jobs that require emotional labor.

Plentiful job resources are assumed to encourage higher work commitment, engagement, motivation, and greater job satisfaction from employees. When job resources are scarce, either because the organization does not have sufficient resources to satisfy what is needed to perform the job, or because employees lack the personal resources—emotive, cognitive, or physical—workers may be unable to cope with job demands or complete job goals. The inability to perform satisfactorily is theorized to affect their physical and psychological well-being (Bakker and Demerouti 2017).

The JD-R theory produces a typology of work circumstances that can be characterized as a two-axis model of high and low job demands and high or low resources. This produces four quadrants depicting conditions of high demands and low resources, high demands and high resources, low demands and high resources, and low demands and low resources. Bakker and Demerouti (2007) discuss how each of these conditions affects motivation and levels of strain. High motivation and low strain results when job resources are high and job demands are low. Average strain and high motivation results when resources are high and demands are high. Low strain and average motivation results when resources are low but demands are also low. And the most non-productive condition exists when demands are high and resources are low. This results in high strain and low motivation. With this in mind, discussion now applies JD-R theory to the subject of employee emotional labor.

The first point of discussion is on emotive display rules, for many organizations require workers to behave in scripted ways and to display emotions they may not actually feel. Especially for those in professional jobs, to appear "professional" is defined by each discipline and the definition is accompanied by an emotive presentation. For example, law enforcement officers are expected to appear confident, assertive, and self-assured. Social workers are expected to appear nurturant and caring. Teachers are expected to act with confidence and grace. Doctors are to appear compassionate and confident, and so forth. The social worker who is not feeling nurturant must don a mask, giving the appearance that she is supportive and nurturant. The police officer who does not feel confident and calm must appear that way, regardless. The teacher whose students fail to do their homework and fail to learn is to act with restraint and patience.

Emotive Display Rules

Using facial expressions, body language, tone of voice, and other non-verbal clues, individuals communicate and convey their emotions to one another. This process is subtle, nuanced, embedded in societal culture, and contextualized to each work setting. Ekman and Friesen (1969) describe the phenomenon, explaining that culturally appropriate emotion displays are learned during early childhood. These "emotion rules" contain the codes that circumscribe the conveyance of various emotions in different contexts, such that some emotions that are appropriate to display in the home are not appropriate in the workplace and vice versa. In other words, emotive displays are influenced, even scripted, by the social context.

Emotion display rules reflect the norms that determine what is, and is not, appropriate for individual emotion expression (Saarni 1988). In the context of organizational behaviors, Sutton (1991) posits that emotion display rules are those that define the appropriate expression of emotion by employees in the work environment. For example, in some offices it is appropriate to be subdued and reserved. In others, people are expected to be friendly and outgoing, cheery and welcoming. The variation in rules is determined by the type of work that employees are engaged in, the degree to which the organization is outward-facing, such that the public observes the behaviors, and the climate, or "mood," within the work unit.

In terms of emotional labor, display rules present a job demand that may, or may not, be stressful. And it is possible that while a display rule is non-stressful for one worker, it may be the opposite for another. In other words, display rules are a condition of employment that may be rewarding or may be a negative attribute of the job, consuming workers' energy as they suppress how they honestly feel. For example, the cheery person who enjoys meeting people will find it rewarding to work in an office that rewards such behavior. On the other hand, the zoning inspector, who must appear stern and unyielding but who actually would like to overlook the rules he is employed to enforce, may find the display rule to be arduous and tiring, because it is an act, a pretense, that consumes energy and is not rewarding. Emotion display rules are a type of organizational norm, prescribing appropriate emotions that are to be displayed by employees in accord with organizational demands. The rules, whether explicit or implicit, determine the types of emotions that must be displayed by employees, who have little autonomy in regard to the emotion they display.

Like wearing a uniform, emotive expression sends a message about who the worker is, what the worker does, and what behavior is appropriate when interacting with the person. A cheery countenance invites a cheery response in return. A stern countenance encourages a quiet, deferential response. In the work setting, employees have to conform to emotion display rules just as they must conform to other work norms, such as getting to work on time, following standardized procedures, and so forth.

While emotion display rules are part of job demands, the rules may not be expressly defined. Instead, whether during the onboarding process where comportment is explicitly trained, or through subtle role modeling where the proper display is implicitly taught, employees learn about behaviors that are appropriate and inappropriate, what is desired and what is not.

In most workplaces, norms encourage the expression of positive emotions and concealment of negative emotions, such as anger or sadness, to promote positive interactions. In fact, display rules may require a clear distinction between emotions to display and emotions to conceal. As both manager and subordinates view conformity to display rules as part of the job requirements, compliance with organizational rules results in workers having to actively regulate their emotional state (Liao and Yan 2015).

Dimensions of Display Rules

Emotive display rules most often separate positive emotions, such as happiness, cheeriness, and friendliness, from negative emotions of sorrow, anger, or rage. Workers are expected to display the former while suppressing the latter. The dimensions of display rules can be categorized into three types: expression of positive emotions, suppression of negative emotions, and suppression of positive emotions. These are discussed below.

Expression of Positive Emotions

Modern society advocates friendly treatment of others, sincerity and kindness, and social harmony. These core principles are a part of our daily life, whether in a professional context or personal life. Positive emotions are used to elicit a positive response from others. If there is any doubt in this, consider the experience of an afternoon at Disney World anywhere on the globe. The Walt Disney Company uses motivational speeches, role-playing, and explicit instructions in its training of new employees. The purpose is to ensure that new employees quickly understand that a pleasant, welcoming countenance is a job demand. All employees must convey pleasant emotions and a sense of happiness.

Suppression of Negative Emotions

Anger, disappointment, sorrow, and even rage are normal emotions. However, the workplace treats these as exceptions and rarely encourages their expression. And when expressed, sanctions vary by the rank and position of the person. Someone working at the street-level may have less leeway than someone in the executive suite. But, there are exceptions. In law enforcement, for example, officers may be trained to appear "tougher than tough," in order to frighten someone who has been arrested into admitting to a crime. In other words, negative emotions may be a part of the job and their expression may be constructive in certain circumstances. Emotion expression is part of the job, complies with job demands, and contributes to effectiveness in meeting organizational goals.

In general, rules regarding the suppression of emotions refer to the suppression of negative emotions. The key is the appropriateness of the displayed emotions in terms of the social context, as well as the consistency between the expression of individual emotions and organizational demands with regard to social norms. There are exceptions, however, as explained below in terms of suppression of positive emotions.

Suppression of Positive Emotions

As counterintuitive as it may sound, suppression of positive emotions may also be a job demand. For example, when a team member achieves an accomplishment, the person may have to suppress the expression of positive emotions to avoid being perceived as a braggart and in order to win coworkers' trust. Likewise, the "tougher than tough" police officer will not be perceived as tough if laughing and responding in a joking manner to the offender. Nor will the tax collector be effective if perceived as a live-and-let-live kind of person. Assertiveness, with a twinge of aggressiveness, will serve the purposes of the job better.

Organizational Display Rules

Organizational emotive display rules refer to the emotion expression norms or standards set and defined by the organization in relation to each job. In most jobs, where workers meet the public, they are required to express positive and suppress negative emotions.

There are two main dynamics between the influence of organizational display rules on emotional labor strategies. First, display rules have a direct effect on emotional labor strategies. If an organization has clear rules for emotive expression, employees are likely to use emotional labor strategies to regulate their emotive expression. As they perform emotional labor, employees must constantly compare their own affect to that which is required by the organization. If there is inconsistency between their actual emotion and the display rule, employees must engage emotion management strategies to regulate their expression in order to perform in a way that is consistent with the rules.

Rules regarding emotive expression encourage pretense because employees must perform as actors, displaying the desired emotion regardless of how they actually feel. It has been well established that there is a direct, significant relationship between having to emotively pretend on the job and experiencing burnout on the job (Guy et al. 2008; Hsieh et al. 2012; Mastracci et al. 2012). In most cultures, it is more stressful to have to suppress emotion than it is to authentically express how one is feeling. Furthermore, the correlation between display rules and emotional labor is also influenced by moderating factors.

While there is a significant correlation between display rules and emotional labor, the correlation is significantly weaker if employees do not comply with the organizational emotional display rules. The degree to which employees are committed to work rules affects the degree to which they comply with them, both in terms of performing desired displays and in terms of suppressing undesirable displays (Liu 2013).

Job Characteristics and Emotional Labor

The job characteristics model, developed by Hackman and Oldham (1975), posits that employees' intrinsic motivation is determined by the characteristics of the job itself. The model proposes that any job can be measured in terms of five dimensions: skill variety, task identity, task significance, autonomy, and feedback. The implication of this is that managers can develop intrinsic employee motivation by improving job design. The assumption is that work will be experienced as meaningful to workers to the degree that their contribution significantly affects the overall effectiveness of the organization.

Of the five dimensions, skill variety refers to the extent to which a job requires different activities, which in turn determines the different skills and abilities required from employees. Task identity refers to the degree to which a job requires complete and well-defined work. Task significance refers to how much a job influences other people's life or work. Autonomy refers to the level of autonomy, independence and judgment the employee can exercise in managing his/her work content and job procedures. And, feedback refers to whether the employee can obtain direct and clear feedback on his/her performance throughout the task completion process. These five dimensions are thought to be linked to three psychological states in employees. Skill variety, task identity, and task significance give rise to experienced meaningfulness. Autonomy leads to experienced responsibility. And, feedback contributes to knowledge of results.

Morris and Feldman (1997) were among the first scholars to study the relationship between job characteristics and emotional labor. They found that different dimensions of job characteristics have different influences on emotional labor. For example, task repetitiveness may positively affect the frequency of emotional labor while negatively influencing the latter's duration. Task diversity may positively affect the diversity of emotions required in daily routines. And, job autonomy may inversely affect the amount of emotive dissonance that results from inconsistency between experienced and displayed emotion.

Several empirical studies support the moderating effect of job autonomy. The findings of Grandey et al. (2005) cross-cultural study, for example, show that job autonomy has a significant moderating effect on the positive correlation between deep acting and emotional exhaustion. When workers perceive themselves to have more control over how they perform their job, the emotional exhaustion that would otherwise result from emotive pretending is reduced. The influence of job autonomy on another variable, job satisfaction, is related to frequency. When there is a high frequency of authentically engaging in emotional labor, job autonomy moderates its effect on job satisfaction such that it is experienced as more positive than negative (Grandey et al. 2005). This shows how job autonomy mitigates the negative effects that can result from emotively intense jobs.

Team Emotion Climate

The concept of team emotional climate has led to an "affective storm" in organizational behavior studies in recent years. This affective storm refers to the significant increase in emotion management research at the organizational level. Among these is the work of Weiss and Cropanzano (1996), whose Affective Events Theory has received widespread attention. It posits that, while employees can experience both positive and negative affective events as they perform their jobs, these events may not directly influence the worker's own behavior. That which does influence workers' own behavior is how each responds to the events, much as the timeworn adage says: "It is not what happens to you that matters; it is how you *think* about what happens to you that matters." This theory provides a new perspective on the study of emotions in organizations, relating job satisfaction to worker's own feelings about their job experiences.

Ashkanasy (2003) proposed a graduated five-level model of emotions in organizations, starting from emotions at the within-person level, moving to emotions at the between-persons level, to emotions at the dyadic (relationship) level, then emotions at the group level and, finally, the emotion climate at the organizational level. However, the overall organizational level may be too abstract to affect individual workers. Instead, emotion climate within workgroups should be the highest level of concern, for that is the highest level where a shared climate is likely to exist.

Other concepts similar to team emotional climate are group affective tone and group emotions. The concept of group affective tone has been translated in some studies as group affective climate, but it is essentially different from the concept of team emotional climate. The term "group affective tone" was first proposed by George (1990). It is defined as the shared emotion in a group, further categorized into two dimensions—positive tone and negative tone. It is measured using the Positive Affect/Negative Affect Scale, which contains simple phrases that describe a person's psychological state. Employees are asked to choose the phrase that best describes their present situation. Then, responses are collated at the group level and examined to determine the level of consistency and to derive the group affective tone (Forgas and George 2001).

Team emotion climate is a more encompassing term than group affective tone, because it comprehends more than only positive and negative affects. Group affective tone only exists if there is high consistency in the emotive perceptions of group members. Because team emotion climate is formed by the shared experience of team members, the concept embraces attitudes, expectations, and emotions, producing a more comprehensive way of understanding the emotive status of a work team.

In recent years, the salutary effects of positive emotions have garnered attention. The internal mechanisms whereby positive emotions promote physical and mental health have also been explored. For example, the broaden-and-build theory of positive emotions (Fredrickson 2001) posits that positive emotions can help individuals reconstruct lost personal resources and replenish depleted physical, mental, interpersonal, and psychological resources. Based on resource conservation theory, when individuals experience a loss of physical and psychological resources due to job demands or other reasons and are unable to replenish them, they experience resource depletion, causing them to feel exhausted. A team's positive emotion climate can replenish resources depleted due to emotional labor, and it is thought to have a buffering effect on job burnout caused by emotional labor.

Emotional Labor and Organizational Support

Studies show a complex relationship between perceived organizational support and employee outcomes, whereby perceptions of support promote positive behaviors among employees while minimizing negative behaviors. This leads to the conclusion that organizational support will facilitate the performance of emotional labor, and it is confirmed by Grandey et al. (2015), who found that organizational support is a predictive organizational factor for performing emotional labor.

Riggle et al. (2009) performed a meta-analysis of the impacts of organizational support on organizational commitment, job satisfaction, job performance, and turnover intention. Their findings show that support significantly affects the level of commitment and job satisfaction, to such an extent that it positively influences job performance and reduces turnover intention. Duke et al. (2009) also study organizational support and include emotional labor as a dimension of work performance. Their results show that perceived organizational support buffers the relationship between emotional labor and employee outcomes, such that high levels of support mitigate negative correlations between emotional labor and both job satisfaction and employee performance.

Other studies that treat organizational support as a moderator reveal more insights. For example, Nixon et al. (2011) investigated how organizational support moderates the impact of emotional labor on work outcomes.

They categorized emotional labor into surface acting and deep acting, and measured employee stress according to turnover intention, level of job satisfaction, burnout, and psychological health. The results of their research indicate that organizational support has a moderating effect on these correlations, with a positive effect on employees who engage in authentic displays of emotion. However, organizational support amplifies the negative effect of emotive pretending.

According to the reciprocity principle of Social Exchange Theory, when employees receive support from the organization, they may in turn increase their job effort to reciprocate the support they receive. In other words, when employees perceive a higher level of organizational support, they may be more committed to the organization and their work. Based on this logic, employees with a higher level of organizational support are less likely to experience stress from emotional labor, and they may be more inclined to perform authentically, rather than only pretending to feel the emotion they are displaying.

In sum, several studies have focused on the relationship between perceived organizational support and emotional labor, and their main focus is on the moderating effect of perceived organizational support on factors affecting emotional labor outcomes. Nixon's research shows that perceived emotional support influences employee outcomes by affecting emotional labor strategies. In other words, employees who perceive higher levels of organizational support may put more effort into their work, be committed to it in an authentic way, and in turn display emotion that is consistent with their true feelings. Therefore, the effect of perceived organizational support is beneficial not only to employee emotional labor strategies but also to positive performance outcomes.

External Reputation of the Organization

Previous research has shown that the external reputation of an organization may influence the emotional labor strategy that employees choose. The perceived external reputation of an organization refers to its employees' perceptions of external stakeholders' attitudes toward it. Based on social comparison theory, when employees perceive that their organization has a superior reputation in comparison with other organizations, their self-esteem may significantly increase, and they may work harder. Therefore, when dealing with customers, they are more inclined to "act in good faith." Conversely, when the organization's perceived external reputation is negative, its employees' self-esteem and sense of organizational belonging may significantly decline; in turn, they may be less enthusiastic about their job. Consequently, they may be more inclined to "act in bad faith" as they perform their jobs.

There is empirical evidence that shows that perceived external reputation has a significant positive impact on the performance of authentic emotive expression, also called deep acting (Mishra et al. 2012). The perceived external reputation of an organization also has a mediating effect on emotional labor strategies through organizational identity. Based on social identity theory, when employees perceive that the organization has a positive external reputation, they may identify more with the organization and align their individual goals with organizational goals. Consequently, they are more committed to, and work harder for, the organization (Mael and Ashforth 1992). As such, they may strive to regulate their inner feelings when dealing with customers.

Conversely, when employees perceive that the organization has a negative external reputation, they are less inclined to identify with the organization and more likely to "act in bad faith." The findings of Mishra et al. (2012) show that organizational identity plays a significant partial mediating role in the positive impact of perceived external reputation on authentic emotive expression and a negative impact on emotive pretending. This shows that commitment to the organization and confidence in its mission makes it less stressful as employees perform their jobs.

Organizational Justice and Emotional Labor

In the establishment of service-oriented government, the demands on civil servants in terms of emotional labor cannot be neglected. When it results in occupational stress, it is a negative outcome for civil servants as individuals, for the organization, for government, and, ultimately, for citizens. When it results in job satisfaction and feelings of self-fulfillment, it is a win-win outcome for workers, the organization, government, and citizens. There is an organizational factor that may play a mediating or moderating role in this relationship, and it is organizational justice. This refers to a subjective judgment regarding whether an individual has been treated fairly in the organization. It is generally classified into four dimensions—distributive, procedural, interactional, and informational—and it deeply influences individual attitudes and behaviors (Colquitt et al. 2001; Lu and Guy 2018a).

Organizational justice is an individual's subjective judgment of whether he/she has been treated fairly in the organization, and it is largely determined by the individual's perception of resource allocation. Research indicates that there is a significant relationship between resource allocation outcomes and overall perceptions of justice in organizations in China (Kim and Leung 2007). In fact, organizational justice is not only an indication of the resources an individual is likely to obtain from the organization, but it also triggers individual expectations of potential future gains, such as securing future benefits and position through fair procedures and supe-rior-subordinate interaction. From the perspective of resource conservation theory, organizational justice is a force that motivates individuals in terms of resource acquisition, whether resources are material or are expressed in terms of individual status.

Organizational justice provides multiple forms of resource support for individuals in their encounter with the work environment so the subject has a logical link to JD-R theory. An instrumental model of justice proposed by Erdogan (2003) argues that there is greater justice when individuals have more autonomy. And, individuals have a higher sense of justice when there is greater certainty regarding future resources. In addition, the organization is not merely a place where individuals obtain material resources; individuals also identify with their workgroups. When they experience justice, there is a halo effect that extends to positive feelings toward their work, the work of their peers, and the performance of the organization (Blader and Tyler 2004). Moreover, fair treatment enhances the identity and self-esteem of members of the organization (Flint 1999). The higher the perceived organ-izational justice, the more it can compensate for resource depletion caused by emotive pretending. This, then, reduces the resulting occupational stress. In terms of authentically displaying emotion, organizational justice has a minimal effect on its relationship with work stress because individuals can regenerate psychological resources by themselves.

As the chapters in this book reveal, surveys of workers engaged in public service around the globe engage in both pretending and authentic expression of emotion in their jobs. Demographic variables have little effect on emo-tional labor strategies (Lu and Guy 2018b). In most, but not all, countries, there is a positive relationship between pretending and burnout, indicating that the more employees use emotive pretense in order to perform their jobs, the more job stress they experience. Conversely, deep acting, the authentic expression of emotion, is more likely to correlate with job satisfaction and feelings of personal fulfillment, although there are variations that occur due to culture.

As discussed previously, emotional labor strategies consume psychological resources (Kruml and Geddes 2000). Whether the outcome of emotional labor is positive or negative depends on the balance of resources available. Emotive pretending requires extensive willpower as the individual is displaying an emotion that is contrary to the real feeling he/she is experiencing. It is a condition of emotive dissonance. At such times, workers may experience immense psychological conflict, leading to exhaustion, anxiety, and other symptoms of stress.

While psychological resources are also required for deep acting, the resources differ from that which is required while pretending. Deep acting relies on perception, interpretation, and other psychological processes to achieve consistency between one's internal emotional experience and external displays. This requires little or no intrapersonal conflict and, thus, is not correlated with job stress as often as is pretending. Organizational justice may account for this, as it enhances individual resource gains and lowers stress.

Conclusion

This chapter uses the JD-R theory to explain how emotional labor fits into job demands and how organizational resources mitigate its deleterious effects. The implications for human resource management in public service organizations are threefold: developing worker commitment to the mission; acknowledging the emotive load that employees encounter; and, ensuring that organizational justice is part of the organizational resources offered to employees. Each is summarized below.

1. Most jobs in public service involve emotional labor. The Job Demands-Resources theory helps answer the question of how to help employees perform their duties and achieve job satisfaction from their work. Because authentic emotive displays are less stressful for workers than pretending is, and because authentic displays—deep acting—results in better performance outcomes and lower staff turnover, JD-R instructs that creating a service-oriented government requires internalization of the mission. The more committed to the mission that workers are, the more authentic their emotive responses to the public will be.
2. The goal of creating service-oriented government can become a performance norm. Only through full awareness and understanding of the concept of service can civil servants truly grasp their job demands and the relationship between them (the government) and the public. Hence, the role of human resource management is to provide more in-depth development and training programs for the establishment of a culture of

service-oriented government and to design comprehensive and in-depth organizational socialization processes that take emotional labor demands into account. The more that workers achieve consistency between their emotive state and the emotion that they display on the job, the more that job stress will be alleviated.

3. Perceptions of organizational justice may provide support in the form of organizational resources. While it is colored by subjective individual perceptions, the judgment is formed based on objective resource allocation within the organization. Therefore, in order to increase perceived justice among civil servants, the employer must allocate resources that are fair, encourage constructive interactions between superiors and subordinates, and create a democratic organizational climate. In this way, there is a balance between job demands and resources.

References

Ashkanasy, N. M. 2003. "Emotions in Organizations: A Multi-level Perspective." In *Multi-level Issues in Organizational Behavior and Strategy*. Research in Multi Level Issues, vol. 2, edited by Fred Dansereau and Francis J. Yammarino, 9–54. Bingley, West Yorkshire, UK: Emerald Group Publishing.

Bakker, Arnold B., and Evangelia Demerouti. 2007. "The Job Demands-Resources Model: State of the Art." *Journal of Managerial Psychology* 22 (3): 309–28. https://doi.org/10.1108/02683940710733115.

Bakker, Arnold B., and Evangelia Demerouti. 2017. "Job Demands-Resources Theory: Taking Stock and Looking Forward." *Journal of Occupational Health Psychology* 22 (3): 273–85.

Blader, S. L., and T. R. Tyler. 2004. "What Constitutes Fairness in Work Settings? A Four-Component Model of Procedural Justice." *Human Resource Management Review* 13 (1): 107–26.

Colquitt, J. A., D. E. Conlon, M. J. Wesson, C. O. Porter, and K. Y. Ng. 2001. "Justice at the Millennium: A Meta-Analytic Review of 25 Years of Organizational Justice Research." *Journal of Applied Psychology* 86 (3): 425–45.

Demerouti, E., A. B. Bakker, J. De Jonge, P. P. Janssen, and W. B. Schaufeli. 2001. "Burnout and Engagement at Work as a Function of Demands and Control." *Scandinavian Journal of Work Environment & Health* 27 (4): 279–86.

Duke, A. B., J. M. Goodman, D. C. Treadway, and Jacob W. Breland. 2009. "Perceived Organizational Support as a Moderator of Emotional Labor/Outcomes Relationships." *Journal of Applied Social Psychology* 39 (5): 1013–34. https://doi.org/10.1111/j.1559-1816.2009.00470.x.

Ekman, P., and W. V. Friesen. 1969. "Nonverbal Leakage and Clues to Deception." *Psychiatry-Interpersonal & Biological Processes* 32 (1): 88–106.

Erdogan, B. 2003. "Antecedents and Consequences of Justice Perceptions in Performance Appraisals." *Human Resource Management Review* 12 (4): 555–78.

Flint, D. H. 1999. "The Role of Organizational Justice in Multi-source Performance Appraisal: Theory-Based Applications and Directions for Research. *Human Resource Management Review* 9 (1): 1–20.

Forgas, J. P., and J. M. George. 2001. "Affective Influences on Judgments and Behavior in Organizations: An Information Processing Perspective." *Behavior and Human Decision Processes* 86 (1): 3–34. https://doi.org/10.1006/obhd.2001.2971.

Fredrickson, Barbara L. 2001. "The Role of Positive Emotions in Positive Psychology: The Broaden-and-Build Theory of Positive Emotions." *American Psychologist* 56 (3): 218–26.

George, J. M. 1990. "Personality, Affect, and Behavior in Groups." *Journal of Applied Psychology* 75: 107–16.

Grandey, A. A., G. M. Fisk, and D. D. Steiner. 2005. "Must 'Service with a Smile' Be Stressful? The Moderating Role of Personal Control for American and French Employees." *Journal of Applied Psychology* 90 (5): 893–904.

Grandey, A. A., D. Rupp, and W. N. Brice. 2015. "Emotional Labor Threatens Decent Work: A Proposal to Eradicate Emotional Display Rules." *Journal of Organizational Behavior* 36 (6): 770–85.

Guy, Mary E., Meredith A. Newman, and Sharon H. Mastracci. 2008. *Emotional Labor: Putting the Service in Public Service.* Armonk, NY: M.E. Sharpe.

Hackman, J. R., and G. R. Oldham. 1975. "Development of the Job Diagnostic Survey." *Journal of Applied Psychology* 60 (2): 159–70.

Hsieh, Chih-Wei, Myung Jin, and Mary E. Guy. 2012. "Managing Work-Related Emotions: Analysis of a Cross Section of Public Service Workers." *The American Review of Public Administration* 42 (1): 39–53.

Kim, T. Y., and K. Leung. 2007. "Forming and Reacting to Overall Fairness: A Cross-Cultural Comparison." *Organizational Behavior & Human Decision Processes* 104 (1): 83–95.

Kruml, S. M., and D. Geddes. 2000. "Exploring the Dimensions of Emotional Labor: The Heart of Hochschild's Work." *Management Communication Quarterly* 14 (1): 8–49.

Liao, H. H., and A. M. Yan. 2015. "The Content of Emotional Labor." *Chinese Journal of Management* 12 (2): 306–12.

Liu, C. 2013. *The Effect of Emotion Display Rules and Emotional Labor on Negative Work Behaviors.* Doctoral Dissertation, Hunan University, Changsha, Hunan Province, People's Republic of China.

Lu, Xiaojun, and Mary E. Guy. 2018a. "Political Skill, Organizational Justice, and Career Success in Mainland China." *International Review of Administrative Sciences* 84 (2): 371–88. https://doi.org/10.1177/0020852315619025.

Lu, Xiaojun, and Mary E. Guy. 2018b. "Emotional Labor, Performance Goal Orientation, and Burnout from the Perspective of Conservation of Resources: A United States/China Comparison." *Public Performance & Management Review*. https://doi.org/10.1080/15309576.2018.1507916.

Mael, F., and B. E. Ashforth. 1992. "Alumni and Their Alma Mater: A Partial Test of the Reformulated Model of Organizational Identification." *Journal of Organizational Behavior* 13(2): 103–23.

Mastracci, Sharon H., Mary E. Guy, and Meredith A. Newman. 2012. *Emotional Labor and Crisis Response: Working on the Razor's Edge*. Armonk, NY: M.E. Sharpe.

Mishra, Sushanta Kumar, Deepti Bhatnagar, Premilla D'Cruz, and Ernesto Noronha. 2012. "Linkage Between Perceived External Prestige and Emotional Labor: Mediation Effect of Organizational Identification Among Pharmaceutical Representatives in India." *Journal of World Business* 47 (2): 204–12.

Morris, J. A, and D. C. Feldman. 1997. "Managing Emotions in the Workplace." *Journal of Managerial Issues* 9 (3): 257–74.

Nixon, A. E., L. Q. Yang, P. E. Spector, and X. Zhang. 2011. "Emotional Labor in China: Do Perceived Organizational Support and Gender Moderate the Process?" *Stress & Health* 27 (4): 289–305.

Riggle, R. J., D. R. Edmondson, and J. D. Hansen. 2009. "A Meta-Analysis of the Relationship Between Perceived Organizational Support and Job Outcomes: Twenty Years of Research." *Journal of Business Research* 62 (10): 1027–30.

Saarni, Carolyn. 1988. "Children's Understanding of the Interpersonal Consequences of Dissemblance of Nonverbal Emotional-Expressive Behavior." *Journal of Nonverbal Behavior* 12: 275–94.

Sutton, R. I. 1991. "Maintaining Norms About Expressed Emotions: The Case of Bill Collectors." *Administrative Science Quarterly* 36 (2): 245–68.

Weiss, H. M., and R. Cropanzano. 1996. "Affective Events Theory: A Theoretical Discussion of the Structure, Causes and Consequences of Affective Experiences at Work." *Research in Organizational Behavior* 18 (3): 1–74.

6

Understanding Emotional Labor at the Cultural Level

Sharon H. Mastracci and Ian Tyler Adams

The wide range of policies demanding multinational attention and the problems that brought them about include the globalization of financial markets, global climate change, internal and cross-border conflicts displacing tens of millions of people (UNHCR 2018), and international trade, among others. Understanding the effects of culture on human behavior is more crucial than it has ever been. Cultural worldviews are ideological belief systems that individuals use to both shape and explain their own and others' behavior (Matsumoto 2006). Expressions of emotion are an essential part of the daily work in organizations that are comprised of meaning-making jobs, so public sector work is on center stage. In this chapter, we explore the effect of cultural norms on several dimensions to emotional labor: emotive displays toward others, how people manage their emotive state, and how others "read" emotive displays and respond to them.

Organizational behavior research in the private sector reveals that culture affects individuals' appraisals of situations and this leads to differential expression of emotions (Matsumoto et al. 1988; Mauro et al. 1992; Roseman et al. 1995). Cultures differ in norms surrounding emotional

S. H. Mastracci (✉)
Department of Political Science, University of Utah,
Salt Lake City, UT, USA
e-mail: Sharon.mastracci@poli-sci.utah.edu

I. T. Adams
West Jordan, UT, USA
e-mail: ian.adams@utah.edu

© The Author(s) 2019
M. E. Guy et al. (eds.), *The Palgrave Handbook of Global Perspectives on Emotional Labor in Public Service*, https://doi.org/10.1007/978-3-030-24823-9_6

expression, and they differ in their display rules (Matsumoto 1990, 1993; Matsumoto et al. 1998, 2005). This chapter begins by discussing definitions of culture and the common elements across definitions. We then discuss Hofstede's IBM studies and Project GLOBE: Two of the most well-known and often-cited organizational behavior studies involving survey respondents in dozens of countries. We then discuss research considerations unique to examining human behavior at the level of culture, including reductionism and ecological fallacy. Additional cross-national comparative research projects focusing on the workplace are also discussed. For instance, Mesquita (2001) introduces emotion explicitly into culturally-comparative research. And Matsumoto et al. (2005) examine display rules and emotion regulation, while surface acting lurks throughout Hofstede's research, particularly when he extends into Confucian cultures with their emphasis on face saving (Hofstede and Bond 1988). Emotions and culture are then examined, including analyses of our data by country and data from other multinational research projects including Project GLOBE, Hofstede et al., and additional data sources such as the World Values Survey, the Chinese Values Survey, and the World Economic Forum. We conclude with a summary of our analyses and a discussion of unanswered questions that arise.

Perhaps ominously, our first question pertains to a fundamental definition: What is culture? Although no consensus definition of culture exists among social scientists, research projects focusing on culture advance working definitions from which to operate. Together, these definitions produce a multifaceted concept of culture. First, culture is social: Some concept of membership is fundamental to any definition of it. Second, culture involves sharing: Some set of attitudes or beliefs is transmitted among the members of a culture. In Project GLOBE, Chhokar, Brodbeck, and House emphasize both the social nature of culture and how it at once includes and excludes: Culture is "a set of parameters of collectivities that differentiate the collectivities from each other in meaningful ways. The focus is on the 'sharedness' of cultural indicators among members of the collectivity" (Chhokar et al. 2007, 3). In his IBM studies, Geert Hofstede consistently draws an analogy between the sharing aspect of culture and computer software, with our physical selves being the hardware: Culture is "the collective programming of the mind" that distinguishes group members from one another (Hofstede 1980, 13). This programming is transmitted via societal institutions including the family, school, and social networks: "National cultures are part of the mental software we acquire during the first ten years of our lives in the family, the living environment, and at school, and they contain most of our basic values" (Minkov and Hofstede 2011, 14). The software consists of beliefs about the world and is transmitted via language. "The collective level of mental programming is shared with some but not with all other people; it is common to people belonging to a certain group or category, but different among people belonging to other groups or categories" (Hofstede 1980, 15). The content of collective programming includes "shared attitudes, beliefs, categorizations, expectations, norms, roles, self-definitions, values, and other such elements of subjective culture found among individuals whose interactions were facilitated by *shared* language, historical period, and geographic region" (Triandis 1993, 156, emphasis original).

Universal aspects of collective programming are inherited while unique aspects are learned. Culture characterizes a group of people: "Culture is to a human collectivity what personality is to an individual" (Hofstede and Bond 1988, 21). While individuals can be more uptight or relaxed, so too can cultures be tight (Singapore) or loose (Brazil) in terms of enforcing norms through societal sanctions and number of police per capital, for example (Gelfand 2018).

Time and location are additional elements of culture: "*Language, time,* and *place* are important in determining the difference between one and another culture, since language is needed to transmit culture and it is desirable to have the same historical period and geography to do so efficiently" (Triandis 2001, 908, emphasis original). In Project GLOBE, House et al. (2004) also underscore the role of time and generation in their definition of culture. They make clear that culture is comprised of shared motives, values, beliefs, identities, and interpretations of significant events, all of which result from common experiences of members of collectives and are transmitted across age generations.

Brewer and Venaik define culture simply as "a 'pattern' or 'configuration' of characteristics that is shared by a group of people" (2014, 1080). Likewise, Matsumoto and Yoo emphasize sharing and underscore the importance of those elements to shape members' behaviors: "A shared system of socially-transmitted behavior that describes, defines, and guides people's ways of life" (2007, 336). Culture promotes group survival: "Culture is to society what memory is to individuals" (Kluckhorn 1954, 921) and "includes what has worked in the experience of a society that was worth transmitting to future generations" (Triandis 2001, 908).

Although there is no consensus definition of "culture," the common elements that appear across most definitions include beliefs, values, norms, attitudes, and meanings that lead to behaviors which are shared among a group of individuals. Examples of what is shared among an identifiable group of people range from the intangible to the observable, including race and ethnicity: "The most parsimonious operationalizations of societal culture consist of commonly experienced language, ideological belief systems (including religion and political belief systems), ethnic heritage, and history" (House et al. 2004, 15). And emotional expressions are also part of what is observable and tangible about an identifiable group of people: "Emotional expressions carry information about nationality or culture beyond the information conveyed by permanent differences between cultural groups in their members' physiognomy of facial features, apparel, or other static features" (Marsh et al. 2003, 375). Recognizing in-group members of one's culture is crucial to sustaining a sense of community or society and language is crucial to identifying group status as well as to transmitting that group's values and beliefs through music, stories, and rituals.

In sum, a culture is a group of people who are characterized by shared beliefs, attitudes, and norms, who may or may not be identifiable by observable physical characteristics. These group of people live and perhaps work in close enough proximity to one another to facilitate sharing beliefs, attitudes, and norms, and must possess some means by which to share the defining elements of their culture. Shared language is the most common means by which elements of culture are transmitted, but emotions also communicate information. Moreover, these group of people live and/or work together at a particular point in time such that sharing norms, practices, beliefs, and attitudes—among other elements of culture—is feasible. Emotive expression is also among a culture's defining characteristics. Before we discuss emotions and culture, however, we review two of the most well-known multi-country research projects in organizational behavior: Hofstede's IBM studies and Project GLOBE. We then consider challenges unique to research on human behavior as it is affected by culture, such that the concept is more stable than "I'll know it when I see it" yet flexible enough to apply to multiple groups of people.

The IBM Studies and Project GLOBE

Hofstede's IBM studies (Hofstede et al. 2010) and Project GLOBE (House et al. 2004) are perhaps the most well-known, large-scale projects comparing work and organizations across multiple countries. Geert Hofstede examined responses to workplace surveys on values and beliefs administered to IBM employees in its offices around the world. Surveys were administered in 1968 and 1972, resulting in more than 116,000 responses from 40 countries. Around the same time, Hofstede et al. (2010) also gathered information from managers participating in international management development courses in several countries to augment the results from the

IBM employee surveys. Employing factor analyses to reduce the data into a tractable number of main categories, Hofstede produced four dimensions of culture: Individualism (Collectivism), Uncertainty Avoidance, Masculinity (Femininity), and Power Distance. Hofstede concluded that many national differences in work-related values, beliefs, norms, and self-descriptions, as well as many societal variables, could be explained in terms of their associations with four major dimensions of national culture: Individualism, Uncertainty Avoidance, Masculinity, and Power Distance (Minkov and Hofstede 2011, 11). Dimensions of culture denote the boundaries between them. Hofstede (1980) claimed that his four dimensions were consistent with the results of 38 previous multi-country comparative studies conducted to date.

Around the time the IBM data were gathered, researchers from ten Asian and Pacific universities administered the Chinese Values Survey (CVS) to 100 students at each of their institutions. When data from the IBM studies and CVS "were compared, it appeared that all four dimensions identified in the IBM material, in addition to a fifth ... were also present in the student data" (Hofstede and Bond 1988, 15). Hofstede and Bond (1988) applied the four-dimension model of culture to Asian countries to capture this fifth cultural dimension and to explore the potential effects of rapid economic growth in that region. They reveal a dimension they initially labeled Confucian Dynamism, which was later generalized to Future Orientation. The original IBM studies failed to capture Future Orientation: "The dimension is composed precisely of those elements that our Western instruments had not registered ... it took the Chinese Values Survey—an Eastern instrument—to identify this dimension" (Hofstede and Bond 1988, 19).

An important and influential outcome from this extension of the IBM studies was the emergence of East/West comparisons in cross-cultural comparative research. Uncertainty Avoidance did not emerge in the Chinese Values Survey (CVS) data and it was found to be a distinctly Western construct. Conversely, Future Orientation was not captured at all in Hofstede's original study but only arose in CVS data: "There is a philosophical dividing line in our world that separates Western from Eastern thinking ... Western thinking is analytical, while Eastern thinking is synthetic" (Hofstede and Bond 1988, 19–20).

Taras et al. (2010) conducted a meta-analysis of 598 studies that employ Hofstede's (1980) original four cultural dimensions: Individualism/Collectivism, Power Distance, Uncertainty Avoidance, and Masculinity/Femininity. The authors compare the explanatory power of these four dimensions to that of individual characteristics on organizationally-relevant outcomes: "Amounts of variance explained by cultural values are as much as (and sometimes more than) that explained by individual differences such as the Big Five personality traits and general mental ability with respect to specific outcomes ... such as organizational commitment, organizational citizenship behavior, organizational identification, team-related attitudes and perceptions, receptivity to certain leadership styles and feedback seeking" (Taras et al. 2010, 429). They find that Individualism vs. Collectivism is the most studied of Hofstede's five cultural dimensions, and the East/West divide is mirrored by a very similar split between East/synthetic/Collectivist and West/analytic/Individualist.

Later in this chapter, we revisit this philosophical dividing line between East and West and examine whether emotional labor is more stressful to respondents in the Individualistic West than those in the Collectivist East because the latter culture rewards sensing the affect of others and attuning to others in order to promote interpersonal harmony. Initially, Hofstede defined Masculinity and Individualism as single scales where high index values indicated Masculine and Individualist cultures, respectively, and low index values indicated Feminine and Collectivist cultures, respectively. Project GLOBE created separate scales for masculinity and femininity, and Individualism and Collectivism. Furthermore, Project GLOBE specified two types of Collectivism.

The Global Leadership and Organizational Behavior Effectiveness (GLOBE) project surveyed 17,000 middle managers from 951 organizations operating in 62 societies in three private-sector industries: Telecommunications, financial services, and food processing. The first volume (House et al. 2004) reported results from these surveys. Project GLOBE modified two of the four dimensions originally revealed in the IBM studies, included the fifth cultural dimension added by Hofstede and Bond and then created two new cultural dimensions: Humane Orientation and Performance Orientation. In total, nine cultural dimensions are quantified and used as independent variables: Uncertainty Avoidance, Power Distance, Institutional Collectivism, In-Group Collectivism, Gender Egalitarianism, Assertiveness, Future Orientation, Performance Orientation, and Humane Orientation.

Project GLOBE divides Hofstede's Collectivism dimension into Institutional and In-Group Collectivism. Institutional Collectivism is "the degree to which organizational and societal institutional practices encourage and reward collective distribution of resources and collective action" (House et al. 2004, 12). In-Group Collectivism is "the degree to which individuals express pride, loyalty, and cohesiveness in their organizations or families" (House et al. 2004, 12). Project GLOBE divides Hofstede's Masculinity/ Femininity dimension into Gender Egalitarianism and Assertiveness.

Gender Egalitarianism is "the degree to which an organization or society minimizes gender role differences while promoting gender equality" (House et al. 2004, 12). Assertiveness is "the degree to which individuals in organizations or societies are assertive, confrontational, and aggressive in social relationships" (House et al. 2004, 12).

GLOBE's two new dimensions, Performance Orientation and Humane Orientation, capture the extent to which organizations and societies "reward performance improvement and excellence" and "encourage and reward individuals for being fair, altruistic, friendly, generous, caring, and kind to others," respectively (House et al. 2004, 13). Project GLOBE sought primarily to employ these nine dimensions as independent variables to explain variations in different types of leadership styles in organizations. Other dependent variables included measures of national income and well-being.

The second volume (Chhokar et al. 2007) profiled 25 individual countries and included results from follow-up "focus groups, in-depth ethnographic interviews, media analysis, participant observation, and unobtrusive measurement" (2007, 24). Concerning theories of organizational leadership, Project GLOBE sought to integrate motivation theories with theories on what cultures value—mainly Hofstede (1980)—and theories on organizational performance. Their central contribution to the literature on organizational leadership is to advance their Culturally Endorsed Implicit Theory of Leadership (CLT), which states that the behaviors encouraged and rewarded by a culture predict "organizational practices and leader attributes and behaviors that are most frequently enacted and most effective in that culture" (House et al. 2004, 17). Among the fifteen propositions emanating from their theory of leadership—not detailed here—arguably the most influential was their observation that leadership theories developed and tested in one culture may not effectively predict leadership behavior in a different culture, thereby expanding Markus and Kitayama's (1991) work to an explicit focus on leadership. Project GLOBE sought a "country-specific understanding of culture and leadership" (Chhokar et al. 2007, 2).

Another important contribution of Project GLOBE was the separate articulation of values and practices. Values relate to preferences about what ought to be, and practices capture behaviors. Survey responses were elicited on both "what is" and "what should be" to capture organizational practices day-to-day separately from what ought to be and what is aspired. This way, the extent to which practices diverge from—or align with—values can be captured, as well. Individual responses are aggregated to the level of culture. For most cultures, cultural boundaries are the same as national political boundaries, but given the central role of language to transmitting "What

We Do" and "What *We* Value," a few countries are divided into multiple cultures: English- and French-speaking parts of Canada are examined separately, as are three regions in Switzerland. Language was not the only difference to lead to separating countries into cultures: In Germany and South Africa, historical definitions of the "We" prompted researchers to subdivide those countries into multiple cultures. Unique historical aspects of East and West Germany led those regions to be analyzed separately, and indigenous and white samples from South Africa were likewise examined separately.

Project GLOBE produced a wide range of results related to leadership, culture, and values. For leadership, Project GLOBE identified nearly two dozen attributes, such as Decisiveness and Foresightedness, as universally desirable: "Ninety-five percent of the societal average scores for these attributes were larger than 5 on a 7-point Likert scale" (House et al. 2004, 39). Eight leadership attributes were found to be universally undesirable, including Irritability and Ruthlessness. Many attributes were found to be culturally contingent: "They are desirable in some cultures and undesirable in others" (House et al. 2004, 40). Ambitious leaders are not valued in all countries, nor are democratic workplaces. In certain cultures, leaders are expected to maintain steep hierarchies and divisions among ranks in organizations. In some cultures, reluctant leaders are valued, and open ambition is not rewarded.

Project GLOBE finds evidence to support the Culturally Endorsed Implicit Theory of Leadership, which emerges as six separate leadership styles: Charismatic/Value-Based, Team Oriented, Participative, Autonomous, Humane-Oriented, and Self-Protective. Charismatic/Values-Based leadership is highly endorsed among English-speaking, Individualist countries and least endorsed in the Middle East. Team-Oriented leadership is favored across the board and receives the highest ratings in Latin American countries. Participative leadership is favored in Germanic Europe, but not in the Middle East. Humane-Oriented leadership is highly endorsed among respondents in Southern Asia but is considered paternalistic and undesirable in Nordic Europe. Autonomous leadership is valued in Eastern Europe but not in Latin America. Self-Protective leadership is generally not endorsed and is considered an impediment to outstanding leadership.

With respect to culture, Project GLOBE answers one of its central questions regarding the influence of national culture on the workplace: "Organizations mirror the societies from which they originate" (Javidan et al. 2004, 726). In fact, national culture appears to influence organizations, while industry does not. In other words, responses of middle managers in food processing, financial services, and telecommunications firms in a particular country resembled one another more than they resembled their industry counterparts in other countries. Project GLOBE also refined two of Hofstede's four dimensions of culture—Masculinity and Collectivism—and confirmed the presence of the other three, while adding two new dimensions: Humane Orientation and Performance Orientation. House et al. conclude, however, that "cultures are not a set of independent, self-standing dimensions, but instead are formed as a confluence of cultural attributes" (2004, 729). Future research should examine which dimensions interact, and how they do so, when multiple cultures come into contact. Their results with respect to culture complicate the simpler question pursued by previous researchers on whether cultures tend toward convergence over time or not.

Finally, with respect to values, Project GLOBE produced the counter-intuitive result that practices do not follow from values: "there is a negative correlation between cultural values and practices in seven out of nine cultural dimensions" (House et al. 2004, 729). This finding contradicts much of the literature on practices and values which suggests, "implicitly or explicitly that cultural practices are driven by cultural values and that there is a linear and positive relationship between them" (House et al. 2004, 729). In an attempt to explain their results, House et al. conjecture that the relationship between practices and values may be nonlinear and more complicated than previously suggested, that there may be mediating conditions between the two, or that observed practices actually inspire respondents to articulate values counter to them: "People may hold views on what *should be* based on what they observe in action" (House et al. 2004, 730, emphasis original). In other words, dismay at observed ambition and greed among business leaders and politicians might have inspired respondents to endorse shared prosperity and a more collectivist mind-set as guiding values for their society. Conversely, dismay at perceived passivity in one's culture and associating ambition with economic growth and innovation may have inspired respondents to endorse Individualism and assertiveness as guiding values for society.

In the years since Hofstede's IBM studies and Project GLOBE, there have been a few multiple-country projects examining cultural dimensions and work, including research teams led by David Matsumoto at San Francisco State University and Harry Triandis at the University of Illinois. Triandis (1989) examined aspects of Individualism/Collectivism and Matsumoto et al. (1988) focused on workplace emotions and display rules. Triandis was perhaps the earliest advocate for treating Individualism and Collectivism separately. Matsumoto was the first to recognize the salience of emotion to cultural characteristics. The vast literature borne of the Triandis and

Matsumoto research teams as well as the IBM studies and Project GLOBE has influenced our research immensely as they each articulate central challenges that arise when culture is the unit of analysis.

Culture as the Unit of Analysis

Countries or cultures as units of analysis are referred to as *ecological-level studies* (Matsumoto and Yoo 2007, 337, emphasis original) and Hofstede (1980, 31) counsels: "Cultures are not king-size individuals: They are wholes and their internal logic cannot be understood in the terms used for the personality dynamics of individuals" (Brewer and Venaik 2014, 1069). Hofstede's dimensions of national culture were comprised of aggregated individual responses, but "are meaningless as descriptors of individuals … because the variables that define them do not correlate meaningfully across individuals" (Minkov and Hofstede 2011, 12). The two levels of analysis are easily confused because, while individual responses are aggregated to generate cultural dimensions in both the Hofstede and Project GLOBE studies, the resulting dimensions pertain to the *culture*, not to the individual. For instance, while a culture is characterized as collectivist or individualist, similar traits in individuals are labeled allocentric and idiocentric, respectively. However, not everyone in a collectivist culture is allocentric, and not everyone in an individualist culture is idiocentric. Aggregating across the country or society reveals the effect of context on individual responses and produces the culture-level indicator, but it is the country or society characteristic that emerges, not an individual trait.

Causing further confusion are the instances in which societies can behave like individuals. Equating dimensions of culture to personality characteristics of individuals is one example. Another is the presence of response bias by culture, which is not unlike the phenomenon of individual response bias. Cultural response bias is "the tendency to avoid extreme ends of a scale in Asian countries or a tendency to avoid the midpoint of a scale in European cultures" (Schlösser et al. 2013, 540). Such response bias is also found among members of subcultures: African-American and Hispanic American survey respondents also tend to avoid extreme points of a scale "in congruence with a cultural hesitation to 'stick out' that results in the use of the middle of a scale" (Matsumoto and Yoo 2007, 341).

Use of multiple indicators to generate single index variable s via factor analysis helps to mitigate bias by spreading any systematic error over multiple variables, but these index variables remain relevant only to the higher level of analysis: "A factor analysis starts from a correlation matrix; therefore, ecological (country-level) factors are different from individual factors" (Hofstede 1980, 48). Creating these index variables, or constructs, allows us to capture the effects of complex social phenomena. Constructs are "not directly accessible to observation but inferable from verbal statements and other behaviors and useful in predicting still other observable and measurable verbal and nonverbal behavior" (Levitin 1973, 492). Importantly, it is up to the researcher—relying on previous research and guided by observation—to select individual variables to collapse into more complex constructs.

The dimensions of culture identified by Hofstede in his IBM studies and House et al. in Project GLOBE were products of choices made by the respective research teams. "A construct is a complex mental idea that reflects objectively existing phenomena ... constructs are not the reality itself, but are imaginary models that scholars build in order to organize their impressions of the observed reality in a way that makes sense to them, and hopefully, to others" (Minkov and Hofstede 2011, 17). Importantly, Project GLOBE modified some of Hofstede's four cultural dimensions: "*Construct* refers to the construction of conceptions or ideas by the investigator. A construct is a product of the investigator's creativity" (House and Javidan 2004, 20). The resulting nine dimensions of culture specified in Project GLOBE "are what multilevel researchers call *convergent-emergent constructs*" (Hanges and Dickson 2004, 124, emphases original):

These constructs are *convergent* because the responses from people within organizations or societies are believed to center about a single value usually represented by scale means. They are called *emergent* because even though the origin of these constructs is a function of the cognition, affect, and personality of the respondents, the properties of these constructs are actually manifested at the aggregate or group (organization or society) level of analysis.

Because underlying elements of constructs converge around mean values, "relationships among aggregate data tend to be higher than corresponding relationships among individual data elements" (Kozlowski and Klein 2000, 8). "Elements that are used frequently become habitual. These result in customs and institutions that reflect the habits" (Triandis 1993, 163). Changes in customs and institutions and their overall constructs—dimensions of culture—over time appear to be very slow (Dorfman and House 2004). Brewer and Venaik "show that although the Hofstede and GLOBE dimensions were developed conceptually and empirically only at the national level, they are often incorrectly applied and interpreted at the individual and organizational levels ... ecological fallacy is the error of assuming that statistical relationships at a group level also hold for individuals in the group" (2014, 1064).

Conversely, Hofstede (1980, 30) warns against committing a *reverse* ecological fallacy, which "consists in comparing cultures on indices created for the individual level" (Hofstede 1980, 30). Finally, scholarly opinion concerning scale invariance in cross-cultural research remains divided. Hofstede warns: "It is a doubtful practice to use instruments developed in one country (in this case, the United States) in another cultural environment, assuming they carry the same meaning there" (1980, 22). Yet in a summary of his research, Hofstede's collaborators disagree and conclude: "Concerns that developing a particular instrument in one cultural environment would make it unsuitable in another environment are sometimes exaggerated" (Minkov and Hofstede 2011, 16). In the next section, we see that it likewise remains an open question among scholars of emotional labor, whether models generated in a Western individualist culture can be employed in Eastern collectivist contexts.

In the study of organizational behavior, scholars explain how culture affects organizations through either a structural approach or a values approach. From the values approach, dimensions of culture shape organizational cultures by endorsing and fostering particular leadership traits and these culturally-endorsed traits prove successful and are repeated in that society: "Collective meaning that results from the dominant cultural values, beliefs, assumptions, and implicit motives endorsed by societal culture results in common leadership and implicit organization theories held by members of the culture" (House et al. 2004, 18). Butler, Lee, and Gross further emphasize the endogeneity of values: "Cultural practices embody cultural values, but those values are simultaneously reinforced by daily practices" (2007, 31). A structural explanation examines a society's laws and institutions: "The level and degree of governmental regulation, development of the industry within a society and national economic system are just a few of the many factors that affect the ways in which a given industry is enacted in a given society" (Dorfman 2004, 50).

From either the values or the structural approach, a society's culture is reproduced in its organizations through the daily behaviors and decisions of organization members (Dickson et al. 2004, 77):

Eventually, people will no longer be consciously aware of the fact that there are other ways of perceiving the world or of responding to situations; the culturally-congruent schema have become chronic … in this way, a direct societal effect is created, in that the shared expectations of the society lead directly to patterns of behavior practices and values that characterize organizations in that society.

The influence of culture on organizations—as captured by Hofstede's five dimensions or GLOBE's nine—has been of enduring interest to cross-cultural scholars, although Individualism/Collectivism is the single most studied dimension. Evidence of culture in organizational practices is found in mission statements and objectives: "The most parsimonious operationalizations of organizational culture consist of commonly used nomenclature within an organization, shared organizational values, and organizational history" (House and Javidan 2004, 16). Common questions include how culture affects decision-making: "National culture constrains rationality in organizational behavior and management philosophies in practices, and in society at large" (Minkov and Hofstede 201⁝, 13).

Although the effects of culture on organizational performance are of interest to scholars as well, Project GLOBE finds cultural dimensions do a better job explaining variance in leadership styles across countries than explaining performance. Furthermore, they find organizations in a particular country to be more similar to one another than organizations in the same industry across countries. In other words, organizations resemble their compatriots more than they resemble their competitors in other countries.

In addition to the cultural dimensions of Hofstede or GLOBE, cultural tightness/looseness also determines the explanatory power of cultural dimensions (Gelfand et al. 2006). This dimension is related to the Hofstede and GLOBE dimensions and adds the extent to which members of a society are sanctioned for violating cultural norms. By adding theory related to the enforcement of cultural norms, Gelfand et al. (2006) expand the frameworks created by Hofstede and GLOBE and develop those theories further. Likewise, we expand both comparative organizational behavior theory and emotional labor theory by applying the latter to the former: "The best proof of the reliability of the dimension scores is their validity in explaining related but outside phenomena according to some kind of theory or logic" (Hofstede 1980, 14). The nature of culture as a unit of analysis guides the selection of analytical approach, as well. Taras, Kirkman, and Steel recommend structural equation modeling to examine how dimensions of culture modify antecedents and consequences of organizational phenomena because "culture is an inherently multilevel construct" (Taras et al. 2010, 434). Accordingly, much of the research on the effects of culture on the antecedents and consequences of emotional labor has employed multilevel models (Lee 2018; Mastracci and Adams 2018).

The data featured in this Handbook were gathered following a strategy of matched samples. The subculture in each country from which we match samples is the public-sector workforce, and we obtain sufficient numbers of observations in each country to facilitate comparison: "Cross-national research can only be done on *matched samples*, similar in all respects except nationality. These samples should, moreover, be of sufficient size—at least 20 and preferably 50 per country" (Hofstede 1980, 14, emphasis original). Matching across countries on this subculture allows us to compare organizational behavioral variables cross-culturally: "When we compare cultural aspects of modern nations, we should try to match for subculture … make the samples very narrow, so that we draw from similar subcultures but in different countries" (Hofstede 1980, 38). By sampling narrowly and focusing on individuals who currently or have had paid working experience in government, our samples are "equivalent enough" and our comparisons are valid and meaningful across countries: "Equivalence in cross-cultural research can be defined as a state or condition of similarity in conceptual meaning and empirical method between cultures that allows comparisons to be meaningful … for cross-cultural comparisons to be valid and meaningful, they have to be 'equivalent *enough*'" (Matsumoto and Yoo 2007, 339, emphasis supplied). In the next section, we examine our data for which culture is the unit of analysis. We begin with a discussion of the literature linking emotion and culture.

Emotion and Culture

The interaction between emotion and culture is addressed in a small body of literature that covers a range of topics from display rules (Matsumoto 2006) recognizing others' emotions (Elfenbein and Ambady 2002), appraisal of one's own emotions (Roseman et al. 1995; Russell 1991) and emotional expression (Van de Vliert 2007). Emotion is implied throughout Hofstede's IBM studies and Project GLOBE. In their meta-analysis of nearly 600 studies employing Hofstede's dimensions of culture, Taras et al. note that "the relationship between cultural values and emotions was stronger than that with the other outcomes on three of four dimensions" (2010, 429). Other outcomes include absenteeism, feedback seeking, job performance, organizational citizenship behavior, organizational commitment, organizational identification, receptivity to certain leadership styles, team-related attitudes and perceptions, and turnover. Links between cultural values and emotions were stronger than links between dimensions of culture and all of these other behaviors of individuals within organizations. Emotion, therefore, emerges as an essential factor in cross-cultural comparison research on organizations because its relationship with Individualism/Collectivism, Power Distance, Uncertainty Avoidance, and Masculinity/Femininity is stronger than the relationships of

Hofstede's cultural dimensions and nearly a dozen other behaviors of individuals in organizations. Matsumoto and Yoo locate the roots of social scientists' studies of emotions and culture in the natural sciences (2007, 332, emphasis original):

> Most modern-day studies of emotion and culture are rooted in the work of Darwin, who in *The Expression of Emotion in Man and Animals* (1872) suggested that emotions and their expressions had evolved across species and were evolutionarily adaptive, biologically innate, and universal across human and nonhuman primates … We also know, however, that people modify their expressions on the basis of *cultural display rules* … Today, the existence of both universality and cultural display rules is well accepted in mainstream psychology.

In the late nineteenth century, Charles Darwin put forth the idea that emotions and emotional expressions, like physical traits, allowed human and nonhuman primates to adapt and evolve. Matsumoto and Yoo (2007) leave room for societies to create and shape norms surrounding emotional displays, as well. In these ways, emotion and emotional expressions are part nature and part nurture. The "nature" effect on emotive expression is both internal and external, meaning that the effect is due to both biology and climate: "Self-expression is higher in wealthy countries with harsh climates (cold or hot) than in countries with temperate climates, whereas self-expression is lower in poor countries with harsh climates than in poor countries in temperate climates" (Triandis and Gelfand 2012, 504; see also Van de Vliert 2007). Emotions arise from biological conditions as deviations from homeostasis (Damasio 1994), signaling that something is wrong or something is right (i.e., Hobbes' pleasures and pains). Maintaining homeostasis through emotional fine-tuning makes emotions evolutionarily adaptive.

The "nurture" effect on emotional expression is the subject of research on recognizing one's own and others' emotions and on organizational and cultural display rules. Cultural display rules indicate how one is supposed to behave in various contexts. Emotion work is the day-to-day effort to feel, or at least appear to feel, appropriate to one's context: Happy at weddings, sad at funerals, concerned about a friend in trouble, and supportive of a loved one's decision. Sometimes that requires no effort, other times it does, but in all cases, emotion *work* is done for the benefit of personal relationships. Emotional *labor*, in contrast, is the effort to feel or appear to feel context-appropriate on the job in accordance with occupational display rules. It is done for the benefit of the employer to conform to professional expectations and to keep the customer happy.

Organizational and occupational display rules invoke emotional labor. When it comes to emotional labor and culture, however, "much of what we know about emotional labor comes from one specific cultural context" (Mesquita and Delvaux 2013, 251). Display rules are foundational to emotional labor, for it is a norm about appropriate behavior that invokes the demand for emotional labor. Individuals in organizations can modify their emotive behaviors to comport with display rules through deep acting or surface acting. In other words, they can authentically express the emotion they are feeling, or they can pretend by expressing an emotion that they do not actually feel.

Research has established a "robust sequence from surface acting to burnout" (Allen et al. 2014, 21) but that well-worn path was developed using North American—mostly US—research participants. We have reason to expect differences in emotional labor by culture based on differences between cultures in the ways that people perceive themselves in relation to others. The few cross-cultural studies of emotion regulation that exist have demonstrated that it is more stressful for people in Individualist compared to Collectivist cultures (Butler et al. 2007, 2009). People in Collectivist cultures regulate their emotions continually to attune themselves to others around them. Regulating emotion to conform to occupational display rules—engaging in emotional labor—is just an extension of day-to-day behavior. Eid and Diener observe "in China, there is a general attitude to consider emotions as dangerous, irrelevant, or illness causing. The moderation or suppression of emotions is generally highly valued in China" (2009, 883).

Broadening the argument to encompass Collectivist and Individualist countries generally, Butler et al. (2007, 44) conclude, "Asian cultures encourage norm conformity and are willing to sacrifice individual consistency in order to encourage social cohesion" because restraint of the inner self is valued far more than is expression of the inner self (Markus and Kitayama 1991). Individualist cultures, on the other hand, prioritize the expression of the inner self: "For those with independent selves, emotional expressions may literally 'express' or reveal the inner feelings, such as anger, sadness, and fear. For those with interdependent selves, however, an emotive expression may be more often regarded as a *public instrumental action* that may or may not be related directly to the inner feelings" (Markus and Kitayama 1991, 236).

In Collectivist cultures, emotion regulation is a tool to achieve and maintain harmony. "Collectivists value harmony within the in-group, whereas

Individualists accept confrontation within the in-group" (Triandis 1993, 177). Because people in Collectivist cultures are accustomed to emotional restraint in their interpersonal interactions in order to sustain harmony, work-based emotional labor "may be more automatic and require fewer cognitive resources to execute" (Butler et al. 2007, 31).

Emotion regulation in Individualist cultures is expected to exact a higher psychological cost. Individualist cultures trace their emphasis on individual liberty to the Enlightenment's triumph of man over institutions, such as the behemoth of the Catholic church in that era, and the ascendance of individual reason over institutional norms. Rousseau (1750, 6), criticizing the modern age in his romanticism of the noble savage, hails authentic self-expression as "genius" and adherence to manners and norms of behavior as nothing less than *immoral*:

> Today … a base and deceptive uniformity prevails in our morals, and all minds seem to have been cast in the same mold. Incessantly politeness requires, propriety demands, incessantly usage is followed, never one's own genius. One no longer dares to appear as he is, and in this perpetual constraint, the men who form this herd called society, placed in the same circumstances, will all do the same things unless stronger motives deter them. Therefore, one will never know well those with whom he deals … suspicions, offenses, fears, coldness, reserve, hate, betrayal will hide constantly under that uniform false veil of politeness.

Politeness, manners, social norms—all inhibit authentic expression and prevent genuine connection between people. The USA came to being amidst the Enlightenment zeitgeist and the impact of that founding context is apparent today. In Western cultures, "high levels of expressiveness are seen as signs of competence and likeability and suppressing emotional behavior is associated with increased psychological responding and reduced affiliation" (Butler, Lee and Gross 2009, 511). In other words, people in Collectivist cultures with interdependent self-construals employ emotion management on a day-to-day basis as a tool to achieve and sustain group harmony, while people in Individualist cultures with independent self-construals value authentic self-expression. Van de Vliert (2007, 157) also demonstrates a link between socioeconomic status of a culture and norms surrounding self-expression: "In poorer countries with more demanding thermal climates, lower household incomes are related to stronger endorsement of survival values at the expense of self-expression values." Day-to-day norms governing individual self-expression extend into the workplace. Work display rules are more restrictive than day-to-day interpersonal display rules.

Few of us are free from presentational expectations at work: Like dress codes and uniforms, workplace display rules standardize individuals within occupations, foster an organizational identity, and shape expectations of the customer. Emotional labor is part of the exchange of work effort for pay between employee and employer. In public service jobs, which are quintessential meaning-making jobs (Guy et al. 2008), to fail to engage in emotional labor is to fail to do the job. A police officer cannot betray anxiety or fear to suspects or victims. A social worker cannot express disgust in front of her clients. An emergency responder cannot panic or recoil from a patient's gruesome injuries as she arrives on the scene of an accident. Public service occupations are quintessential meaning-making jobs because a substantial part of the product is what the citizen feels. The symbolism embedded in public service work begins with the American flag flying in front of government buildings and extends to the insignia on uniforms worn by police officers and firefighters (Mastracci et al. 2012).

Whether in the private or public sector, emotional laborers can pursue one of two approaches: They can convince themselves that the display rules are objectively right and true (deep acting) or they can fake it (surface acting). Emotional labor research on private-sector workers shows that surface acting is more stressful and produces more negative outcomes in the form of burnout and emotional exhaustion compared to deep acting (Hulsheger and Schewe 2011). Emotional labor research on public-sector workers has revealed much about public service work. First, emotional labor is fundamental to quality public service and is undertaken during face-to-face and voice-to-voice interactions. Second, both new and long-tenured employees engage in emotional labor; neither exerts more nor less. Years on the job improves one's capacity for emotional labor, not unlike how consistent exercise improves one's capacity for physical labor. Emotional labor is not specific to an agency or department; it is located in the job and not the jobholder, and the frequency and intensity of emotional labor varies by job. Third, emotions in the workplace are *not* antithetical to professionalism or to reasoning. On-the-job emotion regulation takes skill, significant effort, is key to getting the job done, and is the very expression of professionalism. Another inheritance from the American origin in Enlightenment thinking is the divorce of emotion from reason. Results from research in neurobiology demonstrate the integral role of emotion in the reasoning process (Damasio 1994). Finally, research on emotional labor in the public sector mainly uses US samples much like its private-sector counterpart, but that is changing.

Recent research on emotional labor in public service has emerged from outside the USA: Lu and Guy (2014) survey Chinese public servants and determine that ethical leadership moderates the effects of surface acting on job engagement. Mastracci (2017) confirms the moderating effect of ethical leadership on surface acting and burnout among new nurses in England's National Health Service. Interestingly, gender appears to matter in contexts outside the USA but not within the USA: Yang and Guy (2015) survey municipal government employees in Seoul and confirm the relationship between authentic emotive expression and job satisfaction. Faking emotion decreases job satisfaction and increases turnover intention for women but not for men. Evidence in a forthcoming publication by Yun et al. (forthcoming) similarly finds an effect of supervisor gender on the emotional labor-burnout link for subordinates, using data from Korea. Also studying Korean public servants, Wilding et al. (2014) find varying effects of the frequency and variety of emotive expressions on job satisfaction and burnout. Hsieh et al. (2016) reveal complex and counterintuitive relationships between emotional labor efficacy and job satisfaction among government workers in Taiwan. The relative absence of cross-cultural comparisons means that the effects of emotional labor—that it can lead to stress and burnout if unsupported but can also contribute to job satisfaction and fulfillment—may be generalized across national and cultural boundaries without empirical support. Differences between cultures on Hofstede's (1980) Individualism index are particularly relevant to emotional labor research (Ashkanasy and Daus 2013; Taras et al. 2010; Triandis 2001).

Matsumoto notes: "Individualism-Collectivism has been identified by several writers as a stable dimension of cultural variability" (1990, 197). The mechanism by which cultural differences manifest in individual responses to display rules is the cultural difference in self-construals (Eid and Diener 2009, 172, emphases added):

> In cultures where an *independent* self is predominant, people are expected to become independent from others and pursue and assert individual goals … people with an independent self are found in individualistic (e.g., Western) cultures more often than in collectivist ones (e.g., Eastern cultures). The *interdependent* (relational) self, on the other hand, is characterized by the belief that the self cannot be separated from others or from the social context … in collectivist cultures, in which this construal of the self is predominant, the social norm is to maintain harmony with others.

With respect to self-construals, "The independent view is most clearly exemplified in some sizeable segment of American culture, as well as in many Western European cultures. The interdependent view is exemplified in

Japanese culture as well as in other Asian cultures, Latin American cultures, and many southern European cultures" (Markus and Kitayama 1991, 225). Recall that a society is individualistic while an individual with an independent self-construal is idiocentric. Triandis (2001, 914) observes: "Idiocentrics think of the self as stable and the environment as changeable whereas allocentrics think of the social environment as stable (duties, obligations) and the self as changeable (ready to fit into the environment)." We suspect that this explains why surface acting—faking it—is more stressful and more strongly linked to burnout in individualist cultures than in collectivist cultures: Feelings are part of one's identity in individualist cultures so to ignore or suppress them is to betray one's identity. "Lying is an acceptable behavior in collectivist cultures, if it saves face or helps the in group" (Triandis 2001, 917). Lying—to oneself or another—is not acceptable in Individualist cultures. Faking expression—surface acting—is more stressful in Individualist cultures than it is in Collectivist cultures and face saving is not a priority in individualist cultures as it is in Collectivist cultures.

Differences in emotional labor experiences should manifest in Individualist and Collectivist cultures. Interestingly, Matsumoto (1990) finds no differences between US and Japanese subjects when they were alone, but results confirm an anticipated East/West split when research participants are in the presence of others. This "suggests the importance of display rules as *social* phenomena" (Matsumoto 1990, 210, emphasis supplied) and therefore influenced by broader culture. Allen et al. (2014) confirm the link between display rules, emotional labor, and burnout for US service workers but not those in China. Hofstede and Bond (1988, 19–20) observe "a philosophical dividing line in our world that separates Western from Eastern thinking … Western thinking is analytical, while Eastern thinking is synthetic."

To date, comparisons across cultures—including East versus West—have examined private-sector workers. We focus on public servants in several countries due to the unique circumstances in which citizens encounter public servants and the emotional labor involved in, for instance, children's services, emergency response, and criminal justice (Guy et al. 2008; Mastracci et al. 2012). The public-sector context holds further interest because while cross-cultural comparisons of the effects of emotional labor on private sector service workers have been conducted, no such comparison in public services has been done to date.

Studying the private sector, Allen et al. find that emotive pretending leads to burnout in the USA but not in China, and that some links between surface acting and outcomes are significantly weaker in the Chinese sample and others' relationships with the opposite direction (2014, 21–22). This important result suggests emotional labor is easier for workers in collectivist cultures compared to those in individualist cultures. Mastracci and Adams (2018) use samples of public-sector workers from five countries and find weaker relationships between surface acting and burnout in Collectivist countries compared to Individualist countries and locate inverse relationships between deep acting and burnout in Collectivist countries. The models fit well in both contexts, further suggesting that the predictions from emotional labor theory may be applied across cultures, contrary to researcher concerns arising from the parochial contexts within which emotional labor models have been developed.

In this handbook, we are able to draw conclusions about emotional labor in public service in a number of countries because we define our target population narrowly and we have a sufficient number of observations from a sufficient number of countries, according to prior research. First, our sample is defined narrowly: Individuals with current or past experience working full time for a government office or public-serving nonprofit organization. This approach is consistent with Matsumoto and Yoo, who recommend that "a sound cross-cultural comparison would entail the collection of data from multiple sites within the same cultural group" (2007, 339). While we can claim our results describe public service in each of our respective countries, we do not claim to have drawn representative samples from each country, as "it is impossible to obtain representative samples within each nation of such multicultural nations such as China, India, or the United States" (House and Hanges 2004, 97).

Second, we obtain at least 45 responses from each country because Project GLOBE researchers found that "the *average* number of respondents needed for a cross-cultural construct of a target reliability of 0.85 is 45" (Javidan et al. 2004, 725, emphasis original). We obtain approximately 200 cases per country for the purpose of analyzing the data using structural equation models (Iacobucci 2010). Third, from our subculture, which is comprised of government workers, we sample across a dozen countries. And the number of countries from which we obtained data is within the range of that recommended by Hofstede to accurately capture and describe dimensions of culture: "Ecological dimensions can more clearly be detected when we have data from more—for example, 10 or 15—societies" (Hofstede 1980, 31). Furthermore, our team is comprised of researchers who were brought up, lived, and worked in their subject countries, many of whom have also lived in more than one cultural environment. This is consistent with recommended practice as well (Hofstede 1980).

Finally, our approach to this project follows Hofstede's recommendations with respect to analyzing data from multiple cultures in that it uses "matrices of ecological correlations for a factor analysis or similar multivariate technique subsuming the original variables into dimensions which can enter laws of the greatest generality, but which are at the same time least sensitive to the uniqueness of each culture" (1980, 42). Using multi-group confirmatory factor analysis (MGCFA), we follow the approach employed in Project GLOBE to create six ecological dimensions: Power Distance, Societal Collectivism, In-Group Collectivism, Masculinity/Femininity, Uncertainty Avoidance, and Future Orientation. Recall that these six dimensions of culture are modifications and extensions of Hofstede's (1980) original four dimensions of culture.

Ten of the twelve countries surveyed in this study were also included in the Project GLOBE study and Appendix B provides a graphical display of our data against Project GLOBE data. The charts demonstrate that the two samples array themselves similarly across ecological indicators. To test whether, in fact, the samples are comparable, we conduct tests of significance. Table 6.1 provides detail of these data as well as results from difference-of-means t-tests. None of the t-statistics in any country are significantly different from zero at the 95% level—two are significant at the 90% level—indicating that the GLOBE data and our data are drawn from the same overall populations and can therefore be reliably compared.

Table 6.1 shows that the ecological dimensions for each country generally conform to expectations based on prior research. India and the Philippines rank highest on Power Distance in the current study while Taiwan, UK, and the USA rank lowest. The China and India indexes on both types of Collectivism are the highest of all countries, while Taiwan, UK, and USA are lowest on Societal Collectivism and Taiwan and Bolivia rank lowest on In-Group Collectivism. Korea ranks highest on Masculinity while the USA ranks lowest. China takes the top spot in Uncertainty Avoidance and in Future Orientation, while index scores for the USA are the lowest in both. In sum, results from t-tests that compare our surveys of public service workers compared to results reported by Project GLOBE reveal negligible differences. Only two comparisons, UK data and Australia data, reach a significance of $p \leq 0.10$. This information allows us to analyze data on emotional labor in public service using culture as the unit of analysis.

Table 6.1 Ecological dimensions by country: Current data versus Project GLOBE

	Australia	GLOBE Australia	China	GLOBE China	Bolivia	GLOBE Bolivia	India	GLOBE India	Korea	GLOBE Korea	Philippines	GLOBE Philippines
Power Distance	3.90	4.74	4.04	5.04	4.04	4.51	4.94	5.47	3.71	5.61	4.73	5.44
Societal Collectivism	4.54	4.29	5.46	4.77	4.11	4.04	5.09	4.38	4.42	5.20	4.72	4.65
In-Group Collectivism	4.86	4.17	5.90	5.80	4.42	5.47	5.61	5.92	4.43	5.54	4.93	6.36
Masculinity/ Femininity	4.21	3.40	4.25	3.05	3.81	3.55	3.93	2.90	4.73	2.50	4.17	3.64
Uncertainty Avoidance	4.55	4.39	5.05	4.94	4.21	3.35	4.85	4.15	4.52	3.55	4.69	3.89
Future orientation	5.00	4.09	5.68	3.75	4.58	3.61	5.53	4.19	4.70	3.97	5.53	4.15
t Statistic (p value)	1.35 (0.10)*		0.99 (0.17)		0.36 (0.36)		0.98 (0.18)		0.04 (0.48)		0.23 (0.41)	

Summary and Open Questions

Research using culture or country as the unit of analysis is much less common than individual-level analyses and poses unique challenges to researchers, including the ecological fallacy and reverse ecological fallacy problems. Individualism and Collectivism are the most studied of the dimensions of culture established by Hofstede and later reinforced in Project GLOBE. Organizational behavior research using culture or country as the unit of analysis has produced very promising results: "Researchers interested in better understanding variance in certain employee outcomes now have evidence that cultural values are just as meaningful explanatory factors as are other individual differences such as personality traits, demographics, or general mental ability" (Taras et al. 2010, 429). That is, national culture explains work-relevant outcomes just as well as demographic characteristics explain work-relevant outcomes. These characteristics include educational attainment and the so-called Big 5 personality traits: extraversion, agreeableness, openness, conscientiousness, and neuroticism. Emotion is a key aspect of organizational behavior explained by national culture. Our results are consistent with those of Project GLOBE, which expanded upon the work of Hofstede's IBM studies. Project GLOBE and the IBM studies are perhaps the most cited multiple-country comparisons of work experiences in the organizational behavior literature. Our contribution to this literature is to expand cross-cultural research into public service.

Open questions remain, however, with respect to the question of cultural convergence, the unique influence of culture on human resource management (to which emotional labor most applies), the unique aspects of public service delivery that are affected by dimensions of culture, and the extent to which one can know one's own and others' emotions. First, questions remain whether work-based norms across countries are converging due to the similarities among public servants in their education and training in universities. In an earlier chapter, the role of Weberian bureaucracy was discussed as a national cultural norm that has been transmitted via professional training for public servants. Hofstede "considered education as one of the key institutions that perpetuates culture at a national level" (Taras et al. 2010, 409). Norms among countries with public servants educated in Weberian bureaucratic ideals in government instill those ideas into others—especially subordinates. Examining leadership worldwide, Project GLOBE observes that "there are some leader behaviors that are universally or near universally accepted and effective" (Dorfman 2004, 65). And governments increasingly interact as policies transcend national borders: "As cultures interact, acculturation is likely to result in changes in some domains, such as job behaviors, and not in other domains, such as religious or family life" (Triandis 2001, 920). How governments interact and shape each other's ecological dimensions could be the focus of future research using culture or country as the unit of analysis. Questions remain as to how the exportation of Weberian ideals has been tempered by the uniqueness of each country. It is important to note that there is no single model of administration and understanding the differences is important in comparative research.

Second, emotional labor and the role of emotions in organizations are most salient to human resource management. As Hofstede and Bond argue, "conflicts are less likely to occur in technology and finance, which are relatively culture-independent, and more likely in marketing and personnel, where cultural diversity is largest" (Hofstede and Bond 1988, 19–20).

Third, and in a similar vein as the argument above that human resource management is more influenced by culture than, say, budgeting and public finance, the nature of public goods fosters interdependent relationships and not simply exchange relationships, as is observed in the private sector. It might even be established that public service organizations are inherently more Collectivist or communal (Triandis 1989) than private-sector organizations. "The prototypical Individualist social relationship is the market. You pay your money and you get something" (Triandis 1993, 160). However, definitions of private and public goods vary by culture: "Utilities are an obvious example, with some countries having government-run monopolies, others having nongovernmental monopolies, others having state or province or regional monopolies, and still others having varying forms and levels of competition" (Dorfman 2004, 76). While public service may be more Collectivist than the private sector and its exchange relationships, the very definition of public service is determined by a culture's norms and values.

The fourth and final open question moves away from culture as the unit of analysis and involves issues fundamental to the study of emotions in general. How well do we know our own emotional states, much less those of another? When researching organizations in different cultures, Hofstede notes, "We will always be subjective, but we may at least try to be 'intersubjective,' pooling and integrating a variety of subjective points of view of different observers" (1980, 15). Hofstede advises researchers to gather information from diverse sources for the purpose of capturing multiple facets of a culture. Research on emotional labor assumes survey respondents can interpret their own emotive states and others' emotions and assumes respondents are aware of display rules and how display rules affect behavior. To this, we add a cross-cultural component and assume members of one culture can interpret embodied emotions of members of other cultures. Finally, we employ models developed using US samples and apply them in other cultural contexts without clear guidance on whether exported explanations of organizational behavior make sense in other countries. In the next chapter, we discuss emotional labor in various situational contexts, particularly the potentially communal situation involving the bond between citizen and government. We also discuss mistreatment of public servants, benevolence, and reciprocity.

References

Allen, Joseph A., James M. Diefendorff, and Yufeng Ma. 2014. "Differences in Emotional Labor Across Cultures: A Comparison of Chinese and US Service Workers." *Journal of Business and Psychology* 29 (1): 21–35.

Ashkanasy, Neal M., and Catherine S. Daus. 2013. *Emotional Labor Across Five Levels of Analysis: Past, Present, Future.* Abingdon, UK: Routledge.

Brewer, P., and S. Venaik. 2014. "The Ecological Fallacy in National Culture Research." *Organization Studies* 35 (7): 1063–86. http://dx.doi.org/10.1177/0170840613517602.

Butler, Emily A., Tiane L. Lee, and James J. Gross. 2007. "Emotion Regulation and Culture: Are the Social Consequences of Emotion Suppression Culture-Specific?" *Emotion* 7 (1): 30–48. https://doi.org/10.1037/1528-3542.7.1.30.

Butler, Emily A., Tiane L. Lee, and James J. Gross. 2009. "Does Expressing Your Emotions Raise or Lower Your Blood Pressure? The Answer Depends on Cultural Context." *Journal of Cross-Cultural Psychology* 40 (3): 510–17.

Chhokar, J. S., F. C. Brodbeck, and R. J. House. 2007. *Culture and Leadership across the World: A GLOBE Report of In-Depth Studies of the Cultures of 25 Countries.* Mahwah, NJ: Lawrence Erlbaum Associates.

Damasio, Antonio R. 1994. *Descartes' Error: Emotion, Reason and the Human Brain.* New York, NY: Penguin Putnam.

Dickson, Marcus W., Renee S. BeShears, and Vipin Gupta. 2004. "The Impact of Societal Culture and Industry on Organizational Culture: Theoretical Explanations." In *Culture, Leadership, and Organizations: The GLOBE Study of 62 Societies,* edited by Robert J. House, Paul J. Hanges, Mansour Javidan, Peter W. Dorfman, and Vipin Gupta, 74–90. Thousand Oaks, CA: Sage.

Dorfman, Peter W. 2004. "Prior Literature." In *Culture, Leadership, and Organizations: The GLOBE Study of 62 Societies,* edited by Robert J. House, Paul J. Hanges, Mansour Javidan, Peter W. Dorfman, and Vipin Gupta, 49–50. Thousand Oaks, CA: Sage.

Dorfman, Peter W., and Robert J. House. 2004. "Cultural Influences on Organizational Leadership: Literature Review, Theoretical Rationale, and

GLOBE Project Goals." In *Culture, Leadership, and Organizations: The GLOBE Study of 62 Societies,* edited by Robert J. House, Paul J. Hanges, Mansour Javidan, Peter W. Dorfman, and Vipin Gupta, 51–73. Thousand Oaks, CA: Sage.

Eid, Michael, and Ed Diener. 2009. "Norms for Experiencing Emotions in Different Cultures: Inter- and Intranational Differences." In *Culture and Well-Being,* edited by E. Diener, 169–202. New York, NY: Springer. https://doi.org/10.1007/978-90-481-2352-0_9.

Elfenbein, Hillary A., and Nalini Ambady. 2002. "On the Universality and Cultural Specificity of Emotion Recognition: A Meta-Analysis." *Psychological Bulletin* 128: 205–35.

Gelfand, Michele. 2018. *Rule Makers, Rule Breakers: How Tight and Loose Cultures Wire Our World.* New York, NY: Scribner.

Gelfand, Michele, L. H. Nishii, and J. L. Raver. 2006. "On the Nature and Importance of Cultural Tightness-Looseness." *Journal of Applied Psychology* 91 (6), 1225–44. http://dx.doi.org/10.1037/0021-9010.91.6.1225.

Guy, Mary E., Meredith A. Newman, and Sharon H. Mastracci. 2008. *Emotional Labor: Putting the Service in Public Service.* Armonk, NY: M.E. Sharpe.

Hanges, Paul J., and Marcus W. Dickson. 2004. "The Development and Validation of the GLOBE Culture and Leadership Scales." In *Culture, Leadership, and Organizations: The GLOBE Study of 62 Societies,* edited by Robert J. House, Paul J. Hanges, Mansour Javidan, Peter W. Dorfman, and Vipin Gupta, 122–51. Thousand Oaks, CA: Sage.

Hofstede, Geert, and Michael Harris Bond. 1988. "The Confucius Connection: From Cultural Roots to Economic Growth." *Organizational Dynamics* 16 (4): 5–21.

Hofstede, Geert, G. J. Hofstede, and M. Minkov. 2010. *Cultures and Organizations: Software of the Mind.* 3rd ed. New York: McGraw-Hill.

Hofstede, Geert. 1980. *Culture's Consequences.* Beverly Hills: Sage.

House, Robert J., and Mansour Javidan. 2004. "Overview of GLOBE." In *Culture, Leadership, and Organizations: The GLOBE Study of 62 Societies,* edited by Robert J. House, Paul J. Hanges, Mansour Javidan, Peter W. Dorfman, and Vipin Gupta, 9–48. Thousand Oaks, CA: Sage.

House, Robert J., and Paul J. Hanges. 2004. "Research Design." In *Culture, Leadership, and Organizations: The GLOBE Study of 62 Societies,* edited by Robert J. House, Paul J. Hanges, Mansour Javidan, Peter W. Dorfman, and Vipin Gupta, 95–101. Thousand Oaks, CA: Sage.

House, Robert J., Paul J. Hanges, Mansour Javidan, Peter W. Dorfman, and Vipin Gupta. 2004. *Culture, Leadership, and Organizations: The GLOBE Study of 62 Societies.* Thousand Oaks, CA: Sage.

Hsieh, Chih-Wei, Jun-Yi Hsieh, and Irving Yi-Feng Huang. 2016. "Self-Efficacy as a Mediator and Moderator between Emotional Labor and Job Satisfaction: A Case Study of Public Service Employees in Taiwan." *Public Performance & Management Review* 40 (1): 71–96.

Hülsheger, Ute R., and Anna F. Schewe. 2011. "On the Costs and Benefits of Emotional Labor: A Meta-Analysis of Three Decades of Research." *Journal of Occupational Health Psychology* 16 (3): 361–89.

Iacobucci, Dawn. 2010. "Structural Equations Modeling: Fit Indices, Sample Size, and Advanced Topics." *Journal of Consumer Psychology* 20 (1): 90–98. https://doi.org/10.1016/j.jcps.2009.09.003.

Javidan, Mansour, Robert J. House, Peter W. Dorfman, Vipin Gupta, Paul J. Hanges, and Mary Sully de Luque. 2004. "Conclusions and Future Directions." In *Culture, Leadership, and Organizations: The GLOBE Study of 62 Societies,* edited by Robert J. House, Paul J. Hanges, Mansour Javidan, Peter W. Dorfman, and Vipin Gupta, 723–32. Thousand Oaks, CA: Sage.

Kluckhorn, K. 1954. "Culture and Behavior." In *Handbook of Social Psychology,* Vol. 2, edited by G. Lindzey, 921–76. Cambridge, MA: Addison-Wesley.

Kozlowski, S. W. J., and K. J. Klein, K. J. 2000. "A Multilevel Approach to Theory and Research in Organizations: Contextual, Temporal, and Emergent Processes." In *Multilevel Theory, Research and Methods in Organizations: Foundations, Extensions, and New Directions,* edited by K. J. Klein and S. W. J. Kozlowski, 3–90. San Francisco, CA: Jossey-Bass.

Lee, Hyun Jung. 2018. "Relation Between Display Rules and Emotive Behavior Strategies and Its Outcomes Among South Korean Public Service Employees." *Public Performance & Management Review* 41 (4): 723–44, https://doi.org/10.10 80/15309576.2018.1464479.

Levitin, T. 1973. "Values." In *Measures of Social Psychological Attitudes,* edited by J. P. Robinson and P. R. Shaver, 489–502. Ann Arbor, MI: Institute for Social Research.

Lu, Xiaojun, and Mary E. Guy. 2014. "How Emotional Labor and Ethical Leadership Affect Job Engagement for Chinese Public Servants." *Public Personnel Management* 43 (1): 3–24.

Markus, H. R., and Kitayama, S. 1991. "Culture and the Self: Implications for Cognition, Emotion, and Motivation." *Psychological Review* 98 (2): 224–53.

Marsh, Abigail A., Hillary Anger Elfenbein, and Nalini Ambady. 2003. "Nonverbal 'Accents' Cultural Differences in Facial Expressions of Emotion." *Psychological Science* 14 (4): 373–76.

Mastracci, Sharon. 2017. "Beginning Nurses' Perceptions of Ethical Leadership in the Shadow of Mid Staffs." *Public Integrity* 19 (3): 250–64.

Mastracci, Sharon, and Ian Adams. 2018. "Is Emotional Labor Easier in Collectivist or Individualist Cultures? An East-West Comparison." *Public Personnel Management.* https://doi.org/10.1177/0091026018814569.

Mastracci, Sharon H., Mary E. Guy, and Meredith A. Newman. 2012. *Emotional Labor and Crisis Response: Working on the Razor's Edge.* Armonk, NY: M.E. Sharpe.

Matsumoto, David. 1990. "Cultural Similarities and Differences in Display Rules." *Motivation and Emotion* 14 (3): 195–214.

Matsumoto, David. 1993. "Ethnic Differences in Affect Intensity, Emotion Judgments, Display Rule Attitudes, and Self-Reported Emotional Expression in an American Sample." *Motivation and Emotion* 17 (2): 107–23.

Matsumoto, David. 2006. "Are Cultural Differences in Emotion Regulation Mediated by Personality Traits?" *Journal of Cross-Cultural Psychology* 37 (4): 421–37.

Matsumoto, David, and Seung Hee Yoo. 2007. "Methodologica Considerations in the Study of Emotion Across Cultures." In *Handbook of Emotion Elicitation and Assessment*, 332–48.

Matsumoto, David, Sachiko Takeuchi, Sari Andayani, Natalia Kouznetsova, and Deborah Krupp. 1998. "The Contribution of Individualism vs. Collectivism to Cross-National Differences in Display Rules." *Asian Journal of Social Psychology* 1 (2): 147–65.

Matsumoto, David, S. H. Yoo, S. Hirayama, and G. Petrova. 2005. "Validation of an Individual-Level Measure of Display Rules: The Display Rule Assessment Inventory (DRAI)." *Emotion* 5 (1): 23–40.

Matsumoto, David, Tsutomu Kudoh, Klaus Scherer, and Harald Wallbott. 1988. "Antecedents of and Reactions to Emotions in the United States and Japan." *Journal of Cross-Cultural Psychology* 19 (3): 267–86.

Mauro, Robert, Kaori Sato, and John Tucker. 1992. "The Role of Appraisal in Human Emotions: A Cross-Cultural Study." *Journal of Personality and Social Psychology* 62 (2): 301–17.

Mesquita, Batja. 2001. "Emotions in Collectivist and Individualist Contexts." *Journal of Personality and Social Psychology* 80 (1): 68–74.

Mesquita, Batja, and Ellen Delvaux. 2013. "A Cultural Perspective on Emotion Labor." In *Emotional Labor in the 21st Century*, 271–92. Abingdon, UK: Routledge.

Minkov, M., and Hofstede, G. 2011. "The Evolution of Hofstede's Doctrine." *Cross Cultural Management* 18 (1): 10–20. http://dx.doi.org/10.1108/1352760111110 4269.

Roseman, Ira J., Nisha Dhawan, S. Ilsa Rettek, R. K. Naidu, and Komilla Thapa. 1995. "Cultural Differences and Cross-Cultural Similarities in Appraisals and Emotional Responses." *Journal of Cross-Cultural Psychology* 26 (1): 23–48.

Rousseau, J. J. 1750. *A Discourse on the Moral Effects of the Arts and Sciences, Online Library of Liberty.* https://oll.libertyfund.org/titles/rousseau-the-social-contract-and-discourses?q=discourse+on+the+moral+effects+of+the+arts+and+sciences#lf0132_head_057.

Russell, James A. 1991. "Culture and the Categorization of Emotions." *Psychological Bulletin* 110 (3): 426–50.

Schlösser, Oliver, Michael Frese, Anna-Maria Heintze, Musaed Al-Najjar, Thomas Arciszewski, Elias Besevegis, George D. Bishop, Mirilia Bonnes, Chris W. Clegg, and Ewa Drozda-Senkowska. 2013. "Humane Orientation as a New Cultural Dimension of the Globe Project: A Validation Study of the Globe Scale and

Out-Group Humane Orientation in 25 Countries." *Journal of Cross-Cultural Psychology* 44 (4): 535–51. https://doi.org/10.1177/0022022112465671.

Taras, Vas, Bradley L. Kirkman, and Piers Steel. 2010. "Examining the Impact of Culture's Consequences: A Three-Decade, Multilevel, Meta-Analytic Review of Hofstede's Cultural Value Dimensions." *Journal of Applied Psychology* 95 (3): 405–39. https://doi.org/10.1037/a0018938.

Triandis, Harry C. 1989. "The Self and Social Behavior in Differing Cultural Contexts." *Psychological Review* 96 (3): 506–20. http://dx.doi.org/10.1037/0033-295X.96.3.506.

Triandis, Harry C. 1993. "Collectivism and Individualism as Cultural Syndromes." *Cross-Cultural Research* 27 (3–4): 155–80.

Triandis, Harry C. 2001. "Individualism-Collectivism and Personality." *Journal of Personality* 69 (6): 907–24.

Triandis, Harry C., and Michele J. Gelfand. 2012. "A Theory of Individualism and Collectivism." In *Handbook of Theories of Social Psychology: Volume 2*, edited by Paul A. M. Van Lange, Arie W. Kruglanski, and E. Tory Higgins, Chapter 51. Thousand Oaks, CA: Sage. http://dx.doi.org/10.4135/9781446249222.n51.

UNHCR. 2018. *Figures at a Glance*. June 19. https://www.unhcr.org/protection/resettlement/593a88f27/unhcr-projected-global-resettlement-needs-2018.html.

Van de Vliert, Evert. 2007. "Climatoeconomic Roots of Survival Versus Self-Expression Cultures." *Journal of Cross-Cultural Psychology* 38 (2): 156–72.

Wilding, Mark, Kyungjin Chae, and Jiho Jang. 2014. "Emotional Labor in Korean Local Government: Testing the Consequences of Situational Factors and Emotional Dissonance." *Public Performance & Management Review* 38 (2): 316–36.

Yang, Seung-Bum, and Mary E. Guy. 2015. "Gender Effects on Emotional Labor in Seoul Metropolitan Area." *Public Personnel Management* 44 (1): 3–24.

Yun, C., Y. Lee, and Sharon H. Mastracci. Forthcoming. "The Moderating Effect of Female Managers on Job Stress and Emotional Labor for Public Employees in Gendered Organizations: Evidence from Korea." *Public Personnel Management*. https://doi.org/10.1177/0091026019829163.

7

Understanding Emotional Labor in Situational Contexts: How Mistreatment Matters

Chih-Wei Hsieh

Thanks to the pioneering work of Hochschild (1983), there is a growing recognition that emotional labor—the act of expressing appropriate emotions—is crucial for the functioning of service work. Considerable scholarly attention has been drawn to workplaces where employees are required to show desirable emotions in order to induce a positive emotional state in the people they serve, that is, that they are satisfied with services rendered. Akin to colleagues in generic management, public administration scholars have also realized that successful completion of public service jobs depends on emotional labor. However, unlike usual business services, public service workers are not always required to provide service with a smile. Instead, they may speak with authority and/or benevolence because the power and legitimacy of the state is manifested in the provision of government services (Guy et al. 2008; Mastracci et al. 2012). For example, in the midst of public disorder, police officers employ calmness and toughness and expect citizens to be deferential. To assist a victim of abuse, social workers express warmth and empathy to open up a conversation with the troubled heart. In both cases, public service workers are expected to present themselves in a professional manner, and job-inappropriate feelings, such as anger, fear, sadness, fatigue, and annoyance, must be hidden from the citizen's sight. Through emotional labor, public service organizations

C.-W. Hsieh (✉)
Department of Public Policy, City University of Hong Kong,
Kowloon, Hong Kong SAR
e-mail: cwhsieh@cityu.edu.hk

© The Author(s) 2019

M. E. Guy et al. (eds.), *The Palgrave Handbook of Global Perspectives on Emotional Labor in Public Service*, https://doi.org/10.1007/978-3-030-24823-9_7

can change the dynamics of the worker–citizen interaction "so that people cooperate, stay on task, and work well together" (Guy et al. 2008, 3).

Regardless of how the demand of emotional labor is applied in public service jobs (Guy et al. 2008), neither worker nor citizen should expect every interaction to be harmonious and peaceful. Many, if not all, public service workplaces are fraught with tension and often conflict. This is because workers often rely on their own beliefs and value systems in deciding and rationalizing their actions (Maynard-Moody and Musheno 2003). When interacting with the public, they thus have a diffuse comprehension of appropriate modes of behavior and a diffuse awareness of consequences of behavioral violations (Lipsky 1980). As a result, workers may deviate from generally accepted norms of demeanor and abuse or misuse their power against those whom they serve.

Public service workers, on the other hand, can also become targets of abuse from the public. As Lipsky (1980) observed, street-level service providers may have to work under conditions of limited resources, such as time, information, staffing, and money. In the wake of neoliberal administrative reforms, heightened citizen demands coincide with budget constraints to force public servants to do more with less (Hood 1991), and the expectations can be overwhelming. When facing citizens who desperately need public assistance, resource inadequacy not only dampens workers' ability to offer an adequate service but also places them at high risk for mistreatment by aggressive clients (Newhill 2003; Virkki 2008). The tension in public service encounters is, therefore, not simply an issue of interaction difficulties between workers and citizens, but rather a phenomenon stemming in many ways from institutional and organizational deficiencies. When workers are ill-prepared to cope with structural deficiencies, frustration, and anger may instigate citizens to turn aggressive. In the end, there are no winners in negative service encounters because service recipients' aggressive behavior may create a vicious cycle, resulting in workers who sabotage service delivery (Shao and Skarlicki 2014; Skarlicki et al. 2008; Wang et al. 2011). This results in decreased service quality (Arnetz and Arnetz 2001; Rupp and Spencer 2006).

The interplay of contextual elements affects the process and outcome of public service encounters. The aim of this chapter is to shed light on the situational dynamics of the worker–citizen interaction. It first delineates two behavioral principles, the moral base of benevolence and the norm of reciprocity, both of which drive the exertion of emotional labor, or lack thereof, on every occasion of public service provision. Against the backdrop of relevant theories, I hypothesize that there will be an association between citizen mistreatment and worker attitudes toward the public service job (job satisfaction), the self (emotive capacity), and citizens (trust in citizens). Using data collected from public service workers in China, Pakistan, Rwanda, South Korea, Taiwan, the UK, and the USA, hypotheses are tested and implications of the findings are discussed.

The Moral Base of Benevolence

Perhaps the most distinctive feature that separates public service from for-profit enterprises is the increasing emphasis on *caring for others*. In his book, *The Spirit of Public Administration*, H. George Fredrickson (1997) said, "The spirit of public administration is dependent on a moral base of benevolence to all citizens." He elaborated on how benevolence defines public administration: "Without benevolence, public administration is merely governmental work. With benevolence, our field has a meaning and purpose beyond just doing a good job; the work we do becomes noble—a kind of civic virtue" (234). These remarks revive the caring tradition of public administration (Stivers 1995) and signify a paradigm shift from the "orthodox" doctrine developed during the early establishment of the discipline.

Woodrow Wilson (1887) is widely considered the father of public administration, for he legitimated it as a field of study in his renowned essay, "The Study of Administration." In it, he stated, "It is the object of administrative study to discover, first, what government can properly and successfully do, and, secondly, how it can do these proper things with the utmost possible efficiency and at the least possible cost either of money or of energy" (p. 197). Rooted in this perspective, "orthodox" public administration theorists have embraced efficiency and economy as the primary values of public administration. For instance, Leonard D. White (1946, 1) contended, "The objective of public administration is the most efficient utilization of the resources at the disposal of officials and employees." The "orthodox" perspective advocates that public administration should distance itself from political considerations by only addressing the production side of government. Under this doctrine, government agencies are advised to develop best available tools to earnestly implement policies. They should thus focus on "the application of scientific methodology to the resolution of public issues and building an identity of neutral expertise" (King and Stivers 1998, 106).

However, if public administration is only concerned with instrumental issues, how can this utilitarian mind-set help government and its administrators become attentive and responsive to the needs of *all* citizens—both men and women, rich and poor, strong and weak, young and old? Dwight Waldo (1980, 45) thus pointedly questioned, "Why would an instrument [bureaucracy] designed to be impersonal and calculating be expected to be effective in delivering sympathy and compassion?" Likewise, Hummel and Stivers (1998, 29) criticized public administration for becoming "a specialized enterprise increasingly devoted to the exercise of technical rules and procedures, whether or not these take care of real-life problems."

Scholars have gradually realized that the function of public administration is much more than producing the optimal input-output ratio in government operations (Frederickson 2015). Benevolence to citizens is the civic virtue expected of all public servants (Lynch and Lynch 2009). This moral foundation reflects not only what public administration ought to be but also what it really is, especially when it comes to the provision of public services. Mastracci et al. once portrayed the role of government as "harbor of refuge" (2012, 6). Because the aim of public service is to serve citizens often in their desperate time of need, altruism in the form of caring is required much more in the public sector than the private sector (Perry and Wise 1990). This view is supported by recent research on public service motivation (PSM). Findings overwhelmingly indicate that individuals are drawn to public service jobs by a desire to care for others, particularly the disadvantaged and vulnerable (Christensen and Wright 2011; Clerkin and Coggburn 2012; Liu et al. 2011; Vandenabeele 2008). Thus, benevolence to all citizens becomes an essential requirement for public service workers. This lays the foundation for nurturing emotional labor in the public sector.

The work of Hsieh et al. (2012) illuminates the role of benevolence as it pertains to the performance of emotional labor. Working in the PSM research stream, they focus on its effect on emotional labor. Perry and Wise (1990) suggested that PSM can fall into three distinct categories: rational, normative, and affective. Among the three, affective motives are closely related to the notion of benevolence for they are perceived as triggers of behavior that are grounded in emotional responses to various social contexts, such as active love of others, and therefore Perry (1996) labeled it as "compassion." Hypothesizing that it is linked to emotional labor, Hsieh and associates surveyed midcareer public managers and found that compassion is positively associated with deep acting and negatively associated with surface acting. Deep acting denotes a strong sense of commitment to the public service role because it captures the attempt of a worker to match the required emotional displays at work. Conversely, surface acting is the passive form of emotional labor for workers. They merely pretend to feel the appropriate emotion and conform to display rules in order to keep the job but they do not "buy into" the feelings they are expressing. All in all, the finding of Hsieh, Yang, and Fu helps us understand the connection between the moral base of benevolence and emotional labor.

The Norm of Reciprocity

Although civic-minded public service workers are expected to be benevolent (Jun 1999), it may be unrealistic to ask them to maintain their composure, regardless of how they are treated by service recipients. The saying, "it takes two to tango," hints that the norm of reciprocity is a powerful force that shapes person-to-person interactions, including public service exchanges between workers and citizens. Conceptually speaking, reciprocity is "a pattern of mutually contingent exchange of gratifications" (Gouldner 1960, 161). Both folk beliefs and theoretical arguments regard reciprocity as a necessity of life. Thousands of years ago, for example, Confucius (2015) promoted reciprocity to be a rule of practice for all one's life. A modern theoretical perspective, Social Exchange Theory, also prescribes reciprocity, in terms of receiving services and goods from others in return for their giving (Molm et al. 2006).

Reciprocity is also a predominant social norm (Gouldner 1960). Due to the norm's prevalence, the vast majority of us frequently engage in social exchanges by alternating between "giving" and "taking" to satisfy our needs and wants. We therefore become the so-called *matchers* (Grant 2013). Matchers are those who strive to achieve and sustain a balance between giving and taking (Fiske 1992). Adhering to the principle of fairness, matchers expect to be repaid in kind when they benefit others; when others have benefited them, they are obliged to return the favor.

However, social exchanges do not always have to involve positive, gratifying actions. People may exchange hostile actions as the old saying, "an eye for an eye and a tooth for a tooth," suggests. The principle of exchanging hostility is known as *the law of retaliation* or the norm of *negative reciprocity* (Eisenberger et al. 2004). Taken together, positive and negative reciprocity are two sides of the same coin because both manifest the characteristic of matchers. As mentioned, matchers embrace the principle of "quid pro quo." That is, for them, a positive action will elicit another positive one and a negative action shall bring another negative one. Because of this, positive reciprocity develops and maintains a continuing relationship that produces mutual benefits for both parties, whereas negative reciprocity can easily ruin an established relationship.

The Government–Citizen Bond

To put it another way, the norm of reciprocity can be regarded as the terms and conditions of a *relational contract*. Despite not being written, a relational contract is a set of expectations that stipulate the interpersonal aspects of exchanges (Macneil Macneil 1983). Through this conceptual lens, we can better put the bonding between public service workers and citizens into perspective. In general, service exchanges tend to be inherently relational for they require interpersonal contact (Paulin et al. 1997). Public service falls within this framework, for it strives to be caring and responsive to citizens (Guy et al. 2008). Moreover, workers also require citizen collaboration and cooperation in their production and delivery of public services.

Because citizens are essentially interactive co-producers, workers must establish a cooperative relationship with them in order to get the job done. "Service with a smile" or a similar demeanor is therefore expected, as is reciprocity from citizens. When one party perceives that the norm of reciprocity is violated, breach of the relational contract undermines mutual collaboration between parties and, in the worst-case scenario, impels people to return hostility for hostility.

Research has substantiated the association between aggression of service recipients and worker sabotage, thereby demonstrating that negative reciprocity in service exchanges exists. For example, in relation to emotional labor, Rupp and Spencer (2006) find that service workers who are exposed to unfair treatment have difficulty adhering to organizational rules that require appropriate emotive displays. They also report that mistreatment of service recipients will result in inauthenticity in service delivery. This means that workers fake work-appropriate emotions and hide—not resolve—negative ones. This finding has been replicated and confirmed by Sliter et al. (2010) and Grandey et al. (2012).

In conclusion, the public service workplace is expected to create a service climate marked by connectedness with the public (Guy et al. 2008) and this is why emotional labor is deemed indispensable. Yet, how emotional labor is done is at the discretion of those who perform such work. For public service workers, benevolence and reciprocity are two important norms that govern their interactions with citizens—the former is the moral base of public service, and the latter is customary in social exchanges. These norms guide workers to determine appropriate behavior in public service delivery, but a dilemma arises when the two are not congruent, particularly in the case of citizen mistreatment.

Hypothesized Effects of Citizen Mistreatment of Public Service Workers

This chapter explores how supposed-to-be benevolent workers react when they are mistreated by citizens. Mistreatment occurs when citizens treat the targeted worker in disrespectful, demeaning, impolite, or unreasonable ways. Even though the intent may not be to harm the target, citizen mistreatment can be expected to trigger a counterproductive effect on the part of the affected worker. Thus, it is theorized that the effect of citizen mistreatment on workers' work attitudes can be threefold: decrements in positive attitudes toward the job (job satisfaction), the self (emotive capacity), and citizens (trust in citizens). First of all, we know that unfavorable work events and conditions will diminish the joy of work (Landy and Conte 2013). One study, in particular, reported that the effect of negative work events on employee mood is stronger than the effect of positive events (Miner et al. 2005), implying that positive experiences at work may not easily offset the damage negative events bring. Constant mistreatment is believed to be detrimental to job satisfaction for it makes it hard for workers to perform at a high level, both cognitively and emotionally, and increases the risk of interpersonal conflicts at work. Additionally, for a civic-minded public service worker, aggression by citizens due to unmet service needs also signals personal failure regarding the pursuit of the public welfare. Feelings of frustration, confusion, and anger may develop, causing job satisfaction to plummet.

To explain the effect of citizen mistreatment on the self, Ego Depletion and Social Cognitive Theories are helpful. According to Ego Depletion Theory, exerting self-control will consume individual strength (Muraven and Baumeister 2000). Keeping one's cool in the midst of interpersonal mistreatment requires a significant amount of self-control, and it is reasonable to anticipate that continuous self-control strength will likely degrade. The decrement in individual stamina should be evident in the worker's emotive capacity, which is the person's ability to deal with emotions in the workplace. This assumption is bolstered by Social Cognitive Theory, which suggests that personal efficacy in specific situations is influenced by the dynamic interaction between the person and the environment (Bandura 1977). In the public service workplace, employees are expected to exert emotional labor, whether being "nicer than nice" for the social worker, "more patient than Job" for the teacher, or "tougher than tough" for the police officer. However, the challenging behavior of citizens can be irritating. When workers confront frequent and intense mistreatment, they may feel overwhelmed by inter- and intra-personal emotion regulation demands—which means managing the emotions of others as well as their own—and thus begin to doubt whether they are capable of performing such work.

Finally, based on the norm of reciprocity, it is reasonable to anticipate that workers will retaliate in response to troublesome provocations on the part of service recipients. As trust is a product of social interactions, we then expect that trust in citizens will decrease as a result of perceived citizen mistreatment. Yang (2005) explained, "…because administrators frequently interact with different citizens, the quality of their experience is more important to their trust in citizens. If administrators have had pleasant experiences, they should be more likely to trust citizens" (276). However, when experiences turn hostile, trust in citizens should deteriorate accordingly.

Based on the above discussions, the following hypotheses are tested:

Hypothesis 1: Citizen mistreatment is negatively related to workers' job satisfaction.
Hypothesis 2: Citizen mistreatment is negatively related to workers' personal capacity to perform emotional labor.
Hypothesis 3: Citizen mistreatment is negatively related to workers' trust in citizens.

Four measures are used to test these hypotheses, and they are described below.

Mistreatment by Citizens

The measurement is derived from the customer incivility scale developed by Skarlicki et al. (2008). The original scale contains eight items that capture distinctive aspects of mistreatment by service recipients. Six of them are applicable to most public service jobs and are used for this study. They are listed below. Cronbach's alpha coefficient for this measure, 0.871, shows the presence of a high degree of internal consistency.

- Clients/customers make demands that I cannot deliver.
- Clients/customers generally raise irrelevant discussion.
- Clients/customers generally doubt my ability.
- Clients/customers often yell at me.
- Clients/customers often use condescending language (e.g., "you are an idiot").
- Clients/customers generally speak aggressively to me.

Job Satisfaction

The concept denotes one's joy of work and is measured by four items selected from previous studies (Guy and Lee 2015; Spector 1985; Yang and Guy 2015). The four-item scale yields a reliability alpha of 0.743, demonstrating acceptable internal consistency. Items of this scale include:

- My job provides career development and promotion opportunities.
- I feel I am being paid a fair amount for the work I do.
- I feel satisfied with my supervisor.
- Overall, I am satisfied with my job.

Emotive Capacity

This construct reflects one's belief in his or her ability to deal with emotions in the workplace. It is measured by respondents' self-report of their capacity to perform emotional labor. We adopted items from the emotional labor questionnaire developed by Guy et al. (2008). The result of reliability test, 0.740, shows that this scale has acceptable internal consistency. Items of this scale are listed below:

- I am good at expressing how I feel.
- I am good at getting people to calm down.
- In my job, I am good at dealing with emotional issues.

Trust in Citizens

This concept is operationalized by a single item that measures the degree to which workers perceive citizens to be trustworthy in their interactions with them at work. This survey item, as well as each of the items mentioned above, is measured on a seven-point Likert-type scale (1 = strongly disagree, 7 = strongly agree).

- When I have contact with clients/customers in my job, I can rely on them to tell the truth.

Respondents

Public service workers were surveyed in China, Pakistan, Rwanda, South Korea, Taiwan, the UK, and the USA during 2015–2016 to test the hypothesized effect of citizen mistreatment on workers' job satisfaction, emotive capacity, and trust in citizens. The survey collected 1746 valid responses from these countries, and respondents were those who either currently worked, or had prior work experience, in public service organizations. Evidence gleaned from this analysis will lead us to answer whether public service workers remain committed to the public service role in spite of unpleasant interpersonal provocations caused by citizens.

Findings

Table 7.1 reports the mean scores of variables that capture respondents' perceptions of citizen mistreatment, job satisfaction, emotive capacity, and trust in citizens. Notable among the findings is that the mean score for citizen mistreatment is 3.3 on a seven-point scale, which is close to the neutral point of "neither agree nor disagree" with the items in the variable. This indicates that the existence of citizen misbehavior toward public service

Table 7.1 Mean scores of variables by country

	Citizen mistreatment	Job satisfaction	Emotive capacity	Trust in citizens
All	3.302	4.787	5.201	4.670
	(1.400)	(1.317)	(1.146)	(1.622)
China	3.595	5.082	5.592	5.420
	(1.234)	(1.128)	(1.004)	(1.367)
Pakistan	3.331	4.882	5.265	4.930
	(1.540)	(1.544)	(1.134)	(1.765)
Rwanda	2.398	4.896	5.983	5.440
	(1.424)	(1.506)	(.917)	(1.692)
South Korea	4.398	4.581	4.360	3.980
	(.999)	(.973)	(.940)	(1.430)
Taiwan	3.775	4.197	4.482	4.270
	(1.239)	(1.313)	(1.161)	(1.406)
UK	2.920	4.849	5.332	4.370
	(1.153)	(1.120)	(.942)	(1.440)
USA	2.948	4.798	5.288	4.420
	(1.279)	(1.331)	(1.180)	(1.588)

Note Standard deviations in parentheses

workers was not particularly severe in the countries surveyed. However, there were some noticeable variations by country. For instance, respondents in South Korea scored the highest at 4.398, whereas Rwandans scored only 2.398—a full two points lower. All other comparisons between countries are fairly uniform with the next greatest divergence occurring for trust in citizens, where it is lower in South Korea than in any other nation.

The stacked histogram plotted in Fig. 7.1 gives a visual presentation of responses in each country pertaining to mistreatment by citizens. Values ranged from a low of 1 (strongly disagree with statements of mistreatment) to a high of 7 (strongly agree with statements of mistreatment). The figure further reveals that a considerable portion of Rwandan, as well as Pakistani, respondents had little experience with citizen mistreatment. Additionally, workers in the UK and the USA, on average, scored below the mean. The discrepancy in sample distribution between South Korea and these countries is noticeable. By comparison, there was a higher proportion of respondents in South Korea whose responses fell above the mean.

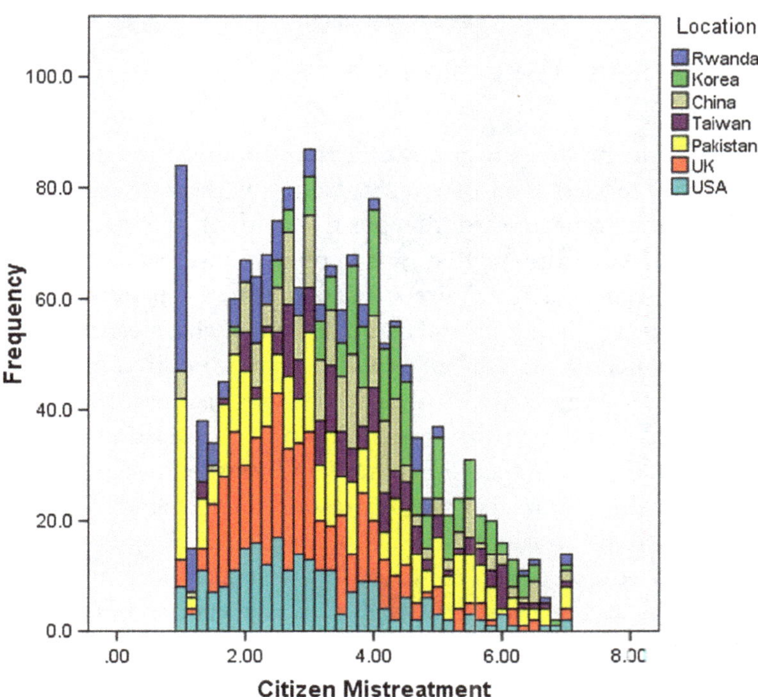

Fig. 7.1 Stacked histogram by country (citizen mistreatment)

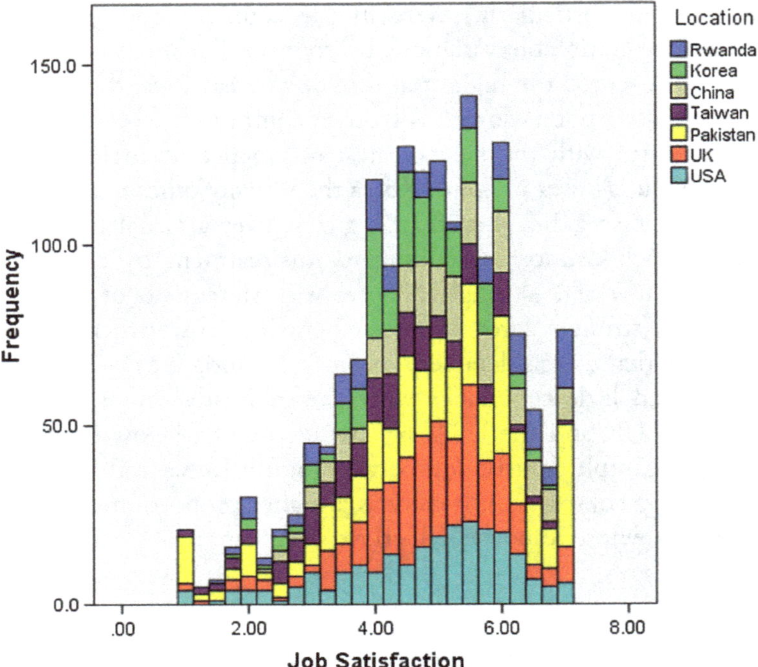

Fig. 7.2 Stacked histogram by country (job satisfaction)

Next, we turn the focus to job satisfaction. On average, survey respondents reported a modest level of job satisfaction with an overall mean score of 4.787, which leans toward the positive end of the seven-point scale (7 = strongly agree). The highest was China, 5.082, whereas the lowest occurred in Taiwan, 4.197. Figure 7.2 shows that the pattern of responses is fairly consistent across nations. In other words, the measure's variability among the seven countries was not as wide as that for citizen mistreatment.

As studies have suggested that individuals vary in their capacity to cope with job-related emotions (Bhave and Glomb 2009; Mastracci et al. 2012), we are intrigued by whether differences also exist between cultures. Are workers in certain cultures good at expressing their feelings and others are not? Are workers in certain cultures good at getting people to calm down and others are not? Are workers in certain cultures good at dealing with emotional issues at work and others are not? Evidence shows that there are noteworthy differences between countries. In general, respondents were high in emotive capacity as the mean score was 5.201. Rwandans led the group of seven countries with a mean score of 5.983. While most scores were above 5,

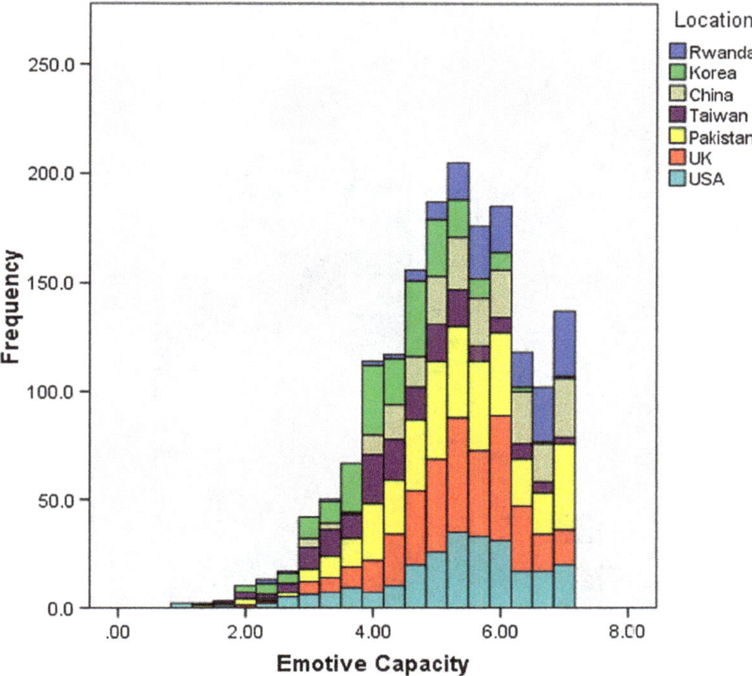

Fig. 7.3 Stacked histogram by country (emotive capacity)

South Korea and Taiwan were 4.360 and 4.482, respectively. In Fig. 7.3, compared with other countries, sample distributions for South Korea and Taiwan slightly tilt toward the middle point instead of the positive end of the scale.

The last variable to be discussed is trust in citizens, which is operationalized and measured by a single item. As shown in Table 7.1 and Fig. 7.4, survey respondents reported a modest level of trust in citizens (mean score = 4.670). Akin to the variable of emotive capacity, Rwanda scored highest among the seven countries and South Korean respondents had lowest trust in citizens. These findings hint at a negative correlation between citizen mistreatment and trust in citizens, as well as emotive capacity. Next, we test hypotheses using correlation analysis.

Table 7.2 presents the results of correlation analysis. At first glance, citizen mistreatment was indeed negatively related to job satisfaction, emotive capacity, and trust in citizens, as hypothesized. These correlations were significant in the aggregate worldwide survey data but varied widely from country to country. For instance, the hypothesized effect of citizen

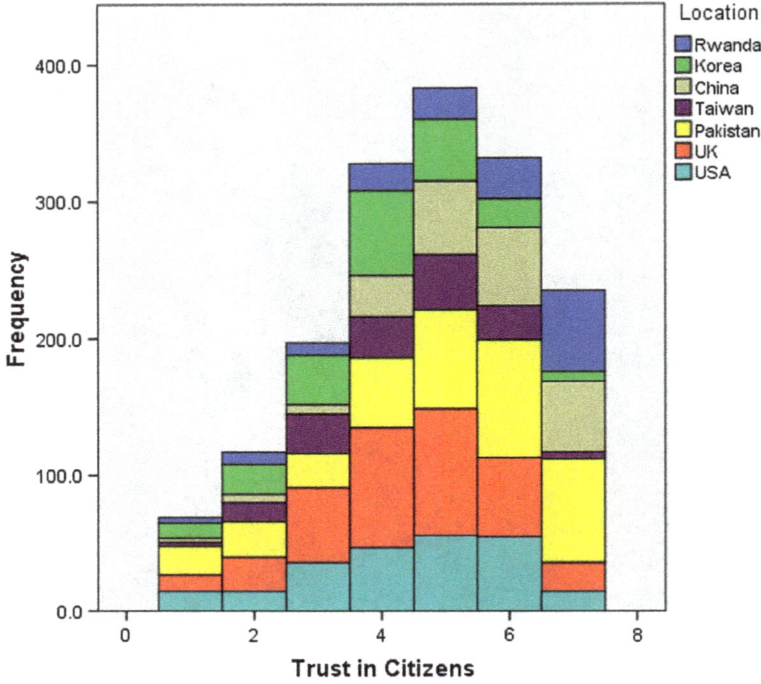

Fig. 7.4 Stacked histogram by country (trust in citizens)

mistreatment on job satisfaction (Hypothesis 1) was successfully upheld by the sub-samples of China, Rwanda, Taiwan, the UK, and the USA. However, although the correlation appeared to be negative in the South Korean sub-sample, the statistic failed to achieve the desired significance level. Even more surprisingly, among Pakistani respondents, the direction of the correlation was actually positive, though the test result was not significant.

As for Hypothesis 2, all of the seven countries showed a negative correlation between citizen mistreatment and workers' emotive capacity. However, only Pakistani and Taiwanese sub-samples could actually lend support to the hypothesis as the test result in both datasets was statistically significant. The rest of the worldwide survey data could not uphold Hypothesis 2.

Last but not least, we postulated that there is a negative correlation between citizen mistreatment and workers' trust in citizens (Hypothesis 3). Six out of the seven countries did show a correlation that was in line with the hypothesis, but only two sub-samples, the UK and the USA, reached

Table 7.2 Correlation matrix

	1	2	3
All sub-samples			
1. Citizen mistreatment			
2. Job satisfaction	−0.151**		
3. Emotive capacity	−0.207**	0.255**	
4. Trust in citizens	−0.164**	0.173**	0.266**
China			
1. Citizen mistreatment			
2. Job satisfaction	−0.176*		
3. Emotive capacity	−0.041	440**	
4. Trust in citizens	−0.107	0.340**	0.318**
Pakistan			
1. Citizen mistreatment			
2. Job satisfaction	0.094		
3. Emotive capacity	−0.149**	0.222**	
4. Trust in citizens	−0.072	0.182**	0.200**
Rwanda			
1. Citizen mistreatment			
2. Job satisfaction	−0.465**		
3. Emotive capacity	−0.084	0.190*	
4. Trust in citizens	0.256**	−.139	0.304**
South Korea			
1. Citizen mistreatment			
2. Job satisfaction	−0.034		
3. Emotive capacity	−0.061	0.243**	
4. Trust in citizens	−0.134	0.251**	0.199**
Taiwan			
1. Citizen mistreatment			
2. Job satisfaction	−0.252**		
3. Emotive capacity	−0.198*	0.327**	
4. Trust in citizens	−0.132	0.315**	0.395**
UK			
1. Citizen mistreatment			
2. Job satisfaction	−0.199**		
3. Emotive capacity	−0.056	0.243**	
4. Trust in citizens	−0.152**	0.095	0.122*
USA			
1. Citizen mistreatment			
2. Job satisfaction	−0.174**		
3. Emotive capacity	−0.013	0.018	
4. Trust in citizens	−0.550**	0.09	0.009

Note *significant at $p < 0.05$; **significant at $p < 0.01$

statistical significance. The Rwandan data also yielded a significant result, but against our prediction, the correlation between citizen mistreatment and trust in citizens was, in fact, positive rather than inverse among Rwandan respondents.

Discussion and Conclusion

Everyday around the globe, there are thousands of men and women working toward the betterment of the general public. They take charge of delivering a wide range of services—police, fire, social work, health care, education, transportation, shelter, to name just a few. Although the great variety of public services are fairly distinctive from one another, successful completion of these jobs uniformly requires not only high intensity but also harmonious coordination of physical, cognitive, and emotional efforts. However, public administration scholars and practitioners alike used to pay heed to only the physical and cognitive aspects of public service work. Now we know that emotional labor is another important component in service delivery.

We all know that workers have to induce a positive emotional state in the people they serve, and therefore, many administrative reforms have focused on how to polish and improve public service tactics, such as "service with a smile." While the pursuit of citizen satisfaction is important, there is ample research that suggests dealing with the public comes with a cost in terms of employee well-being (Guy et al. 2008; Hsieh et al. 2011; Hsieh 2012). This is primarily because people who work in public services are often exposed to the emotions of those they serve. While some service encounters may be pleasant, other interactions can easily become hostile.

Citizen aggression, disrespect, or rudeness can be detrimental to the emotional state of public service workers. Drawn from theories of job satisfaction, ego depletion, social cognition, and reciprocity, we hypothesized that citizen mistreatment would eradicate the drive and passion that workers rely on to deliver high-quality services to the general public, leading to decrements in positive attitudes toward the job (job satisfaction), the self (emotive capacity), and citizens (trust in citizens). Hypothesis testing of this study was performed using survey data collected in China, Pakistan, Rwanda, South Korea, Taiwan, the UK, and the USA. Results generally support these hypotheses, although differences emerge between the countries. These findings have profound implications for the management of public service exchanges as well as the understanding of cultural differences in the emotional aspects of public service work.

First of all, in the aftermath of citizen mistreatment, ways to recuperate from the stressful event and regain the joy of one's work are important (Sonnentag et al. 2008). Unlike business service organizations which demand emotional labor because it affects the bottom line, public service organizations demand emotional labor because it connects government and its people. The rapport developed through service exchanges facilitates successful completion of public services, which comes back to strength the continuing government–citizen relationship. From beginning to end, public service workers play a critical role in relationship building with citizens. Therefore, it really matters whether they are happy with their jobs or not. According to the Conservation of Resources Theory (Hobfoll 2002), the investment of organizational resources in workers (e.g., supervisor support, recognition, rewards, employee assistance programs, and self-care plans) may mitigate the harmful impact of citizen mistreatment on job satisfaction.

Organizations can also take preventive measures to sustain worker job satisfaction. For workers who struggle with service interactions with citizens, training and development can nurture the worker skills and abilities required to provide "service with a smile" or other appropriate forms of emotional labor. However, citizen mistreatment may be a result of resource deficiencies rather than interaction difficulties between workers and citizens. Thus, public service organizations must avoid making workers a scapegoat for structural deficiencies. The PSM literature has suggested that the propensity to care for others is a unique characteristic of public service workers (Perry and Wise 1990). While workers are determined to cater to the needs of citizens, they must have the capacity to do so. Resource deficiencies result in unmet service needs of citizens, and, in turn, provoke worker perceptions of conflicting role expectations (to serve the interest of citizens versus to preserve the resources of the organization). And, research shows that conflicting or ambiguous roles imposed by organizations reduce job satisfaction (Landy and Conte 2013).

Indeed, when workers are hired to perform public service jobs, organizations are obligated to position them to survive and thrive in the workplace. As these findings show, even when workers are not to blame for citizen mistreatment, the unpleasant service encounter can lead them to doubt their emotive capacity. To mitigate this negative effect, managers' emotional support of public service workers through *cognitive reframing* is highly recommended as this strategy can effectively improve self-concepts (Lachman et al. 1992). Cognitive reframing, also known as cognitive restructuring (Beck 1997), "involves taking the facts and critical elements of the situation and formulating a plausible narrative that will have a different emotional impact"

(Williams 2007, 606). Simply put, it is an attempt to direct a targeted individual to adopt a new perspective on stressful events and reframe his or her beliefs in a good light. For example, managers may cultivate workers' confidence in their personal efficacy by encouraging a positive service transformation from the past experience. Focusing on lessons learned instead of on personal failures prepares workers for their next encounter.

Finally, managers need to address the effect of citizen mistreatment on trust in citizens. Influenced by the social norm of reciprocity, most people have the tendency to return kindness for kindness and hostility for hostility. Thus, public service workers may turn from being benevolent into agonizing over citizen mistreatment. Consequently, their trust in citizens will plummet, as our findings indicate. Negative reciprocity only escalates interpersonal conflict in the worker–citizen interaction. If negative reciprocity is not the solution to the difficult circumstance where service exchanges are out of control, what is *the* solution? There is no easy answer. Because public service workers are the agents of government, they exercise state power and are expected to be just, reasonable, and considerate. One may argue that it is too much to ask workers to have unfailing care of citizens. Indeed, there is no endless benevolence, nor is there endless hostility. Both are actions of social exchange that are fluid and dynamic; both may change from situation to situation. In such a case, returning benevolence for citizen mistreatment may help workers soften the tension between them and recipients. A constructive and productive service interaction can therefore be re-built.

There are also ways to help civic-minded workers develop perseverance in spite of citizen mistreatment. Although the majority of humans are so-called matchers, there are still individuals who have the propensity to put others' interests before their own. They are called *givers* because they give to others more than they take (Grant 2013). Givers are self-sacrificing. Givers are agreeable. Givers are attentive to the needs of others. And, givers are motivated by public service values (Perry and Wise 1990). Thus, the employment of individuals with such qualities may help public service organizations minimize the risk of citizen mistreatment. Even when confronted with an uncivil citizen, these workers can adhere to organizational display rules and make every effort to calm things down (Hsieh et al. 2012). Thus, they can maneuver emotional labor and turn citizens' concerns and complaints into a desirable service outcome. In addition to selection strategies, managers may also utilize organizational socialization. Research indicates that workers often internalize organizational norms that specify appropriate work behavior through social learning (Weber and Murnighan 2008). The development of a service climate that recognizes and encourages benevolence to all citizens is the first step to reduce workers' acts of retaliation against citizens. Formal and informal learning opportunities, such as seminars and coaching, should also help workers "buy in" to service expectations.

However, we should be mindful of the fact that there are two sides in every public service exchange. If organizations would like to transform the service experience from confrontational to mutually respectful, citizens have to cooperate as well. Organizational support is the most needed resource that workers can rely on to cope with citizen mistreatment. Thus, organizations are advised to have well-developed policies and procedures in place to prevent and handle troublesome provocations against their valuable human assets—the workers. The message sent to citizens must be clear and consistent—no verbal and physical violence will be tolerated.

To conclude, citizen mistreatment is found to be negatively correlated with workers' job satisfaction, emotive capacity, and trust in citizens. However, there are notable differences among the countries surveyed, differences for which later chapters will shed more light. For example, we do not know why some of the correlations were more significant in some countries than others. We also do not know why citizen mistreatment was positively related to trust in citizens among Rwandan respondents, although the chapter detailing Rwanda helps to reveal an explanation. Deeper investigation into the complexion of each nation reveals more of the pieces in these puzzles.

References

Arnetz, Judith E., and Bengt B. Arnetz. 2001. "Violence Towards Health Care Staff and Possible Effects on the Quality of Patient Care." *Social Science & Medicine* 52 (3): 417–27.

Bandura, Albert. 1977. "Self-Efficacy: Toward a Unifying Theory of Behavioral Change." *Psychological Review* 84 (2): 191–215.

Beck, Aaron T. 1997. "The Past and Future of Cognitive Therapy." *The Journal of Psychotherapy Practice and Research* 6 (4): 276–84.

Bhave, Devasheesh P., and Theresa M. Glomb. 2009. "Emotional Labour Demands, Wages and Gender: A Within-Person, Between-Jobs Study." *Journal of Occupational and Organizational Psychology* 82 (3): 683–707.

Christensen, Robert K., and Bradley E. Wright. 2011. "The Effects of Public Service Motivation on Job Choice Decisions: Disentangling The Contributions of Person-Organization Fit and Person-Job Fit." *Journal of Public Administration Research and Theory* 21 (4): 723–43.

Clerkin, Richard M., and Jerrell D. Coggburn. 2012. "The Dimensions of Public Service Motivation and Sector Work Preferences." *Review of Public Personnel Administration* 32 (3): 209–35.

Confucius. 2015. *The Analects of Confucius*. Translated by Robert Eno. http://www.indiana.edu/~p374/Analects_of_Confucius_(Eno-2015).pdf. Accessed August 1, 2018.

Eisenberger, Robert, Patrick Lynch, Justin Aselage, and Stephanie Rohdieck. 2004. "Who Takes the Most Revenge? Individual Differences in Negative Reciprocity Norm Endorsement." *Personality and Social Psychology Bulletin* 30 (6): 787–99.

Fiske, Alan P. 1992. "The Four Elementary Forms of Sociality: Framework for a Unified Theory of Social Relations." *Psychological Review* 99 (4): 689–723.

Frederickson, H. George. 1997. *The Spirit of Public Administration*. San Francisco: Jossey-Bass Publishers.

Frederickson, H. George. 2015. *Social Equity and Public Administration: Origins, Developments, and Applications*. New York: Routledge.

Gouldner, Alvin W. 1960. "The Norm of Reciprocity: A Preliminary Statement." *American Sociological Review* 25 (2): 161–78.

Grandey, Alicia, S. C. Foo, M. Groth, and R. E. Goodwin. 2012. "Free to Be You And Me: A Climate of Authenticity Alleviates Burnout From Emotional Labor." *Journal of Occupational Health Psychology* 17 (1): 1–14.

Grant, Adam M. 2013. *Give and Take: Why Helping Others Drives Our Success*. New York: Penguin Books.

Guy, Mary E., and Hyun Jung Lee. 2015. "How Emotional Intelligence Mediates Emotional Labor in Public Service Jobs." *Review of Public Personnel Administration* 35 (3): 261–77.

Guy, Mary E., Meredith A. Newman, and Sharon H. Mastracci. 2008. *Emotional Labor: Putting the Service in Public Service*. Armonk, NY: M.E. Sharpe.

Hobfoll, Stevan E. 2002. "Social and Psychological Resources and Adaptation." *Review of General Psychology* 6 (4): 307–24.

Hochschild, Arlie R. 1983. *The Managed Heart: Commercialization of Human Feeling*. Berkeley, CA: University of California Press.

Hood, Christopher. 1991. "A Public Management for All Seasons?" *Public Administration* 69 (1): 3–19.

Hsieh, Chih-Wei. 2012. "Burnout Among Public Service Workers: The Role of Emotional Labor Requirements and Job Resources." *Review of Public Personnel Administration* 34 (4): 379–402.

Hsieh, Chih-Wei, Myung H. Jin, and Mary E. Guy. 2011. "Consequences of Work-Related Emotions: Analysis of a Cross-Section of Public Service Workers." *American Review of Public Administration* 42 (1): 39–53.

Hsieh, Chih-Wei, Kaifeng Yang, and Kaijo Fu. 2012. "Motivational Bases and Emotional Labor: Assessing the Impact of Public Service Motivation." *Public Administration Review* 72 (2): 241–51.

Hummel, Ralph P., and Camilla Stivers. 1998. "Government Isn't Us: The Possibility of Democratic Knowledge in Representative Government." In *Government is Us: Public Administration in an Anti-Government Era*, edited by Cheryl S. King and Camilla Stivers, 28–48. Thousand Oaks, CA: Sage.

Jun, Jon S. 1999. "The Need for Autonomy and Virtues: Civic-Minded Administrators in a Civil Society." *Administrative Theory & Praxis* 21 (2): 218–26.

King, Cheryl S., and Camilla Stivers. 1998. *Government is Us: Strategies for an Anti-Government Era.* Thousand Oaks, CA: Sage.

Lachman, Margie E., Suzanne L. Weaver, Mary Bandura, Elaine Elliot, and Corinne J. Lewkowicz. 1992. "Improving Memory and Control Beliefs Through Cognitive Restructuring and Self-Generated Strategies." *Journal of Gerontology* 47 (5): 293–99.

Landy, Frank J., and Jeffery M. Conte. 2013. *Work in the 21st Century: An Introduction to Industrial and Organizational Psychology.* 4th ed. Hoboken, NJ: Wiley.

Lipsky, Michael. 1980. *Street-Level Bureaucracy: Dilemmas of the Individual in Public Services.* New York, NY: Russell Sage Foundation.

Liu, Bangcheng, Chun Hui, Jin Hu, Wensheng Yang, and Xinli Yu. 2011. "How Well Can Public Service Motivation Connect With Occupational Intention?" *International Review of Administrative Sciences* 77 (1): 191–211.

Lynch, Thomas D., and Cynthia E. Lynch. 2009. "Democratic Morality: Back to the Future." In *Ethics and Integrity in Public Administration: Concepts and Cases*, edited by R. W. Cox, 5–25. Armonk, NY: M.E. Sharpe.

Macneil, Ian R. 1983. "Values in Contract: Internal and External." *Northwestern University Law Review* 78: 340–418.

Mastracci, Sharon H., Mary E. Guy, and Meredith A. Newman. 2012. *Emotional Labor and Crisis Response: Working on the Razor's Edge.* Armonk, NY: M.E. Sharpe.

Maynard-Moody, Steven, and Michael Musheno. 2003. *Cops, Teachers, Counselors: Stories from the Front Lines of Public Service.* Ann Arbor: University of Michigan Press.

Miner, Andrew, Theresa Glomb, and Charles Hulin. 2005. "Experience Sampling Mood and its Correlates at Work." *Journal of Occupational and Organizational Psychology* 78 (2): 171–93.

Molm, Linda D., Jessica L. Collett, and David R. Schaefer. 2006. "Conflict and Fairness in Social Exchange." *Social Forces* 84 (4): 2331–52.

Muraven, Mark, and Roy F. Baumeister. 2000. "Self-Regulation and Depletion of Limited Resources: Does Self-Control Resemble a Muscle?" *Psychological Bulletin* 126 (2): 247–59.

Newhill, Christina E. 2003. *Client Violence in Social Work Practice: Prevention, Intervention, and Research.* New York, NY: Guilford Press.

Paulin, Michele, Jean Perrien, and Ronald Ferguson. 1997. "Relational Contract Norms and the Effectiveness of Commercial Banking Relationships." *International Journal of Service Industry Management* 8 (5): 435–52.

Perry, James L. 1996. "Measuring Public Service Motivation: An Assessment of Construct Reliability and Validity." *Journal of Public Administration Research and Theory* 6 (1): 5–22.

Perry, James L., and Lois R. Wise. 1990. "The Motivational Bases of Public Service." *Public Administration Review* 50 (3): 367–73.

Rupp, Deborah E., and Sharmin Spencer. 2006. "When Customers Lash Out: The Effects of Customer Interactional Injustice on Emotional Labor and the Mediating Role of Discrete Emotions." *Journal of Applied Psychology* 91 (4): 971–78.

Shao, Ruodan, and Daniel P. Skarlicki. 2014. "Service Employees' Reactions to Mistreatment by Customers: A Comparison Between North America and East Asia." *Personnel Psychology* 67 (1): 23–59.

Skarlicki, Daniel P., Danielle D. Van Jaarsveld, and David D. Walker. 2008. "Getting Even For Customer Mistreatment: The Role of Moral Identity in the Relationship Between Customer Interpersonal Injustice and Employee Sabotage." *Journal of Applied Psychology* 93 (6): 1335–47.

Sliter, Michael, Steve Jex, Katherine Wolford, and Joanne McInnerney. 2010. "How Rude! Emotional Labor as a Mediator Between Customer Incivility and Employee Outcomes." *Journal of Occupational Health Psychology* 15 (4): 468–81.

Sonnentag, Sabine, Carmen Binnewies, and Eva J. Mojza. 2008. "Did You Have a Nice Evening?" A Day-Level Study on Recovery Experiences, Sleep, and Affect." *Journal of Applied Psychology* 93 (3): 674–84.

Spector, Paul E. 1985. "Measurement of Human Service Staff Satisfaction: Development of the Job Satisfaction Survey." *American Journal of Community Psychology* 13 (6): 693–713.

Stivers, Camilla. 1995. "Settlement Women and Bureau Men: Constructing a Usable Past for Public Administration." *Public Administration Review* 55 (6): 522–29.

Vandenabeele, Wouter 2008. "Government Calling: Public Service Motivation as an Element in Selecting Government as an Employer of Choice." *Public Administration* 86 (4): 1089–105.

Virkki, Tuija 2008. "Habitual Trust in Encountering Violence at Work: Attitudes Towards Client Violence Among Finnish Social Workers and Nurses." *Journal of Social Work* 8 (3): 247–67.

Waldo, Dwight. 1980. *The Enterprise of Public Administration*. Novato, CA: Chandler & Sharp Publishers.

Wang, Mo, Hui Liao, Yujie Zhan, and Junqi Shi. 2011. "Daily Customer Mistreatment and Employee Sabotage Against Customers: Examining Emotion and Resource Perspectives." *Academy of Management Journal* 54 (2): 312–34.

Weber, J. Mark, and J. Keith Murnighan. 2008. "Suckers or Saviors? Consistent Contributors in Social Dilemmas." *Journal of Personality and Social Psychology* 95 (6): 1340–53.

White, Leonard D. 1946. *Introduction to the Study of Public Administration*. Rev. ed. New York, NY: Macmillan.

Williams, Michele 2007. "Building Genuine Trust Through Interpersonal Emotion Management: A Threat Regulation Model of Trust and Collaboration Across Boundaries." *Academy of Management Review* 32 (2): 595–621.

Wilson, Woodrow. 1887. "The Study of Administration." *Political Science Quarterly* 2 (2): 197–222.

Yang, Kaifeng. 2005. "Public Administrators' Trust in Citizens: A Missing Link in Citizen Involvement Efforts." *Public Administration Review* 65 (3): 273–85.

Yang, Seung-Bum, and Mary E. Guy. 2015. "Gender Effects on Emotional Labor in Seoul Metropolitan Area." *Public Personnel Management* 44 (1): 3–24.

Part III

International Comparisons
of Emotional Labor

This part describes the methodology for survey development and administration, provides a description of the public service context for each nation surveyed, and presents findings. Chapter 8 describes the challenge of achieving measurement invariance when administering a survey in twelve countries located on six continents. Translation and back translation are used to ensure language compatibility but linguistic subtleties remain in how meaning is interpreted. The research model is described, and the questionnaire is included in Appendix C. Chapters 9 through 20 detail political dynamics, cultural traditions, and the governmental system in each nation surveyed. The relationship between public service, the performance of emotional labor, and its effect on job outcomes is reported for Australia, Bolivia, China, India, South Korea, Pakistan, Philippines, Rwanda, Taiwan, Thailand, the UK, and the USA. Chapter 21 compares findings across nations, teasing out patterns of similarities and differences.

8

Measuring Emotional Labor: Survey Construction, Measurement Invariance, and Structural Equation Model

Seung-Bum Yang, Mary E. Guy, Sharon H. Mastracci, Aisha Azhar, Chih-Wei Hsieh, Hyun Jung Lee and Xiaojun Lu

International comparative research is hampered by linguistic hurdles and measurement issues. Similar to comparing apples (English) and manzanas (Spanish) that which appears different may be similar, and vice versa. Extending the metaphor to international surveys, researchers must not assume that wording of items means the same in different cultures. To do so can result in findings that may be statistically significant but meaningless. This is especially the case when it comes to measuring emotional labor, a nebulous concept that is very real in practice but elusive in theory.

Another way to think about this is by using the example of how shoes are sized in different cultures. The same shoe is denoted by different measures around the globe. A man's shoe size of 9 in the USA is equivalent to a size 42 in France, 8.5 in the UK, and 270 in South Korea. In a comparative

Much of this chapter was first published as Seung-Bum Yang, Mary E. Guy, Aisha Azhar, Chih-Wei Hsieh, Hyun Jung Lee, Xiaojun Lu, and Sharon H. Mastracci. 2018. "Comparing Apples and Manzanas: Instrument Development and Measurement Invariance in a Cross-National Analysis of Emotional Labor in Public Service Jobs." *International Journal of Work Organization and Emotion* 9 (3): 264–82. https://doi.org/10.1504/IJWOE.2018.10015953.

S.-B. Yang (✉)
Department of Public Administration, Konkuk University, Seoul, South Korea
e-mail: sbyang@konkuk.ac.kr

M. E. Guy
School of Public Affairs, University of Colorado Denver, Denver, CO, USA
e-mail: mary.guy@ucdenver.edu

study between the USA and France, it would be wrong to conclude that 42 is greater than 9. In fact, they are equivalent. Thus, the assumption of measurement invariance enters the discussion.

As we focus on the emotive demands of public service work around the globe, the survey developed for this research overcomes the "apples and manzanas" and "shoe size" problems. Awareness of the emotive component in work performance is mounting, the perspectives on it are increasing and the need for knowledge about its relationship to national culture is overwhelming (see, for example, Atkinson and Lucas 2013; Jenkins and Conley 2007; Komporozos-Athanasiou and Thompson 2015). Public management researchers have identified it as a subject of critical inquiry (e.g., Guyand Lee 2015; Guy et al. 2008; Hsieh 2012; Hsieh et al. 2012; Mastracci et al. 2012; Yang and Guy 2015). To accommodate growing interest in the subject, the survey instrument developed for this book enables comparison across culture and nation.

First, definitions used to develop the survey items are specified, and then the procedure for conducting the pilot survey and analysis of the data is explained. This is followed by a description of the final survey, data collection technique, and report of tests for measurement equivalence.

S. H. Mastracci
Department of Political Science, University of Utah, Salt Lake City, UT, USA
e-mail: Sharon.mastracci@poli-sci.utah.edu

A. Azhar
School of Governance and Society, University of Management and Technology, Lahore, Pakistan
e-mail: aisha.azhar@umt.edu.pk

C.-W. Hsieh
Department of Public Policy, City University of Hong Kong, Kowloon, Hong Kong SAR
e-mail: cwhsieh@cityu.edu.hk

H. J. Lee
Department of Public Administration, MyongJi University, Seoul, South Korea
e-mail: Tweety06@mju.ac.kr

X. Lu
Department of Public Administration, School of International and Public Affairs, Shanghai Jiao Tong University, Shanghai, China
e-mail: xjlv@sjtu.edu.cn

Measuring Emotional Labor

Emotional labor is the management of one's own emotional state as well as the emotional state of the other in order to do one's job. Although particularly notable in emotionally intense jobs, such as emergency response, child protective services, and law enforcement, it is a required component in most jobs that require person-to-person interaction. It is the emotive component of the job that directly contributes to job satisfaction and a sense that one's work is worthwhile and makes a difference (Guy et al. 2008). To a lesser, but important degree, it is the emotive component that also contributes to burnout.

Emotional labor was initially conceptualized as a bipolar construct, where workers either pretend to feel the emotion they display while suppressing how they actually feel, or they actually feel the emotion they are expressing (Hochschild 1979, 1983). Rather than adopt this binary explanation, Morris and Feldman (1996) operationalized it as "the effort, planning, and control needed to express organizationally desired emotion during interpersonal transactions" (987). They parse the effort into four dimensions: (1) frequency of emotional display, (2) attentiveness to required display rules, (3) variety of emotions to be expressed, and (4) emotional dissonance. Of these four dimensions, the first, frequency of emotional display, refers to the frequency of interactions between workers and customers. The job demand for emotional labor increases as the requirement for appropriate emotional displays increases. The second dimension is attentiveness to required display rules. This aspect includes both the duration and intensity of the emotional display. Duration refers to how long the interaction lasts between worker and customer. Compared to a short interaction, a longer duration requires a higher level of sustained emotional labor. Intensity refers to the depth of feeling, whether displayed by pretense or authentically experienced, during the interaction. For example, the emotional intensity that police officers must display during an apprehension will be far higher than that of receptionists or sales clerks, even though all engage in emotional labor daily. The third dimension is the variety of emotions that are required to be expressed. The level of emotional labor increases as the variety of emotions required to be expressed increases. Their fourth dimension is emotional dissonance, which is the conflict between one's own feelings and the feeling that must be displayed. More emotional labor is expended when workers must express emotions they do not actually feel, as compared to when they are required to express emotions that reflect their true feelings.

As more has become known about emotional labor, Guy et al. (2008) applied the concept to public service work. As much as it is a part of customer service—being friendly and understanding—it is much more important in public service due to the nature of the work. Rather than a benign retail exchange, public service workers deal not only with routine exchanges, but also extreme events. When the child protective service worker must remove an injured infant from the arms of an abusive parent, when rescue workers must respond to horrific accidents, and when public information officers must keep their cool while giving factual information to harried reporters and frightened citizens, emotional labor is part of the job. The work cannot be done without it. And because emotional labor in the public service context involves regulating one's own emotional state as well as calming the citizen, Guy et al. conceptualize the work from three perspectives: the performance of emotional labor itself; the worker's skill at performing it; and the degree to which workers must suppress their true feelings in order to display an opposite feeling, that is, to pretend.

Understanding emotional labor is a work in progress: Whether discussed in terms of its dimensions as Morris and Feldman do, or whether from perspectives, as Guy et al. do, there is much more to be learned. Terminology varies from study to study depending on the specific focus of attention (see, for example, Ashkanasy et al. 2017; Brotheridge and Grandey 2002; Gabriel et al. 2015; Grandey 2000, 2015; Grandey et al. 2013; Hulsheger and Schewe 2011; Rayner and Lawton 2018; Roh et al. 2015). In the past, the derogation of emotional labor to a lesser status than cognitive or physical labor has meant that too little attention has been paid to it. It is far more than simply coping with job demands. It is a "comes with" of employment—it is part of the job.

The instrument developed for the research in this handbook paves the way for scholars to investigate emotional labor and to include it in the knowledge bank of job requirements and job performance across countries and cultures. The study is restricted to those who work in public service for that is the population of interest and it embraces a panorama of job experiences, from frontline work involving face-to-face exchanges to executive office work that involves policy-setting. The goal of the work—whether it is policing, teaching, firefighting, health care, emergency response, regulating, or planning—is to be responsive to laws and to advance safety and quality of life.

Construct Definition of Emotional Labor

For the purposes of this survey instrument, we define emotional labor as the worker's potential to perform the emotive component of the job and to express job-appropriate emotions whether one actually feels them or not, by either pretending or by authentically reflecting their true feelings. This definition is operationalized by three variables: *Emotive capacity* refers to the extent to which individuals sense and respond to emotional issues. *Pretending* means hiding true feelings while expressing and displaying other feelings. It occurs when there is emotive dissonance between the emotion that the worker experiences and the emotion that the worker expresses. *Deep acting* is the opposite of pretending. It refers to authentically experiencing the emotion that is displayed. Each is elaborated below.

Emotive Capacity

The first variable, emotive capacity, reflects employees' positive or negative perception of their level of abilities and skills to deal with emotions in the workplace. This includes sensitivity to their own emotional state as well as responsiveness to that of other people. Some workers are good at expressing their feelings and others are not (Bhave and Glomb 2009; Mastracci et al. 2012). Some are good at sensing how others are feeling and others are not. Likewise, there are employees who are good at getting people to calm down, while others are more like accelerants. In other words, individuals vary in their capacity to respond emotively. Some of the variability may be attributable to professional training and staff development, and some is unique to individuals regardless of training (Guy et al. 2008; Guy and Lee 2015).

Two ethnographic studies highlight the role of emotive capacity. A study of how detectives do their work revealed distinctive differences in emotive capacity (Stenross and Kleinman 1989, 444). While detectives enjoyed playing verbal judo with criminals and could easily don a gameface, they found their interactions with victims to be emotionally trying and resented having to "hold their hands." Similarly, an investigator with the Chicago Office of Public Guardian described his detective work as that of being an emotional chameleon, displaying whatever emotion was likely to elicit the most information during his interviews (Guy et al. 2008). He was proud of his ability to sense how a person is feeling and to instantaneously display the emotive behavior that would achieve his ends. Both of these cases are examples of emotive capacity. The detectives enjoyed being "tough" but did not like that part of the job that required them to show sadness or caring. In other words, their emotive capacity varied according to the emotive demand. On the other hand, the investigator prided himself on displaying whatever emotion was called for at the moment.

Researchers have identified numerous psychological constructs to explain the significance of emotive capacity on work performance. Self-efficacy or personal efficacy is an important variable in psychology and management. It is an individual's belief in their capabilities, and this contributes to behavioral change (Bandura 1977). It has been found that people with higher levels of self-efficacy are more capable of performing emotive work (Guy et al. 2008). Locus of control is another psychological term that explains one's belief in personal capacity, consequence, and destiny (Rotter 1966). Employees who score high on measures of internal locus of control believe they can control the situation. Employees who score low, on the other hand, believe they have no control over the situation.

Pretending Expression

The second variable is pretending. Under conditions of emotive dissonance, employees hide how they actually feel in order to express a different one that is job-appropriate, such as the cheery receptionist who actually feels aggravated. Or, the self-confident firefighter who actually is filled with fright. These are situations in which they wear a "mask" to express emotions they do not actually feel. The intensity of emotional labor is higher for employees whose work requires them to engage in emotive pretense (Yang and Guy 2015).

Researchers have discussed emotive pretending from various perspectives. "Surface acting" is one of the terms that is popularly used. Hochschild (1983) defines surface acting dramaturgically: "To show through surface acting the feelings of a Hamlet or an Ophelia, the actor operates countless muscles that make up an outward gesture" (Hochschild 1983, 37). Grandey (2000) also uses surface acting as a dimension of emotional labor, but she looks it as a process of "managing observable expressions." Guy et al. (2008) interviewed employees who worked in prisons, social services, and emergency response call centers and suggested a different terminology after learning how workers describe their own surface acting. In the workers' words, they suppress their own emotions in a way that is different from being an actor on stage. What the employees say they do is that they don a false face, a mask, to express the emotion they do not actually feel. In police work, it is often referred to as verbal judo or wearing a gameface. In social work, it is demonstrated by the caseworker who must show compassion even when she does not feel compassionate. It is demonstrated by the first responder who displays an aura of neutrality despite experiencing feelings of horror. Rather than calling it "surface acting," they view it as behavior, not theater art. Thus, it is a *pretending expression* instead of surface acting.

Table 8.1 Dimensions of emotional labor

	Dimensions	Guiding framework
Hochschild (1983)	Surface acting Deep acting	Dramaturgy
Morris and Feldman (1996)	Frequency of emotional display Attentiveness to required display rules – Duration of emotional display – Intensity of emotional display Variety of emotions to be expressed Emotional dissonance	Interaction
Grandey (2000)	Surface acting Deep acting	Emotion regulation
Guy et al. (2008)	Emotional labor, per se Personal efficacy False face	Emotion management
Current study	Emotive capacity Pretending expression Deep acting	Emotion management

Deep Acting

The third variable is authentically feeling the emotion that is expressed and displayed. Hochschild (1983) and Grandey (2000) call this deep acting, to contrast it to the superficial display that occurs when the worker is merely pretending to feel the emotion being displayed. Similar to actors on a stage who invoke emotions through trained imagination, when on the job, workers are experiencing the feelings that they display to their clients. Deep acting is authentic, such that there is consistency between how workers feel and the emotion they display (Grandey 2000).

Table 8.1 displays the chronological variation in terminology from Hochschild's work, to Morris and Feldman's, to Grandey's to Guy, Newman, and Mastracci's, to the present study. The evolution reflects the developing knowledge base around the subject and the linguistic translation from retail work to the more emotionally intense jobs of public service.

The Pilot Survey

In order to create the pilot survey, items were adapted from previous research. The final version of the pilot questionnaire contained fifteen items and was completed in October 2014. The questionnaire used a seven-point Likert-type scale (1 = strongly disagree, 7 = strongly agree) for each item.

Back-Translation

The original questionnaire was scripted in English. For the non-English speaking countries where the pilot was to be administered (China, Korea, Taiwan), the questionnaire was translated into their languages before the survey was conducted. To validate the translated questionnaire, two experts in each language were involved in the translation process, back-translating and cross-checking each other's translation.

Data Collection Pool for Pilot

Pilot data were collected from public service workers in five countries: the UK, the USA, South Korea, China, and Taiwan, between October 2014 and January 2015. These countries provided convenience samples of varied cultures. At least one researcher was native to each country and administered the survey there. Respondents were comprised of public employees or students enrolled in public administration classes who already had public sector work experience. Their work covered a broad array of jobs, from health and human services, to law enforcement, to education, to lawyers and accountants. Some of these jobs emphasize "service with a smile" and some do not; some emphasize intense daily contact with the public and some do not. That which is in common across all the respondents is that the ultimate goal of their job is not to achieve a sale but to deliver a service or enforce a law. A total of 145 usable responses from the pilot survey were obtained for the pilot data analysis.

Pilot Data Analysis

Collected data were merged into one SPSS file and reviewed to detect coding errors and missing values. Outliers were removed from the data set. This occurred in a few cases in which the respondents consistently provided extreme answers (1 or 7) for all questions, including those that were reverse worded. Then, descriptive statistics such as mean, standard deviation, skewness, and kurtosis were examined. Next, factor analyses were conducted and principal component analysis was used to test whether measurement items were composed of only one factor. The analyses were performed country by country and variable by variable, using the 1.0 eigenvalue threshold. Factor loadings and the content/meaning of survey items were examined. Based on the factor analysis, items were deleted or revised as necessary, taking into

Table 8.2 Survey items

Emotive capacity	1. I am good at expressing how I feel
	2. I am good at getting people to calm down
	3. In my job I am good at dealing with emotional issues
Pretending expression	4. I hide my true feelings so as to appear pleasant at work
	5. In my job I act confident and self-assured regardless of how I actually feel
	6. I wear a "mask" in order to deal with clients/customers in an appropriate way
Deep acting	7. I try to actually experience the emotions that I must show to clients/customers
	8. I work hard to actually feel the emotions that I need to show to clients/customers
	9. I work at developing the feelings inside of me that I need to show to clients/customers

consideration nuances of language and cultural differences. Additionally, Cronbach's alpha coefficients were used to test for the level of internal consistency of each measurement item. All variables produced alpha levels of 0.7 or higher, indicating that the items achieved sufficient interitem reliability.

The goal in designing the questionnaire was to make it as short, as reliable, and as valid as possible. For statistical analysis purposes, we aimed to have a minimum of three survey items for each variable in order to meet the requirements of confirmatory factor analysis (CFA) (Hair et al. 2014). Evaluation of the pilot data showed that this was achieved. Six items from the pilot questionnaire were deleted, yielding a final questionnaire with three items per variable, for a total of nine items. Table 8.2 displays items for each variable. The resulting questionnaire maximizes efficiency while ensuring reliable measurement.

The Cross-National Survey

The worldwide survey began in Spring 2015 in the UK, China, South Korea, Taiwan, Rwanda, USA, and Pakistan (note: Australia, Bolivia, the Philippines, and Thailand joined the study later). A researcher native to each country secured a convenience sample of public officials. As with the pilot survey, a seven-point Likert-type scale (1 = strongly disagree, 7 = strongly agree) was used for each item. The English version of the questionnaire is in Appendix C.

Demographic Characteristics of Respondents

The selection process was similar to that for securing respondents for the pilot. The criterion for inclusion was that survey participants either currently worked, or had prior work experience, in public service organizations. Anyone who had participated in the pilot study was excluded from the survey. A total of 1746 respondents responded to the survey. The number in each country, their gender, years of experience, and educational level are displayed in Table 8.3.

The number of responses obtained in each country ranged from 154 (Rwanda) to 386 (Pakistan).[1] Female respondents (55.3%) comprised a higher percentage than male respondents (42.3%), which is usual in the public service workforce. Most of the respondents have college degrees or higher (84.2%). Again, this is usual because public service is predominantly knowledge work. In terms of their tenure in public service, a majority of respondents (60.1%) have worked less than 10 years.

Descriptive Statistics

Table 8.4 displays means and standard deviations for each survey item in each country. The mean score for all items in all countries is greater than 4. The standard deviations for all survey items are greater than 1, with the exception of item 2 of the Pretending variable for Rwandans, which has a standard deviation of 0.89.

Reliability Tests

Table 8.5 shows Cronbach's alpha coefficients for variables by country. For Emotive Capacity, alpha coefficients ranged from 0.614 (Pakistan) to 0.773 (China). For Pretending, alpha coefficients ranged from 0.612 (China) to 0.729 (Korea). For Deep Acting, alpha coefficients ranged from 0.792 (UK) to 0.924 (Korea).

Tests for Measurement Invariance

To examine the factor structure of the model, confirmatory factor analyses (CFA) for each country were conducted, as depicted in Fig. 8.1. Multi-group confirmatory factor analysis (MGCFA) was performed across

Table 8.3 Background of respondents (percentage in parentheses)

Variables	Category	China $n = 211$	Korea $n = 208$	Pakistan $n = 386$	Rwanda $n = 154$	Taiwan $n = 173$	UK $n = 360$	USA $n = 254$	Total $n = 1746$
Gender	Male	58 (27.5)	93 (44.7)	267 (69.2)	72 (46.8)	73 (42.2)	76 (21.1)	99 (39.0)	738 (42.3)
	Female	153 (72.5)	115 (55.3)	115 (29.8)	71 (46.1)	80 (46.2)	278 (77.2)	154 (60.6)	966 (55.3)
	N/A	0 (0.0)	0 (0.0)	4 (1.0)	11 (7.1)	20 (11.6)	6 (1.7)	1 (0.4)	42 (2.4)
Length of Public	Less than 10	179 (84.8)	113 (54.3)	220 (57.0)	114 (74.0)	76 (43.9)	200 (55.5)	147 (57.9)	1049 (60.1)
Service	10–19 years	32 (15.2)	30 (14.4)	77 (20.0)	36 (23.4)	52 (30.1)	72 (20.0)	57 (22.4)	356 (20.4)
	20–29 years	0 (0.0)	55 (26.5)	52 (13.5)	3 (2.0)	19 (11.0)	45 (12.5)	27 (10.6)	201 (11.5)
	30 or more	0 (0.0)	3 (1.4)	28 (7.2)	0 (0.0)	3 (1.7)	37 (10.3)	20 (7.9)	91 (5.2)
	N/A	0 (0.0)	7 (3.4)	9 (2.3)	1 (0.6)	23 (13.3)	6 (1.7)	3 (1.2)	49 (2.8)
Education	High school or less	169 (80.1)	19 (9.1)	18 (4.7)	27 (17.5)	10 (5.8)	9 (2.5)	1 (0.4)	253 (14.5)
	College	42 (19.9)	163 (78.4)	45 (11.6)	93 (60.4)	155 (89.6)	211 (58.6)	37 (14.6)	746 (42.7)
	After college	0 (0.0)	18 (8.7)	241 (62.4)	27 (17.5)	0 (0.0)	132 (36.7)	215 (84.66)	633 (36.3)
	Other	0 (0.0)	8 (3.8)	76 (19.7)	5 (3.3)	0 (0.0)	0 (0.0)	1 (0.4)	90 (5.2)
	N/A	0 (0.0)	0 (0.0)	6 (1.6)	2 (1.3)	8 (4.6)	8 (2.2)	0 (0.0)	24 (1.4)

Table 8.4 Mean scores for survey items

	China		Korea		Pakistan		Rwanda		Taiwan		UK		USA		Total	
	Mean	SD	Mean	SD	Mean	SD	Mean	SD	Mean	SD	Mean	SD	Mean	SD	Mean	SD
Emotive capacity																
Item1	5.52	1.22	4.22	1.34	5.25	1.56	5.98	1.19	4.41	1.43	4.89	1.39	5.18	1.46	5.06	1.48
Item2	5.68	1.16	4.53	1.12	5.43	1.39	6.01	1.15	4.49	1.34	5.56	1.10	5.47	1.30	5.34	1.32
Item3	5.53	1.28	4.33	1.22	5.03	1.55	5.95	1.10	4.47	1.43	5.53	1.18	5.18	1.47	5.16	1.43
Pretending																
Expression																
Item1	5.51	1.45	5.06	1.29	5.35	1.65	5.90	1.26	5.22	1.39	5.10	1.58	4.53	1.70	5.20	1.56
Item2	6.15	1.05	4.80	1.23	5.59	1.44	6.19	0.89	5.18	1.22	5.49	1.24	5.39	1.25	5.53	1.30
Item3	4.56	1.76	4.72	1.41	4.53	2.05	5.92	1.36	5.17	1.52	4.99	1.69	4.67	1.64	4.86	1.75
Deep acting																
Item1	5.95	1.09	4.83	1.30	4.87	1.55	6.11	1.15	5.28	1.25	4.75	1.44	4.51	1.53	5.07	1.48
Item2	5.87	1.08	4.91	1.31	4.74	1.70	6.18	1.23	5.33	1.10	4.43	1.60	4.13	1.57	4.93	1.59
Item3	5.77	1.18	4.83	1.32	4.80	1.69	6.18	1.20	5.24	1.20	4.25	1.59	4.18	1.55	4.88	1.60
n	211		208		386		154		173		360		254		1746	

Table 8.5 Cronbach's alphas for emotional labor variables

Country	Alpha coefficients		
	Emotive capacity	Pretending	Deep acting
China	0.773	0.612	0.853
Korea	0.643	0.729	0.924
Pakistan	0.614	0.665	0.824
Rwanda	0.720	0.715	0.816
Taiwan	0.744	0.704	0.887
UK	0.653	0.624	0.792
USA	0.771	0.671	0.852
Total ($n = 1746$)	0.736	0.667	0.867

countries. This is important because cross-national research requires measurement invariance in order for comparisons to be valid. This means that items must mean the same thing to respondents in different countries. In other words, it requires that a size 9 shoe in one country has the same dimensions as a size 9 shoe in another country. In the MGCFA model, emotional labor is explained by three latent variables: emotive capacity, pretending, and deep acting. Three items were loaded on each latent variable, as shown in Fig. 8.1.

Measurement indicators for each construct should be equivalent across countries. Three types of measurement invariance are recommended: configural, metric, and scalar (Jilke et al. 2015; Kim et al. 2013; Milfont and Fischer 2010; Steenkamp and Baumgartner 1998). Tests for configural invariance are used to determine whether the basic model has the same factorial structure across countries. Configural invariance does not guarantee comparisons across the countries, but it serves as the baseline model for establishing measurement invariance. Tests for metric invariance indicate

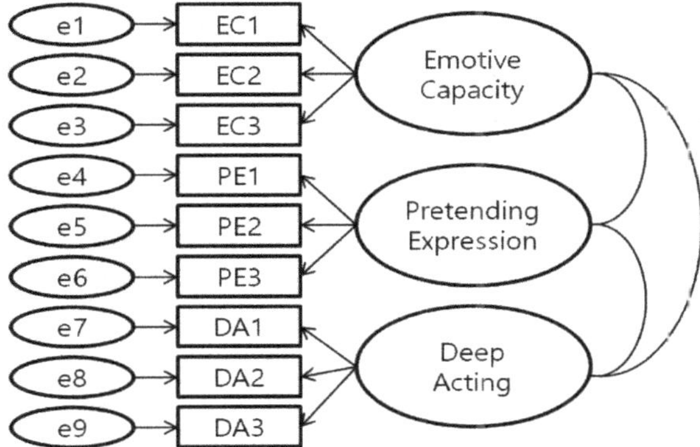

Fig. 8.1 Confirmatory factor analysis model

Fig. 8.2 Configural, metric, and scalar invariance (*Source* Adapted from Jilke et al. [2015, 38])

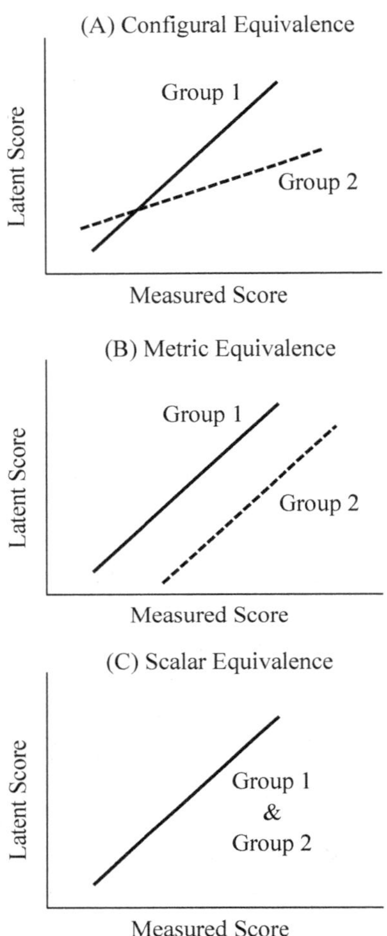

whether factor loadings of the measurement items are equivalent across countries. The third type of measurement invariance is scalar invariance, and it indicates whether the intercepts of the measurement items are the same across the countries.

Jilke et al. (2015) provide a helpful graphical expression of these three types of measurement invariance. The graphs in Fig. 8.2 provide intuitive illustrations of the meaning of these three types of invariance. The first graph depicts configural equivalence where the two lines exist, but the slope coefficients as well as the two intercepts are different. In the second graph, metric equivalence, the slope coefficients of the two lines are the same but the intercepts are not. The third graph shows scalar equivalence where not only the slope coefficients but also the intercepts are same. While metric invariance enables comparisons of regression coefficients, comparison of latent means requires scalar invariance.

Multi-group Confirmatory Factor Analysis

This section reports findings from analyses that tested for measurement invariance across China, Korea, Pakistan, Rwanda, Taiwan, UK, and the USA (Tables 8.4 and 8.5 display summary data). The three measurement invariance models to be tested are nested models, where the configural invariance model is less restricted than the metric invariance model, and the metric invariance model is less restricted than the scalar invariance model. In applications of MGCFA, the chi-square difference test for nested models can be used to assess differences between the models (Schermelleh-Engel et al. 2003).

Configural Invariance

A test for configural invariance was done with Maximum Likelihood estimation. All parameters are estimated without any constraints for the seven groups at the same time. All factor loadings are statistically significant across the group at the 0.001 level. Indices for the configural invariance test are: $\chi^2(\mathrm{df} = 168, n = 1746) = 587.396$, $p < 0.001$, $\chi^2/\mathrm{df} = 3.496$, CFI $= 0.920$, RMSEA $= 0.038$. The model fits the data across the seven nations. Configural invariance is achieved and this indicates that the factor structures are equivalent across the seven groups.

Metric Invariance

Next, the test for metric invariance was conducted using Maximum Likelihood estimation constraining the factor loadings (the regression weights) of the nine indicators to be equal across the seven countries. All factor loadings are statistically significant across the group at the 0.001 level. Indices for the metric invariance test are: $\chi^2(\mathrm{df} = 204, n = 1746) = 638.596$, $p < 0.001$, $\chi^2/\mathrm{df} = 3.130$, CFI $= 0.917$, RMSEA $= 0.035$. This is the full metric invariance test and the Chi-square difference test shows that the full metric invariance model is significantly different from the configural invariance model. Thus, full metric invariance is not achieved.

We then conducted a partial metric invariance test with Maximum Likelihood estimation relaxing one constraint. Partial metric invariance is acceptable as long as at least one indicator is invariant across the groups (Bryne et al. 1989; Steenkamp and Baumgartner 1998). All factor loadings are statistically significant across the groups at the 0.001 level. Indices for the partial metric invariance test are: $\chi^2(df = 198, n = 1746) = 609.988$, $p < 0.001$, $\chi^2/df = 3.081$, CFI $= 0.922$, RMSEA $= 0.035$. The Chi-square difference test shows that the partial metric invariance model is not significantly different from the configural invariance model. Thus, partial metric invariance is achieved.

Scalar Invariance

Finally, a test for scalar invariance was conducted with Maximum Likelihood estimation. All factor loadings were statistically significant across the groups at the 0.001 level. Indices for the scalar invariance test are: $\chi^2(df = 246, n = 1746) = 1602.425$, $p < 0.001$, $\chi^2/df = 6.514$, CFI $= 0.743$, RMSEA $= 0.056$. The model does not fit the data well, and the Chi-square difference is statistically significant. Thus, scalar invariance is not achieved. Tables 8.6 and 8.7 display the fit indices and chi-square tests.

Table 8.6 Summary of fit indices: seven nations

	χ^2	df	χ^2/df	RMSEA	CFI
Configural invariance	587.396	168	3.496	0.038	0.920
Metric invariance	638.596	204	3.130	0.035	0.917
Partial metric invariance	609.988	198	3.081	0.035	0.922
Scalar invariance	1602.425	246	6.514	0.056	0.743

Table 8.7 Chi-square difference tests: seven nations

	χ^2 difference	df difference	RMSEA difference	CFI difference	Decision
Test of configural invariance	Baseline	Baseline	Baseline	Baseline	Accept
Test of metric invariance	51.2	36	−0.003	−0.003	Reject
Test of partial metric invariance	22.592	30	0	0.005	Accept
Test of scalar invariance	992.437	48	0.021	−0.179	Reject

After the MGCFA, we combined all the datasets and conducted CFA with Maximum Likelihood estimation. In the CFA model, emotional labor is explained by three latent variables: emotive capacity, pretending, and deep acting. Three measurement items were loaded on each latent variable. The CFA analysis showed that all factor loadings are statistically significant at the 0.001 level. Indices are: χ^2(df $= 24$, $n = 1746$) $= 351.514$, $p < 0.001$, χ^2/df $= 14.646$, CFI $= 0.940$, RMSEA $= 0.088$.

Although the ideal of overall measurement invariance is not achieved, the fact that configural and partial measurement variance were achieved enables the research to go forward and to administer the survey around the globe. Data were gathered and are presented in the chapters that follow. Although the means cannot be compared from country to country, the patterns of results can be compared and this is done through structural equation modeling. This provides more insight than has hitherto been possible while still embracing the reality that there are cultural and linguistic nuances that subtly alter the meanings of emotive terminology (Guy and Azhar 2018). Moreover, it allows researchers to move a step beyond the current dilemma of being left to our assumptions and theories or, worse, to assume total measurement invariance when, in fact, it does not exist.

Structural Equation Model

The structural equation model (SEM) shown in Fig. 8.3 was run for all countries and path coefficients were standardized. (The numbered questionnaire items may be found in Appendix C.) Note that there is a covariance path between PRETENDING and DEEP ACT in the model. This is due to the theoretical assumption that there is a relationship between the two approaches that workers can take in order to respond to job demands (Kline 2010). In Hochschild's (1983) terminology, workers decide whether to engage in superficial emotional labor by pretending to feel the emotion they display (surface acting) or they can authentically respond by displaying the emotion they actually feel (deep acting).

In the chapters that follow, SEM results are shown for each nation surveyed. Chapter 21 then provides a cross-national comparison that highlights similarities and differences.

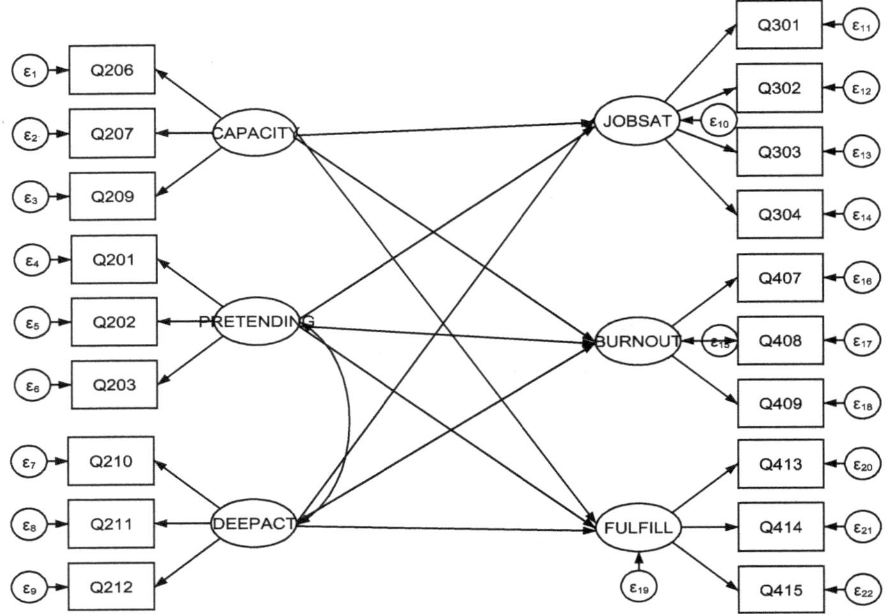

Fig. 8.3 Structural equation model

Conclusion

The measurement scale that enables cross-national comparisons of emotional labor uses three variables: emotive capacity, pretending expression, and deep acting. With only nine items, it is brief, translates well into other languages, and the responses are easily analyzed. Moreover, the items overcome a major stumbling block to comparative analyses in that they achieve two of the three forms of measurement invariance.

The survey instrument was developed by collecting data in seven countries on four continents. CFA shows that the measurement indicators represent theoretical constructs well. MGCFA confirms that configural and partial measurement invariance across the countries is achieved.

Like apples and manzanas, the achievement of configural and partial measurement invariance means that it is possible to meaningfully compare the relationships and patterns of the three emotional labor variables in a variety of countries. Like the shoe size problem, however, the fact that scalar invariance is not achieved means that a meaningful comparison of latent mean scores of the three emotional labor variables across the countries cannot be reliably done. Although frustrating, this fact does not prevent studying patterns within each country and comparing the patterns to that which prevails in other countries.

The upshot is that the combined effect of cultural and linguistic nuances to the meaning of words and scale values complicates cross-national research but it does not prevent it. This survey can be used to study patterns of relationships as responses in one country are compared to responses in another country. However, data cannot be merged in such a way that a mean of 3 on emotive capacity, for example, in one country is assumed to indicate the same level as a mean of 3 in another country.

The measurement items evaluated here can be used in modeling causal relationships and comparing patterns across nations in regard to emotional labor and other variables. In doing so, research opens a window to better understanding of the differences and similarities of the public service experience in varied cultures. Just as Kim et al. (2013) conclude in their work on public service motivation, the failure to achieve scalar invariance does not preclude the ability to compare patterns of relationships across countries, even though it is unlikely that one singular scale can achieve uniform meaningfulness around the globe.

The contribution of this instrument is that it enables comparative empirical study to examine causal effects of emotional labor variables across countries. Does emotive capacity contribute to job satisfaction in China, similar to how it does in the USA? Does pretending contribute to burnout in the UK, similar to its effect in the USA? Does deep acting correlate with job performance in China similar to how it correlates in Taiwan? So much is yet to be learned about the relationship between worker traits and emotional labor as they are nested in the context of national culture. In the workplace, the effects of emotional labor may, or may not be, the same from country to country. The variables reported here provide a means for investigating these interesting questions. Results are in the chapters that follow.

Note

1. The UK sample includes 360 respondents, 159 of whom are nurses who work for the National Health Service. All respondents were included in the analysis reported in this chapter. However, to ensure that one profession did not bias the data in Chapter 19, nurses were excluded from the analyses reported there. This prevents data from one frame of reference—professionally trained nurses—from dominating the variety of public service jobs in the UK. This also allows for more meaningful comparability across nations, as is presented in Chapter 21.

References

Ashkanasy, N. M., A. C. Troth, S. A. Lawrence, and P. J. Jordan. 2017. "Emotions and Emotional Regulation in HRM: A Multi-level Perspective." *Research in Personnel and Human Resources Management* 35: 1–52.

Atkinson, C., and R. Lucas. 2013. "Policy and Gender in Adult Social Care Work." *Public Administration* 91 (1): 159–73.

Bandura, Albert. 1977. "Self-Efficacy: Toward a Unifying Theory of Behavioral Change." *Psychological Review* 84 (2): 191–215.

Bhave, D. P., and T. M. Glomb. 2009. "Emotional Labour Demands, Wages and Gender: A Within-Person, Between-Jobs Study." *Journal of Occupational and Organizational Psychology* 82 (3): 683–707.

Brotheridge, C. M., and Alicia A. Grandey. 2002. "Emotional Labor and Burnout: Comparing Two Perspectives of 'People Work'." *Journal of Vocational Behavior* 60 (1): 17–39.

Bryne, B. M., R. J. Shavelson, and B. Muthen. 1989. "Testing for the Equivalence of Factorial Covariance and Mean Structures: The Issue of Partial Measurement Invariance." *Psychological Bulletin* 105 (3): 456–66.

Gabriel, A. S., M. A. Daniels, J. M. Diefendorff, and G. J. Greguras. 2015. "Emotional Labor Actors: A Latent Profile Analysis of Emotional Labor Strategies." *Journal of Applied Psychology* 100 (3): 863–79.

Grandey, Alicia A. 2015. "Emotional Labor Threatens Decent Work: A Proposal to Eradicate Emotional Display Rules." *Journal of Organizational Behavior* 36 (6): 770–85.

Grandey, Alicia A., J. M. Diefendorff, and D. E. Rupp, eds. 2013. *Emotional Labor in the 21st Century: Diverse Perspectives on Emotion Regulation at Work.* New York, NY: Routledge.

Grandey, Alicia A. 2000. "Emotion Regulation in the Workplace: A New Way to Conceptualize Emotional Labor." *Journal of Occupational Health Psychology* 5 (1): 95–110.

Guy, Mary E., and Aisha Azhar. 2018. "Emotional Labor Meanings, Gender, and Culture: A Comparative Assessment." *Administrative Theory & Praxis* 40 (4): 289–303. https://doi.org/10.1080/10841806.2018.1485452.

Guy, Mary E., and Hyun Jung Lee. 2015. "Emotional Intelligence and Emotional Labor: How Related Are They?" *Review of Public Personnel Administration* 35 (3): 261–77.

Guy, Mary E., Meredith A. Newman, and Sharon H. Mastracci. 2008. *Emotional Labor: Putting the Service in Public Service.* Armonk, NY: M.E. Sharpe.

Hair, J. F., W. C. Black, B. J. Babin, and R. E. Anderson. 2014. *Multivariate Data Analysis.* 7th ed. Essex, UK: Pearson Publishing.

Hochschild, Arlie R. 1983. *The Managed Heart: Commercialization of Human Feeling.* Berkeley, CA: University of California Press.

Hochschild, Arlie R. 1979. "Emotion Work, Feeling Rules, and Social Structure." *The American Journal of Sociology* 85 (3): 551–75.

Hsieh, Chih-Wei. 2012. "Burnout Among Public Service Workers: The Role of Emotional Labor Requirements and Job Resources." *Review of Public Personnel Administration* 20 (2): 1–24.

Hsieh, Chih-Wei, Myung Jin, and Mary E. Guy. 2012. "Managing Work-Related Emotions: Analysis of a Cross Section of Public Service Workers." *The American Review of Public Administration* 42 (1): 39–53.

Hulsheger, U. R., and A. F. Schewe. 2011. "On the Costs and Benefits of Emotional Labor: A Meta-Analysis of Three Decades of Research." *Journal of Occupational Health Psychology* 16 (3): 361–89.

Jenkins, S., and C. Hazel. 2007. "Living with the Contradictions of Modernization? Emotional Management in the Teaching Profession." *Public Administration* 85 (4): 979–1001.

Jilke, S., B. Meuleman, and S. Van de Walle. 2015. "We Need to Compare, But How? Measurement Equivalence in Comparative Public Administration." *Public Administration Review* 75 (1): 36–48.

Kim, S., W. Vandenabeele, B. E. Wright, L. B. Andersen, F. P. Cerase, R. K. Christensen, and Céline Desmarais. 2013. "Investigating the Structure and Meaning of Public Service Motivation Across Populations: Developing an International Instrument and Addressing Issues of Measurement Invariance." *Journal of Public Administration Research and Theory* 23 (1): 79–102.

Kline, Rex B. 2010. *Methodology in the Social Sciences: Principles and Practice of Structural Equation Modeling.* New York, NY: The Guilford Press.

Komporozos-Athanasiou, A., and M. Thompson. 2015. "The Role of Emotion in Enabling and Conditioning Public Deliberation Outcomes: A Sociological Investigation." *Public Administration* 93 (4): 1138–51.

Mastracci, Sharon H., Mary E. Guy, and Meredith A. Newman. 2012. *Emotional Labor and Crisis Response: Working on the Razor's Edge.* Armonk, NY: M.E. Sharpe.

Milfont, T. L., and R. Fischer. 2010. "Testing Measurement Invariance Across Groups: Applications in Cross-Cultural Research." *International Journal of Psychological Research* 3 (1): 111–21.

Morris, J. A., and D. C. Feldman. 1996. "The Dimensions, Antecedents, and Consequences of Emotional Labor." *Academy of Management Review* 21 (4): 986–1010.

Rayner, Julie, and Alan Lawton. 2018. "Are We Being Served? Emotional Labour in Local Government in Victoria, Australia." *Australian Journal of Public Administration* 77 (3): 360–74. https://doi.org/10.1111/1467-8500.12282.

Roh, C. Y., M. Jae Moon, Seung-Bum Yang, and K. Jung. 2015. "Linking Emotional Labor, Public Service Motivation, and Job Satisfaction: Social Workers in Health Care Settings." *Social Work in Public Health* 31 (2): 1–15.

Rotter, Julian B. 1966. "Generalized Expectancies for Internal Versus External Control of Reinforcement." *Psychological Monographs: General & Applied* 80 (1): 1–28.

Schermelleh-Engel, K., H. Moosbrugger, and H. Müller. 2003. "Evaluating the Fit of Structural Equation Models: Tests of Significance and Descriptive Goodness-of-Fit Measures." *Methods of Psychological Research* 8 (2): 23–74.

Steenkamp, J.-B. E. M., and H. Baumgartner. 1998. "Assessing Measurement Invariance in Cross-National Consumer Research." *Journal of Consumer Research* 25 (1): 78–90.

Stenross, B., and S. Kleinman. 1989. "The Highs and Lows of Emotional Labor: Detectives' Encounters with Criminals and Victim." *Journal of Contemporary Ethnography* 17 (4): 435–52.

Yang, Seung-Bum, and Mary E. Guy. 2015. "Gender Effects on Emotional Labor in Seoul Metropolitan Area." *Public Personnel Management* 44 (1): 3–24.

9

Australia

N. Emel Ganapati and Meredith A. Newman

On October 9, 2012, the Leader of the Opposition Party, Tony Abbott, put in a motion of no confidence in the Speaker of the Australian Parliament, Peter Slipper. The motion asked for Slipper to be fired "immediately" as Slipper sent a staffer text messages with sexual content, which were characterized by Abbott as "vile" and "derogatory" (Lester 2012). In the end, there was a motion of no confidence and Peter Slipper resigned. What made this particular day memorable in Australia, however, was the speech made by the country's first female prime minister, Julia Gillard, in response to Abbott's motion regarding the unsuitability of Slipper for high office due to his sexist and misogynist views. It was also how this speech was portrayed in the Australian media in its aftermath.

In her speech, often referred to as the "sexism and misogyny speech" (*The Sydney Morning Herald* 2012), Gillard reminded the members of Parliament and the public about Abbott's past statements regarding women and their place in Australian society. This is a man, she said, who responded to a question about underrepresentation of women in institutions of power in

N. Emel Ganapati (✉)
Public Policy and Administration,
Florida International University, Miami, FL, USA
e-mail: ganapat@fiu.edu

M. A. Newman
Florida International University, Miami, FL, USA
e-mail: newmanm@fiu.edu

© The Author(s) 2019
M. E. Guy et al. (eds.), *The Palgrave Handbook of Global Perspectives on Emotional Labor in Public Service*, https://doi.org/10.1007/978-3-030-24823-9_9

Australia by saying, "If it's true…that men have more power generally speaking than women, is that a bad thing?" She added Abbott's comments about the differences between men and women: "what if men are by physiology or temperament, more adapted to exercise authority or issue command?" She highlighted Abbott's characterization of Australian women as "housewives" doing "the ironing" at home and who choose "the easy way out" when it comes to abortion. She explained how he called her "a man's bitch," "yelled at" her "to shut up," and insulted her family. She concluded her speech by saying, "the Leader of the Opposition should think seriously about the role of women in public life and in Australian society because we are entitled to a better standard than this" (*The Sydney Morning Herald* 2012).

Gillard was calling out the Opposition Party Leader for his hypocrisy, asking him to take some responsibility for his past statements about Australian women, and demanding an apology. Although her speech was well received by media outlets outside Australia (Lennard 2012), there was a domestic media backlash (Wright and Holland 2014). It was framed by the Australian national and local media, among others, as Gillard's "uncontrolled emotional outpouring" (455). Wright and Holland (2014, 463) explained the media's framing of Gillard's speech as follows:

> The media acted as a gendered mediator through their framing of her delivery as driven by (female) emotion(s). Gillard was framed as having lost control of any rational façade she had put on and pretended. In this framing, her speech on misogyny saw her stripped back to an emotional feminine self, as she exposed her true nature as reactive, emotional, irrational and ultimately unsuitable for and incapable of leadership.

The framing of Gillard's speech by the media in this way raises a number of questions for public servants in Australia and their performance of emotional labor, including: What are the norms and values that define the relationship between the government, its public servants and its citizens? Is public service gendered? Are there different expectations for male and female public servants? What are the consequences of emotional labor for public servants? Does managing of emotions lead to job satisfaction and personal fulfillment or burnout? These are the questions we will explore in this chapter.

There is a growing literature on Australia that acknowledges the importance of emotions in the public sector. Most of this literature, however, focuses on emotional intelligence rather than on emotional labor. Examples include Brunetto et al.'s (2012) study that examines emotional intelligence's positive consequences—for example, job satisfaction, well-being, organizational commitment, and turnover intentions—among police officers (Brunetto et al. 2012) or Hurley et al.'s (2016) study that highlights the need to nurture emotional intelligence to prevent mental health problems and bullying in the Australian public sector. There are several additional studies conducted on emotional intelligence of healthcare personnel (Kozlowski et al. 2018; Pisaniello et al. 2012) and college students (Bhullar et al. 2012; Foster et al. 2017, 2018). One of the rare studies conducted on emotional labor in Australia relates to the private sector (Newnham 2017). It examines the relationship between surface acting and burnout among hotel workers in Australia with comparable workers in the Philippines.

Focusing on emotional labor among public servants in Australia, the format of this chapter is as follows. In the next section, we provide a background on Australia's broader context. We then explain public service delivery in Australia by detailing the governance structures and reforms as well as the political culture in the country. We proceed with presenting our data and methods, followed by our findings on emotional labor and a discussion of findings. We conclude with directions for future research and policy implications of our findings.

The Broader Country Context

Australia has a unique historical, geographical, demographic, religious, economic, human development and political background. It has a colonial past with Great Britain, which made its formal territorial claims in the east coast of Australia in 1770, when Captain James Cook took control of that area. Soon after, Britain took possession of the west coast, claiming all of Australia as its territory in 1829. On January 1, 1901, six self-governing British colonies on the island continent declared independence from the Federation of UK Colonies to become the Commonwealth of Australia.

Australia is the smallest continent. Yet, it is the world's largest island and the sixth largest country in the world after Russia, Canada, China, the USA, and Brazil. Its landmass is slightly smaller than the contiguous USA. Its population is 24.2 million (World Bank 2018a). The country is highly urbanized with 89% of its total population living in urban areas (World Bank 2017). Its population is mainly concentrated along the coast, especially along the east and southwest coast. The interior is referred to as the "outback." It is characterized by its remoteness from urbanized areas, low population density, and largely infertile soils; and it is "one of the wildest and most intact places on earth" (Wolnarski et al. 2014, 2).

Australia is a highly multicultural country, with the largest ethnic groups identifying as English (26%) and Australian (25%) (Central Intelligence Agency 2018). Along with Canada, it is one of "the two most prominent examples of countries with explicit multicultural citizenship policies" (Soutphommasane 2005, 405). It allows "all members of our society [to] have equal opportunity to realise their full potential and must have equal access to programs and services" and "every person … to maintain his or her culture without prejudice or disadvantage" (Curran 2004, 132–33). Some argue that there is a "relative absence of deep social and economic divisions," little dissent among ethnic and racial groups in the country, and only recently has there been politicization of the status of indigenous populations (Butler et al. 1999, 258). While this may be debatable (Zappala 1998), 96% of the population are either very or quite proud to be Australian, compared to 87% in the USA who say they are very or quite proud to be American (Inglehart et al. 2014).[1]

Australia has a reputation for being "the most Godless place under Heaven" (Bellanta 2010, 57). According to the World Values Survey (Inglehart et al. 2014), a majority of Australians (64%) do believe in God. However, 46% in the country do not belong to a religion or a religious denomination. A large majority of the population either do not consider themselves as religious (42%) or are atheists (16%). Sixty-seven percent of Australians report not having much confidence or no confidence at all in churches, compared with 41% in the USA. The largest religious denominations in the country are Protestants and Roman Catholics (Central Intelligence Agency 2018).

Australia is one of the most advanced economies of the world. With a current Gross National Income (GNI) per capita of $54,130, it is within the World Bank's category of high income countries (World Bank 2018b). It has abundant natural resources and energy. In 2016, it was the world's largest net exporter of coal (International Energy Agency 2017). There are increasing concerns, however, regarding unemployment levels (6.1% in 2015) and widening inequalities in the country (OECD 2017). Between 2004 and 2014, the real incomes of the lowest quantile of households in Australia grew by about 25%, compared to 40% for those in the top quantile (OECD 2017).

According to the UNDP (2016), Australia is among the "very high human development" countries, ranking second behind Norway in terms of the Human Development Index (HDI). The HDI is a composite index that takes into account income (estimated GNI per capita), education (expected years of schooling and mean years of schooling), and health (life expectancy at birth). Australia's HDI ranking is much higher compared to the USA and

Canada, which share the tenth rank, and to the UK (#16). The country also ranks as the second behind Norway in terms of the Gender Development Index (GDI) that uses the same variables as the HDI, disaggregated by gender. In terms of the Gender Inequality Index (GII), however, Australia's ranking falls down to 24th behind Norway and many other developed countries. This index is different than the GDI in the sense that it measures gender inequalities in three aspects of human development: reproductive health (maternal mortality ratio and adolescent birth rates), empowerment (proportion of parliamentary seats occupied by females and proportion of adult females and males aged 25 years and older with at least some secondary education) and economic status (labor force participation rate of female and male populations aged 15 years and older).

The current structure of governance in Australia has been greatly influenced by the British Westminster-Whitehall parliamentary system of government developed in the UK. The term Westminster comes from the Palace of Westminster, which is the seat of the British Parliament. Whitehall is a main road in London, along which there are several government departments. It is also used to refer to the British civil service and government. The influence of the UK on Australia's governance is not surprising given that the country remains part of the Commonwealth. Although there was a referendum in 1999 to break ties with the British monarchy and declare Australia as a republic, the referendum was rejected by the majority of the people (BBC News 1999).

Australia is a parliamentary democracy under a constitutional monarchy. Its legislative branch is a bicameral Federal Parliament, which includes the Senate and the House of Representatives. The British monarch is the ceremonial chief of state and is represented by the governor-general. The head of government is the prime minister, who is elected from among the members of the Parliament and sworn in by the governor-general following legislative elections. The governor-general is appointed by the monarch on the recommendation of the prime minister and is an Australian although historically they were British (Parliament of Australia 2018a). The country's legal system is based on the English common law model.

Similar to the USA, Australia has a federal system of government with powers divided between a national government (also referred to as the Australian government or the Commonwealth) and six individual states (New South Wales, Queensland, South Australia, Tasmania, Victoria, and Western Australia). Hence, some scholars refer to the public administration system in Australia as a Washminster or Westington system, a hybrid model between Westminster and Washington models (Johnston 2004; Edwards et al. 2012).

Australia also has two territories (Australian Capital Territory and Northern Territory) that are not claimed by these six states but are within Australia's borders.

The national government in Australia delegates powers to state governments and is responsible for such areas as national defense, trade, commerce, foreign diplomacy, currency, and taxation (Parliament of Australia 2018b). The states have their own constitutions and parliaments. Each state has a Governor, who exercises the powers of the monarch over state matters, and a Premier, the head of the state government (Australian Government 2018a). They are financially dependent on the national government as they have limited taxing powers (Johnston 2000).

Local governments, also known as local councils, are the closest level of government to the people (Grant and Dollery 2012). Their geographical boundaries are determined by the states, and their role and authority differ from state to state. A majority of local governments in the country have the council manager form of government (Tan et al. 2016); that is, all executive functions are handled by professional administrators appointed by the councils. Local governments were first established in Australia during colonial times to help manage geographically dispersed and rapidly growing populations, and they had more of a focus on public health and building codes and regulations (Tan et al. 2016). They currently provide such services to the public as urban planning, waste collection, public recreation, libraries and child care, among others (Dollery et al. 2006; Australian Government 2018b). Yet, their range of services are limited, compared to the services provided by their counterparts in the USA. They typically do not include policing, education, power, public transportation, or affordable housing. A major contributing factor is that state governments exercise a substantial amount of control over local governments, especially in terms of their fiscal base and revenues (Tan et al. 2016).

Public Service Delivery

In this section, we present the context of public service delivery in Australia. We first introduce the Australian Public Service (APS) system. We then explain the strong state tradition in the country and how this tradition has changed the state and the state's relationship with its citizens over the years through NPM reforms undertaken in the country. This is followed by a discussion on Australia's political culture.

The Australian Public Service

Based on the British Westminster-Whitehall system, the public service in Australia "exists as a separate arm of executive government, which impartially implements the policy decisions of the government of the day" (Dann 1996, 28). It is based on the principle of neutral public service independent of politics undertaken by career public servants (Edwards 2012; Johnston 2000). These public servants are expected to be "concerned only with administration, not policy making" (Dann 1996, 28). They are "typically recruited following graduation from secondary or tertiary education and remain with the service for most, if not all, of their working lives. Both recruitment into, and promotion within, the public service is based on merit" (Dann 1996, 28–29).

A fundamental institution in the country's public service is the APS, which has evolved in line with Australia's unique context under different governments (Johnston 2000). The APS is "the public administration arm" of the federal government although the federal government includes non-APS agencies as well (346). It represents a number of government organizations whose personnel are employed under the Public Service Act (PSA) 1999, the principal act that governs the employment, and work on behalf of the federal government (Australian Government 2018c). The responsibility "to position the APS workforce for the future" falls within the responsibility of the Australian Public Service Commission (APSC), a small, central-level agency within the portfolio of the Department of Prime Minister and Cabinet. The APSC's current priorities include modernizing the employment framework, shaping the APS workforce, building workforce capability, and promoting integrity (APSC 2018a).

APS agencies are divided into four categories (APSC 2018b): (1) departments, such as Department of Foreign Affairs and Trade; (2) statutory agencies with all staff employed under the PSA (e.g., Office of the Commonwealth Ombudsman): (3) statutory agencies that have the capacity to employ staff under the PS Act as well as their own enabling legislation, such as the Australian Institute of Health and Welfare; and, (4) executive agencies, such as the Infrastructure and Project Financing Agency. There is also a fifth category of agencies that are part of APS agencies, employ staff under the PSA, but have some degree of independence in terms of their operations, such as the Australian Office of Financial Management under the Department of the Treasury.

According to the APSC's 2016–2017 State of the Service Report (2017a), a majority of the APS workforce (57%) are employed by four agencies: the Department of Human Services, Australian Taxation Office, Department of Home Affairs, and the Department of Defence. The largest proportion of APS employees are from the Australian Capital Territory (37.9%), the country's federal district in the southeast enclaved within the state of New South Wales. It includes Canberra, the capital city. This report also states that the APS had 152,095 employees in 2016–2017 period, the lowest employment levels since 2006. Over the last decade, within APS's workforce, both the percentage of older adults (aged 50 or over) and employees who worked on a part-time basis have increased from 25 to 32% and from 12 to 16%, respectively (APSC 2017a). The number of employees that receive performance bonuses has also been declining steadily over the years. In 2017, 18,199 employees received performance bonuses; this was a 6% decline from 2016 and a 25% decline from 2015 (APSC 2017b).

Women currently make up 59% of the APS workforce (APSC 2017a). The APSC (2017a) report notes that the agency with the highest proportion of women is the Workplace Gender Equality Agency (89.7%). The agencies with the lowest proportion of women include the Bureau of Meteorology, and Australian Transport and Safety Bureau (31.4% each). Since 2008, although the percentage of women holding senior-level positions has increased from 36 to 43%, the majority of such positions continues to be held by men.[2] More specifically, they are held by men of Anglo-Celtic origin. In fact, the percentage of white men at the top of Australia's executive branch and its parliament are greater than the USA, Canada, or New Zealand (Cave 2018). Furthermore, the percentage of women working part time (23.7%) is also significantly higher than men (4.7%). Women represent approximately 88% of all employees working part time, compared with 12% for men. According to the APS Remuneration Report 2017 (APSC 2017b), although the gender pay gap continues to exist in the public sector, it has declined to 8.4% in 2017, slightly down from 8.6% in 2016 and 9.6% in 2013.

It is also important to note that there is a nationwide professional organization, the Institute of Public Administration Australia (IPAA), which brings together those involved in public service in Australia, either through the APS or non-APS agencies at the federal level or state and local levels (Podger 2018). This organization was established in 1927 in South Australia and has been adding divisions in each state and territory in Australia since 1985 (IPAA 2018). The IPAA produces the quarterly *Australian Journal of Public Administration* and holds a national public administration conference every year.

Another notable aspect of public service in Australia is that the country did not have a public administration focused school until 2003, when Australia and New Zealand School of Government (ANZSOG) was established (Podger 2018). ANZSOG is a school network which includes a number of universities across the two countries. Prior to the establishment of ANZSOG, those interested in joining public service received an education that had more of a focus on political science, as opposed to a focus on management. Many civil servants were also sent abroad for degrees in business and public administration.

The Strong State Tradition and the Aftermath of NPM Reforms

Historically, Australia has had a strong state tradition. Starting from the beginnings of European settlement in 1788, the government played an important role in nation-building by building infrastructure, developing land for settlements, and providing services to the public (Aulich 2011; Butler et al. 1999). "A lack of suitable resources, isolation from European centres of capital, the demands of relatively concentrated urban populations and the general inhospitable nature of the land all necessitated an activist government with the capacity to successfully promote the infrastructure needed for development" (Butler et al. 1999, 256).

In the words of Bland (1945, 203, cited in Aulich 2011, 204), "[T]he first two or three decades after 1788 saw State activity *in excelsis*. The Government fed, clothed and employed everyone. It cleared and cultivated farms; it bred and reared flocks; it built and ran mills; it discovered and developed mines." In many ways, the government transformed the Australian economy to "a system of monopoly capitalism" (Encel 1970, 322; cited in Aulich 2011, 204). By the 1980s, the government had ownership of a number of enterprises, ranging from typically privately owned sectors, such as banking, to sectors that typically require monopolies, such as telecommunications.

The government's monopoly in the economy started to change when the Australian Labor Party Government (ALPG) came to power in 1983. Influenced by the NPM reforms that were already being implemented under Thatcher's and Reagan's governments in the UK and USA (Johnston 2000), the ALPG initiated Australia's transformation toward greater reliance on the private sector, albeit with a "cautious" approach (Boston and Uhr 1996, 61, in Johnston 2000, 347). According to some, these reforms were also shaped by a group of conservative bureaucrats who were dedicated to neo-classical economic ideas and who were in positions of power in agencies in charge of financial and economic policy, such as the Department of Finance (Johnston 2000; Kelly 1994).

The NPM reforms implemented in the country have evolved differently under different governments that followed the ALPG, depending on the priorities of the electorate (Johnston 2000). However, each government embraced the basic principles of NPM, including "a commitment to markets and global competition" and a "belief in the private business sector as the guiding light for the public sector" (362). The NPM reforms ranged from deregulating the markets and downsizing and privatizing the public sector, to making the regulatory framework less restrictive to businesses, to industrial relations reforms and introduction of private sector management techniques such as performance contracting, among others (Johnston 2000). The scope of the reforms even reached provision and funding of key social services, including health care and education, primarily through introduction of user fees or tax incentives. The government's role has changed from "sole or primary service provider" to "a role as enabler or facilitator of individual and community choice" (Aulich 2011, 209).

Australia's transformation under the NPM reforms has exhibited several unique characteristics. First, these reforms had bi-partisan support from both right- and left-wing parties, and even from academia in the early years (Johnston 2000). The ALPG was a left-wing party that was headed by the country's most notable trade union leader. The party's decision to move toward reform was driven not by political ideology per se but by "economic pragmatism," in part to address such economic problems as unemployment and in part to increase efficiency and accountability in the public sector (Johnston 2000, 347). Second, the NPM reforms in the country gave Australia an international reputation as "a bold reformer" (Considine et al. 2014, 470). They were more wide-ranging than reforms in most OECD nations, except in the UK and New Zealand (Johnston 2000), transforming Australia into "one of the world's significant privatisers" (Aulich 2011, 200). Third, the reforms took place both at the national level and at state levels. Just like the national government, state governments pursued major privatization reforms and outsourced many of their services (Aulich 2011).

The NPM reforms had mixed results in the country. While some praised how they helped shield Australia from the global economic crisis, increased organizational and program efficiency and streamlined service delivery to customers (Aulich 2011; Podger 2018), others highlighted its failures. Even the former Labor Party Prime Minister noted, "the great neo-liberal experiment of the past 30 years has failed" (Rudd 2009). Some argued that the reforms were without a grand plan (Halligan 2000). Others said publicly owned enterprises, such as airports and the Australian Wheat Board, were transferred to the private sector "without appropriate regulatory changes or guarantees" (Aulich 2011, 210). Some maintained that the reforms increased the amount of bureaucracy by making every action accountable (Johnston and Marshall 1994) and politicized senior executive management positions and policy advice in the public sector (Aucoin 2012; Johnston 2000; Podger 2018). Still others suggested that the reforms turned such objectives as efficiency and accountability into "ends in themselves rather than a means to better outcomes for Government" (Johnston 2000, 351) while giving much less attention to social objectives that have intrinsic value but not easily quantifiable including equality and social justice (Considine 1988, 1990; Lingard 1993; Yeatman 1990). They provided minimal protections for the disadvantaged populations, leading to emergence of an "underclass" (Lingard 1993). They led to the "loss of publicness" (Aulich 2011, 199) and undermined "the ethos of public service" (Johnston 2000, 359). Some blamed it for the decline in public sector employment as a proportion of the workforce (Podger 2018) and argued that "public administration as a formerly popular term is already largely obsolete in Australia" (Johnston 2000, 359).

In the 2000s, Australian public administration continued to build on and adjust the NPM. However, the emphasis shifted more toward new approaches, including "whole-of-government" or "connected government," "citizen-centered services" (Podger 2018, 154), or different forms of governance, including "collaborative" and "network" governance (Considine 2003; Edwards et al. 2012; Fawcett et al. 2011; Gunasekera 2008; Mintrom and Wanna 2006; O'Flynn and Wanna 2008; Pollitt and Bouckaert 2011) and "digital governance" (Dunleavy et al. 2008; Macnamara 2010) or "e-government" (Horsburgh et al. 2011). The governance approach was indeed adopted by the Australian National Audit in 2003 or referred to in the legislation, including the Public Service Act 1999 and the Financial Management and Accountability Act 1997 (Edwards et al. 2012).

These newer discourses on public administration acknowledge that "the role of government in governance has been changing, but it continues to be central" in a network of more horizontal and collaborative relationships that involve nonprofit organizations, private sector, and communities (Halligan 2015, 715). These relationships are in contrast to more traditional vertical relationships that continue to exist throughout public service

(Edwards et al. 2012). In many ways, the old principles of public administration are blended with the new ones rather than being replaced by NPM and others. Several different approaches co-exist in one way or another (Edwards et al. 2012). In the words of Rhodes et al. (2008), "it is not a question of 'in with the new, out with the old', but of 'in with the new alongside key components of the old'" (474).

Political Culture

Like Almond and Verba (1989), we define political culture as "attitudes toward the political system and its various parts, and attitudes toward the role of the self in the system" (12). It is naïve to assume that political culture in a country as unique as Australia is static or uniform. It is dynamic and constantly changing, and it varies from place to place, especially in regard to urbanized versus rural areas. Yet, there are widely shared norms, values, and beliefs that define the relationship between the Australian government and its citizens. We examine these under four headings in this section: acceptance of big, yet federalist government; politically disengaged yet civically engaged citizens; low trust and perceived corruption; the national identity narratives and the gendered terrain of public service.

Acceptance of Big, yet Federalist Government

As discussed earlier, Australia historically has had a strong state tradition since the beginnings of European settlement in 1788. In line with this tradition, Australians have an "instrumental view of government," acknowledging "the need for, and acceptance of, big government" (Butler et al. 1999, 257). In a recent survey conducted worldwide, 91% of Australians reported that greater respect to authority is a good thing or that they would not mind it (Inglehart et al. 2014). Despite their tolerance of big government and respect for authority, Australians predominantly value federalism and federalist values (Brown 2013; Robbins 1978). Based on analysis of data from Australian Constitutional Values Survey, Brown (2013) finds that 66% of adult citizens in the country are classified as strong federalists. This is in contrast to 25% of citizens who are non-federalists. There are varying opinions within the population, however. Women, for instance, on average, are stronger federalists than men "while also being somewhat less likely than men to consider that Australia's present system delivers adequately on these [federalist] values." (297). Federalism also has stronger support in some parts of the country than others. For example, 51% support strong federalist policies in Western Australia while only 40% support such policies in New South Wales.

Politically Disengaged, yet Civically Engaged Citizens

Closely related to the acceptance of big government, there is a subject-participant culture in Australia (Butler et al. 1999). This culture not only refers to citizens being less informed about the government and its institutions (Butler et al. 1999; Emy and Hughes 1988; Jaensch 1997), but also to a "poorly developed sense of political responsibility among its citizens," especially the younger populations (Aitkin 1986, 9). Australia Curriculum, Assessment and Reporting Authority (ACARA) (2017) shows that only 38% of Year 10 students achieved at or above the proficient standard in being an informed citizen in terms of government and democracy; laws and citizens; and citizenship, diversity, and identity. World Values Survey (Inglehart et al. 2014) indicates that only 43% of Australians consider politics as very or rather important in their lives, and 91% of Australians think that greater respect for authority is a good thing or that they would not mind it.[3]

Until the 1960s, the subject-participant culture, which left policy making decisions to senior-level bureaucrats (Butler et al. 1999; Emy and Hughes 1988; Payne 1973), was coupled with limited opportunities for citizen participation. Starting from the 1960s and the 1970s, however, there has been a greater involvement of citizens in the government's policy making processes (Butler et al. 1999). This in part had to do with movements led by students and women against the Vietnam war, pollution and gender issues, and with greater opportunities provided by the government for citizen involvement (Butler et al. 1999; Milo 1984). Newer technologies also have enabled participation. Young people, for instance, exhibit limited interest in traditional forms of electoral participation. They have, however, considerable engagement in non-electoral types of political participation, including engaging online (e.g., through social media) as well as signing petitions, boycotting products, and attending demonstrations (Gauja 2015; Loader et al. 2014; Martin 2012; Vromen 2003).

Despite being politically disengaged, Australians are extremely active in civic life. In Gauja's (2015) words, they are a "nation of joiners" of voluntary organizations (31). According to the 2016 State of Volunteering in Australia Report (PwC 2016), 94% of the population volunteers formally in the context of a formal organization or informally outside the context of a formal organization. Formal and informal volunteering account for 48 and 6% respectively while a combination of both types of volunteering account for 40% in the country. The volunteering patterns vary across the states and across age groups and gender. Formal volunteering, for instance, was highest in Western Australia (51%) and lowest in Tasmania (35%). In terms of informal volunteering, Northern Territory had the highest rate (65%) while New South Wales had the lowest rate (44%). Furthermore, the groups that were most likely to be volunteers were those who were 15- to 17-year-old individuals as well as women (Australian Bureau of Statistics 2015).

Low Trust and Perceived Corruption

Trust in government, its agencies and officials is complicated in Australia. One would expect higher levels of trust in a country like Australia, given the ability of its political system to adjust to the electorate's changing demands and expectations and a relatively low level of corruption in government (Gauja 2015). Transparency International (2018) ranks Australia as the 13th least corrupt country among 180 countries and territories based on perceived levels of public sector corruption according to experts and businesspeople. Public service employees in Australia also report low levels of corruption in their workplace. According to the 2017 APS Employee Census (APSC 2018c), a majority of the employees agree that they work in a high corruption-risk work environment and were positive that their colleagues would report corrupt behavior if they experienced it (76%). They were confident about what to do if they identified corruption in the workplace (82%). Only 5% of public service employees actually witnessed corrupt behavior. Of this 5%, 64% reported the incident to authorities.

McAllister's (2014) study, which found that Australians have had negligible experiences of corruption among public officials, confirms Transparency International's and APS Employee Census's findings on trust. According to the same study, however, three in four Australians believe that there is some corruption among politicians, and half of the population perceive corruption to be on the rise. McAllister (2014) explains this discrepancy between people's experiences and perceptions of corruption by noting that (1) citizens report few bribery experiences by public officials (only one in ten); and, (2) high level rather than low level corruption, together with collective judgements rather than personal judgements about it, affect citizens' perceptions. It is important to understand people's perception of corruption as it shapes how they view the government's performance and to what extent it serves their interests (Gilley 2009; Uslaner 2008).

Australia is a low level trust society, where trust seems to be in decline (Martin 2010). The 2004 International Social Survey Program (ISSP) Citizenship survey places Australia in the middle range of 18 advanced democracies (Martin 2010). A study conducted on six Asia Pacific countries—Australia, Hong Kong, Japan, South Korea, Taiwan, and Thailand—also categorizes Australia as a lower trust country, along with South Korea and Taiwan (Ward et al. 2016). According to the World Values Survey (Inglehart et al. 2014), a majority of Australians do not trust political parties (85%), the Parliament (69%), or the civil service (54%). Among the government institutions in Australia, only the police enjoy high levels of confidence (83% with high trust).

McAllister (2014) notes that Australians trust local government the most, which is the closest level to them, followed by the state and the federal government. In another study, Meyer and colleagues (2013) add that trust in all levels of government is the lowest among population groups that typically have the poorest access to government services, specifically populations that are older (people aged 60+), have lower income, and who live in inner and outer regional areas (as opposed to major cities).

National Identity Narratives and the Gendered Terrain of Public Service

There are a number of "national identity narratives" that define what it means to be an "Aussie" (Holland and Wright 2017, 588). The most notable such narrative is mateship. Mateship is a term that refers to friends, usually men, providing unconditional support to one another and having shared experiences amid the toughest conditions. It has deep historical roots in Australia, where early settlers needed one another to survive in often adverse environments. When asked to "define what makes a typical Australian," their top answer was "mateship" (Burin 2015). It is important to note that mateship is not simply a cultural idiom in Australia. It is also an important part of Australia's political culture (Holland and Wright 2017). Prime Minister Howard, for instance, wanted to include the term mateship into the Constitutions' preamble in the 1990s. Although this did not materialize, mateship was included in the citizenship test for migrants (*The Sydney Morning Herald* 2006). Prime Minister Gillard used the same term as she was asking the nation to work together following the Queensland floods in 2011 (Burin 2015, para 5): "This Australia Day, more than anything else, we know mateship lives… We will hang on to our Aussie mateship and our Aussie fair go, in the worst of times and in the best, because we're Australian."

Another important national identity narrative includes the ANZAC legend. The term ANZAC stands for Australian and New Zealand Army Corps, whose first international military action involved fighting on the side of the British Commonwealth against the Ottoman Empire during World War I in the Gallipoli peninsula in modern Turkey. Although ANZAC soldiers lost the battle in Gallipoli and more than 8000 of them lost their lives, they are remembered for their remarkable courage. Their legend symbolizes "the birth of the Australian nation through sacrifice in war" (Holland and Wright 2017, 593). ANZAC is an important part of national identity in both Australia and New Zealand. In Australia, April 25 is the national Anzac Day, initially declared to commemorate the lives of ANZAC soldiers who lost their lives in Gallipoli and was broadened later to commemorate the lives of all Australians who lost their lives in Australia's military and peace-keeping operations abroad and to reflect on the meanings of war (Australian War Memorial 2018).

There are other national identity narratives such as the Aussie Digger, the Larrikin, the Ocker, and the Bushmen (Holland and Wright 2017). The Aussie Digger typically refers to an Australian soldier and is closely related to mateship and the ANZACs. The myth is that Australian soldiers who fought during World War I were mainly working-class miners and were digging trenches at Gallipoli. The Larrikin symbolizes youthful rowdyism. The roots of this term date back to the late nineteenth and early twentieth centuries when rowdy young men who banded together in gangs defied the authorities and assaulted citizens in urban areas such as Sydney and Melbourne. The Ocker is a term used for those who are rough and uncultivated in their talk and behavior. It "encompasses a broader group of 'everyday Australians,' enjoying simple pursuits outside of sophisticated urban centres" (593). Both the Larrikin and the Ocker project a feeling of "conviviality: comradeship with a touch of good-hearted sexism" (Chipperfield 2001). The Bushmen is used for men who live in or have experience in the Australian bush or outback. Such men are seen as "fiercely capable, self-reliant, but affable" (594). It is not uncommon to notice references to these narratives in the political discourse. "John Howard and Tony Abbott, in particular, made frequent appeals to the ANZAC myth and narratives of mateship, at times attempting to embody the qualities of the Larrikin, the Ocker, and even the Bushman, albeit in a modern form" (594).

Holland and Wright (2017) highlight an important commonality of Australia's national identity narratives: they are highly "exclusivist" and gendered (588). McTernan (2013) notes, "the belief that everyone should be given a 'fair go' runs deep [in Australia], but at the same time there exists a very powerful sense of mateship, of male values and a male-inscribed culture." In this particular culture, women are referred to as the "sheila," an often derogatory slang that "serves to put 'women' in their place" (True 2013, 115) by depicting them as "sexual objects of desire, the ruin of men and mateship" and "good for nothing" individuals (116).[4] Holland and Wright (2017) make it clear that they do not say that "all of the Australian population is sexist," but that, as a nation, Australia "has been built upon a series of exclusions, the maintenance of which are necessary prerequisites for the preservation of national identity in lieu of a national conversation on the role of women within the state" (601).

Perhaps the most notable example on the role of women within the state was the APS's implementation of a "marriage bar," a policy that is "difficult to comprehend" today (Sawer 1996, 1). This policy prevented recruitment and continued employment of married women in public service. It required that female employees resign upon marriage. "Women who were discovered attempting to keep their marriages secret were sacked from the civil service; a salutary lesson for others seeking to do the same" (Chappel and Waylen 2013, 606). The marriage bar applied even to widows with children. There were some exceptions made, however, "when it suited the government and the public service" (Colley 2018, 230). A prime example occurs in times of labor market shortages.

The marriage bar was justified on different grounds (Colley 2018). One justification was that women did not need jobs as men should be the main bread-winners in the household (Anker 1997; Connell 2006). Another argument was that married women had limited capabilities and were more likely to miss work, and therefore less reliable than men. The third argument was an economic one, focusing on organizational needs for productive workers. Employees represented "good value in the early years" while their productivity was increasing "with years of service" and before it flattened out "in later years" (Colley 2018, 230). Hence, young girls were recruited to public service jobs that they were thought to be capable of doing, such as typewriting, before their marriage with the understanding that they were to resign upon marriage. There was also a historical need-based justification for the marriage bar. After World War II, there was a need to accommodate men who returned from the battlefield and needed work.

The marriage bar in Australia was removed in 1966, right before a federal election and twenty years after the UK had removed its version of the policy (Sawer 1996). Legislation on equal employment opportunities was introduced in the 1980s to address further discrimination in the public sector (Colley 2018). Although the public service system is based on the "seemingly neutral" merit system, the merit system was "introduced in a far from neutral work environment characterised by extensive occupational segregation and combined political and societal patronage that favoured men" (Colley 2018, 232). Hence, public service in Australia remains gendered (Colley 2018; Connell 2006; Dann 1996). Men hold jobs that are "relatively good in terms of pay, security and opportunities for advancement" whereas women continue to occupy certain positions "with lesser pay, opportunities and security" (Colley 2018, 231).

Debates about women's place in the public service are ongoing in Australia. Connell (2006) argues that there is widespread belief among public service employees that women and men have "different physical capacities (men stronger), character traits (women more patient, men more ambitious), interests (men technical, women human relations), and skills (men understand machinery)" (845). Yet, public service employees acknowledge that gender relations are changing as a result of equal employment and sexual harassment regulations. Connell (2006) adds that these changes bring about "emotions of gender transition" (e.g., resentment, distrust, anger, and exasperation) among a group of public service employees (837). Especially, some men feel that they are not appreciated as much or that they are being sidelined in the workplace. And some still have a hard time accepting orders from women and feel that some women are promoted in public service simply because of their gender. It is important to note, however, that each organization has its own gender regime, which is "produced by a different organizational history and associated with a different configuration of personal experience and consciousness" (845).

The Australian Study on Emotional Labor

Now that we have a better understanding of the broader Australian context, public service, and political culture, we present the emotional labor study conducted with public service employees in Australia. The next section provides the descriptive statistics of the study. This is followed by a discussion of the variables, presentation of the structural equation model employed for the study, the results, and the discussion of findings.

Demographic Statistics

We recruited participants for our study in Australia via post-card, which provided the link to an online survey. We distributed our recruitment post-cards at the IPAA's annual national conference that was held in Melbourne, Australia in September 2012 and through the IPAA's President's Office. A total of 80 public servant employees completed the survey. Table 9.1 exhibits the characteristics of our respondents.

A considerable majority of our respondents were 40 years of age or older (75%), female (69%), and had less than 20 years of experience in public service (60%). They were highly educated, with 88% having a college degree

Table 9.1 Demographic characteristics: Australia

	Frequency	Percent
Age		
Less than 30	4	5.0
30–39 years	16	20.0
40–49 years	22	27.5
50–59 years	28	35.0
60 or more	9	11.3
N/A	1	1.3
Gender		
Female	55	68.8
Male	25	31.3
N/A	0	0.0
Public service experience		
Less than 10	26	32.5
10–19 years	22	27.5
20–29 years	12	15.0
30 or more	20	25.0
N/A	0	0.0
Educational level		
Less than high school	0	0.0
High school graduate	2	2.5
Some college	1	1.3
2-year associate degree	1	1.3
College graduate	10	12.5
Some graduate school	16	20.0
Master's degree	27	33.8
Law degree (J.D., LL.B.)	5	6.3
Doctorate degree (Ph.D., M.D., Ed.D.)	12	15.0
Other (please specify)	0	0.0
N/A	6	7.5

or higher. In fact, half of the respondents had a graduate degree. The ones with a master's and doctorate degree were 34 and 15%, respectively. Six percent of our respondents had a law degree. While our sample was similar to the current public service employees within the APS system in terms of age (74%), it had a higher percentage of female employees than the APS system (59%) and a lower percentage of public service employees with less than 20 years of experience than the APS system (98%) (APSC 2017a).[5]

As shown in Table 9.2, in terms of occupational characteristics, 36% of the respondents have chosen the "other" category.[6] The service area of work for this group ranged from international aid/development, correctional services, environment, and social security to risk and performance management. Approximately 13% of the respondents worked in administration, and information/communication service areas. Eleven percent were in law enforcement. Public service employees involved in health care and education were 9 and 8%, respectively. The remaining employees were distributed across the categories of community development/neighborhood, finance or accounting, human resource management, military, public works, social services and transportation.

Table 9.2 Occupational characteristics: Australia

Occupation	Frequency	Percent
1. Administration	10	12.5
2. Community development/neighborhood services	3	3.8
3. Engineering, manufacturing, or production	0	0.0
4. Education	6	7.5
5. Disaster response	0	0.0
6. Finance or accounting	1	1.3
7. Firefighter	0	0.0
8. Health care	7	8.8
9. Housing	0	0.0
10. Human resource management	2	2.5
11. Information & communication	10	12.5
12. Law enforcement	9	11.3
13. Military	2	2.5
14. Public relations	0	0.0
15. Planning	0	0.0
16. Public works: streets, sanitation, utilities	4	5.0
17. Purchasing	0	0.0
18. Recreation and parks	0	0.0
19. Research and development	0	0.0
20. Social services	1	1.3
21. Transportation	1	1.3
22. Support services (such as equipment maintenance)	0	0.0
23. Other	29	36.3

Emotional Labor Variables

Our survey gathered information on three different dimensions of emotional labor, emotive capacity, pretending, and deep acting. (1) Emotive capacity refers to "certain basic, conventional, learned, affective-relational communicative skills that help them interact smoothly, negotiate potential interpersonal conflicts, and reach different ends in speech" (Caffi and Janney 1994, 327). (2) Pretending expression, also referred to as surface acting or "faking in bad faith," occurs when a person modifies a display of emotion without actually changing one's inner feelings because such displays are required in the work environment (Hochschild 1983; Rafaeli and Sutton 1987). And, (3) deep acting, which is also referred to as "faking in good faith," refers to modifying one's inner feelings to match the required display rules with the intent of seeming authentic to the audience (Hochschild 1983; Rafaeli and Sutton 1987).

We had three dependent variables that focused on consequences of performing emotional labor: job satisfaction, burnout, and personal fulfillment. As seen in Table 9.3, two out of three of our emotional labor variables had a Cronbach's alpha level above the generally acceptable level of 0.70 (between the range of 0.731 and 0.836). The only one that was below this threshold—albeit not by much—was pretending expression. This could be interpreted as "low number of questions, poor inter-relatedness between items or heterogeneous constructs" (Tavakol and Dennick 2011, 54). The three items in the pretending expression variable were: "I hide my true feelings so as to appear pleasant at work," "In my job I act confident and self-assured regardless of how I actually feel," and "I wear a 'mask' in order to deal with clients/customers in an appropriate way." All our dependent variables reported a Cronbach's alpha level that was above 0.80 (between the range of 0.812 and 0.918).

Table 9.3 Descriptive statistics and Cronbach's alpha: Australia

	Mean	SD	Cronbach's alpha
Emotive capacity	5.15	1.08	0.731
Pretending expression	4.59	1.14	0.672
Deep acting	4.50	1.33	0.836
Job satisfaction	5.05	1.29	0.812
Burnout	4.06	1.59	0.910
Personal fulfillment	5.09	1.50	0.918

Results

We used structural equation modeling (SEM) to test the direct effect of the three emotional labor variables for all our respondents—emotive capacity, pretending expression, and deep acting—on the outcome variables: job satisfaction, burnout, and personal fulfillment. Table 9.4 presents the standardized path coefficients.

Figure 9.1 displays the paths. Solid arrows indicate statistical significance at $p \leq 0.05$. Dotted arrows indicate nonsignificant relationships. A "+" represents a positive relationship. A "−" represents a negative relationship. Explanation of these results is provided below.

Table 9.4 Structural model results: Australia

Hypothesized paths	Coefficients	p-value
Emotive capacity → Job satisfaction	0.273*	0.049
Emotive capacity → Burnout	−0.184	0.141
Emotive capacity → Personal fulfillment	0.200	0.107
Pretending expression → Job satisfaction	−0.184	0.311
Pretending expression → Burnout	0.417*	0.003
Pretending expression → Personal fulfillment	−0.090	0.597
Deep acting → Job satisfaction	0.305*	0.036
Deep acting → Burnout	−0.260*	0.035
Deep acting → Personal fulfillment	0.566*	0.000

Model fit: χ^2= 287.663 (df= 126), CFI= 0.800, RMSEA= 0.127, SRMR= 0.159

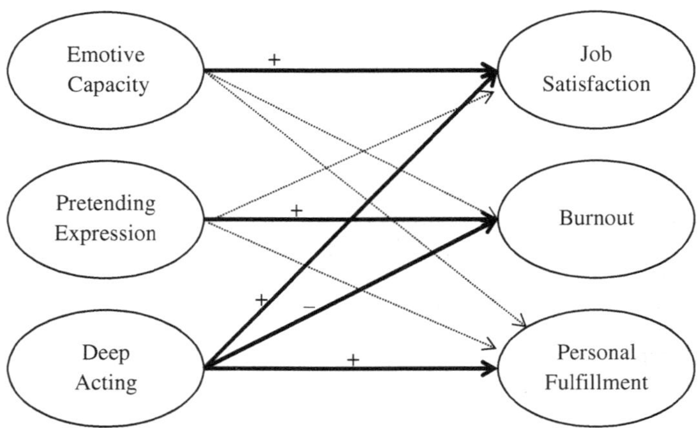

Fig. 9.1 Path diagram for Australia

Emotive Capacity

Emotive capacity includes three items: "I am good at expressing how I feel," "I am good at getting people to calm down," and "In my job I am good at dealing with emotional issues." As shown in Table 9.4, emotive capacity has a direct, positive effect on job satisfaction ($p = 0.049$). The relationships between emotive capacity and the other two variables, burnout, and fulfillment, do not achieve statistical significance.

Pretending Expression

This variable included the following items: "I hide my true feelings so as to appear pleasant at work," "In my job I act confident and self-assured regardless of how I actually feel," and "I wear a 'mask' in order to deal with clients/customers in an appropriate way." Pretending expression has a statistically significant direct effect on one variable: burnout ($p = 0.003$). Its relationship to the other two variables does not achieve significance.

Deep Acting

Items in the deep acting variable are: "I try to actually experience the emotions that I must show to clients/customers," "I work hard to actually feel the emotions that I need to show to clients/customers," and "I work at developing the feelings inside of me that I need to show to clients/customers." The model establishes a statistically significant relationship with all three of the outcome variables. It has a positive and statistically significant effect on job satisfaction ($p = 0.036$) and personal fulfillment ($p = 0.000$), and it has a significant negative effect on burnout ($p = 0.035$).

Discussion

The results on deep acting are consistent with the earlier literature in public administration, which suggests that authentic expression of emotion has positive outcomes for public service employees: it increases their job satisfaction and personal fulfillment (Jin and Guy 2009) while reducing their work-related burnout (Guy et al. 2008). These effects are possible as public service employees may have a stronger motivation to help the public, compared with private sector employees (Houston 2005; Perry 1996), or as they may feel that they are making a difference in the lives of the public that they serve. The broader literature on emotional labor also suggests that employees who perform emotional labor could feel empowered, as their work involves managing the emotions of the other—whether the other is a co-worker or the public (Leidner 1999; Stenross and Kleinman 1989; Tolich 1993).

The results on pretending expression among public service employees in Australia are also largely in agreement with previous studies in public administration. This literature suggests that pretending expression increases burnout among public servants (Guy et al. 2008; Hsieh et al. 2012). In other words, performing emotional labor is exhausting and stressful for public service employees who feel one way but pretend to feel another way in order to perform their jobs.

The unexpected part of our study relates to emotive capacity, which has a significant direct effect only on job satisfaction and no such effect on fulfillment or burnout. This finding is partially consistent with earlier studies conducted in Australia, which suggest that emotional intelligence leads to job satisfaction and well-being among public service employees. See, for example, Brunetto et al. (2012).[7] As noted by several scholars (Guy and Newman 2004; Guy et al. 2008), however, emotional labor is considered as "women's work" as it involves managing of emotions through nurturing and caring. Hence, it is often invisible and under-valued in public service. For example, emotive skills are rarely included in performance appraisals. Accordingly, we believe that there is a negative relationship between emotive capacity and personal fulfillment among public service employees in Australia because they are aware of the fact that their emotive capacity, which they tap into at work on a regular basis, is neither recognized nor appreciated. This might be especially true for female employees, who comprised 69% of our sample. They must perform in the gendered terrain of public service in Australia and in the midst of "emotions of gender transition" (Connell 2006, 837). Another possible explanation for the lack of a significant relationship between emotive capacity and personal fulfillment might be that public service employees have to deal with a public that is less informed about the government and its institutions, and that is less engaged and less responsible (Aitkin 1986; Butler et al. 1999), as detailed in the political culture section. Public service employees who employ their emotive capacity might find their jobs less fulfilling if they have to deal with a public that seems not to care.

Conclusion

The results of our study suggest that performance of emotional labor has both upsides and downsides among public service employees in Australia. Those with higher levels of emotive capacity achieve greater job satisfaction. And, when able to display authentic emotions, emotional labor is rewarding. Public service employees receive job satisfaction and personal fulfillment and do not experience frustration or helplessness when their emotive expressions are sincere as they interact with the public and their co-workers. However, they experience burnout when there is emotive dissonance at work. This occurs when they must mask how they honestly feel in order to perform their jobs. In such cases, they force themselves to display whatever emotion is appropriate for the circumstance.

There are a number of limitations in this study. For instance, as in any other studies that use self-report surveys, there may be common source bias. Furthermore, the study was limited to 80 public service employees, most of whom were women. It will be incorrect to assume that the responses reported here represent the perceptions of all public service employees in Australia, which is a highly unique country. Therefore, there is a need for further studies using a larger and more diverse sample. Given the gendered terrain of public service in Australia, we especially recommend studies that distinguish between the emotional labor of female and male employees and the consequences of such labor. Future studies might also be conducted in different agencies and different locations, such as coastal urban versus rural areas, because they have different local political cultures. A supplement to the results of this study would be an examination of factors that reduce burnout in public service. And, studies that employ qualitative methods—interviews, focus groups, and participant observation—could provide deeper insights into emotional labor and its consequences than can be captured by surveys.

As noted by public administration scholars (Guy and Newman 2004; Guy et al. 2008; Mastracci et al. 2012), given the centrality of emotional labor in public service, there is a need to make it more visible and appreciated. One suggestion is to incorporate emotional labor into hiring practices. Jin and Guy (2009), for instance, note that the job descriptions could categorize jobs as emotionally intense, moderate or having a light level of emotive demands. Another suggestion is to ensure that public service employees who perform emotional labor have access to job resources that would help ease their work-related burden and reduce their burnout. Examples include increased job autonomy, co-worker support, and formal or informal psycho-social support (Hsieh 2014). Moreover, emotive skills could be evaluated and rewarded in performance appraisals (Hsieh and Guy 2009). In countries like Australia where the public seems to be disengaged with the government and its institutions, there might also be opportunities for building the capacity of the public.

Notes

1. The majority (51%) agreed with the statement that Australian people should get priority over immigrants when jobs are scarce (Inglehart et al. 2014).
2. By senior-level positions, we are referring to Senior Executive (SES) category. This category includes Senior Executive (SES) Bands 1, 2, and 3 (or equivalent).
3. The following question was asked of participants: "I'm going to read out a list of various changes in our way of life that might take place in the near future. Please tell me for each one, if it were to happen, whether you think it would be a good thing, a bad thing, or don't you mind?: Greater respect for authority" (Inglehart et al. 2014, 26–27).
4. The term is also used in New Zealand.
5. We are unable to provide data from the APSC report (2017a) on the educational level of APS employees as 68% of data is missing in the report.
6. The respondents were allowed to select more than one category of work.
7. We would like to note that Brunetto et al. (2012) measure emotional intelligence using Wong and Law's (2002) scale, which includes sub-scales on emotion appraisal of oneself and others as well as use and regulation of emotion. Our measure of emotive capacity includes three items: "I am good at expressing how I feel," "I am good at getting people to calm down," and "In my job I am good at dealing with emotional issues."

References

Aitkin, D. 1986. "Australian Political Culture." *Australian Cultural History* 5: 5–11.

Almond, G. A., and S. Verba. 1989. *The Civic Culture: Political Attitudes and Democracy in Five Nations*. 2nd ed. Newbury Park, CA: Sage.

Anker, R. 1997. "Theories oaf Occupational Segregation by Sex: An Overview." *International Labour Review* 136 (3): 315.

Aucoin, P. 2012. "New Political Governance in Westminster Systems: Impartial Public Administration and Management Performance at Risk." *Governance* 25 (2): 177–99.

Aulich, C. 2011. "It's Not Ownership That Matters: It's Publicness." *Policy Studies* 32 (3): 199–213.

Australia Curriculum, Assessment and Reporting Authority (ACARA). 2017. *National Report on Schooling in Australia 2016.* Sydney: ACARA. Accessed October 31, 2018. https://www.acara.edu.au/docs/default-source/default-document-library/national-report-on-schooling-in-australia-2016fe9f12404c94637ead88ff00003e0139.pdf?sfvrsn=0.

Australian Bureau of Statistics. 2015. *4159.0—General Social Survey: Summary Results, Australia, 2014.* Accessed October 31, 2018. http://www.abs.gov.au/ausstats/abs@.nsf/Latestproducts/4159.0Main%20Features152014?opendocument&tabname=Summary&prodno=4159.0&issue=2014&num=&view=.

Australian Government. 2018a. *State and Territory Government.* Accessed October 31, 2018. https://www.australia.gov.au/about-government/how-government-works/state-and-territory-government.

Australian Government. 2018b. *Local Government.* Accessed October 31, 2018. https://www.australia.gov.au/about-government/how-government-works/local-government.

Australian Government. 2018c. *About the Australian Public Service (APS).* Accessed October 31, 2018. https://www.apsjobs.gov.au/about.aspx.

Australian Public Service Commission (APSC). 2018a. *What We Do.* Accessed October 31, 2018. https://www.apsc.gov.au/what-we-do.

Australian Public Service Commission (APSC). 2018b. *APS Agency Listing.* Accessed October 31, 2018. https://www.apsc.gov.au/aps-agency-listing-agencies-covered-public-service-act-1999.

Australian Public Service Commission (APSC). 2018c. *APS Values and the Code of Conduct.* Accessed October 31, 2018. https://stateoftheservice.apsc.gov.au/2018/01/aps-values-code-conduct-2/.

Australian Public Service Commission. 2017a. *2016–17 State of the Service.* Accessed October 31, 2018. https://stateoftheservice.apsc.gov.au/blog/2016-17-state-service/.

Australian Public Service Commission. 2017b. *APS Remuneration Report 2017.* Accessed October 31, 2018. https://www.apsc.gov.au/aps-remuneration-report-2017.

Australian War Memorial. 2018. *The Anzac Day Tradition.* Accessed October 31, 2018. https://www.awm.gov.au/commemoration/anzac-day/traditions.

BBC News. 1999. "Australia Rejects Republic." November 6. Accessed Octber 31, 2018. http://news.bbc.co.uk/onthisday/hi/dates/stories/november/6/newsid_2514000/2514833.stm.

Bellanta, M. 2010. "A Hard Culture? Religion and Politics in Turn-of-the-Century Australian History." *Australian Journal of Politics & History* 56 (1): 55–65.

Bhullar, N., N. S. Schutte, and J. M. Malouff. 2012. "Associations of Individualistic-Collectivistic Orientations with Emotional Intelligence, Mental

Health, and Satisfaction with Life: A Tale of Two Countries." *Individual Differences Research* 10 (3): 165–75.

Bland, F. A. 1945. *Planning the Modern State*. 2nd ed. Sydney: Angus & Robertson.

Boston, J., and J. Uhr. 1996. "Reshaping the Mechanics of Government." In *The Great Experiment*, edited by F. Castles, R. Gerritsen, and J. Vowles, 48–67. St. Leonards, Australia: Allen & Unwin.

Brown, A. J. 2013. "From Intuition to Reality: Measuring Federal Political Culture in Australia." *Publius: The Journal of Federalism* 43 (2): 297–314.

Brunetto, Y., S. T. T. Teo, K. Shacklock, and R. Farr-Wharton. 2012. "Emotional Intelligence, Job Satisfaction, Well-being and Engagement: Explaining Organisational Commitment and Turnover Intentions in Policing." *Human Resource Management Journal* 22 (4): 428–41.

Burin, M. 2015. "Aussie Mateship: Tracing the History of a Defining Cultural Term." *ABC Ballarat*, January 23. http://www.abc.net.au/local/stories/2015/ 01/23/4167572.htm.

Butler, C., C. Rissel, and F. Khavarpour. 1999. "The Context for Community Participation in Health Action in Australia." *Australian Journal of Social Issues* 34 (3): 253–65.

Caffi, C., and R. W. Janney. 1994. "Toward a Pragmatics of Emotive Communication." *Journal of Pragmatics* 22 (3–4): 325–73.

Cave, Damien. 2018. "In a Proudly Diverse Australia, White People Still Run Almost Everything." *New York Times*, April 10. Accessed at https://www.nytimes. com/2018/04/10/world/australia/study-diversity-multicultural.html.

Central Intelligence Agency (CIA). 2018. *The World Factbook: Australia*. Accessed October 31, 2018. https://www.cia.gov/library/publications/the-world-factbook/ geos/as.html.

Chappell, L., and G. Waylen. 2013. "Gender and the Hidden Life of Institutions." *Public Administration* 91 (3): 599–615.

Chipperfield, M. 2001. "Ockers Against Wowsers Stand Up for Their Skimpies." *Daily Telegraph*, February 4. Accessed October 31, 2018. https:// www.telegraph.co.uk/news/worldnews/australiaandthepacific/australia/1321069/ Ockers-against-wowsers-stand-up-for-their-skimpies.html.

Colley, L. 2018. "For Better or for Worse: Fifty Years Since the Removal of the Marriage Bar in the Australian Public Service." *Australian Journal of Politics & History* 64 (2): 227–40.

Connell, R. 2006. "The Experience of Gender Change in Public Sector Organizations." *Gender, Work & Organization* 13 (5): 435–52.

Considine, M. 1988. "The Corporate Management Framework as Administrative Science: A Critique." *Australian Journal of Public Administration* 47 (1): 4–18.

Considine, M. 1990. "Managerialism Strikes Out." *Australian Journal of Public Administration* 49: 166–78.

Considine, M. 2003. "Governance and Competition: The Role of Non-profit Organisations in the Delivery of Public Services." *Australian Journal of Political Science* 38 (1): 63–77.

Considine, M., S. O'Sullivan, and P. Nguyen. 2014. "New Public Management and Welfare-To-Work in Australia: Comparing the Reform Agendas of the ALP and the Coalition." *Australian Journal of Political Science* 49: 469–85.

Curran, J. 2004. *The Power of Speech: Australian Prime Ministers Defining the National Image.* Carlton, VIC: Melbourne University Publishing.

Dann, S. 1996. "Public Sector Reform and the Long-Term Public Servant." *International Journal of Public Sector Management* 9 (2): 28–35.

Dollery, B., J. Wallis, and P. Allan. 2006. "The Debate That Had to Happen But Never Did: The Changing Role of Australian Local Government." *Australian Journal of Political Science* 41 (4): 553–67.

Dunleavy, P., H. Margetts, S. Bastow, and J. Tinkler. 2008. "Australian E-Government in Comparative Perspective." *Australian Journal of Political Science* 43: 13–26.

Edwards, M., J. Halligan, B. Horrigan, and G. Nicoll. 2012. *Public Sector Governance in Australia.* Canberra: Australian National University (ANU) E Press.

Emy, H., and O. Hughes. 1988. *Australian Politics: Realities in Conflict.* 2nd ed. Melbourne: Macmillan Australia Pty Ltd.

Encel, S. 1970. *Equality and Authority: A Study of Class, Status and Power in Australia.* Melbourne, Australia: Cheshire.

Fawcett, P., R. Manwaring, and D. Marsh. 2011. "Network Governance and the 2020 Summit." *Australian Journal of Political Science* 46: 651–67.

Foster, K., J. Fethney, D. Kozlowski, R. Fois, F. Reza, and A. McCloughen. 2018. "Emotional Intelligence and Perceived Stress of Australian Pre-registration Healthcare Students: A Multi-Disciplinary Cross-Sectional Study." *Nurse Education Today* 66: 51–56.

Foster, K., J. Fethney, H. McKenzie, M. Fisher, E. Harkness, and D. Kozlowski. 2017. "Emotional Intelligence Increases Over Time: A Longitudinal Study of Australian Pre-registration Nursing Students." *Nurse Education Today* 55: 65–70.

Gauja, A. 2015. "The State of Democracy and Representation in Australia." *Representation* 51 (1): 23–34.

Gilley, B. 2009. *The Right to Rule: How States Win and Lose Legitimacy.* New York, NY: Columbia University Press.

Grant, B., and B. Dollery. 2012. "Autonomy Versus Oversight in Local Government Reform: The Implications of 'Home Rule' for Australian Local Government." *Australian Journal of Political Science* 47(3): 399–412.

Gunasekera, C. 2008. "Network Governance Amidst Local Economic Crisis." *Australian Journal of Political Science* 43: 207–23.

Guy, Mary E., and Meredith A. Newman. 2004. "Women's Jobs, Men's Jobs: Sex Segregation and Emotional Labor." *Public Administration Review* 64 (3): 289–98.

Guy, Mary E., Meredith A. Newman, and Sharon H. Mastracci. 2008. *Emotional Labor: Putting the Service in Public Service.* Armonk, NY: M.E. Sharpe.

Halligan, J. 2000. "Public Service Reform Under Howard." In *The Howard Government,* edited by G. Singleton, 49–64. Sydney, Australia: University of New South Wales Press.

Halligan, J. 2015. "Public Administration in the Australian Journal of Political Science: A Review." *Australian Journal of Political Science* 50 (4): 707–18.

Hochschild, Arlie. 1983. *The Managed Heart.* Berkeley, CA: University of California Press.

Holland, J., and K. A. M. Wright. 2017. "The Double Delegitimatisation of Julia Gillard: Gender, the Media, and Australian Political Culture." *Australian Journal of Politics & History* 63 (4): 588–602.

Horsburgh, S., S. Goldfinch, and R. Gauld. 2011. "Is Public Trust in Government Associated with Trust in E-Government?" *Social Science Computer Review* 29 (2): 232–41.

Houston, David J. 2005. "Walking the Walk of Public Service Motivation: Public Employees and Charitable Gifts of Time, Blood, and Money." *Journal of Public Administration Research and Theory* 16 (1): 67–86.

Hsieh, Chih-Wei. 2014. "Burnout Among Public Service Workers: The Role of Emotional Labor Requirements and Job Resources." *Review of Public Personnel Administration* 34 (4): 379–402.

Hsieh, Chih-Wei, and Mary E. Guy. 2009. "Performance Outcomes: The Relationship Between Managing the Heart and Managing Client Satisfaction." *Review of Public Personnel Administration* 29 (1): 41–57.

Hsieh, Chih-Wei, Myung H. Jin, and Mary E. Guy. 2012. "Consequences of Work-Related Emotions: Analysis of a Cross-Section of Public Service Workers." *American Review of Public Administration* 42 (1): 39–53.

Hurley, J., M. Hutchinson, J. Bradbury, and G. Browne. 2016. "Nexus Between Preventive Policy Inadequacies, Workplace Bullying, and Mental Health: Qualitative Findings from the Experiences of Australian Public Sector Employees." *International Journal of Mental Health Nursing* 25 (1): 12–18.

Inglehart, R., C. Haerpfer, A. Moreno, C. Welzel, K. Kizilova, J. Diez-Medrano, M. Lagos, P. Norris, E. Ponarin, and B. Puranen, et al., eds. 2014. *World Values Survey: Round Six—Country-Pooled Datafile Version.* Accessed October 31, 2018. http://www.worldvaluessurvey.org/WVSDocumentationWV6.jsp. Madrid: JD Systems Institute.

Institute of Public Administration Australia (IPAA). 2018. *About Us.* Accessed October 31, 2018. http://www.ipaa.org.au/about-us/.

International Energy Agency. 2017. *Key World Energy Statistics.* Accessed October 31, 2018. https://www.iea.org/publications/freepublications/publication/KeyWorld2017.pdf.

Jaensch, D. 1997. *The Politics of Australia.* Melbourne, Australia: Macmillan Education Australia Pty Ltd.

Jin, Myung H., and Mary E. Guy. 2009. "How Emotional Labor Influences Worker Pride, Job Satisfaction, and Burnout: An Examination of Consumer Complaint Workers." *Public Performance & Management Review* 33 (1): 88–105.

Johnston, Judy. 2000. "The New Public Management in Australia." *Administrative Theory & Praxis* 22 (2): 345–68.

Johnston, Judy. 2004. "An Australian Perspective on Global Public Administration Theory: Westington Influences, Antipodean Responses and Pragmatism?" *Administrative Theory & Praxis* 26 (2): 169–84.

Johnston, Judy, and N. Marshall. 1994. "Performance Evaluation and Accountability in Australian Public Sectors: Have the Means Become the Ends?" In *Public Sector Reform*, edited by I. Scott and I Thynne, 169–92. Hong Kong: AJPA.

Kelly, P. 1994. *The End of Certainty: Power, Politics and Business in Australia.* St. Leonards: Allen & Unwin.

Kozlowski, D., M. Hutchinson, J. Hurley, and G. Browne. 2018. "Increasing Nurses' Emotional Intelligence with a Brief Intervention." *Applied Nursing Research* 41: 59–61.

Leidner, R. 1999. "Emotional Labor in Service Work." *Annals of the American Academy of Political and Social Science* 561: 81–95.

Lennard, N. 2012. "Australian PM Takes on Misogyny." *Salon*, October 9. Accessed October 31, 2018. http://www.salon.com/2012/10/09/australian_pm_takes_on_misogyny.

Lester, A. 2012. "Ladylike: Julia Gillard's Misogyny Speech." *New Yorker*, October 9. Accessed October 31, 2018. https://www.newyorker.com/news/news-desk/ladylike-julia-gillards-misogyny-speech.

Lingard, B. 1993. "Managing Democracy in the Public Sector." *Social Alternatives* 12 (2): 10–14.

Loader, B. D., A. Vromen, and M. A. Xenos. 2014. "The Networked Young Citizen: Social Media, Political Participation and Civic Engagement." *Information, Communication & Society* 17 (2): 143–50.

Macnamara, J. 2010. "The Quadrivium of Online Public Consultation: Policy, Culture, Resources, Technology." *Australian Journal of Political Science* 45: 227–44.

Martin, A. 2010. "Does Political Trust Matter? Examining Some of the Implications of Low Levels of Political Trust in Australia." *Australian Journal of Political Science* 45 (4): 705–12.

Martin, A. 2012. "Political Participation Among the Young in Australia: Testing Dalton's Good Citizen Thesis." *Australian Journal of Political Science* 47 (2): 211–26.

Mastracci, Sharon H., Mary E. Guy, and Meredith A. Newman. 2012. *Emotional Labor and Crisis Response: Working on the Razor's Edge.* Armonk, NY: M.E. Sharpe.

McAllister, I. 2014. "Corruption and Confidence in Australian Political Institutions." *Australian Journal of Political Science* 49 (2): 174–85.

McTernan, J. 2013. "Julia Gillard: Australian Blokes Have Done Their Country Down." *The Telegraph*, 28 June. Accessed October 31, 2018. https://www.

telegraph.co.uk/news/worldnews/australiaandthepacific/australia/10148550/Julia-Gillard-Australian-blokes-have-done-their-country-down.html.

Meyer, S. B., L. Mamerow, A. W. Taylor, J. Henderson, P. R. Ward, and J. Coveney. 2013. "Demographic Indicators of Trust in Federal, State and Local Government: Implications for Australian Health Policy Makers." *Australian Health Review* 37 (1): 11–18.

Milo, N. 1984. "The Political Anatomy of Community Health Policy in Australia, 1972–1982." *Politics* 19 (2): 18–33.

Mintrom, M., and J. Wanna. 2006. "Innovative State Strategies in the Antipodes: Enhancing the Ability of Governments to Govern in the Global Context." *Australian Journal of Political Science* 41: 161–76.

Newnham, M. P. 2017. "A Comparison of the Enactment and Consequences of Emotional Labor Between Frontline Hotel Workers in Two Contrasting Societal Cultures." *Journal of Human Resources in Hospitality & Tourism* 16 (2): 192–214.

O'Flynn, J., and J. Wanna, eds. 2008. *Collaborative Governance: A New Era of Public Policy in Australia?* Canberra: Australian National University (ANU) E Press.

OECD. 2017. "OECD Economic Surveys: Australia-Overview." Accessed October 31, 2018. http://www.oecd.org/eco/surveys/economic-survey-australia.htm.

Parliament of Australia. 2018a. "Australian System of Government." Accessed October 31, 2018. https://www.aph.gov.au/About_Parliament/House_of_Representatives/Powers_practice_and_procedure/00_-_Infosheets/Infosheet_20_-_The_Australian_system_of_government.

Parliament of Australia. 2018b. "The Australian Constitution." Accessed October 31, 2018. https://www.aph.gov.au/About_Parliament/Senate/Powers_practice_n_procedures/Constitution/chapter5.

Payne, R. 1973. "Public Participation in the Urban Planning Process." *Australian Planning Institute Journal* 11 (1): 25–30.

Perry, James L. 1996. "Measuring Public Service Motivation: An Assessment of Construct Reliability and Validity." *Journal of Public Administration Research and Theory* 6 (1): 5–22.

Pisaniello, S. L., H. R. Winefield, and P. H. Delfabbro. 2012. "The Influence of Emotional Labour and Emotional Work on the Occupational Health and Wellbeing of South Australian Hospital Nurses." *Journal of Vocational Behavior* 80 (3): 579–91.

Podger, Andrew. 2018. "PAR's (and ASPA's) Contribution to Public Administration Internationally." *Public Administration Review* 78 (1): 151–55.

Pollitt, Christopher, and Geert Bouckaert. 2011. *Public Management Reform*. 3rd ed. Oxford: Oxford University Press.

PricewaterhouseCoopers Australia (PwC). 2016. "State of Volunteering in Australia: Help Create Happiness." Accessed October 31, 2018. https://www.volunteeringaustralia.org/wp-content/uploads/State-of-Volunteering-in-Australia-full-report.pdf.

Rafaeli, A., and R. I. Sutton. 1987. "Expression of Emotion as Part of the Work Role." *Academy of Management Review* 12 (1): 23–37.

Rhodes, R. A. W., J. Wanna, and P. Weller. 2008. "Reinventing Westminster: How Public Executives Reframe Their World." *Policy & Politics* 36 (4): 461–79.

Robbins, J. 1978. "Localism and Local Government in South Australia." *Australian Journal of Political Science* 13: 81–91.

Rudd, K. 2009. "The Global Financial Crisis." *The Monthly*, February. Accessed October 31, 2018. http://www.safecom.org.au/rudd-global-crisis.

Sawer, M. 1996. *Removal of the Commonwealth Marriage Bar: A Documentary History*. Canberra, Australia: Centre for Research in Public Sector Management, University of Canberra.

Soutphommasane, T. 2005. "Grounding Multicultural Citizenship: From Minority Rights to Civic Pluralism." *Journal of Intercultural Studies* 26 (4): 401–16.

Stenross, B., and S. Kleinman. 1989. "The Highs and Lows of Emotional Labor: Detectives' Encounters with Criminals and Victims." *Journal of Contemporary Ethnography* 17 (4): 435–52.

Tan, S. F., A. Morris, and B. Grant. 2016. "Mind the Gap: Australian Local Government Reform and Councillors' Understandings of Their Roles." *Commonwealth Journal of Local Governance* 19: 19–39.

Tavakol, M., and R. Dennick. 2011. "Making Sense of Cronbach's Alpha." *International Journal of Medical Education* 2: 53–55.

The Sydney Morning Herald. 2012. "Transcript of Julia Gillard's Speech." October 10. Accessed October 31, 2018. https://www.smh.com.au/politics/federal/transcript-of-julia-gillards-speech-20121010-27c36.html.

The Sydney Morning Herald. 2006. "Migrants Need to Learn Mateship: PM." December 13. Accessed October 31, 2018. https://www.smh.com.au/national/migrants-need-to-learn-mateship-pm-20061213-gdp18m.html.

Tolich, M. B. 1993. "Alienation and Liberating Emotions at Work." *Journal of Contemporary Ethnography* 22 (3): 361–81.

Transparency International. 2018. "Corruption Perceptions Index 2017." Accessed October 31, 2018. https://www.transparency.org/news/feature/corruption_perceptions_index_2017.

True, J. 2013. "'Fit Citizens for the British Empire?': Class-ifying Racial and Gendered Subjects in 'Godzone' (New Zealand)." In *Women Out of Place: The Gender of Agency and the Race of Nationality*, edited by B. F. Williams, 103–28. New York, NY: Routledge.

UNDP. 2016. "Human Development Report: Human Development for Everyone." New York, United Nations Development Programme. Accessed October 31, 2018. http://hdr.undp.org/sites/default/files/2016_human_development_report.pdf.

Uslaner, E. M. 2008. *Corruption, Inequality and Trust*. New York: Cambridge University Press.

Vromen, A. 2003. "'People Try To Put Us Down …' Participatory Citizenship of 'Generation X'." *Australian Journal of Political Science* 38 (1): 79–99.

Ward, P. R., E. Miller, A. R. Pearce, and S. B. Meyer. 2016. "Predictors and Extent of Institutional Trust in Government, Banks, the Media and Religious

Organisations: Evidence from Cross-Sectional Surveys in Six Asia-Pacific Countries." *PLOS One* 11 (10): e0164096.

Wolnarski, J., B. Traill, and C. Booth. 2014. *The Modern Outback: Nature, People and the Future of Remote Australia.* PEW Charitable Trusts. Accessed October 31, 2018. https://www.pewtrusts.org/en/research-and-analysis/reports/2014/10/the-modern-outback.

Wong, C. S., and K. S. Law. 2002. "The Effects of Leader and Follower Emotional Intelligence on Performance and Attitude: An Exploratory Study." *The Leadership Quarterly* 13: 243–74.

World Bank. 2017. *World Development Indicators 2017.* Washington, DC: World Bank.

World Bank. 2018a. "Australia: Country Profile." Accessed October 31, 2018. http://databank.worldbank.org/data/views/reports/reportwidget.aspx?Report_Name=CountryProfile&Id=b450fd57&tbar=y&dd=y&inf=n&zm=n&country=AUS.

World Bank. 2018b. *World Development Report: Learning to Realize Education's Promise.* Washington, DC: World Bank.

Wright, K. A. M., and J. Holland. 2014. "Leadership and the Media: Gendered Framings of Julia Gillard's 'Sexism and Misogyny' Speech." *Australian Journal of Political Science* 49 (3): 455–68.

Yeatman, A. 1990. "Reconstructing Public Bureaucracies: The Residualisation of Equity and Access." *Australian Journal of Public Administration* 49: 17–21.

Zappala, G. 1998. "Clientelism, Political Culture and Ethnic Politics in Australia." *Australian Journal of Political Science* 33 (3): 381–97.

10

Bolivia

Pamela S. Medina

Bolivia, officially known as the Plurinational State of Bolivia, is a landlocked country in the heart of South America and one of the least-developed countries on the continent (UNICEF 2003). Approximately two-thirds of Bolivian adults identify as ethnically indigenous and the country recognizes 37 official languages, making Bolivia one of the most culturally diverse countries in South America (Madrid 2008). With a tumultuous political history that frequently excluded the indigenous majority, Bolivia has suffered from dictatorships and attempted coups marking an unstable political climate. In 2005, citizens elected the country's first indigenous president, resulting in a number of significant changes in governing structure, culminating with the approval of a new constitution in 2009. Faced with serving a diverse population in a highly decentralized government system, Bolivian public servants confront unique challenges. This chapter begins by reviewing essential parts of Bolivian history that have affected the work of public servants, including an introduction to the structure of government and the state of public management. Next, key features of the national culture are presented to contextualize the social environment. In the final sections, results of a study of Bolivian public servants are presented to demonstrate the practice of emotional labor in the country.

P. S. Medina (✉)
California State University, San Bernardino, CA, USA

M. E. Guy et al. (eds.), *The Palgrave Handbook of Global Perspectives on Emotional Labor in Public Service*, https://doi.org/10.1007/978-3-030-24823-9_10

From Independence to the Rise of the MAS

Formerly consisting of a number of indigenous empires primarily descendant from the Incas, Bolivia gained independence from Spain in 1825. Although at independence Bolivia was one of the largest countries in South America, the country would lose approximately half of its territory by the 1900s. In the years following independence, a series of conflicts with neighboring countries resulted in the loss of a significant portion of crucial territories including access to the coast and Bolivia's most important port at Atacama, now part of Chile (Henderson 2013). While rich in natural resources including silver, tin, and oil, Bolivia has long struggled to maintain economic prosperity without cheap access to maritime routes for shipping (Morales 2003). These territorial losses have hampered development and contributed to the country's economic instability.

Among the battles for territory, the loss of the Chaco war with neighboring Paraguay in 1935 set into motion a series of political struggles that served as a turning point in the country's political history. The unexpected loss of the war was particularly distressing for Bolivians who lost 60,000 people in just three years (Morales 2003). Citizens questioned the capability and motives of their political leaders, which changed hands four times during the short war. Formerly accustomed to mistreatment and exclusion from political representation, indigenous men who returned from war demanded social justice. As a result, a number of new political factions were established.

Emergence of Party Politics

Party politics in Bolivia are important in understanding the nature of public service, as parties do not typically represent ideology, but rather "exist as vehicles to distribute patronage for the middle class" (Harten 2011, 15). One of the most significant modern Bolivian political parties to emerge out of the loss of the Chaco war was the Nationalist Revolutionary Movement (MNR), which would become a major actor in the 1952 National Revolution. Running on a platform slogan of "land to the Indian, mines to the state" (133), the MNR was the first party to establish universal suffrage (Morales 2003). A major goal of the MNR was to unify the country under one national culture. This unification strategy aimed to make Spanish the dominant language and committed to social justice by modernizing the indigenous and rural identity (Harten 2011). This assimilationist approach, while aiming to improve conditions for the indigenous majority, failed to consider the needs of the diverse indigenous population. This theme persists as a primary debate in Bolivian politics. By the 1960s, the MNR was viewed as corrupt and after a series of demonstrations against them, a successful military coup replaced the MNR in 1964.

Military Dictatorships and Political Turmoil

From 1964 through 1982, Bolivia faced its longest period of military dictatorship. During this time, Bolivia gained a reputation for the highest number of attempted coup d'états in the world (Morales 1992). This period of chaos, instability, and repression was promulgated by nine different presidents in just four years, from 1978 to 1982 (Morales 2003). Although civilian rule was re-established in 1982, the country was still reeling with poverty, distrust of government, and the rise of illegal drug production in response to the collapse of the economy. In 1993, President Gonzalo Sanchez de Lozada was elected, putting the MNR back in power and characterizing a new era of neo-liberal Bolivian politics. Most notably, the Sanchez de Lozada administration was responsible for the Law of Popular Participation (LPP) which heavily decentralized the government. Among the most significant aspects of the LPP were the division of the country into 311 municipalities from only approximately thirty municipalities prior (Harten 2011). Additionally, the LPP allowed for legal recognition of indigenous communities, and the transfer of ten percent of the national budget to regional development groups in the country's nine departments (Kohl 2003). Through the LPP, the number of local elected officials increased from 262 to 2900, with an estimated 1624 newly elected municipal mayors coming from the indigenous population (Klein 2011). In addition to the LPP, Sanchez de Lozada was responsible for the privatization of the oil and gas industry, a strategy which would prove to be contentious in the coming years.

Following Sanchez de Lozada, former dictator Hugo Banzer was elected in 1997 and heavily emphasized further privatization of state owned enterprises, and the eradication of the coca plant, used in the production of cocaine (Morales 2003). In 1994, cocaine export accounted for approximately six percent of Bolivia's GDP (Painter 1994, 49). The coca plant has been a controversial political topic since the 1970s. As a predominantly indigenous country, the coca plant is traditionally used for ceremonial and medicinal purposes and has been part of Andean culture for over 4000 years (Kohl 1996). With strong support and investment from the USA, coca eradication policies during this time were associated with arbitrary arrests, human rights abuses, and little effect on high-level traffickers, instead causing the most damage to small farmers (Farthing and Kohl 2001). President Banzer's militarized eradication program was met with heavy resistance and protest, and among other issues, helped to cement the popularity of the current administration led by the Movement toward Socialism (MAS).

The Rise of the MAS

Banzer resigned due to illness in 2001 and Sanchez de Lozada was elected for a second term in 2002. However, Sanchez de Lozada only carried the election with less than a quarter of the votes. Foreshadowing the changes in the dominant parties, the second highest number of votes were cast for Evo Morales, an indigenous leader of the Coca Growers Foundation representing the MAS (Klein 2011). Sanchez de Lozada's second term was characterized by social unrest, mostly in response to the sustained push to privatize oil, gas, and water, and the continued eradication of the coca plant. Known as "Black October," deadly strikes in 2003 led Sanchez de Lozada to resign. Vice President, Carlos Mesa, took over for a short period, only to resign in 2005 marking the demise of the MNR. In 2005, Evo Morales was elected to the presidency winning 54% of the votes (Harten 2011).

Soon after his election, Morales and the MAS began working on their primary campaign promise: to re-found the country with a new constitution. The new constitution was approved in 2009, with significant changes including a major effort at further decentralizing the government. Currently, "the constitution identifies four levels of autonomy: departmental, regional, municipal, and indigenous…the constitution then defines no less than nine different types of territorial entities, as well as [provides] for additional local variations" (Harten 2011, 219). In addition, prosecutorial immunity was taken from members of congress, indigenous judicial functions were legitimized, means for referendum and citizen-led initiatives were added, and a number of rights were incorporated into the constitution including rights to water, food, free health care, education, and housing. Furthermore, the constitution established natural resources as belonging to the Bolivian people. As a result of nationalization of oil and gas, revenues to the state increased from US$173 million in 2002 to an estimated US$1.57 billion in 2007 (Harten 2011). Symbolizing the new acknowledgment of the country's many ethnic groups, the country's name was changed from the Republic of Bolivia to the Plurinational State of Bolivia.

The State of Public Management

Taking into account the 1994 LPP and the 2009 Bolivian Constitution, the country is now highly decentralized with substantial resources and authority in the hands of lower levels of government (Boulding and Gibson 2009). Thus, Bolivian public servants, especially at the local level, are tasked with administering a diversity of services. This section will highlight important characteristics of the Bolivian public service.

Among Latin American countries, Bolivian public servants experience one of the largest gaps in salaries between the public and the private sectors, leading many qualified public servants to seek jobs in the private sector (Cornell 2014). Prior evidence has noted that salary supplements are used to retain certain employees through the use of discretionary funds or assignments which "enjoy access to rents (licenses, inspections, procurement, etc.)" (UNPAN 2000, 25). Furthermore, cronyism and politicized recruitment are persistent problems, contributing to low levels of consistency in salaries across similar positions (UNPAN 2000).

Politicized recruitment of public servants in Bolivia is among the highest in Latin America, most comparable to Venezuela and Honduras which are considered fragile states (Cornell 2014; Messner et al. 2018). This lack of a merit-based hiring system is associated with several enduring issues including a lack of technically skilled public servants, lack of job security, and a lack of continuity in program implementation. A study by the United Nations Public Administration Network (UNPAN 2000) notes that patronage appointments, known as *confianza*, or trust, hires, are used regardless of an individual's qualifications, leading to issues with public sector efficiency (UNPAN 2000). The report remarks that

> …even if we assume that patronage appointees are always technically qualified for their positions, [their] incentive is to be responsive to their political patrons… Of course, a well-known problem arising from clientelism is that technical competence is often given a secondary consideration in appointment decisions…According to this logic, public employment's primary function is to serve as a mechanism of political control; its role as an instrument to carry out policy programs is secondary. (UNPAN 2000, 69)

Although policies are in place to protect employees from arbitrary discharge, employees may be pressured by blackmail, threats of poor performance appraisal, freezing out, and physical threats if they do not leave their positions when asked. A 2000 survey of Bolivian public servants revealed that these political pressures were more prevalent among ministry workers and occurred less frequently in autonomous units (UNPAN 2000).

With the 2005 election of the MAS, considerable turnover occurred within the public sector (Gingerich 2010). However, the MAS has now been in power for more than 12 years and turnover has not stabilized, indicating a persistent problem. Turnover in public service remains high at all levels, and public servants note difficulties in implementing programs because of a lack of bureaucratic stability and discontinuity in leadership (Cornell 2014).

Safeguards have been put into place to contend with many of these issues. These include a merit-based Civil Service Program (PSC) in 1992 and the Financial Administration and Control System (SAFCO). Both of these laws attempt to hinder corruption and ensure the protection of use of government resources by public servants (OAS 2009). However, existing data notes that these reforms have had little effect on combating patronage (UNPAN 2000).

Bolivian citizens are aware of issues of corruption in government. A 2014 public opinion survey revealed that 43% of Bolivians view corruption as commonplace among public officials, and 8% of respondents noted that a public servant had solicited a bribe from them (LAPOP 2014). Furthermore, respondents indicated a moderate level of confidence in the municipal government to complete required tasks (3.8/7) (LAPOP 2014). Generally, public servants are faced with low pay, job insecurity, and poor perceptions from citizens.

Given the nature of public management, Bolivian public servants operate in a fragile space. Patronage appointments contribute to feelings of job insecurity, but given the country's historically poor economic performance, fear of being able to find another job may also prevent public servants from leaving stressful positions. Moreover, citizens have poor perceptions of public servants, which can be discouraging to public servants who desire to take pride in their work.

Bolivian National Culture

Bolivian national culture emphasizes mutual aid through cooperative relationships with little confrontation. As noted in the review of the Bolivian public sector, informality is commonplace, although structure and rules are viewed positively. This section describes Bolivian national culture using data from mid-level managers and executives collected as part of the 2004 GLOBE Project.

Like most countries in Latin America, Bolivia has a highly collectivist national culture, rooted in the traditions of many of the countries' indigenous groups. Native cultures in Bolivia are founded on structures of communal labor, emphasizing cooperation, and responsibility in the sustainability of their communities (Hardman 1976). These traditions are reflected in data noting that Bolivians highly value both in-group collectivism and institutional collectivism. Based on data from the GLOBE Project, in-group collectivism, referring to "the degree to which individuals express pride, loyalty, and cohesiveness in organizations or families" is rated high (House et al. 2004, 12). Additionally, institutional collectivism, referring to "the degree to which organizational and societal institutional practices encourage and reward collective distribution of resources and collective action," is also highly valued when compared to other nations (House et al. 2004, 11).

Bolivian national culture values rules, consistency, structure, and formal procedures. GLOBE Project data reveal that uncertainty avoidance in Bolivia is roughly comparable to the worldwide average, demonstrating a moderate preference for alleviating unpredictability. Additionally, Bolivians value a centralized and structured power distance (House et al. 2004), likely resulting from the centralized power structures that have historically been present. The concept of *respeto*, or respect for hierarchical authority, is common among Hispanics (Garza and Watts 2010). However, there is a disconnect between value and practice. While Bolivians highly value rules, GLOBE data suggest that this does not translate directly into practice, with an uncertainty avoidance score at the worldwide average (House et al. 2004). These findings are also reflected in studies of the bureaucratic system, which note that "evidence of informality suggests that formal policies, rules and procedures that are meant to serve as institutional restraints are not effective" (UNPAN 2000, 27).

Perhaps given the importance of cooperation, Bolivians tend to be slightly less assertive than citizens of other countries. GLOBE data report that Bolivians value and practice assertiveness defined as "the degree to which individuals are confrontational and aggressive in their relationships with others", at a lower level than the worldwide average (House et al. 2004, 12). This behavior is common in Hispanic cultures, which value harmony, empathy, expression of positive emotions, and avoidance of conflict, known as *simpatía* (Sanchez-Burks and Lee 2007). Finally, humane orientation, or, "the degree to which a collective encourages and rewards individuals for being fair, altruistic, generous, caring and kind to others" although highly valued, is practiced at about the same level as the rest of the world, falling into the "medium" category (House et al. 2004, 13).

In the following sections, data, methods, and results from a survey of public servants working in Bolivia are presented. The study explores the practice of emotional labor, and its direct effect on burnout, job satisfaction, and personal fulfillment.

Sample Characteristics

Bolivia is divided into nine departments and various municipal and regional governments, while indigenous self-government is also permitted in designated ancestral territory, per the 2009 constitution. The data for this chapter were collected from a sample of public servants working for the municipal level government in the country's administrative capital, La Paz. Participants included career civil servants as well as lower level frontline service providers. The total sample included 201 participants. Overall, participants were relatively young and female with a mean age of 36 years. Given the age range of the sample, most respondents (74%) had less than 10 years of experience in the public sector. Only 19 participants were male, and all male employees were career civil servants. A majority of participants had completed at least some higher education and a technical diploma was common, with 38% of the sample holding either a *tecnico medio* or a *tecnico superior* diploma, equivalent to 1–2 years of vocational training. Additionally, 28% of respondents had earned a Bachelor's Degree. Full sample characteristics are provided in Table 10.1.

Occupational Characteristics

Based on the nature of the sample, a majority of participants (74.1%) cited education as their primary occupational area. Social Services (10.4%), Administration (8.5%), and Community Development/Neighborhood Services (7.5%) were next most cited occupation categories, respectively. Additional occupational data are provided in Table 10.2.

Variables

The study collected data for three dimensions of emotional labor including emotive capacity, pretending expression, and deep acting. Outcome variables included dimensions of job satisfaction, burnout, and personal fulfillment. Scales were developed for each variable to test the internal consistency of the latent variables. As noted in Table 10.3, only Burnout and Personal

Table 10.1 Demographic characteristics: Bolivia

	Frequency	Percent
Age		
Less than 30	52	25.9
30–39 years	83	41.3
40–49 years	38	18.9
50–59 years	13	6.5
60 or more	5	2.5
N/A	10	5
Gender		
Female	135	67.2
Male	19	9.5
N/A	47	23.4
Public service experience		
Less than 10	149	74.1
10–19 years	36	17.9
20–29 years	7	3.5
30 or more	2	1.0
N/A	7	3.5
Educational level		
Less than high school	0.0	0.0
High school graduate	3	1.5
Some college	77	38.3
2-year associate degree	12	6.0
College graduate	56	27.9
Some graduate school	16	8.0
Master's degree	7	3.5
Law degree (J.D., LL.B.)	2	1.0
Doctorate degree (Ph.D., M.D., Ed.D., etc.)	0	0
Other (please specify)	13	6.5
N/A	15	7.5

Fulfillment reached the preferred alpha of 0.7 or higher. This inconsistency can be explained in two primary ways. First, existing research has noted that reliability is dependent on sample heterogeneity (Lehmann 1985; Anastasi 1982). Due to the homogeneous nature of the sample with respect to gender, public service experience, and occupation, low response variances could contribute to the lower Cronbach's alpha scores, overall. Second, due to the fear of dismissal and low job security, it is possible that there was an underreporting bias (see, for example, Moloney and Chu 2016). Respondents inconsistently answered questions, particularly those that related to their ability to do their jobs well.

Of particular note among the variables is the fact that the Pretending Expression variable was somewhat problematic. Initially, it included three survey items: (1) "I hide my true feelings so as to appear pleasant at work," (2) "In my job I act confident and self-assured regardless of how I actually feel,"

Table 10.2 Occupational characteristics: Bolivia

Occupation	Frequency	Percent
1. Administration	17	8.5
2. Community development/neighborhood services	15	7.5
3. Engineering, manufacturing, or production	1	0.5
4. Education	149	74.1
5. Disaster response	3	1.5
6. Finance or accounting	9	4.5
8. Health care	8	4.0
10. Human resource management	5	2.5
11. Information and communication	7	3.5
12. Law enforcement	2	1.0
14. Public relations	2	1.0
15. Planning	8	4.0
18. Recreation and parks	1	0.5
19. Research and development	1	0.5
20. Social services	21	10.4
21. Transportation	1	0.5
23. Other	2	1.0

Table 10.3 Descriptive statistics and Cronbach's alpha: Bolivia

	Mean	SD	Cronbach's alpha
Emotive capacity	5.515	0.210	0.641
Pretending expression	3.614	0.423	0.546
Deep acting	4.584	0.838	0.596
Job satisfaction	4.734	1.118	0.601
Burnout	4.391	0.402	0.804
Personal fulfillment	5.668	0.2	0.724

and (3) "I wear a 'mask' in order to deal with clients/customers in an appropriate way." A Cronbach's Alpha score of 0.2 was discovered upon initially testing these three items for internal consistency. Additionally, a problematic negative relationship was discovered between the item related to acting confident and self-assured and the items related to hiding true feelings and wearing a 'mask' at work. Upon further review, it is notable that there was more variation present in both items 1 (standard deviation = 2.105) and 3 (standard deviation = 2.278), while item 2 had a much stronger level of agreement (standard deviation = 1.602). Therefore, item 2 was removed in order to proceed with the analysis. This action resulted in a Cronbach's Alpha to 0.546. It is possible that respondents identified acting confidently and self-assured as positive behaviors, and associated acting, hiding true feelings, and wearing a "mask" negatively. Because this is an exploratory study in a nation rarely surveyed, these variables provide a reasonable starting point for analysis.

Results

This study uses Structural Equation Modeling (SEM) to estimate the effect of three dimensions of emotional labor on job satisfaction, burnout, and personal fulfillment. The results of the structural model are presented in Table 10.4.

For the purpose of this exploratory study, relationships that achieve a statistical significance level of $p \leq 0.05$ are treated as notable and highlighted in the path diagram in Fig. 10.1.

The findings are described below.

Table 10.4 Structural model results: Bolivia

Hypothesized paths	Coefficients	p-value
Emotive capacity → Job satisfaction	0.132	0.190
Emotive capacity → Burnout	−0.020	0.823
Emotive capacity → Personal fulfillment	0.435*	0.000
Pretending expression → Job satisfaction	−1.01*	0.000
Pretending expression → Burnout	0.734*	0.000
Pretending expression → Personal fulfillment	−0.502*	0.000
Deep acting → Job satisfaction	0.986*	0.001
Deep acting → Burnout	−0.065	0.671
Deep acting → Personal fulfillment	0.348*	0.034

Model fit: $\chi^2 = 289.443$ (df = 142), CFI = 0.776, RMSEA = 0.078, SRMR = 0.097

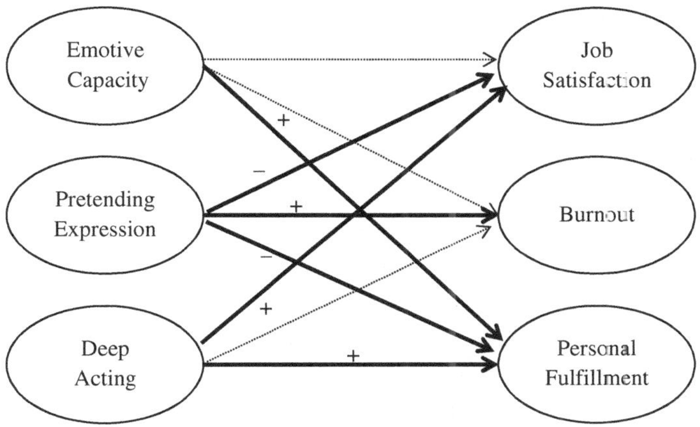

Fig. 10.1 Path diagram for Bolivia

Emotive Capacity

Results demonstrate that emotive capacity has a statistically significant positive relationship with personal fulfillment ($p = 0.000$). The SEM model reports no effect of emotive capacity on job satisfaction or burnout. Emotive capacity includes the survey items: "I am good at expressing how I feel", "I am good at getting people to calm down," and "In my job I am good at dealing with emotional issues".

Pretending Expression

Pretending expression has a statistically significant positive relationship with burnout ($p = 0.000$), and a statistically significant negative relationship with job satisfaction ($p = 0.000$) and personal fulfillment ($p = 0.000$). Pretending expression included the survey items "I hide my true feelings so as to appear pleasant at work," and "I wear a 'mask' in order to deal with clients/customers in an appropriate way".

Deep Acting

Deep acting was positively associated with job satisfaction ($p = 0.001$) and personal fulfillment ($p = 0.034$). It was not associated with burnout. Items included in this variable included: "I try to actually experience the emotions that I must show to clients/customers," "I work hard to actually feel the emotions that I need to show to clients/customers," and "I work at developing the feelings inside of me that I need to show to clients/customers".

Discussion

This study examined the effect of a series of emotional labor variables upon outcomes including job satisfaction, burnout, and personal fulfillment among a sample of Bolivian public servants. Findings revealed that emotional labor had a significant impact on each outcome variable. This section will discuss the implications of these findings within the Bolivian context.

Like public servants in other parts of the world, Bolivian public servants are tasked with delivering a variety of services to a demanding public. However, the influence of political parties and corruption place an additional strain on the public servant. Patronage appointments require individuals to respond to their political appointer while simultaneously operating under a persistent fear of losing their jobs. This limits their ability to use the discretion that is an important feature of their work (Lipsky 2010). With a desire to maintain respect for hierarchy in a structured setting, public servants also have to navigate a largely informal system while earning salaries much lower than those in the private sector. Combined, these characteristics depict a scenario in which any employee may feel dissatisfied and burnt out as a result of their organizational environment.

Among the sampled population, emotional labor in the form of deep acting was directly related to higher levels of job satisfaction and personal fulfillment, consistent with existing literature (Mastracci et al. 2012). In contrast to emotive pretending, in which an individual must display a "false-face," deep acting refers to convincingly displaying an emotion. It is associated with a feeling of pride in one's work (Guy et al. 2008, 5). Deep acting was positively related to both job satisfaction and personal fulfillment among this sample, despite the fact that political constraints limit public servants from using discretion as they might choose. And, deep acting was not associated with burnout. Cultural and demographic features of the sample are important in interpreting these results. Existing research has noted that women are more likely to seek social support in stressful situations (Simon and Nath 2004). With males comprising less than 10% of the sample, it is possible that burnout is mitigated through maintenance of positive relationships in the workplace. The impact of gender in this context requires further exploration.

As a collectivist culture, *simpatía*, or the preference for harmony, avoidance of conflict and preference for positive emotions (Sanchez-Burks and Lee 2007) is an important feature of Hispanic culture. As such, individuals take pride in their ability to interact with others in positive ways. Related to this, emotive capacity measured the extent to which an individual perceived their ability to cope with their own emotions and those of others. Among the sampled population, public servants who were better at coping with their own emotions and those of others felt more personal fulfillment in their work. Interestingly, emotive capacity was not associated with job satisfaction as is common in the literature (Mastracci et al. 2012).

Finally, those who reported higher levels of emotive pretending were more likely to report lower levels of job satisfaction and personal fulfillment, and higher levels of burnout. Consistent with the literature, inauthentic expression is often associated with higher levels of emotional exhaustion leading to burnout, especially among women (Mastracci et al. 2012). Furthermore, existing research notes that when workers engage in authentic emotive expression on the job, they are more likely to be engaged and experience less burnout (Lu and Guy 2014).

Conclusion

The preceding study serves to illuminate the influence of context in the practice of emotional labor. Bolivia's political context both permits and constrains public servants from exercising discretion, characterizing an environment that is, at best, unpredictable. Perhaps in response to this, informality in public management has become commonplace. Citizen perceptions of public management are reflective of this instability, maintaining little confidence in those responsible for delivering public service. Nevertheless, employees operate in a culture that values harmonious interaction, presenting public servants with an incongruous challenge. Taking into account these cultural nuances, expression of emotional labor among Bolivian public servants largely reflects existing research in other countries. Further exploration of context could explore how the combination of informality and collectivism manifest in organizational culture and individual coping strategies.

References

Anastasi, A. 1982. *Psychological Testing*. 5th ed. New York, NY: Macmillan.

Boulding, Carew E., and Clark C. Gibson. 2009. "The Effects of Nongovernmental Organizations on Local Politics in Bolivia." *Comparative Political Studies* 42 (4): 479–500.

Cornell, Agnes. 2014. "Why Bureaucratic Stability Matters for the Implementation of Democratic Governance Programs." *Governance: An International Journal of Policy, Administration, and Institutions* 27 (2): 191–214.

Farthing, Linda, and Kohl, Benjamin. 2001. "Bolivia's New Wave of Protest." *NACLA Report on the Americas* 34 (5): 8–11.

Garza, Yvonne, and Richard E. Watts. 2010. "Filial Therapy and Hispanic Values: Common Ground for Culturally Sensitive Helping." *Journal of Counseling & Development* 88 (1): 108–13.

Gingerich, Daniel W. 2010. "Bolivia: Traditional Parties, the State, and the Toll of Corruption." *Corruption and Politics in Latin America: National and Regional Dynamics*. London, UK: Lynne Rienner.

Guy, Mary E., Meredith A. Newman, and Sharon H. Mastracci. 2008. *Emotional Labor: Putting the Service in Public Service*. Armonk, NY: M.E. Sharpe.

Hardman, Martha James. 1976. *Andean Women*. New York, NY: American Universities Field Staff.

Harten, Sven. 2011. *The Rise of Evo Morales and the MAS*. London, UK: Zed Books.

Henderson, Peter V. N. 2013. *The Course of Andean History*. Albuquerque, NM: University of New Mexico Press.

House, Robert J., Paul J. Hanges, Mansour Javidan, Peter W. Dorfman, and Vipin Gupta, eds. 2004. *Culture, Leadership, and Organizations: The GLOBE Study of 62 Societies.* Thousand Oaks, CA: Sage.

Klein, Herbert S. 2011. *A Concise History of Bolivia.* New York, NY: Cambridge University Press.

Kohl, Benjamin. 1996. "Coca/Cocaine Control Policy in Bolivia and the United States." *Colloqui* 11 (Spring): 1–7.

Kohl, Benjamin. 2003. "Democratizing Decentralization in Bolivia: The Law of Popular Participation." *Journal of Planning Education and Research* 23 (2): 153–64.

Latin American Public Opinion Project (LAPOP). 2014. *The Americas Barometer.* Accessed March 1, 2019. https://www.vanderbilt.edu/lapop/about-americasbarometer.php.

Lehman, Donald R. 1985. *Market Research and Analysis.* Homewood, IL: Irwin.

Lipsky, Michael. 2010. *Street-Level Bureaucracy: Dilemmas of the Individual in Public Services.* New York, NY: Russell Sage Foundation.

Lu, Xiaojun, and Mary E. Guy. 2014. "How Emotional Labor and Ethical Leadership Affect Job Engagement for Chinese Public Servants." *Public Personnel Management* 43 (1): 3–24.

Madrid, Raul. 2008. *The Rise of Ethnopopulism in Latin America.* New York, NY: Cambridge University Press.

Mastracci, Sharon H., Mary E. Guy, and Meredith A. Newman. 2012. *Working on the Razor's Edge: Emotional Labor in Crisis Response.* Armonk, NY: M.E. Sharpe.

Messner, J. J., Nate Haken, Patricia Taft, Ignatius Onyekwere, Hannah Blyth, Charles Fiertz, Christina Murphy, Amanda Quinn, and Mckenzie Horwitz. 2018. "Fragile States Index 2018—Annual Report." *Fragile States Index*, April 24. fundforpeace.org/fsi/2018/04/24/fragile-states-index-2018-annual-report/.

Moloney, Kim, and Hyo-Youn Chu. 2016. "Linking Jamaica's Public Service Motivations and Ethical Climate." *The American Review of Public Administration* 46 (4): 436–58. https://doi.org/10.1177/0275074014557022.

Morales, Waltraud Q. 1992. *Bolivia: Land of Struggle.* Boulder, CO: Westview Press.

Morales, Waltraud Q. 2003. *A Brief History of Bolivia.* New York, NY: Lexington Books.

Organization of American States (OAS). 2009. *Corruption in Bolivia.* Accessed September 12, 2018. http://www.oas.org/juridico/english/bolivia_corruption.htm.

Painter, James. 1994. *Bolivia and Coca: A Study in Dependency.* Vol. 1. New York, NY: United Nations University Press.

Sanchez-Burks, J., and F. Lee. 2007. "Culture and Workways." In *Handbook of Cultural Psychology*, edited by S. Kitayama and D. Cohen, 346–69. New York, NY: Guilford Press.

Simon, Robin W., and Leda E. Nath. 2004. "Gender and Emotion in the United States: Do Men and Women Differ in Self-Reports of Feelings and Expressive Behavior?" *American Journal of Sociology* 109 (5): 1137–176.

United Nations Public Administration Network (UNPAN). 2000. *From Patronage to a Professional State: Bolivia Institutional Governance Review.* Report No. 20115-BO. Accessed March 1, 2019. http://siteresources.worldbank.org/INTEM POWERMENT/Resources/10060_bolivia.pdf.

UNICEF. *Resources.* 2003. Accessed September 13, 2018. https://www.unicef.org/bolivia/resources_2332.htm.

11

China

Xiaojun Lu

China is an ancient country whose norms and traditions are rooted in Confucianism. This chapter describes Confucian prescriptions at three levels: individual, interpersonal, and political. It then discusses the civil service system and explains how emotional labor is performed and perceived. Survey data gathered from government employees are then presented and discussed in terms of how findings reflect public service practice in China.

At the Individual Level

There are three ideals that guide individual behavior: benevolence, rites, and righteousness. A benevolent person loves people and this means loving everyone, not merely some—it is a "big love." Those who are benevolent are loving in their interpersonal relations and practice kindness in their interactions (Zhang 2009, 21). Additionally, self-restraint and restoration of rites are attributes of benevolence. Self-restraint means "Do unto others as you want others to do unto you." In other words, people must not force someone to do something that they would not want to have done to them. Additionally, self-consciousness is an important characteristic, being aware of one's own actions and their effects.

X. Lu (✉)
Department of Public Administration, School of International
and Public Affairs, Shanghai Jiao Tong University, Shanghai, China
e-mail: xjlv@sjtu.edu.cn

M. E. Guy et al. (eds.), *The Palgrave Handbook of Global Perspectives
on Emotional Labor in Public Service*, https://doi.org/10.1007/978-3-030-24823-9_11

Rites refer to the social order and norms that have been established by custom. "Restoration of rites" means that people should behave in accordance with norms and customs and it is thought to be a prerequisite for personal self-improvement. It is expected that people will refrain from improper desires, and inordinate ambitions (Chen 2005). Rites mean that the relationships among people are governed by common understandings. Couples, fathers and sons, brothers, seniors and juniors, and friends all have corresponding rights and obligations. Everyone should be in the right place, know exactly where he/she is positioned when dealing with his/her family and the outside world, and fulfill his/her duties and responsibilities that correspond to his/her position (Liu 2006).

Righteousness means upholding the proper way to behave. It is commonly understood that to be righteous is to be proper and is thought of as a well-accepted moral foundation. While it is understood that wherever humans interact, there will be both acceptable and unacceptable behaviors, righteousness must prevail (Cao 2017).

At the Interpersonal Level

Confucian directives that focus on interpersonal relations emphasize kinship, the human touch, reciprocal feelings, and individual feelings. These emphases extend to the spirit of harmony and the golden mean, which, in turn, link the fate of individuals and families to the fate of the country and the world.

Emphasis on Human Feelings

Chinese culture emphasizes kinship and feelings in a way that humanizes interactions. Treasuring the human touch and appreciating the reciprocal nature of interactions are important to the culture and to interpersonal relationships. Feelings are heavily emphasized between friends, family, and acquaintances. For example, norms of conduct include not rejecting requests from others lightly, being zealous in helping friends, and choosing self-sacrifice to make things easier for friends (Guo 2007).

Emphasis on Harmony

The pursuit of harmony, union, and cooperation is foundational to group interactions, with harmony being the highest goal. In terms of rites, harmony is thought to be the most precious and its sequel, coordination, is also prized. In getting along with one another, the advocated approaches include seeking a peaceful solution to disagreement, adopting the golden mean, and avoiding being too difficult to please. This is expressed metaphorically as "If the water is too clear, there will be no fish. If a person is too critical, there will be no partners." There is also emphasis on tolerance to the extent that people should be willing to sacrifice their interests in order to serve others, to seek common ground while reserving differences, and to advocate for unity (Yu 2007).

The Art of the Golden Mean

Impartiality is the essence of the doctrine of the golden mean. This doctrine requires taking the midpoint of extremes and treasuring peace. It is the highest proposition of Confucian philosophy, and it contains the basic methodology of Confucian doctrine. In team building, human relations, and customer relationships, attention must be paid to the art of the golden mean. This art is to govern speaking about and coping with issues, advancing or retreating one's point of view as appropriate. All things should be handled properly, leaving room for modification. Only by doing this can one's behavior be "invincible" (Fan 2007).

At the Political Level

Confucianism advocates for a national spirit of unity between the state and the family and teaches that people must assume responsibility for their country. This leads to a close linkage between the fate of individuals and families and the fate of China and, by extension, the world. This means that each person bears personal responsibility for oneself, family, locality, country, and the world (Zhu 2015).

Confucius believed that the top priority for government is to define properly a positive social hierarchy. Each level has its own title, responsibility, and interests, and no one should be allowed to trespass on others' property to pursue their own interests. This allows the ruler and his ministers, as well as fathers and sons, to have a proper position, each handling their own business and enjoying their own benefits without interfering with each other (Liu 2006).

Fast forward to now, in the midst of record-breaking economic reforms and these Confucian principles remain as guideposts for Chinese culture and individual behavior.

Impact of Traditional Culture on the Development of Public Management

In order to integrate the nation into the international economy, China has made major changes since 1978 to implement what is called its "reform and opening-up." Economic reforms have incorporated market principles into a socialist system of government, with de-collectivization of agriculture and selective welcoming of foreign investment and market-based entrepreneurialism. Large-scale government planning programs alongside market reforms have propelled the national economy, leading to its current Belt and Road Initiative. This program is developing markets and trade routes with China's Asian neighbors. It is one of the largest infrastructure and investment projects in history, involving trade partnerships with more than 68 countries (Campbell 2017).

During these remarkable economic and social advancements, China's public management system has provided the necessary support for these achievements while maintaining the nation's social structure (He 2016). The country's governance structure and public management system show the following characteristics.

1. Continuous Reform, Innovation, and Adaptability

Ever since its reform and opening up, China's public management system has been adapting to changes by undergoing constant reforms and innovations. The basic trend has been to loosen the economic and social systems in order to allow this large, ancient country to integrate with the modern world economy.

2. Self-Driven Continuous Improvement

Since ancient times, China has been motivated to pursue the ideal system of governance. Government initiatives have been the backbone of modernization throughout these reforms.

3. Flexibility and Adaptability in Decision-Making

Central government is formally a unitary hierarchical system, having an entrenched "order-execution" system from the top down. However, this process is not as rigorous and rigid as it may sound. In fact, there are numerous flexible feedback loops, and these render the entire system more adaptable to constant change and growing complexity.

4. The "Ruling Party—Government" Linkage and Inter-Development

The joint development of the Communist Party of China and Chinese government is the core feature and logic of China's public administration system. China's party-government relationship is neither a mode of party-in-place-of-government, as is often misunderstood, nor is it a mode that can be generalized as one of party-government integration. Rather, it is a mode of joint development that includes simultaneous separation and integration.

The rich ideology of coexistence and co-prosperity between man and nature in traditional Chinese culture has become increasingly prominent in the country's governance structure. First, group principles and holistic values combine to promote economic and social development of Chinese society. Li Yun in the Book of Rites says, "When the great principle prevails, the world is a commonwealth." Embraced within this is the worth of working for the welfare of the world. This holistic concept and public ideology assists in cultivating the concept of collectivism and serving the public whole-heartedly. It is the basis for guaranteeing healthy development of the socialist market economy to properly balance the relationship between the public and private sectors and the relationship between social and individual values.

The idea of "harmony is most precious" is conducive to a harmonious society. The thoughts of "harmony with difference" and "harmony is most precious" in Confucian culture are similar to principles in modern public relations that emphasize the importance of interpersonal interaction, communication and collaboration, and creation of a good public relations environment. For example, the theory of public relations prescribes continuous effort on the part of organizations to gain the trust and goodwill of the public. This is to be done by adapting to their interests and adjusting policies and service guidelines to be responsive.

Discussion turns now to the human factor in Chinese government. The evolution of the civil service system is described and this is followed by an explanation of how cultural values guide the work of civil servants.

Evolution of the Civil Service System

In conjunction with China's other reforms over the past forty years, there have also been profound changes in its civil service system. Numerous practical breakthroughs and theoretical innovations have been achieved.

Borrowing from Western public personnel systems, China has established a civil service system that comports with Chinese culture and governance. It has evolved in three stages, roughly 1978–1986, 1993–2005, and since 2006. These periods are described below.

Conversion to a Formalized Civil Service System (1978–1986)

As China entered the initial stage of its civil service reform, it first abolished the tenure system for leading positions and established a mandatory retirement age for many posts, along with retirement benefits. This meant that the lifetime sinecure for high ranking employees was replaced with a retirement system that allowed them to retire from their jobs with financial security, thus creating an infusion of new job opportunities for younger workers. Simultaneously, a human resource management system with a classification and compensation schedule was developed. These reforms have now become a well-accepted dimension of the political system.

Maturing of the Civil Service System (1993 Through Early 2005)

On August 14, 1993, promulgation of the "Provisional Regulations on State Civil Servants" marked the implementation of the national civil service system in China and the further standardization of personnel categories. Based on the spirit of the "Guideline on Deepening the Reform of the Personnel System for Cadres in 2000," China then accelerated development of its civil service system and formulated laws for personnel management in the party and in government organizations.

Development of the Civil Service System (Since 2006)

The promulgation of the civil service law had marked a significant development for government employees in China. As the first comprehensive law on the management of personnel, the law is a milestone in moving the management of civil servants toward a scientific, standardized, and legalized approach (Yan and Wu 2010).

Cultivation of Civil Servants' Spirit of Public Service

China is currently building a service-oriented government. This goal requires improving both worker ability and level of services provided by each individual civil servant. Traditional notions of civil servants are that they are employees who are motivated by hierarchical authority, structured jobs, and employment security. New Public Management considers civil servants to be market participants. In contrast, New Public Service teaches that civil servants should emphasize service for citizens and should delegate power to citizens while managing public organizations and implementing policies. Their work should not be focused on piloting government ships, nor should it be on paddling government ships. Instead, civil servants should establish public institutions with perfect integration and responsiveness. This assumes that their motives and rewards are more than just about salary and security; they are about delivering public services in a way that has a positive effect on the lives of citizens and achieves harmony. This public service motivation includes such values as loyalty, responsibility, civil rights, fairness, opportunity, and justice (Tang 2007).

The public service spirit of China's civil servants includes the following seven imperatives:

1. Use power for positive ends. In the process of delivering public services, civil servants enjoy the power and support that citizen trust enables. In return, their actions should advance citizens' interests and should reflect their wishes within the context of law and supervision.
2. To act as agents. As in a principal-agent relationship, there is a contractual relationship between civil servants and citizens. Citizens entrust them to use their positions and the resources at their disposal—rules, funding, authority—to provide services and to produce public goods.
3. To provide public services. The primary activity of the government and its civil servants is to provide all citizens with comprehensive, high-quality public products. In public service, civil servants should represent the voices of those who do not otherwise have the means to participate in the policy process. Workers are obligated to be mindful of public interests and greater goodness, to respect the personal dignity of citizens, and to spare no effort to uphold citizens' rights.
4. Realize public interest. Civil servants are providers and implementers who satisfy public needs and realize public interests. The goal of China's new

public service is to transcend one's own interests to discover common interests, i.e., public interests, and to act in accordance with those interests. In contrast to corporate managers, who attempt to treat public funds as their own property, civil servants should be committed to contributing meaning to society, so that the public interests can be better distributed.

5. Handle public affairs. The core of civil servants' work is to handle public affairs. These include political, economic, social, and cultural management. Civil servants should serve and care about others as they handle these affairs.

6. Take public responsibility. Civil servants must be mindful of their responsibility to the public while they are providing services. This obligation differs from the responsibilities of political officials and it also differs from dictates of New Public Management, which in contrast, focuses on responsiveness to efficiency, cost-benefit, and market forces.

7. Cultivate citizen participation. Among the responsibilities of civil servants are that they interact with citizens, listen and delegate power to them. The goal of this is to strengthen the citizen's role in democratic governance.

Emotional Labor in China's Public Sector

Attention to emotional labor has been developing rapidly in retail sales and customer service. And recognition for its role in public service is now gaining traction as appreciation for its essential role increases. For example, employees at a rescue station are expected to show sympathy and concern for the citizens requiring assistance, and employees of a marriage registry are expected to show enthusiasm and happiness for couples who register to marry. Guy et al. (2008; Mastracci et al. 2012) were the first scholars to apply the concept of emotional labor to public service work, arguing that it is an important element in citizen–state transactions and is essential for improving public services.

In order to build a service-oriented government in China, the quality of public work is garnering increasing attention. When providing services to citizens, public sector employees must interact actively with citizens, display the emotion expected by their organization, and exhibit a positive image, all while serving people whole-heartedly. The goal is for citizens to place additional trust in, and become more satisfied with, public services. Thus, the emotional labor demands for government employees are high. The following cases demonstrate this.

Two Case Studies of Emotional Labor in Government Agencies

The first case involves Secretary Zhu, a member of the National People's Congress in a street office in a district of Shanghai. This case demonstrates the relationship between public service providers and citizens. On a summer day several years ago, a heavy rain poured down, accompanied by loud thunder; with a flash, a lightning bolt suddenly struck. The lightning strike damaged thirteen televisions, telephones, DVD players, and other household appliances of the eight families who lived in building number 11 of the Hongchu residential area. Residents rushed to the property management company. A staff member of the company responded, "This is none of my business." Then, they went to the cable station, only to be told "This is none of my business." By then, residents were becoming anxious. Upon learning about the incident, Secretary Zhu immediately rushed to building number 11 and said, without hesitation, "It is my business and the business of our general Party branch." While calming the residents, she sent a team to contact various agents to determine why the household appliances were damaged and in doing so, she upheld the rights of the residents.

Another example of Secretary Zhu's work occurred with a resident of her district. Resident Manggen Zhang had lung cancer and was hospitalized for surgery. "When I was in the hospital, my neighbors came to visit me every day, and some even brought fish soup to me. Some of my neighbors looked familiar to me, but I couldn't even remember their names. The patients in my room thought that I was a big deal, but I was simply an ordinary man on the welfare program." In fact, these visits were all arranged by Secretary Zhu, and any resident of Hongchu who is hospitalized with a serious illness receives the same treatment. Similar to many other residents' experiences, Manggen Zhang remarked emotionally, "What a blessing to live in this community!" And a year prior, Secretary Zhu had also helped Manggen Zhang and his daughter finds jobs.

On another occasion, Secretary Zhu heard from residents that a man from building 19 sounded a little unusual and would, to whomever he saw, close every conversation with "Take care" and "Goodbye." Secretary Zhu learned that the man's wife had been laid off from her job. His factory was not doing well either. The Secretary visited the man's home and saw only five bundles of cotton sweaters and pants in the room. The kitchen was full of bags of fish and vegetables. It turned out that the head of the household had also been laid off. He had to sell a backlog of cotton fabrics to receive 300 Chinese yuan for living expenses. Seeing that the bundles of cotton sweaters and pants could not be sold and there was no way to pay his son's tuition, the family was determined to commit suicide by opening the gas valve after finishing their final dinner. Secretary Zhu's heart was deeply hurt. This family had run into such enormous difficulties without her finding out in a timely manner, so she felt deeply guilty and uneasy. She contacted various departments and helped them open a small store in the community to solve their financial problems. Later, she helped the head of the household locate a job. Now, the family lives a stable life, and their son has found a job after graduating from a three-year college. The household head said movingly, "We fell to the lowest valley of our lives and into the most desperate dilemma, but we have returned to a better life. Our gratitude to Secretary Zhu is greater than we can express."

The second case involves a group of medical workers and a doctor-patient relationship. In the emergency room of a hospital in Shanghai, people were packed so tightly together they could barely move. The emergency room was originally designed to accommodate thirty-six beds, but it was stuffed with more than sixty beds. Additional beds would not fit and had to be moved to the lobby, hallways, or any corner where they would not impede walking. The head nurse of the emergency room, Jinxia Jiang, said while inspecting the patients, "This is not too bad. As there are no outpatient clinics on weekends, more than eighty beds will be in the emergency room. The registration lobby has literally become the second emergency room."

Meanwhile, the information desk was being bombarded with questions: "The street office told me to get my medical record card stamped here. Why did you refuse to do it?" "My child fell in the elevator and got injured. Which department should I go to?" "What happened to the migrant worker who just arrived?" A woman carrying a medical record card, a mother holding her child, and a police officer writing a record were simultaneously bombarding the information desk with questions. "For pediatrics, go to Xinhua Hospital. We don't have a special child injury department here." "To get your record stamped, go and find 120 behind the hospital." "What's the name of the migrant worker? Let me check it out…" There was no pause.

Qing Zhu, who was on duty at the pre-screening desk, spoke quickly and, evidently, the patient who came for the consultation was not satisfied with these simple answers. "We only need to bandage it up. It is nothing serious. There is no need to go to Xinhua." The woman holding the child was anxious. "All I saw was the emergency room; where do you expect me to go in such hot weather?" The woman who had asked for a stamp was unhappy and seemed to be uneasy. The police officer saw that Qing Zhu was occupied, so he wrote the name on a piece of paper, knocked on the desk, and handed over the paper.

The first three customers had barely moved when other patients and their families pushed their way through to the information desk. Finding that it was too much for Qing Zhu to handle alone, Jinxia Jiang helped explain to the mother holding the child, while Qing Zhu was still explaining to the woman who wanted to get her record stamped. The 120 and the hospital emergency room belong to two different organizations. The 120 had mistyped her name, so it had to be stamped to be valid. It may be that the nurse's voice sounded too loud when answering questions, or it could be that it is annoying to have to go multiple places to accomplish a task. The woman who wanted her record stamped murmured, "I am here to ask because I have no idea. Who knew it's so troublesome here? Damn it!" and she left, very unhappy.

During Qing Zhu's eight hours on duty, Zhu barely had time to breathe. And Jinxia Jiang's 24-hour shift in exchange for time off would remain on the schedule. The nurses in the emergency room had to remain on high alert all the time and respond to all types of unexpected situations, and this is not even the worst part. "It is common for doctors and nurses to be cursed at. It's understandable. If you are sick, you have a bad temper, but oddly, some extreme family members will resort to fighting, which is hardly acceptable. Some time ago, one of our nurses was washing her hands when a patient's family member knocked her on the head." Jinxia Jiang sighed deeply.

Both of these cases demonstrate the emotive load of employees' jobs. With both expected and unexpected demands coming at them throughout their shifts, they must be emotively agile while also being responsive to job demands. Managing their own emotive state, as well as managing how the citizen is feeling, is part of the job.

Study of Emotional Labor Based on Investigation

The survey was administered to full-time community employees working in frontline government departments in China. Data collection occurred in June 2015. With the assistance of personnel managers, 218 questionnaires were delivered and 211 valid responses were received, yielding a response rate of 96.8%. All those who were surveyed worked in community affairs. Their jobs required them to engage in either face-to-face or voice-to-voice communication with citizens in their daily work. Table 11.1 displays sample characteristics. It shows that the vast majority are between the ages of 30 and 59, over two-thirds are women, most have less than ten years of work experience in public service, and two-thirds hold college degrees.

Table 11.1 Demographic characteristics: China

	Frequency	Percent
Age		
Less than 30	10	4.7
30–39 years	71	33.6
40–49 years	45	21.3
50–59 years	79	37.4
60 or more	6	2.8
N/A	0	0.0
Gender		
Female	153	72.5
Male	58	27.5
Public service experience		
Less than 10	179	84.8
10–19 years	32	15.2
20–29 years	0	0.0
30 or more	0	0.0
N/A	0	0.0
Educational level		
Less than high school	0	0.0
High school graduate	70	33.2
Some college	0	0.0
2-year associate degree	0	0.0
College graduate	99	46.9
Some graduate school	42	19.9
Master's degree	0	0.0
Law degree (J.D., LL.B.)	0	0.0
Doctorate (Ph.D., M.D., Ed.D., etc.)	0	0.0
Other (please specify)	0	0.0
N/A	0	0.0

In regard to their occupations, all respondents are employed in community development and neighborhood services jobs.

In order to investigate emotional labor and its effects, the following variables and items were employed in the analysis:

For *pretending expression*, the following survey items were used.

I hide my true feelings so as to appear pleasant at work
In my job I act confident and self-assured regardless of how I actually feel
I wear a "mask" in order to deal with clients/customers in an appropriate way

For *emotive capacity*, the following survey items were used.

I am good at expressing how I feel
I am good at getting people to calm down
In my job I am good at dealing with emotional issues

For *deep acting*, the following survey items were used.

I try to actually experience the emotions that I must show to clients/customers
I work hard to actually feel the emotions that I need to show to clients/customers
I work at developing the feelings inside of me that I need to show to clients/customers

For *job satisfaction*, the following survey items were used.

My job provides career development and promotion opportunities
I feel I am being paid a fair amount for the work I do
I feel satisfied with my supervisor
Overall, I am satisfied with my job

For *burnout*, the following survey items were used.

I leave work feeling tired and run down
I leave work feeling emotionally exhausted
I feel "used up" at the end of the workday

For *personal fulfillment*, the following survey items were used.

I gain a strong sense of personal fulfillment at my job
I feel like my job is something I want to do rather than something I have to do
My work is a source of personal meaning in my life

Results

Descriptive statistics and correlations are shown for the variables and then structural equation model testing follows.

Descriptive Statistics and Correlations

Descriptive statistics for emotive capacity, pretending expression, deep acting, job satisfaction, burnout, and personal fulfillment are displayed in Table 11.2. Cronbach's alpha, which indicates the level of internal reliability for each variable, exceeds the desirable level of 0.70 for all except Pretending and Job Satisfaction. For these two—0.621 and 0.692, respectively—the values are nevertheless high enough to use them for exploratory purposes.

Table 11.2 Descriptive statistics and Cronbach's alpha: China

	Mean	SD	Cronbach's alpha
Emotive capacity	5.59	1.00	0.776
Pretending expression	5.43	1.09	0.621
Deep acting	5.87	0.98	0.851
Job satisfaction	5.09	1.11	0.692
Burnout	3.67	1.71	0.878
Personal fulfillment	5.87	1.08	0.887

Table 11.3 Structural model results: China

Hypothesized paths	Coefficients	p-value
Emotive capacity → Job satisfaction	0646*	0.000
Emotive capacity → Burnout	0.147	0.144
Emotive capacity → Personal fulfillment	0.485*	0.000
Pretending expression → Job satisfaction	−0.106	0.357
Pretending expression → burnout	0.212	0.056
Pretending expression → Personal fulfillment	−0.003	0.979
Deep acting → Job satisfaction	0.139	0.261
Deep acting → Burnout	−0.312*	0.005
Deep acting → Personal fulfillment	0.433*	0.000

Model Fit: $\chi^2 = 400.600$ (df = 142), CFI = 0.855, RMSEA = 0.100, SRMR = 0.174

Structural Equation Modeling (SEM) is used to estimate the effect of the three dimensions of emotional labor on job satisfaction, burnout, and personal fulfillment. Results are presented in Table 11.3.

For purposes of this exploratory study, those relationships that achieve a statistical significance of $p \leq 0.05$ are treated as noteworthy and are highlighted in the path diagram in Fig. 11.1.

These results are similar to those found in other cultures in that emotive capacity has a positive relationship with job satisfaction and personal fulfillment. Moreover, the authentic expression of emotion is positively related to feelings of personal fulfillment, and it is inversely related to burnout. It is noteworthy that, as Table 11.3 shows, emotive pretending is positively related to burnout ($p = 0.056$) but falls slightly outside this study's criterion level of $p \leq 0.050$. This finding is consistent with meta-analyses of Western samples, which have shown that surface acting, which involves pretending to feel an emotion one does not actually feel, is often associated with stress and impaired well-being (Hülsheger and Schewe 2011; Kammeyer-Mueller et al. 2013). To summarize the findings from China, the following results are highlighted:

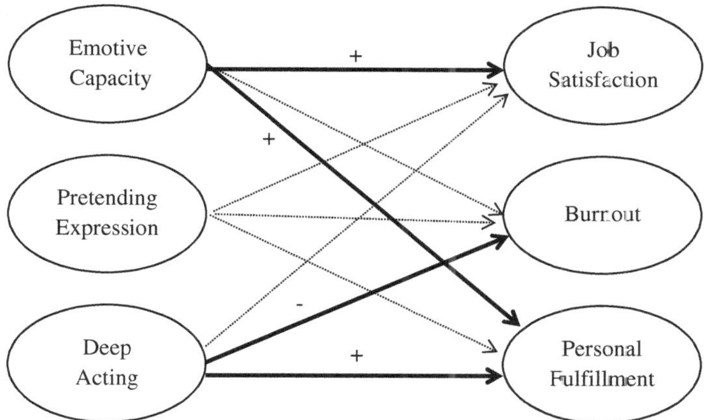

Fig. 11.1 Path diagram for China

Emotive Capacity: The ability to perform emotional labor has a positive relationship with job satisfaction and personal fulfillment and has no relationship to burnout.

Pretending Expression: Having to display an emotion that one does not actually feel, in other words, emotive pretense, is not significantly related to job satisfaction or personal fulfillment. It is close to being positively related to burnout, but does not reach the criterion level of the other significant findings.

Deep Acting: The authentic display of emotion results in higher levels of personal fulfillment and reduces the likelihood of burnout.

So How Does National Culture Matter?

There are hints as to how national culture factors into these findings. Interpersonal activities require emotional labor and maintaining harmony acts as a super-goal during interactions. Based on the positive relationships between emotive capacity and job satisfaction and between emotive capacity and personal fulfillment, the results for Chinese workers indicate that this super-goal leads civil servants to have a sense of achievement when harmony is maintained.

Because of the strength with which Confucian principles imbue expectations, higher ability to perform emotional labor leads to higher personal fulfillment. In China, people's self-constructions depend on their relationship with those around them. Being able to maintain harmonious relations with others helps people boost their self-esteem and emotional labor is the tool they use to achieve this end. It follows, then, that their interactions with citizens boost their own self-esteem and thereby facilitate job satisfaction. This is demonstrated by the positive relationship between deep acting and personal fulfillment.

The fact that inauthentic emotive expression—pretending—is not related to the outcome variables may be explained by this. Emotive pretending is sometimes necessary in order to maintain harmonious relationships. The norms that Chinese conform to during interpersonal exchanges shed light on this and are enumerated below in the Confucian principles of Ren, Yi, and Li.

> *Ren*: The philosophy of Confucianism elevates the value of benevolence to others (Ren), over one's own feelings.
> *Yi*: Engaging in pretending expression is done to achieve a harmonious relationship, and this is considered as a right behavior (Yi).
> *Li*: Following emotive display rules is prescribed by organizational expectations, so following them is consistent with socially desirable norms (Li).

The guidance of Ren, Yi, and Li help workers accept the importance of emotive expression in various forms and help to minimize the effect of having to display emotions one does not actually feel. Thus, the relationship between pretending and outcome variables does not rise to the level of being significant.

Emotional Labor Management Strategies and Suggestions

Given the findings reported from this survey of China's civil servants, this chapter concludes with a discussion of how emotional labor factors into public performance and how it should be integrated into human resource management for the nation's civil service. In the 1970s as China was embarking on reforms, researchers proposed the theory that government is a living organism. This theory has come to be interpreted as relational administration, which implies caring, awareness, collaboration, courage, and intuition. A caring perspective places emphasis on wholeheartedness, responsiveness, and the importance of relationships and emotional connections. The most serious challenge for public administrators in the twenty-first century is not to make their work more efficient but to make it more humane and more caring. To that end, the current need is to adjust practice so that caring becomes a highly valued goal at the street level just as it is in theory.

Public satisfaction with government is achieved via the active interactions between citizens and the state. The bridge between them is the civil servant, who must be competent, experienced, administratively positive, and must derive pride from the work. In the pursuit of public satisfaction, the worker's job satisfaction is an important variable. As the case of Secretary Zhu demonstrates, emotional labor provides meaning and value to the communications between civil servants and citizens. Conversely, too much emotion work, which is not reflected in the reward system, will give rise to emotional exhaustion, as demonstrated by the case of Qing Zhu and Jinxia Jiang. This is why it is necessary for the human resource system to be sensitive to emotional labor and to incorporate recognition of it in personnel functions: job analysis, job description, classification, and compensation, employee career development, and selection and promotion.

Within China's current personnel structure, these human resource functions do not reflect or may even hinder the recognition of emotional labor. It would be beneficial to transform the functions such that they incorporate awareness of emotional labor as a skill worthy of compensation, just as other job skills are. This is because the essence of public-sector human resource management is to improve the quality of public services and to satisfy the public. In the relationship between emotional labor and satisfaction of the public, job satisfaction of the civil servant is the mediating variable. Public satisfaction means accomplishment of the mission, and this, in turn, reinforces motivation of civil servants and their own personal satisfaction.

A durable human resource management strategy would be two-pronged. It would emphasize the importance of emotional labor's role in achieving satisfaction on the part of the public, and it would emphasize the personal benefits for employees as their own job satisfaction and feelings of self-worth increase. Awareness of their own emotions and of their psychological state will enhance their own lives both on the job and off.

Current human resource functions fail to reflect the value of emotional labor in job descriptions, recruitment, and selection. Job descriptions only describe the formal job requirements, without defining the emotional skills and competencies required of the employee, meaning that they only provide the cognitive task requirements of the job. It is the job description that forms the basis for all the other links to human resource functions, because all other functions are dependent on the information contained in the job description. No attention to emotional labor in the job description indicates that it is overlooked everywhere else in the human resource chain. Because emotional labor is indispensable in the process of public service and in the shaping of government's image, the challenge for human resource management is to use emotive skills as a criterion for performance evaluation and as a basis for compensation.

References

Cao, Xixi. 2017. *Research on Confucian Moral Education Thoughts in the Pre-Qin Dynasty.* Master's thesis, Jiangxi University of Science and Technology. Accessed November 30, 2018. http://www.cnki.net/KCMS/detail/detail. aspx?dbcode=CMFD&QueryID=19&CurRec=3&dbname=CMF-D201801&filename=1017111840.nh&urlid=&yx=&v=MDY5MDBWR-jI2R2JLNUg5bklyNUViUElSOGVYMUx1eFlTN0RoMVQzcVRyV00xRnJD-VVJMS2ZiK2RwRnl2bVY3L0E=.
Campbell, Charlie. 2017. "It's Building the New Silk Road: Here Are Five Things to Know Ahead of a Key Summit." *Time*, May 12. Accessed http://time.com/4776845/china-xi-jinping-belt-road-initiative-obor/.
Chen, Lai. 2005. "Giving Priority to the Other Party: Shuming Liang's View of Confucian Ethics." *Zhejiang Academic Journal* (1): 5–14.
Fan, Hao. 2007. "Confucian Ethics of Harmony and Its Moral and Philosophical Significance." *Morals and Civilization* (6): 4–10.
Guo, Weihua. 2007. "Interpretation of Confucian Humanistic Philosophy." *Theory Monthly* (12): 53–55.
Guy, Mary E., Meredith A. Newman, and Sharon H. Mastracci. 2008. *Emotional Labor: Putting the Service in Public Service.* Armonk, NY: M.E. Sharpe.
He, Zhe. 2016. "The Dialogue Between the Core Logic of China's Public Management System and Other Systems." *Journal of Gansu Administration Institute* (1): 47–54.
Hülsheger, U., and A. Schewe. 2011. "On the Costs and Benefit of Emotional Labour: A Meta-Analysis of Three Decades of Research." *Journal of Occupational Health Psychology* 16 (3): 361–89.
Kammeyer-Mueller, J. D., A. L. Rubenstein, D. M. Long, M. A. Odio, B. R. Buckman, Y. Zhang, and M. D. K. Halvorsen-Ganepola. 2013. "A Meta-Analytic Structural Model of Dispositional Affectivity and Emotional Labor." *Personnel Psychology* 66 (1): 47–90.
Liu, Zhaowei. 2006. "On Confucianism and Harmonious Society." *Journal of Shenyang Normal University* (Social Science Edition) 30 (1): 5–9.
Mastracci, Sharon H., Mary E. Guy, and Meredith A. Newman. 2012. *Emotional Labor and Crisis Response: Working on the Razor's Edge.* Armonk, NY: M.E. Sharpe.

Tang, Xinglin. 2007. "Public Service: The Essence of the Civil Servant Spirit." *Journal of Jiangsu Administration Institute* (2): 102–106.

Yan, Weijing, and Leichun Wu. 2010. "Review of Sixty Years of Changes and the Development Trend of the Civil Service System." *Proceedings of the Socialist Administration System with Chinese Characteristics Seminar and the Annual Meeting of China's Administration Society*, February 2. Beijing, China.

Yu, Chunmei. 2007. "The Basic Content and Modern Significance of Confucian Harmony." *Theoretical Investigation* (3): 66–68.

Zhang, Jing. 2009. *Research on the Relationship Between Contemporary College Students' Confucian and Traditional Values and Mental Health*. Jilin University. Doctoral dissertation. Accessed November 30, 2018. http://www.cnki.net/KCMS/detail/detail.aspx?dbcode=CDFD&QueryID=11&CurRec=1&dbname=CDFD0911&filename=2009098187.nh&urlid=&yx=&v=MDg1Nzg3TVYxMjdGN094RnRERXFFKRWJQSVI4ZVgxTHV4WVM3RGgxVDNxVHJXTTFGGckNVUkxLZmIrZHBGGeWpsVmI=.

Zhu, Li. 2015. *Research on the Cultivating Effect of Pre-Qin Confucianism on Socialist Core Values*. Doctoral dissertation, Shandong University. Accessed August 15, 2008. http://www.cnki.net/KCMS/detail/detail.aspx?dbcode=CDFD&QueryID=3&CurRec=1&dbname=CDFDLAST2015&filename=1015371013.nh&urlid=&yx=&v=MDc3MzdyM0FWRjI2RzdDL0g5SE5ySkViUElSOGVYMUx1eFFlTN0RoMVQzcVRyV00xRnJDVVJMS2ZiK2RwRnlqbFY.

12

India

Pallavi Awasthi

The cultural history of India is about 4500 years old with foundations in classical Sanskrit literature, the Vedic period, and the Indus Valley civilization (1500 BCE–500 BCE). During this period, a distinctive classical culture and philosophy emerged which is largely referred to as Hinduism today. The Hindu tradition encompasses a polytheistic system of divinity with various rituals to seek the ultimate truth (Central Intelligence Agency 2019). For centuries—until the seventh century CE—the people of the Indian subcontinent enjoyed a rich intellectual and cultural life and lived in peace without any invasive external influences. However, toward the end of the seventh century CE, Turkish, Persian, and Arab invaders raided and occupied a large part of the Indian territory. By the thirteenth century, the majority of the Indian subcontinent was under Muslim rule. The integration of Islamic religious ideology became a major challenge as this ideology was based on Arabic rather than Sanskrit cultures. This resulted in a deeper level of complexity and sophistication in the cultural life of India.

In the early seventeenth century, the British East India Company established a foothold in India, resulting in the decline of Muslim supremacy. This laid the foundation of the British colonial empire. The main objective of the British East India Company was business and trade but gradually they became powerful rulers. By midway through the nineteenth century,

P. Awasthi (✉)
Public Policy and Administration, Florida International University,
Miami, FL, USA
e-mail: Pawas001@fiu.edu

© The Author(s) 2019
M. E. Guy et al. (eds.), *The Palgrave Handbook of Global Perspectives
on Emotional Labor in Public Service*, https://doi.org/10.1007/978-3-030-24823-9_12

India came under the direct control of Britain. The British ruled until the mid-twentieth century, creating a deeper religious rift in Indian society. For the first time, the country was forced into subordination by the imposition of industrial mass production, causing many indigenous craft and cottage industries to suffer. Most Indian institutions, universities, technologies, and railroad systems served British rather than Indian economic interests. The country that had contributed about 23% of the GDP in the world economy during the early eighteenth century was left to a meager 4.2% share by 1950 (Maddison 2003). India's share of the industrial output in the world economy declined from 23% in 1750 to only 3% in 1900 and around the same time UK's share increased from 2% in 1700 to 9% in 1870 (Tharoor 2016).

Many historians blame British colonial rule for the abysmal state of India's economic performance. During the British Raj, as some called it, India suffered a major deindustrialization of native manufacturing industries. A massive decline in demand and increasing unemployment in India's handicraft and handloom industry occurred during this time. This led to a significant transfer of capital and drain of revenue from India to England (Banerjee and Iyer 2005). The British administration left India underdeveloped, over-populated, and wrought with unprecedented poverty and complex social problems. It also left it with an inherited governmental structure. India's governmental structure is British parliament ary system with three government branches: the legislative, judiciary, and the executive. The type of government is a federal parliamentary republic in India.

The Indian freedom movement led by Mahatma Gandhi eventually provided independence from the British Empire in 1947. However, it resulted in the partition of India, creating two nations: India (the Hindu majority) and Pakistan (the Muslim majority). The partition of India was based on a two-nation theory grounded in the belief that the primary identity of Muslims in India was not their language and ethnicity but religion. Eventually, India was divided into two nations based on distinct religious ideologies: Pakistan, a Muslim majority nation, and India, a Hindu majority nation. The Partition was a cataclysmic event affecting the social, political, economic, and cultural lives of millions of people. As Indian historians relate, no other country in the twentieth century endured two such simultaneous, contrary movements. One was a popular nationalist movement unique in the annals of world history for ousting colonizers through nonviolent means while the other was the counter-movement of Partition, which was marked by violence, cruelty, bloodshed, displacement, and massacres. (Hasan 2005; Kaul 2001). Even today, Partition remains a controversial topic and is the cause of ongoing tension and terrorism in the Indian subcontinent.

The twenty-first-century Indian society is multi-religious, and multilingual, with numerous castes and tribes. Certainly, Hindu religious thought, which traces its roots to the Vedas and Upanishads, remains central to the spiritual and philosophical foundation of India even today. However, many other religions and schools of thought emerged at different times in history and found their place. This laid the foundation for pluralistic acceptance and the multicultural nature of India, making room for many different faiths and beliefs to evolve. Even though Islam had a presence in India for about 800 years, Hinduism was not the only religion before Islam. Buddhism predominated from 450 BCE to the thirteenth century CE, so much so that Chinese scholars labeled India as a Buddhist kingdom. However, both Buddhism and Hinduism drew from Vedic values. Similarly, Jainism has a long history, tracing its beginning from 599 BCE. Additionally, atheistic and agnostic beliefs found their place in the Vedic philosophical texts. From the tenth century CE onward, Christians, Jews, and Persians came to India. Likewise, Sikh ism flourished since the fifteenth century CE and has many followers across India, with the largest concentration in the State of Punjab.

Pundit Jawaharlal Nehru, the first Prime Minister of India, described India's past as a palimpsest. Each dominant culture left its traces of interwoven ideologies but never eliminated what came before it. Such is the image of India's deep civilizational history. The Indian subcontinent is also the only place where the four largest religions of the world—Hinduism, Buddhism, Christianity, and Islam—coexist. Khilnani (2016, 4) notes:

> Through religious collisions and philosophical and ethical explorations, many … [have taken part] in intense arguments that have been kept going for millennia: about what kind of life is worth living, what kind of society is worth having, which hierarchies are morally legitimate, what role religion has in the political and legal order, and what kind of place India should be. Such arguments have kept India in a permanent (and, on balance productive) state of openness about what the country and its people are.

This rich, complicated history, and the creative energy that it accompanies, has produced an India that seeks to catalyze the nation into a singular cultural concoction. This is especially notable in that India is home to the world's second largest number of languages. There are about 780 languages and 66 different scripts with numerous major and minor linguistic groups and dialects (Biswas 2017). However, the Indian constitution identifies 22 scheduled languages excluding English (India, n.d.). Sen and Blatchford (2001) reported about 1600 "mother tongues" and 18 major languages in

India. Although the national language is Hindi, English is prevalent due to India's colonial past. Hindi and English are recognized as official languages by the Department of Official Languages, Government of India (Ministry of Home Affairs, n.d.).

There are six classical languages of Dravidian and Indo-Aryan origin. Hindi is spoken by the largest number of people with its roots in classical Sanskrit and Indo-Aryan descent. The ethnic, religious, and linguistic diversity sets India apart from the rest of the world. The language diversity in India is a manifestation of its long history and culture. The diversity makes India a phenomenon among the major world civilizations in its entirety and peculiarity. Amartya Sen (2004) describes India as an immensely diverse country with many different pursuits, vastly disparate convictions, widely divergent customs, and a veritable feast of viewpoints. Any attempt to talk about the culture of the country, or about its history or contemporary politics, must inescapably involve considerable selection.

Despite so many distinct religious ideologies, attempts have been made to unify Indian brethren. However, conflicts remain along the religious lines. Communal violence has erupted at various times in Indian history. For example, the Hindu–Muslim riots were at their peak during the partition of India in 1947, in the 1980s, the early 1990s, and again in 2002. Parallel with the predominance of deep religious differences across the society, the practice of non-violence was symbolic of the Indian freedom movement led by Mahatma Gandhi. Non-violence is based on Vedic and Yogic principles that emphasize the relationship of humanity with the universe (Klitgaard 1971). In fact, the philosophical life of the Indian Muslim community is influenced by shared traditions of spirituality and Yogic culture. This has evolved into the popular Sufism practices among Muslims. Yogic philosophy is the hallmark of the unity and co-existence of India's multi-ethnic, multilingual, and multi-religious society even today. Social reformer Bipin Chandra Pal (1911) commented that unity of India is neither racial nor religious, neither political nor administrative. It is a peculiar type of unity, which, at best, can be described as cultural. During an early period in history, India fully realized a very deep though complex kind of organic unity that supports all the apparent diversity and multiplicity of our land and its people.

Regardless of the countless complex challenges, India of today is extraordinarily diverse, both ethnically and culturally. It is the sixth largest economy and the youngest country thriving as a global power in the twenty-first century (Central Intelligence Agency 2019). It is also the largest democracy in the world with a population nearing 1.33 billion (World Bank 2016).

It has a well-developed industrial infrastructure and the largest pool of scientists, engineers, and most of the world's information technology professionals. A recent International Monetary Fund (2018) report concludes that India is the fastest growing economy and has lifted millions out of poverty. In recent years, the Government of India has initiated important structural reforms to build infrastructure and catch up with advanced economies in the world. These policies continue to bear fruit with a growth forecast of 7.3% of the GDP in FY 2018–2019 and 7.5% in the FY 2019–2020.

With the aforementioned context, the discussion now sketches how emotional labor has been interwoven and immersed in the country's spiritual, cultural, and governance traditions. First comes a description of the historical evolution of India's public sector from British Colonial times until now. This section also reviews the impact of India's national culture on the public service delivery system. This is followed by a description of the survey data obtained from public servants who work in the education sector. Discussion is provided of how their emotional labor experiences affect their job attitudes. The chapter concludes by discussing the findings in view of the cultural and historical context of the public service system in India.

History of Public Administration

The history of public administration in India can be traced back to 563 BCE. Presumably, the oldest classical literature "Arthashastra" (written in Sanskrit language) in the Indian subcontinent on public administration was written by Acharya Vishnugupta, sometime between 321 and 296 BCE. Contained in Arthashastra are lessons on statecraft, state administration, and effective governance. The lessons of Arthashastra in the practice of public administration are still relevant today (Boesche 2002). At present, public administration in India is suffused with ancient cultural philosophy, colonial heritage, and globalization.

The colonial legacy of India's public administration is largely Weberian: centralized and hierarchical with differentiated ranks. The erstwhile Indian Civil Service (ICS) during British colonial rule was set up as a "steel frame" to serve the colonial masters. Its members belonged to the elites of society. The ICS was organized strictly to fulfill imperialistic goals by exploiting and subjugating the people of India. Segregated from the rest of the citizenry due to their exclusive class and superior background, officers in ICS were selected based on nominations of the directors of the British East India Company and were mostly English. Representation of Indians in the ICS was limited since the British Government wanted to keep control and hence did not allow many Indians to participate and succeed in the civil service selection process. The ICS promoted exclusiveness of the elite and was distant from the people. With no accountability toward people, the ICS primarily existed for the purposes of tax collection and maintaining law and order (Misra 1977; Tummala 1996).

The Indian freedom movement kept its distance from the officials of the ICS due to its imperialistic character. This was so much the case that the Congress party leader and the first Prime Minister of independent India, Pandit Jawaharlal Nehru, asserted that values of ICS violated the public service spirit and needed restructuring to create a new order in independent India. At the time, the reactions to whether ICS should be retained were mixed. One group of leaders in the freedom movement felt that ICS should be demolished and the others felt that the "steel frame" of the administrative system should be retained (Srivastava 1965). As a result, the civil service in post-independence India inherited British governance with the exception that it must function under the parliamentary system and accept the supremacy of the elected political executive. Although imperialistic ICS transitioned into the Indian Administrative Services (IAS), its influence remains to this day.

Several other national centralized services, such as the Indian Police Service (IPS), Indian Forest Service (IFS), and Indian Foreign Service (IFS), gradually came into existence. The IAS was bestowed with the crucial role of meeting the developmental needs of India after independence. However, it remained authoritarian, infected by status-consciousness, and was largely dissociated from the masses. The attitude and behavior of IAS officials left them ill-equipped to pursue the massive development goals of India post-independence. The Indian bureaucracy continued as staid, hierarchical, and regulatory in character.

Following independence, the Government of India came up with many recommendations for changes in the civil service (Tummala 2002). In the wake of federal restructuring and the democratic setup, a planning commission was created in the 1950s. The first five-year plan suggested ways to improve public services and strengthen the district administration at the grassroots level. To cope with the changing nature of administration and recommendations of the five-year plans, the First Administrative Reforms Commission (ARC) was established in 1966 (Mehta 2000). The first ARC report (Government of India 1966, 1) included an appendix that stated its charge:

The Commission will give consideration to the need for ensuring the highest standards of efficiency and integrity in the public services, and for making public administration a fit instrument for carrying out the social and economic policies of the Government and achieving social and economic goals of development, and also one which is responsive to the people.

Furthermore, the ARC went on to add that a new approach is necessary for governmental administration. It asserted that there should be an integration of specialists from outside the hierarchy and that administration should become a direct enabler in the process of policy formulation. The goal of these recommendations was to enhance task performance throughout the bureaucracy. The fundamental emphasis of the first ARC was, essentially, to create the ideal civil servant—one who is a model citizen, ever ready to serve, and one who serves with civility. Innumerable suggestions were made to change the IAS ethos toward service-orientation. However, the implementation of ARC suggestions faced resistance from senior executives in government, who took umbrage with the implication that they were averse to change and disposed to maintaining the status quo. As a result, administrative reforms were incremental in nature, did not alter the power and authority bestowed within the IAS, and did not advance the ethos of service.

In the early 1990s, India was going through an economic depression. Increased public spending had led to a fiscal deficit and external debt. The condition was further exacerbated by the Gulf War and an increase in oil prices. Policies from the Nehruvian era that had been designed to lift India out of poverty had instead left about 330 million people living below the poverty line with plummeting life expectancy. This left India with no choice other than to delicense industrial corridor projects, liberalize imports, and increase foreign investment. As a result, in June 1991, during the leadership of Mr. P. V. Narasimha Rao, the then Prime Minister, India embarked on a new liberal economic policy, easing the control of government and giving more autonomy to the private sector and to entrepreneurs. While the new economic policy initially looked promising, it only resulted in adjusting a few control mechanisms. It failed to produce a fundamental social and economic transformation.

Post-liberalization, India made tremendous economic growth, but this progress did not trickle down to the grass roots. Instead, it created huge income gaps between rich and poor. Infrastructure in the key areas of education and health could not touch the poorest. Scholars cited poor quality of governance as the bottleneck that prevented India from moving to the next level of development and growth (Moharir 2000). Amartya Sen, Nobel laureate in economics, echoed the failure of inadequate investment in human capital by successive governments in India (1998). Sen points out that even after fifty years of independence, half the adults in India remain illiterate and two-thirds of women cannot read or write. Compared to other East and Southeast Asian countries, India's human capital growth trajectory lagged. He faults reformist leaders for failing to acknowledge how literacy and other forms of social achievement provide opportunities for shared, participatory processes that will contribute to India's economic expansion. Despite the fact that India has raised its overall rate of economic growth, a large part of Indian society remains excluded from economic opportunities and participation.

As the post-liberal economy transitioned to the neo-liberal era, the need for restructuring the civil service was obvious. Neoliberalism served as an interface between the state and the citizen and demanded improved accountability, transparency, and an entrepreneurial and customer-oriented culture in public service delivery. The advent of globalization and information technology increased pressure on the Government of India for revamping the civil service structure and culture. The need for self-governance, decentralization, and community development was clearly defined across various levels of the administrative milieu. The Government of India established the Second Administrative Reforms Commission in 2005 to cope with market changes and to suggest measures for a proactive, responsive, sustainable, and accountable administration at all levels of the Government. Fifteen reports were drafted by the second commission, providing guidelines for transforming governance in India (Department of Administrative Reforms n.d.). Out of the fifteen reports, the recommendations of four of them were central to the reforms needed for twenty-first-century India. Their topics include (1) the right to information as a master key to good governance, (2) organizational restructuring of the government, (3) refurbishing personnel administration, and (4) governance built on a citizen-centric model. These are described below.

1. The Right to Information as a Master Key to Good Governance. This report led to the Right to Information Act of 2005, a pathbreaking legislation (Second Administrative Reforms Commission 2006). It was a paradigm shift from the colonial time's Official Secrets Act 1923, which denied access to information for the public. The commission recommended that implementation of the Act would be a harbinger of a new

era of transparency, responsibility, accountability, and participatory democracy. The Prime Minister of India at the time, Dr. Manmohan Singh, said that civil servants must see the Right to Information Act as instrumental in improving the government–citizen interface. This, he argued, would result in a caring and effective government for our people.

2. Organizational Restructuring of the Government. This report highlighted the need for core principles of reinventing the government. The recommendations in this report included decentralization to state and local government, infrastructure and human development, separation of policy making from execution, citizen–customer orientation, and appropriate delegation of responsibilities.

3. Refurbishing Personnel Administration. This report suggested that the civil service in India is not yet prepared to keep pace with a competitive and dynamic economy. It argued for a culture of meritocracy, where promotions would be based on performance evaluations rather than on non-job-related factors. Accordingly, the report included specific recommendations for reforms needed in the recruitment, training, and performance appraisal system within the civil service.

4. Governance Built on a Citizen-Centric Model. During India's struggle for freedom, Mahatma Gandhi epitomized the central philosophy of the "customer being the most important visitor in our premises" (Second Administrative Reforms Commission 2009, Master 17). Underpinning this philosophy, the Commission issued a report, *Citizen Centric Administration—The Heart of Governance*. This report emphasized several barriers to efficient delivery of public services, and one of the most important among them is attitudinal problems of the public servants. Specifically, the report recommended key issues to address if citizen-centric administration is to be achieved. These include strengthening citizen-centric decision-making, creating citizen charters, setting up consultative mechanisms for receiving suggestions, and ensuring greater representativeness of the community in the conceptualization and execution of policies and programs.

Although seven decades have passed since India achieved independence from British colonial rule, the dream of civil service reform is yet to be realized. In a recent statement, policy analyst Yamini Aiyar (2018) wrote that India's bureaucracy needs to look beyond the rules to institutionalize a new culture of trust and deliberation. She refers to Prime Minister

Modi's statement that India's bureaucracy is a nineteenth-century administrative system, struggling to manage a twenty-first-century economy with eighteenth-century laws. Building a twenty-first-century bureaucracy requires changing the frame of the current debate on reforms. It requires moving beyond rules and procedures to a focus on institutionalizing a culture of trust and deliberation. For too long, there has been a trust deficit between the citizens and the bureaucracy.

Recent interest in civil service restructuring has, once again, spurred the debate on the need for changing the recruitment process and in-service training systems. However, the debate on recognizing bureaucracy as a social entity has been largely ignored. This has led to a willful disregard for the fact that norms and culture play a significant role in shaping bureaucratic behavior and subsequent government performance (Mangla 2015). Unless there is a fundamental change in the underlying norms and culture in which the civil service system is embedded, transformation at the grassroots level in the civil service is a far-fetched reality. Indian historian Ramachandra Guha (2017) argues that in no other democracy do generalists so comprehensively corner the top jobs at the higher levels of administration. He criticizes the current system, which advantages those who achieved high scores on entry-level examinations decades ago. He argues that officeholders should have the skills to perform their current job, not the entry-level job they were hired into when their careers began.

Regardless of the recommendations of multiple commissions, successive governments have failed to address civil service reforms. Citizens perceive civil servants as wooden, inflexible, self-perpetuating, and inward looking. The trust deficit is high between citizen and government. There has hardly been any foundational improvement in the public service work culture and there are no meaningful guidelines on how to perform work effectively. Consequently, the attitude of a civil servant is one of indifference and insensitivity to the needs of citizens. The majority of the citizens are not satisfied with the delivery of need-based services (Joshi 2013).

This raises two key questions: What is the commonly held notion of public service work in twenty-first-century India, considering that it fails to serve the needs of its citizens? And what does it take to perform it well? Analysis of attitudes and behaviors of public servants in relation to the citizen taxpayer is important in a democratic and diverse nation like India. Underpinning the norms of gender, identity, and national culture in modern India, this study sheds light on emotive aspects of public service work, referred to as "emotional labor," and how it impacts satisfaction, burnout, and personal fulfillment while performing the public service job.

National Culture, Emotion, and Public Service Delivery

Prior research suggests that the culture of a nation affects every aspect of human behavior (Christie et al. 2003; Javidan et al. 2006). Cultural expressions through arts, music, and literature are integral to the well-being and enrichment of human life. Since times immemorial, cultural influences were visible in human desires, frustrations, ambitions, and freedoms alike.

Cultural foundations account for major differences in work ethic, responsibility, entrepreneurialism, risk propensity, and dynamic management of human behavior (Fukuyama 1995; Sen 2004). A nation's culture is defined as software of the mind and it is based on the values, beliefs, and assumptions learned in early childhood, all of which distinguish one group of people from the other (Hofstede 1984). Culture is embedded deeply in the everyday life of people and is relatively impervious to change. Such influences frame the cultural conditioning of a society and are continuously transferred from generation to generation.

In cross-cultural psychology, Western and Eastern cultures are treated dichotomously with opposing value systems (Nakamura 1964). Western cultures, such as the USA and Germany, are considered highly individualistic, and people value autonomy in work and personal life. The self-construal s of individuals from Western cultures are independent from others and shaped by a focus on personal needs and desires. In contrast, Eastern cultures, such as India, Japan, and China, are collectivistic and value the interdependent "self." Persons in these cultures prioritize interpersonal harmony and see "self" in relation to others (Singelis et al. 1995; Markus and Kitayama 1991). As described by Nakamura (1964), the cultures of both the "oriental" and the "occidental" are diverse, with each one being extremely complex. Each is a composite formed from a range of narrower concepts.

Widely used in cross-cultural studies, Hofstede's (2010) five cultural dimensions, applied to any nation's workforce behavior, are power distance, individualism-collectivism, masculinity-femininity, uncertainty avoidance, and long-term vs. short-term orientation. Power distance is the extent to which the less powerful member in any organization of a country accepts that it is normal for power to be distributed unequally. In power distant societies, hierarchy and inequality are the norms. On Hofstede's scale, China (80) and India (77) scored the highest in power distance with Japan (54) and the USA (40) falling far lower. Next on Hofstede's scale is the dimension of individualism versus collectivism. Individualistic societies are those in which the interest of an individual prevails over the interest of a group. In contrast, collectivist societies are those in which interest of the group prevails over the interest of an individual. Hofstede (2010) found that the USA (91) was ranked highest on individualism followed far behind by India (48), Japan (46), and China (20).

Hofstede's scale also touches on masculinity versus femininity, which describes the dominant gender role patterns in understanding gender equality in society. Masculine cultures value ambition, performance, and assertiveness. Clear gender roles are the norms in masculine cultures, which prize decisiveness. Conversely, feminine cultures endorse beauty, nurturance, and aesthetics and gender roles are more ambiguous. Japan (95) scored highest on masculinity, followed by China (66), the USA (62), and India (56). The fourth dimension on Hofstede's scale is uncertainty avoidance. It is the extent to which members of a culture are risk averse and feel threatened by ambiguity and unknown situations. Japan (92) ranks highest on uncertainty avoidance, followed far behind by the USA (46), India (40), and China (30). The last dimension is long-term versus short-term orientation. Long-term-oriented cultures look toward the future and value perseverance, while short-term-oriented cultures give importance to the past and present and focus on quick results. Japan (88) and China (87) rate highest on long-term orientation, followed far behind by India (51) and the USA (26).

Likewise, the GLOBE study (House et al. 2004) identified differences in leadership styles among managers in Western and Eastern cultures. Indian culture rated highly on team oriented and humane leadership behavior, while China, Japan, and South Korea rated highly on self-protective and autonomous leadership behavior. Likewise, Indian culture, compared to Western (USA, Canada, Europe, and Latin America excluding Scandinavian countries) is less performance oriented and more participative.

As useful as Hofstede's and House's classifications are for understanding multifaceted cultures within and across nations, the categories are too simplistic to capture the deeper dynamics of the ways of feeling and thinking of people from the East or West. There are many variations of culture, just as there are many sub-cultural dimensions unique to each country.

Local cultures differ from nation to nation. For example, Singh, Zhao, and Hu (2005) analyzed the Web site content for three countries: Japan, China, and India. They found a considerable variation of values within these three Asian cultures. For instance, China and Japan were higher in collectivistic and family values in comparison with India. Masculinity was more a prominent value in India and Japan than in China.

Similarly, studies have shown that Indian culture is more argumentative and dialogue oriented than in its East Asian counterparts, such as China, Japan, and South Korea. Additionally, due to the historical, religious, and philosophical foundations of centuries-old systems, the cultural frame is more visible and dominant in the East than in the West. East Asian countries like China, Japan, and South Korea are heavily influenced by Confucianism. The family unit is central to Confucians. While these countries embraced modern science and technology as the means for progress in the twenty-first century, the underlying Confucian faith drives the ethical basis and mutual trust in interpersonal relationships. It drives a belief in education and hard work. In this regard, Indian culture is similar to other Asian countries.

Indians trace their roots in Vedic philosophical traditions. According to the Vedic worldview, the world order is a part of eternal cosmos. This view advocates the belief that life is an illusion, Maya, and the only pursuit worth chasing is spiritual enlightenment through inner transformation. The personal life is not just one but a succession of many lives existing repeatedly in limitless time. For Indians, an individual phenomenon is insignificant and the idea of collective oneness with the universal is foremost. Time is cyclical, and opportunities never end but are recurring. Success or failure in any endeavor is attributable to one's Karma, and the events in this life are pre-determined by our actions in past lives. Such a worldview in India dominates the work ethic, trade, and business.

Underpinning stark cultural differences between India and the West, Sen (2005) uses three distinct approaches to describe how the West views India: curatorial, exoticist, and magisterial. The West's view has emerged mainly due to India's colonial past and lingers still. Of the three, the curatorial approach is the most diverse yet comprehensive in assimilating the intellectual and cultural aspects of India. The exoticist view is narrowly concerned with the wondrous aspects embedded in spirituality. The magisterial view sees India mainly as a territory with a colonial history and imperialistic past. These approaches have resulted in a distinct image of India, with increasing emphasis on the arcane non-material (spiritual wonders) aspects. The rationalistic perspective that accounts for India's achievements in mathematics, science, and analytical pursuits is diminished when this point of view is used.

Likewise, Western perceptions of how emotion is framed in India are shallow. Lynch (1990) noted that the way people in India lead their emotional lives and their conception of emotions is different from the West. The wisdom of reason over emotion has been central in Western philosophy.

However, the Indian philosophy recognizes reason and emotion as intertwined realities and never distinct from each other.

The language in a culture significantly affects and reflects emotion recognition. Matsumoto and Assar (1992) studied the difference in emotion recognition among Indian college students using Hindi and English languages. They found that expressions of anger, sadness, and fear were recognized more intensely in the English language than in Hindi, with the exception of anger when expressed by women in Hindi. And, sadness among women was more intense in English.

In the English language, the verb "to feel" is central to the expression of any type of emotion, but in Hindi—the official language of India, spoken by more than 50% of all people in India—the expression of emotion has no such equivalent verb. Many Hindi language words, such as "Ullaas" (exuberance, jubilation, glee, fun), evoke an emotion that many English language words do not encompass. Similarly, "Samvedna" (feel, feeling, compassion, sensitivity, condolence) brings to notice many English words; however, none of them encompass the holistic understanding of the nuances associated with the word. The emotions and the essence these Hindi words evoke are far from any equivalent in English. Therefore, emotive expression in the Hindi language is comprehensive of depth and diversity of nuances and has very little in common with English translations. Cross-cultural comparisons of emotive expressions in India, therefore, are necessary for a deeper understanding of the work environment in a globalized world and particularly in the West.

The expression or suppression of emotions is interwoven in a nation's culture (Kitayama, Markus, and Matsumoto 1995). The social dynamic in different cultures creates different situational experiences, which in turn affects how people regulate their emotions. Therefore, one responds to a certain situation with emotions appropriate to one's cultural model. Researchers who emphasize the role of culture in shaping emotive expression anticipate differences in the emotion-based lexicons of various cultures (see, e.g., Averill 1997; Kitayama et al. 2000; Lutz and White 1986; Russell 1991). For example, people living in individualistic and collectivistic cultures respond to emotional cues differently (Markus and Kitayama 1991; Matsumoto 1991). In collectivistic cultures, group norms, harmony, and cooperation are more important than expressing personal emotions. Emotions are experienced and learned during interactive social encounters, are relationship focused, and therefore are controlled in collectivistic cultures (Mesquita and Karasawa 2004; Safdar et al. 2009). While individualistic cultures promote expression of a wide range of emotions, such expression is perceived as good for the individual's well-being and independence. For instance, Wilson et al. (2012) found that school children in the USA were more open to expressing emotions such as anger, sadness, or physical pain than children in India. This is consistent with individualistic cultures promoting emotional expression and collectivistic cultures promoting emotional moderation (Eid and Diener 2009).

Analogous to how cultural norms affect emotive expression, cultural norms also impact the service delivery experience of customers and employees (Chase and Tansik 1983; Winsted 1997). Western cultures expect direct, unambiguous, and explicit communication in a service encounter. In contrast, Asian cultures endorse less verbal communication and stress the quality of interpersonal relations during a service delivery encounter (Knapp et al. 2013; Pan and Schmitt 1996). Translating this to the public service context, Guy et al. (2008) posit that expression of desired emotion and suppression of undesired emotion while performing public service work are necessary to enhance the service delivery experience of citizens. The management of emotion, including non-verbal cues, as well as expression or suppression of emotion, while performing a job is labeled "emotional labor."

It has been well established that emotional labor influences customer interaction and service delivery (Grandey et al. 2005; Hochschild 1983). But, a discussion of emotional labor is incomplete without highlighting the idiosyncratic cultural influences within a country. Emotional labor requires that workers suppress their private feelings in order to show "desirable" job-related emotion. Unlike physical work, emotional labor is "invisible" and not measurable in the way that number-of-widgets-produced can be counted. Jobs that require emotional labor have three distinct categories in common: First, they require face-to-face or voice-to-voice contact with the public; second, they require workers to manage the emotional state of another person; and third, they allow the employer to exercise a degree of control over the emotional activities of employees (Hochschild 1983, 147).

As mentioned earlier in this chapter, ancient cultural traditions and its colonial history have a major influence on India's public service delivery system (United Nations Development Program 2015). However, the nation's development needs are redefining the public service landscape. The Weberian style of bureaucratic behavior is no longer acceptable. Citizens are not ready to accept complacent bureaucratic behavior. The need for relational, caring, and emotive behavior is strongly pronounced and is inevitable. Today's India demands a responsive public administration, which is empathic and nurturing (Stivers 1995). The diminishing awe once inspired by the public servant of yesteryear is perceived now as indifferent and insensitive to the needs of the citizens.

In a joint initiative by Government of India and the United Nations Development Program, a program to strengthen human resource management has been developed. Working jointly, the project developed a civil service competency dictionary to facilitate the transition from a rule-based to a competency-based public administration (Government of India UNDP 2014). There are four main competencies listed in the dictionary, namely: ethos, ethics, equity, and efficiency. The main competencies are divided into subgroups, and in them, there is emphasis on the emotive competencies needed for efficient public service delivery. Primary among these are empathy, self-awareness, and self-control. For example, emotive skills included under empathy are the following: recognizes body language, facial expression, and tone of voice to understand the unspoken message; and recognizes unspoken thoughts, feelings, and concerns. Other subgroups include additional emotive competencies such as:

- public servant should have the ability to pick up signals when others are not feeling comfortable and display consideration;
- understands both what is being said by a person and underlying reasons for the emotional state of the person;
- understands and appreciates others' feelings and concerns;
- probes to understand people's unspoken issues, thoughts, and feelings;
- makes inferences that go beyond the explicitly stated content and emotion;
- demonstrates empathy by correctly understanding reactions or emotions of others;
- and encourages others to read deeper into others' emotions by providing practical tips.

Likewise, emotive competencies enlisted in the subgroups of self-awareness and self-control behavior include:

- aware of own feelings and emotions;
- aware of the connection between own feelings and the impact on one's own actions and performance;
- resists the temptation to act impulsively;
- remains calm during stressful situations;
- aware of how one's emotions and actions impact others;
- conducts oneself rationally even under strong internal emotions;
- and calms others during stressful situations.

Even though emotive competencies are a significant part of the civil service competency dictionary, there is no mention of explicit "emotional labor" requirements of public service work and in what ways it is different in Indian culture. To address this lacuna, this study uses the public service context to untangle emotional labor among public servants and reveal how it is unique in the Indian setting. It brings attention to the nuances of citizen-centric administration. If not comprehensive, this study is at least the first step to understand the intricateness of emotional labor experiences rooted in a remarkably distinct public service culture.

The Confluence of Gender, Identity, Culture, and Emotion Work

Emotive expression and suppression among public servants in India are entwined in its ancient culture, colonial past, and contemporary globalization influences. At present, Western influence is stronger and more visible than ever before among the youth and India's middle class. In the Vedic system, roles of men and women were not inferior to each other. Women participated equally in political and intellectual pursuits. The intellectual argumentative tradition was not the preserve of men only, but rather traversed the boundaries of gender, class, and caste. However, Muslim rule for many centuries and later British colonization set divisions between genders, castes, and religions. Specifically, the gender culture division was about bolstering male power and subjugating women. The Indian family system considered the man to be the breadwinner, and the woman to be the householder. Unlike American men, who usually see their actions dependent on their personal and individual choices, Indian men see their actions as determined by the social group, which also affects their family life (Bellah et al. 1985; Derne 1995). However, these trends are changing, mostly in urban and semi-urban areas. Women are contesting men's entitlement to power and seek to discover their identity. Indian women, at present, bear a conflicting identity, because it is interwoven in the shifting boundaries of modern and traditional cultures. The identity conflicts and struggles of modern Indian women are depicted in a recently released courtroom drama film titled "Pink" (Sircar 2016). The essence of the film is translated thus:

Start a journey to find yourself, why are you depressed? Start walking, even time is searching for your existence. The chains that cuff you, don't think of them as your clothes. Melt these chains and make them your weapon. Why are you in such a state, when your character is pure? Those sinners don't have a right to examine or judge you. Burn and incinerate the web of atrocity and social norms around you. You aren't the holy flame of worship, but a firelight of anger. Fly your scarf like a flag, even the sky will shake. And if your scarf falls, it will cause an earthquake. (Ghazi 2016)

Such are the fault lines of struggle for identity and equality among women in India at present. The complex issues associated with emotions, gender, culture, and identity affect the way emotional labor is shaped for public servants. Studying emotional labor among public servants, most of whom are women working as public-school teachers in this study, is a complex issue. A deeper analysis of nuances associated with the experience of emotional labor of public-school teachers is needed, and admittedly, a quantitative survey to untangle the subject of emotions in Indian public service is cursory at its best. Nevertheless, this study is a beginning for understanding emotional labor among public servants in India.

The Study

This study highlights the emotional labor experience of public-school teachers and its impact on the outcomes of job satisfaction, burnout, and personal fulfillment. This section is organized as follows: First, a description of the public-school teaching environment in India is provided in the context of the emotional labor requirements of public service work. Second, demographic characteristics of the sample are presented. Third, a description of emotional labor variables is shown along with the structural equation modeling. Finally, the discussion of findings contextualized in the Indian public service environment is presented.

Public-School Teaching and Emotional Labor

The post-colonial status of education and literacy in India was grim. After independence from British rule, India found itself besieged with illiteracy and lack of public education. The 1951 census of India reported that only 9% of women and 27% of men were literate (Ministry of Home Affairs 2011). In subsequent decades after independence, some progress was made in terms of increasing school enrollment. In 1986, the first national policy on education was drafted and it stressed that universal education was fundamental if India was to undergo social transformation (Ministry of Human Resource Development 2018). More recently, two policies, the Sarva Shiksha Abhiyan in 2001 and the Right to Education Act in 2009, brought a significant rise in enrollment as well as an increase in the quality of education. Apart from an increase in the number of children going to school, parents who are poor and illiterate now understand why education is mandatory in the modern society.

Despite the positive picture with regard to student enrollment and parent's willingness to send their children to school, the situation is appalling in terms of working conditions for the school teachers. One-room schoolhouses, fifty to sixty students per teacher, and one teacher teaching multiple grades are not unusual. In the rural areas, schools do not have basic facilities such as chalkboards, toilets, drinking water, and enclosed buildings. In addition, many schools are understaffed, which results in poor quality of teaching and high teacher absenteeism. Mooij (2008) reported low motivation, dissatisfaction, and ambiguous feelings among public-school teachers with their profession and work environment.

Public-school teaching is highly centralized, with almost no decision-making power given to teachers either collectively or individually. Moreover, senior officials in government frequently fault teacher's work and rarely give any words of appreciation. There is no system in place to motivate teachers to work more effectively, nor are there structured teacher training sessions to strengthen teaching based on the student needs (Cheney et al. 2008). To make matters worse, the performance appraisal system is left to a simple set of measurable indicators that put no emphasis on measuring the qualitative aspects of teacher-student quality of interaction and classroom practices. Constructive feedback is rarely given to teachers and there is almost no accountability. The paradox is that the teachers are simultaneously controlled and neglected (Majumdar and Mooij 2012).

The public-school education system is largely based on the traditional public administration processes that were described earlier in this chapter. The system is highly centralized and bureaucratic, while the decentralization and delegation prescribed under New Public Management reforms are missing. To put it bluntly, Sharma and Jyoti (2006) report that job satisfaction among public-school teachers is abysmal. The reasons they cite for low job satisfaction include the behavior of superiors, their colleagues' behavior, social perceptions about their job, low pay, and lack of promotion and recognition. Likewise, Shukla and Trivedi (2008) report that teachers feel physically and emotionally exhausted and suffer high levels of burnout. To quote from the study:

They think that their job has taken up all the energy and 'life' which was theirs and so they feel drained and used up. They feel ineffective in their job environment and are losing confidence in themselves. They have apprehensions about any new assignment or project given to them and feel they will never be able to complete it properly. This has developed a sense of alienation and escapism in them and they have started working in isolation; maintaining a psychological distance from everyone related to their job. (330)

Teachers use various emotional labor strategies to bring effectiveness into their teaching delivery (Hargreaves 1995) and studies suggest that emotional labor demands are the primary cause of burnout and dissatisfaction among school teachers (Yin et al. 2013; Zembylas and Shutz 2009). Additional factors that contribute to increased emotional labor in the Indian context is poor school infrastructure, a centralized education system embedded in a high power distance culture, and a high teacher-student ratio. For these reasons, it is expected that public-school teachers in India will experience intense emotional labor in their work. This study sheds light on emotion work of public-school teachers and its impact on their job satisfaction, burnout, and personal fulfillment. The uniqueness of Indian culture and its public service work context adds to the environmental milieu within which teachers' emotional labor, gender, and cultural identity intertwine.

Demographic Characteristics

Table 12.1 represents the demographic characteristics of respondents in the study. About 206 public service workers completed the survey, and most of them work in the public education sector. The age, gender, public service experience, and level of educational attainment are presented. About 80% of the survey respondents are between 30 and 50 years old, and about 12% are younger than 30 years. The clear majority of respondents are women (90%) and most hold master's degrees (77%). To conclude, the sample is comprised of middle-aged, highly educated women teachers, working in the public education sector in India.

Occupational characteristics of the survey respondents are shown in Table 12.2. The categories are not mutually exclusive, which means that out of the 206 respondents, a few also wear multiple hats, perhaps as educators who work in administration, planning, health care, human resource management, information and communication technology, public works, and so forth. None of the participants come from high-risk jobs such as firefighters or disaster response. Similarly, no one among the survey respondents has experience in the technical fields of engineering or in the manufacturing sector.

Table 12.1   Demographic characteristics: India

	Frequency	Percent
Age		
Less than 30	25	12.1
30–39 years	80	38.8
40–49 years	78	37.9
50–59 years	19	9.2
60 or more	1	0.5
N/A	3	1.5
Gender		
Female	184	89.3
Male	21	10.2
N/A	1	0.5
Public service experience		
Less than 10	35	17.0
10–19 years	18	8.7
20–29 years	4	2.0
30 or more	0	0.0
N/A	149	72.3
Educational level		
Less than high school	0	0.0
High school graduate	0	0.0
Some college	0	0.0
2-year associate degree	1	0.5
College graduate	26	12.6
Some graduate school	8	3.9
Master's degree	159	77.2
Law degree (J.D., LL.B.)	4	1.9
Doctorate degree (Ph.D., M.D., Ed.D., etc.)	3	1.5
Other (please specify)	0	0.0
N/A	5	2.4

Emotional Labor Variables

Survey participants responded to the three dimensions of emotional labor: deep acting, emotive capacity, and pretending expression. The three dependent variables (see Table 12.3) are burnout, job satisfaction, and personal fulfillment. All the emotional labor variables and the dependent variables reported a Cronbach's alpha level above 0.60, which denotes an acceptable level of inter-item consistency. Among emotional labor variables, the Cronbach's alpha for pretending expression and emotive capacity dimensions is slightly lower (0.60 and 0.62) than it is for deep acting (0.75). This may have resulted because the present context in India is in transition. Some women come from educated, open-minded families and are more assertive

Table 12.2 Occupational characteristics: India

Occupation	Frequency	Percent
1. Administration	1	0.5
2. Community development/neighborhood services	0	0.0
3. Engineering, manufacturing, or production	0	0.0
4. Education	206	94.1
5. Disaster response	0	0.0
6. Finance or accounting	0	0.0
7. Firefighter	0	0.0
8. Health care	3	1.4
9. Housing	0	0.0
10. Human resource management	3	1.4
11. Information and communication	3	1.4
12. Law enforcement	0	0.0
13. Military	0	0.0
14. Public relations	1	0.5
15. Planning	1	0.5
16. Public works: streets, sanitation, utilities	1	0.5
17. Purchasing	0	0.0
18. Recreation and parks	0	0.0
19. Research and development	0	0.0
20. Social services	0	0.0
21. Transportation	0	0.0
22. Support services (e.g., plants and equipment maintenance)	0	0.0
23. Other	0	0.0

Table 12.3 Descriptive statistics and Cronbach's alpha: India

	Mean	SD	Cronbach's alpha
Emotive capacity	5.66	1.00	0.624
Pretending expression	5.15	1.32	0.604
Deep acting	5.10	1.23	0.750
Job satisfaction	5.33	1.21	0.727
Burnout	3.63	1.76	0.765
Personal fulfillment	5.94	0.97	0.683

about their emotive expression while others belong to patriarchal, conservative families and perhaps they interpret pretending and hiding emotions differently. On the other hand, the alpha level for deep acting is markedly higher, so perhaps the dynamic social context and ancient spiritual traditions in India made women capable of creating and developing certain emotional experiences at a deeper level.

The three items in the pretending expression variable are "I hide my true feelings so as to appear pleasant at work"; "In my job I act confident and self-assured, regardless of what I actually feel"; "I wear a mask in order to deal with clients/customers in an appropriate way." "I hide my true feelings so as to appear pleasant at work."

Likewise, the three items which measure the deep acting variable are "I try to actually experience the emotions that I must show to the clients and customers"; "I work hard to actually feel the emotions that I need to show to clients/customers"; "I work at developing the feelings inside of me that I need to show to clients/customers." Based on the mean scores, the teachers in their job do not interpret wearing an emotive mask or hiding their true feelings as consistently as they interpret working hard to create certain emotional expressions appropriate for the job.

Results

This study uses structural equation modeling (SEM) to test the relationship between the emotional labor variables (emotive capacity, pretending expression, and deep acting) and the dependent variables included in this study (job satisfaction, burnout, and personal fulfillment).

In this exploratory study, the relationships that are statistically significant at $p < 0.05$ are treated as notable and highlighted in the path diagram in Fig. 12.1.

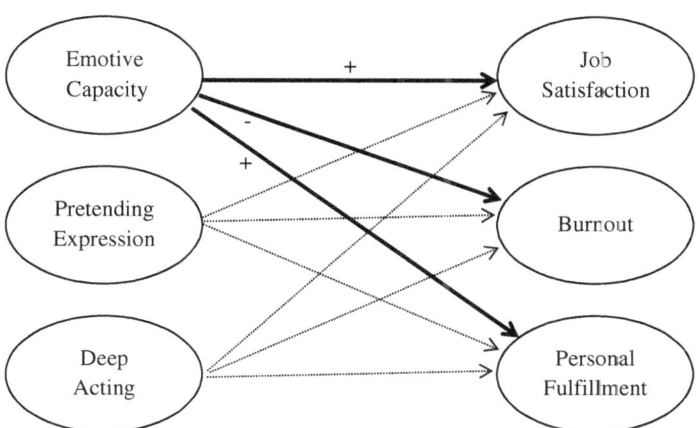

Fig. 12.1 Path diagram for India

Interpretation of Findings

The findings are summarized in terms of the relationship between the independent and dependent variables.

Emotive Capacity

The SEM results shown in Table 12.4 suggest that emotive capacity is positively related to two outcome variables: job satisfaction ($p = 0.000$) and personal fulfillment ($p = 0.000$). In addition, emotive capacity has an inversely significant relationship with the third outcome variable burnout ($p = 0.000$). These results are consistent with prior research on emotional labor in public service with respect to emotive capacity (Guy et al. 2008). The items for the emotive capacity variable include "I am good at expressing at how I feel," "I am good at getting people to calm down," and "In my job I am good at dealing with emotional issues."

Pretending Expression

Pretending expression measures the aspect of emotive behavior when workers suppress their true feelings in order to display whatever emotion is appropriate for the task at hand. This study finds no significant relationship between emotive pretending and outcome variables. The items measuring emotive pretending are "I hide my true feelings so as to appear pleasant at work," "In my job I act confident and self-assured regardless of how I actually feel," and "I wear a 'mask' in order to deal with clients/customers in an appropriate way."

Table 12.4 Structural model results: India

Hypothesized paths	Coefficients	p-value
Emotive capacity → Job satisfaction	0.571*	0.000
Emotive capacity → Burnout	−0.546*	0.000
Emotive capacity → Personal fulfillment	0.799*	0.000
Pretending expression → Job satisfaction	−0.076	0.424
Pretending expression → Burnout	0.124	0.143
Pretending expression → Personal fulfillment	0.074	0.399
Deep acting → Job satisfaction	−0.020	0.838
Deep acting → Burnout	0.822	0.371
Deep acting → Personal fulfillment	−0.050	0.632

Model fit: $\chi^2 = 313.299$ (df = 142), CFI = 0.794, RMSEA = 0.087, SRMR = 0.098

Deep Acting

Table 12.4 shows that none of the three path coefficients relating deep acting to outcome variables achieve significance. Items for deep acting are: "I try to actually experience the emotions that I must show to the clients/customers," "I work hard to actually feel the emotions that I need to show to the clients/customers," and "I work at developing the feelings inside of me that I need to show to the clients/customers."

Discussion

This chapter examines the effect of emotional labor of public-school teachers, most of whom are women, on their level of job satisfaction, burnout, and personal fulfillment. The objective of this chapter is to understand the direct effect of three dimensions of emotional labor—emotive capacity, pretending, and deep acting—on three job outcomes: job satisfaction, burnout, and personal fulfillment. The method utilized to analyze this relationship was structural equation modeling. Findings reveal that emotive capacity has a significant effect on all three outcome variables. It is positively related to job satisfaction and personal fulfillment and negatively related to burnout. Neither Pretending nor Deep Acting shows a significant relationship to outcome variables.

The history of public administration in India is influenced by its rich cultural heritage and colonial past. An analysis of India's national culture elucidates the current public service environment, which is a result of the multicultural ideologies embedded within it. The post-colonial impact of Weberian bureaucracy has influenced the service delivery approach for public servants. The national culture permeates the service delivery system with high power distance and uncertainty avoidance on the one hand, and a sense of collectivism, harmony, and group-supporting behaviors on the other. The high power distance is visible in the public-school teaching environment too, which is centralized with almost no decision-making powers given to school teachers even though a culture of collectivism behooves the teachers to build a sense of engagement, openness, and relationship with the community.

Despite acknowledgment of the importance of education and the relative progress over the last few decades, most of the teachers are demotivated and dissatisfied in their profession. They complain about a lack of open feedback mechanisms, no appreciation from superiors, and poor infrastructure and working conditions. As a result, teachers experience a high level of burnout. Additionally, the changing nature of teaching in government schools now is putting a heavy emotional burden on teachers. The expectation is that a good teacher is supposed to not only teach well but also be affectionate toward children, satisfy their needs, and be a role model. They should be dedicated to the teaching profession and perform well even in difficult situations, which means children should be able to trust and have confidence in their teachers.

These results illustrate that the nature of a teaching job in India's public-school system is highly emotion laden. Moreover, it is culture specific and enmeshed with gender identification. The absence of a relationship between authentic emotive expression as measured by Deep Acting and the outcome variables may be an indicator that work conditions place such constraints on teachers that the usual dynamics between emotional labor and work outcomes are absent. In other words, teachers' efforts to emotively engage students in an authentic way may be overshadowed by work conditions. India's collectivist culture, which values group norms and being socially supportive, may create a feeling of oneness within the community. However, the impact of power distance, poor working conditions, and lack of appreciation by their superiors is taking a toll. This reflects the changing societal perceptions about the teaching profession. It is as if teaching is not as important a job as it used to be in ancient times in India, when teachers were given the status of a "Guru" (teachers are equivalent to God).

The results for emotive capacity are as anticipated. Collectivist norms provide social security and support, which results in better emotion management abilities among the teachers. This is reflected in the positive relationship between emotive capacity with job satisfaction and with personal fulfillment. However, there is a gender undertone associated with this finding. The general belief is that women are better at understanding and expressing emotions, so they are expected to have higher levels of emotive capacity and to experience less burnout. The data show, in fact, that higher levels of emotive capacity are related to lower burnout.

In sum, the diversion of gender role orientations in India, especially now that more women are participating in the workplace, is creating additional emotional burdens for women. India's history and diverse culture have a built-in environment that structures women's identity around the qualities of relatedness, cooperation, and emotionality (Prasad 2003; Thomas and Sudhakar 1994). Thus, women teachers have agency to build emotive connections with their students, as the results illustrate, but the work creates a stressful, demotivating environment. In the future, exploring the nuances of emotional labor and gender identity in India is an exciting area of research for study.

Conclusion

Regardless of India's tumultuous colonial past and the deeper impressions of it in the culture and lifestyle of Indian people, India of today is looking ahead as a global frontrunner. India has been a success story in sustaining democracy within a nation with a huge population, multiple religions, and linguistic diversity. India has successfully traversed the path of modernity, and it was not possible without an extraordinary will of the people of India along with the democratic and administrative state. The administrative state in India, although functioning under the garb of modernity, has a deeper aesthetic, cultural, and emotional overtone of thousands of years of history, creating a culture that unifies the nation.

An all-encompassing thought captures the aesthetic and emotional character of India. It is visible in a recent effort by the Ministry of External Affairs when it engaged in a project to bring singers from 124 countries together to sing "Vaishnav Jana to Tene Kahiye Je" to pay homage to Mahatma Gandhi on his 150th birth anniversary (Khurana 2019). It is a devotional poem written by the Gujarat poet Narsinh Mehta in the fifteenth century and was included in Mahatma Gandhi's daily prayer sessions. The English translation goes like this:

> Call those people Vaishnavas who
> Feel the pain of others,
> Help those who are in misery,
> But never let self-conceit enter their mind.

> They respect the entire world,
> Do not disparage anyone,
> Keep their words, actions and thoughts pure,
> The mother of such a soul is blessed.

> They see all equally, renounce craving,
> Respect other women as their own mother,
> Their tongue never utters false words,
> Their hands never touch the wealth of others.

They do not succumb to worldly attachments,
They are firmly detached from the mundane,
They are enticed by the name of God (Rama),
All places of pilgrimage are embodied in them.

They have forsaken greed and deceit,
They stay afar from lust and anger,
Narsi says: I'd be grateful to meet such a soul,
Whose virtue liberates their entire lineage. (Natarajan 1996, 100)

Therefore, a sense of commitment among public-school teachers for the public service is not surprising, nor is the high emotional load. The results in the study reinforce the perspective that India at present is confronting multiple ideologies and the changing nature of administration. This study opens a door to see through the emotive aspects of public service work in India. However, a qualitative study in the future is a worthy endeavor, for it can explore the deeper dimensions of the emotional lives of public servants while taking into consideration India's cultural and historical background.

References

Aiyar, Yamini. 2018. "Look Beyond Rules to Reform India's Bureaucracy". *Hindustan Times*. https://www.hindustantimes.com/opinion/look-beyond-rules-to-reform-the-bureaucracy/story-9UNqqyjR8MNNJjEVo00350.html. Updated June 1, 2018.

Averill, James R. 1997. "The Emotions: An Integrative Approach." In *Handbook of Personality Psychology*, edited by Robert Hogan, John Johnson, and Stephen Briggs, 513–41. Amsterdam, Netherlands: Elsevier. https://doi.org/10.1016/B978-0-12-134645-4.X5000-8.

Banerjee, Abhijit, and Lakshmi Iyer. 2005. "History, Institutions, and Economic Performance: The Legacy of Colonial Land Tenure Systems in India." *American Economic Review* 95 (4): 1190–213.

Bellah, Robert N., Richard Madsen, William M. Sullivan, Ann Swidler, and Steven M. Tipton. 1985. *Habits of the Heart: Individualism and Commitment in American Life*. Berkeley, CA: University of California Press.

Biswas, Soutik. 2017. "The Man Who 'Discovered' 780 Indian Languages." October 27. https://www.bbc.com/news/world-asia-india-41718082.

Boesche, Roger. 2002. *The First Great Political Realist: Kautilya and His Arthashastra*. Lanham, MD: Lexington Books.

Central Intelligence Agency. 2019. "India Country Overview." *World FactBook*. https://www.cia.gov/library/publications/the-world-factbook/geos/in.html. Updated February 5, 2019.

Chase, Richard B., and David A. Tansik. 1983. "The Customer Contact Model for Organization Design." *Management Science* 29 (9): 1037–50.

Cheney, Douglas, Andrea Flower, and Tran Templeton. 2008. "Applying Response to Intervention Metrics in the Social Domain for Students at Risk of Developing Emotional or Behavioral Disorders." *The Journal of Special Education* 42 (2): 108–26. https://doi.org/10.1177/0022466907313349.

Christie, P. Maria Joseph, Ik-Whan G. Kwon, Philipp A. Stoeberl, and Raymond Baumhart. 2003. "A Cross-Cultural Comparison of Ethical Attitudes of Business Managers: India, Korea and the United States." *Journal of Business Ethics* 46 (3): 263–87.

Department of Administrative Reforms and Administrative Grievances. n.d. *Second Administrative Reforms Commission: Reports.* https://darpg.gov.in/arc-reports. Updated February 13, 2019.

Derné, Steve. 1995. *Culture in Action: Family Life, Emotion, and Male Dominance in Banaras, India.* Albany, NY: SUNY Press.

Eid, Michael, and Ed Diener. 2009. "Norms for Experiencing Emotions in Different Cultures: Inter- and Intranational Differences." In *Culture and Well-Being*, edited by Ed Diener, 169–202. Switzerland: Springer, Dordrecht. https://doi.org/10.1007/978-90-481-2352-0_9.

Fukuyama, Francis. 1995. "I. The Primacy of Culture." *Journal of Democracy* 6 (1): 7–14.

Ghazi, Tanveer. 2016. *Tu Khud Ki Khoj Mein Nikal, Tu Kis Liye Hataash Hai.* (trans: "Start a Journey to Find Yourself, Why are You Depressed?") Accessed February 16, 2019 at https://www.youtube.com/watch?v=YZGfZjAOgs0.

Government of India. 1966. *"Resolution."* New Delhi, India. January 5. Accessed February 7, 2019 at https://darpg.gov.in/sites/default/files/resolution.pdf.

Government of India UNDP. 2014. *Civil Services Competency Dictionary.* Accessed February 16, 2019 at http://persmin.gov.in/otraining/competency%20diction-ary%20for%20the%20civil%20services.pdf.

Grandey, Alicia A., Glenda M. Fisk, Anna S. Mattila, Karen J. Jansen, and Lori A. Sideman. 2005. "Is 'Service with a Smile' Enough? Authenticity of Positive Displays During Service Encounters." *Organizational Behavior and Human Decision Processes* 96 (1): 38–55.

Guha, Ramachandra. 2017. *India After Gandhi: The History of the World's Largest Democracy.* New York, NY: HarperCollins.

Guy, Mary E., Meredith A. Newman, and Sharon H. Mastracci. 2008. *Emotional Labor: Putting the Service in Public Service.* Armonk, NY: M.E. Sharpe.

Hargreaves, David H. 1995. "School Culture, School Effectiveness and School Improvement." *School Effectiveness and School Improvement: An International Journal of Research, Policy and Practice* 6 (1): 23–46.

Hasan, Mushirul. 2005. *India Partitioned: The Other Face of Freedom.* 4th ed. Delhi, India: Roli Books.

Hochschild, Arlie. 1983. *The Managed Heart.* Berkeley, CA: University of California Press.

Hofstede, Geert. 1984. "Cultural Dimensions in Management and Planning." *Asia Pacific Journal of Management* 1 (2): 81–99.

Hofstede, Geert, Gert Jan Hofstede, and Michael Minkov. 2010. *Cultures and Organizations: Software of the Mind.* New York, NY: McGraw Hill.

House, Robert J., Paul J. Hanges, Mansour Javidan, Peter W. Dorfman, and Vipin Gupta, eds. 2004. *Culture, Leadership, and Organizations: The GLOBE Study of 62 Societies.* Thousand Oaks, CA: Sage.

India. n.d. *Constitutional Provisions Relating to Eighth Schedule.* Accessed February 17, 2019 at https://mha.gov.in/sites/default/files/EighthSchedule_19052017.pdf.

International Monetary Fund. 2018. India's Strong Economy Continues to Lead Global Growth. August 8. https://www.imf.org/en/News/Articles/2018/08/07/NA080818-India-Strong-Economy-Continues-to-Lead-Global-Growth.

Javidan, Mansour, Robert J. House, Peter W. Dorfman, Paul J. Hanges, and Mary Sully De Luque. 2006. "Conceptualizing and Measuring Cultures and Their Consequences: A Comparative Review of GLOBE's and Hofstede's Approaches." *Journal of International Business Studies* 37 (6): 897–914.

Joshi, Anuradha. 2013. "Do They Work? Assessing the Impact of Transparency and Accountability Initiatives in Service Delivery." *Development Policy Review* 31: s29–s48.

Kaul, Suvir, ed. 2001. *The Partitions of Memory: The Afterlife of the Division of India.* Delhi, India: Permanent Black.

Khilnani, Sunil. 2016. *Incarnations: A History of India in Fifty Lives.* New York, NY: Farrar, Straus and Giroux.

Khurana, Suanshu. 2019. "An Ode from the World." *The Indian Express,* February 17. https://indianexpress.com/article/world/an-ode-from-the-world-music-gandhi-birthday-music-tribute-global-artists-5383490/.

Kitayama, Suanshu, Hazel Rose Markus, and Hisaya Matsumoto. 1995. "Culture, Self, and Emotion: A Cultural Perspective on 'Self-Conscious' Emotions. In *Self-Conscious Emotions: The Psychology of Shame, Guilt, Embarrassment, and Pride,* edited by J. P. Tangney and K. W. Fischer, 439–64. New York, NY: Guilford Press.

Kitayama, Shinobu, Hazel Rose Markus, and Masaru Kurokawa. 2000. "Culture, Emotion, and Well-Being: Good Feelings in Japan and the United States." *Cognition & Emotion* 14 (1): 93–124.

Klitgaard, Robert E. 1971. "Gandhi's Non-violence as a Tactic." *Journal of Peace Research* 8 (2): 143–53.

Knapp, Mark L., Judith A. Hall, and Terrence G. Horgan. 2013. *Nonverbal Communication in Human Interaction.* Stamford, CT: Cengage Learning.

Lutz, Catherine, and Geoffrey M. White. 1986. "The Anthropology of Emotions." *Annual Review of Anthropology* 15 (1): 405–36.

Lynch, Owen, ed. 1990. *Divine Passions: The Social Construction of Emotion in India.* Berkeley, CA: University of California Press.

Maddison, Angus. 2003. *The World Economy: Historical Statistics*. Paris, France: Organisation for Economic Cooperation and Development (OECD). https://doi.org/10.1787/19900295.

Majumdar, Manabi, and Jos Mooij. 2012. *Education and Inequality in India: A Classroom View*. Abingdon, UK: Routledge.

Mangla, Akshay. 2015. "Bureaucratic Norms and State Capacity in India: Implementing Primary Education in the Himalayan Region." *Asian Survey* 55 (5): 882–908.

Markus, Hazel R., and Shinobu Kitayama.1991. "Culture and the Self: Implications for Cognition, Emotion, and Motivation." *Psychological Review* 98 (2): 224–53. https://doi.org/10.1037/0033-295X.98.2.224.

Matsumoto, David. 1991. "Cultural Influences on Facial Expressions of Emotion." *Southern Journal of Communication* 56 (2): 128–37.

Matsumoto, David, and Manish Assar. 1992. "The Effects of Language on Judgments of Universal Facial Expressions of Emotion." *Journal of Nonverbal Behavior* 16 (2): 85–99.

Mehta, Vinod, ed. 2000. *Reforming Administration in India*. New Delhi, India: Har-Anand Publications.

Mesquita, Batja, and Mayumi Karasawa. 2004. "Self-Conscious Emotions as Dynamic Cultural Processes." *Psychological Inquiry* 15 (2): 161–66.

Ministry of Home Affairs, Government of India. n.d. "Constitutional Provisions: Official Language Related Part-17 of the Constitution of India." Retrieved July 1, 2018. http://www.rajbhasha.nic.in/en/constitutional-provisions.

Ministry of Home Affairs, Government of India. 2011. *Census Digital Library*. Accessed October 5, 2018. http://www.censusindia.gov.in/DigitalLibrary/Archive_home.aspx.

Ministry of Human Resource Development, Department of School Education and Literacy. 2018. *School Education*. http://mhrd.gov.in/rte. Updated May 8, 2018.

Misra, Bankey Bihari. 1977. *The Bureaucracy in India: An Historical Analysis of Development Up to 1947*. Oxford, UK: Oxford University Press.

Moharir, Vasant. 2000. "Education and Training in Public Policy for Developing Countries: Some Perspectives." *Africanus* 30 (1): 7–21.

Mooij, Jos. 2008. "Primary Education, Teachers' Professionalism and Social Class About Motivation and Demotivation of Government School Teachers in India." *International Journal of Educational Development* 28 (5): 508–23.

Nakamura, Hajime. 1964. *Ways of Thinking of Eastern Peoples: India, China, Tibet, Japan*, revised English translation, edited by Philip P. Wiener. Honolulu, HI: East-West Center Press.

Natarajan, Nalini, ed. 1996. *Handbook of Twentieth-Century Literatures of India*. Westport, CT: Greenwood Publishing Group.

Pal, Bipin Chandra. 1911. *The Soul of India: A Constructive Study of Indian Thoughts & Ideals*. Calcutta, India: Choudhury & Choudhury.

Pan, Yigang, and Bernd Schmitt. 1996. "Language and Brand Attitudes: Impact of Script and Sound Matching in Chinese and English." *Journal of Consumer Psychology* 5 (3): 263–77.

Prasad, Anshuman, ed. 2003. *Postcolonial Theory and Organizational Analysis: A Critical Engagement.* New York, NY: Palgrave Macmillan. https://dx.doi.org/10.1057/9781403982292.

Russell, James A. 1991. "Culture and the Categorization of Emotions." *Psychological Bulletin* 110 (3): 426–50. http://dx.doi.org/10.1037/0033-2909.110.3.426.

Safdar, Saba, Wolfgang Friedlmeier, David Matsumoto, Seung Hee Yoo, Catherine T. Kwantes, Hisako Kakai, and Eri Shigemasu. 2009. "Variations of Emotional Display Rules Within and Across Cultures: A Comparison Between Canada, USA, and Japan." *Canadian Journal of Behavioural Science/Revue Canadienne des Sciences du Comportement* 41 (1): 1–10. http://dx.doi.org/10.1037/a0014387.

Second Administrative Reforms Commission. 2006. *Right to Information: Master Key to Good Governance,* June. New Delhi: Government of India. http://unpan1.un.org/intradoc/groups/public/documents/cgg/unpan045200.pdf.

Second Administrative Reforms Commission. 2009. *Citizen Centric Administration: The Heart of Governance,* February. New Delhi, India: Government of India. http://unpan1.un.org/intradoc/groups/public/documents/cgg/unpan045780.pdf.

Sen, Amartya. 1998. "Mortality as an Indicator of Economic Success and Failure." *The Economic Journal* 108 (446): 1–25.

Sen, Amartya. 2004. "How Does Culture Matter." In *Culture and Public Action,* edited by Vijayendra Rao and Michael Walton, 37–58, Stanford, CA: Stanford University Press.

Sen, Amartya. 2005. *The Argumentative Indian: Writings on Indian History, Culture and Identity.* London, UK: Macmillan Publishing.

Sen, Reena, and Peter Blatchford. 2001. "Reading in a Second Language: Factors Associated with Progress in Young Children." *Educational Psychology* 21 (2): 189–202.

Sharma, R. D., and Jeevan Jyoti. 2006. "Job Satisfaction Among School Teachers." *IIMB Management Review* 18 (4): 349–63.

Shukla, Anil, and Tripta Trivedi. 2008. "Burnout in Indian Teachers." *Asia Pacific Education Review* 9 (3): 320–34.

Singelis, Theodore M., Harry C. Triandis, Dharm P.S. Bhawuk, and Michele J. Gelfand. 1995. "Horizontal and Vertical Dimensions of Individualism and Collectivism: A Theoretical and Measurement Refinement." *Cross-Cultural Research* 29 (3): 240–75.

Singh, Nitish, Hongxin Zhao, and Xiaorui Hu. 2005. "Analyzing the Cultural Content of Web Sites: A Cross-National Comparison of China, India, Japan, and US." *International Marketing Review* 22 (2): 129–46.

Sircar, Shoojit. 2016. *Pink.* Accessed February 16, 2019 at https://www.imdb.com/title/tt5571734/.

Srivastava, G. P. 1965. *The Indian Civil Service*. Delhi, India: S. Chand and Company.

Stivers, Camilla. 1995. "The Listening Bureaucrat: Responsiveness in Public Administration." *Public Administration Review* 54 (4): 364–69.

Tharoor, S. 2016. *An Era of Darkness: The British Empire in India*. New Delhi, India: Aleph Book.

Thomas, Sophy, and U. Vindhya Sudhakar. 1994. "Gender Role Orientation and Coping Repertoire of Women in the Management of Military Induced Stress." *Journal of Indian Psychology* 12 (1–2): 49–61.

Tummala, Krishna K. 1996. *Public Administration in India*. Singapore: Allied Publishers. United Nations Development Program. 2015. *Human Development Report*. Accessed February 16, 2019 at http://hdr.undp.org/sites/default/files/2015_human_development_report.pdf.

Tummala, Krishna K. 2002. "Administrative Reform in India." In *Administrative Reform in Developing Nations,* edited by Ali Farazmand, 29–48. Westport, CT: Praeger Publishers.

Wilson, Stephanie L., Vaishali V. Raval, Jennifer Salvina, Pratiksha H. Raval, and Ila N. Panchal. 2012. "Emotional Expression and Control in School-Age Children in India and the United States." *Merrill-Palmer Quarterly* 58 (1): 50–76.

Winsted, Kathryn Frazer. 1997. "The Service Experience in Two Cultures: A Behavioral Perspective." *Journal of Retailing* 73 (3): 337–60.

World Bank. 2016. *India Development Update*. Accessed July 27, 2018. https://data.worldbank.org/country/india.

Yin, Hong-Biao, John Chi Kin Lee, and Zhong-hua Zhang. 2013. "Exploring the Relationship Among Teachers' Emotional Intelligence, Emotional Labor Strategies and Teaching Satisfaction." *Teaching and Teacher Education* 35: 137–45.

Zembylas, Michalinos, and Paul A. Schutz. 2009. "Research on Teachers' Emotions in Education: Findings, Practical Implications and Future Agenda." In *Advances in Teacher Emotion Research*, edited by Paul A. Schutz and Michalinos Zembylas, 367–77. New York, NY: Springer.

13

Republic of Korea

Hyun Jung Lee

The culture of South Korea is rooted in traditional Confucianism but modifications have evolved in response to the country's position in the global economy, international travel and trade, and the global homogenization that accompanies the proliferation of social media. This chapter describes governmental initiatives in recent decades and relates cultural attributes to public service jobs and the performance of emotional labor. First comes a discussion of Korean culture.

Korean Culture

All Confucian cultures, while imbued with similarities, also differ from one another. Similarly, individualism and collectivism are not diametrically opposed conditions. Rather, they are cultural characteristics that can be marked on a multidimensional continuum. At the most extreme ends, individualism and collectivism represent the most significant cultural difference among nations (Triandis 1996, 2001). However, among Asian countries where collectivist cultures and Confucian values are strongly rooted throughout, differences are nuanced, with subtle variations in the extent to which they are manifested. These nuances result from historical events,

H. J. Lee (✉)
Department of Public Administration,
Myongji University, Seoul, South Korea
e-mail: Tweety06@mju.ac.kr

301

M. E. Guy et al. (eds.), *The Palgrave Handbook of Global Perspectives on Emotional Labor in Public Service*, https://doi.org/10.1007/978-3-030-24823-9_13

colonial pressures, and economic influences, all of which combine to affect perceptions of the self, one's obligations to others, and norms about how to interact with others (Kwon et al. 2013; Matsumoto 1990; Scherer 1997).

In the case of South Korea, its contemporary culture is influenced by traditional Confucianism. Public opinion is also shaped as a result of Japan's control of the country from 1905 until 1945. First as a protectorate of Japan, and then formally annexed by Japan, Korea was deprived of being able to administer its internal affairs until it returned to self-government in 1945. During Japanese rule, Korean traditions and culture were suppressed. Joined by a common enemy, this had the effect of uniting Koreans, resulting in a homogeneous population with strong emotional bonds and relatedness.

The importance of emotional relatedness can be found in the Korean word, *woori*, which represents a strong collectivist identity attached to South Korean society. For instance, when South Korean people refer to their mothers, they say *woori* mom, instead of "my mom." Instead of saying "my school," South Korean people call it a *woori* school, and instead of saying my wife, they say *woori* wife (Cho 2004). The word *woori* translates as *our* or *we* in English, but those words do not capture the deep meaning of *woori*.

In South Korea, the meaning of *woori* goes beyond relatedness and implies the following: "we are family who don't betray each other," and "we live together and die together." The word *woori* implies a tight bond between people. *Woori* is amplified when strangers meet by asking about each other's hometown, school, or blood relations. The goal is to find a commonality between each other and the connection serves to build the *woori* relationship. This, in turn, creates an in-group versus out-group feeling, in which those who share *woori* are the in-group. Consistent with other collectivist cultures, the expression of negative emotion, such as anger, is thought to break harmony (Matsumoto 1990). Thus, one of the strategies that Korean people use to sustain a *woori* relationship with others is to display more positive emotions to members of in-groups and reserve more negative emotions for those of out-groups.

This separation of in-group from out-group membership is found most notably in families and contributes to strong familism. *Familism* means the subordination of personal interest and prerogatives to the values, interests, and demands, of the family. It means placing the family above anything else and represents the family as the basic unit of society and the source of human identification and moral discipline (Chang 2010; D. Lee 2018; Park 2004). Familism is also associated with patriarchy, a benchmark of Confucianism.

Familism and Neo-Familism

The ideology of familism in South Korea, while rooted in tradition, has been in transition in recent decades. According to tradition, government viewed families as being responsible for caring for their own needs, leaving such matters to be resolved by family units. This included everything from gender relations, where patriarchy governed, to childcare and eldercare. When familism was at its height, families were seen as the bulwark of society and more important than government.

Through the process of colonization, the Korean War (1950–1953), military rule followed by industrialization, and the country's entry into the international economy, the South Korean people have gradually moved from distrust of the state for material, physical, and psychological protection (D. Lee 2018) to what is now called neo-familism. This term captures government's move toward a blend of Confucianism, with its family-centered focus and a more democratic and gender-equal society. The paradigm of male breadwinner—female care-giver has given way to dual-career couples and paid family leave policies for both fathers and mothers. *Hojuje*, the system that legally approved unequal status between men and women, was abolished in 2005 when the National Assembly amended the Civil Act to ensure equality between men and women and to prohibit discrimination against women. Passage of the bill marks the transition of familism from the traditions of the early postcolonial period to its instrumental use as a means for economic development in the 1970s, to a catalyst for democracy in the late 1980s (Shin 2006).

In traditional familism, families relied on themselves for social identity and safety. Support and cooperation were the common elements that made the system work. Culturally, the admixture of democratic and gender-equal relations based on liberalist notions, coupled with family-centeredness that is rooted in Confucianism, means that the centrality of the family remains as an essential characteristic of Korean culture but it has transitioned into neo-familism. Even in neo-familism, the South Korean people place "family" as a core value and consider it as

a. the key provider of social protection;
b. the force that makes all family members stay together and commit to each other, regardless of circumstances; and
c. the most important social unit, with the well-being of the family group having priority over the interests and necessities of each one of its members (D. Lee 2018).

A famous Korean proverb, "The habits of three year olds run to age eighty," and "Eighty year olds have habits that were formed when they were three year olds," reminds everyone that the family exercises a socializing influence over personal thought, value, and belief that lasts a lifetime (Park 2004). Likewise, familism insists on loyalty, trust, and cooperative attitudes within the family group. In general, a society with strong familism is organized by interpersonal network s which mediate events and needs that might otherwise be seen as the responsibility of government (Lande 1977).

In addition, familism plays a significant role in determining appropriate behavior for members of the family. There is a family hierarchy, set by gender and age, and the structure provides definition for all members in terms of who oversees and leads the family. Following Confucian custom, parents are superior to children, and, more specifically, the father ranks above the mother, who ranks above the son, who ranks above the daughter (Chang 2010). The assumption is that male members of the family provide financial support, and female members are caregivers for the rest of the family, including parents-in-law. This traditional family hierarchy lingers in the cultural psyche as well as in the Korean bureaucracy (S. Choi and C.-O. Park 2014).

The idea of familism extends to social relationships in a modified way. Called *quasi-familism*, it is defined as the belief that persons who are acquainted with each other via social ties should be treated like a family (Park 2004; Shin 2006). As already explained, a *woori* relationship builds quasi-familism. As soon as people engage with one another, they find common factors that unite them and build a *woori* relationship, which grows into quasi-familism.

When people are strongly tied to one another over the course of time, they feel *cheong*, a word that represents a degree of relatedness and closeness (Choi 2006). It is a psychological state that takes a long period of time to develop. For instance, married couples in South Korea not only live with love but *cheong* as well, and when a person works for an employer for a long time with the same co-workers and supervisors, they may feel *cheong* toward each other. The point of this discussion is to show that there are many words in the Korean language that capture the emotive element in interpersonal relationships and reveal strong collectivistic characteristics.

South Korea in Comparison

Another way to understand South Korea's culture as compared to other countries is provided by Hofstede's dimensions of national cultures (2001). Four dimensions are most useful in this regard: *power distance, individualism* versus *collectivism, masculinity* versus *femininity*, and *uncertainty avoidance*. Power distance deals with inequality, such that a score of 0 indicates total equality, meaning no power distance. At the other extreme, a score of 100 means total deference to those perceived to have more power. In high power distance countries, the less powerful members of organizations within a country expect and accept that power is distributed unequally. On this dimension, Hofstede scores South Korea at 60, implying that it is a moderately hierarchical society where people accept some degree of inherent inequality between superiors and subordinates. This compares to scores of 94 in the Philippines, 80 in China, 64 in Thailand, 58 in Taiwan, and 40 in the USA.

For the dimension of individualism, which measures the degree to which interests of the group prevail over interests of the individual, a score of 0 indicates total collectivism and 100 indicates total individualism. Hofstede assigns a score of 18 to South Korea, as compared to scores of 32 in the Philippines, 20 in China and Thailand, 17 in Taiwan, and 91 in the USA. Thus, it is one of the most collectivist states, valuing long-term commitment to the "in-group" and fostering strong relationships where everyone takes responsibility for fellow members of their group. People are less willing to reveal their own personal opinions and tend to conform to those around them. In addition, the relationships between employer and employee are perceived in moral terms (like a family) and hiring and promotion decisions take account of the employee's in-group (Hofstede 2001). Moreover, people who live in collectivist countries emphasize the importance of remaining united, lest everyone fail (House et al. 2006).

The masculinity dimension relates to how the society is driven by competition, assertiveness, toughness, and material success versus what Hofstede calls feminine characteristics of modesty, achievement, and success in school and workplace (Hofstede 2001). A low score is called femininity and means that the dominant values are tenderness, concern for quality of life, and caring for others. South Korea is scored 39 and is thus considered on the feminist end of the continuum. This implies a focus on "working in order to live" rather than "living in order to work." Korea's score compares to 64 in the Philippines, 66 in China, 34 in Thailand, 45 in Taiwan, and 62 in the USA.

Lastly, Uncertainty Avoidance has to do with the way that a society deals with ambiguous or unknown situations. Countries that score high on this dimension feel threatened by the unknown and those that score low on it see ambiguity and the unknown as not threatening. South Korea ranks high on this dimension, scoring 85, as compared to 44 in the Philippines, 30 in China, 64 in Thailand, 69 in Taiwan, and 46 in the USA (Hofstede 2001).

This score helps to explain Korea's collectivism, because it serves to overcome the uncertainties associated with threats (House et al. 2006). The score may also be at least partially attributable to its current geographic situation, where the Korean peninsula is divided into two regions, with the saber-rattling of the North being a threat to the South.

Considering these scores as a whole, they depict South Korea as a collectivist culture that is more similar to Taiwan and Thailand than to China or the Philippines. And it differs on all measures, as one would expect, from the USA. Having said that, many of the governmental reforms adopted in recent decades originated in the USA and UK. How they have been adapted to the Korean context and their degree of their success are discussed next.

Public Sector Reforms

New Public Management (NPM) reforms were instituted in South Korea after the Asian financial crisis of 1997 wrought a devastating impact on the Korean economy (Boo 2010). It was the worst recession since the 1950s and caused many socioeconomic problems, including huge layoffs, record-high unemployment, and record-low GDP growth (−5.8% in 1998). The public blamed the financial crisis on an inefficient government bureaucracy and, thus, supported reform of the entire system, including the financial system, labor, the business sector, and the public sector (Boo 2010).

President Kim Dae-Jung took office at the beginning of the crisis and adopted NPM initiatives that were focused on cutting the cost of government and downsizing the bureaucracy through privatization (Han and Kim 2017). The reforms resulted in drastic reductions in the size of the government workforce, and many state-owned enterprises were privatized in a short period of time (Kim and Park 2005).

Following President Kim's administration, President Rho Moo-Hyun assumed office in 2004. During this time, Rho's administration focused on small government with a results-oriented focus (Han and Kim 2017). The theme of the reform was to meld the public, private, and nonprofit segments of the economy and to think of citizens as customers, just as in passive commercial transactions (J. Lee 2014; Ryan 1995). The nation's economy soared and rose to one of the world's ten largest, but his administration was beset by criticism that the economic views were obsolete and that quality-of-life issues were not being given sufficient attention.

After President Roh's administration, President Lee Myung-Bak assumed office in 2008, only to be confronted with an economic downturn caused by the financial crisis in the USA and Europe. Because of their interconnected economies, economic growth in South Korea fell from 2.8% in 2008 to 0.7% in 2009, increased to 6.5% in 2010, but fell again to 3.7% in 2011, and 2.3% in 2012 (Korea Statistics 2014). To address this instability, another reform was initiated with the slogan of "more efficient and competitive." Although this served to stabilize the economic situation, it also did away with much of the decentralization that had been implemented during the NPM reforms. This had the effect of strengthening the executive center, marking a return to more traditional public administration processes (Han and Kim 2017). Reforms continued, with heightened attention to collaboration among ministries and an initiative labelled "Government 3.0."

Government 3.0

Following President Lee's administration (2008–2013), President Park Geun-Hye assumed office and announced the Government 3.0 initiative as a new paradigm for government operations. Its goal was to promote active sharing of public information and to remove the barriers that existed between ministries. The initiative was designed to advance four core values: openness, sharing, communication, and collaboration and to harness the capabilities of information and communication technology (ICT) in the process. Its objective was to provide individualized public services through intra- and intergovernmental cooperation and public-private partnerships.

The initiative required sweeping changes to the administrative paradigm, shifting the focus from a government-centered to a citizen-centered approach. The goal was to provide customized services for citizens, generate more jobs, and support a creative economy (J. W. Lee 2014; Park and Lee 2015). To reach the goals, President Park's administration designed three strategies: transparent government, competent government, and service-oriented government. The third strategy, service-oriented government, aimed at providing high-quality services to citizens by tailoring them to individual needs by using ICT (Nam 2013).

From the implementation of NPM with its focus on results-oriented, customer-friendly services, to the demands that accompanied Government 3.0 initiatives, additional burdens were placed on government employees. Increased demands for information disclosure-related tasks were not a priority for public agencies and not part of the regular work routine. Thus, workers have been beset with additional demands on their time. Faced with more technical tasks to perform while still being expected to be responsive and engaging with citizens, their hurried performance puts authentic engagement with citizens at risk. When sensing that workers are only pretending to please them, citizens become dissatisfied and complain about their work, which puts even more pressure on employees. This brings an emotive burden to their work that is above and beyond the usual stressors.

As seen, reforms accompany each incoming President's administration, from traditional public administration practices to NPM, post-NPM, Government 3.0, and beyond. Each reform brings additional service and time demands on workers, and this, in turn, increases the emotive burden for workers. The challenge for them is to balance their employer's demands for greater responsiveness to citizen needs, their own desire to perform well, and citizen's expectations for excellent public service. This confluence of work demands brings the subject of emotional labor into focus.

Emotional Labor in South Korea

Attention to emotional labor has been on the rise in the popular media in recent years. Among the most well-known stories is that of "nut gate" because it demonstrates the abuse of power by someone in power against a person in a lower position. Called "gapjil," the abuse is an arrogant display of authoritarian actions by those who hold power over others. The nut rage incident occurred when an airline passenger showed "gapjil" to a flight attendant and crew chief. A brief summary of the incident is as follows.

The incident happened in 2014 on a plane at John F. Kennedy International Airport in New York City. Before take-off, a flight attendant served macadamia nuts to first-class passengers in a closed packet. One of the passengers was Ms. Cho, the Korean Air vice president. She was dissatisfied with the way the attendant served the nuts to her because she preferred them on a plate, rather than in a sealed packet. Cho verbally and physically abused the attendant and called the cabin crew chief to her seat to complain. Ms. Cho ordered the crew chief to kneel down and beg for forgiveness. She repeatedly struck his knuckles with the edge of a digital tablet and ordered the chief to get off the plane. The pilots taxied back to the airport's gate so that he could deplane (Park and Hancocks 2015). Because of "gapjil" behavior by Cho, the flight attendant and the cabin crew chief had to suppress their own emotions and beg Cho for forgiveness. The outrageous story went viral, and the public outcry was enormous. It was obvious that Cho's treatment of the attendant and the crew chief was inappropriate and damaging to their emotional well-being.

Being a flight attendant has been a popular occupation in South Korea, but after this incident, people have reconsidered whether it is wise to hold such a job. This incident is a microcosm of tensions in Korean society, whether reflected in business or government. When workers are treated as if they are servants, the emotional challenge of frontline work is enormous (Jeong and Berlinger 2018). There is a social perception in Korea that friendly services are a must. Rooted in the hierarchical system, people tend to perceive a customer and a seller as a king and a servant relationship. Because customers are the ones who pay for services, they tend to show "gapjil" behavior to the sellers. To meet expectations, sellers obey customer requests and show great respect to them. This relationship has been a long-standing social norm. This even extends to standard performance in department stores. For example, when stores first open their doors to customers each morning, all sales associates line up at the entrance, bow their heads, and smile as a sign of respect as customers enter the store.

The transference of gapjil to government work is not unexpected. Performing emotional labor includes not only face-to-face interaction, but also voice-to-voice interaction as well. At the 114 call center, the nationwide number for directory service in South Korea, customers are greeted saying "Dear customer, I love you" at the beginning of conversation. Why? Because this romantic phrase makes customers happy. Since 2009, South Korean Call Centers have changed greetings from "Hi, this is 114 call center" (2009) to "Be happy," to "Yes" (2013) to "Greetings" (2015), to "Dear customer, I love you" (2016 and current) (Park 2017). It is problematic for call center operators to have to say "I love you" each time they answer the call. Even worse, many callers respond by saying "Sorry, I have a girlfriend," or "Let's go out if you love me that much" (Park 2017), which indicates the vulnerability of call takers to verbal abuse. Over 90% of call takers are women, and this job expectation requires them to deliver lovely greetings while suppressing their true feelings. Many female call operators report experiencing depression, burnout, and loss of appetite (Park 2017). Because many call center operators complained about verbal abuse by customers, a policy has been implemented allowing them to hang up if a caller swears three times. According to a recent study by the Korea Institute for Occupational and Environmental Health, 87% of South Korean workers whose jobs require emotional labor have been verbally harassed by customers (C. Lee 2018).

In November 2017, the Ministry of Employment and Labor published a health protection handbook for workers engaged in this form of emotional labor. The handbook contains the definition of emotional labor, explains why it is necessary to manage it, provides health protection measures, and suggests best practices. It even includes measures to lower stress among emotional laborers, such as a customer service manual, displaying a message asking people not to do any act that might cause stress and allowing more work autonomy. Translating from the business sector to government, discussion turns now to the public service context.

Emotional Labor in Public Service

Given the status quo in the private sector, it comes as no surprise that the Korean people tend to treat government employees more disrespectfully than respectfully. Many people perceive public employees as a hippopotamus eating the people's taxes, a frequent caricature in cartoons. Citizens believe that they are not being well-served and believe that they have a right to receive better public service. As a result, many public service employees are experiencing negative consequences, such as increased depression, increased turnover, and even higher incidents of suicide. As such, public service workers are encountering more emotional difficulty than one might anticipate. Thus, it is a problem that requires a solution.

According to the studies of awareness of public service in South Korea in 2007 and 2010, the majority of people are aware of services that are provided by government and they want to have even more services provided (S. Choi and H. W. Park 2014; Hwang and Ham 2001). However, most are oblivious to the emotive demands of the work. Among sixteen public service categories, the top four that Koreans perceive to be the most important are firefighting, security, public education, and social welfare. Those who work in these jobs are required to perform emotional labor. In other words, these jobs require understanding one's own emotional state as well as others' emotions, managing one's own emotions while responding to the situation at hand, and being responsive to citizens' demands. This is especially the case for services that are delivered by police officers, firefighters, emergency call takers, and social workers, all of which involve jobs that directly influence people's lives (Guy and Lee 2015; Hsieh 2014; Resh 2010). In other words, the public service jobs that Koreans value the most are the very definition of emotional labor jobs.

In addition, because of NPM reforms and Government 3.0 initiatives in South Korea, government organizations have transformed from a strong bureaucratic system into a competitive and market-oriented structure. As a result, customer satisfaction in the public sector is now recognized as an important factor for achieving higher performance (Song et al. 2017). The standards of assessment for public service performance have gravitated toward citizen satisfaction, and this puts pressure on public service workers to perform in such a way that their work is evaluated positively by a demanding public. Further, public service employees who work in administrative jobs must deliver services as quickly as possible due to people's impatience with waiting and receiving slow service. However, the faster that service workers are required to perform, the more likely it is that they engage in emotive pretending, having to suppress their true feelings. This produces emotive dissonance and negative effects on workers' well-being.

According to a study by the National Human Rights Commission in 2015, 37.9% of firefighter s experienced verbal violence during the study period, and 81.2% of them report performing emotional labor. This is especially the case for emergency rescue personnel. Moreover, for firefighters who worked in disaster response, 40% of them suffered post-traumatic stress disorder (PTSD) in the form of depression or panic disorder after the accident. Further, based on 2016 data from the Ministry of Interior and Safety, there were 27 firefighters who died while rescuing people and there were 41 who died by committing suicide during a five year period (Lee 2016). In addition, the number of people who call the emergency dispatch center (the 119 number in Korea, similar to 911 in the USA) has mushroomed from 8,549,511 in 2010 to 18,778,105 in 2014, an increase of 247%, but the number of police officials and firefighters has increased by only 8.2% in the same period. As these numbers show, there are many emotional labor issues in public service at the same time that there are inadequate therapeutic clinics or public management systems that can help public service workers deal with the emotive demands of their jobs (Song 2018).

The Survey

Discussion turns now to the survey of government workers. Respondents for the present study are drawn from government employees who are currently working at five *Gu* in South Korea. *Gu* is the word for municipal government; a gu is similar to a borough in the USA. As of December 31, 2016, there were 1,029,528 employees working in all Korean governments, including central and local government (but not including armed forces personnel). About 38% (374,755) of these were employed in local governments throughout the country.

Table 13.1 Demographic characteristics: Korea

	Frequency	Percent
Age		
Less than 30	48	23.3
30–39 years	75	36.4
40–49 years	53	25.7
50–59 years	30	14.6
60 or more	0	0
N/A	0	0
Gender		
Female	115	55.3
Male	93	44.7
N/A	0	0
Public service experience		
Less than 10	113	54.3
10–19 years	30	14.4
20–29 years	55	26.5
30 or more	3	1.4
N/A	7	3.4
Educational level		
Less than high school	0	0
High school graduate	19	9.1
Some college	11	5.3
2-year associate degree	18	8.7
College graduate	134	64.4
Some graduate school	7	3.4
Master's degree	10	4.8
Law degree (J.D., LL.B.)	0	0
Doctorate degree (Ph.D., M.D., Ed.D., etc.)	1	0.5
Other (please specify)	8	3.8
N/A		0

There were 208 respondents who completed the survey. As shown in Table 13.1, most of the respondents ranged in age from 30 to 50 years of age. There are slightly more women than men in the sample (women 55.3% and men 44.7%). While about 42% of the respondents have worked for government for more than ten years, the remainder have worked less than ten years. Regarding education, almost two-thirds of respondents are college graduates (64.4%), while another 8% hold graduate degrees. To summarize the demographics of the group, it is a highly educated group of younger workers.

Table 13.2 lists the occupational areas of the respondents. About two-thirds of them (68.9%) work in administrative jobs. Finance, housing, and social services are additional areas where larger percentages of respondents work. The frequency adds to more than the number of respondents because

Table 13.2 Occupational characteristics: Korea

Occupation	Frequency	Percent
1. Administration	153	68.9
2. Community development/neighborhood services	4	1.8
3. Engineering, manufacturing, or production	2	0.9
4. Education	2	0.9
6. Finance or accounting	10	4.5
7. Firefighter	2	0.9
8. Health care	1	0.5
9. Housing	11	4.9
11. Information and communication	1	0.5
12. Law enforcement	8	3.6
16. Public works: streets, sanitation, utilities	4	1.8
17. Purchasing	1	0.5
20. Social services	13	5.8
21. Transportation	8	3.6
22. Support services	2	0.9

Table 13.3 Descriptive statistics and Cronbach's alpha: Korea

	Mean	SD	Cronbach's alpha
Emotive capacity	4.361	0.940	0.643
Pretending expression	4.861	1.059	0.729
Deep acting	4.857	1.224	0.924
Job satisfaction	4.570	0.965	0.746
Burnout	4.571	1.453	0.873
Personal fulfillment	4.532	1.209	0.895

these categories are not mutually exclusive. One may work in administration for housing, for example.

Descriptive statistics for the variables used in this study are shown in Table 13.3, along with Cronbach's alpha, a measure of interitem reliability for each variable.

All items were answered on a 7-point Likert-type scale that ranged from 1 (strong disagreement) to 7 (strong agreement). All latent variables were tested using factor analysis with Varimax rotation, and all showed good convergent validity and had reliability higher than 0.60.

Structural equation modeling was selected to examine the relations among emotive capacity, pretending expression, deep acting, burnout, job satisfaction, and personal fulfillment. The model fit indices are shown in Table 13.4. The overall model fit was assessed using goodness-of-fit indices, including absolute fit indices (CMIN/DF and RMSEA) and incremental fit indices (TLI, CFI, NFI). The research model is not fully satisfied because

Table 13.4 Structural model results: Korea

Hypothesized paths	Coefficients	*p*-value
Emotive capacity → Job satisfaction	0.237*	0.015
Emotive capacity → Burnout	−0.103	0.228
Emotive capacity → Personal fulfillment	0.326*	0.000
Pretending expression → Job satisfaction	0.152	0.086
Pretending expression → Burnout	0.403*	0.000
Pretending expression → Personal fulfillment	−0.017	0.812
Deep acting → Job satisfaction	0.245*	0.004
Deep acting → Burnout	−0.083	0.275
Deep acting → Personal fulfillment	0.487*	0.000

Model fit: $\chi^2 = 380.848$ (df $= 142$), CFI $= 0.884$, RMSEA $= 0.092$, SRMR $= 0.130$

the commonly accepted thresholds of the fit indices are not all met. However, for an exploratory study of this type, which uses constructs of emotional labor designed for application around the globe, it is satisfactory.

The relationship between each of the emotional labor variables and outcomes are shown in Table 13.4. The findings reveal that emotive capacity is significantly and positively related to job satisfaction and personal fulfillment and is not significantly related to burnout. Pretending expression is significantly and positively related to burnout, but it is not related to personal fulfillment or job satisfaction. Deep acting, the authentic expression of emotion, has a significant, positive relationship with both job satisfaction and personal fulfillment, but no significant relationship with burnout (Fig. 13.1).

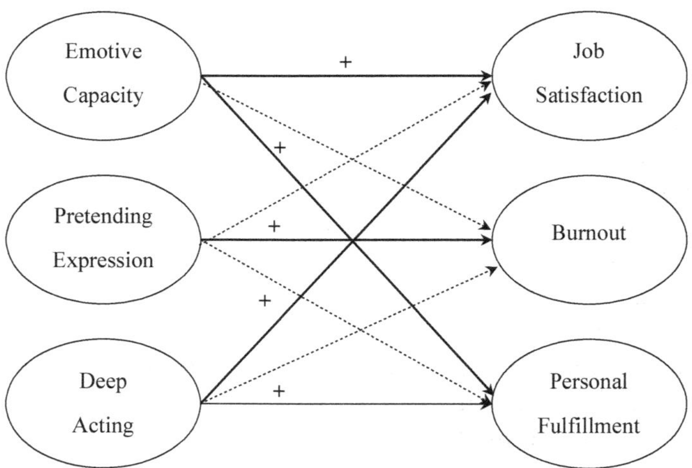

Fig. 13.1 Path diagram for Korea

Discussion

These results show that emotional labor significantly affects how workers feel about their jobs. The business literature has shown an inconsistent relationship, perhaps focusing more on the negative aspects than on the positive. Although burnout, depression, and turnover occur, it is clear from these data that there are positive consequences, including job satisfaction and a sense of personal fulfillment. The only deleterious condition is when workers must suppress their true feelings and pretend to feel another way. That is the one circumstance that produces burnout.

More specifically, South Korean public service employees who are good at facilitating their own emotive expression and know how to use their emotive skills achieve greater job satisfaction and find their jobs fulfilling. The findings reveal that greater emotive capacity results in more positive relationships with job satisfaction and personal fulfillment. Those whose emotive capacity is high succeed in emotive work because they know how to sense how citizens are feeling and respond constructively.

In addition to emotive capacity, deep acting, which is the authentic expression of emotion, also shows positive relations with job satisfaction and personal fulfillment. When employees are able to express the emotion they truly feel, they experience personal fulfillment (Grandey 2003). This has a beneficial effect for the worker, the citizen being served, as well as the employer, because it generates more job commitment (Lazanyi 2011). Moreover, higher commitment to the organization also generates more altruistic behavior. This positive cycle regenerates itself, producing better service to citizens and more job commitment on the part of employees.

There is a downside to emotional labor. Consistent with the findings from prior studies, South Korean public service workers who must suppress how they feel and, instead, express a different emotion are more likely to experience burnout. This is because emotive pretending consumes personal resources and, thus, causes stress and eventually brings burnout. When public service employees use emotive pretending over a prolonged time, depersonalization sets in and results in emotional exhaustion (Hochschild 1983). In order to address these negative consequences, organizational support and social support are necessary as well as training to help employees learn strategies to deal with emotive demands (Lee 2018a, b). In the South Korean context, people's perceptions toward public service workers urgently need to change. Just as with the implementation of procedures that protect private sector workers from abusive work behaviors, workplace rules that can offer protection to those engaged in frontline public service jobs will be beneficial.

Conclusion

This chapter has described the Korean culture and how it shapes the delivery of public services and citizen expectations of government workers. After describing the coverage of emotional labor in private sector jobs, survey data of government workers show that, despite the media attention that is focused on its negative consequences, in fact, the emotive aspects of their jobs significantly contribute to job satisfaction and feelings of self-fulfillment. With this in mind, the cultural pressure to deliver "service with a smile" is having deleterious effects. It is this aspect of the job—emotive pretending—that produces negative experiences.

To the degree that government can devise a means for more clearly establishing reasonable expectations on the part of the public for what government workers can produce, the work environment will be healthier for workers. Perhaps the reforms that have been strongly "customer" focused should be reined in so that expectations match capacity. The deleterious effects on workers of not being able to accommodate citizen demands are demotivating. A more accurate match between what workers can produce and what citizens should expect will point the way forward.

References

Boo, Hyeong-Wook. 2010. "Korea's Experience with NPM-Based Reform: Applying the Policy Fashion Concept." *The Korean Journal of Policy Studies* 25 (1): 19–33.

Chang, K. S. 2010. *South Korea Under Compressed Modernity: Familial Political Economy in Transition.* London, UK: Routledge.

Cho, Kyuhoon. 2004. *Religion in Diaspora: The Transformation of Korean Immigrant Churches in Global Society.* Unpublished M.A. Thesis, Religious Studies, University of Ottawa.

Choi, Sang. J. 2006. *Psychology of Korean People.* Seoul: Chung-Ang University Press.

Choi, Sujin, and Han Woo Park. 2014a. "An Exploratory Approach to a Twitter-Based Community Centered on a Political Goal in South Korea: Who Organized It, What They Shared, and How They Acted." *New Media & Society* 16 (1), 129–48. https://doi.org/10.1177/1461444813487956.

Choi, Sungjoo, and Chun-Oh Park. 2014b. "Glass Ceiling in Korean Civil Service: Analyzing Barriers to Women's Career Advancement in the Korean Government." *Public Personnel Management* 43 (1): 118–39. https://doi.org/10.1177/0091026013516933.

Grandey, Alicia A. 2003. "When 'The Show Must Go On': Surface Acting and Deep Acting as Determinants of Emotional Exhaustion and Peer-Related Service Delivery." *Academy of Management Journal* 46 (1): 86–96.

Guy, Mary E., and Hyun Jung Lee. 2015. "How Emotional Intelligence Mediates Emotional Labor in Public Service Jobs." *Review of Public Personnel Administration* 35 (3): 261–77.

Han, Chong H., and Sun H. Kim. 2017. "The Changing Modes of Administrative Reform in South Korea." *Transylvanian Review of Administrative Sciences* 50: 54–72.

Hochschild, Arlie. 1983. *The Managed Heart: Commercialization of Human Feeling*. Berkeley, CA: University of California Press.

Hofstede, Geert. 2001. *Culture's Consequences: Comparing Values, Behaviors, Institutions, and Organizations Across Nations*. 2nd ed. Thousand Oaks, CA: Sage.

House, Robert J., Paul J. Hanges, Mansour Javidan, Peter W. Dorfman, and Vipin Gupta. 2006. *Culture, Leadership, and Organizations: The GLOBE Study of 62 Societies*. Thousand Oaks, CA: Sage.

Hsieh, Chih-Wei. 2014. "Burnout Among Public Service Workers: The Role of Emotional Labor Requirements and Job Resources." *Review of Public Personnel Administration* 34 (4): 379–402.

Hwang S. W., and J. S. Ham. 2001. Public Employees' Perception and Attitudes Toward Public Administration. Seoul, South Korea: Korean Institute of Public Administration (KIPA) Research Report 01-18-2.

Jeong, Sophie, and Joshua Berlinger. 2018. "Korean Air 'Nut Rage' Scandal: Flight Attendant Awarded $18,000 Settlement." CNN, December 20. Accessed April 4, 2019 at https://www.cnn.com/2018/12/19/asia/korea-air-nut-rage-settlement-intl/index.html.

Kim, B.-S., and S.-H. Park. 2005. *Hankuki Jungbu Gaehyuk: Sunggwa, Munjae Kuriko Gwajae [History of Government Reform in Korea: The Good, the Bad, and the Ugly]*. Seoul, South Korea: Korean Association for Public Administration Summer Symposium Series.

Korea Statistics. 2014. *Composite Economic Indexes*. Accessed March 31, 2019 at http://kostat.go.kr/portal/eng/surveyOutline/2/1/index.static.

Kwon, Hoin, K. Lira Yoon, Jutta Joormann, and Jung-Hye Kwon. 2013. "Cultural and Gender Differences in Emotion Regulation: Relation to Depression." *Cognition and Emotion* 27 (5): 769–82.

Lande, C. H. 1977. "Networks and Groups in Southeast Asia". In *Friends Followers and Factions: A Reader in Political Clientelism*, edited by Steffen W. Schmidt, 103–127. Berkeley, CA: University of California Press.

Lazanyi, K. 2011. "Organizational Consequences of Emotional Labour in Management." *Applied Studies in Agribusiness and Commerce* 5:125–30.

Lee, Claire. 2018. "Government Introduces Measures to Protect Workers in Service Sector." *KoreaHerald.com*, October 18. Accessed April 4, 2018 at http://www.koreaherald.com/view.php?ud=20181018000783.

Lee, Dayoon. 2018. "The Evolution of Family Policy in South Korea: From Confucian Familism to Neo-Familism." *Asian Social Work and Policy Review* 12: 46–53.

Lee, Hyun Jung. 2018a. "Relation Between Display Rules and Emotive Behavior Strategies and Its Outcomes Among South Korean Public Service Employees." *Public Performance & Management Review* 41 (4): 723–44. https://doi.org/10.10 80/15309576.2018.1464479.

Lee, Hyun Jung. 2018b. "How Emotional Intelligence Relates to Job Satisfaction and Burnout in Public Service Jobs." *International Review of Administrative Sciences* 84 (4): 729–45. https://doi.org/10.1177/0020852316670489.

Lee, Jooha. 2014. "What Happens After the Passage of Reform Initiatives? Two Dimensions of Social Policy Reform in Korea." *International Review of Administrative Sciences* 80 (1): 193–212. https://doi.org/10.1177/0020852313513873.

Lee, Jung Hee. 2016. "Tears of 119 Firefighters: Let's Not Be a Firefighter." April 25. Accessed April 10, 2019 at http://star.ohmynews.com/NWS_Web/ OhmyStar/at_pg_m.aspx?CNTN_CD=A0002204039#cb.

Lee, J. W. 2014. "A Study on the Correspondence Between Government Paradigm and Information Disclosure Paradigm." *Journal of the Korean Association for Regional Information* 17 (2): 147–72.

Matsumoto, David. 1990. "Cultural Similarities and Differences in Display Rules." *Motivation and Emotion* 14 (3): 195–214.

Nam, T. W. 2013. "Government 3.0 in Korea: Fad or Fashion?" *Proceedings of the 7th International Conference on Theory and Practice of Electronic Governance,* October. Accessed March 30, 2019 at https://www.researchgate.net/publica-tion/266657140_Government_30_in_Korea_Fad_or_fashion. https://doi.org/ 10.1145/2591888.2591896.

Park, Eun Hyung, and Jea-Wan Lee. 2015. "A Study on Policy Literacy and Public Attitudes Toward Government Innovation: Focusing on Government 3.0 in South Korea." *Journal of Open Innovation: Technology, Market, and Complexity* 1 (23): 1–13. https://doi.org/10.1186/s40852-015-0027-3.

Park, Madison, and Paula Hancocks. 2015. "Korean Air Executive Jailed over 'Nut Rage' Incident." February 12. Accessed March 30, 2019 at https://www.cnn. com/2015/02/12/world/asia/korean-air-nut-rage-verdict/index.html.

Park, Seohoi S. 2017. "Dear Customer, I Love You: Emotional Labor at South Korean Call Centers." May 29. Accessed March 29, 2019 at https://www.korea-expose.com/emotional-labor-korean-call-centers.

Park, Tong H. 2004. "The Influences of Familism on Interpersonal Trust of Korean Public Officials." *International Review of Public Administration* 9 (1): 121–35.

Resh, William G. 2010. "Book Review of *Emotional Labor: Putting the Service in Public Service.*" *Review of Public Personnel Administration* 30 (2): 257–62.

Ryan, N. 1995. "Unravelling Conceptual Developments in Implementation Analysis." *Australian Journal of Public Administration* 54 (1): 65–80.

Scherer, Klaus R. 1997. "The Role of Culture in Emotion-Antecedent Appraisal." *Journal of Personality and Social Psychology* 73: 902–22.

Shin, Ki-Young. 2006. "The Politics of the Family Law Reform Movement in Contemporary Korea: A Contentious Space for Gender and the Nation." *Journal of Korean Studies* 11 (1): 93–125. https://doi.org/10.1353/jks.2006.0005.

Song, L. R. 2018. "If You Swear, We'll Report It." May 9. Accessed April 10, 2019 at http://www.edaily.co.kr/news/read?newsId=03017606619207280&mediaCodeNo=257.

Song, Min Hye, Seung-Bum Yang, and Hyun Jung Lee. 2017. "A Study on the Management of Emotional Labor and Social Exchange of Public Servants: Perceived Organization Support and Leader-Member Exchange. *Modern Society & Public Administration* 27 (1): 163–91.

Triandis, Harry, C. 1996. "The Psychological Measurement of Cultural Syndromes." *American Psychologist* 51 (4): 407–15.

Triandis, Harry, C. 2001. "Individualism-Collectivism and Personality." *Journal of Personality* 69 (6): 907–24.

14

Pakistan

Aisha Azhar

Pakistan's culture has been described as a mixture of religion, Indian origins, British inheritance, and American influences (Khilji 2001). The vast majority of the Pakistani population—96%—is Muslim (Pakistan Bureau of Statistics 2019) and religion is a prominent, although nuanced, factor in everyday life. In other countries where the population is predominantly Muslim, Islam is embedded in the national culture and it influences organizations in terms of their policies and processes (Tayeb 1997). However, in Pakistan, Islamization of macro-institutions is more limited than one would expect. Due to the overwhelming impact of other factors, such as Indian origins, British legacies, and American influences, Islamization in Pakistan is argued to have penetrated only the outer shell of its culture (Ahmad 1996; James 1993; Lyon 1993; Malik 1996).

Because of Pakistan's unique history, the Islamic value system is not as much of a guiding norm for society in general (Khilji 2001). For example, the creation of elite classes in society, notably feudal and civil servants, is a function of the British colonial legacy, which remained dominant on the sub-continent for more than a century. Despite the fact that an educated middle class is now represented sufficiently among the elites, it has not been able to sway attitudes toward greater Islamization. The elites continue to cling to the love of power, status, and money, with too little concern for

A. Azhar (✉)
School of Governance and Society,
University of Management and Technology, Lake City, Pakistan
e-mail: aisha.azhar@umt.edu.pk

© The Author(s) 2019
M. E. Guy et al. (eds.), *The Palgrave Handbook of Global Perspectives on Emotional Labor in Public Service*, https://doi.org/10.1007/978-3-030-24823-9_14

the needs of the people. Laws protect the powerful and affluent and the rule of law is not implemented properly. The powerful and the rich can commit a crime and go unpunished, thanks to bribes or nepotism (Hussain 1999; Khilji 1999, 2001).

From an economics perspective, Pakistan has not paid sufficient attention to education in the past and, consequently, has failed to benefit from significant income gains. This has resulted in the nation having a lack of competitiveness in international markets (Amjad 1992; Khan and Marvi 1993). However, this does not mean that Pakistan has a shortage of educated manpower. The fact is that the proportion of the budget allocated to higher education has been spent disproportionately on colleges and universities in urban areas (Korson 1993). Khilji (2000) argued that this lack of attention to the power of education, coupled with population growth and reduced job opportunities for both the educated and uneducated citizenry, resulted in a contradictory situation that produced an abundance of unemployed graduates and illiterate workers.

The Work Environment

Economic policies in Pakistan have remained liberal and thus are designed in accord with market mechanisms. Public investment has been used to enhance private investment. After the 1971–1977 period of nationalization, an era of aggressive privatization began that undertook the denationalization of public enterprises and provided motivation for the private sector to invest.

Privatization initiatives sparked investors' interests and led to the development of many new enterprises, particularly in the banking sector. The government also embarked on initiatives to foster a business-driven culture designed to encourage the use of professional and modern management practices. As a consequence, a healthy and competitive business environment was created, with the private sector being more progressive than the public sector (Khilji 1999, 2002).

Culture and Human Resource Management

The culture of Pakistan has been described as being a collectivist one that is associated with high uncertainty avoidance and high power distance (Hofstede 1991, 2001; Khilji 1999, 2001; Trompenaars and Hampden-Turner 1999). There is a tacit understanding of respect for authority as a function of high power distance, and people are seen as being emotively connected and integrated into cohesive groups. People are found to be in the mid-range on the masculine to feminine continuum (Hofstede et al. 2010, 139). This dimension ranks countries according to the importance attached to work and life goals. At the masculine end are high importance attached to earnings, recognition, advancement, and challenge. At the feminine end are having a good working relationship with one's superior, cooperation, living in a desirable area, and employment security. Pakistan's rating indicates that both women and men attach importance closer to the middle of the continuum on these various aspects. Regardless of Hofstede's ratings, however, people are more inclined to value behaviors associated with masculine qualities.

In the past two decades, the increasing foreign direct investment and the influence of multinationals have induced several changes in the traditional management practices in Pakistan. Pakistani organizational culture is categorized as a distinct culture with high power distance, high collectivism, and high uncertainty avoidance (Hofstede 1980; Khilji 1999, 2002; Trompenaars and Hampden-Turner 1999). These issues pose unique problems for organizations as they address the convergence of Western parent-company practices with local culture. Because of the distinctiveness of local culture, global principles of management and human resource management practices must adapt to what is an uneasy fit.

Khilji (2000) explains how the local culture requires divergence from foreign practice. The conflation of contextual variables—economic, legal, and socio-cultural—produces changes that do not fit the script of parent companies and of management theories developed in other contexts. For example, House et al. (2004) report that in Pakistan, people in positions of authority are expected to act like parents and take care of their employees and their families. Regardless of whether this is judged as paternalistic or as a holistic view of employees that rises above a task-based point of view, it directs the behavior of managers and workers alike, modifying expectations and the relationship between superior and subordinate.

Despite being in a high power distance culture, Pakistani organizations have made progress toward a more participatory style of management among employees and managers. Contextual forces have prevented full adoption of this, however (Khilji 2000, 2001). Pakistani organizations resist alternative practices and attempt to maintain or preserve their traditional practices.

Khilji (2001), in her analysis of human resource practices in Pakistan, characterizes the bureaucracy as having a formal and centralized hierarchical structure. According to her, policies are formulated at the top and authority and delegation flow down to each office in a uniform fashion that fits within cultural expectations. Employees are given little autonomy and they are not encouraged to take new initiatives or learn new things. There is a notable communication gap between management and employees. Top to bottom communication is minimal and bottom-up communication rarely occurs. Management practices are made in isolation and employee involvement remains an alien concept. Hence, employee commitment and loyalty to their employers are rare.

In a typical Pakistani organization, managers have little autonomy. They are expected to hire employees not on the basis of merit but on the recommendation of government-appointed committees or unions (Khilji 1999, 2001). Salary is awarded based on seniority and creativity is not encouraged. In fact, it is rare due to rigid rules and regulations. Moreover, employee initiatives are not encouraged and hence not rewarded. Wages and salaries are not compatible with competitive-market rates of other countries (Khilji 2000). Despite the presence of training institutes that have been established to provide for employee development, organizations fail to benefit from their programs due to poor strategic planning, faulty implementation, and inadequate human resource management practices. Training programs are generally not designed according to individual needs, and they are not aligned with career development plans of individual employees. Consequently, training has produced little real impact. This lack of strategic focus has resulted in diminishing the motivational level of employees.

The unhealthy work context has resulted in a cadre of employees who have little trust in one another (Jamal 1998; Khilji 1999). Despite the nation's collectivist culture, employees adopt an idiosyncratic relationship with their workplace. Khilji (1999) describes how employees develop a clear distinction between in-group and out-group membership (Triandis 1995), where employees see organizations as out-groups, while families or co-workers form in-groups. Whenever conflict arises, the latter is always given preference over the former.

Human Resource Management: Control and Change

In both business and government, the presence of multinationals influence, or, more accurately, attempt to influence, the human resource practices in Pakistani offices. Whether a multinational corporation or a governmental recipient of US Agency for International Development (USAID) dollars, the human resource practices as prescribed by headquarters are adapted to fit the local Pakistani context. Regardless of how strictly defined the policy structures are, and how specific the administrative manual is, actual practice is still influenced by local norms when it comes to implementing global mandates. Hence, HRM practices are not applied fully according to universal standards. Khilji (2002) reports how this differential is manifested in terms of policy and implementation. For example, while employees are encouraged to contribute ideas, they are not given the authority to make decisions or implement them. Policies are approved after consultation with headquarters, rather than after consultation with workers at the street level. The point of view of local organizations is not valued. The work of human resource managers, then, is more one of bookkeeping than one of developing the necessary human capital. HR managers are reduced to keeping track of recruitment, selection, and training of workers.

Khilji (2002) reports that in Pakistani organizations, changes to the top-down management style are frequently initiated by senior managers, but implementation of these changes is arduous. Line managers often resist because they perceive threats to their authority. Employees, on the other hand, feel positive about the initiative because they are encouraged to offer their points of view on issues and areas that need attention. While those at the street level think of this style of management as forward-looking, professional, and proactive, their superiors resent it. When policies are formulated at the top and implementation is dependent on line managers, Khilji observed a visible gap between policy formulation and its implementation. The primary reason for this is the preservation of core cultural tenets that expect there to be a formal, hierarchical structure. Because cultural norms require deference to authority, the system perpetuates itself.

Public Service in Pakistan: The Inherited Legacy

The nature and quality of public service and management in Pakistan face numerous challenges. Since independence, the government bureaucracy that was inherited from the British colonial system has continued to grow and has remained insensitive to the needs of the public. Although some efforts have been made by various groups to respond to the calls for incorporating a disciplined and market-oriented approach to public management, successive governments have remained comfortable with the traditional approach. A considerable amount of resources have been wasted in examining the systems and proposing recommendations. Implementation of proposed changes has been met with inaction rather than action. Non-conformance to the latest approaches to public management has resulted in a low level of productivity and poor quality of services. Despite this, some advances have been made since independence, especially in terms of labor laws and updates to other laws.

In recent years, particularly after the deregulation of the economy over the course of the past thirty years, American influences have diluted the impact of the British legacy and have significantly influenced the educational institutions and workplaces in Pakistan. The best reputed business schools are now managed like the top business schools in North America (Khilji 1999, 2000, 2001). The renowned training institutes, such as the Pakistan Institute of Management, were established with aid from Harvard University and the Ford Foundation. Much of the training content has a special focus on American practices and is designed to align with US management style.

Given the choice, Pakistani managers prefer to follow American management practices because it is perceived as progressive and performance oriented. British managers are considered to be more bureaucratic and slow, very similar to how Pakistani civil servants are perceived. In fact, those who work for Pakistan's government are criticized as having inherited their management habits from the British. Just as in businesses, government organizations are caught in a bind, halfway between knowing they need to modernize according to global standards and halfway wanting to preserve their core cultural values and behaviors.

Administrative Reforms

Administrative reforms emerged as a central theme after independence (1947) in Pakistan. The post-independence administrative history of Pakistan is marked by a series of stages. Jadoon and Jabeen (2010) describe three reform models in Pakistan. First came the development administration reform model, which occurred from 1947 until 1977. It focused mainly on civil service reforms. Although these reforms did not bring structural change, they did bring procedural changes. These included creation of training institutions and establishment of special autonomous or semi-autonomous bodies. During the Zulfikar Ali Bhutto regime, the government did a commendable job of implementing reforms by reorganizing the Civil Service of Pakistan (CSP) into occupational groups. The main aim of these reforms was to weaken the iron grip that the bureaucracy had on governing processes.

The second stage brought the development management reform model. It occurred from 1977 until the late 1990s and happened under the military rule of Zia-ul-Haq, followed by two civilian governments. Consistent with New Public Management, decentralization processes were initiated that were later transformed into aggressive privatization of state-owned enterprises. The public sector reforms made under this development management model were started in the 1980s under the structural adjustment programs (SAP) of the International Monetary Fund (IMF). Their main focus was on privatization and reduction of the size of government. However, less attention was paid to improvements in public sector management.

The third stage is the development governance reform model. It was initiated in 1999 and continues now. During this stage, a number of initiatives have been undertaken to promote good governance. Among these are the promotion of local democracy as well as structural reforms designed for self-sustainable growth. A new local government system was introduced that changed the structure of district governments. A number of other reform initiatives have been undertaken during this stage, as well, including agencification, under which regulatory and service delivery agencies were created within respective ministries.

Public Organizations

On the wave of New Public Management, a government privatization program was introduced that boosted interest of investors. Several new enterprises were set up and multiple initiatives were taken by the government to promote a business-driven culture and encourage modern management practices. This wave developed a competitive business environment where the private sector was more strengthened than the public sector (Bokhari 1996).

Political instability coupled with the radical change from civil bureaucracy to parliamentary democracy caused unrest. Moreover, it engendered an atmosphere of insecurity and pessimism among the public (Burki 1993; Khilji 2001). Due to hollow claims made by politicians who failed to deliver on their promises, the public developed a distrustful attitude toward government. The same attitude of distrust carried over to private sector organizations, where employees lost trust in management.

Khilji (2001) couples problems associated with the large number of unemployed citizens and their limited job opportunities with economic uncertainty and unwise budgeting priorities. This maelstrom of forces exaggerated the frustration and insecurity already felt by the working class in

Pakistan. One of the major issues with Pakistan's labor force has always been its growing population rate. As a result, the increased national output has never been proportional to the needs of its growing populace. Khilji (2001) credits the unstable political system, growing income disparity, and social disparities as major reasons for further deterioration of the situation. She cited Jamal (unpublished), who argues that traditional and cultural values associated with collectivism have weakened in the past ten to twenty years due to economic hardship. Factors like competition for scarce jobs, job retention, and motivation to excel in a status-conscious and materialistic society have paved the way for individualistic attitudes toward organizations (Khilji 1999). This inculcates a negative animus between citizen and state and between employee and employer.

This negative spiral lowers organizational commitment and increases turnover. Employees primarily build an economic relationship with organizations but treat their employer as an out-group. This means that investment in their own work performance is not as strong as their job description demands. On the other hand, good relationships with managers are considered important in order to pursue professional or individual goals. This leads to the development of in-groups in the form of connections between workers and their superiors. This two-sided coin raises questions about the emotive load of public jobs and how workers manage the dissonance they experience.

Emotional Labor

The scholarship concerning emotional labor in Pakistan is scant. One exception is a study by Syed and Ali (2013), who explored the nature and extent of contextual emotional labor associated with women's decisions to step into the male domain of the workplace. Contextual emotional labor is identified as an integral part of Muslim female employees' work in the formal employment sector. In Pakistan, organizational and societal display rules seem to be more incongruent than in Western countries. Syed et al. (2005) posited that countries with a Muslim majority show inconsistency between societal orientations primarily based on Islamic norms of modesty and organizational display rules. Some emotions, such as guilt, fear, and shame, are thought to arise as a result of encountering immoral or corrupt behaviors (Aronfreed 1968). This is theorized to lead to depression, anxiety, and self-degradation (Lutwak et al. 2001). Syed (2008) emphasized the significance of examining "the aversive states that may follow one's transgression" and how employees should handle these situations (Syed 2008, 194). To probe the subject further in the context of public service work, questionnaires were distributed to government workers in Lahore, Pakistan.

The Study

The survey was administered between August 2015 and November 2015. After removing outliers and unusable data, there were 386 survey responses to analyze. Demographic characteristics (gender and age) of the respondents are listed in Table 14.1. In terms of age, a majority of the respondents (43.3%) were below 30 years of age. The next larger group comprises employees (27.5%) between 30 and 39 years of age, followed by 15.4% falling between 40 and 49 years old. Most of the respondents were females

Table 14.1   Demographic characteristics: Pakistan

	Frequency	Percent
Age (missing=85)		
Less than 30	143	43.3
30–39 years	25	27.5
40–49 years	69	15.4
50–59 years	53	12.2
60 or more	11	1.6
Gender (missing=3)		
Female	269	69.7
Male	114	29.5
Public service experience (missing=9)		
None	29	7.5
Less than 10	191	50.7
10–19 years	77	20.4
20–29 years	52	13.8
30–39	25	6.6
40 and above	3	0.8
Educational level (missing=8)		
Less than high school	7	1.8
High school graduate	10	2.6
Some college	6	1.6
2-year associate degree	6	1.6
College graduate	33	8.5
Some graduate school	19	4.9
Master's degree	184	47.7
Law degree (J.D., LL.B.)	14	3.6
Doctorate degree (Ph.D., M.D., Ed.D., etc.)	22	5.7
Other (please specify)	77	18.9

Table 14.2 Occupational characteristics: Pakistan

Occupation	Frequency	Percent
1. Administration	165	42.7
2. Community development/neighborhood services	181	46.9
3. Engineering, manufacturing, or production	135	35
4. Education	28	7.3
5. Disaster response	24	6.2
6. Finance or accounting	25	6.5
7. Firefighter	171	44.3
8. Health care	134	34.7
9. Housing	134	34.7
10. Human resource management	129	33.4
11. Information and communication	116	30.1
12. Law enforcement	114	29.5
13. Military	92	23.8
14. Public relations	87	22.5
15. Planning	74	19.2
16. Public works: streets, sanitation, utilities	73	18.9
17. Purchasing	71	18.4
18. Recreation and parks	64	16.6
19. Research and development	38	9.8
20. Social services	29	7.5
21. Transportation	25	6.5
22. Support Services (e.g., equipment maintenance)	19	4.9
23. Other	19	4.9

(69.7%). The most commonly reported education level is Master's degree (47.7%), followed by the second largest category of respondents, who hold college degrees (8.5%). Not quite half of the respondents (42%) had ten years or more of work experience.

Table 14.2 shows the occupational characteristics of employees. The majority of respondents are associated with community development/neighborhood services (46.9%). The second largest association is found to be with the firefighting group (44.3%) followed by the third type, which are administrative jobs (42.7%). The categories are not mutually exclusive, such that one may work in an administrative capacity in law enforcement, for example.

Results

Table 14.3 displays the variables used in the analysis, their descriptive statistics, and their alpha coefficients. As shown, Cronbach alpha coefficients ranged from 0.856 to 0.614, with most above 0.700, indicating acceptable interitem reliability.

Table 14.3 Descriptive statistics and Cronbach's Alpha: Pakistan

	Mean	SD	Cronbach's alpha
Emotive capacity I am good at expressing how I feel I am good at getting people to calm down In my job I am good at dealing with emotional issues	5.23	1.13	0.614
Pretending expression I hide my true feelings so as to appear pleasant at work In my job I act confident and self-assured regardless of how I actually feel I wear a "mask" in order to deal with clients/customers in an appropriate way	5.16	1.34	0.664
Deep acting I try to actually experience the emotions that I must show to clients/customers I work hard to actually feel the emotions that I need to show to clients/customers I work at developing the feelings inside of me that I need to show to clients/customers	4.80	1.41	0.824
Job satisfaction My job provides career development and promotion opportunities I feel I am being paid a fair amount for the work I do I feel satisfied with my supervisor Overall, I am satisfied with my job	4.87	1.53	0.845
Burnout I leave work feeling tired and run down I leave work feeling emotionally exhausted I feel "used up" at the end of the workday	4.30	1.59	0.763
Personal fulfillment I gain a strong sense of personal fulfillment at my job I feel like my job is something I want to do rather than something I have to do My work is a source of personal meaning in my life	5.05	1.48	0.856

These variables were then used in confirmatory factor analysis to assess the measures in the model. Six latent constructs were developed in order to test the model. Several fit indices were evaluated to assess the fit of the measurement model to the data. The chi-square statistic was significant ($p < 0.000$). It is noted that large sample sizes or more complex models are more likely to result in a significant chi-square (Bearden et al. 1982; Fonnel and Larker 1981; Hu and Bentler 1999).

Structural Equation Model

Analysis then proceeded to structural equation modeling, which was employed with Maximum Likelihood Estimation (MLE). Table 14.4 displays the significance and direction of the path coefficients for the structural model. In addition to chi-square, measures used to test for goodness of fit include RMSEA, SRMR, and CFI, all of which are shown at the bottom of Table 14.4.

The paths are illustrated in Fig. 14.1. The bold lines indicate statistically significant paths.

Table 14.4 Structural model results: Pakistan

Hypothesized paths	Coefficients	p-value
Emotive capacity → Job satisfaction	0.265*	0.004
Emotive capacity → Burnout	−0.017	0.841
Emotive capacity → Personal fulfillment	0.252*	0.004
Pretending expression → Job satisfaction	−0.016	0.823
Pretending expression → Burnout	−0.066	0.387
Pretending expression → Personal fulfillment	0.025	0.745
Deep acting → Job satisfaction	0.238*	0.001
Deep acting → Burnout	0.159*	0.027
Deep acting → Personal fulfillment	0.222*	0.001

Model fit: $\chi^2 = 656.475$ (df = 142), CFI = 0.820, RMSEA = 0.097, SRMR = 0.141

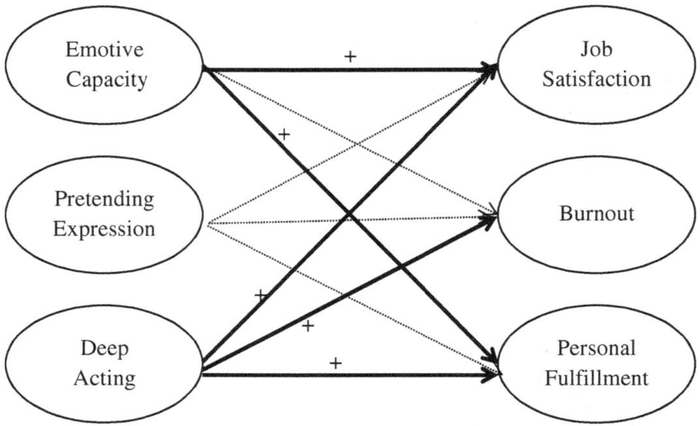

Fig. 14.1 Path diagram for Pakistan

Discussion

This study examined the impact of three dimensions of emotional labor in public service jobs—emotive capacity, pretending expression, and deep acting—on three primary work outcomes, including job satisfaction, burnout, and personal fulfillment, in Pakistan. The purpose of this is to explore how the Pakistani context factors into the impact of emotional labor on those who provide public service.

Results from the structural equation model indicate that emotive capacity has a positive relationship with both job satisfaction and feelings of personal fulfillment. Deep acting—the authentic expression of how one is feeling—is also associated positively with feelings of job satisfaction and personal fulfillment and it is also associated with burnout. Interestingly, pretending expression's relationship with the three outcome variables is not significant with any of them. The relationships between emotive capacity and outcome variables as well as between deep acting and outcome variables are consistent with expectations. The fact that pretending does not produce an effect is of particular interest, because in many countries it has a significant deleterious effect.

Building upon previous studies of emotional labor, we assumed that the capacity to be emotively responsive on the job (emotive capacity) and to engage in authentic displays of emotion (deep acting) would have a positive relationship with job satisfaction and personal fulfillment, and they do. It was further hypothesized that emotional labor would be positively associated with burnout, and it is. That which differs in the Pakistani context compared to research elsewhere is the lack of a relationship between pretending (surface acting) and any of the outcome variables. Of special interest is the lack of a relationship between it and burnout.

Studies conducted elsewhere usually show a positive relationship between pretending and burnout as well as exhaustion (Brotheridge and Grandey 2002; Judge et al. 2009) and depersonalization (Brotheridge and Grandey 2002; Diefendorff et al. 2011). Job satisfaction and personal fulfillment, being positive outcomes, are assumed to be the opposite of burnout. So, it is not unusual for emotional labor to produce both constructive work outcomes as well as a personally destructive outcome, in the form of burnout, when emotive pretending is required. In Pakistan, the context helps to explain this study's counter-intuitive results.

The findings reported here indicate that public employees in Pakistan who must display emotions that they do not actually feel do not suffer the usual consequences that those in most countries do. Employees still are able to feel worthwhile, useful, valuable, and able to give themselves to their organizational work roles. This means when employees wear a fake smile, displaying emotions they do not actually feel, they are not experiencing the angst that usually accompanies having to suppress true feelings in order to comply with organizational display rules. Thus, the emotive incongruency of pretense does not put the individuals in an uncomfortably dissonant state. According to previous studies on emotional labor, when employees stay in a state of discomfort for a prolonged period of time, they can neither associate themselves with their work role nor discover meaningfulness and value in their work. This generally results in reduced organizational outcomes such as diminished satisfaction and personal fulfillment. Public employees in Pakistan, in contrast, demonstrate no such deleterious outcomes, perhaps because they are so accustomed to pretending as they perform their jobs and reconcile their work lives with their personal lives.

People learn to interpret their feelings according to the values, norms, and expectations of the cultural context in which they reside. As mentioned previously, organizational and societal display rules in Pakistan are more incongruent than in Western societies. These findings show that government employees in Pakistan generally see their emotive display as separate from their personal lives and are able to adapt to job demands.

The findings related to emotive capacity and deep acting are more consistent with what is found elsewhere. Since emotive capacity is about personal efficacy rather than about acting, its positive association with job satisfaction and personal fulfillment is quite understandable. And, personal efficacy in dealing authentically with others, in other words, deep acting, contributes to job satisfaction and feelings of self-fulfillment, as is expected.

Conclusion

This is not the first study to demonstrate the flaw in assuming that cultural differences are inconsequential when it comes to public administration. Previous research on the transferability of administrative models from Western to developing countries has shown controversial results. In this regard, scholars have shown disagreements with the myth of value-free administrative systems, and they have highlighted the ineffectiveness of the borrowed Western administrative models in societies with different sets of value systems (Dwivedi and Henderson 1990; Haque 1997; Lammers and Hickson 1979; Martin 1991; Monavvarian 2014).

Since the overall norms and principles of bureaucracy in developing countries are shaped and influenced by the colonial administrative heritage, the post-independence administrative norms borrowed from Western designs and Western trained local experts are often inconsistent with local social norms (Haque 1997). Traditional societal display rules may contradict organizational display rules. Having adapted to this incongruence, it is logical to assume that the adaptation works well in the workplace, equipping workers with the ability to practice emotive pretending, without it affecting their psyche and how they feel about the job. They are accustomed to differentiating between their life experiences in their "in-groups" of friends, family, or religious groups, and they effectively distance themselves from feeling shortchanged when they must suppress their true emotion and express a different emotion in order to perform their jobs.

In this study, public employees showed the ability to achieve feelings of job satisfaction and fulfillment from performing authentic emotional labor. And they showed the ability to don a mask—to emotively pretend—without it affecting how they feel about their work. In other words, as a culture, they have adapted to workplace demands and they accommodate them in a constructive fashion. The work context, characterized by colonial administrative habits, styles, and values, demands that they remain indifferent in their dealings with the public. Haque (1997) categorized this incongruity as formalism, which is described as the incompatibility of the exogenous administrative norms with the indigenous social culture. Adaptation to this disparity between the codes of conduct in private life and codes of conduct on the job is an occupational survival technique.

References

Ahmad, Mumtaz. 1996. "The Crescent and the Sword: Islam, the Military, and Political Legitimacy in Pakistan, 1977–1985." *The Middle East Journal* 50 (3): 372–86.

Amjad, Rashid. 1992. "The Employment Challenges for Pakistan in the 1990s." Accessed March 24, 2019. https://mpra.ub.unimuenchen.de/39265/1/The_Employment_Challenges_for_Pakistan.pdf.

Aronfreed, Justin. 1968. *Conscience and Conduct: The Socialization of Internalized Control over Behavior.* New York, NY: Academic Press.

Bearden, William O., Subhash Sharma, and Jesse E. Teel. 1982. "Sample Size Effects on Chi Square and Other Statistics Used in Evaluating Causal Models." *Journal of Marketing Research* 19 (4): 425–30. https://doi.org/10.1177/002224378201900404.

Bokhari, F. 1996. "Loss of Faith?" *The Banker* 146 (842): 73–76.

Brotheridge, Céleste M., and Alicia A. Grandey. 2002. "Emotional Labor and Burnout: Comparing Two Perspectives of 'People Work'." *Journal of Vocational Behavior* 60 (1): 17–39.

Burki, Shahid Javed. 1993. "Pakistan's Economy in the Year 2000: Two Possible Scenarios'." In *Contemporary Problems of Pakistan*, edited by J. Henry Korson, 1–15. Lahore, Pakistan: Pak Book Corporation.

Diefendorff, James M., Rebecca J. Erickson, Alicia A. Grandey, and Jason J. Dahling. 2011. "Emotional Display Rules as Work Unit Norms: A Multilevel Analysis of Emotional Labor Among Nurses." *Journal of Occupational Health Psychology* 16 (2): 170–86.

Dwivedi, O. P., and Keith M. Henderson. 1990. "State of the Art: Comparative Public Administration and Development Administration." In *Public Administration in World Perspective*, edited by O. P. Dwivedi and Keith M. Henderson, 9–20. Ames: Iowa State University Press.

Fornell, Claes, and David F. Larcker. 1981. "Structural Equation Models with Unobservable Variables and Measurement Error: Algebra and Statistics." *Journal of Marketing Research* 18 (3): 382–88.

Haque, M. Shamsul. 1997. "Incongruity Between Bureaucracy and Society in Developing Nations: A Critique." *Peace & Change* 22 (4): 432–62.

Hofstede, Geert. 1980. *Culture's Consequences: International Differences in Work-Related Values*. Beverly Hills, CA: Sage.

Hofstede, Geert. 1991. *Cultures and Organizations: Software of the Mind*. London, UK: McGraw-Hill.

Hofstede, Geert. 2001. *Culture's Consequences: Comparing Values, Behaviors, Institutions and Organizations Across Nations*. Thousand Oaks, CA: Sage.

Hofstede, Geert, Gert Jan Hofstede, and Michael Minkov. 2010. *Cultures and Organizations: Software of the Mind*. 3rd ed. New York, NY: McGraw Hill.

House, Robert J., Paul J. Hanges, Mansour Javidan, Peter W. Dorfman, and Vipin Gupta. 2004. *Culture, Leadership, and Organizations: The GLOBE Study of 62 Societies*. Thousand Oaks, CA: Sage.

Hu, Li-tze, and Peter M. Bentler. 1999. "Cutoff Criteria for Fit Indexes in Covariance Structure Analysis: Conventional Criteria Versus New Alternatives." *Structural Equation Modeling: A Multidisciplinary Journal* 6 (1): 1–55.

Hussain, Irfan. 1999. "Democracy in the Doldrums." *Dawn*, October 16. Accessed March 24, 2019. https://www.dawn.com/news/1074373.

Jadoon, Muhammad Zafar Iqbal, and Nasira Jabeen. 2010. "Public Administration Education in Pakistan: Issues, Challenges, and Opportunities." *Pakistan Vision* 11 (1): 120–41. Accessed at http://pu.edu.pk/images/journal/studies/PDF-FILES/Artical%20No-6.pdf.

Jamal, A. 1998. "Can We Learn Something from the Perceptions and Consumption Practices of Transnational South Asia Communities Living in the West?" Paper presented at the Inaugural Conference of the Asia Academy of Management, Hong Kong, December 28–30.

James, Morrice. 1993. *Pakistan Chronicle*. London: Hurst.

Judge, Timothy A., Erin Fluegge Woolf, and Charlice Hurst. 2009. "Is Emotional Labor More Difficult for Some Than for Others? A Multilevel, Experience-Sampling Study." *Personnel Psychology* 62 (1): 57–88.

Khan, F. A., and J. Marvi. 1993. "Building Pakistan's International Competitiveness." *Pakistan and Gulf Economist*, 40–50.

Khilji, Shaista E. 1999. *An Empirical Study of Human Resource Management in Pakistan: The Case of Pakistan*. PhD Unpublished Thesis, University of Cambridge.

Khilji, Shaista E. 2000. "East is East: A Culture Sensitive View of HRM in Pakistan." Paper presented at the second Conference of the Asia Academy of Management, Singapore, December 15–18.

Khilji, Shaista E. 2001. "Human Resource Management in Pakistan." In *Human Resource Management in Developing Countries*, edited by Pawan S. Budhwar and Yaw A. Debrah, 102–20. New York, NY: Routledge.

Khilji, Shaista. E. 2002. "Modes of Convergence and Divergence: An Integrative View of Multinational Practices in Pakistan." *International Journal of Human Resource Management* 13 (2): 232–53. https://doi.org/10.1080/09585190110102350.

Korson, J. Henry, ed. 1993. *Contemporary Problems of Pakistan*. Boulder, CO: Westview Press.

Lammers, Cornelis J., and David Hickson, eds. 1979. *Organizations Alike and Unlike: International and Interinstitutional Studies in the Sociology of Organizations*. New York, NY: Routledge.

Lutwak, Nita, Jacqueline B. Panish, Joseph R. Ferrari, and Brian E. Razzino. 2001. "Shame and Guilt and Their Relationship to Positive Expectations and Anger Expressiveness." *Adolescence* 36 (144): 641–53.

Lyon, P. 1993. "Epilogue." In *Pakistan Chronicle*, edited by Morrice James, 242. London: Hurst.

Malik, Iftikhar H. 1996. "The State and Civil Society in Pakistan: From Crisis to Crisis." *Asian Survey* 36 (7): 673–90.

Martin, Denis-Constant. 1991. "The Cultural Dimensions of Governance." *The World Bank Economic Review* 5 (suppl_1): 325–42.

Monavvarian, Abbas. 2014. "A Model of Strategic Thinking: Islamic and Iranian Perspective." *International Journal of Business, Economics and Management* 1 (10): 316–28.

Pakistan Bureau of Statistics. 2019. *Population by Religion*, March 22. Accessed March 25, 2019. http://www.pbs.gov.pk/sites/default/files//tables/POPULATION%20BY%20RELIGION.pdf.

Syed, Jawad. 2008. "From Transgression to Suppression: Implications of Moral Values and Societal Norms on Emotional Labour." *Gender, Work & Organization* 15 (2): 182–201.

Syed, Jawad, Faiza Ali, and Diana Winstanley. 2005. "In Pursuit of Modesty: Contextual Emotional Labour and the Dilemma for Working Women in Islamic Societies." *International Journal of Work Organisation and Emotion* 1 (2): 150–67. https://doi.org/10.1504/IJWOE.2005.008819.

Syed, Jawad, and Faiza Ali. 2013. "Contextual Emotional Labor: An Exploratory of Muslim Female Employees in Pakistan." *Gender in Management: An International Journal* 28 (4): 228–46. https://doi.org/10.1108/GM-01-2013-0007.

Tayeb, Monir. 1997. "Islamic Revival in Asia and Human Resource Management." *Employee Relations* 19 (4): 352–64.

Triandis, Harry Charalambos. 1995. *Individualism & Collectivism*. Boulder, CO: Westview Press.

Trompenaars, Fons, and Charles Hampden-Turner. 1999. *Riding the Waves of Culture: Understanding Diversity*. New York, NY: McGraw-Hill.

15

Philippines

Ador R. Torneo

Emotional labor in the public sector is an emerging topic raising significant interest not only in the USA but also elsewhere in the world. The concept emotional labor was coined by Hochschild (1983) and is defined as "the process by which workers are expected to manage their feelings in accordance with organizationally defined rules and guidelines" (Wharton 2009, 147). Emotional labor is typically described in terms of two types: surface acting, or pretending to feel a certain emotion, and deep acting where workers experience the emotions they are required to show. The interest in emotional labor in the public sector stems partially from the realization that many, if not most, public service jobs require interpersonal contact with the public (Guy et al. 2008). This means that most government employees must manage their emotions in order to perform their jobs effectively.

While public administration in the Philippines often follows the trends and developments in American public administration, there is often a delay before these take root. For example, reforms influenced by the Reinventing Government and New Public Management movements in the USA were adopted in the Philippine civil service only in the late 1990s and early 2000s. Recent initiatives focus on the harmonization of performance evaluation systems and the adoption of new performance management systems (see, e.g., Torneo et al. 2017a, b). While discussions of emotional labor in

A. R. Torneo (✉)
De La Salle University, Manila, Philippines
e-mail: ador.torneo@dlsu.edu.ph

© The Author(s) 2019
M. E. Guy et al. (eds.), *The Palgrave Handbook of Global Perspectives on Emotional Labor in Public Service*, https://doi.org/10.1007/978-3-030-24823-9_15

the public sector have gained significant traction elsewhere, it has not yet taken root in the Philippines. As of this writing, there is no publicly available research on emotional labor in the Philippine public sector.

A handful of studies and a thesis pertaining to emotional labor in the Philippines have been conducted, but they focus on service industries in the private sector. For example, Barcebal et al. (2010) unpublished research examined the effect of emotional labor on the burnout level of 159 frontline employees from several types of service organizations in the Philippines, including airline, food, academe, and call center work. Additionally, Ruppel et al. (2013) research examined emotional labor in the context of a call center in the Philippines. Sia's (2016) work focused on the influence of emotional labor on the work and personal life of employees in a franchise industry setting in the Philippines. Newnham's (2017) more recent study examines and compares the enactment and consequences of emotional labor among frontline hotel workers in the Philippines and Australia.

Barcebal et al. (2010) found that surface acting, but not deep acting, is related to burnout and exhaustion of Filipino service sector employees. These workers engage in more deep acting than surface acting. Ruppel et al. (2013) found that Filipino "call centre employees reported emotional stress, leading to job dissatisfaction, reduced organization commitment and ultimately increased intention to turnover" (246). Newnham (2017) found that both Australian and Filipino workers report higher levels of burnout when using surface acting and lower levels of burnout when using deep acting more often. Respondents in both countries experience similar levels of deep acting and burnout, and those who report high job autonomy also report lower levels of burnout. Higher levels of burnout are reported by individualists who use surface acting more frequently.

The growing global interest in emotional labor in public sector organizations is a significant development since public service delivery often involves the management of emotions. However, the general lack of awareness on emotional labor in the Philippine civil service is regrettable. This aspect of the work is not acknowledged, compensated, or rewarded, and mechanisms to help government employees deal with this aspect of their work are not in place. Thus, Filipino government employees tend to deal with consequences of emotional labor such as stress and burnout on their own. This chapter is an attempt to add to the literature on this topic and to contribute for improving human resource policy in the Philippine public sector.

Overview of the Philippine Civil Service

The Philippines is an archipelagic country of 7641 islands in the Pacific with an estimated national population of 107.7 million as of 2019. It is a developing country with a medium-sized economy and is a founding member of the Association of Southeast Asian Nations (ASEAN). Geographically, it is divided into three major island groups called Luzon, Visayas, and Mindanao and has seventeen administrative regions. It has a presidential and unitary form of government largely patterned after the American system with powers divided among the executive, the bicameral legislature, and the judiciary. The official languages are Filipino and English, but there are eight major languages spoken and at least 120 languages and dialects in use. The country has a significant diaspora resulting in around 10.2 million people of Filipino descent living outside of the country. At least 2.3 million Filipinos are overseas migrant workers.

Modern-day Philippine civil service is guided by the Administrative Code of 1987. The civil service was shaped by American traditions of public administration, and there is a strong emphasis on the principles of merit and professionalism. Applicants need to pass the Civil Service Examinations (CSE) to be eligible for government employment and tenure. Those aspiring to senior career service positions need to pass rigorous exams to attain Career Executive Service Officer (CESO) eligibility and/or need to possess recognized graduate degrees or qualifications. Many top-level positions, however, are appointed at the discretion of the President, and the number of direct and indirect appointees exceeds 7500 (Hodder 2009). Senior officials, such as cabinet and sub-cabinet members and local chief executives, can also freely appoint people in confidential positions involving personal trust. The government also hires temporary consultants and contractual personnel to fill its staffing needs.

Given its substantial population, archipelagic geography, and rapidly growing economy, the size of the Philippine civil service is also proportionally large. The bureaucracy is composed of around 2,420,892 employees distributed among various national government agencies, state universities and colleges, local water districts, local government units, and government-owned and controlled corporations (Civil Service Commission 2017). Of this number, 1,569,585 are career service personnel, 190,917 are noncareer service personnel, and 660,390 are Job-Order or Contract of Service personnel. National government agencies are

Table 15.1 Inventory of human resources of the Philippine Government (as of August 2017)

Major subdivision	1st Level	2nd Level	Total
National government agencies	138,076	1,008,261	1,146,337
Government owned and controlled corporations	19,718	46,859	66,577
State universities and colleges	15,260	42,190	57,450
Local water districts	10,493	4128	14,621
Local government units	177,202	107,398	284,600
Total	360,749	1,208,836	1,569,585

Source Data provided by Civil Service Commission (2017)

estimated to employ a total of 1,146,337 first and second level employees. Table 15.1 shows the distribution of first and second level employees. First level jobs are clerical, trades, crafts, and custodial service positions which involve non-professional or sub-professional work. Qualifications for first level jobs require less than a college degree. Second level jobs are professional, technical, and scientific positions. Qualifications for these jobs require at least a college degree.

Among the national agencies, the largest share of employees can be found in the Department of Education, which employs nearly 600,000 public-school teachers and non-teaching personnel. Beyond that department, the Department of Interior and Local Government and attached agencies employ approximately 170,000 police and non-police personnel in the Philippine National Police, along with 4247 civilian employees. There are 22,062 personnel in the Bureau of Fire Protection, along with 11,217 personnel in the Bureau of Jail Management and Penology. Additionally, there are thousands of personnel in other units according to the Civil Service Commission's 2017 human resources inventory.

Government-owned and controlled corporations employ 66,577 personnel, state universities, and colleges employ 57,450 personnel, and local water districts employ around 14,621 personnel. Local government units also employ large numbers of personnel since they are at the frontline of public service delivery. The total number of personnel employed by local governments is estimated at around 284,600. As of 2017, these personnel are distributed among the Philippines' 81 provinces, 145 cities, 1489 municipalities, and 42,036 barangays at the village level. The official estimated number of personnel for local government units is likely at the conservative side given the common practice of hiring contractual workers and volunteer workers (e.g., Barangay Health Workers) to fill shortages in staffing at the local level.

History of the Philippine Civil Service

Much of the modern-day Philippine civil service systems and structures are patterned after that of the USA, but traces of its pre-colonial history and colonial influences from Spain remain. Prior to Spanish occupation in the seventeenth century, the various islands of the Philippines may be described as autonomous proto-states governed by native leaders called *sultans, datus,* and *rajas* under a politico-administrative system with Islamic and Indian influences. The basic political and administrative unit at the village level was called a *balangay* headed by a village leader or *datu.* As well, native kingdoms and sultanates also existed under the leadership of more powerful leaders of which there were several. Without a single ruler and with varying languages and culture, relationships between the island proto-states were fluid and were characterized by trade, competition, cooperation, and conflicts.

Political and administrative leadership in the villages were held by the *datu* and supported by a council of elders. The *datu* had near unlimited authority and was responsible for defending the community, administering justice, arbitrating conflicts, deciding on the use of communal lands, collecting tributes, and delivering services. A legal system also existed governing ownership of property, inheritance, marriage, rights and obligations, and individual behavior (Abueva 1988; De la Torre 1986). Some regions in Mindanao acquired more power, wealth, and territory and developed into sultanates. Reyes (2011), however, notes that these communities were not able to lay down the foundations of an established bureaucracy, even when these cohesive communities were governed by internal rules and practices and demonstrated political and economic organization and relatively mature culture and institutions.

Spain established a colonial form of government when it gained control over most of the Philippine islands in the seventeenth century. During this period, Spaniards were a privileged class and held the top political and administrative positions in the colonial government. Spanish mestizos also occupied privileged positions well above most natives and migrants in the colony. The colonial government was headed by a *Gobernador-General* representing the Spanish monarchy. A variety of colonial positions such as those of viceroy, members of the supreme court, and provincial executives were also granted based on grants or favors from the monarchy. Catholic friars held very strong influence over not only the religious and socio-cultural life, but also the political and administrative life in the colony (e.g., see Corpuz 1957; Endriga 2003).

During this time, many positions in the colonial government were sold to the highest bidder (Corpuz 1957). The administrative system that Spain established was primarily designed with the "practical objective of increasing the royal estate through tributes, monopolies, fees and fines" (Endriga 2003, 394). The highest position that natives could attain was the *gobernadorcillo*, which fused political, economic, administrative, and judicial leadership. At the village level were units called *pueblos* or *barrios* (Abueva 1988) headed by *cabeza de barangay* or *teniente del barrio*. Spain ruled the islands, which it named Las Islas Filipinas, after the Spanish King Felipe II, for 333 years, until the impending threats of the Philippine Revolution and the challenge of rising US colonial ambitions forced it to cede the colony to the latter in exchange for twenty million dollars in the 1898 Treaty of Paris.

Prior to American colonization, natives waged war against Spain and had established a revolutionary form of government. Filipino revolutionaries had already surrounded the capital of the Spanish colonial government in Intramuros, Manila, before the surprise landing of American troops in 1898. Their arrival was followed by the outbreak of the Philippine-American War in 1899 as the colonial intentions of the USA became clear. In the same year, Filipino revolutionaries promulgated the Malolos Constitution, out-lining in detail the political and administrative system for the new government, even as the war raged (Abueva 1988). These never fully materialized as most of the Philippine revolutionary forces either fell or surrendered to the Americans by 1902, even as small pockets of resistance remained.

The foundations of the modern-day political and administrative systems of the Philippines were established under the direction of the USA from 1898 to 1946. The USA initially established a colonial military government followed by the civilian Insular Government of the Philippine Islands. In contrast to Spain, Americans established a secular government with republican and democratic characteristics, established a public educational system, and allowed increased political participation of Filipinos. Emerging ideas about the "science of administration" influenced their establishment of a professional civil service influenced by merit principles. Additionally, there was a very strong drive for the American colonial government to replace the graft-ridden Spanish civil service with one that is professional and selected based on merit (Reyes 2011). The Commonwealth of the Philippines was established under Filipino political leaders in the presidential elections of 1935, following passage of the Philippine Independence Act of 1934. The Commonwealth was intended to be a transition government in preparation for eventual independence (Hutchcroft 2000; Karnow 1989; Reyes 2011).

Preparation for Philippine independence was interrupted by the outbreak of World War II in 1941 and occupation by the Japanese Imperial Army from 1942 to 1945. In place of the Commonwealth government, whose leaders fled the country with American forces, Japan installed a puppet government with conscripted Filipino leaders under the command of the occupying forces. This period was marked by disruption in the political, economic, and social life as well as in the bureaucracy (Reyes 2011). Filipinos occupying administrative positions were torn between trying to maintain government services and covertly supporting resistance forces fighting Japan. Supporters of Japan were branded as traitors and collaborators. Scholars note that it was common then for bureaucrats to engage in acts of corruption and deliberate sabotage, partially as a form of resistance and an expression of nationalism (Corpuz 1957). Japan's occupation ended when the USA reclaimed the Philippines in the 1945 Battle of Manila.

The period after 1945 involved massive rebuilding of both infrastructure and the political and administrative systems destroyed during the war. Manila, the capital, is often cited as the second most devastated city in the world during World War II after Warsaw, Poland. Most of the destruction attributed to carpet bombing by American forces against Japanese Imperial forces. The war destroyed infrastructure, killed a substantial part of the population, and left the economy and the bureaucracy in shambles. On the 4th of July 1946, the USA granted independence to the Philippines while the country was still struggling to recover from the destruction of the war. New leaders were elected, and rehabilitation and rebuilding began. Many bureaucrats who served under the Japanese were ostracized as collaborators (Corpuz 1957). The civil service was weakened, traumatized, and lost much of its previous prestige (Reyes 2003).

In 1950, the Bell Mission was sent to assess the situation of the Philippines. Part of the mission involved assessing political and administrative capability. The mission concluded that "only the most far-reaching program of reform and self-help, supported by economic and technical assistance from this country [United States] could save the Philippines from total collapse" (Eggan 1951, 16). To rebuild the bureaucracy, and consistent with the mission's recommendations, the Institute of Public Administration (IPA) was established on June 15, 1952, at the University of the Philippines. Its mission was to provide training, teaching, and research in public administration. Filipinos were sent to the USA and trained in American government and public administration. Gradually, the bureaucracy was rebuilt in line with the structures, systems, and principles of American public administration as the country recovered (Reyes 2011).

Before World War II, civil servants in the Philippines enjoyed job security, competitive wages, attractive hours, and generous benefits under the American regime (Endriga 2003). The civil service was a prestigious career.

Political events during and after World War II led to economic hardship and a general distrust toward the government. Rampant corruption and graft in the 1950s and 1960s, along with the declaration of Martial Law under the Marcos Regime, took away the prestige and privileges associated with the civil service (Reyes 2011).

While he was elected democratically in 1965 to a four-year term and reelected in 1969 for a second four-year term, Ferdinand Marcos' declaration of Martial Law from 1972 to 1981 established an authoritarian government. It stayed in power until it was ousted by the People Power Revolution of 1986. Marcos controlled the armed forces, centralized both executive and legislative powers under the Presidency, and effectively ruled by decree. The judiciary was weakened, mass media were largely controlled by the regime, the opposition was restrained, and protests and dissent were suppressed by the authorities, often violently (Thompson 1995).

In this period, many private enterprises were nationalized or transferred to accomplices of the regime (Celoza 1997). Internally, the bureaucracy also experienced conflicting directions. On the one hand, Marcos initiated efforts to reorganize, professionalize, rid the civil service of unqualified personnel, and codify a new civil service code. On the other hand, tenured members of the civil service were summarily dismissed and replaced by accomplices of the regime. The civil service became both a "willing and unwilling" collaborator of the regime (Reyes 2011, 348). Graft and corruption at the highest levels became rampant under the Marcos regime. The economy also spiraled downward, and the Philippines was buried in debt. By 1986, Philippine debt had ballooned from only $600 million in 1965 when Marcos was first elected to $26 billion.

Marcos was ousted in the People Power Revolution of 1986. The new President, Corazon C. Aquino, initially established a Revolutionary Government in 1986 and then a new government under a new Philippine Constitution in 1987. The separation between the executive, legislative, and judiciary was restored, and safeguards were adopted with the intention of preventing the abuses that had happened under the Marcos regime. The period was also marked by the new regimes' attempt to reorganize, rationalize, and cleanse the government of the vestiges of Marcos. The job security of civil servants was once again challenged with the removal of tenured personnel as the new regime attempted to "de-Marcosify" the government. New people were appointed in political and administrative positions and a new code of conduct and ethical standards for public officials and employees were passed. The new regime sought to reinvigorate the civil service and undo the legacies of the Marcos regime (Cariño 1989; Reyes 2011, 349).

After 1986, the bureaucracy was characterized by a period of relative normalcy. A major change in the civil service came in 1992 when the Philippines adopted the Local Government Code of 1991 and the national government embarked on a process of deconcentrating, decentralizing, and devolving many of its powers and functions to local government units. Instead of the previous system of appointments, elections were restored at the local level. Local government units—provinces, cities, municipalities, and barangays—were established to serve both political and administrative functions. These enjoyed a measure of autonomy from the national government. Personnel from national agencies were devolved to, and absorbed by, local government units (Brillantes and Sonco 2011).

The post-1987 period in the Philippines also followed developments in political and administrative thought in the West, albeit with some delay. Reinventing Government, New Public Management, and associated ideas shaped much of the administrative policies adopted by the Philippine government. The government embarked on privatization of public enterprises, outsourced and contracted services, adopted performance management systems, and even adopted e-government. Succeeding administrations carried forward these public-sector reform programs. For example, during the presidency of Fidel V. Ramos (1992–1998), the bureaucracy was reengineered with the goal of achieving better governance. During the rule of Joseph Estrada (1998–2001), effective governance was emphasized. Gloria Macapagal Arroyo's administration engaged in the streamlining of the bureaucracy (Domingo and Reyes 2011). In 2012, the administration of President Benigno Simeon Aquino Jr. also adopted a results-based approach toward performance management. It was called the Strategic Performance Management System (SPMS) and was accompanied by a Performance-Based Incentive System (PBIS) to rationalize the bonuses granted to public sector personnel (Torneo et al. 2017a, b).

Dimensions of National Culture and the Philippine Bureaucracy

The history, experiences, and development of Philippine public administration have allowed it to develop a culture that varies somewhat from the broader societal culture. Reyes (2011) argues that public administration in the Philippines observes and pursues administrative values that are a mixture of three major sometimes compatible, sometimes conflicting, influences.

He enumerates these influences as: the wider Filipino societal culture, the norms of Weberian bureaucracy, and the influences of the colonial periods. These result in a civil service that is in many ways similar in form to the USA after which it was patterned, but with a distinct character and unique set of challenges particular to its culture and context.

Based on his intensive study of how workers' values are shaped by national culture, Geert Hofstede (1984) argued that national cultures could be grouped into four dimensions: power distance, individualism, masculinity, and uncertainty avoidance. These four perspectives came to be known as Hofstede's Dimensions of National Culture. These dimensions have since increased to include long-term orientation and indulgence, bringing the total to six dimensions. These provide a better understanding of the values, beliefs, and norms of a country as well as its workers' values. They can also help put the workings of a country's civil service into context.

The power distance index describes how workers from lower ranks accept that power is distributed unequally throughout an organization. Individualism classifies societies into individualist and collectivist societies. People in collectivist societies tend to gravitate toward each other and are taught at an early age that both immediate and extended family ties are very important. Individualistic societies, on the other hand, tend to be independent of one another, and they focus on taking care of themselves and their immediate family (Hofstede 1984).

Masculinity describes the extent to which a country values achievement and success as compared to valuing nurturing behaviors and equality. Masculine countries tend to strive for achievement and gains in material wealth. Feminine countries are more concerned with quality of life rather than personal gain. Uncertainty avoidance, on the other hand, is the extent to which societies try to deal with the unknown. Countries with high uncertainty avoidance would be more likely to enforce strict laws and behavioral codes in order to minimize uncertainty. Those that score low on uncertainty imposes fewer restrictions are more lenient with laws and their enforcement, and they tend to believe more in change and innovation (Hofstede 1984).

Based on Hofstede's (n.d.-a) dimensions of national culture, the Philippines scores 94/100 in the power distance index, which exemplifies its hierarchical social structure and the people's acceptance of the culture of dualism that is pervasive throughout society. The hierarchical nature of Philippine society, while not as pronounced as in Confucian Asian societies, does have overt manifestations that link to social, political, and economic factors. Children are taught from a young age to respect their elders. Both children and adults perform an honoring gesture called "mano" with elder family, kin, or family friends. Filipino language also adds the polite modifier "po" or "opo" at the end of sentences to signify respect to elders, people perceived to be of high standing, superiors within an organization, religious authority, and even strangers.

In the context of the civil service, hierarchy may be observed in the prevalence of top-down decision-making in public organizations. Unlike in more egalitarian cultures, Filipino employees look up to, and defer to, their superiors and people in authority. They have come to expect that those in higher positions enjoy privileges that may go beyond those that are accorded to their own positions. This phenomenon is called dualism and is a manifestation of the unequal power distribution prevalent in Philippine society.

Varela (2003) argues that dualism has been alive in the islands even before Spanish colonization. Reyes (2003) argues that dualism was further ingrained in Filipino culture during the Spanish and American regime. Under Spain, the caste system was largely erased, and the status of natives was relegated to below the Spanish and Spanish *mestizos*. Then came the Americans, who looked down on Filipinos as "little brown brothers" who needed to be civilized (Wolff 1961). In more recent history, dualism manifests in the better treatment accorded to those in the higher levels of society relative to those in lower positions. Elite officials who are found to be involved in corrupt practices or scandals are often exonerated by presidents while lower-ranking employees suffer more severe consequences. According to Varela (2003), "… these cases of bureaucratic dualism are replicas of the double standard in society covering all aspects of life: familial, social, political, economic, and even religious" (463).

The Philippines scores 32 out of 100 in the individualism dimension. This indicates that it is a collectivist society. This dimension is exemplified by three major traits that Jocano (1981) argues, greatly influences Filipino behavior and decision-making: personalism, familism, and particularism or popularism. Personalism refers to the value Filipinos place in interpersonal communication. Familism refers to the importance, in terms of welfare and interest, given to family over the community. Lastly, particularism or popularism refers to the importance of being well-liked and widely accepted by a group, a community, or an organization. Cultural values such as *utang-na-loob* (related to debt of gratitude), and *pakikisama* (related to maintaining camaraderie) are held in high regard.

These traits can be seen both positively and negatively, depending on the context. On the one hand, they contribute to the smooth interpersonal relations of Filipinos, who can get along with others without showing signs of conflict. They emphasize "being agreeable even under difficult circumstances, sensitive to what others are feeling, and willing to adjust one's behaviour accordingly" (Jocano 1973, 274). On the negative side, it can also contribute to the unwillingness of civil servants to engage in confrontation or outright conflict and instead may result in compromising policies and procedures to avoid disagreements or differences (Reyes 2011, 349). It can also contribute to nepotism and patronage within the bureaucracy (Varela 2003).

The culture of patronage is influenced by the values, beliefs, and norms associated with familism, *utang-na-loob, pakikisama*, nepotism, and favoritism (Varela 2003). Reyes (2003) notes that the policies and practices of filling public offices during Spanish colonization were conceivably the start of the culture of patronage within the Philippine civil service. The practice has become so ingrained within the Philippine culture that it has developed into a societal and administrative norm. De Guzman (2003, 6) best describes the acceptance of this norm within the bureaucracy this way: "Administrators generally accept civil service eligibility as a minimum requirement, but between two or three civil service eligible, they could then choose the one recommended by a politician, a compadre, or a relative."

The Philippines scores 64 out of 100 on the masculinity dimension, making it a masculine country in Hofstede's typology. This denotes a strong value for achievement and gain of material wealth. This is exemplified in economic migration as an accepted way of life in the Philippines. Altogether, almost 10.2 million people of Filipino descent are working and living overseas with many living as permanent residents or having citizenship in other countries. Officially, 2.3 million Filipinos work as Overseas Filipino Workers (OFWs) or migrant workers overseas, primarily in order to improve the lives of their families. These numbers do not take into account the rural to urban migrants or the workers that leave their family in the province to find jobs in the cities. Varela (2003) also notes that most Filipino rank and file employees work multiple jobs or have multiple sources of income to provide for their family.

The strong value for achievement and material wealth may be further reinforced by the link between economic standing and social status. While the Philippines does not have a formal caste system in place, there are high levels of economic inequality and poverty. Those with higher economic status enjoy higher social standing. At the top of the hierarchy are a handful of elite families who hold both economic and political positions at the national and local levels (McCoy 2009). Well-to-do families still typically employ maids from poorer families to do household and menial chores. Because economic mobility is associated with social status, many parents strive and sacrifice to provide their children a good education to improve their socio-economic position and, in the hope, that it will help them lift their families out of poverty.

The Philippines scores 44 out of 100 in the uncertainty avoidance dimension. This reflects the low preference for avoiding uncertainty, a relaxed attitude in which practice counts more than principles, and deviation from rules is tolerated. The Philippines has numerous laws to address graft and corruption, which include, among others, the Anti-Graft and Corrupt Practices Act, the Code of Conduct and Ethical Standards for Public Officials and Employees, and the Procurement Reform Act. Despite these laws, anti-corruption measures have shown little success and very few high-level officials have been convicted for graft and corruption.

Despite promises of reforms, 2017 data from Transparency International show that the Philippines still ranks 111th out of 180 countries in the Corruption Perceptions Index. Varela (2003) argues that a lot of the laws, orders, and decisions conflict with each other, which renders transparency within the system difficult. The challenge of navigating the legal jungle has led to increased ambiguity and acceptance of uncertainty. Furthermore, laws are often not strictly enforced, and implementation is uneven and sometimes follows a case-by-case basis.

The Survey

In this section, we report the data analysis of the survey on emotional labor conducted among public sector employees in the Philippines. The survey was conducted in Pasay City during August and September 2015. Pasay City is located in Metropolitan Manila, the National Capital Region of the Philippines. The city's total population was 417,000 in 2015. We contacted the Pasay City government personnel office, distributed, and recovered 252 survey questionnaires to city employees. Of the total questionnaires, we obtained 209 usable responses, which yielded an 81.7% response rate. Table 15.2 summarizes demographic characteristics of the respondents. A majority, approximately 63%, are in their 40s and 50s. There are more female respondents (60%) than male respondents. In terms of the education level, most of the respondents (87.5%) are college graduates or higher.

The respondents are from various occupations (see Table 15.3). The top five occupations claim about half of the total occupations (52.7%). In descending order, they are health care (16.1%), administration (12.2%),

Table 15.2 Demographic characteristics: Philippines

	Frequency	Percent
Age		
Less than 30	21	10.0
30–39 years	44	21.5
40–49 years	72	34.4
50–59 years	60	28.7
60 or more	7	3.3
N/A	5	2.1
Gender		
Female	125	59.8
Male	83	39.7
N/A	1	0.5
Public service experience		
Less than 10	65	31.1
10–19 years	77	36.8
20–29 years	40	19.1
30 or more	19	9.1
N/A	8	3.9
Educational level		
Less than high school	0	0.0
High school graduate	4	1.9
Some college	7	3.3
2-year associate degree	12	5.7
College graduate	113	54.1
Some graduate school	12	5.7
Master's degree	31	14.8
Law degree (J.D., LL.B.)	9	4.3
Doctorate degree (Ph.D., M.D., Ed.D.)	18	8.6
Other (please specify)	1	0.5
N/A	2	1.1

finance or accounting (8.9%), community development/ neighborhood services (8.0%), and education (7.5%).

This study employs structural equation modeling (SEM) to investigate the effect of emotional labor on behavioral outcome variables. Emotional labor in this study is composed of three dimensions (Yang et al. 2018). The three constructs of emotional labor are emotive capacity, pretending expression, and deep acting. The three behavioral variables included in the model are job satisfaction, burnout, and personal fulfillment. Table 15.4 summarizes the mean scores, standard deviations, and Cronbach's alpha coefficients. In terms of the reliability test, all of the variables achieve a Cronbach's alpha level of above 0.7.

Table 15.5 summarizes the results of the structural equation modeling analysis.

Table 15.3 Occupational characteristics: Philippines

Occupation	Frequency	Percent
1. Administration	44	12.2
2. Community development/neighborhood services	29	8.0
3. Engineering, manufacturing, or production	21	5.8
4. Education	27	7.5
5. Disaster response	16	4.4
6. Finance or accounting	32	8.9
7. Firefighter	0	0.0
8. Health care	58	16.1
9. Housing	1	0.3
10. Human resource management	18	5.0
11. Information and communication	12	3.3
12. Law enforcement	2	0.6
13. Military	0	0.0
14. Public relations	24	6.6
15. Planning	17	4.7
16. Public works: streets, sanitation, utilities	6	1.7
17. Purchasing	5	1.4
18. Recreation and parks	2	0.6
19. Research and development	9	2.5
20. Social services	22	6.1
21. Transportation	1	0.3
22. Support services (such as equipment maintenance)	2	0.6
23. Other	13	3.6

Table 15.4 Descriptive statistics and Cronbach's alpha: Philippines

	Mean	SD	Cronbach's alpha
Emotive capacity	5.43	1.05	0.734
Pretending expression	5.20	1.29	0.709
Deep acting	5.25	1.07	0.778
Job satisfaction	5.20	1.28	0.760
Burnout	4.48	1.46	0.800
Personal fulfillment	5.71	1.12	0.841

Figure 15.1 depicts a path diagram showing relationships between the emotional labor variables and the behavioral variables. The bold paths are statistically significant at $p \leq 0.05$. As shown, the emotive capacity variable has a significant effect on the three behavioral variables. It is positively related to both job satisfaction and personal fulfillment, while it is negatively related to burnout. In the Philippine context, as workers perceive that they are good at dealing with emotional issues in their workplace, they are more likely to be satisfied with their job. Likewise, the more an employee feels a high level of emotive capacity, the higher the level of his or her personal

Table 15.5 Structural model results: Philippines

Hypothesized paths	Coefficients	p-Value
Emotive capacity → Job satisfaction	0.534*	0.000
Emotive capacity → Burnout	−0.259*	0.005
Emotive capacity → Personal fulfillment	0.550*	0.000
Pretending expression → Job satisfaction	0.000	0.996
Pretending expression → Burnout	−0.011	0.916
Pretending expression → Personal fulfillment	0.043	0.681
Deep acting → Job satisfaction	−.080	0.541
Deep acting → Burnout	0.398*	0.000
Deep acting → Personal fulfillment	−0.004	0.973

Model fit: $\chi^2 = 417.501$ (df = 142), CFI = 0.827, RMSEA = 0.096, SRMR = 0.168

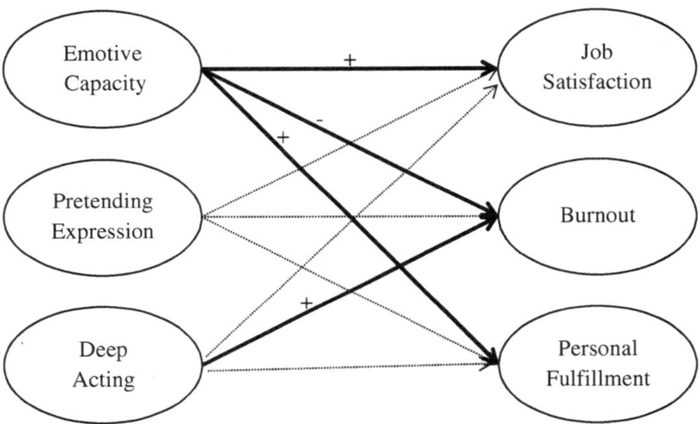

Fig. 15.1 Path diagram for Philippines

fulfillment is. As well, high emotive capacity diminishes the likelihood of burnout.

In terms of the effect of pretending expression, this variable shows no significant effect on job satisfaction, burnout, or personal fulfillment. Traditionally, analysts believe that suppressing individual's true feelings to appear pleasant in a workplace causes burnout as well as decreases job satisfaction and personal fulfillment (Hochschild 1983; Morris and Feldman 1996). However, this is not true in the case of the Philippines. It seems the intensity of emotive pretending, whether it is high or low, does not lead to any meaningful difference in job-related behavior for Philippine public sector employees. The idea that emotive pretending has a negative effect was primarily developed in the US work environment. The finding from the Philippine data implies that emotive pretending is experienced differently in this culture and context.

The results also reveal that deep acting has a statistically significant positive impact on burnout. The direction of the relationship between deep acting and burnout is not consistent with findings in the US. Hochschild (1983) posits that deep acting among US workers can lessen burnout while strengthening job satisfaction and personal fulfillment. The Philippine survey shows a different result, with authentic emotive expression increasing, rather than decreasing, burnout. This leads to the question of whether there are cultural differences in emotive expression that are specific to the Philippines (Matsumoto and Yoo 2008).

Discussion of Results

It is possible that the differences in the impact of emotional labor in the Philippines and the USA may partially reflect differences in culture and context. Using the latest data on Hofstede's dimensions of national culture, we find that the two countries have similar scores in the masculinity and uncertainty avoidance dimensions, but they differ in the power distance and individualism dimensions (*Hofstede Insights* n.d.-a, n.d.-b). The Philippines is a highly collectivist society with a score of 32 in the individualism dimension whereas the USA is a highly individualist society with its score of 91. The Philippines tends to be more accepting of hierarchy with its score of 94 in the power distance index while the USA is more egalitarian with a score of 40. In the masculinity dimension, the Philippines scored 62 and the USA scored 64, indicating the strong value the culture in both countries place on material well-being. In the uncertainty avoidance dimension, the Philippines scored 44 while the USA scored 46, suggesting both cultures have a relaxed attitude toward rules and regulations and that deviating from the rules is tolerated.

We do not have enough data at this point to definitively resolve how much of the differences in the Philippine and the US cases can be explained by cultural or contextual differences. We note that among the countries covered in the study reported in this handbook, the effect of emotional labor on behavioral outcome variables in the Philippines is most similar to Thailand and India. It is identical to Thailand and differs with India on only one relationship. While there is a significant positive relationship between deep acting and burnout in the Philippines, there is no relationship between these two variables in India. Why this is the case requires further exploration, especially since these three countries have very distinct cultures and public administration traditions.

Interestingly, the results also reveal that the impact of some dimensions of emotional labor in the Philippines also differs between public and private sector employees. The impact of deep acting on burnout among the government employees surveyed in this study is different from its impact on those in the private sector in previous studies. Barcebal et al. (2010) found that surface acting, but not deep acting, is related to exhaustion and burnout among employees of service organizations. These employees tended to engage in more deep acting rather than surface acting, but this did not correlate significantly with exhaustion and burnout. Newnham (2017), on the other hand, found that Filipino hotel frontline service workers report higher levels of burnout when using surface acting and lower levels of burnout when using deep acting more often.

The difference in the impact of surface and deep acting between Philippine public and private organizations merits further investigation. It may reflect differences in methodology and measurement between the studies, differences in the organizations where the surveys were conducted, or even fundamental differences in the culture and context of Philippine private sector and public sector organizations. It is difficult to resolve this question without a deeper study, but preliminary information provides some leads worth investigating.

As noted earlier, government employees in the Philippines operate in an environment where values are a mixture of three sometimes compatible, sometimes conflicting, influences. These include the broader Filipino societal culture with its idiosyncrasies which include personalism, familism, and debt of gratitude among others; the formalities dictated under the norms of Weberian bureaucracy, which include strict adherence to rules; and colonial influences, which include merit and fitness among others (Reyes 2011, 349).

The mixture of values means that Filipino government employees must navigate their mandates along with a complex set of cultural expectations that may vary from case to case and from time to time. These can conceivably take a toll in terms of job satisfaction, personal fulfillment, and burnout. An employee might take on the role of an impersonal and strict rule-abiding civil servant when dealing with the general public one moment and then switch into a more sympathetic, personalistic, and flexible persona when dealing with "very important persons" (VIPs), friends, or relatives the next moment. The latter may also have to deal with requests for favors which on occasion may entail deviating from established policies and procedures which is likely to be stressful. This is likely to occur in local governments since employees will generally be dealing with people from their own communities.

Another factor to consider is that Filipino government employees are expected to meet public expectations in an environment of scarce resources and low pay. When the survey was conducted, the average pay of Philippine government employees was generally lower than their private sector counterparts. In the local setting, government employees must deal with all kinds of requests ranging from routine public services to sometimes desperate pleas for assistance for hospitalization, medicine, scholarships, weddings, jobs, and even burials. Expectations are from womb to tomb. The resources of local governments, however, are often very limited. Even when employees sincerely want to extend help, they may not always have enough resources or the best means to do so. Plausibly, this requires significant emotional labor on their part.

Lastly, Philippine government employees often have to deal with political pressure and navigate the sometimes-turbulent waters between politics and administration. In addition to complying with legal and administrative rules, they also must be sensitive to the expectations of political principals. This is especially true in local governments since the distance between elected officials and their constituents tend to be very narrow. A local government employee must be highly sensitive to political cues. For example, they cannot simply just invoke the rules and turn away "special requests." They must be careful lest they offend supporters, friends, or relatives of incumbent local officials and affect their chances for reelection.

Private sector employees in the Philippines generally do not have to navigate the same set of complex rules and expectations as public sector employees. Overall, they tend to have narrower and better-defined performance targets, enjoy better pay, serve only a select group of clienteles, and are able to treat all clients in a similar manner: as customers whose business is important and whose satisfaction is of paramount importance. They do not have to switch roles as often, do not have to deal with political pressure and political principals, have a limited set of public expectations, and are less likely to deal with situations involving breaking with established rules or procedures when compared to local government employees.

We end this chapter with the proposition that the effect of emotional labor on behavioral outcome variables including job satisfaction, personal fulfillment, and burnout in the Philippine public sector may be tempered by cultural and contextual factors whose mechanisms we do not yet fully understand, and which should be subject to further study. Culture and context may potentially explain the similarities in the findings between the Philippines, Thailand, and India, the notable differences in the USA and Philippines, and the differences in the emotional labor between Philippine private and public sector employees. Future studies should consider integrating measurable social and cultural dimensions in the empirical model and complement this with comparative or cross-case analysis to gauge how these dimensions relate to aspects of emotional labor between and within country cases. Mixed methods research can also probe more deeply the particularities, the context, and the relationship among the various dimensions of emotional labor in the context of Philippine public and private sector organizations.

References

Abueva, J. V. 1988. "Philippine Ideologies and National Development." In *Government and Politics of the Philippines*, edited by Raul P. de Guzman and M. A. Reforma, 8–73. Singapore: Oxford University Press.

Barcebal, M., M. Chua, K. A. Dulay, and G. Hechanova. 2010. "Emotional Labor and Burnout Among Filipino Service Workers." *Philippine Daily Inquirer*, June 21. Retrieved from https://www.pressreader.com/philippines/philippine-daily-inquirer/20100621/283631051282797.

Brillantes, A., and J. T. Sonco. 2011. "Decentralization and Local Governance in the Philippines." In *Public Administration in Southeast Asia: Thailand, Philippines, Malaysia, Hong Kong, and Macao*, edited by Evan M. Berman, 355–79. Boca Raton, Florida: CRC Press.

Cariño, L. V. 1989. "Bureaucracy for a Democracy: The Struggle of the Philippine Political Leadership and the Civil Service in the Post-Marcos Period." *Philippine Journal of Public Administration* 33 (3): 2017–252.

Celoza, A. F. 1997. *Ferdinand Marcos and the Philippines: The Political Economy of Authoritarianism*. Santa Barbara, CA: Greenwood Publishing Group.

Civil Service Commission. 2017. *Inventory of Government Human Resource (as of August 31, 2017)*. Retrieved from http://www.csc.gov.ph/phocadownload/IGHR/2017/IGHR%20Manual%20FY2017_asofAugust31.pdf.

Corpuz, Onofre D. 1957. *The Bureaucracy in the Philippines*. Manila, Philippines: Institute of Public Administration.

De Guzman, Raul P. 2003. "Is There a Philippine Public Administration?" In *Introduction to Public Administration in the Philippines: A Reader*. 2nd ed., edited by V. A. Bautista, M. P. Alfiler, D. R. Reyes, and P. D. Tapales, 3–11. Quezon City, Philippines: National College of Public Administration and Governance.

De la Torre, Visitacion R. 1986. *History of the Philippine Civil Service*. Quezon City, Philippines: New Day Publishers.

Domingo, M. O. Z., and D. R. Reyes. 2011. "Performance Management Reforms in the Philippines." *Public Administration in Southeast Asia: Thailand, Philippines, Malaysia, Hong Kong, and Macao*, edited by Evan M. Berman, 397–402. Boca Raton, FL: CRC Press.

Eggan, F. 1951. "The Philippines and the Bell Report." *Human Organization* 10 (1): 16–21.

Endriga, J. N. 2003. "Stability and Change: The Civil Service in the Philippines." In *Introduction to Public Administration in the Philippines: A Reader*. 2nd ed., edited by V. A. Bautista, M. P. Alfiler, D. R. Reyes, and P. D. Tapales, 393–414. Quezon City, Philippines: National College of Public Administration and Governance.

Guy, Mary E., Meredith A. Newman, and Sharon H. Mastracci. 2008. *Emotional Labor: Putting the Service in Public Service*. Armonk, New York: M. E. Sharpe.

Hochschild, Arlie. 1983. *The Managed Heart*. Berkeley, CA: University of California Press.

Hodder, R. 2009. "Political Interference in the Philippine Civil Service." *Environment and Planning C: Politics and Space* 27 (5): 766–82.

Hofstede, Geert. 1984. "Cultural Dimensions in Management and Planning." *Asia Pacific Journal of Management* 1 (2): 81–99.

Hofstede Insights. n.d.-a. *Philippines*. Accessed April 13, 2019. https://www.hofstede-insights.com/country/the-philippines/.

Hofstede Insights. n.d.-b. *United States*. Accessed April 13, 2019. https://www.hofstede-insights.com/country/the-usa/.

Hutchcroft, P. D. 2000. "Colonial Masters, National Politicos, and Provincial Lords: Central Authority and Local Autonomy in the American Philippines, 1900–1913." *The Journal of Asian Studies* 59 (2): 277–306.

Jocano, F. Landa. 1973. *Folk Medicine in a Philippine Community*. Quezon City, Philippines: Punlad Research House.

Jocano, F. Landa. 1981. *Folk Christianity: A Preliminary Study of Conversion and Patterning of Christian Experience in the Philippines*. Quezon City, Philippines: Trinity Research Institute, Trinity College of Quezon City.

Karnow, S. 1989. *In Our Image: America's Empire in the Philippines—Headlines Series 288*. New York, NY: Foreign Policy Association.

Matsumoto, D., and S. H. Yoo. 2008. "Methodological Considerations in the Study of Emotion Across Cultures." In *Handbook of Emotion Elicitation and Assessment*, edited by J. A. Coan and J. J. B. Allen, 332–48. Oxford, UK: Oxford University Press.

McCoy, A. W., ed. 2009. *An Anarchy of Families: State and Family in the Philippines*. Madison, WI: University of Wisconsin Press.

Morris, J. A., and D. C. Feldman. 1996. "The Dimensions, Antecedents, and Consequences of Emotional Labor." *Academy of Management Review* 21: 986–1010.

Newnham, M. P. 2017. "A Comparison of the Enactment and Consequences of Emotional Labor Between Frontline Hotel Workers in Two Contrasting Societal Cultures." *Journal of Human Resources in Hospitality & Tourism* 16 (2): 192–214.

Reyes, D. R. 2003. "Public Administration in the Philippines: History, Heritage, Hubris." In *Introduction to Public Administration in the Philippines: A Reader.* 2nd ed., edited by V. A. Bautista, M. P. Alfiler, D. R. Reyes, and P. D. Tapales, 38–65. Quezon City, Philippines: National College of Public Administration and Governance.

Reyes, D. R. 2011. "History and Context of the Development of Public Administration in the Philippines." In *Public Administration in Southeast Asia: Thailand, Philippines, Malaysia, Hong Kong, and Macao,* edited by Evan M. Berman, 355–80. Boca Raton, FL: CRC Press.

Ruppel, C. P., R. L. Sims, and P. Zeidler. 2013. "Emotional Labour and its Outcomes: A Study of a Philippine Call Centre." *Asia-Pacific Journal of Business Administration* 5 (3): 246–61.

Sia, L. A. 2016. "Emotional Labor and Its Influence on Employees' Work and Personal Life in a Philippine Franchise Dining Industry Setting." *International Journal of Applied Industrial Engineering (IJAIE)* 3 (1): 74–85.

Thompson, M. R. 1995. *The Anti-Marcos Struggle: Personalistic Rule and Democratic Transition in the Philippines.* New Haven, CT: Yale University Press.

Torneo, Ador R., Georgeline B. Jaca, Jose Ma Arcadio C. Malbarosa, and Jose Lloyd D. Espiritu. 2017a. *Impact of the PBIS on the Productivity and Morale of Employees of the Department of Interior and Local Government (DILG): A Quantitative Assessment.* Unpublished Report Submitted to Philippines-Australia Human Resources and Organisational Development Facility (PAHRODF).

Torneo, Ador R., Georgeline B. Jaca, Jose Ma Arcadio C. Malbarosa, Jose Lloyd D. Espiritu. 2017b. *Preliminary Assessment of the Performance-Based Incentives System (PBIS) on Selected Agencies: Policy Recommendations.* Accessed March 2, 2019. https://www.pahrodf.org.ph/prgs/final-policy-notes/pbis-policy-note-final.pdf.

Varela, A. 2003. "The Culture Perspective in Organization Theory: Relevance to Philippine Public Administration." In *Introduction to Public Administration in the Philippines: A Reader,* 2nd ed., edited by V. A. Bautista, M. P. Alfiler, D. R. Reyes, and P. D. Tapales, 438–72. Quezon City, Philippines: National College of Public Administration and Governance.

Wharton, Amy S. 2009. "The Sociology of Emotional Labor." *Annual Review of Sociology* 35: 147–65.

Wolff, L. 1961. *Little Brown Brother: How the United States Purchased and Pacified the Philippine Islands at the Century's Turn.* Quezon City, Philippines: Wolff Productions.

Yang, Seung-Bum, Mary E. Guy, Aisha Azhar, Chih-Wei Hsieh, Hyun Jung Lee, Xiaojun Lu, and Sharon H. Mastracci. 2018. "Comparing Apples and Manzanas: Instrument Development for Cross-National Analysis of Emotional Labor in Public Service Jobs." *International Journal of Work Organization and Emotion* 9 (3): 264–82. https://doi.org/10.1504/IJWOE.2018.10015953.

16

Rwanda

Sebawit G. Bishu

Rwanda is one of the forty-eight countries in the sub-Saharan Africa (SSA) region. It is located in the Central/Eastern part of the sub-Saharan Africa region and is a landlocked country with a population of 11.9 million people (World Bank, n.d.a). While a small country, Rwanda has the highest population density in the African continent. Less than three decades ago, Rwanda went through a dramatic social and political crisis that culminated in genocide. Despite the social, economic, and political upheaval that followed, the country has rehabilitated itself and developed stable economic growth. Its economic and structural reforms succeeded in making major changes to its social, economic, and political landscape (Arndt et al. 2016).

In the last two and half decades, Rwanda has reported steady economic growth and has improved poverty conditions, including achieving food security (IMF 2011). By the end of 2015, it was one of the few sub-Saharan nations that had succeeded in achieving most of the United Nations' Millennium Development Goals (World Bank, n.d.a). It is one of the most agriculture-dependent economies in the sub-Saharan region, with approximately 89% of the population involved in work related to farming (McMillan and Headey 2014).

Rwanda's economic growth and stability have been consistently improving since the 1994 civil war. Data show that by the year 2012, eighteen years after the genocide, Rwanda's gross domestic product (GDP) per capita was

S. G. Bishu (✉)
School of Public Affairs, University of Colorado Denver, Denver, CO, USA
e-mail: sebawit.bishu@ucdenver.edu

© The Author(s) 2019
M. E. Guy et al. (eds.), *The Palgrave Handbook of Global Perspectives on Emotional Labor in Public Service*, https://doi.org/10.1007/978-3-030-24823-9_16

50% larger than it was before the genocide (Arndt et al. 2016). Steady economic growth is also evident in the improved day to day living conditions of the people. Today, Rwanda is often cited as Africa's success story.

This chapter has two main sections. The first provides a review of key social, political, and institutional events that have taken place in Rwanda. This historical review provides insight into forces that continue to shape public service delivery in the country. Discussed here is the national war recovery and rehabilitation strategy that yielded extraordinary results, making Rwanda a socially and economically progressive country. The second section cites survey data collected from public servants in Rwanda and describes how they report emotional labor in their jobs and the outcomes this produces in terms of their everyday work experience. Implications of the findings are discussed in light of the country's social and institutional context.

From Colonization to Independence

Rwanda was colonized by Germany from 1887 to 1919 and later by Belgium until independence in 1962. The German colonial administration was short-lived and left comparatively little impression on the social, economic, and political structure of the country. Belgium's colonial administration, on the other hand, stamped a significant impression on Rwanda's social, economic, and political structures (Powley 2003). Essentially, Belgian colonial powers planted the roots that gave rise to ethnic division and group superiority (Powley 2005). Powley (2003) argues that when Belgian colonizers "consolidated local power in the hands of Tutsi chiefs and privileged Tutsi over Hutu with regard to land rights, education, socioeconomic opportunity, and access to power," that introduced the concept of ethnic group superiority and led to the genocide that occurred in the 1990s (10). Historian Prunier (1995) also reports that colonialism introduced the "systematic violence" that lead to the genocide (25). Colonialism disrupted the existing social harmony and promoted an economic and social structure where one ethnic group dominated others.

The Genocide

Rwanda's history is marked by ethnic violence that took 800,000 lives in just 100 days. The genocide disrupted the social, economic, and physical fabric of the country (Powley 2005). In its aftermath, Clark (2018) reports that:

When the Rwandan Patriotic Front (RPF), the rebel movement led by Paul Kagame, captured control of Rwanda and halted the genocide in July 1994, it inherited not so much a state as a cemetery. In the preceding 100 days, 800,000 people out of a national population of seven million had been murdered, the majority by their neighbors and other civilians. Seventy percent of all Tutsis, the ethnic minority that had been the target of the Hutu *génocidaires*, were dead, along with 30% of all Twas, the smallest of Rwanda's ethnic groups. Throughout Rwanda, roads, rivers, and pit latrines were clogged with rotting corpses. The infrastructure of the country—houses, roads, hospitals, offices, schools, power stations, and reservoirs—lay in ruins. Nearly all government workers—politicians, judges, civil servants, doctors, nurses, and teachers—had died or fled. Looters had emptied the banks, leaving the national treasury without a single Rwandan franc. (Clark 2018, para. 1)

The genocide was fueled by bipolar ethnic conflict that left citizens traumatized and the country's infrastructure devastated. The conflict ended in 1994 when the Tutsi-dominated ethnic group (Rwandan Patriotic Front) gained military power. To date the Rwandan Patriotic Front (RPF) is the party that governs the country. The genocide impacted men, women, young, and old alike. Many men were killed in the genocide, and women lost their husbands and children and survived rape and physical abuse (Powley 2003). Communities were displaced, and livelihoods were destroyed. Powley (2005) reports that in addition to the violence that communities experienced, many were displaced, families were disintegrated, and livelihoods were destroyed. Survivors were traumatized. Besides material loss, the genocide shattered existing social structures and support networks that played central roles in sustaining communities. The genocide also caused significant loss of the male population, with 70% of the country's population reportedly being women in the immediate aftermath (Powley 2003).

War and Reconstruction

The World Bank reports that during the genocide period, the life expectancy of the Rwandan people was less than 30 years (World Bank, n.d.b). The majority of men who engaged in the war never returned, leaving women with the responsibility of providing for their families. At the war's conclusion, the new government that took power functioned under dire circumstances. Hunt (2017) reports that:

With no running water, erratic electricity, and offices looted to the last piece of paper, the new Rwandan Patriotic Front government went to work, focusing first on the fetid cleanup and then on reestablishing political structures. They had little institutional knowledge to draw on: previous leaders had fled or been killed; new leaders had minimal governance experience. Of some 785 judges before the genocide, twenty survived. When the transitional National Assembly was created in November 1994, none of the seventy-four new members and only five staff members had participated in the prewar parliament. (70)

Rwanda's recovery is yet to be over. As of 2016, life expectancy had more than doubled from twenty years prior, such that it was now 67 years (World Bank, n.d.b). But in addition to rebuilding social, economic, physical, and political infrastructure, the country still struggles to re-establish social norms and order. Uwamaliya and Smith (2017) report that, to date, significant numbers of genocide survivors lack access to education, including access to basic primary education. Individuals with war-related disabilities lack access to basic services (Uwamaliya and Smith 2017). Over 23 years after the genocide, rehabilitation remains a public health challenge. Along with delivering basic needs, many also argue that holistic rehabilitation requires that government and other service providers tackle justice issues (Siegert and Ward 2010; Uwamaliya and Smith 2017).

Rebuilding the Public Sector

After the civil war, government was faced with the challenge of rebuilding its public sector workforce. With a significant part of the population deceased or dislocated, recruiting public servants was a costly and time-consuming effort. Applying a large-scale hiring effort proved to be expensive and depleted limited resources. Hausman (2011) reports that after the genocide, surviving public servants who returned to their positions did so out obligation to their country. Upon return, many served in exchange for food assistance. Despite large-scale efforts to restore governmental functions, public institutions lacked proper recruitment and staffing procedures. In the absence of proper procedures, performance monitoring lacked a system of evaluation. This meant that little was known regarding whether government was effectively executing its work. Essentially, for a long time the civil service simply operated in a state of emergency. A few years after the civil war, systems began to be put in place and a civil service reform was launched with the goal of improving effective delivery of services.

The civil service reform aimed at decentralizing public service delivery. In this effort, the Ministry of Local Government employed over 4000 civil servants who were engaged in hospitals, schools, and other reconstruction efforts (Hausman 2011). During its early implementation, the reform faced several challenges. Some of them involved recruiting skilled laborers, inflated salaries and lack of proper staffing inventory. Hausman (2011) reports that "civil servants often lacked basic qualifications…in 1998, 80% of civil servants lacked secondary school qualifications, and many had not finished primary school" (3). The reform was latter followed by establishment of the Public Service Commission, whose mission was to address government ineffectiveness and build a skilled public-sector workforce. The commission was later successful at restoring core governmental services. To this date, civil service reform is seen as a successful undertaking in the country's post-conflict reconstruction.

Decentralization and Rebuilding Local Governments

A large undertaking of the reform effort involved decentralizing power from the central government to lower levels of government. This process was initiated in the effort to promote public participation at local levels. The reform itself fostered local elections, citizen participation in matters of local governance, and organizing local communities to engage in local policy decisions. Besides decentralization of service delivery, the Rwandan government educated citizens and public servants about the changing roles of local governments. The government decentralization process was implemented in phases.

> The first stage, between 2000 and 2003, included the sector- and cell-committee elections and a campaign to publicize the decentralization program. In the second stage, the central and provincial governments would shrink while district and sector governments grew and took on new responsibilities. (Hausman 2011, 4)

The decentralization effort was focused on developing autonomy and capacity building. Establishing civil service accountability was also a part of the reform (Hausman 2011). As part of the newly established system, local leaders were made accountable for participating in public performance contracts that ensure delivery of set outcomes. The newly introduced system instilled a need for collaboration with local communities, such that they became a vital part of policy implementation plans.

The Psychology of War

In the Rwandan culture, natural death is celebrated when it is expected (Bagilishya 2000). However, when death is unexpected and comes as a surprise, Bagilishya (2000) reports that:

> Rwandan tradition imposes a strict code of behavior when confronted with great sorrow. Self-control, discretion and the patience to wait for a favorable moment to exact restitution or revenge for wrongs suffered are a part of the attitudes and behaviors highly valued by Rwandan culture. (347–48)

When death is caused by an adversary, Bagilishya (2000) reports:

> …traditional Rwandan law is clear: vengeance is the family's obligation. Revenge can be carried out without distinction on any male relative of the murderer's family. If the family does not satisfy this obligation, the spirits of the victim will take over by troubling the family in diverse ways in order to remind them of their duty. (348)

With the civil war, vicious cycles of vengeance and adversity became the norm. Social norms that promoted harmony were lost. Ethnic groups were hostile to each other. Groups that lost family members retaliated in return. The genocide left a permanent mark on the psychological well-being of the Rwandese people. For the Rwandan government, healing the wounds caused by war has been a process that demands time, effort, and resources. Trauma recovery necessitated that communities, government, and civil society organizations mobilize resources. Where order was lost, community leaders and public servants acted as mediators. They mobilized resources to help break cycles of retribution. Healing and reconciliation therefore became an integral part of the public service that community leaders and members of civil societies delivered.

Reconciliation

In the aftermath of the genocide, reconciliation and rebuilding trust among social groups was necessary but challenging. Rwanda's social conflict stemmed from ethnic segregation and polarization promoted by ethno-centric nationalism. Diffusing ethnic conflict was therefore an essential component of the reconstruction effort. A nationwide, government-initiated effort to reestablish social harmony was known as "Umuganda." "Umuganda" means once a month day of service (Specia 2017). It is explained this way:

> The premise is simple and extraordinary in its efficient enforcement: Every able-bodied Rwandan citizen between the ages of 18 and 65 must take part in community service for three hours once a month. The community identifies a new public works problem to tackle each month. (Specia, 2017, para. 3)

"Umuganda" was introduced to foster a culture of collaboration. The program, led by the National Unity and Reconciliation Commission, was a means to facilitate social healing and to rebuild social cohesion. In 2015, several years after the commission's initial launch, it reports that reconciliation in Rwanda was at 92.5% (Specia 2017). Besides government-initiated programs like "Umuganda," civil society organizations played a critical role in reconciliation efforts. They provided socio-economic rehabilitation as well as peace and reconciliation services. Government depended on civil society organizations to provide reconciliation trainings and to provide counseling services to victims and perpetrators of the genocide. Since the war, civil society organizations have aided in restoring society's trust in communities and in government.

The Emotive Work of War Recovery

Rwanda's genocide is one of the grimmest man-made crises of the twentieth century. In its aftermath, Rwanda was left to ruins and the country was devastated. The task of recovery was immense. Hunt (2017) reports:

> Rwanda lay in ruins: churches and schools turned into massacre sites, roadsides turned into open graves. Those who managed to survive faced the herculean task of rebuilding when every semblance of normalcy had vanished. (70)

Guy and Newman (2004) argue that emotion work is an integral part of the service that bureaucrats deliver, and it has been well-established that such work impacts program outcomes and citizen satisfaction (Remington 2017). Studies that explore post-war recovery echo this refrain and reveal the emotional demand inherent in engaging with war victims (Byrski 2012). Research on the emotive work of war recovery mainly focuses on the role that aid and medical care providers play in rehabilitation efforts. Frontline service providers who engage in war rehabilitation nurture citizens back to life after their traumatic experiences. Mastracci et al. (2012) report that emotional labor in public service delivery necessitates that public servants:

> … suppress, exaggerate, or otherwise manipulate their own and/or another's private feelings in order to comply with work-related display rules …. Public service jobs require emotional labor because they involve working directly with people and, more crucially, because they target vulnerable populations or people in vulnerable situations. This is due to the nature of the services provided by government and the role of government as harbor of refuge. (6)

In the Rwandan context, restoring social, economic, physical, and psychological order was the imperative for everyone who engaged in service delivery. Their effectiveness was crucial for the country to regain its civil order. The burden of restoring and nurturing society back to life therefore became a daily responsibility. For bureaucrats whose lives and families were personally affected by the genocide, the act of providing rehabilitation occurred while they themselves underwent trauma recovery.

Mothering and Mobilizing Change

Pre-colonization, Rwandan culture was embedded in norms that promoted division of roles for men and women. Despite their separate roles, the social fabric for a long time promoted harmony. Most importantly, the contribution that individuals made to society was respected and valued (Hunt 2017). Women often engaged in household responsibilities in the private sphere, and men engaged as bread-winner in the public sphere. Hunt (2017) reports that men and women in the Rwandan culture "filled distinct functions within family and community (24)".

The genocide introduced social change that impacted gender relations. After the war, women became heads of household and providers, engaging in previously male domains. Women also engaged in rebuilding communities. Moreover, they were faced with responsibilities of caring for 500,000 orphans (Powley 2003). In the absence of a functioning government, women mobilized grassroots organizations that provided services to communities. The national crisis opened a window of opportunity for women to engage in public service (Hunt 2017). Rehabilitation services that focused on peace and reconciliation became critical areas and women engaged in them. During this time, women-led community efforts that were backed by support from government and civil society organizations. Hunt (2017) reports that:

Once again, the grassroots push was met with a pull from the top. The government also insists on reconciliation, so we were involved in public programs to make those who had killed and those who were targeted work together and talk to one another. (168)

Women's participation in traditionally male roles included community governance and opened new frontiers for them to impart policy changes (Powley 2004). Such circumstances not only changed the opportunity landscape for women to engage in the formal economy, but also provided an opportunity to advocate for policy agendas that were responsive to the needs of women and families. Demonstrating how women actively mobilized to effect policy change through cooperation with civil society organizations, Powley (2003) reports that during the post-conflict era, the Rwandan Women's Movement initiated a ratification of the new constitution. To identify policy agendas that were important to women, the Women's Movement consulted with civil society organizations as well as women and families at grassroots levels. By doing so, the Women's Movement was able to bring to light issues and concerns that were important to women and families in their communities.

Powley (2003) reports that once the Women's Movement ensured drafting of the constitution, it engaged in mobilization campaigns to persuade elected officials and government leaders to support its implementation. This approach to civil society mobilization and participation proved to be effective in bringing policy concerns to the attention of legislators. And this, in turn, led to the feminization of policy outcomes. Feminization of policy outcomes in Rwanda focused on bringing to attention those policy issues that had been neglected in the past and are important to women and their families.

Rwanda's recent abortion and land ownership laws are tangible examples of feminization of policy outcomes. For example, up until 2009 Rwanda's abortion policy was one of the strictest anywhere, making the procedure lawful only when two physicians certified that it was necessary to protect her health. In 2012, more latitude was built into the law, allowing it for cases of incest, rape, forced marriage, or fetal impairment. In terms of land policy, in 2004 a new policy was adopted that allowed widows and female orphans to retain their land, rather than it being given to a male relative.

Rwanda's bottom-up governing strategy aided in strengthening the role that grassroots organizations played in the reconstruction. As of May 2018, Rwanda leads the world with the most share of women in parliament (Inter-Parliamentary Union 2018). Women represent 61.3% of the lower or single house seats in parliament. And as of 2016, women represented nearly half (47.4%) of the appointed ministerial positions in government.

With all the changes that the nation has undergone in the recent past, and the extraordinary role that government has played in bringing reforms and reconciliation about, these questions beg to be addressed: How does the emotive dimension reflect these demands? Do the everyday work experiences of Rwandan public servants reflect this? And to what degree is the emotive dimension in their daily work heightened? Findings reported in Chapter 7 show that Rwandan workers respond less negatively when citizens mistreat them when compared to other nations. Might this be because of the context outlined here?

The Study

Introduced here are data, method, and findings using survey data from public servants who work in Rwandan public institutions. This section explores the direct effect of emotional labor on workers in the study population. The organization of this section is as follows: First, descriptive statistics of the study participants are presented. Second, a discussion of the emotional labor variables is presented along with analysis of the structural equation model. Finally, contextual interpretation of the results is presented along with summary comments.

Demographic Statistics

Demographic characteristics of respondents are shown in Table 16.1. There were 154 public service workers who completed the survey, most of whom work in the Gatsibo area. Their age, gender, public service experience, and level of educational attainment are listed. The descriptive statistics shows that 80% of the survey participants are younger than 39 years old. The age group of 40 years and older—those who would have been most personally engaged in the civil war—are represented only in small numbers. Both genders are evenly represented (at 46% each) in the survey. Almost all survey participants (97%) have less than 19 years of experience in public service, again representing the decimation of the public service during the war. The majority (74%) of respondents have 10 years or less of work experience. Over 55% have a college degree or higher. In sum, this is a youthful, well-educated cohort of workers.

Table 16.2 displays occupational characteristics of survey participants. Nearly two-thirds of them work in positions that directly provide service to

Table 16.1 Demographic characteristics: Rwanda

	Frequency	Percent
Age		
Less than 30	47	30.5
30–39 years	77	50.0
40–49 years	25	16.2
50–59 years	4	2.6
60 or more	0	0
N/A	1	0.6
Gender		
Female	71	46.1
Male	72	46.8
N/A	11	7.1
Public service experience		
Less than 10	114	74.0
10–19 years	36	23.4
20–29 years	3	2.0
30 or more	0	0.0
N/A	1	0.6
Educational level		
Less than high school	6	3.9
High school graduate	21	13.6
Some college	18	11.7
2-year associate degree	13	8.4
College graduate	62	40.3
Some graduate school	13	8.4
Master's degree	10	6.5
Law degree (J.D., LL.B.)	3	1.9
Doctorate degree (Ph.D., M.D., Ed.D.)	1	0.6
Other (please specify)	5	3.2
N/A	2	1.3

the public. They work in education (40.3%), health care (13%), community development/neighborhood services (3.9%), law enforcement (2.6%), social services (3.2%), and disaster response (2.6%). Slightly more than a fifth of the participants engage in human resource management, finance/accounting and administrative roles (22.6%). Very few survey participants engage in technical and supportive roles (approximately 6%).

Emotional Labor Variables

The survey gathered information on three dimensions of emotional labor: emotive capacity, pretending expression, and deep acting. Job satisfaction, burnout, and personal fulfillment are the three dependent variables

Table 16.2 Occupational characteristics: Rwanda

Occupation	Frequency	Percent
1. Administration	16	10.4
2. Community development/neighborhood services	6	3.9
3. Engineering, manufacturing, or production	5	3.2
4. Education	62	40.3
5. Disaster response	4	2.6
6. Finance or accounting	15	9.7
8. Health care	20	13.0
9. Housing	2	1.3
10. Human resource management	1	0.6
11. Information and communication	3	1.9
12. Law enforcement	4	2.6
13. Military	2	1.3
14. Public relations	3	1.9
15. Planning	1	0.6
20. Social services	5	3.2
21. Transportation	2	1.3
22. Support services (e.g. plants and equipment maintenance)	1	0.6
23. Other	2	1.3

Table 16.3 Descriptive statistics and Cronbach's alpha: Rwanda

	Mean	SD	Cronbach's alpha
Emotive capacity	5.99	0.92	0.720
Pretending expression	6.00	0.95	0.715
Deep acting	6.16	1.02	0.816
Job satisfaction	4.90	1.51	0.721
Burnout	6.12	0.82	0.536
Personal fulfillment	6.31	0.89	0.784

(see Table 16.3). All of the emotional labor variables reported a Cronbach's alpha level above the generally acceptable level of 0.70, and of the dependent variables, all except burnout also achieve this level of interitem consistency. The fact that burnout achieves only a level of 0.536 raises questions about the meanings of the items in this variable for these respondents. In many other nations, the alpha level for this variable is markedly higher, so perhaps the Rwandan context and the nature of the effort that goes into restoring a nation riven by war changes the way workers interpret their experience. The three items in the Burnout variable are "I leave work feeling tired and run down"; "I leave work feeling emotionally exhausted"; "I feel "used up" at the end of the workday." Perhaps it is that workers leave work feeling tired and emotionally exhausted, but not "used up."

Results

This study applies structural equation modeling (SEM) to test the direct effect of emotional labor variables (emotive capacity, pretending expression, and deep acting) on the outcome variables included in this study (job satisfaction, burnout, and personal fulfillment). Table 16.4 displays the results.

For purposes of this exploratory study, those relationships that achieve a statistical significance level of $p \leq 0.05$ are treated as notable and highlighted in the path diagram in Fig. 16.1.

The diagram shows the relationships between emotive capacity, pretending, and authentic emotive displays and the outcome variables of job satisfaction, burnout, and personal fulfillment. These relationships are explained below.

Table 16.4 Structural model results: Rwanda

Hypothesized paths	Coefficients	p-value
Emotive capacity → Job satisfaction	0.213	0.090
Emotive capacity → Burnout	−0.021	0.885
Emotive capacity → Personal fulfillment	0.245*	0.044
Pretending expression → Job satisfaction	0.212	0.131
Pretending expression → Burnout	0.084	0.577
Pretending expression → Personal fulfillment	0.188	0.158
Deep acting → Job satisfaction	0.087	0.505
Deep acting → Burnout	0.368*	0.011
Deep acting → Personal fulfillment	0.315*	0.012

Model fit: $\chi^2 = 440.930$ (df = 142), CFI = 0.721, RMSEA = 0.117, SRMR = 0.163

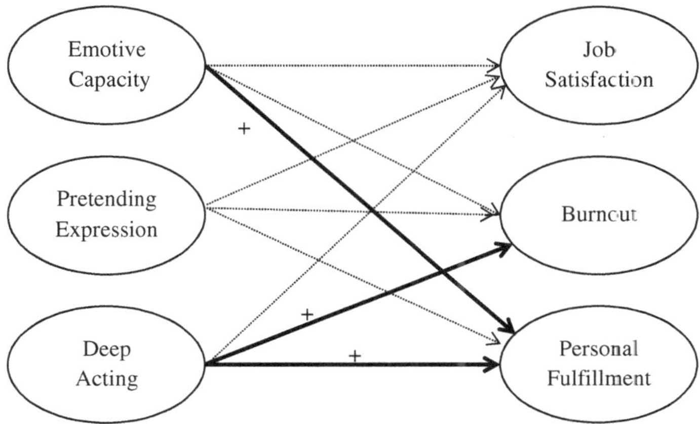

Fig. 16.1 Path diagram for Rwanda

Emotive Capacity

Table 16.4 shows that emotive capacity has a positive relationship with personal fulfillment ($p = 0.044$). The SEM model does not produce a direct effect on the other two outcome variables. Emotive capacity includes these items: "I am good at expressing how I feel," "I am good at getting people to calm down," and "In my job I am good at dealing with emotional issues."

Pretending Expression

Pretending expression is that form of emotional labor that involves suppressing how one actually feels in order to display an emotion appropriate to the circumstances of the task. It occurs when workers suppress how they actually feel while displaying a "work appropriate" emotion. The items in this variable include "I hide my true feelings so as to appear pleasant at work," "In my job I act confident and self-assured regardless of how I actually feel," and "I wear a 'mask' in order to deal with clients/customers in an appropriate way." Prior research reports that pretending is associated with employee burnout (Erickson and Ritter 2001; Hochschild 1983). In the case of Rwandan workers, this is not the case. There are no close associations between pretending and any of the outcome variables. This is a distinctly different finding than in many other countries.

Deep Acting

The results displayed in Table 16.4 show that deep acting has a positive and statistically significant direct effect on two outcome variables: personal fulfillment ($p = 0.012$) and burnout ($p = 0.011$). Items within the deep acting variable include "I try to actually experience the emotions that I must show to clients/customers," "I work hard to actually feel the emotions that I need to show to clients/customers," and "I work at developing the feelings inside of me that I need to show to clients/customers."

Discussion

This chapter explores the direct effect of emotional labor variables on individual outcomes in terms of job satisfaction, personal fulfillment, and burnout, for public service workers in Rwanda. The objective of the analysis is to investigate the direct effect of three dimensions of emotional labor:

emotive capacity, pretending, and deep acting. Structural equation modeling was used to reveal the association. The results show that deep acting, in other words, the authentic expression of emotion, has a direct effect on personal fulfillment and on burnout. Second, it demonstrates that emotive capacity has a direct effect on personal fulfillment. Equally important is the absence of a significant direct relationship between emotive pretending and the outcome variables.

Rwanda's history of post-genocide reconstruction is marked by a national collaborative effort aimed at rebuilding the country's social and institutional infrastructure. A review of Rwandan history illustrates that the public service sector played a significant role in the country's recovery from the civil war. The work of service delivery post-disaster proves to have an impact on those who engage in rehabilitation processes. National rehabilitation efforts have imbued the work culture with a sense of collaboration and shared responsibility among the Rwandan people. This culture was demonstrated when, for several months after the war, public servants returned to work without pay. Many worked simply in return for food. Public servants and community leaders who engaged in the recovery provided services while they, too, tried to reconstruct their families and homes. Although it has been over two decades since the genocide and the country demonstrated an exceptional level of social, economic, and physical recovery, the national mantra of collaboration still remains evident.

The direct effect of emotive capacity on bureaucrats' sense of personal fulfillment sheds light on our understanding of the effects of emotional labor beyond organizational outcomes to personal outcomes. The SEM result showing the direct effect of authentic expression of emotion—deep acting—demonstrates the double-edged sword that emotive demands of the job create. They bring both fulfillment and burnout. Pretending—surface acting—only requires bureaucrats to "alter visible emotive displays" (Remington 2017, 42). Authentically expressing how one is feeling involves the actual experience of inner emotions and goes beyond pretense. But even in the best of circumstances, where one's work is making obvious, substantive change for the better, and is contributing to feelings that one's work is worthwhile, it still risks burnout.

Considering Rwanda's history of national commitment to public service, study participants' display of deep acting does not come as a surprise. The association between their emotion work and burnout perhaps traces to the gravity of the work they are engaged in. This result could also suggest that burnout manifests itself as a result of the conflicting emotional experience that bureaucrats go through as they engage in altering their own emotional state to "present oneself as trustworthy" (Remington 2017, 42). This resonates with the findings in Chapter 7 and demonstrates that workers in Rwanda have a much higher tolerance level for citizens who treat them abusively than workers in other countries.

In the Rwandan context, the genocide became a force that resulted in a national commitment to rehabilitation. Public servants, community organizations, civil society organizations, and citizens working collectively played a central role in the recovery process. National rehabilitation, including reconstruction, economic development, and recovery from war trauma, has been the mantra of public institutions for over two decades. Evidence of personal fulfillment is yet a testament to the commitment of the Rwandan bureaucracy to public service.

Conclusion

Despite the experience of a civil war that claimed over 800,000 lives in 100 days, Rwanda has become a beacon of hope for the sub-Saharan Africa region. Rwanda's gender equity achievement in political representation gives the rest of the world hope that gender equity is a possibility and not a myth. Rwanda has also made remarkable progress in the economic front with 7–8% growth since 2003 (United Nations Foundation 2014). As of 2015, Rwanda succeeded in achieving most of the United Nations' Millennium Development Goals (World Bank, n.d.a). The country's national reconstruction strategy succeeded in bringing various stakeholders together, including the public sector, non-governmental organizations, communities, and citizens.

In the months after the civil war, public servants who survived the genocide willingly returned to service. The post-war civil service reform centered on decentralization and more autonomy for local governments. This strategy was successful in fostering collaboration at the community level and has led to a remarkable recovery.

National recovery efforts instilled a sense of commitment and individual responsibility among communities, bureaucrats, and citizens. The findings in this chapter reinforce the story that is conveyed about Rwanda's national commitment to public service. While results reported in the analysis are no surprise, further investigation can help us discover whether emotional labor manifests differently for bureaucrats engaged in different roles. Also, further investigation of generational differences in emotional labor experience and outcomes may capture differences in the sentiment and commitment to public service after the civil war.

References

Arndt, Channing, Andy McKay, and Finn Tarp. 2016. *Growth and Poverty in Sub-Saharan Africa*. Oxford, UK: Oxford University Press.

Bagilishya, Dogratias. 2000. "Mourning and Recovery from Trauma: In Rwanda, Tears Flow Within." *Transcultural Psychiatry* 37 (3): 337–53.

Byrski, Liz. 2012. "Emotional Labour as War Work: Women Up Close and Personal with McIndoe's Guinea Pigs." *Women's History Review* 21 (3): 341–36.

Clark, Pill. December. 2018. "When Remembrance Is Official Policy." *Foreign Affairs*, January/February. Accessed June 10, 2018. https://www.questia.com/read/1P4-1980695237/rwanda-s-recovery-when-remembrance-is-official-policy.

Erickson, Rebecca J., and Christian Ritter. 2001. "Emotional Labor, Burnout, and Inauthenticity: Does Gender Matter?" *Social Psychology Quarterly* 64 (2): 146–63.

Guy, Mary, E., and Meredith A. Newman. 2004. "Women's Jobs, Men's Jobs: Sex Segregation and Emotional Labor." *Public Administration Review* 64 (3): 289–98.

Hausman, David. 2011. "Rebuilding the Civil Service After War: Rwanda after the Genocide, 1998–2009." *Innovations for Successful Societies*. Accessed July 30, 2018. https://successfulsocieties.princeton.edu/publications/rebuilding-civil-service-after-war-rwanda-after-genocide-1998-2009.

Hochschild, Arlie. 1983. *The Managed Heart: The Commercialization of Human Feeling*. Berkeley, CA: University of California Press.

Hunt, Swanee. 2017. *Rwandan Women Rising*. Durham, NC: Duke University Press.

International Monetary Fund. 2011. *Rwanda: Poverty Reduction Strategy Paper—Progress Report Country Report*. Washington, DC: International Monetary Fund.

Mastracci, Sharon H., Mary E. Guy, and Meredith A. Newman. 2012. *Emotional Labor and Crisis Response: Working on the Razor's Edge*. Armonk, NY: M. E. Sharpe.

McMillan, Margaret, and Derek Headey. 2014. "Introduction—Understanding Structural Transformation in Africa." *World Development* 63 (November): 1–10.

Powley, Elizabeth. 2003. "Strengthening Governance: The Role of Women in Rwanda's Transition." The Hunt Alternative Fund. Accessed June 10, 2018. https://www.inclusivesecurity.org/publication/strengthening-governance-the-role-of-women-in-rwandas-transition/.

Powley, Elizabeth. 2004. *Strengthening Governance: The Role of Women in Rwanda's Transition: A Summary*. New York, NY: United Nations. Accessed March 1, 2019. http://www.un.org/womenwatch/osagi/meetings/2004/EGMelectoral/EP5-Powley.PDF.

Powley, Elizabeth. 2005. "Rwanda: Women Hold Up Half the Parliament." In *Women in Parliament: Beyond Numbers*, edited by Julie Ballington and Azza Karam, 154–63. Stockholm, Sweden: International IDEA.

Prunier, Gerard. 1995. *The Rwanda Crisis: History of a Genocide*. New York, NY: Columbia University Press.

Remington, Christa. L. 2017. *The Cultural Competence of Response and Recovery Workers in Post-Earthquake Haiti*. Doctoral Dissertation, FIU Electronic Theses and Dissertations. 3455. Miami, FL: Florida International University. https://doi.org/10.25148/etd.fidc001939.

Siegert, Richard J., and Tony Ward. 2010. "Dignity, Rights and Capabilities in Clinical Rehabilitation." *Disability and Rehabilitation* 32 (25): 2138–46.

Specia, Megan. 2017. "How a Nation Reconciles After Genocide Killed Nearly a Million People." *The New York Times*. Accessed June 13. https://www.nytimes.com/2017/04/25/world/africa/rwandans-carry-on-side-by-side-two-decades-after-genocide.html.

United Nation Foundation. 2014. "20 Years After the Genocide: 5 Remarkable Achievements Made in Rwanda." Accessed June 10, 2018. http://unfoundationblog.org/20-years-after-the-genocide-5-remarkable-achievements-made-in-rwanda/.

Uwamaliya, Philomene, and Grahame Smith. 2017. "Rehabilitation for Survivors of the 1994 Genocide in Rwanda: What Are the Lessons Learned?" *Issues in Mental Health Nursing* 38 (4): 361–67.

World Bank. n.d.a. *Rwanda Country Overview*. Accessed June 10, 2018. http://www.worldbank.org/en/country/rwanda/overview#1.

World Bank. n.d.b. *Rwanda*. Accessed June 10. https://data.worldbank.org/country/rwanda.

Taiwan

Chih-Wei Hsieh, Mao Wang and Yue Zhang

Taiwan is an island country located in the East Asia region of the Pacific Rim. It neighbors are Japan to the northeast through the Ryukyu Arc and the Philippines to the south across the Luzon Strait. On the west, it is separated from Mainland China by the 100-mile-wide Taiwan Strait. From a geographical standpoint, Taiwan connects Northeast and Southeast Asia as well as Southern China and the Pacific Ocean. Due to its pivotal location, Taiwan was successively colonized by several sovereignties, including China, Spain, the Netherlands, and Japan. Following the surrender of Imperial Japan in 1945, the Republic of China (ROC) took control of Taiwan and its surrounding islands—and continues to do so today. In 1949, ROC was defeated by communists who later established the People's Republic of China and ROC retreated to Taiwan. Hence, Taiwan is synonymous with ROC in many ways, for the island comprises 99% of ROC's territory since the Chinese Civil War.

C.-W. Hsieh (✉) · Y. Zhang
Department of Public Policy, City University of Hong Kong,
Kowloon Tong, Hong Kong
e-mail: cwhsieh@cityu.edu.hk

Y. Zhang
e-mail: yzhang297-c@my.cityu.edu.hk

M. Wang
Department of Political Science, National Taiwan University,
New Taipei City, Taiwan, Republic of China

© The Author(s) 2019
M. E. Guy et al. (eds.), *The Palgrave Handbook of Global Perspectives
on Emotional Labor in Public Service*, https://doi.org/10.1007/978-3-030-24323-9_17

The ROC government's relocation from the mainland to Taiwan marked the beginning of the martial law era (1949–1987). Under martial law, the government imposed press censorship, banned the establishment of new political parties, and restricted the freedoms of speech, publication, assembly, and association (Executive Yuan 2016). The oppression caused notorious abuses and violations of human rights but also stabilized the society in a turbulent time. Then, industrialization in the 1960s and massive infrastructure projects in the 1970s stimulated rapid economic growth that extended into the 1990s. The Taiwan Economic Miracle made Taiwan one of the "Four Asian Tigers," alongside Hong Kong, Singapore, and South Korea. The gross domestic product (GDP) per capita since that period has soared. In contrast to its valuation in 1961, which was US $15, GDP reached over US $22,000 by 2015. This economic blossoming facilitated political transformation. Martial law was rescinded in 1987, and a new democracy began to emerge. Less than ten years later, the Taiwanese people voted for their own president, and the first change-of-party occurred in the second presidential election in 2000.

The population of 23 million people in Taiwan is predominantly comprised of Han Chinese (over 95%), while indigenous Austronesian people make up only 2% (Executive Yuan 2016). Thus, Taiwan's national culture is deeply influenced by Chinese traditions and Confucianism in particular. With more than 2000 years of development, Confucian ethics, the essence of traditional Chinese culture (Lin and Ho 2009), has served as the cultural foundation in the Greater China region. Compared with Mainland China, however, Taiwan has been on a different historical path, including Japanese colonial rule from 1895 to 1945 and the rule of ROC since 1949. Thus, Taiwan exhibits both distinctive cultural features and similarities that it shares with other Greater China jurisdictions. According to Hofstede (1991), Taiwanese in general are more collectivistic than people in China and Hong Kong. They also show a stronger sense of adherence to Confucian values such as "benevolence, righteousness, and independent ethical judgment" (Lin and Ho 2009, 2407).

Discussion turns now to the development and current state of public service in this island country. Particular attention is paid to the expectations and attitudes toward public servants. We will also give a detailed account of the cultural setting in which emotional labor is performed. Such background information helps to better explain the survey results collected from Taiwanese public servants. Finally, the second half of the chapter reports research findings that shed light on emotional labor and its consequences among Taiwanese participants. Implications of these findings are discussed.

The Development and Current State of Public Service

The Taiwanese people used to be influenced by traditional Chinese culture and the legacy of authoritarian regimes (including Imperial China, Imperial Japan, and early ROC rule) and therefore heavily relied on services the government provided. Historically, officials who represent the government and wield public power were regarded as *fu-mu-guan* (father/mother-like officials) or *da-ren* (superior men). Public service was therefore the result of mercy or benevolence from officials, which of course could be fleeting and capricious—changing from one administration to another.

For most of the martial law period, public service languished in even deeper obscurity. Due to the lack of checks and balances, public administration was meant to serve the interests of the ruling class instead of the public interest. But, in the 1970s, which is considered the grounding stage of Taiwanese public administration, some measures were undertaken to address political corruption and to increase the bureaucracy's competence to offer high-quality services (Jan 2010). Public servants were thus urged to embrace the spirit of anti-bribery and to avoid accepting gifts of money or valuable items from citizens. Meanwhile, public service was streamlined and became more accessible and convenient for the general public.

After political and economic developments in the 1980s, public administration went through another wave of transformation. Reforms first focused on the size and breadth of government (Su et al. 2013), including restructuring the Taiwan Provincial Government to a three-layered government, reducing the number of cabinet-level organizations, and downsizing the civil service. Later, the principles of New Public Management (NPM) were adopted by the government and led to several reform projects, such as developing performance assessment systems and organizational innovations. These were primarily in the domains of deregulation, corporatization, decentralization, and outsourcing (Jan 2010). As of today, the government reinvention movement has been underway in Taiwan for two decades. The focal point of the NPM initiatives is to rebuild the image of the government and public servants, facilitate public participation, regulate the financial system, and increase public satisfaction with the government (Kuo 2001). Taiwan also established a dedicated unit, the Government Reinvention Promotion Committee, to coordinate and oversee inter-agency reform efforts. In general, NPM has brought significant changes to the government, and these are reflected in various aspects of public service, including the devolution of

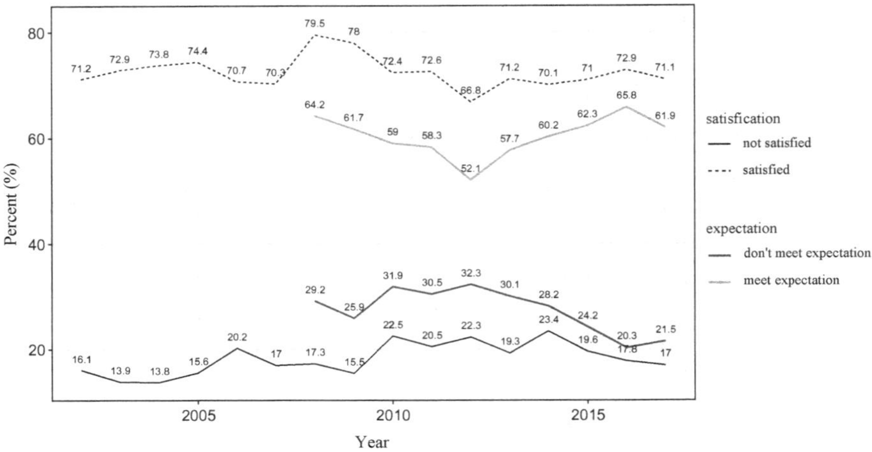

Fig. 17.1 The trend of citizen satisfaction

authority; provision of flexibility and the assurance of performance, control, and accountability; development of competition and choice; and increases in the responsiveness of public services (Kuo 2001).

Since the government has put enormous effort into improving service quality, particularly in regard to responsiveness and accountability, the question arises as to whether these efforts have brought success. When it comes to measuring public service performance, citizen satisfaction is the way to measure this. Accordingly, the National Development Council (NDC) (2017) has conducted annual surveys to evaluate citizen satisfaction since 2002.[1] The survey results presented in Fig. 17.1 show two interesting findings. First, the percentage of citizen satisfaction has been constantly high, ranging between 66.8 and 79.5%. Second, the fluctuation in citizen satisfaction has paralleled the extent to which citizen expectations are met.

To pursue continuous service excellence, the government has also initiated a new project called the Government Service Quality Award. Since 2008, the goal has been to use competition for the award as a means to improve service quality. For frontline service agencies, service quality is evaluated based on a list of key performance indicators such as customer service, online information service, and innovative value-added service. This new initiative is highly customer-oriented, and the overall win rate is around 18% (262 out of 1471). Awardees help the government set benchmarks for similar types of agencies and provide best practices for the rest to follow.

Political developments have also been changing the public service landscape. In Taiwan, the process of democratization is gradually cultivating a

Table 17.1 Citizen attitudes toward public servants

	Enthusiasm		Diligence		Trust	
Year	1984	1991	2004	2014	2006	2016
Agree	70.54%	74.71%	63.45%	66.88%	29.51%	43.85%
Not agree	12.77%	16.94%	30.43%	27.89%	39.91%	41.91%
Other	16.69%	8.34%	6.12%	5.23%	30.58%	14.24%
N	4307	1139	1781	1875	1972	1966

Data Source Fu (2017)

populist culture (Shyu 2008). Regular elections offer opportunities for constituents to not only exercise their civil rights but also express their policy preferences. To win elections, politicians often choose to side with *popular* opinion instead of the *right* opinion. As a result, bureaucrat bashing is rampantly used by them to gain public support (Berman et al. 2013). In this political atmosphere, a new power dynamic between administrators and citizens is taking shape as citizens move from thinking of themselves as the oppressed to thinking of themselves as valued customers. They, thus, become influential and sometimes demanding, particularly in how they evaluate the performance of services they receive from government.

Citizen-oriented reforms fundamentally alter citizen attitudes toward public servants. Although anti-administration criticisms can be hard to swallow (Borst and Lako 2017), self-determined public servants must be ready to embrace this challenge and strive to restore public trust and confidence. The Taiwan Social Change Survey conducted by Academia Sinica (Fu 2017) constantly monitors citizen attitudes toward public servants, including enthusiasm (which was measured in 1984 and 1991), diligence (which was measured in 2004 and 2014), and trust (which was measured in 2006 and 2016). Results are summarized in Table 17.1.

The survey offers insight into citizen expectations and changes in their opinions over time. In general, most citizens believe that enthusiasm is a required personal trait for public servants (70.54% in 1984 and 74.71% in 1991) and that those employed by government are, indeed, diligent (63.45% in 2004 and 66.88% in 2014). Additionally, citizens have found public servants to be more trustworthy (from 29.51% in 2006 to 43.85% in 2016). The statistics are certainly encouraging. Yet, there are still a large proportion of citizens (41.91%) who do not trust that public servants will do their best to maximize the interests of the country.

To summarize, citizens in the modern era demand high-quality services from public servants, which means an ideal public servant must be not only diligent but also polite and enthusiastic. However, it is difficult—if not impossible—for public servants to please everyone. In spite of indisputable evidence showing how service outcomes have improved, politicians and the media have never stopped criticizing the government and public servants. For example, research of Hung and Huang (2016) shows that the overall image of public servants presented in newspaper headlines tends to be more negative than ever before. This finding reflects the prevalence of bureaucrat bashing and also indicates that citizens are putting more responsibilities and higher expectations on public servants. Through the eyes of the general public, there remains considerable room for public service improvement.

Work Culture that Shapes Emotional Labor

In light of heightened citizen expectations, the government enacted the Code of Conduct for Public Servants in 2010 to regulate attitudes and behaviors of those who are called upon to deliver services to the general public. One of the requirements asks public servants to be sympathetic and to offer friendly, warm, convenient, and proactive service in order to gain public trust and respect. This demeanor is expected throughout the process of public service delivery, whether answering phones and handling routine tasks or responding to unprogrammable events, such as emergency situations. To successfully perform this work, obviously, requires emotional labor. Defined as the behaviors, planning, and control to express organizationally desired emotions during service transactions, emotional labor plays an important role in soliciting citizen cooperation. This, in turn, eventually affects organizational performance (Morris and Feldman 1996; Chen and Lin 2009).

Emotional labor is relational in nature (Guy et al. 2008), and such work seamlessly matches the national culture of Taiwan. Akin to other Chinese sub-cultures, Taiwan's society is characterized by *guanxi* (relationship). People commonly believe that success, in any form, must rely on timing (*tianshi*), location (*dili*), and harmony among those involved (*renhe*). The ability to maintain interpersonal harmony is considered the most precious skill. For example, forbearance (*ren*) can avoid confrontation and conflict. There is an idiom in Taiwan which promotes the virtue of forbearance: *With a little forbearance, you will find calm and peace; take a little step back, and you will find more space around you.* Additionally, during the colonial period, the Taiwanese inherited the Japanese spirit of politeness (Hwang 2010) and turned it into a daily practice, for it can smooth interpersonal relationships.

With the emphasis on *guanxi*, the pursuit of harmony naturally becomes the highest principle in interpersonal relationships. Regardless of the

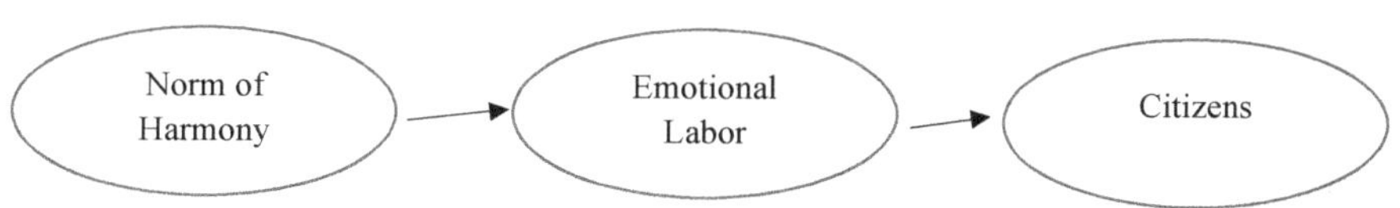

Fig. 17.2 The cultural framework of emotional labor in Taiwan

rightfulness of one's position, who breaks the harmony first is considered morally wrong (Yang 1992). As a result, people tend to deliberately control and manipulate their emotions to avoid harming interpersonal harmony with members of the social group (Triandis 2000).

Figure 17.2 illustrates how public service jobs require workers to engage in emotional labor (Fig. 17.2). Influenced by the social norm of interpersonal harmony, Taiwanese public servants are expected to suppress their personal feelings in order to maintain a professional demeanor. Inappropriate emotional displays could damage the rapport with citizens. However, the political culture, characterized by populism, is reshaping the administrator–citizen relationship. As a result, the workplace is becoming increasingly demanding and challenging for public servants. They are asked to process a large number of routine tasks while being responsive to citizen demands. In the wake of bureaucrat bashing, they receive little appreciation in return. This aggravates emotional labor, for it intensifies the need to practice emotion regulation at work. Moreover, it complicates workers' mental state, especially in regard to the depletion of self-esteem and professional pride. According to conservation of resources theory (Hobfoll 1989), this could lead to job stress and dissatisfaction. Over time, employee recruitment and retention would also be adversely affected.

In Taiwan, being a public servant is a popular choice for university graduates. Every year, the pursuit of employment that provides job security (known as the *iron rice bowl* mentality) draws thousands of people to compete for public sector jobs (Su 2010). Taiwan uses civil service entrance examinations for admission to the civil service. As illustrated in Fig. 17.3, the number of people who take the Civil Service Examination has increased rapidly between 1980 and 2010. In addition to job permanency, the impetus for recruits to seek public sector employment is referred to as the "golden hello." This term is indicative of the compensation package for new hires, which is more munificent than that of their private sector peers.

In recent years, however, the number of examination participants has dropped significantly and the resignation rate of public servants is climbing, as Fig. 17.4 shows (Ministry of Civil Service 2018). Many have attributed the recent challenges in civil service recruitment and retention to reduced pension

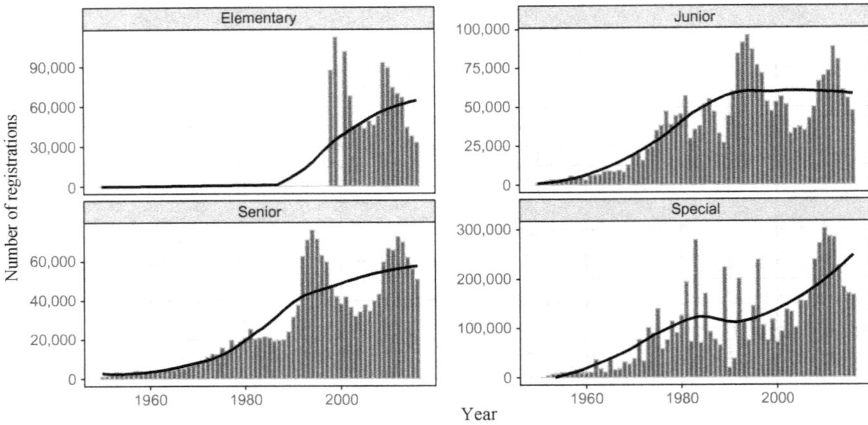

Fig. 17.3   The number of participants in civil service examination by year

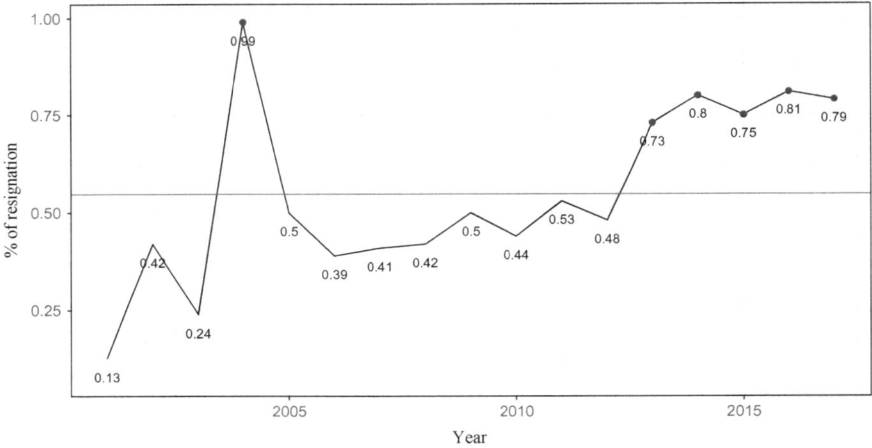

Fig. 17.4   The trend of resignation by public servants

benefits (Wu 2017). However, it could also be affected by increased emotional labor demands because, according to a recent government report, there has been an increasing number of public servants requesting Employee Assistance Programs to help them relieve work pressure and deal with difficulties they encounter at work (Directorate-General of Personnel Administration 2017).

In sum, the emotional labor demands of public service work in Taiwan are intense. Because maintaining interpersonal harmony is deemed necessary in Taiwanese society, emotional labor is therefore not merely a job demand; it is also a cultural task. In recent years, however, people have become less enthusiastic about public service work. It is a human capital crisis that warrants further investigation. In particular, there is an urgent need to thoroughly understand the effects of emotional labor in the Taiwanese public sector. Yet, such research remains scarce and largely overlooked. Only a few studies have addressed emotional labor among Taiwanese public servants (see, e.g., Grandey et al. 2013; Hsieh et al. 2016; Chen and Lin 2009). Thus, the chapter aims to contribute to this understudied terrain. Research findings are presented in the sections that follow.

The Study

Presented here are data, method, and analytical results based on the survey of public servants in Taiwan. This section first displays descriptive statistics of a set of demographic variables that serve to profile the characteristics of the study sample. Next, we offer a discussion of emotional labor variables and employ structural equation modeling (SEM) to test the effect of emotional labor on employees' mental state, including job satisfaction, burnout, and personal fulfillment. This is followed with a contextual interpretation as well as discussion of the implications of these results.

Demographic Statistics

This study reports a survey of 173 public servants that was administered in Taiwan in 2015. Table 17.2 displays demographic characteristics of the sample, including age, gender, public service experience, and educational level. The age of respondents varies from 20 to 68 years old, and the average age is 37.5 years old. The results show that the 30- to 39- and 40- to 49-year-old age groups have 63 and 55 respondents, comprising roughly 36.4 and 31.8% of the sample respectively. In addition, there are 23 respondents from ages 20 to 29, making up 13.3% of the sample. As such, the majority of the respondents fall in the range of 20–49 years old, while there are only 11 respondents aged 50 or more (6.4%). With regard to gender distribution, there are 73 male and 80 female respondents, making up 42.2 and 46.2% of the sample, respectively, suggesting that gender attributes are nearly equally distributed. For those who did report public sector work experience, their work tenure in the public sector ranges from 0 to 35 years, and the mean tenure is 10.73 years. Nearly half (43.9%) of respondents have less than ten years of public service experience. There are 52 respondents who

Table 17.2 Demographic characteristics: Taiwan

Variable	Frequency	Percent
Age		
Less than 30	23	13.3
30–39 years	63	36.4
40–49 years	55	31.8
50–59 years	10	5.8
60 or more	1	0.6
N/A	21	12.1
Gender		
Female	80	46.2
Male	73	42.2
N/A	20	11.6
Public service experience		
Less than 10	76	43.9
10–19 years	52	30.1
20–29 years	19	11
30 or more	3	1.7
N/A	23	13.3
Educational level		
Less than high school	1	0.6
High school graduate	9	5.2
Some college	117	67.6
2-year associate degree	35	20.2
College graduate	3	1.7
Some graduate school	0	0.0
Master's degree	0	0.0
Law degree (J.D., LL.B.)	0	0.0
Doctorate degree (Ph.D., M.D., Ed.D., etc.)	0	0.0
Other (please specify)	0	0.0
N/A	8	4.6

have worked in the public sector for 10–19 years, comprising 30.1% of the sample. There are only a few people who have worked in the public sector more than 20 years: 19 respondents (11%) have worked in the public sector for 20–29 years, and three (1.7%) have worked for more than 30 years. In terms of educational level, 117 out of 173 respondents have a college degree, making up the largest proportion (67.6%). Another 35 respondents hold a 2-year associate degree, which constitutes 20.2% of the sample. Overall, it is a relatively youthful, less experienced, and well-educated cohort of public servants.

We tabulate the occupation distribution of the sample in Table 17.3. As the table shows, respondents are employed by a broad range of public organizations. A quarter (39 respondents) of them performs administrative duties. Many also work in fields such as human resource management (11%),

Table 17.3 Occupational characteristics: Taiwan

Occupation	Frequency	Percent
1. Administration	39	25.2
2. Community development/neighborhood services	1	0.6
3. Engineering, manufacturing, or production	2	1.3
4. Education	16	10.3
5. Disaster response	3	1.9
6. Finance or accounting	5	3.2
7. Firefighter	2	1.3
8. Health care	1	0.6
10. Human resource management	17	11
12. Law enforcement	13	8.4
14. Public relations	4	2.6
15. Planning	2	1.3
16. Public works, streets sanitation, utilities	10	6.5
17. Purchasing	5	3.2
18. Recreation and parks	15	9.7
19. Research and development	6	3.9
20. Social services	1	0.6
21. Transportation	5	3.2
22. Support services (e.g. plants and equipment maintenance)	2	1.3
23. Other	6	3.9

education (10.3%), recreation and parks (9.7%), law enforcement (8.4%), and public works, streets sanitation, and utilities (6.5%). Employees in these public sector jobs make up the majority of the sample. Other respondents come from research and development (3.9%), finance or accounting (3.2%), purchasing (3.2%), transportation (3.2%), public relations (2.6%), and disaster response (1.9%). Jobs such as engineering, manufacturing or production, planning, and support services respectively have two representatives (1.3%) in the sample, and community development/neighborhood services, health care, and social services have only one (0.6%).

Emotional Labor Variables

There are three emotional labor variables to be examined, namely emotive capacity, pretending expression, and deep acting. Before exploring how these variables affect job satisfaction, burnout, and personal fulfillment, this study first checks Cronbach's alpha level of each study variable. As previously mentioned, these variables are comprised of multiple survey items, and each item is measured on a seven-point Likert-type scale (1 = strongly disagree, 7 = strongly agree). Therefore, scale reliability should be examined using a

Table 17.4 Descriptive statistics and Cronbach's alpha: Taiwan

	Mean	SD	Cronbach's alpha
Emotive capacity	4.482	1.161	0.745
Pretending expression	5.276	1.104	0.688
Deep acting	5.384	1.055	0.884
Job satisfaction	4.197	1.313	0.802
Burnout	4.700	1.451	0.889
Personal fulfillment	4.488	1.410	0.872

measure of internal consistency, such as Cronbach's alpha. Cronbach's alpha for the three emotional labor variables is 0.745 (emotive capacity), 0.688 (pretending expression), and 0.844 (deep acting). And, Cronbach's alpha level is 0.802 for job satisfaction, 0.889 for burnout, and 0.872 for personal fulfillment. Taken together, all except pretending expression report a Cronbach's alpha value above the generally acceptable level of 0.7. Even though pretending expression has a marginally lower score, it does not fall too much behind as the value is 0.688. Therefore, we contend that all of the variables have achieved internal consistency.

Table 17.4 presents means and standard deviations of the study variables. Concerning three emotional labor variables, the mean score is 4.482 for emotive capacity (SD = 1.161), 5.276 for pretending expression (SD = 1.104), and 5.384 for deep acting (SD = 1.055). The result indicates that respondents, on average, give their emotive capacity a modest assessment and they also actively exert emotional labor at work by using pretending expression and/or deep acting. As for the three dependent variables, the mean score is 4.197 for job satisfaction (SD = 1.313), 4.7 for burnout (SD = 1.451), and 4.488 for personal fulfillment (SD = 1.410). Compared to other countries in this book, the level of job satisfaction as well as personal fulfillment is relatively low, whereas the level of burnout is slightly high.

SEM Results

This study employs SEM to analyze the data. To address a relatively small sample, the SEM estimation specifies a 95% bias-corrected confidence interval and 500 times bootstrap resamples to test effects of emotional labor variables (emotive capacity, pretending expression, and deep acting) on dependent variables (job satisfaction, burnout, and personal fulfillment). As shown in Table 17.5, a set of fit indexes suggest that this hypothesized model fits the survey data (χ^2 [142] = 369.940; $p < 0.001$; CFI = 0.859;

Table 17.5 Structural model results: Taiwan

Hypothesized paths	Coefficients	p-value
Emotive capacity → Job satisfaction	0.571	0.000
Emotive capacity → Burnout	−0.417	0.000
Emotive capacity → Personal fulfillment	0.557	0.000
Pretending expression → Job satisfaction	−0.436	0.000
Pretending expression → Burnout	0.308	0.003
Pretending expression → Personal fulfillment	−0.445	0.000
Deep acting → Job satisfaction	0.099	0.269
Deep acting → Burnout	−0.006	0.950
Deep acting → Personal fulfillment	0.100	0.241

Model fit: $\chi^2 = 369.940$ (df = 142) $p < 0.001$, CFI = 0.859, RMSEA = 0.097, SRMR = 0.120

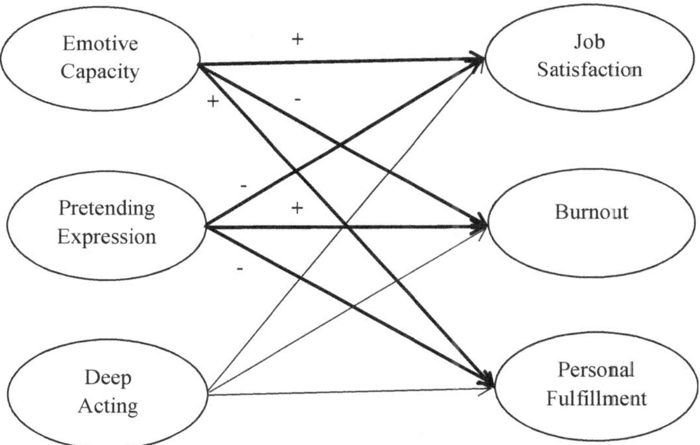

Fig. 17.5 Path diagram for Taiwan

RMSEA = 0.097 [0.085; 0.109]; SRMR = 0.120). The table reports the parameter estimates with standardized regression weights.

These results are graphically displayed in Fig. 17.5. Significant paths are highlighted in bold.

Explanation of Findings

Emotive Capacity. Previous studies based on US samples (Guy et al. 2008; Hsieh et al. 2012) have shown that public servants' emotive capacity can enhance job satisfaction and pride in work on the one hand and reduce the risk of burnout on the other hand. In the same vein, our study of Taiwanese respondents also indicates that emotional capacity has a statistically significant effect on three dependent variables. Specifically, emotional capacity is positively related to job satisfaction ($\beta = 0.571$, $p < 0.001$) and personal fulfillment ($\beta = 0.557$, $p < 0.001$), and it is negatively related to burnout ($\beta = -0.417$, $p < 0.001$).

Pretending Expression. Since Hochschild (1983) introduced the concept of emotional labor, ample evidence has suggested that pretending expression (theoretically referred to as surface acting) is the most detrimental form of emotional labor because it generates a discrepancy between displayed and felt emotions. To appear to be warm and friendly, workers are instructed to hide or suppress job-inappropriate feelings such as anger, fear, sadness, fatigue, and annoyance. To keep negative feelings in check requires physiological resources, and these resources are not infinite. Therefore, prevailing wisdom is that pretending expression will deplete one's stamina and mental energy, and this contributes to burnout and job dissatisfaction. Our SEM results are consistent with the existing literature as we found that pretending expression is negatively related to job satisfaction ($\beta = -0.436$, $p < 0.001$) and positively related to burnout ($\beta = 0.308$, $p < 0.01$). In addition, pretending expression is negatively related to personal fulfillment ($\beta = -0.445$, $p < 0.001$). These results suggest that masking one's feelings generate discernible effects on public servants in Taiwan.

Deep Acting. While pretending expression denotes faking work-related emotions, deep acting implies that one accepts the work role and makes the effort to align his/her feeling with the role expectation. Therefore, it is believed that deep acting can generate positive job experiences and, in turn, result in job satisfaction (Hsieh et al. 2016). However, empirical evidence has been fairly inconsistent (Hülsheger and Schewe 2011). In this study, the SEM analysis also fails to establish any significant relationship between deep acting with job satisfaction, burnout, and personal fulfillment. Demystifying the reasons behind this result will advance our knowledge of cultural differences in the emotional labor experience.

Discussion

Public administration scholars have recognized emotional labor as an integral part of public service performance (Guy et al. 2008). Insofar as Taiwan is concerned, however, scholars and practitioners alike have not yet paid close attention to this important topic. To contribute to this relatively unknown subject, this study explores the effect of emotional labor variables, namely emotive capacity, pretending expression, and deep acting, on job satisfaction, burnout, and personal fulfillment. To reveal the association, SEM was performed using the survey data collected from 173 Taiwanese public servants in 2015. The results show that emotive capacity is positively related to job satisfaction and personal fulfillment and inversely related to burnout. On the opposite, pretending expression is negatively related to job satisfaction and personal fulfillment and is positively related to burnout. Deep acting generates no discernible effect on employees' mental state. In general, findings derived from the Taiwan sample vary from those found in most other countries, particularly when considering the relationship between deep acting and outcome variables. Taiwan's unique culture may help to explain these differences.

There may be reasons to believe that, in terms of culture, Taiwan and China have much in common. On the one hand, the national culture of Taiwan contains inherited Chinese traditions that have been rooted in a shared history. Yet, on the other hand, Taiwan has distinctive cultural characteristics regarding political and social values due to the fact that it has developed into a liberal-democratic regime, quite separate from that of Mainland China. For over a century, the separation between the two countries has grown, first because of Japanese colonial rule from 1895 to 1945 and then due to the rule of ROC since 1949 (Chun 1996). As a result, cultural heritage mixed with recent political and social developments has made Taiwan a unique case (Shi 2001; Shyu 2008).

The norm of interpersonal harmony remains a dominant force that shapes the interactive dynamics between public servants and citizens in Taiwan. Practices that can smooth interpersonal relationships and avoid confrontation and conflict are highly valued in the public service workplace as well as in other segments of society. Normally, those who bring disturbance to interpersonal harmony will be condemned. However, recent anti-administrative criticisms, coupled with the rise of the populist culture, require public servants to shoulder more responsibilities to develop and maintain a cooperative relationship with citizens. For these public servants, emotional labor legitimizes public service because it is an occupation designed to offer care for the people. Emotional labor is also embedded in socialization to the culture and workers are subject to the influence of social norms, such as the importance of interpersonal harmony.

As emotional labor is also a cultural task, Taiwanese public servants may bring personal skills to employment that they acquired through cultural socialization. In the process of socialization, public servants modify their inner feelings to comply with social norms inculcated by the unique Taiwanese culture. As Triandis (2000) suggests, people in a collectivistic culture are accustomed to controlling and manipulating their emotions in order to avoid damaging interpersonal harmony. Therefore, it is understandable that deep acting has little to no effect on Taiwanese public servants because this form of emotional labor is an integral part of life, whether in their personal lives or their work lives.

The explanation for findings related to deep acting begs for an answer to this question: Why is pretending expression detrimental to the well-being of Taiwanese civil servants? Although deep acting and emotive pretending are considered different emotional labor strategies, they are by no means mutually exclusive. To actually experience work-related emotions requires workers to, first, put aside their personal feelings. However, Hsieh (2014) contended that pretending expression requires more strenuous effort than deep acting because "the worker needs to pay conscious attention to the outward expression and exert considerable effort to control inner feelings" (395). As the "work" continues, personal energy spent regulating emotions will eventually be exhausted. Therefore, compared to deep acting, pretending expression is deemed more detrimental as it will erode one's sense of work-related well-being.

Emotive capacity is also a significant predictor of job satisfaction, burnout, and personal fulfillment but yields a different effect than pretending expression. Individuals with better emotive capacity are more likely to experience high levels of job satisfaction and personal fulfillment and a low risk of burnout. However, our Taiwan sample does not show confidence in their emotive capacity. These findings have important implications for solving the emerging human capital crisis in the Taiwanese public sector.

As previously mentioned, there is a troubling trend facing public employers as job seekers are hesitant to enter the public sector and an increasing number of incumbents choose to quit their jobs. Therefore, it is suggested that, for jobs that constantly require emotional labor, employers promote and cultivate workers' emotive capacity through recruitment and selection as well as through training and development. As job satisfaction and personal fulfillment improve and the likelihood of burnout decreases, problems of employee recruitment and retention shall be alleviated accordingly.

Conclusion

Finding a "one size fits all" practice to manage emotional labor across cultural boundaries can be an exercise in vanity. In this chapter, we have found that, although there is indeed common ground, there are also undeniable differences between the Taiwan sample and other countries. We believe that this finding is a result of Taiwan's national culture. As people are accustomed to regulating their emotions in order to avoid harming interpersonal harmony, they become immune to its effects. However, masking one's inner feelings can by all means deplete one's emotional resources, leading to counterproductive work outcomes. Recently, political and social developments have changed the dynamics between public servants and citizens. This has made emotional labor increasingly overwhelming for those responsible for delivering public services. Bit by bit, their job demands and how they experience their work is adversely affecting civil service recruitment and retention. There may be a legitimate solution, based on our findings, only if public employers can effectively improve public servant's emotive capacity so that they can regain the joy and meaningfulness at work—without burning out.

Note

1. NDC conducted two surveys every year before 2014 but only one since 2014. For the 2002–2013 data, we choose the first survey to report. Additionally, note that the information concerning citizen expectations of public service is only available in surveys conducted after 2008.

References

Berman, Evan M., Don-Yun Chen, Chung-Yuang Jan, and Tong-Yi Huang. 2013. "Public Agency Leadership: The Impact of Informal Understandings with Political Appointees on Perceived Agency Innovation in Taiwan." *Public Administration* 91 (2): 303–24.

Borst, R. T., and C. J. Lako. 2017. "Proud to Be a Public Servant? An Analysis of the Work-Related Determinants of Professional Pride Among Dutch Public Servants." *International Journal of Public Administration* 40 (10): 875–87.

Chen, Ling-Hsiu, and Shang-Ping Lin. 2009. "Reducing Service Agents' Emotional Labor By Emotion-Focused Human Resource Management Practices." *Social Behavior and Personality* 37 (3): 335–42.

Chun, Allen. 1996. "Discourses of Identity in the Changing Spaces of Public Culture in Taiwan, Hong Kong and Singapore." *Theory, Culture & Society* 13 (1): 51–75.

Directorate-General of Personnel Administration, Executive Yuan. 2017. *Promoting Employee Assistance Programs 2.0 in the Public Sector: Manual.* Directorate-General of Personnel Administration, Executive Yuan. Accessed March 23, 2019. https://www.dgpa.gov.tw/FileConversion?filename=dgpa/files/201801/166097 ca-3b1c-4680-977f-11e2a0f52243.pdf&nfix=&name=%e9%9b%bb% e5%ad%90%e6%9b%b8.

Executive Yuan, Republic of China (Taiwan). 2016. *The Republic of China Yearbook 2016.* Taipei: Executive Yuan.

Fu, Yang-Chih. 2017. *2016 Taiwan Social Change Survey (Round 7, Year 2): Citizen and Role of Government (C00321_2).* Taipei: Survey Research Data Archive, Academia Sinica. Accessed March 23, 2019. https://srda.sinica.edu.tw/data-search_detail.php?id=2224.

Grandey, Alicia A., Nai-Wen Chi, and Jennifer A. Diamond. 2013. "Show Me the Money! Do Financial Rewards for Performance Enhance or Undermine the Satisfaction from Emotional Labor?" *Personnel Psychology* 66 (3): 569–612.

Guy, Mary E., Meredith A. Newman, and Sharon H. Mastracci. 2008. *Emotional Labor: Putting the Service in Public Service: Putting the Service in Public Service.* Armonk, NY: M. E. Sharpe.

Hobfoll, Stevan E. 1989. "Conservation of Resources: A New Attempt at Conceptualizing Stress." *American Psychologist* 44 (3): 513–24.

Hochschild, Arlie R. 1983. *The Managed Heart: Commercialization of Human Feeling.* Berkeley, CA: University of California Press.

Hofstede, Geert. 1991. *Cultures and Organizations: Intercultural Cooperation and Its Importance for Survival—Software of the Mind.* London: McGraw-Hill.

Hsieh, Chih-Wei. 2014. "Burnout Among Public Service Workers: The Role of Emotional Labor Requirements and Job Resources." *Review of Public Personnel Administration* 34 (4): 379–402.

Hsieh, Chih-Wei, Jun-Yi Hsieh, and Irving Yi-Feng Huang. 2016. "Self-Efficacy as a Mediator and Moderator Between Emotional Labor and Job Satisfaction: A Case Study of Public Service Employees in Taiwan." *Public Performance & Management Review* 40 (1): 71–96.

Hsieh, Chih-Wei, Myung H. Jin, and Mary E. Guy. 2012. "Consequences of Work-Related Emotions: Analysis of a Cross-Section of Public Service Workers." *American Review of Public Administration* 42 (1): 39–53.

Hülsheger, Ute R., and Anna F. Schewe. 2011. "On the Costs and Benefits of Emotional Labor: A Meta-Analysis of Three Decades of Research." *Journal of Occupational Health Psychology* 16 (3): 361–89.

Hung, Mei-Jen, and Chien-Shih Huang. 2016. "Bureaucracy Bashing: A Content Analysis of Newspaper Headlines About Civil Servants in Taiwan." *Taiwan Democracy Quarterly* 13 (3): 45–92.

Hwang, Yih-Jye. 2010. "Japan as 'Self' or 'the Other' in Yoshinori Kobayashi's on Taiwan." *China Information* 24 (1): 75–98.

Jan, Chung-Yuang. 2010. "History and Context of Public Administration in Taiwan." In *Public Administration in East Asia: Mainland China, Japan, South Korea, and Taiwan*, edited by Evan M. Berman, M. Jae Moon, and Heungsuk Choi, 497–516. Boca Raton, FL: CRC Press.

Kuo, Yu-Ying. 2001. "Chapter 19. New Public Management in Taiwan: Government Reinvention." In *Learning from International Public Management Reform: Part B*, edited by Lawrence Jones, James Guthrie, and Peter Steane, 337–51. Bingley: Emerald Group Publishing.

Lin, Liang-Hung, and Yu-Ling Ho. 2009. "Confucian Dynamism, Culture and Ethical Changes in Chinese Societies—A Comparative Study of China, Taiwan, and Hong Kong." *The International Journal of Human Resource Management* 20 (11): 2402–17.

Ministry of Civil Service, R.O.C. (Taiwan). 2018. *Personnel Turnover Status of All Civil Servants, by Year.* Taipei: Ministry of Civil Service, R.O.C. (Taiwan).

Morris, J. Andrew, and Daniel C. Feldman. 1996. "The Dimensions, Antecedents, and Consequences of Emotional Labor." *Academy of Management Review* 21 (4): 986–1010.

National Development Council, Executive Yuan. 2017. *Citizens' Satisfaction About Public Service Quality Survey.* Taipei: National Development Council. Accessed March 24, 2019. https://www.ndc.gov.tw/News.aspx?n=3146119524BF3BF9.

Shi, Tianjian. 2001. "Cultural Values and Political Trust: A Comparison of the People's Republic of China and Taiwan." *Comparative Politics* 33 (4): 401–19.

Shyu, Huoyan. 2008. "Populism in Taiwan: The Rise of a Populist-Democratic Culture in a Democratising Society." *Asian Journal of Political Science* 16 (2): 130–50.

Su, Tsai-Tsu. 2010. "Civil Service Reform in Taiwan." In *Public Administration in East Asia: Mainland China, Japan, South Korea, and Taiwan*, edited by Evan M. Berman, M. Jae Moon, and Heungsuk Choi, 609–26. Boca Raton, FL: CRC Press.

Su, Tsai-Tsu, Richard M. Walker, and Lan Xue. 2013. "Reform and Transition in Public Administration Theory and Practice in Greater China." *Public Administration* 91 (2): 253–60. https://doi.org/10.1111/padm.12030.

Triandis, Harry C. 2000. "Culture and Conflict." *International Journal of Psychology* 35 (2): 145–52. https://doi.org/10.1080/002075900399448.

Wu, Baiwei. 2017. "The High-Cension Candidates Have Fewer Examinations and Evaluations: Lack of Changes, More Choices for Exams ...." *Taipei Times,* July 6. Accessed March 23, 2019. https://news.ltn.com.tw/news/life/breakingnews/2123423.

Yang, Kuo-Shu. 1992. "Social Orientation of the Chinese: A Social Exchange Perspective." In *Psychology and Behaviors of the Chinese: Ideas and Methods*, edited by Kuo-Shu Yang and An-Bang Yu, 87–142. Taipei: Laureate.

18

Thailand

Amporn Tamronglak

Thailand is located in Southeast Asia and is considered to be a country with a long and rich history of living in harmony amid diversity. It is surrounded by neighboring countries of Myanmar in the West and North, the Lao People's Democratic Republic, Vietnam, and Cambodia in the East, and Malaysia in the South. All of these countries share the great Mekong River of 4909 km, which additionally flows through China. The current population of Thailand is around sixty-five million: 80% of the population are native Thais, 10% are Chinese, and 3% are Malays. The rest of the minorities are Mons, Khmers, and various hill tribespeople in the Northern part of Thailand. The majority of Thai people, approximately 89%, believe in Buddhism of Theravada. Only 10% are Muslims, mostly in the Southern Provinces along the Thai-Malay border, and 0.7% believe in Christianity, particularly Catholicism. There are also a small number of Sikhs and Hindus in the heart of Bangkok. They all have the freedom to express their beliefs without fear of persecution, as protected by the Constitution under his Majesty the King.

A. Tamronglak (✉)
Faculty of Political Science,
Thammasat University, Bangkok, Thailand

M. E. Guy et al. (eds.), *The Palgrave Handbook of Global Perspectives on Emotional Labor in Public Service*, https://doi.org/10.1007/978-3-030-24823-9_18

From Absolute Monarchy to Democracy

Thai bureaucracy has been evolving since 1448. The traditional administration of Thai public services can be traced back to the early established patriarchy during the Sukhothai Kingdom (1238–1350) and autocracy during the Ayutthaya Kingdom (1350–1767).[1] The kings were perceived and considered to be the deva raja (god kings). This image of the king as a sort of deity remains to this day as a demonstration of respect (Neher 1996). The king continued to rule and centralize Thailand's political system during the Chakri Dynasty (1782–present) while fighting against the threat of Western imperialism and maintaining the independence of the monarchy.

As the years progressed, an absolute monarchy could not withstand the highly educated cadre of bureaucrats from Western civilization nor democratic ideology. Thus, power was seized and the country's absolute monarchy became a limited monarchy under constitutional democracy in 1932. The "bureaucratic polity," as coined by Fred Riggs in 1964, began and continues through today. It does not share political power with the majority of the Thai people. Indeed, only the upper classes of the ruling elite have the opportunity to make decisions. The fact that Thailand was never colonized by Westerners, unlike other neighboring countries, has become a point of pride for the country, but it is also a weakness because its political process is run by either bureaucrats or the military. Indeed, the general public is never involved in the process (Neher 1996, 308).

Politics, as described by renowned political scientist Chai-anan Samudavanija (2002), is a "vicious cycle" that is played and fought by various parties from different groups of bureaucrats. Whoever is able to gather the most powerful force wins the fight. In the case of Thailand, it is apparently the army. The junta seized power and control of Thai politics more than ten times between 1932–1973 (Paribatra 1993, 881), each time legitimizing its regime by claiming that it was guarding the nation's security and trying to stay in power as long as possible. As of today, the number of coups d'état outnumber the total number of general elections held since the country became democratic. Not only did the military take control of the government by keeping other political factions, interest groups, and student activists at bay, it also took advantage of several economic opportunities. In the eyes of the military, politicians are threats to the king and are likely to create political instability, social disorder, corruption, and economic recessions (Hirschfeld 1994; Neher 1995, 1996).

In 1973, student uprisings brought an end to authoritarian military rule in Thai politics. However, democracy did not last very long. Due to increasing fear of communist insurgencies, the military reclaimed power in 1976 (Lysa 2000, 31; Hirschfeld 1994; Neher 1996). Several scholars—Charnvit Kasetsiri, Nidhi Eawsriwong, Sujit Wongthes, to name a few—have criticized the emphasis placed on national identity, claiming that it has hampered national progress in all aspects of economic, political, social, and cultural development (Lysa 2000). Despite several turbulent years of political instability, the constitutional system has persisted, although with several changes. The present constitution is the twentieth in Thai history. Western scholars have remarked that Thai people see "democracy" differently. For Thai people, democracy, particularly "semi democracy," means "having individual freedom" while supporting an authoritarian military leadership. In Thailand, sovereignty originates from the king and emanates down to the bureaucracy and then to the citizens, not the other way around as in Western societies. Generally speaking, in Western democracies, citizens select their leaders by candidates competing to win the majority vote. Thus, Western democratic stability depends on its ability to self-perpetuate through gradual reform and renewal (Case 2001). In contrast, Thailand's semi-democracy, like other Asian democracies, has been unable to maintain and enhance stability or institutionalize the regime.

The Rise of the Military State

During the 1980s, the political situation in Thailand was somewhat stabilized under Prime Minister Prem Tinsulanonda, the former army commander in chief, with only a few military coup d'état attempts. Though he led the coalition government of three parties (the Democrat Party, the Social Action Party, and the Chart Thai), he also needed support from the army to balance several military cliques, most notably "the Young Military Officers Group," popularly called "the Young Turks" belonging to Class Seven (1960 graduates) and Class Five (1958 graduates) of the elite Chulachomklao Royal Military Academy. By gaining the trust and support of the king, he was able to survive several attempted coups throughout his eight-year rule. He was also able to institutionalize a political process based on the party system. Thailand's general public believed their political system to be on the verge of full democracy, and there was popular demand for participation, representation, and an industrialized economy. Indeed, an authoritarian and narrowly based military rule was considered unfavorable. Another factor was that military cliques had become scattered and needed new allies in the Senate and in other political parties. Many military leaders had begun to form new political parties, for instance Kriangsak Chamanan of the National Democracy (Chart Prachathipatai). Although Prem was considered an honest and loyal leader, he was also criticized as being indecisive and weak (US Library of Congress, n.d.). However, his sincerity and lack of corruption led him to be considered one of the most influential people in Thai politics. Prem is still considered a statesman and serves as president of the Privy-council.

In the 1990s, a major coup d'état was staged by Army Commander Suchinda Kraprayoon to take control from the democratically elected Chatichai Choonhavan, a leader of the Thai Nation Party (August 1998–February 1991). The junta subsequently appointed Anand Panyarachun as prime minister, and a new constitution was promulgated by Anand with a general election scheduled for March 22, 1992. Although a coalition cabinet was formed, Narong Wongwan was not allowed to be Prime Minister despite the fact that his Justice Unity Party won the most seats in parliament, because he was allegedly linked to a drug scandal. Ex-military Commander Suchinda, who once declared he would allow non-elected persons to lead the country, did not honor his words and, instead, served as prime minister.

The second student riots in Thai history occurred in May 1992 with massive public protests. "Black May," as it was notoriously called, began with the Chamlong Srimuang, Sudarat Keyuraphan, and Dr. San Hatthirat leading protests to demand Suchinda's resignation. On their way to the Government House, protesters were stopped at Phan Fa Bridge, blocked by razor wire created by the police. The confrontations between the nearly 40,000 protesters led by Chamlong and the police, joined by the military, turned the area around Phan Fa Bridge and Democracy Monument into a war zone. A state of emergency was declared in Bangkok and its vicinity, including Samutprakarn, Samutsakhon, Nonthaburi, Pathumthani, and Suchinda. It was illegal for groups of ten or more people to gather. The police were legally allowed to use arms and coercion to stop the opposition. As a result, the protesters moved to the Ramkhamhaeng University in the east of the city. About 50,000 people gathered in the area, and violence escalated between the two sides. Eventually, the royal family had to intervene. First, Princess Sirindhorn and Prince Crown Prince Vajiralongkorn addressed the public via a television broadcast on May 20 to end the violence. The King, though, had to address the leaders of both sides, Suchinda and Chamlong, to put an end to the confrontation. In a television broadcast, King Bhumibol Adulyadej said:

> The Nation belongs to everyone, not one or two specific people. The problems exist because we don't talk to each other and resolve them together. The problems arise from 'bloodthirstiness'. People can lose their minds when they resort to violence. Eventually, they don't know why they fight each other and what the problems they need to resolve are. They merely know that they must overcome each other and they must be the only winner. This no way leads to victory, but only danger. There will only be losers, only the losers. Those who confront each other will all be the losers. And the loser of the losers will be the Nation…. For what purpose are you telling yourself that you're the winner when you're standing upon the ruins and debris? (Bhumibol'Adulyadej, May 20, 1992)

The results of the fight were 39 casualties, an unreported number of missing persons, numerous injuries, over 3500 arrests, and several unofficial reports of torture. A fact-finding committee led by General Pichit Kullawanit was established in the Ministry of Defense, although nothing has yet to be released to the public.[2]

Financial Crisis, People Democracy, and Administrative Reform

Due to the political turmoil of the 1990s, the economy remained stagnant. As a result, at the end of 1990s, Thailand—like many countries in Southeast Asia—faced an economic crisis. Corruption became widespread as many political leaders turned a profit from their offices, receiving government contracts and serving on the executive board of a telecommunications company that received concessions from the government, which created conflicts of interest. Both the World Bank and the International Monetary Fund (IMF) helped Thailand recover not only from the devaluation of its currency but also from the broader Asian Financial Crisis that resulted. However, the aid came with several conditions, specifically government reform and more stringent fiscal policies.

A new constitution was drafted by the Constitutional Drafting Assembly, which comprised popularly elected citizens from all occupations. The "People's Constitution" was the country's sixteenth constitution, and it redesigned the bicameral legislature. As a result, members of the Senate were no longer allowed to be members of any political parties. To lay the foundation for a constitutional parliament, many new independent commissions were established to provide checks and balances for political institutions. Among these were the Election Commission, which was split from the Ministry of Interior and tasked with overseeing public hearings and election activities on both the national and local levels. Also created were Ombudsmen, the National Human Rights Commission, the Constitutional Court, the Administrative Court, the Office of the Auditor-General, the National Anti-Corruption Commission, the Consumers' Protection Organization, and the Environmental Conservation Organization. The power to appoint the members of these committees rested on the Senate. The 500 parliamentary seats were filled by 400 elected individuals and another 100 from the party lists based on the modified proportional representation. The drafters' intention was to guarantee that the next coalition government would comprise two well-established political parties, like Chuan Leekpai's Democrats and Thaksin Chinnawat's Thai Rak Thai Party.

In the past, too many factions in the coalition had caused a great deal of political instability and economic downturn. As expected, the TRT party won the hearts of the grassroots in the 2001 general election with strategic populist policies. Thaksin Shinawatra took control of the government in a landslide victory with 248 parliamentary seats. To prevent a vote of no confidence, a coalition government was formed with the Chart Thai Party, the New Aspiration Party, and the Seritham Party. A series of reforms were enacted for economic, social, education, and healthcare policies. They laid the foundation for the present condition of the Thai bureaucracy and politics by including twelve free years of public education, free and equal access to universal healthcare coverage, One Tambon One Products (OTOP)[3], and so forth. The economy was booming and GDP hit a record high at 6.8% in 2003, up from 2.1% in 2001, when Thaksin first became the premier (*The Economist*, 2005). Non-performing loans also dropped from 50% to 12%, and poverty fell to less than 10%.

Administrative Reform

One of many successful reforms initiated by Thaksin was the restructuring of the nation's bureaucracy. Using funds from the IMF, he completely reformed the hierarchical structure of the nation's outdated bureaucracy and embraced a New Public Management (NPM) concept. He reorganized and redesigned numerous governments, ministries, departments, and agencies.

Indeed, as many as twenty new ministries were established, such as Social and Human Security Development, Tourism and Sports, Natural Resources and Environment, Information and Communication Technology, and Culture. To further streamline bureaucracy, more than thirty Autonomous Public Organizations (APOs) were created. These were created from larger, inefficient departments and each was tasked with its own specific mission. It was expected that some APOs would be terminated once the tasks were fulfilled. However, these APOs were never shut down, even though performance evaluations confirmed either successful completion or failure at achieving their assigned task. In-depth interviews with the directors of several APOs revealed their close relationship with a number of politicians (Tamronglak 2011). Thus, it is clear that these APOs have become sanctuaries for politicians who do not win elections.

New laws, regulations, and practices also laid the foundation for Thailand's current bureaucracy, including the aforementioned APOs, as well as a Special Delivery Unit (SPU), contracting some services out to other parties, public-private-partnerships, and so forth. Indeed, bureaucratic practices were transformed through re-engineering, downsizing, early-retirement, one-stop services, and the use of single-window centers to reduce red-tape.

From his business experience as the CEO of a successful company, Thaksin, in 2001, also initiated the idea of "CEO-governors" in an effort to empower the provincial governors under the Ministry of Interior to implement new results-oriented management practices. By October 2003, the CEO-governor concept was applied to all provinces. Running provincial affairs like a business, CEO-governors were authorized to plan and co-ordinate with provincial developments and other legitimate authorities to issue bonds for fund-raising. The "provincial CFOs" were directly accountable to the CEO-governors. Although this new idea seemed positive in theory, when put in practice, it stumbled because the governing structure was divided into separate ministries, each specializing in different functions. The CEO concept required centralization, thereby absorbing the decision-making power from all other ministries. This consolidation implied centralization of power from national and local administrations into one position. As a consequence, it contradicted the opportunity for localization of administration. This problematic practice did not last very long, as the military staged another coup d'état in 2006 and put a stop to it.

Though the economy was on the upswing during Thaksin's administration, corruption remained rampant. Two distinguished institutions provided contradictory reports on control over corruption: Worldwide Governance Indicators (WGI) by the World Bank gave Thailand a lower score on

Control of Corruption during 2002–2005, while Thailand's Corruption Perceptions Index (CPI) produced by Transparency International (TI) improved its rank from 61 in 2001 to 59 in 2005. Thaksin and his family were accused and later charged for conflict of interests over land purchased from a state agency and a business transaction with a telecom company. Due to the many allegations of corruption, the military was able to rationalize a coup d'état in 2006 while he was attending a UN summit in New York. Another reason given for why they should seize power was lèse majesté, or political interference with state agencies, and the creation of social divisions among Thai people to the "colored politics" of Red-Shirt and Yellow-Shirt bipartisanism. Although Thaksin currently resides in asylum, he was influential within the TRT party and Thai politics and Royalists still consider him a threat to military power and to democratic process.

In terms of administrative restructuring, an important development during Thaksin's era was the attempt to balance his power with the power of the military by transferring control over the Royal Thai Police to the Prime Minister. In this way, he was able to counterattack any military coups. The police force later played a significant role as peacekeepers during a number of protests and movements created by citizens.

Political Turmoil

A new constitution was drafted ten years after the junta in 2006 to fix the unexpected problems and flaws created by the 1997 Constitution. The general election was organized by the Election Commission when the Constitution was promulgated after the national referendum in 2007. It was the 25th election in Thai politics, and over 200,000 soldiers and policemen and 1500 civil servants were employed to maintain the peace and monitor election fraud. The TRT had been dissolved after the coup d'état and the new People's Power Party (PPP) had formed, led by Samak Sundaravej. The PPP won the most seats in this election and was about to form a coalition government with five other parties, when the Election Commission found PPP deputy leader Yongyuth Tiyapairat to be guilty of election fraud. Apparently, he had bought votes and this resulted in the dissolution of the PPP.

Another election was arranged, and this time the Democrat party won. Abhisit Vejjajiva became the Prime Minister and immediately had to tackle the global economic crisis as well as domestic disturbances caused by the Red-Shirts, which were former Thaksin allies and supporters. Abhisit was forced to use military force to maintain the peace in Bangkok. Thaksin's supporters disapproved of Abhisit's premiership, claiming that the December 2008 election had been unfair. The United Front for Democracy Against Dictatorship (UDD), or the Red-Shirts, initiated a series of protests against Abhisit and demanded that he step down. The gathering of 25,000 protesters in Bangkok required a security force of 50,000 men to contain it. Police officers who were assumed to be loyal to Thaksin were placed on duty and not allowed to use guns. However, the UDD pressured them by using bombs, guns, and every means necessary to agitate Abhisit and, thus, challenge his power at the Rajadamnoen protest site and the Rajaprasong intersection. A state of emergency was declared on the evening of April 8. The situation worsened and tensions continued to mount as innocent civilians, including one Italian journalist, were killed by snipers. By the end of May, over 2100 individuals had been injured. An attempt to create a negotiation process between Abhisit and the UDD's leader failed and the conflict could not be reconciled. At the end of the battle, Abhisit decided to dissolve the parliaments and called another election in 2011, which he expected to win.

However, the former PPP members had regrouped to form the Pheu Thai Party, this time led by Thaksin's youngest sister, Yingluck Shinawatra. The turbulent political climate and long political unrest during Abhisit's administration meant that the majority of the public wanted someone new. Yingluck Shinawatra won over those who still supported Thaksin and wanted to see him and his sister improve the economy.

She became the first female premier in Thailand. With little experience in politics, her policies and actions were perceived to come from her big brother abroad. She implemented popular populist policies, including the rice-pledging scheme, a higher minimum wage of 300 THB per day, and the minimum wage for university graduates of 15,000 THB per month. Although these initially earned her popular support, they would later cause her problems.

Her proposal for general amnesty for all juntas was construed as merely a way to get her brother back into country and return to him all of the assets that had been seized from his telecom company. After heavy flooding in 2011, she was accused of being negligent and incompetent at handling the flood disaster.

During her administration, in 2013 and 2014, the People's Democratic Reform Committee (PDRC) staged anti-government protests against her, and the former Democrat Party parliamentary representative (MP), Suthep Thaugsuba, put more political pressure on her. A state of emergency was declared for sixty days in 2014, during which the media was censored, political gatherings of more than five persons were prohibited, and the military was ordered to use force to detain and press charges. Confrontations between protesters and police officers occurred in many areas (Changwattana Road, Prathum Wan, Ratchaprasong, Silom, and Asok) and resulted in injuries and death. While police officers abstained from using shotguns, protestors attacked them with bombs and guns. The fights became more violent when police officers began fighting back with real ammunition, rather than the rubber bullets they had resorted to previously.

The Election Commission was tasked with organizing a general election for February 2, 2014, to mitigate the situation as soon as possible. On the day of the election, 10,000 police officers stood by to ensure the safety of all voters. However, the election was interrupted and not completed within one day. Eventually, the constitutional court was summoned by the ombudsmen to determine whether the election was unconstitutional.

On March 21, 2014, the constitutional court ruled in a 6-3 decision, that a general election must be held on the same day, nationwide, within 45 days of the dissolution of the House of Representatives. As a result of the court's decision, students staged protests. They posted a sign that read, "Respect My Future" on black mourning cloth, which they draped over the Democratic Monument. And they posted a sign that read, "Respect My Vote" in front of Lord Rattanathibet's Mansion. Additionally, they demanded the resignation of all constitutional court judges. Protests and counter-protests led by Red-Shirts were widespread throughout Bangkok and several other provinces. Fights between the two camps were out of control, and M16 rifles were spotted being used by both sides. Suthep announced his intention to not stop until he won the battle to overthrow the government. As political unrest worsened, Prime Minister Yingluck Shinawatra was removed from office by a coup d'état led by army chief General Prayut Chan-o-cha on May 20, 2014.

Thailand Today: What Do We See in Military Government?

The present administration is not that much different from previous governments. The military government of General Prayut Chan-o-cha has been viewed by the public as highly authoritarian. Indeed, government information is closely scrutinized and censored before being revealed to the public through a single gateway of online media. Open access to government policies and information is non-existent, and public criticism of government actions and policies is monitored. Anyone found openly criticizing the government is arrested or taken to a military camp for "attitude adjustment."

For instance, in 2015, fourteen students were arrested for protesting for democracy. They were later released, but only after promising not to foment political unrest or protest the government again. Other land reform activists, who were attempting to march from the north of the country to the capital, were also stopped and detained in the same manner. Political demonstrations and street protests are discouraged by the current administration, and serious military force is used immediately in such cases. Those who support the government argue that such actions are necessary to maintain the peace.

The government's supporters would like General Prayut Chan-o-cha to remain in power after the general election, which was March 24, 2019. However, the path to remain in power may not be a bed of roses because new opposition actors, such as Future Forward Party (FFP), add to the complicated system of mixed-member proportional representation (MMPR). The Future Forward Party (FFP) was founded in March, led by Thanathorn Juangroongruangkit, former Vice President of Thai Summit Group and Piyabutr Saengkanokkul and former lecturer from Law Faculty, Thammasat University. Unexpectedly, the FFP won most trust from the newest generation of voters, gaining 6,330,617 popular votes, behind the military established Palang Pracharath Party (8,441,274) and Phue Thai Party (7,881,006). Exploiting social media like Facebook and Twitter, the FFP came in third in the general election to win a total of about 81 seats in parliament (31 elected representatives and 50 party list representatives).

The Democrat Party was embarrassed to come in fourth in the competition with only 3,959,385 popular votes (Election Commission, May 28, 2019). As a result, Abhisit Vejjajiva resigned from the post as promised for not being able to win the election. With the new calculation of representatives based on the system of mixed-member proportional representation (MMPR), General Prayut Chan-o-cha faces new challenges in finding allies from twenty-six political parties to form a coalition government. Though the general election is now completed with reelection in Constituency 8 of Chiang Mai Province on May 26, 2019, negotiations among allies are still unsettled. The Democrat Party now has a newly elected leader, Jurin Laksanawisit, and decided to join the coalition government. But, the party has apparently split into two sides: those voting for and those voting against General Prayut Chan-o-cha.

The political situation in Thailand has yet to put all cards on the table. Stories continue to unfold regarding the new government. It will be interesting to see how General Prayut Chan-o-cha will strategically negotiate among the parties, balancing their interests and upholding his power against the ambitious and social-media-mastered leader of FFP, who recently announced he would campaign as a Prime Minister candidate against him.

Images of the Government: Through the Eyes of the People and Their Expectations

In a class entitled, Seminar in Public Administration and Policy, students were assigned to ask residents of Bangkok for their opinions on bureaucracy, bureaucrats, public services, and military government. Quick interviews were conducted with those in various walks of life, including street vendors, foreigners living in Bangkok, travelers, foreign students, motorcycle-taxi drivers, unskilled workers, and so forth. The majority of responses expressed dissatisfaction due to problems of inequality in public services, the overall ineffectiveness and inefficiency of the government, the excessive abuse of power of bureaucrats, the increase in corruption, and more. Most notably, the people see government as both good and evil. For the past four years, in the current junta rule, the country has been at peace, although people are treated differently based on their socio-economic class. Street-level bureaucrats are arrested and questioned if any wrong-doing is determined. The convicted bureaucrats are punished harshly and must leave the service. However, those high ranking officials who are close friends to the junta will be left untouched despite rumors of corruption or suspicious wrong-doings.

Twenty-Year National Strategic Plan: Bureaucratic Reform

Thailand was once considered a contender for the "Five Tiger Cubs" in Southeast Asia, a group of countries that included Indonesia, Malaysia, the Philippines, Thailand, and Vietnam. Thailand's GDP was ranked the second largest in all of Southeast Asia. Its economy relies heavily on tourism, especially the hotel and restaurant sectors (about 24.9% of GDP), as well as trade and logistics (13.4%) and agriculture (8.4%) (Nag 2018). Poverty levels, based on the percentage of the population living below the national poverty line, have decreased dramatically from 65.26 to 13.15% (Nag 2018). Nevertheless, the majority of the population, though employed, are trapped in low paying jobs. As a result, the economy is unable to grow significantly due to the country's political instability, rampant corruption, and poor educational system. The country's Human Capital Index score was only 0.6 out of 1.0, which is 65th among the 157 world territories. Singapore, by comparison, scores 0.88 (*The Nation*, 2018). For these reasons, Prayut Chan-o-cha, unlike his predecessors, has designed a long-term plan for the country's national development extending over the next twenty years. The national strategic plan is the first of its kind and was required in the 2017 Constitution, which was ratified by the king on October 13, 2018.

From the perspective of politicians, this new constitution aims to dispose of the old politicians, especially Thaksin, his family, and his supporters, by eliminating all loopholes that benefit him, his family business, or his political empire. Corruption will further be diminished and corrupt individuals will be brought to justice. Nevertheless, this long-term plan has been criticized as a ploy for the junta to continue holding power for at least the next ten years. The main purpose of the new development plan was to achieve stability in all aspects of society—political, economic, environmental, and educational—and improve the nation's wealth. To this end, Prayut established the Super-committee in 2017, officially known as the administrative committee for reform, reconciliation, and national strategy. It is led by him in addition to other deputies, ministers, experts, and representatives from public-private committees.

The national strategic plan, which had been previously studied and proposed by two consecutive assemblies (the National Legislative Assembly [NLA] in 2015 and National Reform Steering Assembly in 2017), will be traced and monitored by the PM's Delivery Unit (PMDU), newly instituted by Prayut. Prayut, himself, serves as chairman on this unit together with three of his trusted friends and several other key persons (Suvit Maesincee, Ampon Kittiampon, and Somkid Jatusripitak). These three close friends recently applied for political party membership that supports Prayut for the next premiership. They all declared their bid to run in the general election scheduled for Spring 2019. The PMDU will focus on ten areas of strategic development in an effort to set Thailand up for success in the next century. Thirty-seven major reform agendas and 138 initiatives will be incorporated into all government ministries, departments, and agencies in coordination with the private sector. The goal is to advance the country's capacity through innovation and digital technology, with new directions for developing the workforce and educating Thai citizens in science, technology, engineering, and mathematics (Prime Minister's Delivery Unit 2018).

The military junta, similar to previous groups of military cadets, participated in the democratic political process and either joined a political party or established a new one to perpetuate its legacy. This time is no different: Prayut recently declared his intention to run for the post next year. Indeed, the cyclical nature of the country's politics is reminiscent of the old Thai saying that, "those who write the rules, will win the game." Against this backdrop of Thai politics, deep cultural traditions continue, as described next.

Thai Culture

Hofstede et al. (2010) examined national culture of countries throughout the world through the lens of six different dimensions: individualism-collectivism, power distance, femininity-masculinity, uncertainty avoidance, short-long-term orientation, and indulgence. Individualism is considered the opposite of egoism and refers to the feeling of being independent. Collectivism, conversely, refers to the idea that a person should know his or her own place. In a family or in society, "I" encompasses the identity in an individual society while "we" is the identifier of a collective society. With regard to Thailand, Hofstede's results find that Thailand scores about mid-range among Asian nations on most cultural variables. On a scale of 0 to 100, the nation scored low (20) on individualism, 64 on power distance, 34 on masculine culture, 64 on uncertainty avoidance, 56 on short versus long-term orientation, and 50 for indulgence versus restraint.

Thai society is comprised of a three-tiered class system: the upper class, the middle class, and lower class. Within the country's lower and middle classes, interpersonal relationships are influenced by Chinese culture and are thus family-oriented (Ramangkul 2017). Indeed, family values are placed above society's values, and Thais are taught to conform to family values. For example, they relate to others by establishing hierarchical family rank using words like "Phi" (older brother or sister), "Nong" (younger brother or sister), uncle, auntie, grandmother, and grandfather. Not only is this considered good manners and shows respect to elders, it also strengthens solidarity and minimizes conflicts (Maisrikrod 1999).

Upper-class Thais are commonly well-educated on Western political ideology because they live in the city, particularly central Bangkok, and consider themselves to be superior to those in the middle and lower classes. They try to maintain their political power and they distance themselves from the rest of the citizenry. The King, as previously noted, adopted the Divine image from Khmer culture as a way of differentiating himself from the common man. Moreover, all decisions are made by those in power or in the higher echelons of bureaucracy, while the masses are not allowed to participate in politics.

The development of the Thai monarchy paradoxically attempts to balance traditional Thai values and modernity. On various occasions, the King has played an important role in stopping bloodshed. This occurred in 1973 when the military overpowered student demonstrations, in 1992 when the military used armed forces to shoot down demonstrators and protesters on the street, and in 1997 when the Asian economic crisis occurred. King Rama IX, also known as King Bhumibol Adulyadej, for example, was cleverly able to resolve major conflicts. He proposed the philosophy of "sufficiency economy" to solve problems of financial mismanagement. Today, the Thai monarchy faces the challenge of being the soul of a nation-state: It strives to simultaneously preserve Thai traditional culture while adopting Western democratic rule. It does so by allowing people from all walks of life to participate in politics and voice their opinions.

The Emotional Labor Survey

For this study, the questionnaire was translated into the Thai language. The survey was then distributed during May and June 2018 to Royal Thai Police Officers in cooperation with the Deputy District Chief in the Ministry of Interior. Respondents were selected from officers currently tasked with enforcing the country's laws and regulations and those who interact with citizens in rural areas in various provinces in Thailand. As for the police officers, the questionnaires were sent to 70 randomly selected officers who were stationed in several Bangkok police stations. The other 150 questionnaires were provided to Deputy District Chiefs from all 77 provinces in Thailand, while they were participating in a one-and-a-half month "Training Program for Deputy District Chiefs" organized by the Ministry of Interior in Bangkok.

Demographic Statistics

Demographic characteristics of the respondents are presented in Table 18.1. Most respondents are less than 49 years old. Indeed, roughly half of them are 30-39 years of age, and 22% are less than 30 years old. Only 20% are 40-49 years old. Moreover, there are more male than female officers (56.8% compared to 40.9%). More than 50% of them are young civil servants in that they have less than 10 years of experience. However, these young cadres are well-educated, with approximately 52.7% holding some type of college degree. An additional 25.5% have a Master's degree.

Table 18.2 reveals the nature of the tasks performed by the respondents. Data show that they are responsible for a variety of activities, from office

Table 18.1 Demographic characteristics: Thailand

	Frequency	Percent
Age		
Less than 30	49	22.3
30–39 years	111	50.4
40–49 years	44	20.0
50–59 years	12	5.5
60 or more	0	0.0
N/A	4	1.8
Gender		
Female	90	40.9
Male	125	56.8
N/A	5	2.3
Public service experience		
Less than 10	125	56.8
10–19 years	22	10.0
20–29 years	11	5.0
30 or more	0	0.0
N/A	62	28.2
Educational level		
Less than high school	0	0.0
High school graduate	3	1.4
Some college	0	0.0
2-year associate degree	2	0.9
College graduate	116	52.7
Some graduate school	20	9.1
Master's degree	56	25.5
Law degree (J.D., LL.B.)	16	7.3
Doctorate (Ph.D., M.D., Ed.D., etc.)	0	0.0
Other (please specify)	1	0.5
N/A	6	2.7

Table 18.2 Occupational characteristics: Thailand

Occupation	Frequency	Percent
1. Administration	87	12.0
2. Community development/neighborhood services	67	9.3
3. Engineering, manufacturing, or production	3	0.4
4. Education	13	1.8
5. Disaster response	25	3.5
6. Finance or accounting	22	3.0
7. Firefighter	7	1.0
8. Health care	12	1.7
9. Housing	17	2.4
10. Human resource management	33	4.6
11. Information and communication	30	4.2
12. Law enforcement	110	15.2
13. Military	8	1.1

Table 18.1 (continued)

Occupation	Frequency	Percent
14. Public relations	33	4.6
15. Planning	65	9.0
16. Public works: streets, sanitation, utilities	16	2.2
17. Purchasing	20	2.8
18. Recreation and parks	10	1.4
19. Research and development	10	1.4
20. Social services	105	14.5
21. Transportation	8	1.1
22. Support services (e.g., plants and equipment maintenance)	6	0.8
23. Other	15	2.1

administration (12.0%) to law enforcement in the field (15.2%) to social services of all kinds (14.5%). Some engage in community development or neighborhood services and thus interact directly with people on-site (9.3%). Close to 30% are responsible for administrative and managerial work, including planning, human resources management, and communication.

Emotional Labor Variables

Designed specifically for this study, the theoretical concept of emotional labor is framed by three dimensions: emotive capacity, pretending expression, and deep acting. The three dependent variables are job satisfaction, burnout, and personal fulfillment. As displayed in Table 18.3, all emotional labor variables exceeded the interitem reliability test with a Cronbach's alpha of more than 0.70, except for emotive capacity. The coefficient for emotive capacity was 0.627, which is lower than the desired level of reliability. Thus, this variable performs differently in the Thai context than in most other nations. The reason may be because Thai civil servants have been working in an unstable political climate for many years. The effects of instability are heightened by the current transition period they are experiencing with the

Table 18.3 Descriptive statistics and Cronbach's alpha: Thailand

	Mean	SD	Cronbach's alpha
Emotive capacity	5.03	0.99	0.627
Pretending expression	4.86	1.35	0.806
Deep acting	4.64	1.22	0.738
Job satisfaction	5.02	1.24	0.817
Burnout	4.29	1.50	0.882
Personal fulfillment	5.50	1.18	0.890

reconciliation of the political ideological divide between two major opposing parties, the Democrat and the Phue Thai. Responses to items within emotive capacity may vary more than usual due to the unpredictability of the contexts within which they work.

Results

Structural equation modeling (SEM) was used to test the direct effect of emotional labor variables (emotive capacity, pretending expression, and deep acting) on the aforementioned outcome variables (job satisfaction, burnout, and personal fulfillment). Results are displayed in Table 18.4.

Table 18.4   Structural model results: Thailand

Hypothesized Paths	Coefficients	p-value
Emotive capacity → Job satisfaction	0.572*	0.000
Emotive capacity → Burnout	−0.123*	0.006
Emotive capacity → Personal fulfillment	0.403*	0.000
Pretending expression → Job satisfaction	−0.131	0.175
Pretending expression → Burnout	−0.012	0.896
Pretending expression → Personal fulfillment	−0.069	0.489
Deep acting → Job satisfaction	−0.032	0.734
Deep acting → Burnout	0.429*	0.000
Deep acting → Personal fulfillment	0.020	0.837

Model fit: $\chi^2 = 382.448$ (df = 142), CFI = 0.861, RMSEA = 0.094, SRMR = 0.130

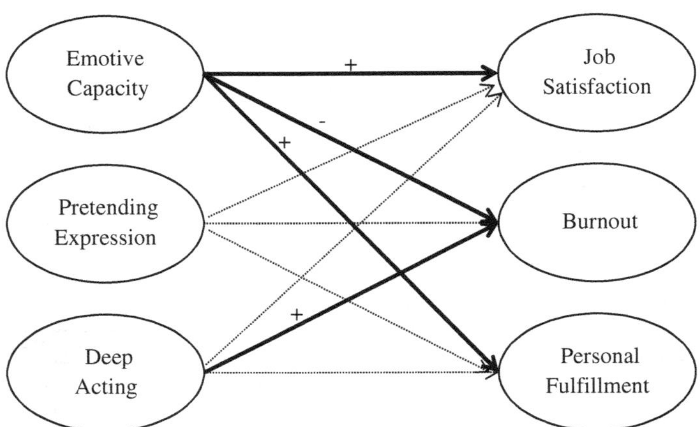

Fig. 18.1   Path diagram for Thailand (*Note* The solid arrows indicate statistically significant relationships. The dotted arrows indicate no significant relationships. A "+" represents a positive relationship. A "−" represents a negative relationship)

As can be seen in Fig. 18.1, the relationships indicated by a solid line between the independent and dependent variables are statistically significant at the level of $p \leq 0.05$. The relationships represented by the dotted lines are not statistically significant. The findings are explained below.

Emotive Capacity

The path coefficients displayed in Table 18.4 indicate that the emotive capacity variable has a direct and strong positive effect on both job satisfaction ($p = 0.000$) and personal fulfillment ($p = 0.000$). The impact of the emotive capacity variable on the dependent variable, burnout, is also statistically significant ($p = 0.006$), but with an inverse relationship. Emotive capacity asks three questions: "I am good at expressing how I feel," "I am good at getting people to calm down," and "In my job, I am good at dealing with emotional issues."

Pretending Expression

Based on the concept of emotional labor proposed by Hochschild (1983), pretending expression, or "surface acting," refers to when someone hides their true feelings while expressing an emotion they do not actually feel (Grandey et al. 2013; Grandey, 2000). In other words, the emotive expression they are displaying is pretense. The outcome of this pretending, in the long-term, will cause stress to the individual, since they must constantly "fake" their true emotions (Grandey 2000). In this study, the statements used for this line of inquiry are quite straightforward: "I hide my true feelings so as to appear pleasant at work," "In my job I act confident and self-assured regardless of how I actually feel" and "I wear a 'mask' in order to deal with clients/customers in an appropriate way." The path coefficients reveal that the pretending expression variable does not have a statistically significant effect on outcome variables. This finding is the opposite of what is found in many other countries, especially in the West (Abraham 1998; Morris and Feldman 1997; Rutter and Fielding 1988).

Deep Acting

The last independent variable used in this study is deep acting, which is a strategy that can be used to regulate one's own feelings to conform with organizational rules or expectations, such as smiling, maintaining eye contact, and speaking in a friendly tone (Hochschild 1983). The feelings displayed are authentic and are perceived to be so by citizens (Grandey et al. 2013, 3–17; Grandey 2000; Diefendorff and Gosserand 2003). The outcomes of this behavior can be both negative (individual stress and health problem) and positive (customer service) (Grandey 2000). The survey used the following statements to determine the effects of the deep acting variable: "I try to actually experience the emotions that I must show to clients/customers," "I work hard to actually feel the emotions that I need to show to clients/customers," and "I work at developing the feelings inside of me that I need to show to clients/customers." Results from the analysis show that the deep acting variable is not related to either job satisfaction or personal fulfillment but it is positively related to burnout ($p = 0.000$).

Discussion

By employing the same framework of analysis to investigate the impact of the three dimensions of emotional labor (emotive capacity, pretending expression, and deep acting) on public servants, particularly police workers and Deputy District Chiefs in Thailand, the findings show how emotive capacity and authentic emotive expression affect job outcomes. The structural equation model used in the analysis confirms that emotive capacity has a direct, positive effect on job satisfaction and personal fulfillment and has a negative effect on burnout. This means that as emotive capacity increases, one's likelihood of experiencing burnout decreases. Moreover, engaging in emotive pretending in order to do a job does not affect outcomes either positively or negatively. Finally, as one engages in authentic emotive expression on the job, the likelihood of experiencing burnout increases.

The respondents chosen for this study were mainly (about two-thirds) the Deputy District Chiefs in Thailand, the Ministry of Interior, and some police workers from the Royal Thai Police. The responsibilities of the Deputy District Chiefs cover a wide range of administrative tasks (notification of birth and death, handling marriage and divorces certificates, receiving complaints on public services, and so forth), as well as ensuring the implementation of government policies, and arresting criminals, among other things. Simply put, Deputy District Chiefs are the ones who have direct contact with citizens from all walks of life in all matters assigned to them by district chiefs. The other respondents include police workers, who are commonly tasked with enforcing laws and regulations, maintaining the peace, protecting citizens from harm, making arrests, and answering and responding to calls for help.

About 72% of the respondents are men under the age of 40 who have been serving the public for less than ten years. As described in the political development of Thailand over the past twenty years, the country is divided into two: those who favor the old-fashioned Democrat Party and those who prefer the newly-formed modern political party Thai Rak Thai (TRT) or Phue Thai Party, led by Thaksin Shinnawatra, a former policeman and business guru who became a politician in 1998. Over the last ten years, the country experienced seventeen coup d'états, thirteen of which were successful. The country has been torn and broken by all of the political unrest. Indeed, political discussions, even among family members, are heated and tend to end in arguments. The societal climate is fragile and full of disagreements, conflicts, and confrontations.

Due to the unstable political climate and the recent death of the beloved King Bhumibol, the Thai people would prefer a peaceful transition in government from authoritarian to constitutional democracy. However, the current PM has been able to maintain his rule through undemocratic means of restricting civil and political rights; violating individual liberty, freedom, and human rights; censoring the media; and restraining the public's ability to criticize the government. The present military junta rule has lasted for more than four years, longer than any other previous elected government in Thai history.

Thai civil servants who have been trained and have developed themselves throughout their career are ready and capable to perform their task at hand. This assertion is strengthened by the theoretical assumption that those who remain in public service for more than ten years are likely to experience job satisfaction and self-fulfillment (Guy et al.Newman 2008). Therefore, it is not surprising that the civil servants in this study take pride in their work—which greatly helps them reduce stress and increase their sense of accomplishment.

Conclusion

Numerous political incidents and periods of turmoil have resulted in the development of semi-democracy in Thailand. The bureaucratic polity is primarily led by the military, which remains prevalent and influential in Thai public services. The current authoritarian military government intends to establish a true and genuine democracy under a constitutional monarchy in the next general election. The role of the King as the soul of the nation helps to preserve the country's traditional values, although this needs to be balanced with Western political ideals. Judging from their responses to survey items, public servants, both police officers and Deputy District Chiefs, feel pride in their work and are quite satisfied with their responsibility. In summary, the results in this study confirm important theoretical assumptions about the effect of emotional labor on its positive correlates, job satisfaction, and personal fulfillment, as well as on its negative correlate, burnout. It would be interesting to explore this connection further for other occupations, such as nurses, doctors, and volunteers. Indeed, according to recent daily news reports, there are frequent disputes between hospital personnel and patients in emergency rooms and provincial hospitals in rural areas.

Thailand is known as the land of smiles, but smiles can convey a multitude of meanings. Thai citizens' ability to endure, keep emotions inside, and put a smile on their face can cause stress and even burnout, and their smiles may not accurately reflect how they actually feel. Thus, this phenomenon requires further investigation. The findings of such studies would be beneficial for human resource departments because it will allow for exploration of the connection between employees' potential and their personal fulfillment in the workplace.

Notes

1. Borommatrailokkanat or Trailok was the king of the Ayutthaya Kingdom from 1448 to 1488.
2. Suchinda was later appointed chairman of Telecom Asia (today known as True Corporation), a company which received a concession to install two million telephone lines in Bangkok during the Anand government. Anand later became Chairman of Saha-Union Group, which had received an independent power producer concession during his government.
3. Thaksin had initiated the policy to increase income in the local areas by encouraging each village to produce one unique product, learning the experience from Japan. The products then are promoted by the Ministry of Commerce.

References

Abraham, R. 1998. "Emotional Dissonance in Organizations: Antecedents, Consequences, and Moderators." *Genetic, Social, and General Psychology Monographs* 124 (2): 229–46.

Bhumibol Adulyadej. 1992. "Royal Intervention." May 20. Accessed August 10, 2018. https://www.youtube.com/watch?v=Rb4Tjs-Qs9o.

Case, William F. 2001. "Thai Democracy 2001 Out of Equilibrium." *Asian Survey* 41 (3): 525–47. Accessed May 10, 2018. https://www.jstor.org/stable/10.1525/as.2001.41.3.525.

Diefendorff, James M., and Robin H. Gosserand. 2003. "Understanding the Emotional Labor Process: A Control Theory Perspective." *Journal of Organizational Behavior* 24 (8): 945–59. Accessed September 20, 2018. https://www.jstor.org/stable/4093748.

Election Commission. 2019. "Criteria and Method in Calculating Party List Representatives." May 28. Accessed May 29, 2019. https://www.ect.go.th/ect_th/download/article/article_20190528140635.pdf.

Grandey, Alicia A. 2000. "Emotional Regulation in the Workplace: A New Way to Conceptualize Emotional Labor." Journal of Occupational Health Psychology 5 (1): 95–110.

Grandey, Alicia A., James M. Diefendorff, and D. Rupp. 2013. *Emotional Labor in the 21st Century: Diverse Perspectives on Emotion Regulation at Work.* London, UK: Routledge.

Guy, Mary, Meredith A. Newman, and Sharon H. Mastracci. 2008. *Emotional Labor: Putting the Service in Public Service.* Armonk, New York: M. E. Sharpe.

Hirschfeld, John. 1994. "Thai Politics." *Culture Mandala: The Bulletin of the Centre for East-West Cultural and Economic Studies* 1 (1): 6368. Accessed August 10, 2018. http://epublications.bond.edu.au/cm/vol1/iss1/10.

Hochschild, Arlie R. 1983. *The Managed Heart: The Commercialization of Feeling.* Berkeley, CA: University of California Press.

Hofstede, Geert, Gert Jan Hofstede, and Michael Minkov. 2010. *Cultures and Organizations: Software of the Mind.* New York, NY: McGraw-Hill.

Lysa, Hong. 2000. "Twenty Years of 'Sinlapa Watthanatham': Cultural Politics in Thailand in the 1980s and 1990s." *Journal of Southeast Asian Studies* 31 (1): 26–47.

Maisrikrod, Surin. 1999. "Joining the Values Debate: The Peculiar Case of Thailand." *Sojourn: Journal of Social Issues in Southeast Asia* 14 (2): 402–13.

Morris, J. A., and D. C. Feldman. 1997. "Managing Emotions in the Workplace." *Journal of Managerial Issues* 9 (3): 257–74.

Nag, Sen Oishimaya. 2018. "The Five Tiger Cub Economies of Southeast Asia." *Economics*, January 27. Accessed October 15, 2018. https://www.worldatlas.com/articles/the-five-tiger-cub-economies-of-southeast-asia.html.

Neher, Clark D. 1995. "Democratization in Thailand." *Asian Affairs: An American Review* 21 (4, Winter): 195–209.

Neher, Clark D. 1996. "The Transition to Democracy in Thailand" (Special Issue on A Peace Regime on the Korean Peninsula) *Asian Perspective* 20 (2): 301–21.

Paribatra, Sukhumbhand. 1993. "State and Society in Thailand." *Asian Survey* 33 (9): 879–93.

Prime Minister's Delivery Unit (PMDU). 2018. "National Strategy." March 20. Accessed October 15, 2018. https://pmdu.soc.go.th.

Ramangkul, Weerapong. 2017. "The Distinguished Characteristics of Thai People." *Prachachatthurakit*, December 16. Accessed October 15, 2018. https://www.prachachat.net/opinion-column/news-88407.

Riggs, Fred W. 1964. *Administration in Developing Countries: The Theory of Prismatic Society*. Boston, MA: Houghton Mifflin.

Rutter, D. R., and P. J. Fielding. 1988. "Sources of Occupational Stress: An Examination of British Prison Officers." *Work and Stress* 2 (4): 291–99.

Samudavanija, Chai-Anan. 2002. *Thailand State-Building, Democracy and Globalization*. Bangkok, Thailand: Institute of Public Policy Studies (IPPS).

Tamronglak, Amporn. 2011. *The Study of Independence and Accountability of Thai Public Organizations*. Bangkok, Thailand: Thammasat University.

The Economist. 2005. Thaksin's way: A Formidable Success Story, Though With Some Worrying Signs." *The Economist*, February 23. Accessed September 2, 2018. https://www.economist.com/special-report/2005/02/03/thaksins-way.

The Nation. 2018. "Weak Education Holds Back Thailand in Worldwide Human-Capital Index." October 15. Accessed October 16, 2018. http://www.nationmultimedia.com/detail/asean-plus/30356417.

U.S. Library of Congress. n.d. "Political Developments, 1980–87." Accessed September 20, 2018. http://countrystudies.us/thailand/81.htm.

19

The UK

Sharon H. Mastracci, Ian Tyler Adams and Ning Kang

> Everybody understands English, but nobody understands England
> —European Commission President Jean-Claude Junker (Lawless 2019, para 10)

Westminster Palace is usually pictured from the East bank of the Thames, along a stretch that runs roughly North/South. It is the meeting place of the UK parliament: The House of Commons and the House of Lords. Big Ben, the clock tower, bookends the immense gothic-revival palace on the right. Farther to the right of Big Ben is a half-mile stretch, called Whitehall. This area runs from Trafalgar Square at its north end to Parliament Square to the south. Several government buildings are located on and around Whitehall, including Scotland Yard, Her Majesty's (HM) Treasury, Revenue, and Customs, the Ministry of Defence, the Old War Office, and the Department for International Development. Just as "Westminster" refers collectively to

S. H. Mastracci (✉)
Department of Political Science,
University of Utah, Salt Lake City, UT, USA
e-mail: Sharon.mastracci@poli-sci.utah.edu

I. T. Adams
Department of Political Science, University of Utah, Salt Lake City, UT, USA
e-mail: ian.adams@utah.edu

N. Kang
Global Development Institute, University of Manchester, Manchester, UK
e-mail: ning.kang-2@manchester.ac.uk

© The Author(s) 2019
M. E. Guy et al. (eds.), *The Palgrave Handbook of Global Perspectives on Emotional Labor in Public Service*, https://doi.org/10.1007/978-3-030-24823-9_19

Parliament, "Whitehall" is shorthand for central government administration in the UK. Compared to the structure of federal government in the USA, Australia, and Canada, UK government remains highly centralized even after several decades of devolution to local authorities as well as to the countries of Scotland, Wales, and Northern Ireland. "Whitehall" is the term used to grumble about "big government" in the UK just as "Washington" is the impersonal embodiment of government in the USA. This introduction describes the post-World War II growth of Whitehall and local governments, and their subsequent reforms.

The UK as a Modern Welfare State

Parliament's passage of the National Insurance Act (1946) and the National Assistance Act (1948) under Prime Minister Clement Attlee established the UK as a modern welfare state. These important laws created the British systems of worker's compensation, social security, and income assistance. These reforms also witnessed the creation of the National Health Service (NHS) in 1948 as a consolidation of all local and charitable hospitals and medical providers. This created a national-level administration for comprehensive, universal healthcare free at the point of service.

British civil service increasingly professionalized with creation of the Civil Service College and the Civil Service Department. These innovations were implemented as a result of the Fulton Report in 1968, which had found that administrators were not professional enough, lacked management skills, and needed more technical and scientific expertise. At the same time, local government management and administration became increasingly professionalized during this period. Concerns about the professional credentials of civil servants were soon eclipsed by concerns over the efficiency of the system overall. "This period of incremental evolution and professionalization in the management of the public sector in the UK was to change during the 1970s, as concerns about the efficiency and effectiveness of government came to transcend all else" (Andrews et al. 2013, 8). The British welfare state had grown too large to meet the demands placed on it: "The *Fulton* reforms of 1968 had largely run out of steam by 1974. The great Heath redesign of central government, announced with a confident flourish in October 1970, was already beginning to be dismantled by the beginning of 1970" (Pollitt 1990, 62). The decade ended with the election of a Conservative government led by Margaret Thatcher, who pledged to reform the UK government.

The story of postwar government in the UK is one of serial reform. While process concerns curb reform efforts in constitutional democracies that have complex federal structures such as in the USA, continual reform is embedded in the UK public service culture. Compared to other Anglophone countries, there are almost no such impediments to government-dictated change in UK civil service: "Much of the UK central government, the civil service, most government departments and civil service agencies have no basis in law and can be changed by executive decision by government ministers ... many other changes can simply be imposed by the government so long as it can command a majority in parliament" (Talbot 2001, 282). In contrast, state and provincial autonomy limit how much change the central government can impose in local government in Australia, Canada, and the USA: "Local government in particular has no guaranteed constitutional status and, as such, has been subject to far-reaching structural and managerial reforms during the past 100 years that would not have been possible in countries with more decentralized political systems" (Andrews et al. 2013, 10).

The absence of such structural and legal obstacles allows UK central government to impose its will on local and national civil service. It is somewhat ironic, however, that reforms emphasizing responsiveness and accountability to the public would resist evaluation: "In the UK, reform has been continual, often intense, and sometimes harsh. Public sector employees have become accustomed to constant restructurings, downsizings, and new 'initiatives' ... Ministers tended to take the line that reform was essential, and *self-evidently desirable*, and that formal, public evaluation might prove a delay and a distraction" (Pollitt and Bouckaert 2000, 274, emphasis supplied).

A culture of continual reform is further supported by the British tradition of generalist, agnostic public service, and an emphasis on results over process. The emphasis on civil servants as generalist administrators, rather than specialist s dedicated to a policy issue, arises again in the 1990s under New Labour and its assumptions about the motivations of professionals in Third Sector organizations. In contrast to dedicated specialists, the UK civil servant is an agnostic generalist. This structure further supports a culture of ongoing reform (Andrews et al. 2013, 11, emphasis supplied):

> Civil servants are regarded as people who work for the public and who are, at the most senior levels, charged with upholding the public interest above narrow sectional interests...rather than being experts in administrative law they are required to be generalists able to appreciate issues from many sides. The pragmatism that this culture produces makes it more open to reforms, in part,

because British civil servants are trained to be responsive to such change, but also because there may be greater acceptance or understanding of the need for change…*results matter more than procedures.*

Results matter more than procedures. Public service in the UK is not bound by statutes governing process and protecting equity and will change (or be changed) to produce desired outcomes. Slow growth in the 1960s and economic crises in the 1970s prompted British lawmakers to challenge the seemingly endless rising costs of the central government. The first Thatcher ministry commenced in 1979 and pledged to address the failings of the state, reduce the size of the public sector, cut costs, and apply the same market discipline and management practices as private-sector business. In 1981, the Civil Service Department was eliminated, "and the Treasury assumed control over Whitehall through the Management and Personnel Office" (Andrews et al. 2013, 9).

Private-sector managerial practices were enforced in public-sector departments: "The UK has been very much part of the Anglophone, US-dominated world of managerialism, management consultants, and management gurus" (Pollitt and Bouckaert 2000, 271). Managerial reforms included the introduction of strategic planning, performance targets, and some pay-for-performance schemes. Managerialism is "the belief that all aspects of organizational life can and should be managed according to rational structures, procedures, and modes of accountability in the pursuit of goals defined by policymakers and senior managers" (O'Reilly and Reed 2012, 24). Bovaird and Russell (2007) characterize the managerialist agenda as little more than a recent vintage of Industrial Age time-and-motion studies: "Reforms in the early 1980s were essentially a crude neo-Taylorist form of managerialism" (307). The managerialist ethos is especially complementary to a generalist civil service responsible for results to the party in charge of a centralized government (Pollitt 1990).

With a few modifications during the New Labour governments under Prime Ministers Blair and Brown in the 1990s, British public service has steadily pursued a managerialist agenda in reaction to the rise of the post-war welfare state. This quest is sustained by the continued centralization of power despite devolutionary pressures and the absence of organizational structures or political counter-pressures that could curb reform efforts. The pursuit of reform since the late 1970s continues through today in an environment of austerity and uncertainty. As this *Handbook* goes to press, the effects on public service provision due to the departure of the UK from the European Union—"Brexit"—remain unclear. At minimum, the EU-funded economic development initiatives that have benefitted former industrial areas of the West Midlands and blighted rural areas will end and become the responsibility of the UK. Whether promised economic growth in other areas, such as British fisheries, will offset the decline in economic supports formerly provided under EU-funded programs, remains unclear, may take years, and will likely never be known with certainty.

Having set the context for the governmental context, this chapter proceeds as follows: First, we explore decades of public service reform in the UK, from public administration, to the management of public funds, to shared governance. Second, we discuss studies that have gauged national culture, including the World Values Survey, Hofstede's IBM studies, and the relationship between national culture and emotional labor. Third, we describe the current study: Survey respondents in the UK, dependent and independent variables, and the structural equation model that analyzes those relationships. Finally, we conclude with a summary of the results.

The chapter focuses on the more recent history of reform in UK government and how it has responded to demands of a modern developed economy. Public administration in what is now the UK has a very long history—long by Western standards, at least. In fact, the administrative state of modern England dates back at least a thousand years to the first English census—the *Domesday Book*—in 1086, under orders from William the Conqueror, King William I. Rather than this chapter trying to capture several centuries of administration, or even a few hundred years of administration under the defined power of a constitutional monarchy, the focus is on twentieth and twenty-first centuries administrative reform, for it is this context that best explains the current administrative culture. The modern history of the administrative state in the UK is a story of faith in the power and promise of reform.

Public-Sector Reform and New Public Management

The unique combination of concentrated power in central government and a faith in private-sector, market-like reforms renders the UK a special example of countries that implemented New Public Management (NPM) reforms. The UK has become "a kind of poster child for NPM and a negative advertisement for its worst excesses" (Andrews et al. 2013, 10). Many of the same factors underpinning rapid establishment of the UK welfare state in the decade following the World War II also underlie the speed and depth with which government can and has pursued its reform agenda: "Given the considerable power that is wielded at the center of the British state, the constitutional and legal flexibility within the system offers the ruling political party in Westminster considerable scope for developing and implementing comprehensive and far-reaching policy programs—and, indeed, for terminating programs deemed unpopular or unsuccessful" (Andrews et al. 2013, 10). That is to say, just as Labour celebrated its landslide victory in the 1945 general elections and proceeded to implement a Post-War Consensus agenda that included general welfare state policies and nationalization of transportation, communications, and health care—largely within the five-year span from 1945 to the 1950 general election—so too would later Conservative governments dismantle much of the welfare state over the three Thatcher ministries from 1979 to 1990.

While the presence of a universally understood "Consensus" agenda in the UK from 1945 through the late 1970s is a matter of debate, the fact that UK government underwent extensive and radical growth and expansion over the period is unquestioned. Centralized power and legal flexibility make rapid change possible. A secure majority in parliament and the absence of legal and institutional barriers, such as strong trade unions, allow changes as quickly and frequently as the majority party wishes: "The unusual dominance of a single party form of executive within the British system gives governments an equally-unusual ability to realize their reform desires, even when these are controversial in Parliament or unpopular in the country … [S]ince 1979, governments have regarded continuing and deep administrative change as perfectly feasible" (Pollitt and Bouckaert 2000, 273).

NPM refers to a public-sector reform agenda in which private-sector competitive mechanisms are introduced to service delivery through performance targets, contracting out, and compensation schemes that mimic private sector pay for performance. Brown and Osborne distinguish between NPM and its predecessor, public *administration* (2005, 50, emphases in original):

New Public *Management* sought to transform public services into more efficient and effective managerial, financial, and operational principles and practices. Public *administration* framed the operation of the public service as requiring the orderly application of rules, decisions, and actions based on consistency and rationality and this approach denoted the traditional model of public service…NPM has been adopted because of an ideological commitment to the economic, market competition model. Administration emphasizes the generalist while management emphasizes the specialist.

Management techniques such as strategic planning and fee-based service delivery are emphasized throughout government organizations, and mission-based activities are managed rather than administered. With its emphasis on results over process, the appeal of NPM transformed from rhetoric to reality: "It was only in 2002, after 20 years of rhetoric, that some central elements of the reform program (particularly business planning and performance management systems) were achieving a significant degree of acceptance and usage, and being regarded as valuable" (Bovaird 2007, 348).

Heralded by advocates of small government as efficient cost-cutting, NPM reforms were not without their critics. Performance-related pay was widely disliked as a market-based reform that would "undermine the basic principles of effective working in the civil service" (Bovaird 2007, 333). Performance targets were similarly derided. The focus on performance targets resulted in at least one high-profile scandal: One example of NPM's worst excesses is found in the hundreds of cases of neglect and premature deaths at the Mid-Staffordshire NHS Foundation Trust hospital, where the pursuit of performance targets and budget cuts took precedence over patient well-being for years (Mastracci 2016).

The NPM reform agenda gained popularity and was adopted by many OECD countries in response to a broad range of significant drivers of institutional change (Brown and Osborne 2005, 55):

> Globalization, a disaffected citizenry, blurring of the boundaries between private, public, and community sector organizations…financial cutbacks, restructuring on a global scale, increasing technological advances and changing labor demographics and higher expectations of services on the part of citizens.

Among several English-speaking countries in particular, "the UK is arguably a critical case for the evaluation of public service performance, since it is often said to have been the 'vanguard state' or at least one of the leading countries, of the New Public Management" (Hood and Dixon 2016, 413; see also Hood 1991). Internal characteristics—a highly centralized national government structure and few legal boundaries to curb reformers' zeal—combined with the external drivers listed above and led the UK to pursue an NPM agenda.

After a decade of postwar rebuilding and robust economic growth in the 1950s, stagnation and trade union strikes characterized the British economy in the 1960s. The period was also marked by violence resulting from ethno-nationalist conflict, called the "Troubles," in Northern Ireland. The number of Troubles-related deaths increased throughout the 1960s, 1970s, and

1980s, punctuated by riots in August 1969, Bloody Sunday in 1972, hunger strike deaths in 1981, and the Brighton Hotel bombing in 1984. To revive its sluggish economy in the 1960s, British lawmakers sought membership in the new European Economic Community (EEC). After failures to gain membership in the EEC in 1963 and 1967, Britain became a member in 1973. Throughout the 1970s, the UK experienced fragile economic growth and escalating inflation captured by the Retail Price Index. The "Winter of Discontent" of 1978–1979 witnessed widespread strikes by public-sector labor unions opposed to wage caps implemented by the Labour Party to control inflationary cost increases. Both major political parties—Labour and the Conservatives—proposed one reform after another (Pollitt 2013, 900):

> Over the past half century, the UK public sector may have been cumulatively the most reformed in the world. It has been in more or less continuous modernization since Mr. Heath became Prime Minister in 1970. Over the long term, it could be argued that the UK outpaces even the famous, radical, but only one-decade-long New Zealand reforms of 1984-1993.

Economic growth due to rebuilding after World War II and the rapid expansion of the welfare state were followed quickly by economic stagnation and complaints about inefficient government and high taxes. Labour governments were criticized for widespread dissatisfaction with the performance of the economy, especially compared to the UK's European counterparts. Crises such as the widespread strikes by public sector trade unions demanding larger pay raises in 1978–1979, called the "Winter of Discontent," and independence movements in both Scotland and Wales, fueled dissatisfaction. Labour's majority soon gave way to the Conservative Party, which won its first of four consecutive parliamentary majorities in the 1979 general election.

1979–1997

Public-sector unions drew the most attention during the Winter of Discontent, as strikes by rail employees, NHS nurses and allied workers, truck drivers, ambulance drivers, trash collectors, and gravediggers severely disrupted economic activity in January and February 1979. Parliament was dissolved shortly thereafter, and a general election was held in May of that year. The Conservative campaign promised to curb inflation and limit the power of labor unions with the very effective campaign slogan against the party in power: *Labour Isn't Working*. After the steady growth of the public sector throughout the decades after World War II, high taxes and high inflation were the targets of both parties. The Conservatives under new Prime Minister Margaret Thatcher won a convincing majority in 1979, followed by victories in the general elections of 1983, 1987, and 1992.

Conservatives privatized several industries that had been nationalized by the Attlee ministry in the late 1940s. The mid-1980s witnessed the selloff of British Telecom, British Gas, the Airports Authority, and water and sewerage systems throughout the country: "about 800,000 employees were transferred from the public sector to the private" (Pollitt and Bouckaert 2000, 273). As mentioned earlier, the unique common-law system of the UK, as well as the absence of autonomous sub-national governments, allows for swift and comprehensive public-sector reform. Because of this expediency, during the Thatcher ministry, reforms to introduce market mechanisms into the public sector accompanied privatization and budget cuts. "The UK stands out for its vigorously-pursued market orientation and the emphasis on the explicitly 'managerial' side of the new public management" (Schroter 2007, 299). Alongside privatization, a focus on efficient service delivery also shrunk public sector headcount: "From 1979 until 1982-83, there was a fierce drive for economies and the elimination of waste. Civil service numbers were cut, first by 14 percent and then, subsequently, by a further six percent" (Pollitt and Bouckaert 2000, 273).

Public-sector reforms continued through the mid- and late 1980s as the Thatcher administration continued to win convincing majorities in general elections. Market mechanisms for the allocation of public resources were implemented on a larger scale, performance measurement systems were expanded, as were contracting-out schemes. An overarching emphasis on "customer service" characterized these reforms, and contracting out and market solutions were touted as the self-evident keys to improving customer service and value for taxpayer money.

The *Citizen's Charter* (Select Committee 1991) was an early, if not the first, formal statement recasting the UK citizen as a customer of public services, and it represents a departure from the traditional deference accorded to career civil servants. The *Charter* reflects a managerial agenda and "reinforced the view that citizens were consumers who needed market-like choice mechanisms, a perspective that had been implanted by some of Mrs. Thatcher's later reforms" (Pollitt 2013, 908). The *Charter* was founded on "six principles of public service which every citizen is entitled to *expect*" (Select Committee 1991, vi):

1. Explicit standards for each service
2. Information and openness
3. Choice and consultation
4. Courtesy and helpfulness
5. Easy-to-use complaints procedures and mechanisms for redress, and
6. Value for money.

The six principles above reveal a new culture, one that involves expectations and a relationship between a buyer and a seller. Among them, "4. Courtesy and helpfulness" is not only subjective and therefore based on the interpretation of the citizen/customer, but is also a clear display rule guiding the behavior of public servants in a modernized and responsive government service environment.

Public management reforms of the early 1990s have proven enduring: "Labels have frequently been changed, but some of the basic ideas of the *Charter* white paper have survived well into the 21st Century" (Pollitt 2013, 908). The citizen-as-customer ethos remains strong in the UK, just as it has remained a guiding principle across NPM-implementing countries. It is a durable concept that remains present in the twenty-first Century Public Servant narrative addressed later. However, other Thatcher-era reforms criticized by opponents were only partially accomplished.

Indeed, for all of the talk about reining in the state and cutting costs, the British welfare state was not dismantled, nor were strict market-based allocation mechanisms imposed throughout the public sector: "Conservatives failed to realize their ambition of 'rolling back' taxation, public expenditure, and public borrowing, although they may have succeeded in halting the long-term trend since WWII for all of these to rise substantially" (Talbot 2001, 286). The upward trajectory of government operating costs and taxes throughout the 1960s and 1970s was very likely curtailed by the measures implemented in the 1980s and 1990s, but any claims about the end of the British welfare state could only be overstatements by Conservatives and fear mongering by the opposition.

Privatization, aggressive contracting, and separating the buyer and provider roles in the public sector effectively hollowed-out certain public service delivery areas. However, relative to other Anglophone countries, the UK civil service maintains an extensive presence in communications and health care as a direct provider of services even today. In other areas such as transportation and economic development, the regulatory apparatus remains robust in the UK, compared to other NPM countries in the Anglosphere.

Even in the hollowed-out service delivery areas, the presence of the public sector remains substantial, even though central government personnel head-counts were slashed. The difference is in the nominal employer of the public servant: "A substantial increase in reported central government running costs in constant-price terms over three decades [is found], even—perhaps especially—in the Margaret Thatcher era, which is often depicted as one of ruthless slashing and burning as far as bureaucracy is concerned" (Hood and Dixon 2016, 420).

Local government operating costs demonstrate a similar increasing trajectory over the 1980s, through the 1990s, and into the present. Although the number of civil servants fell over the three-plus decades from the Thatcher government to the present, operating costs at both the national and the local levels have increased due to increased "consultancy costs and outsourcing contracts for IT and other services" (Hood and Dixon 2016, 424; see also 2015). Contracting out or "commissioning," when conducted properly, "should be cyclical, inclusive, and lead to an improvement in services" as well as lower costs through competition among potential providers (Rees et al. 2017, 179).

Commissioning was assumed to be a self-evident good and cost-effective public management strategy, despite its higher costs to taxpayers and inconsistent evidence of effectiveness (Elkomy et al. 2019). In their examination of commissioning mental health services, Rees, Miller, and Buckingham conclude that this approach to public service delivery still bears characteristics of the earlier large-scale welfare state (2017, 191):

> Neither represents the fulfillment of aspirations for fully marketized services, nor for the holistic or entirely deliberative process advocated by others … [W]e advocate caution therefore in portraying commissioning as either the revolutionary approach heralded by advocates or most feared by critics.

Thatcher-era reforms did, however, curb public-sector growth: "Critics from across the political spectrum concur that it was misguided for the state in the postwar period to have expanded into areas previously occupied by third-sector organizations" (Kelly 2007, 1009). Expansion of the British welfare state may have expanded into too many service delivery areas. Government may have grown too much. While the end of the twentieth century witnessed the end of Conservative majorities, the UK did not return to a big government period of the past. New Labour heralded the rise of the Third Sector in the provision of public services.

1997–2000

A landslide victory for the Labour Party in May 1997 ushered in the first of three ministries under Prime Minister Tony Blair. Although the Conservative Party was swept out of office, its reform narrative remained: "The new Labour government of 1997 reversed very little of what had gone before" (Pollitt and Bouckaert 2000, 274). Kelly concurs in her discussion of the new government's motives: "Driven by its commitment to the market and the conviction of the inevitability of globalization, New Labour's administration has continued down the pathway of withdrawing government from the direct provision of services to the public" (2007, 1008). The tide had turned such that public service cost cutting and efficiencies remained persuasive political arguments, regardless of the party in charge. Central government as the primary provider of services would not return to the big government era of the 1950s (Andrews et al. 2013, 9):

> The 'hard' private sector management tools of contracting out and performance monitoring were still maintained, but were made subordinate to top-down hierarchical models of continuous improvement with often-elaborate, target-based, incentive systems. At the same time, these more conventional modes of governing and managing were supplemented with a greater emphasis on the need to strengthen the relationships between the different stakeholders involved in public-service design and delivery.

The decline of public administration throughout the late twentieth century "is brought into sharper relief by the concomitant rise of management" (Gabriel 1999, 402). UK public service delivery evolved from a somewhat passive administration of taxpayer-funded resources to a more active public management, and finally to the "third way," characterized as cooperative governance among multiple actors. The various stakeholders involved in design and delivery now included the state, the market, and civil society—that is, nonprofit and non-governmental organizations.

A third way of delivering public services depicted a network of relationships among private, public, and charitable sector organizations and introduced the notion of shared governance among them. Citizens have a role in decision-making in this new, mutually empowering system as consumers, where "buying becomes tantamount to voting, and market surveys the nearest we have to collective will" (Gabriel 1999, 405). Coined "New Labour," the Blair Ministry was clearly shaped by the long Conservative period of the 1980s and 1999s but demonstrated marked differences from pre-Thatcher

Labour governments. For example, "trade unions were kept much more in a position of being one amongst a wide variety of 'stakeholders' rather than favored partners as in earlier periods of Labour rule" (Talbot 2001, 298).

Moreover, New Labour retained prior governments' pro-managerialist reform initiatives such as the New Public Management performance targets and budget austerity. Thus, "laying off civil servants to hit headcount-reduction targets and re-hiring them as consultants … was said to have been widespread under the Thatcher government and indeed well into the 2000s" (Hood and Dixon 2016, 426). Victories were declared by slashing public-sector headcount. No victories could be claimed with respect to slashing public-sector budgets, however, because personnel costs to pay workers as consultants were just as high and often higher than when they were on government rolls. New Labour sought to distinguish its reform initiatives from previous ones by highlighting the role of the third sector, which included nonprofit organizations, community organizations, and voluntary organizations across a range of policy areas.

The inspiration for New Labour's embrace of the voluntary sector was the limited role that the third sector had played under previous Conservative administrations, coupled with a romanticized vision of the potential for voluntary organizations to deliver quality public services cheaper and more effectively than the public sector could. Reacting to the implementation of economic development initiatives under the Thatcher and Major governments, New Labour emphasized the untapped potential of third- or voluntary-sector organizations to deliver not only services but also shape policy in true community governance relationships with central government and local authorities (Osborne and McLaughlin 2002).

Voluntary associations were assumed to be better situated to address social needs because they were experts in their fields, not generalists like civil servants. Likewise, it was assumed that because they developed expertise and were meant to care about their subject matter and the clients they served, workers in charitable organizations would provide service superior to that of the objective, disinterested, and administrator. It was further assumed that workers in charitable organizations would not seek self-interest or seek to consolidate or expand their powers and that they would not be corruptible. These aspirations were meant to inspire government: "New Labour's mission for the third sector is a segment of its wider ambitions for the modernization of the UK's public sector" (Kelly 2007, 1004). Third-sector organizations were presumed to hold specialized information on the nature of the policy area and its recipients, a level of knowledge and responsiveness that was unrivaled by the public sector. Third-sector organizations also enjoyed a high degree of public trust and the belief in their inherent ability to deliver better value for money and to do so more ethically than the public sector could.

However, public trust had been earned by these voluntary organizations through their efforts as advocates for their constituents. Closer co-governance with the public sector posed "real dangers for the voluntary sector, which could lead to the negation of its legitimate societal roles as independent watchdog and voice for the marginal and dispossessed … voluntary organizations run the risk of not being able to act independently of the state" (Osborne and McLaughlin 2002, 61). Although the New Labour government was sympathetic with the risks faced by voluntary organizations, "it continue[d] to be highly centralist and use top-down mechanisms such as regulation, inspection, and steering through advice and guidance" to ensure that public funds were being accounted for properly and that providers were responsive to the citizenry (Kelly 2007, 1015).

New Labour's Voluntary Sector Compact was launched in November 1998 (Osborne and McLaughlin 2002) at the national level, but the process of developing compacts at the local level was slow because local governments struggled to contain the boundaries of the scope of these compacts. For example, it remained unclear whether local government compacts with voluntary sector organizations should also include health, public health, environmental services, and police authorities. Voluntary sector compacts were employed in economic development initiatives, but questions arose regarding whether the scope of services should be more ambitious.

Complicating the picture, "New Labour's zeal for frequent initiatives" led to policy overload for both national and local governments, and their partner voluntary sector organizations (Kelly 2007, 1016). Moreover, New Labour did not hand over control to the voluntary sector for public service delivery and the "supposed control freakery of the Labour government's efforts to steer this increasingly-complex system was a target for opposition parties prior to the formation of the Conservative-led coalition government in 2010" (Andrews et al. 2013, 9). Costs were not contained under this approach, but the newfound power of the voluntary sector truly distinguished this period of public sector reform from earlier rounds of managerialist changes.

The continued development and implementation of reform initiatives was New Labour's expression of legitimacy during this time: "Throughout the Labour administration the reform of public services was displayed as a *totemic signifier of the intent and seriousness of the party*" (O'Reilly and Reed 2012, 21, emphasis supplied). It was left to other constituencies to evaluate the effectiveness of these initiatives, and we turn to the limited body of evaluation literature shortly. In brief, problems with scoping these compacts, lines of authority, the limited discretion possessed by voluntary organizations, and fiscal austerity, dampened the potential for joined-up working between the public and third sectors. Public resistance to tax increases limited the ability of the Blair and Brown ministries to provide financial resources to national and local governments to implement the Voluntary Sector Compact or other initiatives undertaken during this period.

A significant weakness of New Labour's emphasis on the third sector was its unquestioned assumption of altruism as the primary, if not sole, motivator of voluntary-sector organizations: "The nature of the third sector's altruistic values are fragile foundations on which to build a new model of social welfare" (Kelly 2007, 1019). Indeed, integration of third-sector organizations into public service delivery through contracting "has not led to the straightforward public sector 'marketization' that advocates desire or that critics fear" (Rees et al. 2017, 175). The pursuit of government reform initiatives to legitimize government carried over from New Labour and was "also discernible in the early days of its successor Conservative-led coalition government" (O'Reilly and Reed 2012, 21). The financial market collapse in the USA and the subsequent worldwide Great Recession took precedence on the UK agenda shortly after Gordon Brown stepped in as Prime Minister after the Blair resignation in 2007. Public service reforms in the early twenty-first century were initiated under a dark cloud of fiscal austerity and glacially-slow economic recovery.

The Twenty-First Century Public Servant

Administration of public monies in the 1950s, 1960s, and 1970s morphed into management of resources in the 1980s and 1990s, and then into shared decision-making and governance in the twenty-first century (Needham and Mangan 2016). A coalition government formed after the 2010 general election, led by the Conservative Party under Prime Minister David Cameron. Governance and co-production across sectors—public, private, and non-profit—characterizes the UK's version of twenty-first-century public service and is a product of all that preceded it. This version is described as "The hybrid form of neoliberal ideology and consumerist discourse that has driven public sector restructuring in the UK" (O'Reilly and Reed 2012, 35). This hybrid form of decision-making and public service delivery is characterized by an environment of low-trust relationships and public sector organizations that are designed according to principal/agent, transactional, and interactions.

Reforms emphasizing management over administration have manifested in the UK as government commissions out public service delivery and create performance targets to properly incentivize third-sector and private-sector organizations to fulfill the public good. From the late 1970s and continuing today, government agencies have been reformed and reorganized from hierarchical bureaucratic organizations with extensive rules, separate from the market, to quasi-market actors (Dunleavy and Hood 1994). This begs the question: Have these reforms improved the quality of public service delivery or at least cut costs?

Findings now show that public sector reforms in the UK—serial reforms—not only failed to cut costs but also diminished the quality of public sector services: "The UK over the three decades analyzed here somehow ended up in a lose/lose situation in which government cost substantially more to run in terms of reported running costs, while there were increasing creaks and groans on the side of perceived fairness and consistency, judged by the incidence of formal complaints and litigation" (Hood and Dixon 2016, 424). Emphasis on cutting headcounts led government agencies to contract out public service delivery and recategorize public servants and private- or third-sector employees. While this cut employment on government rolls, costs were at least as high and often higher than service delivery under the old model. Centralized authority in the UK, extensive growth in commissioning, and very limited devolution to regional governments, local authorities, or municipal governments, led to higher costs overall and little difference in service quality.

With expert knowledge and pre-existing relationships with client populations, third-sector organizations are key players in policy development and decision-making, rather than service-delivery agents responding to incentives. Public service delivery by private- and third-sector organizations in the UK is referred to as the *plural state*: "The evolution of this plural state has also seen a shift, first from the administration of government services to their management, and then from their management to their governance" (Brown and Osborne 2005, 5). One key difference between management "over" in a principal/agent relationship and governance "among" peer entities is found in decision-making and policy development. While as managers, public-sector organizations set targets and terms for non-governmental entities to deliver services, under a governance model, "voluntary and community organizations are now recognized as critical actors in the *development of* social policy within the plural state" (Osborne and McLaughlin 2002, 55, emphasis supplied).

It is believed that the central role of non-governmental actors will make public service delivery more responsive and improve quality. This theory has been severely tested by evidence in a post-recession environment: "The old narrative of public-spirited but under-rewarded public servants was replaced by one of over-privileged public employees, especially after the crisis in public finances in 2008-2009" due to the worldwide Great Recession (Parry 2011, 364). NPM reforms pre-dated the worldwide financial crisis, but scrutiny of the public sector combined with austerity demands following the recession result in a political and social context in which the old UK welfare state of the 1950s will likely never re-emerge.

Even post-NPM reforms do not revive the prior welfare state model. Public leadership finds itself under increasing scrutiny not only as a result of the financial straits caused by the international financial crisis, but also as a result of narratives promulgated by New Public Management and now network governance reforms. These express distrust of civil servants and are coupled with increased pressure for accountability toward clients, employees, and local authorities (Teelken et al. 2012). As the failed promises of NPM were reckoned with, new theoretical propositions emerged: "The alternative to NPM networking is thus not a monolithic and bureaucratic state but a cooperative venture of practice institutions oriented toward the common good" (Overeem and Tholen 2011, 741). Whether the third sector can rescue public service delivery from high costs and low quality arising from NPM, reforms remain to be seen. The romanticized assumptions of the promise and possibility of third-sector delivery in the UK seem ripe only for a letdown.

The reform narrative—particularly the neoliberal, market-based NPM reforms of the Thatcher ministries and into the Blair government—scored political points but failed to improve the production and delivery of public services or cut costs. More often than not, the history of public-sector reforms in the UK is a story of solutions in search of problems: "Most reform exercises in the public services did not begin by looking at what was producing repeated complaints or litigation and taking that as the cue for what needed attention. Rather, those makeovers tended to start from ready-made solutions (such as outsourcing, IT, business methods, or managerial empowerment) looking for problems" (Hood and Dixon 2016, 425).

Reform for the sake of reform had its political uses as well. Compared to other Anglophone countries—even ambitious NPM countries—the UK "was a 'serial reformer' to a particularly marked degree" (Hood and Dixon 2016, 410). Enough policy analyses have now been conducted to conclude that championing reform may no longer yield the political benefits that it used to, even though few political and structural barriers prevent reforms from happening: "It is possible that, in the UK at least, the specifically political payoffs from tales of managerial reform may be dwindling. There have been so many of them that skepticism among both the public and public servants is widespread…[the] stories have become unconvincing" (Pollitt 2013, 919). In other words, the faith in the promise of reform may have reached a saturation point.

Satire must bear at least a passing resemblance to its subject matter, lest it fails in its objective. The tug-of-war between Parliament and government was depicted in the popular BBC television sitcom *Yes, Minister*, where elected officials try to impose changes while the civil service undermines them. That tension continues to this day. Perhaps the most durable inheritance from the market-based reforms that began in the 1980s has been the perceptual switch from citizen to customer. Reforms alone were not responsible for this switch, as larger forces created a supportive environment, including the "increased ease of registering complaints with the advent of the Internet [and] even some long-term social trend toward greater litigiousness or propensity to make formal complaints" (Hood and Dixon 2016, 416). Customers demand responsiveness and quality service, and from the development and growth of the UK welfare state to today, demands on the system remain high.

The UK rapidly developed its welfare state infrastructure as it rebuilt in the 1940s and 1950s. From that time through the present, the British public sector has "gone from being overloaded in the 1960s/1970s to being 'hollowed out' in the 1980s/early 1990s, to 'congested' in the late 1990s/2000s and is now undergoing a period of serious retrenchment" (Andrews et al. 2013, 9). Scholars are divided whether public-sector reform has changed much about government in the UK besides headcount. Although the UK has earned "a reputation as one of the main pathfinders in both the rhetoric and practice of public sector reform" (Bovaird and Russell 2007, 325), "the paradox of public services and management in the UK over the past 20 years or so is that *everything has changed and nothing has changed*" (Talbot 2001, 299, emphasis supplied).

Measuring National Culture

Starting from the premise that national cultures have a notable impact on the dominant styles of management within a society, both private and public organizations are "culture bound" (Schroter 2007, 314). Culture plays a role in organizational practices and in the citizen–state encounter. It is gauged through the study of a people's—usually a nation's—shared values, norms, behaviors, rules, and symbols. What is important? Who is "we" and what do we do? What is rewarded and what is punished? What is communicated and transmitted among "us"? What is ignored?

Data from two large-scale, long-term projects still inform our understanding of national culture to this day: Hofstede's IBM studies and the World Values Survey of Project GLOBE. Hofstede's original four dimensions provided the general framework for Project GLOBE: Power distance (PDI), Individualism vs. collectivism (IDV), Uncertainty avoidance (UA), and Masculinity vs. femininity (MAS). PDI captures a nation's tolerance for inequality: "The extent to which the less powerful members of organizations and institutions accept and expect that power is distributed unequally" (Hofstede 1980, 331). IDV gauges the extent to which people in a nation are integrated into groups; the extent to which the "I" is emphasized over the "we." UA is the degree to which people tolerate ambiguity in a society. A nation that scores high on UA likely enforces strict behavioral norms and endorses strict laws and absolute truth to govern relationships. MAS captures a people's preference for "achievement, heroism, assertiveness and material rewards for success [or] cooperation, modesty, and caring for the weak and quality of life" (Shermon 2016, 135). Two dimensions were added after the initial IBM studies in 1980: Future Orientation and Indulgence.

The UK ranks high on Individualism, low on Future Orientation, and near the middle on other dimensions of culture. Updates on the initial project from Hofstede et al. (2010) also rank the UK very high on Individualism, higher than average on Masculinity, and lower than average on Power Distance. As a country scoring high on Individualism, the UK is a culture where "there are loose ties between individuals, less social cohesion, and a higher responsibility to take care of yourself" (Bouckaert 2007, 47).

While an Individualist culture, the UK is imbued with a strong Collectivist streak via its welfare state and the demands of its citizens for public services. Brits "prove to be much more enthusiastic in their support for established mass welfare services … the NHS [is] part of the 'collectivist' element in British political culture" (Schroter 2007, 307). After decades of reforms that introduce market mechanisms to the allocation of public services, British public service is scaling back in all areas *except* health care: "Despite attempts to 'sell' partial privatization, [the NHS] remains something of a 'sacred cow' to the British electorate" (Andrews et al. 2013, 9).

Lower-than-average PDI seems counterintuitive in light of the British class system and the degree of control of central over local government due to centralized tax distribution. The UK's low PDI contradicts what we know about High-PDI countries: "High power distance countries accept greater inequalities, expressed as salary gaps, privileges, and status symbols.

There is also more centralization of power. This is a very hierarchical society" (Bouckaert 2007, 47). This seems a salient description of at least some dimensions of the UK, and other comparative scholars also observe this contradiction: "The British preference for strong political leadership has often been insufficiently appreciated … intimately linked is the alleged 'deferential' component of political life in Britain, which has eventually become the object of heated debates in political culture studies" (Schroter 2007, 302).

While no definitive resolution of the apparent contradiction is found in comparative-culture literature, we may gain insights from examining which countries score high on PDI: Countries in Latin America, Africa, Asia, and the Arab world score consistently high PDIs. Anglo and Germanic countries score low on PDI. Ultimately unsettled in the literature, PDI may be influenced by IDV, as high-PDI countries also tend to be Collectivist and low-PDI countries tend to be Individualist. Further research would sort out these dimensions.

The UK scores low on Uncertainty Avoidance, which "results in high risk taking, focusing on results even if that includes taking calculated risks. There is no uneasiness with exceptional situations, and ambiguity is considered to create degrees of freedom, which are taken. A culture of risk is part of this" (Bouckaert 2007, 48). It is notable that NPM was adopted widely throughout Anglo countries, where a "cluster of low power distance and low uncertainty avoidance resulted in a mixed cluster of Anglo-Saxon countries, including the so-called NPM countries": Australia, Canada, New Zealand, the UK, and the USA (Bouckaert 2007, 50). While high IDV is both necessary and sufficient for the adoption of NPM reforms, with their emphasis on principal/agent relations, the UK also scores high on MAS, and higher than average on long-term orientation, and indulgence.

The World Values Survey (WVS) ranks the UK high on Secular/Rational Values and Self-Expression, which are analogous to Hofstede's IDV (Inglehart et al. 2014). Like the Hofstede dimensions of culture, WVS ranks the UK high on masculinity and uncertainty avoidance, and near the middle on future orientation. Unlike Hofstede et al. (2010), Project GLOBE and WVS score the UK high on Power Distance. This is a more intuitively supported finding given the British class system and the degree of central control in government. In WVS Wave 5, fully sixty percent of respondents in the UK ($n = 1041$) considered politics "Not Very Important" or "Not At All Important" to daily life (Inglehart et al. 2014). Nearly ninety percent of respondents indicated that they were not members of any political party and nearly eighty percent were not members of labor unions. Respondents tend to believe in the value of hard work for a better standard of living.

Roughly the same number of respondents felt government should take responsibility for providing for its citizens as those who felt individuals should provide for themselves, with the distribution between these two poles skewing slightly toward the individual (Inglehart et al. 2014). When asked about their level of confidence in government, however, about two-thirds responded, "Not Very Much" or "None At All" compared to one-third who answered "A Great Deal" or "Quite A Lot." Interestingly, this 65/35 split is not observed in respondent sentiment about British civil service. Respondents were more evenly split, albeit with a slight negative skew in their confidence in the civil service: 41.6% answered, "A Great Deal" or "Quite A Lot," while 49.3% answered, "Not Very Much" or "None At All."

Emotional Labor and Public Service Delivery

NPM reforms that introduced competitive-market dynamics to public-sector service delivery and emphasized the citizen as customer and a customer-service ethos may have only exacerbated emotional labor demands in public services (Thomas 2013). Mimicking private-sector service delivery, public-sector workers under NPM may experience emotional labor similarly to their counterparts in private-sector customer service. Where public service workers are assessed on customer satisfaction, and customer satisfaction derives from how a citizen perceives her or his interpersonal interaction with public servants, NPM increases the emotional labor demands upon public servants. But the concept of "the customer" is problematic in public services because it raises issues of inequality, oversimplification, and a lack of commitment to the public interest. The increasing demands of responsiveness and "customer satisfaction" may contribute to increasing levels of emotional labor (Rayner and Lawton 2017, 2). Public servants interact with the citizenry in higher-stakes contexts compared to typical consumer interactions with workers in retail settings. Higher-stakes interactions such as well-child visits in foster placements, or considering eligibility for council housing and other benefits, demand emotional labor.

The Study

Data from UK public servants, most of whom work for municipal and county government, are used to determine whether the latent variables of emotive capacity, pretending expression, and deep acting exist, and if so, how they relate to job satisfaction, burnout, and personal fulfillment.

Methodology

In March, April, and May 2015, we surveyed current and former local government employees ($n = 201$) while the first author was a Fulbright scholar hosted by the Institute of Local Government Studies (INLOGOV) at the University of Birmingham. Students in MPA classes with current or prior paid experience in government or nonprofit organizations comprised about a quarter of the sample ($n = 49$). Another one-quarter of the sample came from city government (Manchester $n = 21$; Birmingham $n = 34$), while about half came from county-level governments (Warwickshire $n = 68$; Yorkshire $n = 29$).

Demographic statistics for the respondents are displayed in Table 19.1. Sixty-one percent of respondents are under age 50, 64% are female, 88%

Table 19.1 Demographic characteristics: UK ($n = 201$)

	Frequency	Percent
Age		
Less than 30	15	7.46
30–39 years	46	22.89
40–49 years	62	30.85
50–59 years	65	32.34
60 or more	5	2.49
Not Answered	8	3.98
Gender		
Female	129	64.18
Male	67	33.33
Not Answered	5	2.49
Public service experience		
Less than 10	24	11.94
10–19 years	51	25.37
20–29 years	61	30.35
30 or more	60	29.85
Not Answered	5	2.49
Educational level		
Less than high school	0	0.00
High school graduate	8	3.98
Some college	17	8.46
2-year associate degree	12	5.97
College graduate	50	24.88
Some graduate school	39	19.40
Master's degree	64	31.84
Law degree (J.D., LL.B.)	1	0.50
Doctorate degree (Ph.D., M.D., Ed.D., etc.)	3	1.49
Not answered	7	3.48

have ten or more years of work experience, and concerning educational attainment, 78% have at least a college degree.

Table 19.2 displays the range of occupations claimed by respondents and reflects the local-government representation of this sample. Respondents were able to select multiple occupations. For example, someone may work in education in an administrative capacity or may work in neighborhood services and provide social services or transportation. The leading occupations are human resource management, community development and neighborhood services, general administration, social services, and information and communication.

Table 19.2   Occupational characteristics: UK

Occupation	Frequency	Percent
1. Administration	25	12.44
2. Community development/neighborhood services	28	13.93
3. Engineering, manufacturing, or production	2	1.00
4. Education	7	3.48
5. Disaster response	0	0.00
6. Finance or accounting	2	1.00
7. Firefighter	0	0.00
8. Health care	11	5.47
9. Housing	3	1.49
10. Human resource management	35	17.41
11. Information and communication	15	7.46
12. Law enforcement	3	1.49
13. Military	0	0
14. Public relations	1	0.50
15. Planning	3	1.49
16. Public works: streets, sanitation, utilities	2	1.00
17. Purchasing	0	0
18. Recreation and parks	1	0.50
19. Research and development	7	3.48
20. Social services	15	7.46
21. Transportation	3	1.49
22. Support services (e.g., plant/equip. maintenance)	0	0
23. Other	5	2.49
Not answered	33	16.42
Multiple selections (up to six selections from above)		
Two occupations	31	15.42
Three occupations	16	7.96
Four occupations	8	3.98
Five occupations	4	1.99
Six occupations	2	1.00

Emotional Labor Variables

The survey items used to capture emotional labor are reported below. Each was scored on a seven-point scale from Strongly Disagree (1) to Strongly Agree (7). The items in each variable are listed below.

Emotive Capacity

> I am good at expressing how I feel.
> I am good at getting people to calm down.
> In my job I am good at dealing with emotional issues.

Pretending Expression

> I hide my true feelings so as to appear pleasant at work.
> In my job I act confident and self-assured regardless of how I actually feel.
> I wear a "mask" in order to deal with clients/customers in an appropriate way.

Deep Acting

> I try to actually experience the emotions that I must show to clients/customers.
> I work hard to actually feel the emotions that I need to show to clients/customers.
> I work at developing the feelings inside of me that I need to show to clients/customers.

Job Satisfaction

> My job provides career development and promotion opportunities.
> I feel I am being paid a fair amount for the work I do.
> I feel satisfied with my supervisor.
> Overall, I am satisfied with my job.

Burnout

> I leave work feeling tired and run down.
> I leave work feeling emotionally exhausted.
> I feel "used up" at the end of the workday.

Personal Fulfillment

> I gain a strong sense of personal fulfillment at my job.
> I feel like my job is something I want to do rather than something I have to do.
> My work is a source of personal meaning in my life.

Table 19.3   Descriptive statistics and Cronbach's alpha: UK

	Mean	SD	Cronbach's alpha
Emotive capacity	5.200	1.034	0.6877
Pretending expression	5.025	1.208	0.6549
Deep acting	4.147	1.298	0.8068
Job satisfaction	4.776	1.192	0.6902
Burnout	4.255	1.479	0.8965
Personal fulfillment	5.174	1.321	0.8610

Table 19.3 provides means and standard deviations for these variables, as well as Cronbach's alpha, a measure of internal consistency. Three coefficients are above 0.80 (Deep Acting, Burnout, and Personal Fulfillment), which indicates very good interitem reliability well above the conventional threshold of 0.70. The other three variables achieve coefficients of 0.65 or above. Given the vulnerability of three- and four-item constructs to consistency statistics, as well as their prevalence in the literature, the results for Emotive Capacity, Pretending Expression, and Job Satisfaction are close enough to the ideal to be used in the analysis.

Findings

Table 19.4 displays results from maximum likelihood estimation of the effect of Emotive Capacity, Pretending, and Deep Acting on the workplace outcomes of Job Satisfaction, Burnout, and Personal Fulfillment. The theoretically specified model is an adequate representation of the data collected in a survey of public servants in the UK.

Of the nine relationships described in Table 19.4—relationships with each of three outcomes by three different independent variables—five of these paths are statistically different from zero. Emotive Capacity increases Job Satisfaction and Personal Fulfillment. Pretending Expression decreases Job Satisfaction and Personal Fulfillment, while it increases Burnout. None of the relationships between Deep Acting and the three outcomes are statistically different from zero.

There is no single best measure or approach to assessing SEM model fit. In a comparative study, model specification is driven by theory. Using UK data, this model performs adequately, although it is at the margins of acceptability. Model goodness-of-fit is shown at the bottom of Table 19.4. Root mean squared error of approximation (RMSEA) is just below the 0.08 threshold and therefore indicates a good fit, and is the most accepted fit statistic. Alternative fit statistics present a more marginal picture.

Table 19.4 Structural model results: UK

Hypothesized paths	Coefficients	p-value
Emotive capacity $\rightarrow$ Job satisfaction	0.385*	0.000
Emotive capacity $\rightarrow$ Burnout	0.011	0.897
Emotive capacity $\rightarrow$ Personal fulfillment	0.326*	0.000
Pretending expression $\rightarrow$ Job satisfaction	−0.488*	0.000
Pretending expression $\rightarrow$ Burnout	0.448*	0.000
Pretending expression $\rightarrow$ Personal fulfillment	−0.277*	0.005
Deep acting $\rightarrow$ Job satisfaction	−0.047	0.557
Deep acting $\rightarrow$ Burnout	0.046	0.572
Deep acting $\rightarrow$ Personal fulfillment	0.047	0.554

Model fit: χ^2 = 314.530 (df = 142), CFI = 0.878, RMSEA = 0.079, SRMR = 0.088

The Comparative Fit Index (CFI) is slightly lower than the 0.90 critical value for good model fit, and the Standardized Root Mean Squared Residual (SRMR) is slightly higher than its 0.08 critical value. The p-value accompanying the model chi-squared is lower than its goodness-of-fit threshold, but is sensitive to sample size and model complexity to the degree that most models will not attain the minimum. Overall, the specified theoretical model is assessed as an adequate fit for the observed data.

The path coefficients are standardized and therefore directly comparable to one another. Emotive Capacity is positively and significantly related to Job Satisfaction and Personal Fulfillment, but not Burnout. Pretending Expression reduces Job Satisfaction and Personal Fulfillment while simultaneously increasing Burnout among respondents. Path comparison shows that Pretending Expression has nearly twice the negative effect on Job Satisfaction ($b = -0.490$) as it does on Personal Fulfillment ($b = -0.280$), while the statistically significant effects from Emotive Capacity are nearly equal for both Job Satisfaction ($b = 0.384$) and Personal Fulfillment ($b = 0.326$). Deep Acting is not a significant predictor of any modeled outcome, an interesting result that sets the UK apart from countries which are otherwise culturally similar such as the USA and Australia.

Figure 19.1 is a simplified diagram of the expected and demonstrated fit, with solid lines indicating a statistically significant relationship and dashed lines denoting paths that did not reach significance. The direction of statistically significant relationships is shown with either a positive or a negative sign.

Structural equation modeling allows for a simultaneous solution for all three dependent variables as explained by all three emotional labor covariates. As a whole, this model reinforces the "robust sequence" (Allen et al. 2014, 21) of effects from emotive pretending (also referred to as surface acting in the theoretical literature). Having to "fake it" by suppressing how one actually feels while displaying a different emotion, is positively related to

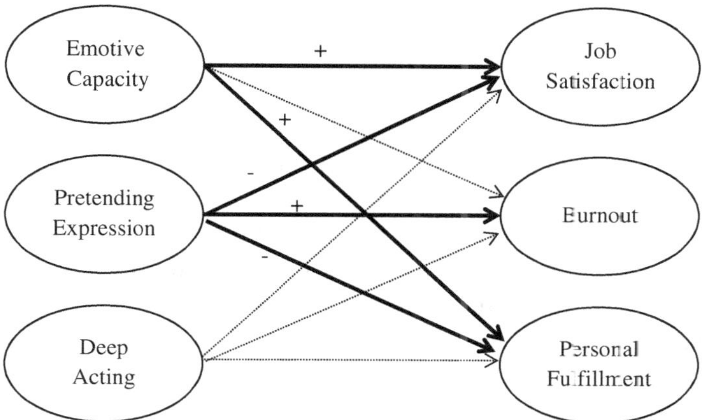

Fig. 19.1 Path diagram for the UK

increased burnout and negatively related to job satisfaction and feelings of personal fulfillment. Although Deep Acting possesses greater internal validity than the other two independent variables do (see Table 19.3), none of its relationships with the workplace outcomes Job Satisfaction, Burnout, or Personal Fulfillment are statistically different from zero.

Among Anglosphere NPM countries, results from the UK vary from those in Australia and the USA. Unlike its cultural cousins, for UK public servants, there is no significant relationship between authentic emotive expression and job outcomes. Instead, the relationships to job satisfaction, personal fulfillment, and burnout are better understood with respect to emotive capacity and emotive pretending and not authentic displays of emotion.

Conclusion

Decades of public-sector reforms and "the encroachment of market relations on political life" (Gabriel 1999, 404) have left their mark on the UK public service. The Individualist culture of the UK with a commitment to reform and a faith in market discipline to bring about efficiency has resulted in a public sector in flux. Centralized governmental power and a secure majority in Parliament allow continual and substantial change in the public sector (Pollitt 1990, 55):

> In Britain, the achievement of a superficially consistent set of decisions concerning civil service management requires little more than a strong executive with a consistent set of prejudices.

From the economic and political turmoil of the 1970s emerged a strong counterpoint to the bureaucratic and centrally-concentrated national government of the UK welfare state. This counterpoint, which Christopher Pollitt describes as the New Right, found fertile ground for reforms rooted in managerialist ideology. This fertile ground is essential to understanding postwar UK public service: "For international public management research, the fact that new organizational practices are adopted to enhance social legitimacy, and not to advance any means-ends efficacy urges scholars to understand the socio-cultural context of any public management reform" (Schedler and Proeller 2007, 15). Although NPM reforms emphasized headcounts and performance targets, promised efficiencies were never realized (Overeem and Tholen 2011). Postwar reforms were meant to implement managerialist ideology. A relatively high UK Individualism fosters a cultural environment in which the citizen easily became a consumer and spending money was accepted as an appropriate form of public action.

That fact that NPM reforms took hold most securely in Individualist cultures such as the UK does not surprise some comparativist researchers (Cheung 2012, 211, emphases supplied):

> Whereas public sector reforms in the West were originally driven by a distrust of the state and its bureaucracy, seeing government *as the problem* (inefficiency, crowding out the market, etc.) and seeking to install market supremacy, government in East Asia is arguably still held *as the solution to problems*, where people expect a competent and selfless bureaucracy to help drive social progress and economic prosperity; this resonates the centuries-old Confucian tradition of harmonious governance.

The Enlightenment emphasis on individual reason and liberty suggests that the solution to problems is neither collective action nor greater power afforded to institutions working on behalf of the collective. Rather, the solution is thought to be more individual freedom. In the UK, however, the central state has remained strong despite the ideological emphasis on devolution and reduced headcount: "Talk of decentralized management and of getting closer to the consumer has not penetrated very far down the hierarchies of our government departments and public services" (Pollitt 1990, 85).

Centralized power allowed the British welfare state to develop and expand rapidly during the Attlee ministry, while it also allowed extensive privatization and implementation of reform in the Thatcher years. Compared to constitutional democracies with federal structures—Australia and the USA—the UK still maintains a large and powerful central government.

Managerialism has left its mark, however, with citizens viewed as consumers and government agencies viewed as sellers. Perhaps this accounts for the lack of a relationship between authentically engaging in emotional labor and job satisfaction or personal fulfillment. There may be less identity with the job itself than would be the case if the citizen—state encounter were more meaningful than a simple customer—seller exchange.

References

Allen, Joseph A., James M. Diefendorff, and Y. Ma. 2014. "Differences in Emotional Labor Across Cultures: A Comparison of Chinese and U.S. Service Workers." *Journal of Business and Psychology* 29 (1): 21–35.

Andrews, Rhys, James Downe, and Valeria Guarneros-Meza. 2013. *Public Sector Reform in the UK: Views and Experiences from Senior Executives: Country Report as Part of the COCOPS Research Project*. Brussels: Coordination for Cohesion in the Public Sector of the Future (COCOPS). Accessed May 11, 2019. www.cocops.eu.

Bouckaert, Geert. 2007. "Cultural Characteristics from Public Management Reforms Worldwide." In *Cultural Aspects of Public Management Reform*, edited by Kuno Schedler and Isabella Proeller, 29–64. London: Elsevier Press.

Bovaird, Tony. 2007. "Triggering Change Through Culture Clash: The UK Civil Service Reform Program, 1999–2005." In *Cultural Aspects of Public Management Reform*, edited by Kuno Schedler and Isabella Proeller, 323–50. London: Elsevier Press.

Bovaird, Tony, and Ken Russell. 2007. "Civil Service Reform in the UK, 1999–2005: Revolutionary Failure or Evolutionary Success?" *Public Administration* 85 (2): 301–28.

Brown, Kerry, and Stephen P. Osborne. 2005. *Managing Change and Innovation in Public Service Organizations*. London: Routledge.

Cheung, A. B. L. 2012. "Public Administration in East Asia: Legacies, Trajectories, and Lessons." *International Review of Administrative Sciences* 78 (2): 209–16.

Dunleavy, Patrick, and Christopher Hood. 1994. "From Old Public Administration to New Public Management." *Public Money & Management* 3 (1): 9–16.

Elkomy, Shimaa, Graham Cookson, and Simon Jones. 2019. "Cheap and Dirty: The Effect of Contracting Out Cleaning on Efficiency and Effectiveness." *Public Administration Review* 79 (2): 193–202.

Gabriel, Yannis. 1999. "Management, Administration, and Critique in the 21st Century." *Administrative Theory and Praxis* 21 (4): 402–8.

Hofstede, Geert. 1980. *Culture's Consequences: International Differences in Work-Related Values*. Thousand Oaks, CA: Sage.

Hofstede, Geert, Gert Jan Hofstede, and Michael Minkov. 2010. *Cultures and Organizations: Software of the Mind*. 3rd ed. New York, NY: McGraw-Hill.

Hood, Christopher. 1991. "A Public Management for All Seasons?" *Public Administration* 69 (1): 3–19.

Hood, Christopher, and Ruth Dixon. 2015. "What We Have to Show for 30 Years of New Public Management: Higher Costs, More Complaints." *Governance* 28 (3): 265–67.

Hood, Christopher, and Ruth Dixon. 2016. "Not What It Said on the Tin? Reflections on Three Decades of UK Public Management Reform." *Financial Accountability and Management* 32 (4): 409–28.

Inglehart, Ronald, Christian Haerpfer, Alejandro Moreno, Christian Welzel, K. Kizilova, Jaime Diez-Medrano, Marta Lagos, Pippa Norris, Eduard Ponarin, and B. Puranen et al., eds. 2014. *World Values Survey: All Rounds—Country-Pooled Datafile Version.* Madrid: JD Systems Institute. http://www.worldvaluessurvey.org/WVSDocumentationWVL.jsp.

Kelly, Josie. 2007. "Reforming Public Services in the UK: Bringing in the Third Sector." *Public Administration* 85 (4): 1003–22.

Lawless, Jill. 2019. "Undone by Brexit, Theresa May Steps Down as Conservative Party Leader." *Chicago Tribune*, June 7. https://www.chicagotribune.com/nation-world/ct-theresa-may-steps-down-conservative-party-leader-20190607-story.html.

Mastracci, Sharon H. 2016. "Beginning Nurses' Perceptions of Ethical Leadership in the Shadow of Mid Staffs." *Public Integrity* 19 (3): 250–64.

Needham, Catherine, and Catherine Mangan. 2016. "The 21st Century Public Servant: Working at Three Boundaries of Public and Private." *Public Money & Management* 36 (4): 265–72.

O'Reilly, Dermot, and Mike Reed. 2012. "Leaderism and the Discourse of Leadership in the Reformation of UK Public Services." In *Leadership in the Public Sector: Promises and Pitfalls*, edited by Christeen Teelken, Ewan Ferlie, and Mike Dent, 21–43. Milton Park: Taylor & Francis.

Osborne, Stephen P., and Kate McLaughlin. 2002. "Trends and Issues in the Implementation of Local Voluntary Sector Compacts in England." *Public Money & Management* 22 (1): 55–64.

Overeem, Patrick, and Berry Tholen. 2011. "After Managerialism: MacIntyre's Lessons for the Study of Public Administration." *Administration & Society* 43 (7): 722–48.

Parry, Richard. 2011. "The UK Civil Service: A Devolving System." In *International Handbook on Civil Service Systems*, edited by Andrew Massey, 3–12. Cheltenham, UK: Edward Elgar.

Pollitt, Christopher. 1990. *Managerialism and the Public Services: The Anglo-American Experience.* Cambridge, MA: Basil Blackwell.

Pollitt, Christopher. 2013. "The Evolving Narratives of Public Management Reform: Forty Years of Reform White Papers in the UK." *Public Management Review* 15 (6): 899–922.

Pollitt, Christopher, and Geert Bouckaert. 2000. *Public Management Reform: A Comparative Analysis*. London: Routledge.

Rayner, Julie, and Alan Lawton. 2017. "Are We Being Served? Emotional Labour in Local Government in Victoria, Australia." *Australian Journal of Public Administration* 77 (3): 360–74.

Rees, James, Robin Miller, and Heather Buckingham. 2017. "Commission Incomplete: Exploring the New Model for Purchasing Public Services from the Third Sector." *International Social Policy* 46 (1): 175–94.

Schedler, Kuno, and Isabella Proeller. 2007. "Public Management as a Cultural Phenomenon: Revitalizing Societal Culture in International Public Management Research." In *Cultural Aspects of Public Management Reform*, edited by Kuno Schedler and Isabella Proeller, 3–28. London: Elsevier Press.

Schroter, Eckhard. 2007. "Deconstructing Administrative Culture: Exploring the Relationship Between Cultural Patterns and Public Sector Change in the UK and Germany." In *Cultural Aspects of Public Management Reform*, edited by Kuno Schedler and Isabella Proeller, 299–322. London: Elsevier.

Select Committee on Public Administration Twelfth Report. 1991. *Citizen's Charter*. https://publications.parliament.uk/pa/cm200708/cmselect/cmpubadm/411/41105.htm. Last updated July 8, 2008.

Shermon, Ganesh. 2016. *Disrupting Human Resources Talent Rules*. Accessed May 11, 2019. http://www.lulu.com/shop/ganesh-shermon/disrupting-human-resources-talent-rules/paperback/product-22982355.html.

Talbot, Colin. 2001. "UK Public Services and Management, 1979–2000: Evolution or Revolution?" *The International Journal of Public Sector Management* 14 (4): 281–303.

Teelken, Christine, Ewan Ferlie, and Mike Dent, eds. 2012. *Leadership in the Public Sector: Problems and Pitfalls*. Milton Park, UK: Taylor & Francis.

Thomas, John Clayton. 2013. "Citizen, Customer, Partner: Rethinking the Place of the Public in Public Management." *Public Administration Review* 73 (6): 786–96.

20

The USA

Geri A. Miller-Fox

The cultural context of a nation affects public service delivery and it also affects how public servants view and experience their work. Although regional, ethnic, and religious differences account for variation among different segments of the population, foundational national values serve as a common substrate for all (Hofstede 1980). This is why national culture is an important factor if we are to understand public service, how it is performed, its emotive load, and its consequences for those whose careers are dedicated to it. Discussion turns first to a description of the American character, followed by a comparison of how the USA ranks among other nations on dimensions of national culture. After the context has been set, a discussion of the public service context in the USA is provided, along with recent reforms. Then, survey findings of public service workers are presented.

The USA

The history of the USA is one of immigrants seeking a land where personal liberty, freedom, and individual opportunity are valued. In the USA, "as the world's most prominent example of people composed of immigrants," there are examples of both assimilation and retention of group identities

G. A. Miller-Fox (✉)
Department of Political Science, University of Utah, Salt Lake City, UT, USA
e-mail: g.a.miller@utah.edu

M. E. Guy et al. (eds.), *The Palgrave Handbook of Global Perspectives on Emotional Labor in Public Service*, https://doi.org/10.1007/978-3-030-24823-9_20

(Hofstede et al. 2010, 45). As embraced by the US Constitution, the nation is founded on the ideals of individual freedoms, liberty, and the pursuit of happiness and opportunity. These values are repeated in the pledge of allegiance to the flag, the national anthem, political rhetoric, and political socialization in early childhood education.

The USA is one of 23 countries and 9 dependent territories in North America, with 80% of the North American landmass belonging to Canada and the USA (Ramos 2018). Bordered by Canada to the north and Mexico and the Gulf of Mexico to the south, the eastern USA is bordered by the Atlantic Ocean and the western USA is bordered by the Pacific Ocean. The northernmost state of the USA (Alaska) borders the shorelines of the Arctic Ocean, the Chukchi Sea, and the Bering Sea. The USA comprises 50 states and several island territories, and as of February 1, 2019, the US Census Bureau estimated the population to be 328,374,269 (2019).

The early days of the USA were heavily influenced by British rule. Declaring its independence from Great Britain in 1776, the USA adopted its constitution in 1787. As one contemplates the founding of the nation, it is noteworthy that the first formal document produced by Americans was entitled the Declaration of Independence. The word "independence" denoted cutting ties with Great Britain but also foretold the cultural emphasis on individual independence. America would soon adopt a Bill of Rights, in the form of ten constitutional amendments, written to ensure individual rights to citizens and to set limits on the power of government.

Those who crafted the Constitution put systems in place that made governing into more of a social contract with citizens than into a power-wielding construction. Implementing checks and balances between the legislative, judicial, and executive branches, and preserving individual rights, meant that government would be slow to act and would be restricted in its powers (Stillman 2010). Attitudes opposed to strong government and in favor of citizen-led initiatives meant that public administration was treated as less important than was the establishment of commerce. Not until the industrial revolution of the late 1800s did attention turn to the machinery of governing and what it takes to "run a constitution," as Woodrow Wilson wrote in 1887. A growing economy, population growth, and migration from farms to cities called for an increase in government services, the necessity for a national income tax, and the organizational infrastructure to administer services.

One of the earliest analyses of the constitutional roots and authority of government comes from the writings of James Madison, Alexander

Hamilton, and John Jay who collectively authored what has come to be called "The Federalist Papers," a collection of 85 essays written between 1787 and 1788 to explain the provisions of the Constitution and to persuade Americans to ratify it (Hamilton et al. 1857/2009). James Madison was a staunch supporter of representative government as critical to a republican form of government, to which he was deeply committed. Alexander Hamilton was an ardent supporter of a strong executive and became Secretary of the Treasury, one of the few departments in the newly formed government. Much of his effort was placed on developing economic structures that remain today, such as a centralized banking system, the US mint, and regulatory, tariff, and taxation policies (Green 2002). Hamilton believed that government was necessary to protect the individual rights of the citizens. His commitment to public administration as fundamental to democracy aligned with his belief that strong institutional structures were necessary to ensure the stability of the government. In order to ensure a thriving economy, Hamilton was also convinced that attention to commerce was essential to the survival of the government. The seeds planted then have grown into what is now ensconced in American political culture as the importance of business, entrepreneurship, and trade. According to Green, "Hamilton's public administration would bear the distinctive marks of a republic bent on commerce" (Green 2002, 543). These early points of view remain today in the form of restrained government, protection of individual rights (Lucaites 1997), and attention to economic prosperity.

For Hamilton writing in the late 1700s and Woodrow Wilson writing in the late 1800s, public administration was the mechanism whereby political life would be realized. The executive functions necessary to support the loosely knit governing structures were designed to be the true strength of the system. Constitutional federalism intended that no branch of government would be so powerful as to seize power over the other branches. Institutional stability was the key to preserving the nation and sustaining the Constitution. Although each branch of government was intended to have separate authority, the dynamic tension between them was designed to maintain an equilibrium. Through leadership and appointment power, each of the institutions has adapted to shifting political winds with a stability that exceeds expectations of many during those founding days. Fast forward to the twenty-first century, and it is obvious that contemporary American culture continues to reflect the values of the founders.

Measuring National Culture

There is a rich literature on national culture. See, for example, Bond (1988), House et al. (2004), and Hofstede et al. (2010). Most notable among these is the work by Geert Hofstede. Started in the 1970s, his work began as a values survey of IBM employees and later developed into the Values Survey Modules, a five-dimensional model (Hofstede 1980; Hofstede et al. 2010) that substantially contributed to the well-known World Values Survey (WVS) databank established in the early 1980s (Buss 1989; Inglehart et al. 1998; Inglehart and Abramson 1994; Hofstede et al. 2010).

National culture is a composite of influences, ranging from historical traditions, religions and ethnic customs, economics, and even geography. While many scholars have contributed to the work of describing national culture, two surveys have, arguably, held the limelight: the GLOBE study by House et al. (2004) and the WVS by Hofstede et al. (2010). The GLOBE study asks participants to respond to how one actually experiences a nation, whereas the WVS uses questions that ask participants to respond to how things *should be*. This difference in phrasing may account for nuanced differences between the two studies' findings.

Gender, generational and social class cultures are not often factored into measurements of national culture. Although demographic subcultures almost certainly account for variation within a culture, this level of analysis is difficult to capture and detail when national culture is analyzed in the aggregate. There are, however, clear gender cultures that emerge within national frameworks (Buss 1989) and a similar argument can be made for generational and social class. Subcultures sculpt norms and expectations within the aggregate national norms and they factor heavily in American history, politics, and assumptions about what is "normal."

The WVS is, nonetheless, a well-respected and useful tool for understanding and evaluating national culture (Hofstede et al. 2010). For the US analysis, scores on six dimensions are most helpful:

1. Power Distance Index
2. Individualism Index
3. Masculinity Index
4. Uncertainty Avoidance Index
5. Long-Term Orientation Index; and
6. Indulgence Versus Restraint Index.

Hofstede et al. score each nation surveyed on each of these dimensions. In terms of categorizing groups of nations, they liken the national culture of the USA with other countries in the global northwest and those of the Anglo world. These kinship countries include Germany, Belgium, Switzerland, Netherlands, Luxembourg, Austria, Sweden, Great Britain, Finland, Canada, Denmark, Norway, New Zealand, Iceland, Ireland, and Australia. Discussion of where the USA ranks on each of these dimensions compared to other nations follows.

Power Distance Index

The USA scored 40 on the power distance index, putting it close to the mid-range on power distance around the globe (Hofstede et al. 2010, 57–59). This index ranks the degree to which inequality is acknowledged and acted upon in a society. The measure estimates "how far away one is from a feeling of power within a cultural framework" (Hofstede et al. 2010, 55).

The PDI is an interesting measurement for this particular study due to the connection between deference to authority and US norms of equality. Just as one perceives or experiences the expectations of what the emotion culture is in the workplace, there are also subtle understandings of the power distance between subordinates and bosses and what is expected of each.

Individualism Index

The second dimension of national culture is the Individualism Index. Of the six dimensions in total, individualism provides the most useful theoretical framework for understanding the effects of emotional labor for the US public service employee. In collectivist societies, individuals and community are linked in tight cohesive groups where interchange, exchange, and loyalty are essential. The interest of the group outweighs the interest of the individual. Conversely, in those cultures where individualism is emphasized, the focus is on an individual's independence and self-reliance (Hofstede et al. 2010).

Individualism versus collectivism is reflected, for example, by differences in how personal priorities are set, how careers are determined, how business relationships are structured, and it even extends to decisions about whom to marry (Buss 1989; Hall 1989). The degree of individualism is revealed by one's selection of pronouns (I versus we), and how one views oneself in relationship to family. In individualist cultures, children and parents distinguish themselves primarily as individuals rather than as members of a unit. Personal identity is stronger and more meaningful than group identity (Hofstede et al. 2010). Individuals are expected to support themselves and make their way in the world independent of others. Additional factors measured for individualism include personal time away from a job, freedom to adopt an individual approach to a job, and work that is personally challenging and fulfilling.

The USA ranks first among all nations on the IDV index (Hofstede Hofstede al. 2010, 95–97). The measure estimates "how far away one is from a feeling of power within a cultural framework" (Hofstede et al. 2010, 55). In this case, respondents report a feeling that they are at the foremost center of power. This represents the ideology that everyone deserves equal treatment (*universalism*), regardless of whom their friends are or what their social status is. Conversely, a collectivist society would think it is natural and ethical to treat one's friends better than strangers, a construct most often thought of as *particularism* or *exclusionism*. In a collectivist society, personal relationships prevail over tasks, whereas in an individualist society, it is not unusual to hear, "this is not personal, it is business" (Hofstede et al. 2010).

Masculinity Index

The third dimension of national culture to consider is masculinity versus femininity, as measured by the Masculinity Index. This index is designed to measure ideas about traditional gender roles. These roles imply generalizations such as men being seen as assertive and achievement oriented while women are seen as more modest, tender, and concerned with quality of life. Cultures are called feminine when emotional gender roles overlap such that both women and men are supposed to be modest, tender and concerned with quality of life. Cultures are called masculine when these roles are distinct, such that men are seen as tough and focused on material success while women are supposed to be modest and tender.

The USA ranked nineteenth from the top, denoting a masculinist culture, very close to Australia but a little less masculinist than Great Britain (Hofstede et al. 2010, 141–43). The masculinity pole looks at opportunities for earnings, workplace recognition, workplace advancement, and a personal sense of accomplishment and challenge. The feminine pole looks at factors such as having a good relationship with the chain of command, cooperation with others, living in a desirable community that is conducive to family life, and employment security (Hofstede et al. 2010).

Uncertainty Avoidance Index

Uncertainty avoidance is a continuum that acknowledges how people handle uncertainty. It denotes the extent to which members of a culture feel threatened by ambiguous or unknown situations. Among other manifestations, this feeling is expressed through nervous stress and in a need for predictability. There is comfort in written rules and even unwritten are viewed as better than no rules (Hofstede et al. 2010, 191). Countries with high tolerance for uncertainty are also those that most commonly respect human rights and political differences.

The USA ranked sixty-fourth on this index, putting it slightly above Great Britain and slightly below Australia, above China and about equal with the Philippines (Hofstede et al. 2010, 192–94). This dimension also looks at people's willingness to openly express frustration in the workplace and show their emotions. Uncertainty avoidance is not the same as risk avoidance. Uncertainty is avoided by a reduction in ambiguity. In the employment setting, ambiguity reduction is achieved by training programs, written policies and procedures, and well understood rules, norms, and processes.

Long-Term Orientation Index

Long-Term Orientation is defined as the fostering of virtues oriented toward future rewards, such as perseverance, thrift, and delaying gratification. Its opposite pole, short-term orientation, stands for virtues related to the past and present, such as respect for tradition, preservation of "face," and fulfilling social obligations (Hofstede et al. 2010, 239). Several factors contribute to determining a cultures' long- or short-term orientation, some of which include the length and quality of marriage, the value of family, consumption habits, and managing personal finances. The USA ranked on the low end at 70, slightly above Australia and below the Philippines and Thailand and well below Great Britain, Pakistan, India, China, Taiwan, and South Korea (Hofstede et al. 2010, 255–58). This denotes a short-term orientation to the American culture.

Indulgence Versus Restraint

Indulgence is a measurement of the degree of freedom people have to make choices about how they spend their time and their resources. Its opposite, restraint, rates the degree to which one is bound by social norms and expectations about the use of personal resources and free time. In other words, this dimension captures the degree of freedom one has to engage in leisurely activities as they choose. The definition for this dimension is that indulgence stands for a tendency to allow gratification of basic human desires related to enjoying life and having fun. Its opposite, restraint, reflects a conviction that such gratification needs to be curbed by strict social norms (Hofstede et al. 2010, 281). The USA ranked at 16, making it a relatively indulgent culture, similar to Great Britain and Australia and markedly more indulgent than Taiwan, Thailand, South Korea, India, or Pakistan (Hofstede et al. 2010, 282–85).

A Composite Picture of US Culture

National culture dimensions are more revealing when used in comparison, rather than as objective truths. Less of a certainty and more of a weathervane that shows which way the wind is blowing, it provides indicators that are useful for understanding how events are interpreted. If the ratings provided by Hofstede et al. (2010) are accurate, the USA as a culture prizes individualism above and beyond all other attributes. It falls in the midrange of countries in terms of power distance; it is a masculinist culture moderately uncomfortable with uncertainty and has a short-term orientation and is self-indulgent. The question of interest for this chapter is how do these cultural characteristics affect the work of those engaged in public service delivery? What are the implications for managing the emotive load of the work? Before addressing this directly, discussion turns to a description of the public administration landscape and to American public management.

The Evolution of US Public Administration and Management

Herbert Kaufman describes the contemporary imperatives of American public administration as "representativeness, political neutral competence, and executive leadership" (1969, 264). Each of these contributes to an understanding of the current work context. The evolution from the nation's founding to current times is revealing. The early years of the republic were characterized by a strong legislature and a weak executive branch (Kaufman 1969/2017). Early public agencies were heavily influenced by legislative guidance as agencies looked to statute and policymakers to establish and institutionalize the bureaucracy. It did not take long for this strong legislative model to develop cracks. Between 1800 and 1900, the young nation's administrative machinery grew rusty, due to numerous systemic and ethical failures (Kaufman 1969/2017). By the late 1800s, Woodrow Wilson (1887) wrote that it had become more difficult to "run a constitution" than to craft one. Heralding the separation between politics and administration as a solution to the corruption that was then occurring, movement started in academic circles to advocate for professionally trained administrators. Graduate training programs were soon established.

At the same time that public administration was professionalizing, the twentieth century also saw a notable expansion of the executive branch, both at the federal level and in the states. As more public services were developed to respond to the needs of a rapidly growing nation, the bureaucracy mushroomed. Management theories that emanated from the success of assembly line production processes produced Scientific Management (Taylor 1912/2017), time and motion studies, and other industrial era initiatives designed to improve efficiency. The Brownlow Commission was created at the behest of President Franklin Roosevelt, who sought advice on how to develop the executive infrastructure of the White House in such a way that the proliferation of executive agencies could be managed. Fundamental transformation occurred among government employees as merit-based employment systems were instituted throughout the states and Hatch Act provisions protected federal workers from political pressures. As oversight commissions, merit systems, procedural hiring practices, professional training programs, and clarification of duties, roles, and responsibilities evolved, a more professionalized public workforce was set in motion.

As the bureaucracy expanded and professional city managers dotted the urban landscape, citizens groused that government was getting too far removed from their control. Public perceptions of government as non-responsive and monolithic gave rise to complaints that the executive branch, whether at the federal, state, or local level, had lost touch with citizens and public values. Although professional training programs taught that Weberian bureaucracy was the best mechanism for ensuring impartial, efficient, skilled, services, the public became impatient (Weber 1922/2017). While traditional views of administration maximized hierarchy and control, it minimized the capacity to make rapid adjustments in processes. Unlike the business environment, which turns quickly as market forces change, governmental infrastructure was cumbersome and unable to accommodate exigencies.

A focus on the structural and hierarchical aspects of administration during the twentieth century is understandable. The government needed infrastructure and this period was heavily focused on establishing organizations that would be capable of delivering services in an accountable fashion. By the latter part of the century, the administrative bureaucracy came to be viewed as one focused on control, rather than on creativity. The paradigm was jolted by initiatives designed to more closely mirror not assembly line production processes but rapidly moving market forces. To trace the evolution of these changes, Stillman (2010) characterizes them as having occurred in four eras. The first is called *POSDCORB Orthodoxy* (1926–1946), a view of public administration as focusing on economy, efficiency, and the politics-administration dichotomy (White 1955; Stillman 2010). This era focused the primary functions of the executive, including planning, organizing, staffing, directing, coordinating, reporting, and budgeting. Stillman calls the second era the *Social Science Heterodoxy* (1947–1989). This era is defined by its focus on interdisciplinary practices, reliance on advances in the social sciences, national and international issues, and institutional effectiveness. See, e.g., Simon (1950) and Waldo (1955). The third era identified by Stillman is *Reassertion of Democratic Idealism* (1968–1988). This era is defined by a focus on policy, representativeness, fairness, legal oversight, and public integrity (Stillman 2010). Finally, Stillman identifies the current era as the fourth in public administration and calls it the *Refounding Movement* (1989–present). It is defined by a focus on legitimacy, democratic values, and public integrity.

Other scholars, such as Jay M. Shafritz and Albert C. Hyde, take a somewhat different approach to framing administrative trends. They classify the past into five eras (Shafritz and Hyde 2012). The first era represents the early voices and first quarter century of self-aware public administration, a period extending from the 1880s to the 1920s. They classify the second era as the New Deal era and mark it from the 1930s to the 1950s. The third era extends from the 1960s and they call it "From JFK to Civil Service Reform" (Shafritz and Hyde 2012). They call the fourth era "From Reagan to Reinvention" and include the 1980s and the 1990s. Finally, Shafritz and Hyde call the current era "Public Administration of the Twenty-First Century." The contrast between Stillman's and Shafritz and Hyde's eras shows that there are different ways of "slicing" the past. Regardless of where dividing lines are drawn, both systems of categorizing eras trace the changing attitudes toward government and its role.

One era that requires more attention is the civil rights movement of the 1950s and 1960s. During this time, Supreme Court decisions reflected predominant public opinion regarding fairness and respect for others. The landmark *Brown v. Board of Education* Supreme Court decision in 1954 ruled that separate schools for African-American children fail to uphold constitutional principles of each person being treated equally. Within a decade, the Civil Rights Act of 1964 outlawed discrimination on the basis of race and gender. These benchmark events, one judicial and the other legislative, reshaped not only the operations of government but also, processes and procedures in every American community and workplace. The civil rights era represented a significant shift in the role of government, and the role of public administrators, from one of sterile attention to management processes to one of being a change agent to effect social equity and a workforce representative of the population being served. The civil rights era fundamentally reshaped the role of government into an arbiter of equal rights in areas such as employment and labor, workplace safety, housing, elections, criminal justice and corrections, public education, health care, and numerous other areas of governmental regulation and oversight.

Just as the civil rights era ushered in health care for the elderly and the poor, fair housing, and equal access to education, the twenty-first century is marked by the initiatives made possible by information and communication technology. From 411 to 911 call systems to twitter accounts and Facebook pages for agencies, to telecommuting, to instantaneous communication around the globe, these developments are having a substantial influence on how public services are delivered and how the public engages with workers, and vice versa. Similar to the changes wrought by the industrial revolution, the effects are yet to be fully understood. One thing is clear, however, and it is that person-to-person communication, whether face-to-face or voice-to-voice, is becoming more precious because it is becoming more scarce. As tweets, texts, and e-mails enable one-dimensional, printed communication, the engagement that accompanies meaningful person-to-person interaction becomes more valuable. A closer look at the economics of the twentieth century helps to reveal dynamics that explain how and why public administration evolved as it did.

Individualism and the Growth of Wealth

The transition of the US economy from agriculture to urban industrialization shaped the nation's politics. From the beginnings of the industrial era in 1790 until it came to fruition on the assembly lines of 1900, this era introduced mass industrialization, mechanization, laborers leaving the home each day to work in factories, the rise of labor unions, and the proliferation of professions and scientific developments. The industrial revolution propelled the USA to its position at the center of the global economy. Hofstede writes, "The strong relationship between national wealth and individualism is undeniable, with the arrow of causality directed, as shown earlier, from wealth to individualism" (2010, 134). A significant shift occurred in the USA as a result of the industrial revolution. Not only did manufacturing and extractive industries rapidly expand, but so did the wealth of the nation and its inhabitants. Several administrative and public management philosophies emerged around this time as well.

During the early 1900s, industrial engineers such as Frederick Taylor (1912/2017) introduced "scientific" methods for managing workers. Asserting that there is one best way to ensure efficient production, Taylor's work emphasized efficiency through process, structure, the "scientific selection of workmen," and watchful supervision of them. Taylor's model of efficiency was significant in shaping the way workers were supervised. His views of the role of frontline employees emphasized efficiency and one best way to achieve outcomes. Taylor's work assumed that through proper application and constant evaluation, production would be greater. He advocated piece rate pay, an early variant of what is now called pay-for-performance. His assumption was that workers were indolent and only motivated by material rewards. Thus, he assumed that piece rate pay was the incentive system that would motivate workers to produce more, an assumption proved wrong by the Hawthorne studies a couple decades later (Mayo 1933).

Taylor emphasized four scientific principles as the foundation of scientific management. First, managers must document how to perform each job, enshrining their expert knowledge such that future workers could walk in the doors and achieve the necessary knowledge at an accelerated pace. One can easily see how this belief translated into such things as policy and procedure manuals, measurements, and performance plans.

The second technique necessary for scientific management is the precise selection, training, and promotion of the right employees. These philosophies would later shape such initiatives such as human resource management, hiring processes, training, and advancement practices. Workers were thought of as interchangeable parts, as if they are bolts and screws to be applied in the production process. When workers leave, they are to be replaced by someone with the same skills. Thus, job descriptions specify the required knowledge, skills, and abilities for each job, with no regard for temperament, personality attributes, or interpersonal skills. Administrators were promoted on the basis of technical expertise rather than on other skills, such as their ability to work effectively with others.

The third technique introduced by industrial thinking was the idea that managers had superior knowledge and it was their responsibility to instruct workers in how to do their jobs, supervise them closely, and correct them when they deviate from the protocol. This would ensure that each employee had the necessary information and knowledge to perform at maximum efficiency. This also required hands-on management with methods for accountability. Respect for the skills and knowledge and ability beyond that which is specified in the job description was deemed to be irrelevant.

Finally, Taylor emphasized the importance of specialization, such that there would be separation between engineers who design mechanical parts from the machinists who actually build the parts. By focusing the efforts of an employee on one thing, it was thought that workers would develop their greatest expertise with greatest efficiency. Combined, these four techniques form the basic theory of scientific management.

Translating these tenets to the work of public administration where judgment and discretion are exercised does not work well. The overall work of the *individual* public administrator is diminished in favor of productivity, output, and efficiency measures. Couple this with the primacy of individualism as a strongly held cultural value and it is easy to see that industrial methods such as prescribed by Taylor are like putting a square peg in a round hole. While rules that constrain discretion and ensure that public officials deliver services neutrally are worthwhile, the consequence is that reliance on rules, standards and performance measurement, also creates frustration and strain for the public employee. Engaging with citizens and making instant judgments about how to respond to the person in order to elicit the desired response requires emotional labor, an invisible set of performances that are missing from job descriptions and performance goals. The contradiction between the emotive skills required to do the job well and the physical and cognitive skills detailed in the job description result in a mismatch. This problem is exacerbated by New Public Management, a market-based approach to delivering public services.

New Public Administration to New Public Management

On the heels of the civil rights era, the 1970s brought a decade of attention to social equity and public administration's role in advancing it. The literature was replete with articles advocating an activist role for administrators.

Called New Public Administration, the question, "Does this service enhance social equity?" drove consideration of practices and policies that heretofore had given only slight, if any, attention to the subject. Thus, social equity gained a toehold as an additional value among the classical objectives of efficient, economical, and effectively managed public services (Frederickson 2002, 295). From this perspective, administrators moved from being neutral administrators to working toward effective, efficient, and equitable management and administration.

New Public Administration soon gave way to New Public Management (NPM), which was a radical departure from public administration of the past. As public opinion turned sour on government's ability to pivot away from traditions of the past and adapt to changing needs, faith in the market principles of supply and demand and competition blossomed. NPM was framed as a way of doing government's "business" according to market principles. Services were outsourced to contractors, competitive bidding drove the procurement process, and the theory holding sway was that competition would drive prices down, which would reduce the cost of services. As a result, workforce reductions occurred in agencies while consultants, non-profits, and businesses contracted to provide services previously provided by in-house staff. As the years rolled by, realization set in that market dynamics often failed to reduce costs and that organizational intelligence was lost as experienced administrators were replaced with contractors who would take their knowledge with them when the contract terminated. By the time Barack Obama left the Presidency in 2016, he had issued an executive order instructing executive agencies to insource rather than outsource services to the degree that was possible. Holdover thinking remains among many, however, and contracted services continue to be relied upon in many areas.

In contrast to reliance on hierarchy and bureaucratic regimens to deliver services, NPM developed from new institutional economics of public choice, transactions cost theory, and principal-agent-theory (Arrow 1963; Niskanen 1971). The principal claim of NPM was that it would provide better public service at lower cost. As if a reversion to the early twentieth century, the focus on efficiency became the predominant value. NPM is linked to four trends: a desire to inhibit government growth, a shift toward privatization and quasi-privatization, the desire to capitalize on information and communication technology, and a more international agenda (Hood 1991). NPM was defined by several doctrines that more often reflect business principles, many of which harken back to scientific management: reliance on benchmarks and outcome measures to ensure accountability; a focus on results with less regard to how they are achieved; faith in the power of competition to keep costs down; and cost cutting.

NPM worked better in theory than in practice (Hood and Dixon 2015). Costs rarely were reduced and service was not better. Enthusiasm for it has paled and an equilibrium has set in whereby insourced services are, in many instances, preferred over outsourced services. The popularity of outcomes measures remains because they serve as a feedback mechanism for determining what is, and is not, working. Decision-making is decentralized to the degree that is possible, but hierarchy remains in place as a control mechanism. Business practices applied to government procurement work in the simplest of domains, such as office supplies, but become problematic when used to guide delivery of human services, such as human services, casework, corrections, emergency medical services, and other services that depend on experienced professionals.

In other words, the whims of fashion have once again given way to dissatisfaction with the latest new idea (Hood 1991). NPM proved to be more hype than substance. The focus on lower costs per unit of service without adequate attention to quality of service turned government agencies into a "performance indicator industry" (Hood 1991, 9). The claim that NPM would have universal application—that one size would fit all—proved to be untrue and was naive.

Tracing the progression through the twentieth century shows the deep roots that the business model has on American government, making evident the power of economic principles whether or not a profit is the goal. The profit motive and supply and demand dynamics are deeply ingrained in administrative processes, obscuring the service function that those who deliver public services are responsible for providing. This attention to economic prosperity and wealth likely accounts for the reasonably high national culture scores in both masculinity and power. At the same time, Americans place a high value on the rights of individuals. While these values are dominant in American national culture, they also create crosswinds. America's capitalism requires inequality, while constitutional values prize equality. The contradiction is omnipresent and it is left to frontline workers to sort out priorities.

Public Values at the Street Level

The degree to which government is able to move its policies into action reflects the degree to which espoused values are actually held as priorities (Krislov 1974/2017). In the American context, this is revealed by the degree to which government actions breathe life into constitutional values.

Representative bureaucracy is a starting point for this. To be representative, those delivering public services must look like those being served. This ideal assumes that those who have common life experiences will have preferences similar to those with shared backgrounds (Krislov 1974/2017, 330). Concerns for representative democracy accelerated after the civil rights movement of the mid-twentieth century, and opened doors to women, African-Americans, and others in traditionally disadvantaged groups. Public values in the USA require power sharing and representative bureaucracy is the vehicle for achieving this.

Statutory provisions determine the nature of authority and functions of public agencies. These provisions outline, describe, and sanction specific functions. Having said that, organizations have cultures, norms, and expectations that systematically shape their duties, priorities, and processes. As a plethora of classic works have documented (see, e.g., Kaufman 1969/2017; Pressman and Wildavsky 1984; Wilson 1889), public administration is as much the delivery of democracy as it is a reflection of democracy (Rohr 1986; Lipsky 1980; Stivers 2000; Waldo 1968).

American government and its actions are imbued with an inherent tension between the rights of individuals and the rights of the collective. In a culture that values power as well as freedoms, it is understandable that those who are not part of the power structure continually clamor for inclusion. It is their birthright. The literature reflects this tension. Normative theorists insist that democratic values are central to the American ideal but there is disagreement over the extent to which the nation actually functions as such. These debates are both current (Lee 2009) and classical (Hamilton et al. 1857/2009).

Administrative actions breathe life into public values. John Rohr (1986) explains that the purpose of the administrative state is to operationalize the Constitution. Rohr argues that public administration is established in the constitutional framework and that documents such as the Brownlow Report, the Federalist Papers, and constitutional case law, establish and support its legitimacy. According to Rohr, "administrators should become active participants rather than feckless pawns in the constitutional struggle" (Rohr 1986, 89). Additionally, he states, "Without some sort of principled autonomy, professionalism in Public Administration can never be taken seriously. A purely instrumental profession is no profession at all" (Rohr 1986, 89). In other words, his argument is that public administrators have the constitutional right and duty to exercise their discretion to ensure constitutional protections and values.

Rohr's conceptualization of public administration is that it is normatively grounded, has constitutional authority, and is a legitimate form of citizen sovereignty. Thus, public administrators have an obligation to deliver democracy. According to Rohr (1986), public administrators should view themselves as the people who run the constitution and are public statesmen in their own right. His argument presents interesting and challenging perspectives. It assumes that the constitution allows for, and intends, a sovereign administrative state. From one perspective, the sovereignty of the populace could jeopardize entire systems if the will of the people is unhindered, just as Madison had opined in the Federalist, worrying that the "passions" of the crowd could overrule good policy. On the other hand, Rohr argues that the framers intended government to understand it exists only because the citizenry allows it to exist. To overcome this contradiction, Frank Goodnow and Woodrow Wilson locate sovereignty within institutions of government and not with the people, themselves, once a government was formed (Rohr 1986, 85). Rohr reconciles his interpretation with that of Goodnow and Wilson by arguing that public administrators ought to act in accordance with constitutional principles, with the knowledge that they are sovereign individuals responsible for the administration of the constitution. Imbued with this imperative, the contrast between the end goal of public administrators and business executives is obvious. The former is to pursue regime values, and the latter is to pursue profits. In both cases, however, the primacy of power and individualism surface.

Discretion

Popular sovereignty allows one to exercise discretion and administrative discretion occurs in a range of settings with varying consequences. Michael Lipsky (1980) provides an in-depth analysis of discretion in his discussion of how public services are delivered. He focuses on the street level, meaning on those bureaucrats who engage in person-to-person contact with the public. This includes public-school teachers, police officers, emergency rescue workers, caseworkers, zoning officers, healthcare professionals, receptionists in public offices, public transportation drivers, public works engineers, public defenders, and so forth. All of these workers make decisions daily, some of which are constrained by law while others allow for discretion. Use of discretion aligns with a culture of individualism.

Lipsky's concern is that public service professionals need discretion in order to perform their tasks due to exigencies of individual circumstances and needs. For example, a police officer will encounter two jaywalkers, one crossing the street in the middle of oncoming traffic and another crossing with no traffic in sight. Both are violating the law, but one is endangering both self and others, while the other is endangering no one. Does each deserve the same penalty for failing to cross the street at a designated crossing point? Autonomy and discretion allow the officer to determine how to allocate effort and perform the job. Strict adherence to law requires the officer to issue a penalty regardless of the danger—or lack of it—caused by the transgressor. How the officer reconciles formal job requirements with personal discretion has emotive consequences. The officer can issue a penalty to the jaywalker who endangered both self and oncoming drivers with authentic assertiveness and confidence. But to issue a penalty to the other jaywalker requires wearing a false face, pretending to be assertive and confident in the judgment of wrongdoing by the offender.

The decision by the officer has consequences for how the public view the work of the bureaucracy. In this case, as warranted and protecting safety, versus as mindless rule-following. Street-level bureaucrats are important because "Citizens directly experience government through them, and their actions *are* the policies provided by government in important respects" (Lipsky 1980, xix–xx). Lipsky's work highlights the quandaries of public service delivery that occur as a result of structural constraints, arguing that it is important to address the tension that street-level bureaucrats face in providing idealized services in less-than-ideal systems.

Street-level bureaucrats develop idiosyncratic processes and strategies for coping with these challenges. Some of this occurs through the approach and attitudes bureaucrats adopt toward rationing of goods and services for specific populations (Schneider and Ingram 1993; Schneider et al. 2014). Approval or denial of benefits is one form of rationing. Another form of rationing is spending more or less time on a case, with a client, or on a task: "important" people or tasks get more time, others get less. Another form of rationing is more psychological in nature. It includes reducing staffing so that citizens must wait longer for services, setting restrictive office hours, or requiring completion of lengthy, complex forms or processes that require multiple time-consuming steps.

Lipsky makes the point that employees become less emotionally attached to their work and its meaning when they do not "own" it. In other words, when they have little authority and discretion, they find themselves being more of a robot, fulfilling requirements but not using their personal skills as unique instruments to effect a desired result, whether it is compliance, agreement, or cooperation. This creates emotional dissonance about one's work and over time, results in alienation. The failure of workers to be able to "express, or need to suppress, their creative and human impulses through work activity" is costly in terms of work productivity and quality and the citizen engagement that results from services well-delivered (Lipsky 1980, 75). Work that is de-motivating results in worker burnout and affects service delivery (Abraham 1998; Austin et al. 2008; Groth et al. 2009). Multiple studies have demonstrated that emotive dissonance contributes to burnout among public servants (Austin et al. 2008; Bhave and Glomb 2013; Brotheridge and Grandey 2002; Pugh et al. 2011; Ciarrochi et al. 2002; Grandey 2000; Guy and Lee 2015; Guy et al. 2008; Hsieh et al. 2012; Mikolajczak et al. 2007; Moradi et al. 2011; Prati et al. 2009; Pugh et al. 2011).

Lipsky argues that how street-level bureaucrats perform their jobs affects how citizens view government. He also claims that the public demand for efficiency results in street-level bureaucrats who adopt routines and practices that influence the outcomes of their efforts. They also adopt practices that allow them to work within the external constraints while balancing their internal struggles in a way that achieves an acceptable balance between public aspirations and requirements of the job or imposed expectations. In other words, workers find a way to achieve congruence between their emotive display and how they actually feel about their work.

In order to ensure fairness and accountability, bureaucratic policies and procedures apply to the collective (target populations) and not specific, individualized circumstances. Lipsky's research highlights the tensions between individualist and collectivist application of rules and it leads him to advocate for an ideal view of service delivery that would allow street-level bureaucrats to exercise discretion with limited external controls. While street-level bureaucrats do not make the policy and do not make the rules, they are held accountable for the delivery, much of which involves emotional labor, which is a form of work separate from, but analogous to, manual or cognitive labor.

Emotional Labor and Public Service Delivery

Only recently has the subject of emotional labor arisen in the context of public service delivery, although it has been a subject in retail sales and customer service for decades, ever since Arlie Hochschild first applied the term to flight attendants and the behaviors they must don to serve airline passengers (Hochschild 1983). Michael Lipsky's *Street-Level Bureaucracy* in 1980, followed by Steven Maynard-Moody and Michael Musheno's *Cops, Teachers, Counselors* in 2003 begged for a deeper understanding of its role in public service delivery. Guy et al. (2008) responded to the call with *Emotional Labor: Putting the* Service *in Public Service.* Since that time, an increasing number of studies have been conducted with the goal of understanding the emotive component in public service work (Mastracci et al. 2012), how it is performed (Guy and Lee 2015), how it relates to job satisfaction (Hsieh et al. 2016; Hsieh et al. 2012), when it results in burnout (Hsieh 2014), and how it can be taught in the classroom (Mastracci et al. 2010).

Emotional labor is required anytime there is person-to-person interaction and the management of emotion is required in order to perform one's job. The steps involved require the rapid sensing of one's own emotional state, sensing the emotional state of the other, and then making a judgment about whether an emotive response is necessary and, if so, what kind. It may involve calming oneself, calming the other, exciting the other, expressing how one is feeling, or suppressing how one is feeling and displaying a different emotion. This sequence requires alterations in facial expression, tone of voice, and physical posture. It consumes energy and is done <u>in order to perform the job</u>. In some occupations, emotive expression is scripted. For example, police officers must appear confident, regardless of whether they feel that way. Social workers are to seem supportive, regardless of how they feel. Receptionists who greet citizens as they enter public buildings are to appear and sound friendly, regardless of whether they feel that way. The public information officer is to sound compassionate, confident, and self-assured in announcements of critical events. In other words, emotional labor and public service work go hand in hand.

Display rules are conveyed to employees through a variety of strategies. Professional training programs teach students about proper presentation of self. Through organizational onboarding, new employees are taught about display rules. While performing a job, accomplished co-workers serve as role models. In sum, display rules are understood as part of the emotive "software" downloading that takes place through cultural and institutional influences.

It has been well established that having to suppress how one feels in order to display a different emotion creates emotive dissonance and contributes to burnout in retail settings (Abraham 1998; Ashforth and Humphrey 1993; Bhave and Glomb 2013; Grandey 2003; Mesmer-Magnus et al. 2012). Emotive pretending is a type of emotional labor where individuals must display emotions that do not match their true feelings. It is also called surface acting. When public service employees use pretense to display an emotion, we can expect it to have similar deleterious effects.

American norms, institutions, structures, and processes influence the degree to which people are culturally programmed regarding the performance of emotional labor. Individual psychological processes are sculpted by these institutions and norms, rendering emotional labor more theoretically complex than when analyzed apart from the context in which it occurs. This study of American public service workers, then, has both theoretical and practical implications.

The central question of this book is to what degree do culture and context produce a collective programming of emotive response such that ways of responding are subtly shaped by life experiences and social environments (Parsons 2007). Institutional and structural explanations of national culture highlight differences in how emotional labor is performed as well the effects it has on work attitudes. While individuals may experience an infinite array of unique life experiences and social interactions, patterns of responding occur. Over time, patterns and modes of action develop into culture by shaping and influencing ideas and values.

Public service in the USA is a two-way street, with citizens expecting to get effective, responsive service and workers expecting to feel good about their work. Employees' roles are shaped by institutional characteristics and the type of work they perform. Some employees may feel more emotionally connected to their work than others, and employees may differ in their emotive sensitivity and expressiveness. Additionally, employees differ in their job attitudes and level of investment in their work. Discussion turns to the study of American public service workers and their experiences related to performing emotional labor on their jobs.

The Study

The focus of this chapter is to explore whether the latent variables of emotive capacity, pretending expression, and deep acting exist, and if so, how they relate to job satisfaction, burnout, and personal fulfillment.

Methodology

Surveys were administered to public service workers across the USA. All had work experience at the federal, state, or local levels of government or in non-profit organizations. Most respondents lived in Denver and Salt Lake City, but others were in Washington, D.C., Atlanta, Miami, Kansas City, and elsewhere. Respondents were a convenience sample, completing the survey at the request of researchers who distributed it in workplaces, at professional conferences, through networks of acquaintances, and in graduate public administration classes where midcareer students were enrolled. The survey resulted in 254 respondents.

Emotional Labor Variables

The survey items are shown below. Each was scored on a seven-point scale from Strongly Disagree (1), to Strongly Agree (7).

Emotive Capacity

> I am good at expressing how I feel.
> I am good at getting people to calm down.
> In my job I am good at dealing with emotional issues.

Pretending Expression

> I hide my true feelings so as to appear pleasant at work.
> In my job I act confident and self-assured regardless of how I actually feel.
> I wear a "mask" in order to deal with clients/customers in an appropriate way.

Deep Acting

> I try to actually experience the emotions that I must show to clients/customers.
> I work hard to actually feel the emotions that I need to show to clients/customers.
> I work at developing the feelings inside of me that I need to show to clients/customers.

Job Satisfaction

> My job provides career development and promotion opportunities.
> I feel I am being paid a fair amount for the work I do.
> I feel satisfied with my supervisor.
> Overall, I am satisfied with my job.

Burnout

> I leave work feeling tired and run down.
> I leave work feeling emotionally exhausted.
> I feel "used up" at the end of the workday.

Personal Fulfillment

> I gain a strong sense of personal fulfillment at my job.
> I feel like my job is something I want to do rather than something I have to do.
> My work is a source of personal meaning in my life.

Demographic statistics for the respondents are displayed in Table 20.1. Eighty percent of respondents are under the age 50, 61% are female, and 41% have ten or more years of work experience, and 97% have at least a college degree if not more education.

Respondents work in a variety of settings, as shown in Table 20.2. The categories are not mutually exclusive, because someone may be in

Table 20.1 Demographic characteristics: USA

	Frequency	Percent
Age		
Less than 30	75	29.5
30–39 years	85	33.5
40–49 years	44	17.3
50–59 years	40	15.7
60 or more	7	2.8
N/A	3	1.2
Gender		
Female	154	60.6
Male	99	39.0
N/A	1	0.4
Public service experience		
Less than 10	147	57.9
10–19 years	57	22.4
20–29 years	27	10.6
30 or more	20	7.9
N/A	3	1.2
Educational level		
Less than high school	0	0.0
High school graduate	1	0.4
Some college	3	1.2
2-year associate degree	3	1.2
College graduate	31	12.2
Some graduate school	131	51.6
Master's degree	67	26.4
Law degree (J.D., LL.B.)	5	2.0
Doctorate degree (Ph.D., M.D., Ed.D., etc.)	12	4.7
Other (please specify)	1	0.4
N/A	0	0.0

administration and be in health care, for example, so the frequency sums to more than the number of respondents.

Descriptive statistics for each of the variables are shown in Table 20.3. The mean of each variable is shown, along with its standard deviation. Cronbach's alpha, a measure of internal consistency, is shown for each variable. Five of the six coefficients exceed 0.700, with only pretending expression being lower than that. At 0.671, it is high enough to warrant inclusion.

Findings

Survey responses were analyzed using Principal Component Analysis (PCA) and Confirmatory Factor Analysis (CFA). Principal component analysis uses orthogonal transformation to convert observations into a set of principal components and explains the variance-covariance structure of a set of variables through linear combinations. As a result, we can interpret the uniqueness of a variable minus its communality. Eigenvalues were used to develop a linear map to measure the distortion induced by the transformation. The

Table 20.2 Occupational characteristics: USA

Occupation	Frequency	Percent
1. Administration	72	14.8
2. Community development/neighborhood services	27	5.6
3. Engineering, manufacturing, or production	19	3.9
4. Education	65	13.4
5. Disaster response	10	2.1
6. Finance or accounting	18	3.7
7. Firefighter	6	1.2
8. Health care	18	3.7
9. Housing	25	5.2
10. Human resource management	2	0.4
11. Information and communication	21	4.3
12. Law enforcement	8	1.6
13. Military	11	2.3
14. Public relations	15	3.1
15. Planning	13	2.7
16. Public works: streets, sanitation, utilities	10	2.1
17. Purchasing	4	0.8
18. Recreation and parks	7	1.4
19. Research and development	27	5.6
20. Social services	33	6.8
21. Transportation	3	0.6
22. Support services (e.g., equipment maintenance)	2	0.4
23. Other	69	14.2

PCA procedures confirmed three latent constructs in the items, consistent with previous research (Yang et al. 2018). CFA procedures demonstrated that latent factors had the expected convergent and discriminant validity. Table 20.4 displays the findings and also includes the goodness of fit measurements for the model. The CFI is 0.880, the p-value RMSEA is 0.088, and the SRMR is 0.093. These values are within acceptable ranges for goodness of fit for research of this nature (Schreiber et al. 2006; Liu 2014).

The relationships between variables reveal interesting findings. While the capacity to experience the emotive content of a job (emotive capacity) has no effect on job satisfaction, or burnout, it has a positive effect on feelings of personal fulfillment. The actual performance of emotional labor in the form of pretending or authentic expression has statistically significant relationships to most outcome variables. Pretending expression has a significant and negative effect on both job satisfaction and personal fulfillment. This finding suggests that in the USA, public service employees suffer deleterious effects when they must suppress how they actually feel in order to display unfelt emotions. This conclusion is supported by the positive relationship between pretending and burnout.

Conversely, the positive relationship between deep acting, the authentic expression of emotion, and job satisfaction and fulfillment indicates

Table 20.3   Descriptive statistics and Cronbach's alpha: USA

	Mean	SD	Cronbach's alpha
Emotive capacity	5.28	1.17	0.771
Pretending expression	4.86	1.20	0.671
Deep acting	4.27	1.36	0.852
Job Satisfaction	4.81	1.31	0.738
Burnout	4.33	1.58	0.913
Personal Fulfillment	5.06	1.48	0.899

Table 20.4   Structural model results: USA

Hypothesized paths	Coefficients	p-value
Emotive capacity → Job satisfaction	0.026	0.723
Emotive capacity → Burnout	0.080	0.282
Emotive capacity → Personal fulfillment	0.155*	0.034
Pretending expression → Job satisfaction	−1.36*	0.000
Pretending expression → Burnout	0.650*	0.000
Pretending expression → Personal fulfillment	−0.992*	0.000
Deep acting → Job satisfaction	0.950*	0.014
Deep acting → Burnout	−0.333	0.065
Deep acting → Personal fulfillment	0.720*	0.005

Model fit: $\chi^2 = 422.686$ (df = 142), CFI = 0.880, RMSEA = 0.088, SRMR = 0.093

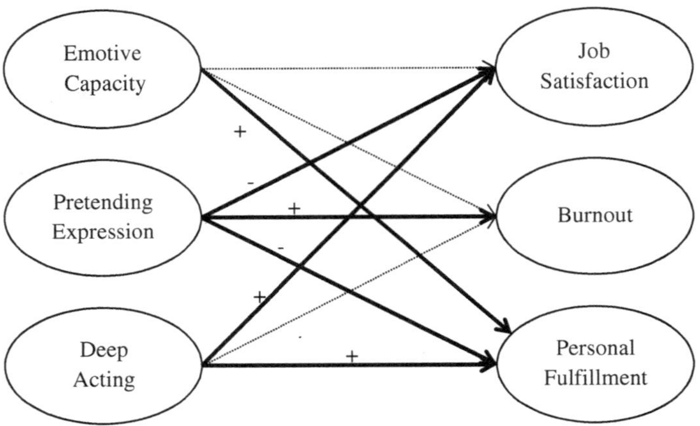

Fig. 20.1 Path diagram for the United States

something quite the opposite. Emotional labor, as long as it allows for the authentic expression of how the worker is feeling, has salutary effects in terms of increasing both job satisfaction and fulfillment.

A path diagram makes it easy to see the relationships. Figure 20.1 displays them. The three independent latent variables are emotive capacity, pretending expression, and deep acting. The three dependent variables are job satisfaction, burnout, and personal fulfillment. Bold arrows denote statistically significant relationships ($p \leq 0.05$).

Discussion

The US sample revealed the presence of latent variables as theorized and results demonstrate the power of a cultural emphasis on individualism. If a national culture of individualism affects public sector employees in such a way that they expect consistency between the emotion they feel and the emotion they display, we should expect to see emotive pretending affecting job satisfaction, burnout, and personal fulfillment. In fact, that is the case. There is a negative relationship between pretending and job satisfaction and between pretending and fulfillment. This is in stark contrast to the positive relationship between the authentic expression of emotion—deep acting—and job satisfaction and personal fulfillment. And, as expected, there is a positive relationship between emotive pretending and burnout.

The negative effect that emotive pretending has on job satisfaction and personal fulfillment suggests that public service employees in the USA experience deleterious effects when they must display an emotion that is incongruent with what they actually feel. In other words, in the USA, public service employees find personal fulfillment when they can express authentic emotions in the workplace. This leaves little room for emotive dissonance and relegates it to a workplace problem.

Conclusion

Findings such as these deepen our appreciation for the emotive content in public service jobs. They also provide useful insights for how to prepare workers to perform their jobs and to prepare them for the most challenging aspects, which arise when emotive dissonance has to be part of the job. Understanding the effect of emotional labor leads to the potential to develop strategies to assist public sector training programs in capitalizing on the benefits of emotional labor as well as to minimize its downside. As citizen engagement and satisfaction with public services looms ever larger on the horizon of concerns in the USA, awareness of emotional labor and its effect on job outcomes also translates into performance outcomes.

Emotive pretending is a required skill set in most jobs. Findings here show that it increases the likelihood of emotional exhaustion so human resource trainers should be providing training and development opportunities to help employees learn constructive strategies when jobs require them to engage in emotive pretending. Human cooperation and professional interactions are expected societal norms and success in this context *requires* acting when authenticity is absent. Emotion regulation, which is a form of emotional intelligence, is a skill that has been found to correlate with the ability to withstand or minimize the threat of burnout under such circumstances (Guy and Lee 2015; Hülsheger et al. 2013; Kotsou et al. 2011; Mikolajczak et al. 2007). Building this into required knowledge, skills, and abilities (KSA) for jobs will provide a more accurate picture of the requirements for each job.

A purposeful appreciation for emotional labor will serve to improve work outcomes for both citizens and workers. As individualist as American culture is, these data confirm that engaging with others on the job in a constructive, manner, produces positive job outcomes. Cognizance of the emotive component in public service jobs provides a deeper, richer understanding of the exchange between citizen and state.

References

Abraham, Rebecca. 1998. "Emotional Dissonance in Organizations: Antecedents, Consequences, and Moderators." *Genetic, Social, and General Psychology Monographs* 124 (2): 229–46.

Arrow, Kenneth J. 1963. *Social Choice and Individual Values.* 2nd ed. New York, NY: Wiley.

Ashforth, Blake E., and Ronald H. Humphrey. 1993. "Emotional Labor in Service Roles: The Influence of Identity." *The Academy of Management Review* 18 (1): 88–115.

Austin, Elizabeth J., Timothy C. P. Dore, and Katharine M. O'Donovan. 2008. "Associations of Personality and Emotional Intelligence with Display Rule Perceptions and Emotional Labour." *Personality and Individual Differences* 44 (3): 679–88. http://dx.doi.org/10.1016/j.paid.2007.10.001.

Bhave, Devasheesh P., and Theresa M. Glomb. 2013. "The Role of Occupational Emotional Labor Requirements on the Surface Acting–Job Satisfaction Relationship." *Journal of Management* 42 (3): 722–41. https://doi.org/10.1177/0149206313498900.

Bond, Michael Harris. 1988. "Finding Universal Dimensions of Individual Variation in Multicultural Studies of Values: The Rokeach and Chinese Value Surveys." *Journal of Personality and Social Psychology* 55 (6): 1009–15. https://doi.org/10.1037//0022-3514.55.6.1009.

Brotheridge, Céleste M., and Alicia A. Grandey. 2002. "Emotional Labor and Burnout: Comparing Two Perspectives of 'People Work'." *Journal of Vocational Behavior* 60 (1): 17–39. http://dx.doi.org/10.1006/jvbe.2001.1815.

Buss, David M. 1989. "Sex Differences in Human Mate Preferences: Evolutionary Hypotheses Tested in 37 Cultures." *Behavioral and Brain Sciences* 12 (1): 1–49.

Ciarrochi, Joseph, Frank P. Deane, and Stephen Anderson. 2002. "Emotional Intelligence Moderates the Relationship Between Stress and Mental Health." *Personality and Individual Differences* 32 (2):197–209. http://dx.doi.org/10.1016/S0191-8869(01)00012-5.

Frederickson, H. George. 2002. "Toward a New Public Administration." In *Classics of Public Administration,* 8th ed., edited by J. Shafritz and Al Hyde, 282–94. Boston, MA: Wadsworth Cengage Learning.

Grandey, Alicia A. 2000. "Emotional Regulation in the Workplace: A New Way to Conceptualize Emotional Labor." *Journal of Occupational Health Psychology* 5 (1): 95–110. https://doi.org/10.1037/1076-8998.5.1.95.

Grandey, Alicia A. 2003. "When 'The Show Must Go On': Surface Acting and Deep Acting as Determinants of Emotional Exhaustion and Peer-Rated Service Delivery." *Academy of Management Journal* 46 (1): 86–96. https://doi.org/10.2307/30040678.

Green, Richard T. 2002. "Alexander Hamilton: Founder of American Public Administration." *Administration & Society* 34 (5): 541–62. https://doi.org/10.1177/009539902237275.

Groth, Markus, Thorsten Hennig-Thurau, and Gianfranco Walsh. 2009. "Customer Reactions to Emotional Labor: The Roles of Employee Acting Strategies and Customer Detection Accuracy." *The Academy of Management Journal* 52 (5): 958–74.

Guy, Mary E., and Hyun Jung Lee. 2015. "How Emotional Intelligence Mediates Emotional Labor in Public Service Jobs." *Review of Public Personnel Administration* 35 (3): 261–77. https://doi.org/10.1177/0734371x13514095.

Guy, Mary E., Meredith A. Newman, and Sharon H. Mastracci. 2008. *Emotional Labor: Putting the* Service *in Public Service.* Armonk, NY: M.E. Sharpe.

Hall, Edward T. 1989. *Beyond Culture.* New York, NY: Anchor Books.

Hamilton, Alexander, James Madison, and John Jay. 1857/2009. *The Federalist Papers: Alexander Hamilton, James Madison, John Jay.* New Haven, CT: Yale University Press.

Hochschild, Arlie R. 1983. *The Managed Heart: Commercialization of Human Feeling.* Berkeley, CA: University of California Press.

Hofstede, Geert. 1980. *Culture's Consequences: International Differences in Work-Related Values.* Beverly Hill, CA: Sage.

Hofstede, Geert, Gert Jan Hofstede, and Michael Minkov. 2010. *Cultures and Organizations: Software of the Mind.* 3rd ed. New York, NY: McGraw-Hill.

Hood, Christopher. 1991. "A Public Management for All Seasons?" *Public Administration* 69 (1): 3–19. https://doi.org/10.1111/j.1467-9299.1991.tb00779.x.

Hood, Christopher, and Ruth Dixon. 2015. "What We Have to Show for 30 Years of New Public Management: Higher Costs, More Complaints." *Governance* 28 (3): 265–67. https://doi.org/10.1111/gove.12150.

House, Robert J., Paul J. Hanges, Mansour Javidan, Peter W. Dorfman, and Vipin Gupta. 2004. *Culture, Leadership, and Organizations: The GLOBE Study of 62 Societies.* Thousand Oaks, CA: Sage.

Hsieh, Chih-Wei. 2014. "Burnout Among Public Service Workers: The Role of Emotional Labor Requirements and Job Resources." *Review of Public Personnel Administration* 34 (4): 379–402.

Hsieh, Chih-Wei, Jun-Yi Hsieh, and Irving Yi-Feng Huang. 2016. "Self-Efficacy as a Mediator and Moderator Between Emotional Labor and Job Satisfaction: A Case Study of Public Service Employees in Taiwan." *Public Performance and Management Review* 40 (1): 71–96.

Hsieh, Chih-Wei, Myung Jin, and Mary E. Guy. 2012. "Managing Work-Related Emotions: Analysis of a Cross Section of Public Service Workers." *The American Review of Public Administration* 42 (1): 39–53.

Hülsheger, Ute R., Hugo J. E. M. Alberts, Alina Feinholdt, and Jonas W. B. Lang. 2013. "Benefits of Mindfulness at Work: The Role of Mindfulness in Emotion Regulation, Emotional Exhaustion, and Job Satisfaction." *Journal of Applied Psychology* 98 (2): 310–25. https://doi.org/10.1037/a0031313.

Inglehart, Ronald, Alejandro Menendez Moreno, Miguel Basáñez, Gabriela Catterberg, Jaime Diez-Medrano, Alejandro Moreno, Pippa Norris, Renata Siemienska, and Ignacio Zuasnabar. 1998. *Human Values and Beliefs: A Cross-Cultural Sourcebook*. Ann Arbor, MI: University of Michigan Press.

Inglehart, Ronald, and Paul R. Abramson. 1994. "Economic Security and Value Change." *The American Political Science Review* 88 (2): 336–54. https://doi.org/10.2307/2944708.

Kaufman, Herbert. 1969/2017. "Administrative Decentralization and Political Power." In *Classics of Public Administration*, 8th ed., edited by J. Shafritz and Al Hyde, 265–77. Boston, MA: Wadsworth Cengage Learning.

Kotsou, Ilios, Delphine Nelis, Jacques Grégoire, and Moïra Mikolajczak. 2011. "Emotional Plasticity: Conditions and Effects of Improving Emotional Competence in Adulthood." *Journal of Applied Psychology* 96 (4): 827–39. https://doi.org/10.1037/a0023047.

Krislov, S. 1974/2017. "Representative Bureaucracy." In *Classics of Public Administration*, 8th ed., edited by J. Shafritz and Al Hyde, 339–43. Boston, MA: Wadsworth Cengage Learning.

Lee, Frances E. 2009. *Beyond Ideology: Politics, Principles, and Partisanship in the U.S. Senate*. Chicago, IL: University of Chicago Press.

Lipsky, Michael. 1980. *Street-Level Bureaucracy: Dilemmas of the Individual in Public Services*. New York, NY: Russell Sage Foundation.

Liu, Baodong. 2014. "Postracial Politics: Counterevidence from the Presidential Elections, 2004–2012." *Du Bois Review: Social Science Research on Race* 11 (2): 443–63. https://doi.org/10.1017/s1742058x14000113.

Lucaites, John Louis. 1997. "Visualizing 'the People' Individualism vs. Collectivism in Let Us Now Praise Famous Men." *Quarterly Journal of Speech* 83 (3): 269–89.

Mastracci, Sharon H., Mary E. Guy, and Meredith A. Newman. 2012. *Emotional Labor and Crisis Response: Working on the Razor's Edge*. Armonk, NY: M.E. Sharpe.

Mastracci, Sharon H., Meredith A. Newman, and Mary E. Guy. 2010. "Emotional labor: Why and How to Teach It." *Journal of Public Affairs Education* 16 (2):123–41.

Maynard-Moody, Steven, and Michael Musheno. 2003. *Cops, Teachers, Counselors: Stories from the Front Lines of Public Service*. Ann Arbor, MI: University of Michigan Press.

Mayo, Elton. 1933. *The Human Problems of an Industrial Civilization*. Cambridge, MA: Harvard.

Mesmer-Magnus, Jessica R., Leslie A. DeChurch, and Amy Wax. 2012. "Moving Emotional Labor Beyond Surface and Deep acting: A Discordance–Congruence

Perspective." *Organizational Psychology Review* 2 (1): 6–53. https://doi.org/10.1177/2041386611417746.

Mikolajczak, Moïra, Emmanuel Roy, Olivier Luminet, Catherine Fillée, and Philippe de Timary. 2007. "The Moderating Impact of Emotional Intelligence on Free Cortisol Responses to Stress." *Psychoneuroendocrinology* 32 (8–10): 1000–12. http://dx.doi.org/10.1016/j.psyneuen.2007.07.009.

Moradi, Afsaneh, Nooshin Pishva, Hadi Bahrami Ehsan, Parvaneh Hadadi, and Farzaneh Pouladi. 2011. "The Relationship Between Coping Strategies and Emotional Intelligence." *Procedia—Social and Behavioral Sciences* 30: 748–51. http://dx.doi.org/10.1016/j.sbspro.2011.10.146.

Niskanen, William A. 1971. *Bureaucracy and Representative Government.* Chicago, IL: Aldine, Atherton.

Parsons, Craig. 2007. *How to Map Arguments in Political Science.* New York, NY: Oxford University Press.

Prati, L. Melita, Yongmei Liu, Pamela L. Perrewé, and Gerald R. Ferris. 2009. "Emotional Intelligence as Moderator of the Surface Acting—Strain Relationship." *Journal of Leadership & Organizational Studies* 15 (4): 368–80. https://doi.org/10.1177/1548051808328518.

Pressman, Jeffrey L., and Aaron B. Wildavsky. 1984. *Implementation: How Great Expectations in Washington Are Dashed in Oakland: Or, Why It's Amazing That Federal Programs Work at All, This Being a Saga of the Economic Development Administration as Told by Two Sympathetic Observers Who Seek to Build Morals on a Foundation of Ruined Hopes.* Berkeley, CA: University of California Press.

Pugh, S. Douglas, Markus Groth, and Thorsten Hennig-Thurau. 2011. "Willing and Able to Fake Emotions: A Closer Examination of the Link Between Emotional Dissonance and Employee Well-Being." *Journal of Applied Psychology* 96 (2): 377–90. https://doi.org/10.1037/a0021395.

Ramos, Juan. 2018. "How Many Countries Are in North America?" *Science Trends.* Accessed October 8, 2018 at https://sciencetrends.com/heres-many-countries-north-america/.

Rohr, John A. 1986. *To Run a Constitution: The Legitimacy of the Administrative State.* Lawrence, KS: University Press of Kansas.

Schneider, Anne, and Helen Ingram. 1993. "Social Construction of Target Populations: Implications for Politics and Policy." *The American Political Science Review* 87 (2): 334–47. https://doi.org/10.2307/2939044.

Schneider, Anne, Helen Ingram, and Peter DeLeon. 2014. "Democratic Policy Design: Social Construction of Target Populations." In *Theories of the Policy Process,* 3rd ed., edited by Paul A. Sabatier and Christopher M. Weible, 105–50. New York, NY: Westview Press.

Schreiber, James B., Amaury Nora, Frances K. Stage, Elizabeth A. Barlow, and Jamie King. 2006. "Reporting Structural Equation Modeling and Confirmatory Factor Analysis Results: A Review." *The Journal of Educational Research* 99 (6): 323–37.

Shafritz, Jay M., and Albert C. Hyde. 2012. *Classics of Public Administration.* 7th ed. Boston, MA: Wadsworth Cengage Learning.

Simon, Herbert A. 1950. *Public Administration.* New York, NY: Knopf.

Stillman, Richard J. 2010. "The Study of Public Administration in the United States: The Eminently Practical Science." In *Public Administration, Concepts and Cases,*9th ed., edited by Richard J. Stillman, 17–29. Boston, MA: Wadsworth Cengage Learning.

Stivers, Camilla. 2000. *Bureau Men, Settlement Women: Constructing Public Administration in the Progressive Era*: Lawrence, KS: University Press of Kansas.

Taylor, Frederick Winslow. 1912/2017. "Scientific Management." In *Classics of Public Administration,* 8th ed., edited by Jay Shafritz and Al Hyde, 56–58. Boston, MA: Wadsworth Cengage Learning.

United States Census Bureau. 2019. *U.S. and World Population Clock.* Accessed April 5, 2019 at https://www.census.gov/popclock/.

U.S. Constitution. Accessed April 5, 2019 at https://www.archives.gov/founding-docs/constitution-transcript, updated December 7, 2018.

Waldo, Dwight. 1955. *The Study of Public Administration.* New York, NY: Random House.

Waldo, Dwight. 1968. "Public Administration." *The Journal of Politics* 30 (2): 443–79. https://doi.org/10.2307/2128449.

Weber, Max. 1922/2017. "Bureaucracy." In *Classics of Public Administration,* 8th ed., edited by J. Shafritz and Al Hyde, 63–67. Boston, MA: Wadsworth Cengage Learning.

White, Leonard Dupee. 1955. *Introduction to the Study of Public Administration.* 4th ed. New York, NY: Macmillan.

Wilson, Woodrow. 1887. "The Study of Administration." *Political Science Quarterly* 2 (2): 197–222.

Wilson, Woodrow. 1889. *The State: Elements of Historical and Practical Politics.* Boston, MA: D. C. Heath.

Yang, Seung-Bum, Mary E. Guy, Aisha Azhar, Chih-Wei Hsieh, Hyun Jung Lee, Xiaojun Lu, and Sharon H. Mastracci. 2018. "Comparing Apples and Manzanas: Instrument Development and Measurement Invariance in a Cross-National Analysis of Emotional Labor in Public Service Jobs." *International Journal of Work Organization and Emotion* 9 (3): 264–82. https://doi.org/10.1504/IJWOE.2018.10015953.

21

Looking for Patterns Across Nations

Mary E. Guy, Sharon H. Mastracci and Seung-Bum Yang

While a century of scholarship in public administration has probed policy process and analysis, implementation and management, institutions, principals and agents, and human, financial, and information resources, readers are left to fill in the blank for what public service *feels* like in terms of everyday experience. The preference for cognition over emotion has produced a tranche of research into tangible, measurable components, to the exclusion of those elements that build job satisfaction, meaningfulness, rapport between citizen and state, and the sparkle that reinforces public service motivation. The data presented in these chapters open the door to a deeper appreciation of how the heart and the head strive to be in harmony in the pursuit of public purposes.

Like turning a prism, comparisons in this chapter are made in three ways, with each shedding light differently on the nations. First, a summary across

M. E. Guy (✉)
School of Public Affairs, University of Colorado Denver, Denver, CO, USA
e-mail: mary.guy@ucdenver.edu

S. H. Mastracci
Department of Political Science,
University of Utah, Salt Lake City, UT, USA
e-mail: sharon.mastracci@poli-sci.utah.edu

S.-B. Yang
Department of Public Administration, Konkuk University, Seoul, South Korea
e-mail: sbyang@konkuk.ac.kr

© The Author(s) 2019
M. E. Guy et al. (eds.), *The Palgrave Handbook of Global Perspectives on Emotional Labor in Public Service*, https://doi.org/10.1007/978-3-030-24823-9_21

nations is provided, which shows overall patterns. Second, bar charts visually contrast path coefficients in each nation, showing the relationship between emotional labor variables and job outcomes. Third, the nations included in this study are compared to Hofstede's categorization of them. This comparison demonstrates the non-linear nature of national characteristics, although this is an arguable point. Finally, the chapter draws conclusions about what the data reveal in regard to how the performance of emotional labor is affected by national culture.

Overall Comparison

The public servants who participated in this survey work in a vast array of policy fields, from education to transportation to social services to public works. Regardless of their occupation, they are highly educated, as evidenced by the fact that over half of the respondents in ten out of the twelve countries surveyed hold at least a bachelor's degree. This demonstrates that public service is largely knowledge work, but it is obvious from the findings that public service is also emotion work.

The analyses in each country used three emotional labor variables. The first, emotive capacity, focuses on the individual's self-reported ability to deal with emotional issues in terms of managing their own emotions, managing the emotional state of the other person, and expressing how they feel. In other words, it is the ability to perform emotional labor. There are three items in the *Emotive Capacity* variable:

- I am good at expressing how I feel
- I am good at getting people to calm down
- In my job I am good at dealing with emotional issues.

The second dimension of emotional labor pertains to how respondents deal with suppressing how they actually feel in order to display a "work appropriate" emotion. There are three items in the *Pretending Expression* variable:

- I hide my true feelings so as to appear pleasant at work
- In my job I act confident and self-assured regardless of how I actually feel
- I wear a "mask" in order to deal with clients/customers in an appropriate way.

The third emotional labor dimension focuses on the authentic expression of emotion in work settings. The three items in the *Deep Acting* variable are:

- I try to actually experience the emotions that I must show to clients/customers
- I work hard to actually feel the emotions that I need to show to clients/customers
- I work at developing the feelings inside of me that I need to show to clients/customers.

There were three variables used to measure outcomes: job satisfaction, burnout, and personal fulfillment. The first, job satisfaction, targets how workers feel about their employment. There are four items used to measure *Job Satisfaction* and they include:

- My job provides career development and promotion opportunities
- I feel I am being paid a fair amount for the work I do
- I feel satisfied with my supervisor
- Overall, I am satisfied with my job.

Burnout results from emotional exhaustion. It is used as a variable that captures the downside of emotional labor and was measured by three items:

- I leave work feeling tired and run down
- I leave work feeling emotionally exhausted
- I feel "used up" at the end of the workday.

The third dependent variable focuses on the upside of emotional labor, that is, the positive feelings that come with performing work that is meaningful. Called *Personal Fulfillment,* three items were used to measure it:

- I gain a strong sense of personal fulfillment at my job
- I feel like my job is something I want to do rather than something I have to do
- My work is a source of personal meaning in my life.

Table 21.1 displays statistically significant positive and negative relationships between emotional labor variables and outcomes in the nations surveyed, as measured by the path coefficients that are provided in each chapter. Only the presence or absence of significant relationships and their direction are noted in the table. This is because we readily concede that coefficients give the illusion of precision when, in fact, it is more accurate to treat them only as useful indicators, especially in exploratory work of a global nature

Table 21.1 Significant SEM paths between emotional labor and job outcomes

	[a]Australia	Bolivia	China	India	Korea	Pakistan	Philippines	Rwanda	Taiwan	Thailand	UK	USA
Emotive capacity → Job satisfaction	+		+	+	+	+	+		+	+	+	
Emotive capacity → Burnout				−			−		−	−		
Emotive capacity → Fulfillment		+	+	+	+	+	+	+	+	+	+	+
Pretending → Job satisfaction		−							−		−	−
Pretending → Burnout	+	+			+				+		+	+
Pretending → Fulfillment		−							−		−	−
Deep acting → Job satisfaction	+	+			+	+						+
Deep acting → Burnout	−		−			+	+	+		+		
Deep acting → Fulfillment	+	+	+		+	+		+				+

Path significance $p \leq 0.05$

[a]The Australian model has alternative model specification (no covariance path) so direct path comparison is cautioned in this table and in Figs. 21.1–21.9

such as this is. A table that serves as a windsock, if you will, is more enduring than one that purports to capture exactness.

The findings are notable. First, there is only one relationship—Deep Acting and Burnout—that changes signs across countries. It is inverse in Australia and China and either nonsignificant or positive in the other nations. Across all other relationships, the direction of the relationship is uniform across countries. Second, the relationship between emotive capacity and feelings of personal fulfillment is the most consistent positive finding across all countries. Only in Australia does it fail to achieve significance. Third, the relationship between emotive capacity and job satisfaction is a close runner-up, showing a positive relationship in every country except Bolivia, Rwanda, and the USA.

The fact that the relationship between emotive capacity and burnout is negative in four countries and not positive in any is also a telling finding. It indicates that emotive capacity is a potent indicator of the power of emotive skills to forestall emotional exhaustion and the burnout that can result from it. Put another way, it speaks to the importance of emotional labor for public service workers, for both its upside of contributing to job satisfaction and feelings of personal fulfillment from the job they perform, as well as the healthful effect of emotive capacity in preventing the emotional exhaustion that leads to burnout. This means that public service professionals who assert that they are good at articulating their emotional state, good at managing the emotional state of others, and generally comfortable dealing with emotional issues are more likely to achieve job satisfaction and feelings of fulfillment from their work and are less likely to suffer burnout.

The positive relationship between emotive pretending and burnout in half the nations is dramatic because it shows the deleterious effect of having to suppress how one actually feels in order to perform the job. At the same time, it is interesting to note that the relationship does not appear in the other half of the nations. It is also interesting to note, although the positive relationship occurs in individualist nations, it also appears in some collectivist nations. This suggests that culture, alone, stops short of explaining the fullness of work performance. The chapters that detail findings for each of these nations speak in more detail about citizens' attitudes toward government and the dynamics that help to explain these results.

A notable commonality revealed by the table is in the relationship between pretending and both job satisfaction and fulfillment. In these cases, there is a statistically significant negative relationship in four countries and a positive relationship in none. In contrast to the uniformity of positive findings for emotive capacity as it relates to job satisfaction and fulfillment, the negative finding in four and the absence of a relationship in the other countries are a harbinger of the deleterious effect that emotive pretending presents. As with other findings, this result is not specific to collectivist versus individualist cultures or for global north versus global south.

The third set of emotional labor relationships targets how authentic emotive expression relates to job satisfaction and feelings of personal fulfillment and how it affects burnout. As the table shows, there is a positive relationship with job satisfaction in five nations, with fulfillment in seven, and there is a negative relationship in none. This is not the case with burnout, which produces mixed results in terms of how authentic emotive expression relates to it. In two countries, there is an inverse relationship, in four countries there is a positive relationship, and in six countries no relationship rises to significance. Again, readers will find explanations for each country's findings in the respective chapters, where descriptions of the culture, political environment, and attitudes toward government shed light on the dynamics that surround public service delivery.

Another way to compare commonalities and differences across nations is by graphing path coefficients for the relationships between emotional labor and job outcomes. The visual representation in Figs. 21.1 through 21.9 shows the commonalities and differences between nations. Coefficients

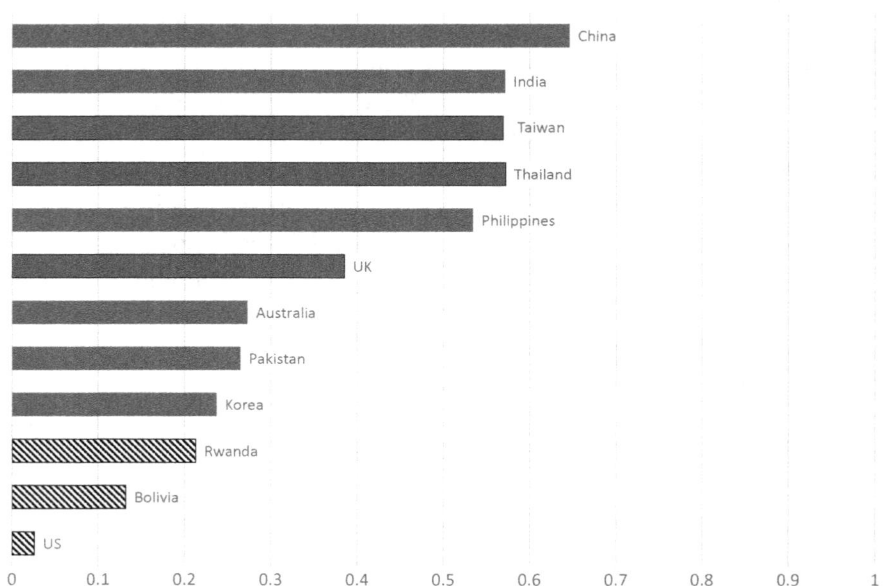

Fig. 21.1 Emotive capacity to job satisfaction

indicate the strength of the relationship. Solid bars denote statistically significant relationships ($p \leq 0.05$), and hash-marked bars denote non-significant relationships. Bars that extend to the right of 0 indicate positive strength and those that extend to the left of 0 indicate negative strengths. To begin, we examine emotive capacity.

Emotive Capacity

Figure 21.1 compares the path coefficients between emotive capacity and job satisfaction. It shows that the relationship is positive in all countries and it is statistically significant everywhere except Rwanda, Bolivia, and the USA. One should use caution in assuming that a shorter bar for one country than another denotes substantive meaning. Due to issues of measurement variance that may be occurring between China and India, for example, the variation may be more indicative of linguistic nuances or response biases than of substantive differences. Nevertheless, the bar chart visually shows the common direction of the relationship.

The next graph shows the relationship between emotive capacity and burnout. It reveals a dramatic difference compared to the relationship with

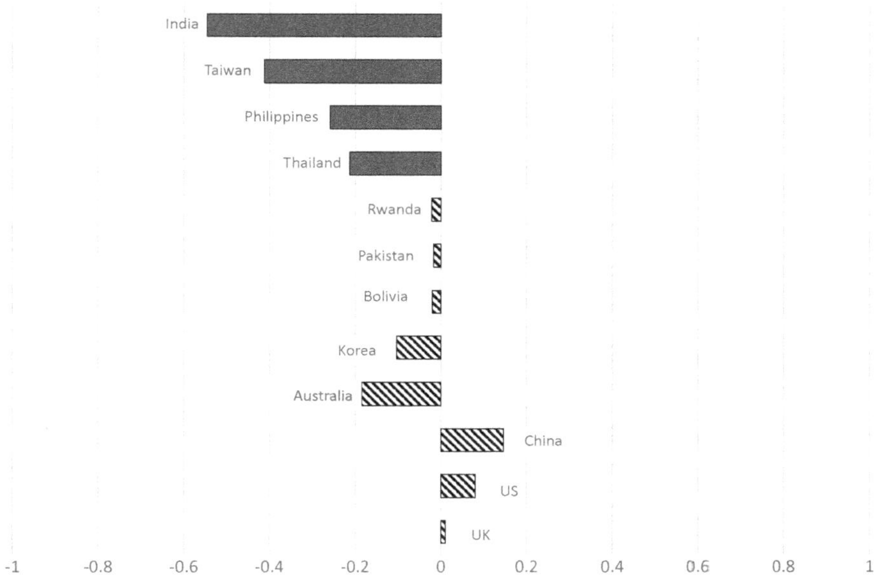

Fig. 21.2 Emotive capacity to burnout

job satisfaction. In fact, Fig. 21.2 shows that there are only four countries where the relationship is significant: India, Taiwan, the Philippines, and Thailand. In each of these, it is inverse, such that the higher that public servants' emotive capacity is, the less likely they are to suffer burnout. In the other eight countries, the relationship varies between positive and negative and does not reach significance.

The third relationship for emotive capacity is with fulfillment. This relationship, shown in Fig. 21.3, is similar to that which is pictured in Fig. 21.1. There is a significant, positive relationship in eleven countries, which means that the higher one's emotive capacity is, the more personal fulfillment workers experience. Only in Australia is the relationship nonsignificant. As pointed out in the discussion in Chapter 9, the degree to which Australians trust government is "complicated." It is possible that Australian public servants protect themselves by not dealing with emotional issues on the job, not expressing how they feel, and not focusing on or managing how citizens feel. This resulting relationship—more accurately, lack of relationship—hearkens back to the discussion in Chapter 7 about mistreatment, either on the part of the employer toward the employee, or on the part of citizens toward public servants. There are two, if not three, sides in every public service exchange: the public servant acting as an agent of the state, the citizen

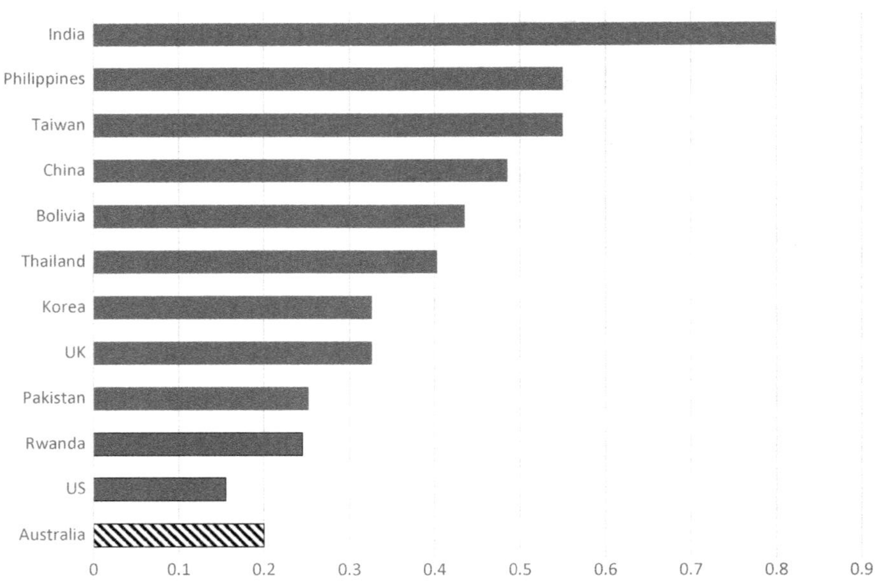

Fig. 21.3 Emotive capacity to personal fulfillment

engaging with the state, and the employing agency. As these data show, in Australia, the interaction among these is not in synchrony.

Unlike the charts for emotive capacity, those that reflect how emotive pretending affects workers show a quite different effect, with many fewer significant relationships.

Emotive Pretending

The first relationship to examine is between pretending and job satisfaction. Pictured in Fig. 21.4, in no country is there a significant, positive, relationship. In four countries—USA, UK, Taiwan, and Bolivia—the relationship is significant and negative and in the others, it does not rise to significance. In other words, in the USA, UK, Taiwan, and Bolivia, the more that workers suppress how they honestly feel in order to display a job appropriate emotion, the more likely they are to experience less job satisfaction. Interestingly, two of these nations are individualist and two are collectivist.

Just as emotive pretending has an inverse relationship to job satisfaction in four countries, it has a positive relationship with burnout in six. Figure 21.5 shows that the three individualist nations, USA, UK, and Australia, show significant relationships to burnout, but so, also, do Bolivia,

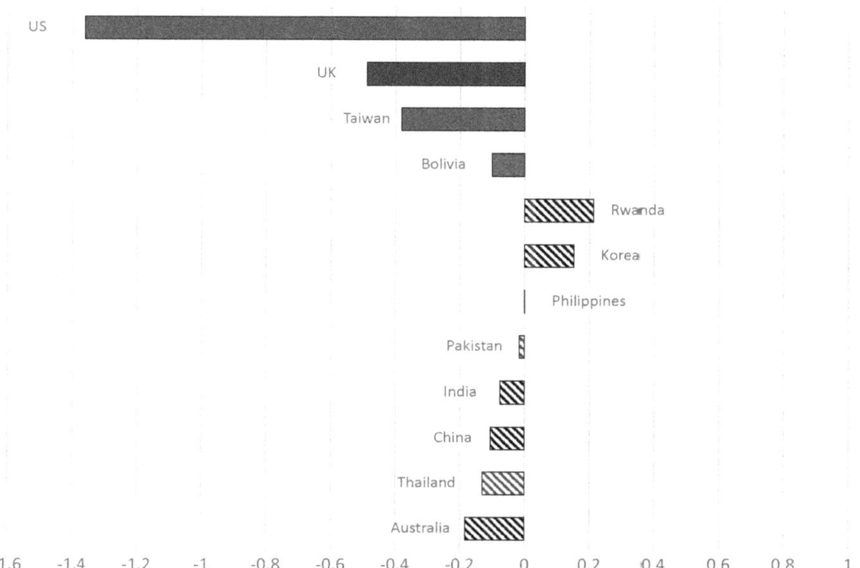

Fig. 21.4 Pretending expression to job satisfaction

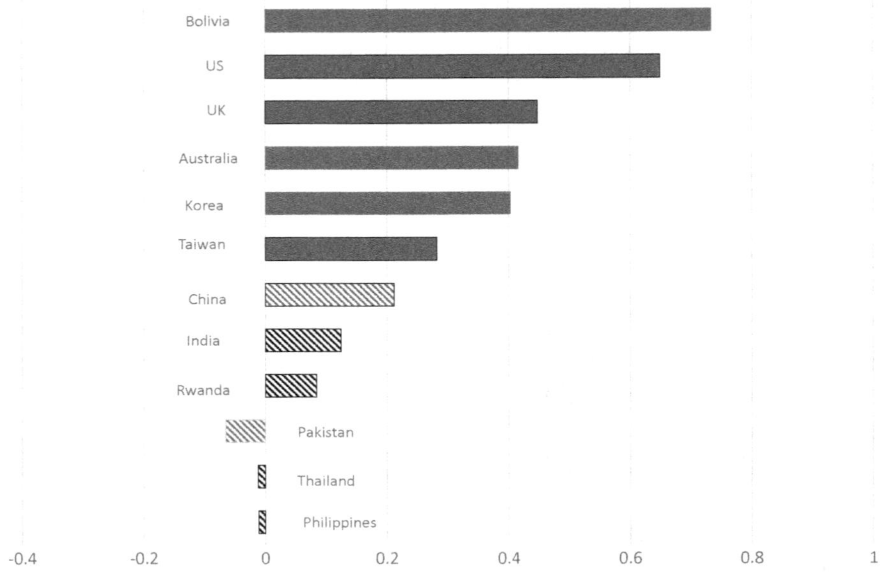

Fig. 21.5   Pretending expression to burnout

Korea, and Taiwan. Half of the nations, however, do not show a significant relationship. As explained in chapters about each of these nations, the personal "price" of emotive pretending is lower in some cultures than others.

The third perspective on the effect of emotive pretending is made possible by looking at its relationship to feelings of personal fulfillment that derive from one's work performance. Figure 21.6 shows how this varies across nations. A quick glance shows that the same countries that produce a significant negative relationship between pretending and job satisfaction also yield a negative relationship with fulfillment. In the other nations, just as in Fig. 21.4, there is not a significant relationship. The USA shows the most extreme effect, but other than that, the presence of a relationship does not draw distinctions between individualist and collectivist societies. The USA's extreme individualism accounts for its score, but it is noteworthy that the strength of the relationship is markedly weaker in the UK and absent in Australia. In other words, once again, the idiosyncrasies of national context, culture, and exigencies of public service delivery combine in a way that demonstrates the disparate effects of emotive pretending around the globe.

The third perspective on how emotional labor affects job satisfaction, burnout, and feelings of personal fulfillment is through the lens of authentic emotive expression, and discussion turns now to that.

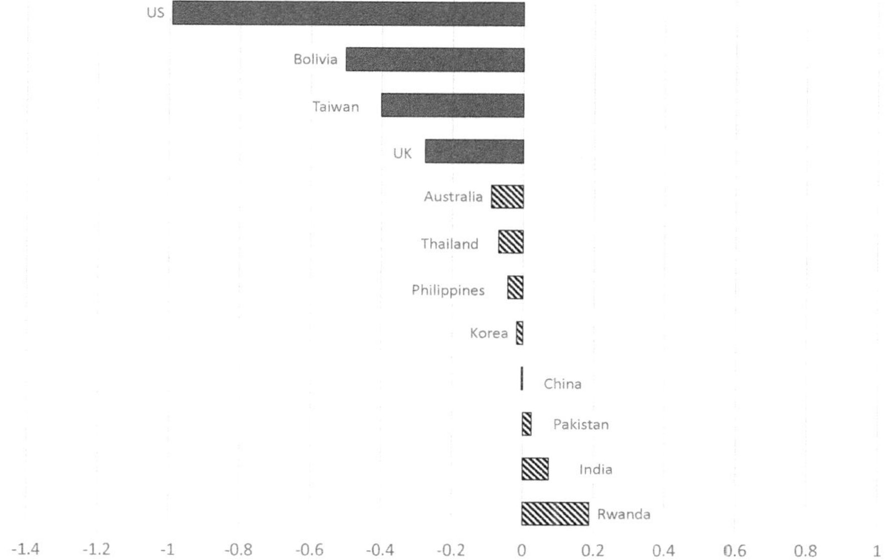

Fig. 21.6 Pretending expression to personal fulfillment

Deep Acting

Deep acting, the authentic expression of felt emotion, is an aspect of emotional labor that is positively impactful in Bolivia, the USA, Australia, Pakistan, and Korea, as shown in Fig. 21.7. In these countries, the more one engages in deep acting, the higher one's job satisfaction is. In other countries, the relationship does not reach statistical significance. These disparate outcomes to the same emotive performance demonstrate the power of context to affect the experience of emotional labor. The behavior, and the feeling, assumes different meanings in different countries. As more public service professionals travel around the globe, it is wise to be sensitive to how differently the same emotion work may be perceived.

As shown in Fig. 21.8, the relationship between deep acting and burnout has widely different effects. In Thailand, the Philippines, Rwanda, and Pakistan, it has a positive effect on burnout, which means that it is problematic from a human resource management perspective. Practitioners are more likely to experience emotional exhaustion, lower morale, and higher turnover when their jobs require it. On the other hand, in China and Australia, deep acting has the opposite effect in that it reduces burnout.

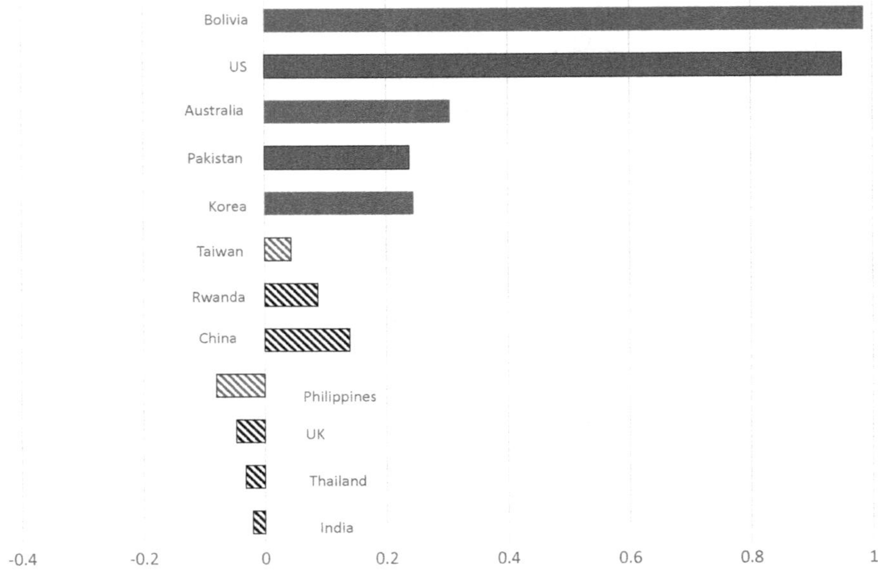

Fig. 21.7   Deep acting to job satisfaction

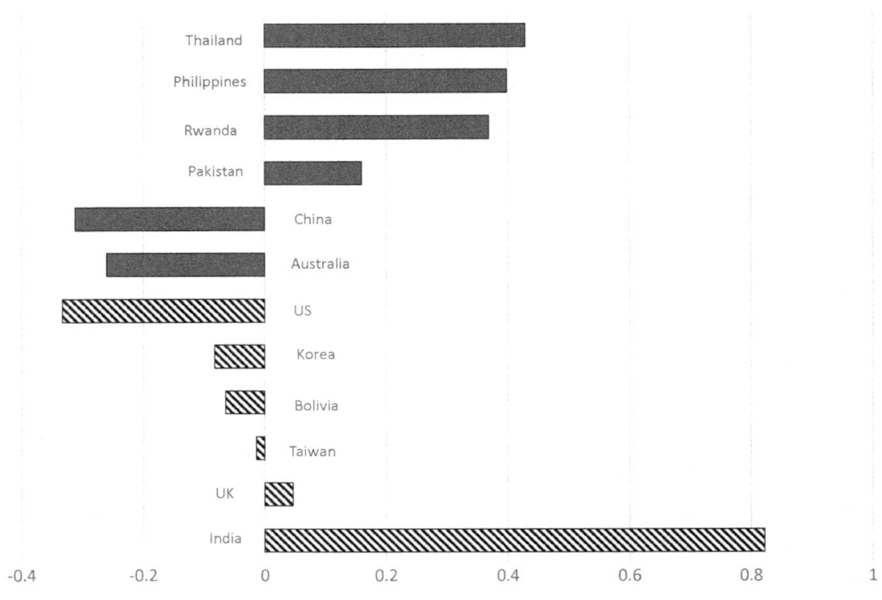

Fig. 21.8   Deep acting to burnout

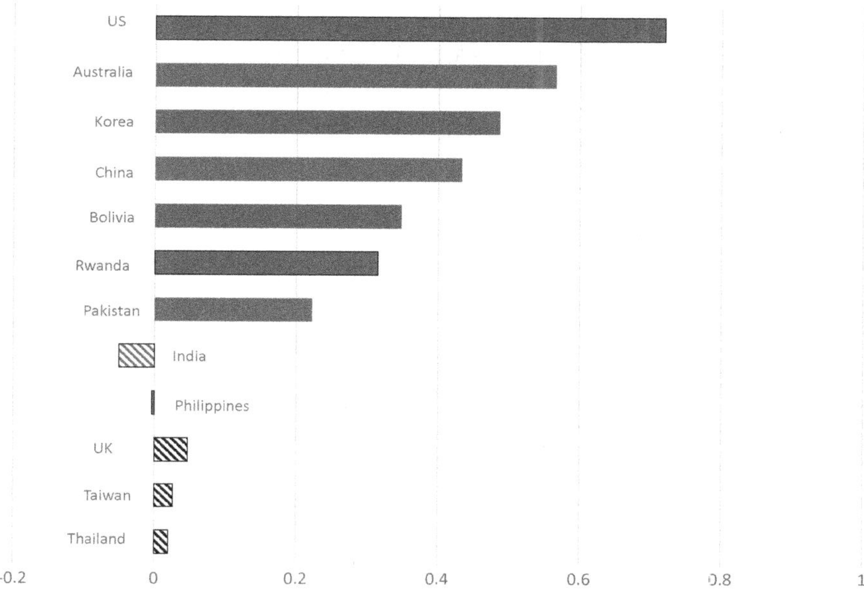

Fig. 21.9 Deep acting to personal fulfillment

Again, the contrast between the effects of the same work performance in different nations demonstrates the behavioral impact of emotional labor. It is work that is taken for granted in most settings but has significant effects on the work environment and the citizen-state encounter.

The third graph, Fig. 21.9, shows the effect of deep acting on feelings of personal fulfillment. It has a positive effect in seven countries and a non-significant effect in the other five nations. This effect is similar, although not in as many countries, as the relationship between emotive capacity and fulfillment.

The comparisons displayed in Figs. 21.1 through 21.9 beg for further consideration in a number of respects. For example, in terms of geographic proximity, ease of travel, and a common language, one would expect China and Taiwan to be more similar than they are. That which differentiates them is not culture, for they are both rooted in Confucianism. One is left to conclude that political dynamics and government—its role and citizens' views of governmental actors—account for the difference. Similarly, one could reasonably expect that there would be more similarity among all collectivist cultures and yet that is not the case, just as there is not as much similarity as one might expect among the individualist nations of USA, UK, and Australia.

The factors that shape and sculpt the emotive component in the citizen-state encounter appear to be an eclectic mix of social and political culture plus the exigencies of current events. For example, the hostility that Australian public servants experience from citizens is reflected in reactions to emotional labor that differ from that in the UK. And, the similar histories of India and Pakistan would seem to produce more similar results than what actually appears. With the same history of having been colonized by England, they have inherited similar bureaucratic systems but now experience them differently. Now, it is religious values that seem to distinguish the countries. Bolivia identifies as a collectivist nation but the relationships between variables are the same as in the USA, the most extreme of individualist nations. Rwanda's history, in which public servants are struggling to rebuild a nation from the ground up, imbues public service delivery with a tone quite different from that of most other nations. The relationship between deep acting and fulfillment as well as with burnout reflects the vigor of a government committed to its work and experiencing emotional exhaustion because of it. One is left to ponder these findings, some of which are intuitive and some of which are counterintuitive.

Another way to understand results is to review the countries in terms of how they are categorized by other authors on dimensions that may provide hints about how public servants do their work. One such dimension relates to whether a culture is "tight" or "loose." Discussion turns now to this avenue of investigation.

Emotional Labor Outcomes vis-a-vis Tight Versus Loose Cultures

Valuing both the emotive <u>and</u> the cognitive is at the vanguard of effective public service and citizen engagement. Citizens must *feel* good about government just as public servants must *care*. Thus, the emotive component is coming into focus, although it takes irregular shapes. This should not come as a surprise. In fact, it is parallel to the work of Michele Gelfand (2018) as she categorized nations according to whether they are "rule makers" or "rule breakers." Using social norms as her focus for categorization, she argued that they are the glue that holds people together, and that the nature of the glue varies by nation.

Social norms shape and sculpt the type of emotional labor that is performed and the effect it has on public servants. For instance, Gelfand (2018) differentiated cultures according to how closely they followed the rules that are established by social norms. She then extrapolates characteristics that are likely to be found in various cultures, noting that there are not linear relationships between tightness versus looseness and economic success, nor between individualism versus collectivism and a variety of sequelae. In fact, there are both loose and tight collectivist cultures as well as loose and tight individualist cultures. In other words, social norms shape behavior within nations in idiosyncratic ways that do not necessarily affect how the nation's economy functions or how the nation's psyche performs.

Gelfand's discussion is consistent with the emotional labor findings summarized above but stops short of having predictive power. Seven of the thirty-three nations that she categorized are also included in this study: the USA, UK, Australia, China, South Korea, India, and Pakistan. She categorizes the USA and Australia as being on the loose end of the continuum while Pakistan anchors the far extreme, being the most stringent of all the nations she rates in terms of following rules. India and South Korea are near Pakistan on the "tight" end of the continuum, and China and the UK approach the mid-range. As Table 21.1 shows, Pakistan, India, and Korea vary in their results just as China and the UK vary. In other words, one template for finding commonalities among nations is only useful for examining one characteristic.

There are as many ways to categorize cultures as there are adjectives available. Similarities can be identified, as well as contrasts. The challenge is to use the categorization that advances understanding of how public service delivery is performed. Trying to associate one set of characteristics with another defies alignment. Tight versus loose cultures is not a meaningful way to draw conclusions about how the emotive component in public service work is experienced or performed.

Another way to categorize national culture is by following the protocol devised by Hofstede et al. (2010). Although intuitively promising, it too has shortcomings, as the comparison below reveals.

Unlikely Cohorts

Regardless of the characteristics analyzed, commonalities among countries are sometimes as anticipated and sometimes counterintuitive. It is not surprising that there is as much variability across countries within a region as there is. Similar variability was found by Hofstede et al. (2010) when investigating cultural traits. For example, Table 21.2 categorizes countries surveyed in this study according to the scores that Hofstede, et al. assigned to

Table 21.2 Countries in this study categorized on Hofstede et al.'s continua

	Power distance[a]	Individualism/ collectivism[b]	Masculine/ feminine[c]	Uncertainty avoidance[d]	Short vs long term orientation[e]	Indulgence vs restraint[f]
75–100	China India Philippines	Australia UK USA		South Korea	China South Korea Taiwan	
50–74	Pakistan South Korea Taiwan Thailand		Australia China India Pakistan Philippines UK USA	Australia Pakistan Taiwan Thailand	India Pakistan UK	Australia UK USA
25–49	Australia UK USA	India Philippines	South Korea Taiwan Thailand	China India Philippines UK USA	Philippines Thailand USA	India Philippines Rwanda South Korea Taiwan Thailand
0–24		China Pakistan South Korea Taiwan Thailand			Australia Rwanda	China Pakistan

[a]*Power distance*: the greater the power distance, the greater the degree of inequality based on age, social status, authority. 0=small power distance; 100=large power distance (Hofstede et al. 2010, 56). [b]*Individualism vs collectivism*: degree to which the interest of the group prevails over the interest of the individual. 0=most collectivist; 100=most individualist (Hofstede et al. 2010, 94). [c]*Masculinity/femininity*: assertiveness, toughness, material success vs modesty, tenderness, concern for quality of life. 0=most feminine, 100=most masculine (Hofstede et al. 2010, 140). [d]*Uncertainty avoidance*: extent to which people feel threatened by ambiguous or unknown situations. 0=weakest uncertainty avoidance, 100=strongest uncertainty avoidance (Hofstede et al. 2010, 191). [e]*Short vs long term orientation*: long term orientation stands for fostering virtues oriented toward future rewards, such as perseverance and thrift. Short-term orientation stands for fostering virtues related to past or present, for example, respect for tradition, fulfilling social obligations, preservation of "face." 0=short term, 100=long term (Hofstede et al. 2010, 239). [f]*Indulgence vs restraint*: Indulgence stands for a tendency to allow relatively free gratification of natural human desires related to enjoying life. Restraint stands for a conviction that such gratification needs to be curbed and regulated by strict norms. 0=most restrained, 100=most indulgent (Hofstede et al. 2010, 281)

them in their study of power distance, individualism versus collectivism, masculinity versus femininity, uncertainty avoidance, short term versus long term orientation, and indulgence versus restraint. (Because Hofstede, et al. did not analyze Bolivia, it is missing from this table and they analyzed Rwanda on only two of the continua).

As the table makes obvious, there are some characteristics, such as power distance and indulgence versus restraint, where Western nations cohere. But, there are also characteristics such as uncertainty avoidance where west and east are as likely to be similar as different. Such is also the case with short- versus long-term orientation.

The categorizations of nations in the table are interesting and to a large degree intuitive based on stereotypes, but many do not comport with the commonalities and differences displayed in Table 21.1. In other words, such broad-ranging categories capture impressions but they fail to capture how public service professionals perform the emotive component of their work. Only somewhat tongue-in-cheek, comparativists assert that culture explains everything and culture explains nothing. Similarly, that is the case here, just as it is the case in so many other comparative studies.

It is tempting to be dismissive of culture as we explain the unique findings of how emotional labor is experienced in public service jobs around the globe. As dissimilar as political traditions are, commonalities arise across all countries. As similar as individualist countries are, some have more in common with collectivist cultures. As much as Confucian cultures share values, there are distinct differences in how emotive pretending is experienced. All this is to say that each nation's culture, dynamics, traditions, political exigencies, and global interconnectedness intertwine, producing unique blends of emotional labor outcomes.

Another way to examine this quandary is by focusing on individual characteristics in the context of culture. Discussion turns now to the Big Five personality traits to learn what they reveal.

Big Five Personality Traits and Emotional Labor

National culture shapes behavior as well as the interpretations of behavior. As demonstrated in Chapter 4, there is significant variation across countries in terms of the Big Five personality traits and how emotional labor is experienced. And, there is significant variation in how emotional intelligence relates to the performance of emotional labor. The findings in this handbook indicate that national context exerts influences above and beyond that which is expected from traditional theories of personality and emotional intelligence, especially when psychological theories are considered without regard to cultural context.

Although personality traits and emotional intelligence are foundational qualities that enable the performance of emotional labor, analyses in these chapters demonstrate that national context sculpts its performance in important ways. Context is shaped not only by culture and political dynamics, but also by organizational characteristics of where the practitioner works, as Chapter 5 explains. The link between emotional labor and its consequences is embedded in a scaffold provided by the organizational setting, where there is an emotion climate that guides performance and its consequences, both positive and negative. Organizational display rules, job characteristics, group dynamics, and the emotion climate within workgroups contribute to how individual emotive performance occurs.

To complicate matters further, it is not only the internal environment of the organization that affects behavior; the external environment does as well. Take the case of Rwanda, for example. In that country, as if in superposition, emotional labor is fulfilling at the same time that it contributes to burnout. What would seem to be incompatible experiences, in fact, are not. Workers must deal simultaneously with mutually exclusive feelings. This is the conundrum that emotional labor presents to workers and to managers who are intent on motivating workers. As Mandell et al. (2013) demonstrated with child welfare workers, it is possible for employees to experience emotional exhaustion and job satisfaction simultaneously. The deciding factor is the commitment that they have to the mission of their work, the belief that they are making a positive difference in people's lives, and the sensitivity they have for the needs of others.

Public perceptions of the organization and its mission influence workers' emotive responses on the job. But these shaping forces do not stop with culture and organizational context. As demonstrated in Chapter 7, the political climate within a country affects the process and outcome of public service encounters. Situational dynamics of the worker-citizen interaction have consequences because they affect workers' view of their own ability to perform and their trust in citizens. This is most notably the case when public servants are treated abusively by citizens. Although there are variations between countries, overall findings show that workers have lower job satisfaction, less trust in citizens, and feel less capable of managing the emotive aspects of their jobs when the citizens they serve are disrespectful. In other words, the emotive burden of the job becomes heavier when citizens are distrustful and disrespectful and this is why political dynamics matter.

Culture and Emotional Labor

Geo-political boundaries are more a fiction than are the cultural, political, organizational, and individual, drivers that shape behavior. But because these constellations of characteristics roughly approximate such boundaries, nation-states become the way of identifying common characteristics. Chapter 6 illuminates the impact that cultural scholarship can have on comparative studies. Informing specific dimensions of emotional labor, it provides a guide for researchers in several ways. First, it is helpful for those who conduct emotional labor research outside their cultural background. Second, it is instructive for those who wish to contrast emotional labor findings between differing cultures. For example, while emotionality and rationality are conceptualized as dichotomous in individualist cultures, they are understood to be continuous processes in eastern cultures. The Chinese expression, "thoughts are felt in the heart" (Young 1994, 118), captures this unity. It is an expression that will not be encountered in Western cultures where thought and emotion are thought to be distinctly different and where it is believed that emotion distracts from cognition.

In collectivist countries, at least to some degree, negative emotions are suppressed in order to maintain harmony, which is seen as a greater good than individual expression. In this case, what might otherwise be viewed as a negative consequence in individualist cultures may be experienced as a positive. This may explain why emotive displays that require pretending do not increase burnout in China and Thailand but they do in the USA and UK.

As tempting as it is to categorize groups of nations into collectivist versus individualist frames, there is not a unitary collectivism or a unitary individualism. For example, in the case above, where emotive pretending increases burnout in the USA and UK, it also increases burnout in Taiwan and South Korea. Simply put, cultures are complex and result from the unique blend of forces that shape each nation-state. There is not a single cultural history of East Asia, for instance (Nakamura 1964). Instead, there is a fascinating diversity of human nature, sculpted by the context of each nation, with more commonalities among nations than one might expect, as well as more differences. For example, one could argue that Taiwan and China would be extraordinarily similar, but as shown in Table 21.1, there are more differences than similarities. For those countries colonized by a culture different from their own, such as Pakistan and India, or the Philippines, the resulting effect is an assimilation of some features while others are discarded. Now these countries are attempting to transform their bureaucracies in ways that hold on to the colonial elements that work for them, while jettisoning the elements that diverge from their own cultural traditions.

Another consideration to take into account when characterizing culture's effect on emotional labor is the role of language. The linguistics of emotion vary from country to country and imbue emotion work with positives and negatives. For example, the English language has far fewer words that capture the emotive exchange and communication between persons than do many Asian languages. Cultures elevate or dismiss emotion and this has an effect on how emotional labor is acknowledged or overlooked in language as well as in the workplace. Political cultures vary in how citizens expect to be treated and whether public service professionals expect to be treated deferentially or to be challenged.

Conclusion

What is one to make of such findings? In this age of global communication, intertwined economies, easy travel, and homogenized tastes, significant differences appear between nations. And in this age of heightened sensitivity to cultural differences, significant commonalities are apparent between nations. While countries are similar in some regards, they differ in others. Neighboring nations, such as Taiwan and China, differ more than one would expect. Distant nations, such as the USA and Australia, are similar but not identical. Bolivia is strikingly similar to the USA but its culture, language, and mores are very different.

Perhaps the best way to think about this is that, foremost, emotional labor is real. It is an easily understood concept that can be surveyed around the world. There may be issues of linguistics that affect how emotion is understood in different cultures and may cause survey items to assume elusively subtle meanings in different contexts, but the nature of its performance can be queried with a series of questions. Emotional labor is a dyadic performance, involving the public service professional and the citizen. Wrapped around this performance is a constellation of attitudes and expectations about compliance, deference, power, help, and support. Emotional labor is performed in most jobs, from police officers to food inspectors, to big city mayors, to social workers, to soldiers. Regardless of the job, the governmental "wrapping paper" of the exchange significantly affects it.

It is important to remain sensitive to national differences and to the fact that there are peculiarities and there are commonalities. Global public administration is an emerging current within public administration scholarship. As challenges become increasingly global in nature—migration, environmental degradation, and cybersecurity threats—international policy is administered by public servants who rely on both their home cultures as well as the meta-culture of international public administration. "Boundary spanning" employees must balance national differences in both display rules and emotive demands. Emotional labor theory applies equally well regardless of culture, but its effects differ according to a complex blend of national traditions, political culture, citizen demands and expectations, and organizational dynamics. Sensitivity to both differences and commonalities falls on the shoulders of the boundary spanners who work across cultures in this diverse, global environment.

The comparisons in this chapter attempt to summarize the findings that are reported in detail in the chapters. There are subtleties to the findings that elude broad characterization, and for these, the individual chapters should be consulted. For the purpose of extrapolating broad lessons, however, the following four points provide a broad overview.

1. Higher levels of emotive capacity are good predictors of job satisfaction, feelings of personal fulfillment, and the ability to resist burnout.
2. The deleterious effect of having to wear an emotive mask—to suppress how one actually feels in order to display a job appropriate emotion—is more potent in some countries than others, and this is only marginally affected by whether a culture is individualist or collectivist.
3. Emotional labor that is performed authentically has salutary effects in most settings in terms of enhancing job satisfaction and feelings of personal fulfillment.
4. Emotional labor does not have a uniform effect across collectivist countries or individualist countries. Instead, its effects are tempered by each nation's culture, traditions, history, and political dynamics. Its effects are best explained by each nation's narratives about how people are supposed to relate to one another.

References

Gelfand, Michele. 2018. *Rule Makers, Rule Breakers: How Tight and Loose Cultures Wire Our World.* New York, NY: Scribner.

Hofstede, Geert, Gert Jan Hofstede, and Michael Minkov. 2010. *Cultures and Organizations: Software of the Mind.* New York, NY: McGraw-Hill.

Mandell, Deena, Carol Stalker, Margriet de Zeeuw Wright, Karen Frensch, and Cheryl Harvey. 2013. "Sinking, Swimming and Sailing: Experiences of Job Satisfaction and Emotional Exhaustion in Child Welfare Employees." *Child & Family Social Work* 18: 383–93.

Nakamura, Hajime. 1964. *Ways of Thinking of Eastern Peoples: India, China, Tibet, Japan*, revised English translation, edited by Philip P. Wiener. Honolulu, HI: East-West Center Press.

Young, Linda W.L. 1994. *Crosstalk and Culture in Sino-American Communication*. Cambridge, UK: Cambridge University Press.

Part IV

Paradigm Shift: Tectonic or Trivial?

This part is like a prism, using findings and theory as a platform for examining the current state of public administration thinking and practice. As if they were primary colors, contrasting assumptions about the best way to pursue public purposes illuminate different approaches to governing. Regardless of perspective, evidence makes it clear that there is a significant emotive component to public service around the globe. Chapters 22–24 argue for a "white" light—a hybridization—between bureaucratic and collaborative strategies that embrace not only cognitive and physical labor, but one that embraces the triumvirate of labors: physical, cognitive, and emotive. In order to provide holistic public service in this interconnected global environment, the emotive component is essential. The book concludes that there is no better time than now to acknowledge emotional labor and to incorporate it into the canon—to make a tectonic shift in how public administration is theorized, taught, and practiced.

22

From Data Dashboards to Human Hearts

Sharon H. Mastracci and Mary E. Guy

Is the responsibility of government to enhance quality-of-life and ensure safe communities? Is it to facilitate individual self-interest but otherwise get out of the way? Is it to stand by, ready with emergency services should disaster strike, but otherwise stay out of sight? Is it the responsibility of government to promote active citizenship, public discourse, and the public interest? Is government the answer to public problems, or is it part of the problem? These questions are answered differently in the twelve countries surveyed. And the answers are based on what a country hopes to be in the future, what it has been in the past, and how it views its relationship to the citizenry. Whatever the point of view, results across all countries demonstrate that there is an emotive component to the citizen–state encounter. This reflects the human element in governing and it is to this that the chapter urges attention as public administration theory evolves.

S. H. Mastracci (✉)
Department of Political Science, University of Utah, Salt Lake City, UT, USA
e-mail: Sharon.mastracci@poli-sci.utah.edu

M. E. Guy
School of Public Affairs, University of Colorado Denver, Denver, CO, USA
e-mail: mary.guy@ucdenver.edu

M. E. Guy et al. (eds.), *The Palgrave Handbook of Global Perspectives on Emotional Labor in Public Service*, https://doi.org/10.1007/978-3-030-24823-9_22

The discussion in this chapter juxtaposes two approaches to understanding government and its processes. To show the contrast, we use New Public Management (NPM) as a shorthand term to refer to marketized government, where supply and demand dynamics are prized as the mechanism for providing services and keeping costs down. In this frame of reference, efficiency and measurable indicators are prioritized. We use New Public Service (NPS) as shorthand to refer to government initiatives that focus on participatory processes, equity, and responsiveness. These two models involve different ways of thinking about (1) the role of government, (2) whose interests matter, (3) how public purposes are pursued, and (4) what the end goal is. In practice, these two frameworks are not mutually exclusive, nor are either implemented in their totality. Instead, they represent opposing "polarities" that reside on a continuum, with nations being situated somewhere between the extremes. The evidence in these chapters argues for positioning closer to NPS than to NPM.

NPM reforms took hold in the 1980s, and arguments to move away from its extreme focus on cost and efficiency have been a strong undercurrent ever since. Concurrently, the rush to implement marketized government has subsided, as the results have failed to produce the efficiencies promised. Counter-reforms in reaction to NPM's shortcomings have been referred to by a number of names: New Public Administration (NPA) to highlight social equity (Ingraham and Rosenbloom 1989), New Public Governance (NPG) or Collaborative Public Management (CPM) to emphasize collaboration and co-production among coordinated networks of interdependent organizations and sectors (Dickinson 2016; Osborne 2006; Zavattaro 2012), and New Public Service, which is rooted in democratic theory and emphasizes a focus on service, engagement with citizens, shared power, and equity (Denhardt and Denhardt 2000, 2015). Bryson et al. attempt to coin "Public Value Governance" as the preferred term of art among post-NPM competitors but ultimately concede that "the Denhardts' label 'New Public Service' has become the leading contender based on citations" (2014, 452).

Of all NPM critiques, NPS has gained the most traction, which is why we use it as the term that signifies the post-marketization phase for public administration theory. NPS also comes closest to capturing the human element, the emotive basis, of the citizen–state encounter. New Public Administration, New Public Governance, and New Public Service each focus on different aspects of service delivery in their critiques of NPM and each represent backlash to the efficiency focus of market-based reforms of the 1980s and 1990s (Rauh 2018).

Emotional Labor and the Citizen–State Encounter

Our interest lies in the embrace of the citizen–state encounter and in the skills and competencies demanded of public servants in this regard. Emotional labor is baked into the role of the public servant and criticism of NPM highlights this shortcoming. Frequent refrains among critical commentary speak to its lack of attention to service, and its failure to comprehend the importance of boundary spanning, brokering, coordinating, and negotiating with counterparts across organizations and sectors (Needham and Mangan 2014). All of these activities demand face-to-face and/or voice-to-voice interpersonal interactions. Emotionally intelligent public servants are needed to fulfill these demands. And NPS makes the most room for the emotive dimensions of these, even though serving, brokering, coordinating, and negotiating remain largely cognitive constructs. When navigating complex hybrid systems, more relational skills and multiple ways of knowing are required of the workforce (Dickinson 2016).

In contrast to NPM, "New Public Service suggests that public administrators must not only share power, work through people, and broker solutions, they must reconceptualize their role in the governance process as responsible participants, not entrepreneurs" (Denhardt and Denhardt 2000, 557). The emphasis on service requires responsiveness and citizen participation even if at the expense of efficiency. Equity and access tend not to be efficient when efficiency is measured only by short-term, tangible markers. "Instead of focusing on targets and measures, citizen participation is concerned with the redesign of decision processes and the integration of citizens therein" (Kroll et al. 2017, 3).

With its emphasis on co-production, NPM gestured in the direction of increasing the participation of the populace in governance processes, but it is not rooted in democratic theory; it is rooted in cost-shifting. Broader participation is not an objective of market-based reforms. In fact, such reforms embellished pre-existing inequalities between those individuals who already had voice and access and those who lacked both.

Efficiency's basis in market competition means that the better-off constituent has more influence and a louder voice. Market competition creates winners and losers, whether in business or government. A return to effectiveness, participation, and democracy are at the heart of a service-minded frame of reference, even when effectiveness and access can only be achieved at the expense of efficiency. With this as backdrop, discussion turns now to the role and structure of government in different countries, because this highlights contemporary governance and reveals how a focus on service provides a meaningful frame of reference for the work that public servants perform regardless of political system.

Countries in the Study

We start by examining the anglophone countries, Australia, UK, and USA. For the past couple of centuries, Australia was a strong central state providing everything for its populace: police, education, housing, transportation, and energy. Its reforms forty years ago were from a position as a centralized state to one that has devolved responsibilities to regional and local governments in order to operate according to a more federal system. It is against this backdrop that New Public Management (NPM) reforms were implemented there in the 1980s. Today, Americans might still characterize Australia as a strong central state, but that would be in contrast to their own federal system that preserves the sovereignty of sub-national entities. Australia, by contrast, would see itself as a more agile governance structure with greater citizen participation and a robust voluntary sector. Importing the Australian approach to the USA would not guarantee similar results, given their dissimilar administrative histories. Likewise, the generally perceived role of government in each country shapes what its citizens expect and what service delivery is thought acceptable.

Government reforms in Australia and the UK started at about the same time, transforming centralized states to a more devolved public service, although not as sub-nationally focused as the USA is with its long tradition of state-level sovereignty. That they started with a strong central government meant that Australia and the UK "drove" radical transformations. At the same time, the USA desired to rely more on non-governmental entities to deliver many public services, but its "shared powers" system meant that reforms would be more tempered. Regardless, Americans were already more accustomed to market provision of public goods—health care remains a for-profit industry in the USA but nowhere else—while Australians and Brits have implemented regulations that govern market allocation of public goods, such as housing.

Moving from anglophone countries to others, different dynamics are noted. For example, in Bolivia, the Philippines, and Thailand, citizens do not trust government to allocate goods and services effectively, so people try to rely on one another and turn toward government as a last resort.

Histories of cronyism and patronage undermine public trust in government and in the transformative power of reform. In the Philippines and Thailand, reforms have been pursued to shore up public confidence in government.

The ethos of public service in Pakistan and India varies from that in many other countries, more closely reflecting the ideals of New Public Service than New Public Management. But both inherited the sterility of British bureaucratic processes from their colonial history, and now find that the bureaucratic apparatus is highly rule-bound and non-responsive. The challenge for each of these countries is to reform government in its own image, to create a public service that reflects the values of the people, after decades of public service culture imported from elsewhere. To some degree, the Philippines is in a similar circumstance, as it breaks free from the systems put in place by the USA during its occupation.

South Korea and Taiwan are pursuing something of a bipolar model of reform: They seek the efficiencies promised by New Public Management with the service promised by New Public Service. In both countries, service is prioritized but against a backdrop of austerity. Strong family cultures in each country lead citizens to look inward for material needs before turning toward the state.

China and Rwanda are centralized states that symbolize their societies: The former by political design and long history, and the latter by necessity post-civil war. Both Chinese and Rwandan citizens look to the state to provide physical protection, material needs, and identity. Chinese see the role of the state as being reflected in each person's interactions with others; the fate of the individual and the fate of the state are one. The Rwandan practice of *umuganda*—mandatory public service for every able-bodied individual—emphasizes and reifies interdependence. In the wake of civil war and genocide, Rwanda re-established local governments to deliver services along the lines of tenets in New Public Service, which advocate decentralization and broad participation. It is little wonder that neither China nor Rwanda ever attempted NPM-style reforms, for market mechanisms do not allocate identity and a sense of interdependence.

Across the twelve countries highlighted in this study, governing strategies have been implemented with varying levels of success. Like a square peg in a round hole, governing systems employed in colonized countries proved to be poorly suited to their populations. Little wonder that public service systems failed to gain sufficient traction because high-level public servants in colonies were mostly from the colonizing power and not indigenous. Unresponsive Indian civil servants were English, not Indian. Alternatively, if elite government posts were awarded to members of the indigenous population, they were granted to select groups and did not represent the overall population, as in the Philippines. Even in Thailand, which has never been colonized by a Western nation, only upper-class Thais participate in politics and administration, while the majority of the population is excluded. And as noted previously, some observers interpret Thailand's history of never having been colonized by a Western power to be something of a drawback, leading to insularity and a comparatively myopic government apparatus.

NPM and NPM-like reforms have been implemented in several of these countries for widely different reasons, with greater efficiency in service delivery being only one of those reasons. Among anglophone nations, pursuing an efficiency strategy demonstrated to their peers that they were on the leading edge of administrative practice, following practices set by the UK. On the other hand, reforms were implemented in Thailand as a condition of World Bank/IMF assistance. Bolivia, Taiwan, and the Philippines have implemented administrative reform as a signal to citizens that each is attempting to clean up government systems that have suffered corruption for generations. Taiwan and Korea have attempted to implement efficiency- and outcomes-based reforms within strong service cultures; in essence, they have sought the best of each—NPM and NPS—with the result being only greater and greater stress on their public servants.

China, India, and Rwanda have not pursued a defined NPM strategy. These three countries catapulted past the NPM movement and follow a public service strategy more akin to that described by New Public Service. It could be argued that these three countries never lost sight of the fact that public service is inherently interpersonal, firmly rooted in the citizen/state encounter and, therefore, reliant upon trust relationships and broad participation by the populace.

The countries included in this study represent only a handful of all the nations on the globe. But the variety among their political dynamics and cultural traditions illustrates the range of contexts and approaches to be found. From ancient countries to those newly founded, from peaceful cultures to those ravaged by civil war, from colonized states to self-governing states, the variety illustrates significantly different contexts. With this in mind, discussion turns now to the transition from reliance on market mechanisms to a renewed emphasis on the human aspect of governance. First, the contrast between measurable outcomes and meaningful outcomes is discussed. Then, the importance of relationship is described. This is followed with a description of the transition from efficiency for its own sake to a frame of reference that prioritizes service. Finally, the importance of emotional labor in this service framework is discussed.

From Measurable Outcomes to Meaningful Outcomes

New Public Management reforms have now been in place long enough in those countries where it was adopted that there is disillusionment with the promise of data dashboards to create more effective government (Hood and Dixon 2015). Governing occurs in an inherently interpersonal milieu, and scholarship and practice are evolving toward a more service-oriented approach, such as that espoused by New Public Service. More correctly, an emphasis on the human factor and a focus on effectiveness have been *re*discovered after a few decades spent chasing the holy grail of efficiency and value-for-money under NPM reforms.

Shortcomings of the efficiency/NPM narrative have led countries to rediscover the fundamentally interpersonal nature of public service. Whether or not it represents a new governance paradigm (Gow and du Four 2000), the return to service exemplified by NPS embraces the broadest constituency and seeks to flatten the bureaucratic hierarchy that alienates people from their government. Organizational humanism, theories of citizen participation, and community and civil society preceded New Public Service and provide the elements for its expression now. Under NPS (Stritch 2016, 348):

> First, the role of the public servant is to help citizens articulate their shared interests, rather than to control or steer society. Second, public interests are the aim, not the by-product, of public administration. Third, public servants do not merely respond to the demands of 'customers' but instead should focus on building collaborative relationships with the citizens they serve. Fourth, instead of valuing productivity, people should be valued in order to establish collaborative processes that can lead to productivity gains in the long term.

A focus on service emphasizes democratic principles and broad citizen participation. This emphasis represents a shift from efficiency to effectiveness, from data dashboards to human hearts. Another way of thinking about this transition is to trace the evolution from a focus on results to a focus on relationships.

From Results to Relationships

Governmental structures, systems, and expectations are in transition. Large, bureaucratic organizations delivering government services at scale have proven slow and cumbersome. The postwar period of rebuilding in the later twentieth century distracted the USA, UK, and Europe from the shortcomings of bureaucracy, but they became obvious as national governments tried to address social problems at scale. The UK created the National Health Service in 1946 and built a bureaucratic apparatus around a network of charitable hospitals and local pharmacies. Nationalized industries sought to meet consumer demands for everything from travel via air, rail, ferry, and coach to communications including telephone and television services, to steel, coal, and petroleum production. The USA continued to implement national-level, social welfare programs, built an interstate highway system, and embarked on the War on Poverty in the 1960s. Both countries confronted stagnating economies—more protracted in the UK than in the USA—and both encountered growing enthusiasm for something different. It came in the form of privatization, decentralization, contracting out, and a citizen-qua-customer orientation.

Managerialism gained popularity as confidence in big government diminished. Across OECD countries, "the evolution of the state created conditions that challenged the prevailing paradigm …. Public Administration underwent a crisis of credibility. It did not work anymore" (Gow and du Four 2000, 585). Reforms were pursued to stem increasing costs of government and to increase efficiency. Advocates for small-government and marketized processes prevailed at the ballot box, which resulted in reforms being implemented to varying degrees in many OECD countries.

Aficionados of reform over-promised results, however, and soon the fundamental interpersonal nature of public service was lost in the pursuit of positive, quantifiable performance indicators. The signifiers became untethered from the signified; *claims about* results become outcomes unto themselves. "Performance measures evolved into—or perhaps always were—more about what a public manager could *claim* to have accomplished, rather than about actual accomplishments: Performance-based management is most fundamentally about communications, not measurement" (Kettl 1995, 64, emphasis original).

Performance management systems evolved into self-evident outcomes and required a bureaucratic apparatus to support them: "Mandates to collect, report, and review performance data have altered existing organizational routines and decision-making processes" (Kroll et al. 2017, 6). Reforms changed the nature of public service delivery from a human endeavor to a large-scale lesson in creative accounting and accountability by spreadsheet: "Traditional social capital is challenged when professional work organizations are reorganized by marketization, when clients become customers, and managerialism and performance management are emphasized" (Svensson,

2006, 585). Helen Dickinson describes the forces that led reformers in different directions over the decades (2016, p. 55, emphasis supplied):

> Market forces were introduced to overcome the inherent limitations of hierarchies. When the inevitable limitations of markets eventuated, a discourse of networks and New Public Governance emerged ostensibly to counter these challenges.… Rather than a wholesale shift to new governance regimes, what happens in practice is that a rather more complex picture emerges of hybrid arrangements comprising features of different forms of governance systems at the same time … paying attention to these factors ultimately affords greater agency *and a sense of humanity to the delivery of public services.*

Bureaucracies gave way to markets as a means for delivering services. Then, markets gave way to governance networks. At some point amidst the frenzy of reforms, public administration lost sight of the inherent complexity of "wicked" human problems, and perhaps even of the inherent humanness of pursuing public purposes. Arguing for a resurrection of the craft of public administration amidst the reign of the generalist, Rod Rhodes exclaims (2016, 638): "The pendulum has swung too far for too long toward the new and the fashionable. It needs to swing back toward bureaucracy and the traditional skills of bureaucrats as part of the repertoire of governing." As this quote makes clear, emphasis on public <u>service</u> is the response to NPM reforms.

Efficiency prioritizes customer satisfaction, while equity prioritizes those who may have been left out of the transaction altogether: those toward whom efficiency is blind. "Too many performance measurement and management regimes and models focus principally on efficiency and effectiveness directly related to the mission and disregard … 'non-mission-based values' such as equity, due process, freedom of information, and citizenship development" (Bryson et al. 2014, 453). A service frame of mind is an approach focused on these "non-mission-based values." It emphasizes access, process, and shared power.

A service orientation is not exactly "anti-outcomes." Rather, it places the citizen at the center in every endeavor, including determinations about desired outcomes and what should be measured: "Public administrators have long struggled with how to measure outcomes of public programs that can have multiple and sometimes conflicting goals coupled with the increasingly intractable and 'wicked' nature of public problems … performance measurement tools have traditionally neglected the potential role of citizens in developing measures that are meaningful and useful as well" (Denhardt and

Denhardt 2015, 669). Performance outcomes can sustain democratic values only when citizens help to determine both desirable outcomes and how they will be measured.

From Efficiency Reforms to Service Reforms

Further contrasts between NPM and NPS are their characterizations of people as customers versus citizens, assumptions about public servants' primary work motivations, and the role of public interest. *Customers* are sources of data whose participation begins and ends with their "purchase" and perhaps some measure of individual satisfaction or dissatisfaction that the organization collects and tracks. The act of purchasing is interpreted as a "vote" of satisfaction (Tiebout 1956). Customers are motivated by self-interest. *Citizens*, on the other hand, have a stake in the community and its interests, and are members of and represent a collective jurisdiction rather than representing individual, idiosyncratic interactions with a service provider.

NPM emphasizes the customer, while NPS emphasizes the citizen (Denhardt and Denhardt 2000). These contrasting views influence, and are influenced by, how the role of government and the public servant is understood. And how we explain the behavior of the public servant shapes how we influence that behavior. Human resource management (HRM) is, in large part, a collection of practices to influence the behavior of workers for the purpose of producing organizational outcomes. If we understand human behavior to be motivated primarily by self-interest, the HRM approach will leverage worker self-interest to shape behavior toward accomplishing organizational goals. If, on the other hand, we trace public servant work motivations to the interests of the collective, then the HRM strategy will leverage collective interests to accomplish the organization's goals.

NPM is based on a worldview variously termed "public choice," "traditional pluralism," or "principal/agent" theory. It assumes that individuals pursue their self-interest. In this scenario, incentives and penalties are employed by policy makers to shape individual behavior. Outcomes emanate from the open competition of individuals acting in their self-interest. At most, government establishes the context for this competition, ensures a level playing field—ensures that the rules are followed—and creates carrots and sticks to shape or "nudge" behavior where the market fails to do so. Otherwise, government allows outcomes to arise from the open interactions of agents following their self-interested motives. The most efficient and therefore optimal outcomes arise from the free play of individual self-interests. And individual public administrators are encouraged to pursue their own self-interest as "entrepreneurs."

Human resource policies that reflect these assumptions are designed to reinforce desired behavior. A principal/agent perspective assumes that individuals pursue their own self-interest and HR systems are built to incentivize and reward that behavior. What is more likely, however, is that workers are motivated by a range of factors. If self-interest is a minor part of what brings public servants to public—and nonprofit—work, then incentivizing self-interested behaviors can backfire. First, it can backfire by addressing only part of public servants' motivations. This produces suboptimal results compared to strategies more accurately targeted. And second, missing the motivational mark can discourage individuals whose motivations are community- or group-based.

Denhardt and Denhardt understand how assuming self-interest can backfire and they implore human resource managers to "nourish and encourage higher-level motivations and values, not extinguish them by treating people as if they were cogs in a machine or as if they were only capable of self-serving behavior ... if we treat people as bureaucrats, as self-serving and self-interested individuals, we encourage them to become just that" (2011, 169). Helen Dickinson observes the same unintended consequences among public servants in nonprofit organizations: "If more market-based models are used, and incentives geared towards satisfying self-interest are embedded, it is no surprise that community sector organizations may begin to behave more like what we would expect from private sector organizations" (2016, 53). Both argue that an NPM-style performance management system can not only miss the motivational mark with public service employees but can, in fact, bring about an increase in self-interested behaviors by placing value on those outcomes.

From Individual Interest to Collective Interest

With respect to the pursuit of the public interest, NPM underplays or denies outright the existence of collective interests. NPM holds that only individual self-interest can be measured and so there exists no separate "collective" or "public" interest or will beyond the aggregation of individual self-interests. NPS, in contrast, accepts the existence of a collective interest beyond the individual's self-interest and its normative approach to the role of government. The role of public administration in the governance system follows suit and places the citizenry and its interests at the center of a system based on democratic ideals. NPS envisions an active role for government and for public administration in order to encourage democratic ideals in pursuit of the public interest.

Three theoretical foundations of NPS are: "(1) theories of democratic citizenship; (2) models of community and civil society; and (3) organizational humanism and discourse theory" (Denhardt and Denhardt 2000, 552). NPS is based on a worldview in which individuals are engaged in governance together with the state as a whole. Individuals are assumed to perceive a broader public interest beyond their own self-interest. Under the aegis of service, public administration maximizes the responsiveness of government and seeks to increase citizen trust in government. In contrast to traditional bureaucracy, organizational humanism is a normative theory of organizations under which public agencies are "less dominated by issues of authority and control and [are] more attentive to the needs and concerns of employees inside public organizations as well as those outside, especially clients and citizens" (Denhardt and Denhardt 2000, 553).

Another dimension to a service frame of reference is that discourse theory is fundamental to it. Discourse operates analogous to competition in managerialism, but unlike competition, individuals are *interdependent,* rather than independent. Therefore, they must communicate with one another in order to accomplish collective ends. Governance, thus, must be rooted in open discourse among citizens and administrators. In this manner, a service framework embodies democratic theory.

A service worldview is expansive, such that "the role of government is transformed from one of controlling to one of agenda setting, bringing the proper players to the table and facilitating, negotiating, or brokering solutions to public problems—often through coalitions of public, private, and nonprofit agencies" (Denhardt and Denhardt 2000, 553). Contrast this to a managerialist worldview that characterizes actors as somewhat mindless but definitely heartless. As if they are agents pursuing individual self-interest akin to pinballs bouncing from incentives to disincentives, the "most efficient" outcomes result from the interplay of individual self-interests on a sterile landscape monitored by a hands-off government. Nowhere are we given to understand that these agents talk to one another or otherwise interact beyond individual, atomized, Lockean reactions to pleasures and pains. New Public Service, on the other hand, is grounded in the "how" of interaction, characterizing NPM's "agents" as humans and emphasizing their humanness.

The "how" of a service orientation emphasizes cooperation and collaboration of groups of people across the public, private, and nonprofit sectors.

They work together to achieve collective purposes. From this point of view, the work of public administration is to help citizens set their agenda and articulate and achieve their shared interests. In other words, public administration serves as a negotiator and broker of solutions. Each of these important roles emphasizes communication and interpersonal relationships.

A focus on service prioritizes the public interest; it is not a residual—a "by product"—of competing self-interested agents. From this perspective, public administration pursues norms of justice, fairness, and equity. These norms are the purpose of the process, and not the presumed product of open competition. Finally, a service perspective eschews citizen-as-customer, because "the relationship between government and its citizens is not the same as that between a business and its customers" (Denhardt and Denhardt 2000, 555). In contrast, the managerialist perspective emphasizes the near term, resulting in a loss of institutional memory, and it embraces marketization or neoliberal beliefs about competition and markets (Rhodes 2016, 640).

Managerialism and the public administration of the Bureau Men (Stivers 2000) envisioned workplace interpersonal dynamics as low-trust relationships based largely on instrumental transactions of carrots and sticks. Managerialism and its predecessor, scientific management, were informed by an explanation of interpersonal relations at work grounded in technical rationality. In contrast, a service perspective places citizens at the center of a responsive public administration that operates with a civic-mindedness and is consistent with organizational humanism (Denhardt and Denhardt 2000). "The elements of human behavior that are at the core of the New Public Service [include] human dignity, trust, belongingness, concern for others, service, and citizenship based on shared ideals and the public interests" (Denhardt and Denhardt 2011, 165). If one takes the Technical Rationality view of human behavior as accurate—that there exists a labor/leisure trade-off where individuals will shirk unless and until they are paid to work—then workplace interventions to achieve organizational objectives will focus on pay and extrinsic rewards. If one takes a view of human behavior that is informed by affective motives rather than strictly economic, then approaches to achieving organizational goals will look different. By focusing on the emotive demands placed upon public servants, we situate their daily experiences at the center of any approach taken to improve workplace processes and pay attention to how to retain those who work in human-focused endeavors.

New Public Service emphasizes "democratic accountability ... social equity, citizen involvement, and bottom-up decision making" (Kroll et al. 2017, 2). Public servants "are viewed not just as employees who crave the security and structure of a bureaucratic job (old public administration) nor as participants in a market (NPM) rather, public servants are people whose motivations and rewards are more than simply a matter of pay or security. They want to make a difference in the lives of others" (Denhardt and Denhardt 2000, 556). And this perspective has broader implications for both worker productivity and overall organizational performance: "If you assume that people are capable of other-mindedness, of service, of acting on shared values as citizens, then it is only logically consistent that you assume public employees are capable of the same motivations and behaviors. We cannot expect public servants to treat their fellow citizens with respect and dignity if they themselves are not treated with respect and dignity" (Denhardt and Denhardt 2011, 165).

In sum, a service orientation rejects the explanation of worker behavior in terms of extrinsic rewards alone. And it subscribes to the assumption that one's choice of occupation and workplace is done purposefully. While job security is an important motivation to work in government, it is no longer as prevalent—thanks in part to decades of NPM reforms—and even so, it remains only one of multiple salient motivations. Our years of working as and with public servants have taught us that individuals are drawn to government to make a difference. While remuneration must be sufficient, it is not the primary driver of worker behavior that public choice theory presumes.

From Stylized Bureaucracy to Relational Bureaucracy

The nature of the citizen–state encounter ranges from the mundane, such as paying a speeding ticket or filing for a building permit, to the life altering, such as applying for an order of protection or appealing a family court's custody decision. A turn toward service in high-stakes circumstances suggests that public servants—those on the government side of the citizen–state encounter—should be ready to handle any human dilemma that arises. Gittell and Douglass refer to these skills as relational competencies: "Hiring and training for relational competence can reflect an organization's valuing of the respect, attentiveness, responsiveness, and concern for others that define caring relations" (2012, 710).

Assumptions about worker motivations incentivize certain behaviors and in fact operate to increase the incidence of such behaviors, just as discussed in terms of performance measures. Similarly, HRM practices encourage some behaviors while discouraging others. Organizations must be mindful of the assumptions underpinning their practices and the worker behaviors they encourage and discourage. By and large, public servants are attracted to service in order to make a difference in society: "Rational attempts to control human behavior are likely to fail in the long term if, at the same time, insufficient attention is paid to the values and interests of individual members of an organization. While these approaches may get results, they do not build responsible, engaged, and civic-minded employees or citizens" (Denhardt and Denhardt 2011, 156).

Theories of workplace motivation evolved from notions about the instrumental trade-off between labor and leisure based on pay. They do not account for the substantial role of personality and emotions to explain why workers work and how much effort they expend. "Feelings and emotions were largely ignored in the study of organizations and management for many decades" (Denhardt and Denhardt 2011, 157). To carry this idea forward, Rhodes (2016) examines "craft skills" of public administrators based on experiential knowledge. These skills are gaining attention because they were missing from managerialism. They include counseling, stewardship, and practical wisdom. Examples of practical wisdom include probity, judgment, diplomacy, and *political nous*, which refers to political intelligence, intellect, or awareness. Awareness of an individual's motivations, alongside HRM practices that encourage civic-mindedness, inspires quality effort from public servants and foster sustainable and humane outcomes in human-centered organizations.

A service orientation resurrects the central role that interpersonal relationships play in order to accomplish agency missions. Managing across organizational boundaries in a networked setting requires "integrating agendas, representing both the agency and the network, setting broad rules of the game that leave local action to network members, developing clear roles, expectations, and responsibilities for all players, agreeing on the criteria for success and sharing the administrative burden" (Rhodes 2016, 640). In contrast, traditional bureaucratic administration emphasizes "conventional notions of professionalism ... characterized by emotional detachment and professional power over the client" (Gittell and Douglass 2012, 716). Managerialism envisions the citizen as a customer, which mischaracterizes the citizen–state encounter as well. The return to a service perspective employs the NPM concept of co-production and governance, but grounds this power-sharing relationship in democratic theory rather than microeconomic theory. The return to service acknowledges that the competitive-market approach creates winners and losers and is not democratic.

NPS seeks to preserve access while also sharing power to accomplish the state's ends. Interpersonal relationships and communicating are fundamental to each of these skills. Boundary spanning is a key skill in governing via networks and working across organizational boundaries involves unique emotional labor demands (Needham et al. 2017).

An operations strategy grounded in relational bureaucracy attempts to obtain the best aspects of two different organizational forms: smaller, relational, or networked organizations and larger bureaucratic organizations. This approach seeks to maintain the integrity of standardized processes and routines in order to maximize access and preserve equity, while also delivering quality public services. It is characterized by "Caring, timely, and knowledgeable responses found in the relational form, as well as the scalability, replicability, and sustainability found in the bureaucratic form" (Gittell and Douglass 2012, 709).

To Denis, Ferlie, and van Gestel (2015), relational bureaucracy is an example of a hybrid organization. Just as Dickinson (2016) observes that old organizational forms and practices are not disappeared or replaced by reform initiatives, so too do Denis et al. (2015) note that public-sector reforms are implemented in spaces that have experienced previous reforms. The result is hybridity, and to Denis et al. (2015), this can happen at the individual level, group level, and organization level. Boundary-spanning occupations exemplify hybridity at the individual occupation level. Relational bureaucracies—both caring and hierarchical—embody hybridity at the organization level. At the group level, work teams that operate with a mix of autonomy as well as oversight provide this example: "Relational competence involves skills such as perspective taking and empathy, which are deeply rooted in personal traits but can also be trained" (Gittell and Douglass 2012, 722). In sum, workplaces and occupations have changed such that the inflexible bureaucrat would not thrive in today's multiple organization, multi-sectoral governance setting.

Although discussed here as a reaction to the biases in managerialism, principles of relational bureaucracy are at least as old as the Human Relations school of thought in organizational theory of the early and mid-twentieth century. In *The Giving of Orders* (1925, 56), Mary Parker Follett places work demands at the center of workplace motivation and worker/manager relationships: "One person should not give orders to another person, but both should agree to take their orders from the situation." The primacy of the situation situates Follett firmly within American Pragmatism, a philosophy that shaped early public administration as well (Stivers 2000).

In his vision of a "post-bureaucratic" public administration, Dwight Waldo (1948) similarly collapses bureaucracy such that everyone in the workplace serves as leaders and followers in turn, as the situation demands. Schon's (1983) Reflection-in-Action places the practitioner—the professional—in the role of curious novice who allows herself to be surprised or puzzled by the situation at hand for the purpose of further honing her craft. In sum, thinking of bureaucracy in relational terms serves to connect public service professionals directly to the work they perform both cognitively and affectively, unlike traditional notions that treat workers as interchangeable parts, divorced from their own feelings and motivations and replaceable by anyone who meets the same minimal qualifications.

From Formalized Contracting to Relational Contracting

A fundamental tenet in managerialism is contracting out the delivery of public services to decrease the size of the state, involve non-governmental service delivery providers, and ultimately lower costs, increase choice, and improve services. But competitive tendering, or contracting out, failed to deliver these benefits on any kind of large scale, in part due to the kinds of services that governments provide. Even some Anglosphere nations—the loudest NPM enthusiasts—have abandoned compulsory commissioning requirements as evidence is increasingly indicating that cost savings and quality improvements are not resulting (see Hood and Dixon 2015, for example).

Even in NPMs' heyday, the market dynamics that were supposed to produce cost savings according to theory did not work in practice. Governments often contracted out to only a single provider, sometimes two, and private-sector firms that won service-provision contracts often insisted on sole-source contract renewals. Sole-sourcing is and always was in the best interests of the private-sector contractor. According to its own theory, sole-source contracting would not be in society's best interest, but NPM is based on theory that does not prioritize or even acknowledge a broader collective interest beyond the aggregation of individual goals. Indeed, according to theory, the contractor's best interest would also comprise society's best interests, yet somehow, citizens did not enjoy lower costs, better quality, or greater choice. Competitive tendering was not, in fact, competitive. Choice neither increased nor decreased and "private delivery does not save money over time [due to] the cost of monitoring ... more contracting generates greater bureaucracy" (Denhardt and Denhardt 2015, 669). This is one more piece of evidence that government should not—and perhaps cannot—run like a business.

Relational contracting is based on high-trust relationships and is often touted as a humanistic means for engaging in a principal/agent relationship. The implicit or unwritten terms of such contracts are of far more interest than the explicit terms, for it is the unwritten aspects of the agreement that sustain compliance. Carson et al. (2006) conclude that formal contracting and relational contracting are imperfect substitutes for one another. This is because, while relational contracting may involve high-trust relationships and perform well when parties are familiar with one another and the environment is certain, in terms of efficiency and cost savings, formal contracts perform better than relational contracts.

Formal contracts also perform better amidst ambiguity. Carson et al. (2006) also challenge previous conclusions that relational contracts resist opportunism. Efficiency and cost savings may suffer due to opportunism arising from uncertainty and flexible terms of relational contracts. Parties may take advantage of the ambiguity, unwritten rules, and trust relationships, all of which can drive up costs. Just because the parties involved will likely work together in the future—relational contracts are treated as "repeated games"—this does not necessarily shield against shirking on either side.

In sum, relational contracting is easier said than done. Trust relationships and negotiating unwritten rules demand interpersonal skills. For our purposes, capturing the importance of emotional intelligence and the role of emotional labor in relational contracts is key. To the extent that public service delivery has moved away from large bureaucracies toward relational contracts and networks, emotional labor skills are all the more crucial for public servants to master.

Emotional Labor and Its Focus on Service

In each instance, each iteration away from managerialism and data dashboards toward a service-oriented way of thinking, relational skills are rediscovered anew. Public servants either figure this out on their own and accommodate relational contracts, relational bureaucracy, or whatever new idea hits their desk, or they fail to figure it out and experience greater stress, greater dissonance between what they feel and what they perceive they "ought" to feel, and leave public service altogether. We think there is a better way.

In the turn away from measuring things and toward serving people, "most commentators agree that now and in the future it will not be sufficient for governments and third-party providers of government services to focus on measures of efficiency and effectiveness, and careful consideration will need to be given to the relational aspects of service delivery" (Dickinson 2016, 54). The relational aspects of service delivery demand emotional labor. Emotional labor is foundational to interpersonal public service and it is as nonverbal as it is verbal: As internal to the public servant as it is external, facing the citizen/client. Trust, rapport, representativeness, empowerment all presume a foundation of emotive competency. "Organizations can foster authentic worker/customer relationships through the use of 'organized emotional care'—specific organizational structures and practices that support rather than restrict or coerce, worker/customer relations" (Gittell and Douglass 2012, 725).

Authenticity in the citizen/state encounter arises naturally when display rules allow it and when empathy is present (Zanetti and King 2013). As example, Schon (1983) describes how granting a rationale to the client's actions leads to understanding, rather than assuming ill intent. He describes an experiment in which schoolteachers observed two boys at a table, both working with colored blocks and triangle shapes but separated from one another by an opaque screen (1983, 67–68):

> The first boy was to tell the second one how to reproduce the pattern. After the first few instructions, however, it became clear that the second boy had gone astray … In their initial reactions to the videotape, the teachers spoke of a 'communications problem.' They said that the instruction giver had 'well-developed verbal skills' and that the receiver was 'unable to follow directions.' Then one of the researchers pointed out that, although the blocks contained no green squares—all squares were orange and only triangles were green— she had heard the first boy tell the second to 'take a green square.' When the teachers watched the videotape again, they were astonished. That small mistake had set off a chain of false moves…. At this point, the teachers reversed their picture of the situation. They could see why the second boy behaved as he did … they were now 'giving him reason.'

To borrow from this experiment in cognition, "giving him reason"— reframing observed behavior to make sense of it—is what Schon calls

Reflection-in-Action. When a client's actions make sense, the public servant understands it and can do something about it. However, one must leave herself open to different explanations, to different theories of another's behavior. Schon describes this as an in-the-moment situation in which "the practitioner allows himself to experience surprise, puzzlement, or confusion in a situation which he finds uncertain or unique. He *reflects* on the phenomena before him, and on the *prior understandings which have been implicit in his behavior*" (1983, 68, emphasis supplied). The practitioner's "prior understandings" are his assumptions, his frame. Analogously, emotive authenticity challenges the public servant to be open to reframing, to empathically comprehending how the other person is feeling, and to respond emotively in a way that is appropriate.

Alluding to organizational display rules, Denhardt and Denhardt define organizational culture in large part as that which creates "the *normative* context for our behavior in organizations" (2011, 162, emphasis supplied). In other words, display rules sculpt how we *should* behave in our occupational roles. At times, this creates an emotional straitjacket when display rules require workers to display confidence when they are unsure, to display calmness when they are excited, to display light-heartedness when they are devastated, to display cheeriness when they are sad. Emotive pretending requires concentration and energy. Over time, in half the countries in this study, this results in workplace stress and burnout.

Emotional labor—managing one's own emotions as well as the emotional state of the other person—is fundamental to interpersonal public service. And increasingly, interpersonal relations are understood to be fundamental to public service. Outcome measures that capture the amount of time a counselor works with a client are a hollow attempt to approximate emotionally laborious exchanges. Each human encounter comes with its own emotive demands.

New Public Service is rooted in organizational humanism, which is an approach to the workplace that celebrates on-the-job learning and acquired knowledge—craftsmanship—and envisions the worker as an integrated whole, not simply a buyer in a market, nor an instrumental actor weighing payoffs in a labor/leisure trade-off (Carnevale and Stivers 2019; Tilman and Brown 1995; Veblen 1914). James C. Scott (1999) contrasts technical knowledge or *techne*—Schon's "technical rationality" (1983, 21)—against craftsmanship, or *metis*. "Organizational humanism has sought to bring a new focus on man and his varied needs, on work as a means of fulfillment, and on the process rather than the structuring of activities" (Wren 1972, 470).

The New Public Service approach is appropriate to meet the needs of workers as well as the needs of citizens. Customers seeking to fulfill their self-interest have a very limited "relationship" with government. Citizen/clients, on the other hand, have a stake in the public interest: "In a world of active citizenship, public officials will increasingly play more than a service delivery role—they will play a conciliating, a mediating, or even an adjudicating role ... these new roles will require new skills ... brokering, negotiating, and conflict resolution" (Denhardt and Denhardt 2000, 554). Making government work more effectively involves community building and citizen engagement, both of which demand public servants who have emotive competency.

Summary

This chapter tracked the ebb and flow of government reforms from service delivery via large bureaucracies, to use of competitive-market mechanisms for the allocation of public goods, to the present return to service in public service. Under managerialist-style market mechanisms, indicators and dashboards have been used to gauge individual and organizational performance. The inherently interpersonal nature of public service, which the return to *service* recognizes, requires that we abandon the illusion that data dashboards provide meaning. One approach that is helpful in this regard is the concept of the Relational Bureaucracy, which is an attempt to capture the best of both previous worlds—the scale and routinization of bureaucracy with the responsiveness and inclusion of networks.

Organizations and networks are comprised of people addressing human problems. In the process of addressing these problems, emotional labor is foundational. Responsiveness and co-production demand emotive competencies. Overlooking the centrality of emotional labor to public service will lead organizations to fall short of their goals and fail to sustain their workforces.

The contrast between an "efficiency" worldview and a "service" worldview makes the point that emotional labor plays a key role in a public service guided primarily by effectiveness and equity concerns. Interpersonal relationships have always been fundamental to effective government and governance. The transition from managerialism to service re-invigorates demands for emotionally intelligent public servants who apply their skills in the pursuit of public purposes.

References

Bryson, John M., Barbara C. Crosby, and Laura Bloomberg. 2014. "Public Value Governance: Moving Beyond Traditional Public Administration and the New Public Management."*Public Administration Review* 74 (4): 445–56. https://doi.org/10.1111/puar.12238.

Carnevale, David, and Camilla A. Stivers. 2019. *Knowledge and Power in Public Bureaucracies: From Pyramid to Circle.* New York, NY: Routledge.

Carson, Stephen J., Anoop Madhok, and Tao Wu. 2006. "Uncertainty, Opportunism, and Governance: The Effects of Volatility and Ambiguity on Formal and Relational Contracting." *Academy of Management Journal* 49 (5): 1058–78.

Denhardt, Robert B., and Janet V. Denhardt. 2000. "The New Public Service: Serving Rather Than Steering." *Public Administration Review* 60 (6): 549–59.

Denhardt, Robert B., and Janet V. Denhardt. 2011. *The New Public Service: Serving, Not Steering.* 3rd ed. New York, NY: Routledge.

Denhardt, Robert B., and Janet V. Denhardt. 2015. "The New Public Service: Revisited." *Public Administration Review* 75 (5): 664–72.

Denis, Jean-Louis, Ewan Ferlie, and Nicolette van Gestel. 2015. "Understanding Hybridity in Public Organizations." *Public Administration* 93 (2): 273–89.

Dickinson, Helen. 2016. "From New Public Management to New Public Governance: The Implications for a 'New Public Service.'" In *Three Sector Solution: Delivering Public Policy in Collaboration with Not-for-Profits and Business,* edited by David Gilchrist and John Butcher, 41–60. Canberra: Australian National University Press.

Follett, Mary Parker. 2017/1925. "The Giving of Orders." In *Classics of Public Administration,* 8th ed., edited by Jay Shafritz and Albert C. Hyde, 76–104. Independence, KY: Cengage Learning.

Gittell, Jody Hoffer, and Anne Douglass. 2012. "Relational Bureaucracy: Structuring Reciprocal Relationships into Roles." *Academy of Management Review* 37 (4): 709–33.

Gow, James Iain, and Caroline du Four. 2000. "Is the New Public Management a Paradigm? Does It Matter?" *International Review of Administrative Sciences* 66 (2): 573–97.

Hood, Christopher, and Ruth Dixon. 2015. *A Government That Worked Better and Cost Less?* Oxford, UK: Oxford University Press.

Ingraham, Patricia Wallace, and David H. Rosenbloom. 1989. "The New Public Personnel and the New Public Service." *Public Administration Review* 49 (2): 116–26.

Kettl, Donald F. 1995. "Building Lasting Reform: Enduring Questions, Missing Reforms." In *Inside the Reinvention Machine: Appraising Governmental Reform,* edited by Donald F. Kettl and John J. DiIulio Jr., 9–86. Washington, DC: Brookings Institution.

Kroll, Alexander, Milena I. Neshkova, and Sanjay K. Pandey. 2017. "Spillover Effects from Customer to Citizen Orientation: How Performance Management Reforms Can Foster Public Participation." *Administration & Society*. https://doi.org/10.1177/0095399716687341.

Needham, Catherine, and Catherine Mangan. 2014. *The 21st Century Public Servant*. Birmingham, UK: University of Birmingham.

Needham, Catherine, Sharon Mastracci, and Catherine Mangan. 2017. "The Emotional Labour of Boundary Spanning." *Journal of Integrated Care* 25 (4): 288–300.

Osborne, Stephen P. 2006. "The New Public Governance?" *Public Management Review* 8 (3): 377–87.

Rauh, Jonathan. 2018. "Ethics Problems in the New Public Service: Back to a Service Ethic?" *Public Integrity* 20 (2): 234–56.

Rhodes, Roderick W. 2016. "Recovering the Craft of Public Administration." *Public Administration Review* 76 (4): 638–47.

Schon, Donald A. 1983. *The Reflective Practitioner: How Professionals Think in Action*. New York, NY: Basic Books.

Scott, James C. 1999. *Seeing Like a State: How Certain Schemes to Improve the Human Condition Have Failed*. New Haven, CT: Yale University Press.

Stivers, Camilla A. 2000. *Bureau Men/Settlement Women: Constructing Public Administration in the Progressive Era*. Lawrence, KS: University of Kansas Press.

Stritch, Justin M. 2016. "A Preliminary Examination of Citizen Orientation and Multiple Dimensions of Organizational Performance." *International Journal of Public Administration* 39 (5): 345–58.

Svensson, Lennart G. 2006. "New Professionalism, Trust, and Competence." *Current Sociology* 54 (4): 579–93.

Tiebout, Charles M. 1956. "A Pure Theory of Local Expenditures." *Journal of Political Economy* 64 (5): 416–24.

Tilman, Rick, and John H. Brown. 1995. "Thorstein Veblen, C. Wright Mills and the Possibilities of a Public Administration." *International Journal of Social Economics* 22 (1): 3–12.

Veblen, Thorstein. 1914. *The Instinct of Workmanship and the State of the Industrial Arts*. New York, NY: Macmillan.

Waldo, Dwight. 2017/1948. *The Administrative State: A Study of the Political Theory of American Public Administration*. New York, NY: Routledge.

Wren, Daniel A. 1972. *The Evolution of Management Thought*. New York: Wiley.

Zanetti, Lisa A., and Cheryl S. King. 2013. "Reflections on Theory in Action: Transformational Public Service Revisited." *Administrative Theory & Praxis* 35 (1): 128–43. https://doi.org/10.2753/atp1084-1806350108.

Zavattaro, Staci M. 2012. "Management Movements and Phases of the Image: Potential for Closing the Loop." *Administration & Society* 45 (1): 97–118.

23

Looking Forward:
Adjusting to the New Paradigm

Sharon H. Mastracci, Mary E. Guy and Seung-Bum Yang

This chapter offers a broadened frame of reference for what constitutes knowledge, extending it beyond the cognitive to embrace the emotive. There is a shift underway from thinking about public service as a thoroughly cognitive practice to thinking about it involving both cognition and embodied knowledge. The term "embodied knowledge" refers to ways of knowing that emerge from feelings and perceptions. Survey responses from public service professionals around the globe make it obvious that there is more to delivering public services than the purely cognitive.

Data from Australia to the USA, and all countries in between, make it obvious that emotional labor is performed in the process of delivering public services. It emanates from a form of embodied knowledge that is foundational in public service practice. How is public administration education adjusting to this shift? This chapter provides examples of both public service

S. H. Mastracci (✉)
Department of Political Science,
University of Utah, Salt Lake City, UT, USA
e-mail: Sharon.mastracci@poli-sci.utah.edu

M. E. Guy
School of Public Affairs, University of Colorado Denver, Denver, CO, USA
e-mail: mary.guy@ucdenver.edu

S.-B. Yang
Department of Public Administration, Konkuk University, Seoul, South Korea
e-mail: sbyang@konkuk.ac.kr

M. E. Guy et al. (eds.), *The Palgrave Handbook of Global Perspectives on Emotional Labor in Public Service*, https://doi.org/10.1007/978-3-030-24823-9_23

practice and education that use embodied knowledge as a starting point. Examples are drawn from human resource management in the Government of India and social care in the UK and the USA. Examples of what embodied knowledge would look like in public service education are based on the required competencies for accreditation from NASPAA, a nonprofit organization that is headquartered in the USA, but represents more than 300 schools of public policy, public affairs, and public administration located in the USA, the UK, Europe, Asia, the Middle East, and South America.

In an effort to gain access to the power afforded to endeavors that claim to be "scientific" and "paradigmatic," the discipline of public administration has embraced a raft of analytical techniques, models, principles, procedures, taxonomies, and measures. What it has avoided is emotion. With apologies to Edward O. Wilson (1998, 294), we are drowning in information, while starving for *meaning*. Public services henceforth will be effectively and equitably delivered by those who possess embodied knowledge, emotionally intelligent people trained to work feelingly and empathically using the right information at the right time, and to make important choices wisely.[1] These effective and fulfilled public servants will be supported and sustained by their organizations through ongoing training and holistic, developmental performance evaluations that recognize and capture emotional labor and reward those who do it well. Early-warning systems will alert public servants and their organizations when occupational stressors are high and/or prolonged. The organization will embrace embodied knowledge, and because public service employers understand the centrality of emotion to effective public service delivery, Master of Public Administration (MPA) degree programs will have abandoned the positivist, Enlightenment-based curriculum of old that prioritizes performance measures and outcome indicators. And the accrediting entities of those MPA programs will have emotive competency at the top of their list of required capabilities and areas of proficiency for every accredited graduate program. And human resource management will be the favorite course in the core curriculum.

Yet the field of public administration remains captive to the positivist worldview. Camilla Stivers (2018) recently took the field to account: "What the world needs now is not science but *meaning*, and science can play a role in getting us to meaning, but only a partial role." The opening line of the previous paragraph accuses the field of pursuing scientific status for other reasons: reputation, legitimacy—access to power that the imprimatur of science affords. But public administration is hardly alone: Social sciences and applied fields study human behavior, yet all lionize the cognitive while downplaying the emotive. Only certain corners of psychology have treated emotion as an integral aspect of knowing rather than a contaminant of knowledge and reason. Public administration proposes to study and serve human behavior yet is content to handle its topic only partially; it is content to stay under the proverbial lamppost where objective outputs can be observed, measured, counted, and compared. But are public administrators better at their jobs with this wealth of measures, systems, and rubrics? Or are they, too, starved for meaning?

For citizens to engage with government, they must care about it. "It is not spreadsheets that cause people to riot in the streets, it is feelings. It is not facts and proverbs that bond citizens to their flag; it is feelings. Emotion factors into the entire administrative continuum, from citizen engagement and participation at the grassroots level to frontline delivery of services, to the symbols of governance at the top of the flagpole" (Guy and Mastracci 2018, 282). Brexiteers in 2016 were motivated by nostalgia and the rhetoric of better times. Later that same year, voters in the USA were drawn to the ballot box, not to Make America More Accurate Again or More Efficient Again, but by the image of a sepia-toned time when America was "Great" and the promise to someday be Great Again.

Stivers argues that theories of administrative behavior should be infused with meaning, because meaning is the glue that holds together the pieces of the State. Our argument is that the field of public administration has doubled down on technical rationality to explain administrative behavior thus far, but that explanation is incomplete. It is not what citizens and residents *think* about the meaning of the State—the collective—but rather, how they *feel* about it. People are public administration. People know information about their jobs, but their decision-making—their administrative behavior—encompasses thoughts *and feelings* (Ljungholm 2014). A person knows a thing *because* he feels it, not in spite of his feelings. We decide and *then* rationalize, not the other way around. Neuroscience has known this for a couple of decades now, but the influence of the Cartesian mind/body dualism deters educators and practitioners of public administration from fully acknowledging and embracing the central role of emotion in learning and in the delivery of public services.

Embodied Knowledge

Embodied knowledge incorporates both cognition and emotion. Rene Descartes' proposition, "I think therefore I am," captured the dualism that he believed existed between mind and body and established reason and emotion as mutually exclusive. Mind thinks, and body feels. Humans think, and animals feel. Thinking is understood to be superior to feeling. This either/or proposition was and is intuitively appealing and durable: Centuries later, emotion is considered inferior to cognition in education, in research, and in everyday living. Even among neuroscientists, emotions were not worthy of study well into the 1980s, because emotions were assumed to have either no role in governing behavior and in rational thought, or they were assumed to impede rational thought: "Emotions were like a toddler in a china shop, interfering with the orderly rows of stemware on the shelves" (Immordino-Yang and Damasio 2007, 4). In the 1980s and 1990s, Antonio Damasio studied patients who had suffered damage to the parts of the brain that process emotion and made a surprising discovery: Their interpersonal awareness seemed to have been lost. And while patients' abilities to know facts and to reason were fully intact, they could not make decisions because they could not value one option over another (2007, 4–5):

> These patients' social behavior was compromised, making them oblivious to the consequences of their actions, insensitive to others' emotions, and unable to learn from their mistakes … failing to show embarrassment when it was due and failing to provide appropriate sympathetic support to those who expected it and who received it in the past. … [And] their reasoning was flawed because the emotions and social considerations that underlie good reasoning were compromised.

Emotion processing in the brain allows a person to perceive feedback from others, to sense social cues that indicate whether norms are followed or violated. Without the ability to process emotions, such an individual is unable to perceive having violated a norm, much less learn from mistakes and avoid committing them in the future. Even in the absence of others, a person still requires emotional information from within the self to weigh options and place value on one option over another in order to decide. With no preferences, with no emotional investment in one outcome over another but with the ability to understand facts and information, a person can reason endlessly. The need for cognition to have a sense-based context—either from within oneself or based on cues from others—led Damasio (1994) to label thoughts that are involved in learning and decision-making "Emotional Thoughts."

Emotional Thought is fundamental not only to decision-making but also to emotional labor. The effort to comply with display rules that dictate what is appropriate and inappropriate according to one's job role—engaging in emotional labor—requires a person to recognize display rules. Recognizing display rules requires assessing the social context and sensing from others or from within whether one's own actions and words follow the rules or not. All of this requires Emotional Thought, and it is therefore fundamental to public service education and practice. This is the particular implication of the role of emotions to decision-making.

Possessing the ability to know a fact but being unable to place value on one piece of information over another reveals "the critical role of emotion in bringing previously acquired knowledge to inform real-world decision-making in social contexts" (Immordino-Yang and Damasio 2007, 5). The ability to place value on one option over others is referred to as the Emotional Rudder and is fundamental to ethical practice. Emotions are essential to public administration because "knowledge and reasoning divorced from emotional implications and learning lack meaning and motivation and are of little use in the real world" (Immordino-Yang and Damasio 2007, 9). Public administration is necessarily and profoundly moored in the real world. Ignoring the role of emotion in delivering public services and learning how to administer them is to do our students and practitioners a grave disservice. The remainder of this chapter provides examples of embodied knowledge in practice and in public service education.

Supporting Embodied Knowledge in Public Service Practice

This section[2] describes a handful of workplace practices that have been adopted to support workers whose jobs require emotional labor. While these interventions have been used in health and social care organizations in the UK and the USA, there are generalizable principles that allow these practices to be adapted and applied in these and other contexts elsewhere. They are presented as potential tools for organizations to consider, rather than turnkey solutions. Moreover, although these interventions differ in a number of ways, the underlying principle for most of them is Reflective Practice (Schon 1983). Each intervention provides practitioners the time and space to Reflect in Action.

Discussed in the previous chapter, Reflective Practice "places an emphasis on learning through questioning and investigation to lead to a development of understanding ... [and] is important in sustaining one's professional health and competence and that the ability to exercise professional judgment is in fact informed through reflection on practice" (Loughran 2002, 34). Reflective Practice has been implemented in one form or another across professions, including medicine, law, engineering, nursing, and teaching. Schon (1987, 233) emphasizes its promise in public organizations: "The enhancement of Reflection-in-Action is part of a larger program, liberating the capacity of human beings to think reflectively and productively about their own work." Each workplace intervention is summarized in Table 23.1.

The practices listed in Table 23.1 take embodied knowledge as its starting point. Supporting the emotive capacities of public servants is embedded in the culture of the organizations that have used them and is not an add-on or an exception to standard operating procedures.

Creating Learning Environments for Compassionate Care (CLECC). CLECC was developed at Southampton University in the UK. The aim of CLECC is to promote compassionate care for older hospital patients by working with ward teams. A practice development practitioner/nurse delivers classroom training, reflective discussions, facilitates action learning sets, and coordinates the practice observations. The focus is on developing the relational capacity of individuals and teams and supporting leaders to create workplace learning environments which support the development of relational practices across the work team. By providing this menu of reflective learning and mutual support, the aim is to embed compassionate approaches in staff/service-user interaction and practice. The implementation program takes place over a four-month period but is designed to lead to a longer-term period of service improvement. Challenges to success include ensuring that the minimum conditions for implementation are met, sustaining the impact of the program once the four-month intervention is complete, and engaging staff in the process. These challenges can be overcome by the strengths of CLECC, which include its team approach, high levels of support, and facilitator involvement.

Relation-Centered Leadership (RCL). RCL was developed at Edinburgh University in partnership with NHS Lothian, a medical center in the UK's National Health Service system. RCL was a three-year participatory action research project to identify and support individuals within teams to develop compassionate care practices. Supporting the development of leadership skills in compassionate care is one of these approaches. The Leadership Program was a year-long program using the principles of appreciative relationship-centered leadership to enable all participants (86 staff, including all clinical nurse managers, charge nurses/ward managers, and other staff nurses across all patient areas in NHS Lothian, approximately ten percent of the nursing workforce) to build on existing skills, knowledge, and experience

Table 23.1 Summary of emotional labor interventions in health and social care, USA and UK

Intervention	Aim	Process	Activities	Conditions for success	Resources required	Impact
Creating Learning Environments for Compassionate Care (CLECC)	To embed compassionate care approaches for older people in the hospital through staff/service-user interaction and practice	Practice development practitioner/nurse delivers classroom training, reflective discussions, facilitates action learning sets, and coordinates practice observations	Action learning sets, team learning activities, peer observations of practice, reflective discussions, and daily 5-minute team clusters	Consistency of lead, ability to release staff, designated room available for reflective discussion, and protected time	Practice development nurse/practitioner post, educational support costs	Developing relational capacity in teams supports the delivery of compassionate care
Relation-Centered Leadership (RCL)	To develop leadership skills in compassionate care	Appreciative relationship-centered leadership	Exploring relationships with self, patients, and families through feedback forms, "feedback fortnight", daily huddles, and observations	Consistent senior staff, engagement from middle managers, focusing on continual reflection, and opportunities for giving feedback and engagement	Room space	Increased self-awareness, enhanced relationships among staff, enhanced reflective thinking, and an enhanced focus on staff and patient needs
Group Supervision	Supports ability to be critical within an environment of substantial uncertainty and change	Focus on three main functions of supervision: education, support, and management	Action learning groups meet every two weeks	Staff released from clinical practice to participate on a regular basis	Facilitator	The process assists in preventing burnout, compassion fatigue, and time off for illness

(continued)

Table 23.1 (continued)

Intervention	Aim	Process	Activities	Conditions for success	Resources required	Impact
Mindfulness	Self-directed practice to focus attention through focusing on present-moment awareness	Can be practiced any time. Formal program might involve 8 two-and-a-half hour weekly group sessions, a daylong silent retreat, and a commitment to practice mindfulness meditation practice outside of work	A range of approaches	Providing time and space to practice; regular practice is needed to develop a "habit" of mindfulness	Time and space	The health and well-being of staff in terms of reduced stress and anxiety. Long-term benefits include reduced employee absences due to stress, anxiety, and depression
Restorative Supervision	Co-coaching approach to process natural responses to complex clinical work to create a solution-focused approach	One-day training on co-coaching. Trained supervisors train others so that the program can become self-sustaining	Six sessions of co-coaching	Releasing staff time for regular supervision	None after initial training	Reduced levels of stress and burnout
Samaritans Volunteer Support System	Support emotional health of volunteers through a focus on their feelings rather than problem solving	At the end of each shift, volunteers "offload" to their shift leader	Volunteers summarize their calls and their feelings about them. Leaders assess the emotional health of the volunteer, and if they feel there is a need, they arrange for further support	Mind-set change including persuading people to stay to debrief at the end of the shift	Protected space; training for shift leaders to assess emotional health	No formal evaluation of approach has taken place

(continued)

Table 23.1 (continued)

Intervention	Aim	Process	Activities	Conditions for success	Resources required	Impact
Schwartz Rounds (Point of Care Foundation: PoCF)	To understand the challenges and rewards that are intrinsic to providing care	Structured forum where all staff, clinical and non-clinical, come together regularly to discuss the emotional and social aspects of working in health care	Rounds take place one time each month, mixed group of staff share their experiences followed by group discussions on emotional impact	Keeping a focus reflection rather than problem solving	Contract with PoCF in the UK to ensure the process is implemented in a consistent and measurable manner; commitment from senior staff	Staff who attend Rounds feel less stressed and isolated, with increased insight and appreciation for each others' roles. They also help to reduce hierarchies between staff and to focus attention on relational aspects of care
Critical Incident Stress Debriefings (CISDs) Self-Care Plans	To support emotional health of staff attending critical incidents	Staff assemble to discuss a call and examine their reactions	In the USA, these are mandatory for some first responders. With self-care plans, employees are required to create a plan and articulate measurable, outcome-oriented goals	Supportive attitude	Mandatory policy ensures full uptake	No formal evaluation of approach has taken place

Source Adapted from Table 3.1 in Mastracci and Sawbridge (2019) and work within a framework of relationships. Within this framework, participants explored relationships with self, patients and families, teams, and the wider organization.

RCL was a large project and funding included five full-time staff. In addition, a Lead Nurse and four Senior Nurses in Compassionate Care were required to support this research. This level of support may be unobtainable for many teams, but as it demonstrated changes in the work environment, some principles and practices may be adaptable for teams to use locally. Challenges to success included staff turnover at the senior level, combating staff time pressures, full engagement and contact with middle managers, which was crucial to sustaining work, sharing good practices and culture change, maintaining the energy of project staff, focusing on continual reflection, taking action, and opportunities for giving feedback and engagement. Despite these challenges, strengths of RCL include an increased self-awareness on the part of staff, enhanced relationships among staff, enhanced reflective thinking, and an enhanced focus on staff and patient needs.

Group Supervision. Group Supervision was developed in 2009 at the University of Birmingham (UK) and is founded on the idea that clinical supervision is fundamental to health and social care practice, underpinned by Reflective Practice. This model of Group Supervision is based on a Reflective Practice process, originally part of a standalone module run by the University of Birmingham and developed to enable staff to share challenges and successes of practice in a safe, supportive, and confidential environment. Practitioners in health and social care professions comprise the target audience for Group Supervision.

A formal evaluation at the end of the program assesses impact, which has consistently emphasized the value of taking part in the Reflective Group, having contact with peers, and sharing issues around the shock of being newly qualified. Informal discussion around the impact on staff retention is positive. Participants value the regular opportunity to meet with peers and share issues relating to practice in a closed group that is facilitated by an experienced practitioner/academic. The initial outlay for an organization is the cost of a facilitator. Challenges include ensuring that staff members are released from clinical practice to participate on a regular basis. Experience has shown that it has been difficult for staff to do this once they have left the program, reinforcing the need for a purposeful and systematic approach to staff support schemes, if they are to be effective. It needs to be built into job descriptions, and time created accordingly, though evidence suggests this is far from reality for many.

Mindfulness. Mindfulness is a self-directed practice for relaxing the body and calming the mind through focusing on present-moment awareness.

Its origins are in Buddhism and are a form of meditation. Mindfulness is a technique that has the potential to help anyone. It is not an approach that has been developed specifically for use in health or social care though it has been introduced in a range of organizations and therapeutic encounters. Through the practice of mindfulness, people are provided with the skills to train themselves to achieve greater maintenance of attention and develop more control in focusing their attention.

Mindfulness meditation practice typically involves sitting with your feet planted on the floor and the spine upright. The eyes can be closed or rest a few feet in front while the hands are in the lap or on the knees. The attention is gently brought to rest on the sensations of the body: feet on the floor, pressure on the seat, and the air passing through the nostrils. As thoughts continue, you return again and again to these physical sensations, gently encouraging the mind not to get caught up in the thought processes but to observe their passage. The development of curiosity, acceptance, and compassion in the process of patiently bringing the mind back differentiates mindfulness from simple attention training. Mindfulness can be practiced for a few moments as a breathing pause in the middle of a busy day or for half an hour in a quiet place first thing in the morning. A program might involve eight 2.5-hour weekly group sessions, a daylong silent retreat, and a commitment to practice mindfulness activities for 45 minutes, 6 days a week. Many variations exist, however. There are also several approaches that can be included under the broad heading of mindfulness including, mindfulness-based cognitive therapy, mindfulness-based relationship enhancement, mindfulness-based wellness education, mindfulness-based eating, and mindfulness-based medical practice. Miller-Fox (2018) discusses the positive potential for mindfulness-based stress-reduction approaches for law enforcement officer training in the USA.

Restorative Supervision. Restorative Supervision was developed in 2013 as a model of supervision designed to support healthcare professionals working within roles in which they have a significant emotional demand. Over 60 NHS Trusts across the UK and Ireland have employed Restorative Supervision. Restorative Supervision involves training both the supervisor and supervisees initially, so that they jointly understand this co-coaching approach to supervision. When professionals undertake complex clinical work, they move between anxiety, fear, or stress. If they can process these natural feelings about work, they can focus on learning needs and development and then enter a creative, energetic, and solution-focused zone. The training program can be varied according to the needs of the organization/staff but generally consists of one-day training supervisors to use co-coaching methods, followed by six sessions. It can also be run as a group session. Trained supervisors can cascade the approach to others so that the program will become self-sustaining using internal resources only. Impact is measured through a combination of qualitative and quantitative measures, the impact on the individual's stress, burnout, compassion fatigue, and compassion satisfaction, and feedback suggests improved levels of confidence and reduced anxiety. A number of studies have found reduced stress and burnout and increased levels of compassion satisfaction due to this approach (Wallbank 2013).

Samaritans Volunteer Support System. Samaritans were established in the UK in 1953 and provided the first 24-hour helpline in the world for people needing to talk confidentially, free from judgment or pressure, with the aim of reducing their isolation. Currently, 15,700 listening volunteers answer a call, email, or text every six seconds. In order to provide emotional support for volunteers, Samaritans have developed a system to reduce the likelihood that they leave a shift feeling anxious or distressed. Every volunteer call handler has access to this support system. Each volunteer undergoes a period of training prior to taking calls. Each shift is between three and five hours, and the volunteers never work alone. Callers are often in a highly distressed state, and the volunteers are actively encouraged to share the last call with their partner in the downtimes between calls. If the volunteer needs longer to debrief, the telephones will be turned off to enable this to happen. It is rare that this action is required, as most debriefs are possible in a few minutes, but the policy signifies the importance with which the organization regards the emotional support of volunteers. It is recognized that if the volunteers are not cared for, they cannot care for the callers. At the end of each shift, the volunteer "offloads" to the shift leader. This process involves the volunteer summarizing the types of calls taken and their feelings about them. The leader makes a judgment about the emotional health of the volunteer, and if they feel they were too strongly affected, they will arrange for further support to be offered, either by doing so themselves, or through the volunteer support team.

Sawbridge and Hewison (2012) created a similar "buddying" scheme on UK hospital wards for nurses, which required some staff time and a project lead. Because it was predominantly a mind-set change, rather than a specific set of actions, it required specific support and role modeling of behavior changes. It also has some logistical barriers: Systematically debriefing at the end of every shift was countercultural for staff, who just wanted to go home. Protected space for this discussion was also an issue, as was enabling nurses to raise issues and discuss their feelings rather than problem solve. The main strength of this system is that it does not require staff to leave the ward for regular periods, as with supervision and in some other models. It requires them to "be with" each other in a different way and have different conversations throughout the day, once the initial training and support have taken place. It does not require large amounts of resources or equipment. Although the program has not undergone formal evaluation, the approach shows considerable promise for a number of settings in which public servants work with colleagues, though without time-out for regular supervision, as colleagues could actively care for each other as well as the people they serve.

Schwartz Rounds. Schwartz Rounds were founded in the UK by the Point of Care Foundation (PoCF) and provide a structured forum where all staff, clinical and non-clinical, come together regularly to discuss the emotional and social aspects of working in health care. They are led by facilitators trained by PoCF. Rounds follow a standard model to ensure that they are replicable across settings and normally take place once a month for an hour at a time with catering provided before the Round. Once the Round starts, a panel comprised of three or four staff share their experiences for the first fifteen to twenty minutes. On each panel, there should ideally be a mix of clinical and non-clinical staff with different levels of seniority. A Round can either be based on different accounts of a case or can explore a theme such as "When things go wrong" or "A patient I'll never forget." Experiences are shared from the perspective of the panel member, not the patient, and the emphasis is on the emotional impact. The remainder of the hour features trained facilitators leading an open discussion. The key skill is for the facilitators to steer the discussion in such a way that it remains reflective and does not become a space to solve problems. The target audience is comprised of all staff, clinical and non-clinical, in a healthcare organization. Rounds are led by a facilitator from within the organization with facilitation experience, but then is trained and supported by PoCF and a senior clinician.

The underlying premise for Rounds is that the compassion shown by staff can make all the difference to a patient's experience of care, but that in order to provide compassionate care, staff must feel supported in their work. Feedback is collected at the end of every Round from all participants using a standardized form provided by PoCF. Over 400 healthcare organizations in the USA use Schwartz Rounds, and feedback has shown that staff who attend Rounds feel less stressed and isolated, with increased insight and appreciation for each other's roles. They also help to reduce hierarchies between staff and focus attention on relational aspects of care.

Critical Incident Stress Debriefings (CISDs) and Self-Care Plans. CISDs have been developed and employed by emergency response organizations in the USA. Target audiences have been police, fire, and emergency medical technicians, but the intervention could be applied in other settings. In a CISD, staff assemble to discuss an emotionally intense—"hot"—call and examine their reactions, very much like the approach taken in Samaritans and Schwartz Rounds. CISDs are mandatory, so no individual feels conspicuous in asking for a session.

Self-care plans were developed in a nonprofit setting in the USA. Within the first 30 days of employment, employees are required to create a plan of personal goals and articulate measurable, outcome-oriented goals. When employees have annual performance appraisals, they are evaluated on their self-care plans as well. A plan can include goals in the areas of physical, emotional, financial, intellectual, or spiritual health and have included goals such as quitting smoking, finishing a university course, or running a marathon. Attending to one's own well-being underpins this approach. An additional resource for managers in US national-level government agencies is from the US Merit Systems Protection Board (MSPB). In its 2016 survey of workers in national government agencies, MSPB gathered data on emotional labor in federal service and has published studies aimed at helping managers learn about the emotive load of the jobs they supervise (US MSPB 2015, 2019). The data are available to the public for further analysis.

Embodied Knowledge in Public Service Education

Embodied knowledge is not, at present, part of the required competencies for NASPAA-accredited programs. NASPAA is a nonprofit organization that was founded in the USA, but reviews and accredits academic degree programs in the USA, the UK, Europe, Asia, the Middle East, and South America. At present, the required competencies for accreditation emphasize cognitive skills. As the organization makes more inroads into program accreditation around the globe, we argue that its standards must keep pace. As our analyses throughout this Handbook have shown, cognition remains reified in many, but not all, national cultures. So-called Western cultures that trace their traditions back through the Enlightenment prioritize cognition, or knowledge of things, over embodied knowledge. NASPAA accreditation standards do not currently represent standards of proficiency in public service across all cultural contexts.

This section discusses how emotive competence underpins and therefore is consistent with current NASPAA accreditation standards. Emotive competence is fundamental to communicating and interacting productively with a diverse and changing workforce, as well as to leading and managing in public governance. We argue that emotive competence should be included along with competencies already required in accreditation standards. India incorporates emotional maturity in its criteria for evaluating public servants. China, Korea, Taiwan, and many other countries are sensitive to the emotive component of public service work.

Given NASPAA's interest in ensuring that accreditation standards are relevant around the globe, attention to the emotive component of public service work is especially crucial. A joint project between the United Nations Development Programme (UNDP) and the Government of India produced the Civil Services Competency Dictionary, a document used in India's civil service today. Emotional Maturity is among these competencies and is defined as "The ability to maintain a sense of professionalism and emotional restraint when provoked, when faced with hostility from others, or when working under conditions of increased stress. It also includes the ability to work effectively under stressful situations, remain resilient and maintain stamina over the long term" (UNDP 2014, 9). Likewise, public service in China and other Confucian countries emphasizes harmony, which demands emotive competence. The newest textbooks now integrate this material into their coverage (see, e.g., Pearce and Sowa 2019; Guy and Ely 2018).

Public service in the twenty-first century demands "the ability to establish and work as part of multi-stakeholder partnerships as well as a mindset of strategic thinking, collaboration, and partnership and the ability to engage in collaborative learning and mutual adjustment" (Rubaii 2016, 472). In the post-bureaucratic environment in which public service currently operates, public servants need persuasion, facilitation, and negotiation skills because they cannot rely on formal lines of authority to accomplish organizational objectives. Emotional Thought is needed to cultivate one's own self-awareness and also to sense the norms and expectations of network partners in shared-power relationships across organizations. These skills must be part of modern public service education.

Making the Affective Turn in Public Service Teaching and Practice

When academic programs build curricula to train students in administrative competencies, much of that which determines student success is emotive while most of the training is cognitive. Whether leadership development, consensual decision-making, employee engagement, team building, or organizational commitment and development, textbooks take the student only a few steps forward, compared to the emotive component of the work. As Stivers asserts, it is *meaning* that is sought, by public servants and citizens alike.

The explosion of interest in public service motivation and human performance are indicators that the field is attempting to expand its focus beyond its mechanical/cognitive heritage. The proliferation of research on public service motivation is evidence of the burgeoning interest in questions of what impels workers to pursue careers in public service. With the exception of Hsieh et al. (2012), however, studies stop short of assessing the emotive challenges and rewards of public service, in terms of how workers experience their joys and their heartaches. Even in reform-minded organizations, Newman and Guy observe (1998, 291) that doctrinaire scientific management remains alive and well in public administration. Taylor's legacy is evident in the reform initiatives of reinvention, right-sizing, restructuring, re-engineering, and pay-for-performance. These are many of the hallmarks of NPM reforms examined throughout these chapters. Each of these practices sets goals to eliminate waste, do more with less, enhance productivity, and make governance more efficient and rational, perhaps effective in a limited sense, but not affective.

Our argument is not a new one; instead, it is one that raises its head but gets drowned out decade after decade. The works of Jane Addams (see Shields 2017), Mary Parker Follett (1919, 1940a, b), and Frances Perkins (1934) all speak to the "laws of human nature" more clearly than currently accepted theory. Their writings make clear that the exercise of power flows in multiple directions and that it is the whole person who comes to work each day, not just that portion of each person that is cognitive and physical. Addams, Follett, and Perkins have confidence in workers' abilities, and all come closer to appreciating the fullness of human capacity, beyond just cognition.

Another way to see the illogic of focusing only on cognitive skills can be found in the popularity of instrumental motivation theories based in Materialism (Inglehart 1971). Maslow's hierarchy is intuitively satisfying and continues to be taught, but it requires Damasio's later theory of Emotional Thought to be comprehensive, and public administration theory has yet to take this extra step. Maslow's hierarchy specifies five levels of needs, the lowest two of which (physiological and safety needs) impel behavior to avoid the fear of being hungry and unsafe. They are based in Materialism, and this is where public administration begins and ends with Maslow. The three higher levels (belongingness, self-esteem, and self-actualization) impel behavior that brings happiness and are all emotion-driven because emotions do what the word implies: *emovere*, which means to move from one state to another or to stir up. Satisfaction of these stages are based in Damasio's (1994) homeostasis theory of emotion: The body sends signals to the brain that something is off, and via Emotional Thought, the brain moves the body to do what is needed to restore homeostasis.

Failure to acknowledge and to incorporate the emotive demands and rewards of work has real consequences. Fragmentation of the labor process means that workers perform discrete tasks without a sense of their contribution to the overall outcome. Their absence of control over work processes, lack of discretion and autonomy, and role ambiguity, leave them feeling more like machines than persons. Alienation is a real risk. An emphasis on extrinsic rewards to the exclusion of intrinsic rewards denies the meaning of work. This dilemma has implications for praxis.

Oblivion to the emotive component of work, in terms of both what workers give and what they get, leaves a black hole where intrinsic rewards are not acknowledged, and the effects of dissatisfaction are not resolved. Engagement, commitment, and job satisfaction are benefits that motivate those in public service to dedicate their careers. Burnout, emotive exhaustion, and discouragement are threats. In public service, alienation has serious consequences because it affects how citizens view government. A public servant alienated from her work alienates citizens from the state because inauthenticity is detectable.

The cognitive logic of effectiveness in organizations obscures the emotive. It is accepted as so natural and right that it seems odd to call it cognitive. This logic of effectiveness suppresses practices that are inconsistent with its basic premises, even when those practices contribute to organizational goals. The result is that organizations adopt the rhetoric of humanism but end up disappearing the very behavior that would embrace emotion work alongside cognitive work. This is why we urge an affective turn—a turn toward affect—in public administration theory.

Public jobs come with both public demands and personal demands. Officials must sense the emotive state of the citizen, analyze what the desired state should be in order to have a successful encounter, determine what actions to take in order to achieve the desired state, and then modify their own behavior in order to achieve this. This instantaneous sensing and responding requires emotional thought and behavior. The whole process is grounded in emotional labor and contributes to how the citizen "feels" during the encounter and how the citizen rates the encounter afterward. The teacher who must mollify angry parents, the caseworker who must investigate family members in response to a child abuse report, the emergency responder who must assure a frightened accident victim, the police officer who must arrest an agitator, the zoning regulator who must reject a waiver request, and the public information officer who must address an uneasy crowd: none of these encounters proceeds in the absence of emotional labor.

Even when the importance of citizen engagement is acknowledged, there is little research into the interpersonal public *encounter*. Blinders prevent the articulation between theory and praxis. Charles Goodsell (1981) identified this gap decades ago, attributing it to the fact that public administration focuses on policy implementation, while leaving the actual encounter to the work of various professions who view it not through the citizen/state lens, but rather through the perspectives of their own disciplinary blinders. Sociologists focus on the bureaucracy, roles, and functions. Social work focuses on the therapeutic exchange; education focuses on the teaching relationship; and healthcare professionals focus on treatment. Lost in this is the overarching importance of the public encounter. It is this nexus that data from Australia to India, from Bolivia to Thailand, from China to Rwanda, reveal. This is precisely where we have trained our sights: The human process in state/citizen encounters that occur every day in the delivery of public services, whether mundane or monumental.

Notes

1. The actual quote by Edward O. Wilson is as follows: "We are drowning in information, while starving for wisdom. The world henceforth will be run by synthesizers, people able to put together the right information at the right time, think critically about it, and make important choices wisely."
2. Portions of the section, "Supporting Embodied Knowledge in Public Service Practice," were previously published in Mastracci and Sawbridge (2019). Portions of the section, "Making the Affective Turn," were previously published in Guy and Mastracci (2018). See the References list for citation details on each.

References

Damasio, Antonio. 1994. *Descartes' Error: Emotion, Reason, and the Human Brain*. London: Penguin Books.
Follett, Mary Parker. 1919. "Community is a Process." *The Philosophical Review* 28 (6): 576–88.

Follett, Mary Parker. 1940a. "The Giving of Orders." In *Dynamic Administration: The Collected Papers of Mary Parker Follett*, edited by Henry C. Metcalf and Lyndall Urwick, 50–70. New York, NY: Harper & Row.

Follett, Mary Parker. 1940b. "The Psychology of Consent and Participation." In *Dynamic Administration: The Collected Papers of Mary Parker Follett*, edited by Henry C. Metcalf and Lyndall Urwick, 210–29. New York, NY: Harper & Row.

Goodsell, Charles T., ed. 1981. *The Public Encounter: Where State and Citizen Meet*. Bloomington: Indiana University Press.

Guy, Mary E., and Sharon H. Mastracci. 2018. "Making the Affective Turn: The Importance of Feelings in Theory, Praxis, and Citizenship." *Administrative Theory & Praxis* 40 (3): 281–88.

Guy, Mary E., and Todd L. Ely. 2018. *Essentials of Public Service: Introduction to Contemporary Public Administration*. Irvine, CA: Melvin & Leigh Publishers.

Hsieh, Chih-Wei, Kaifeng Yang, and Kai-Jo Fu. 2012. "Motivational Bases and Emotional Labor: Assessing the Impact of Public Service Motivation." *Public Administration Review* 72 (2): 241–51.

Immordino-Yang, Mary Helen, and Antonio Damasio. 2007. "We Feel, Therefore We Learn: The Relevance of Affective and Social Neuroscience to Education." *Mind, Brain, and Education* 1 (1): 3–10.

Inglehart, Ronald. 1971. "The Silent Revolution in Europe: Intergenerational Change in Post-industrial Societies." *American Political Science Review* 65 (4): 991–1017.

Ljungholm, Doina Popescu. 2014. "The Role of Emotional Labor in the Delivery of Public Services." *Review of Contemporary Philosophy* 13 (1): 11–16.

Loughran, J. John. 2002. "Effective Reflective Practice: In Search of Meaning in Learning About Teaching." *Journal of Teacher Education* 53 (1): 33–43.

Mastracci, Sharon, and Yvonne Sawbridge. 2019. "Showing You Care: Emotional Labor and Public Service Work." In *(Re)imagining the Future Public Service Workforce*, edited by Helen Dickinson, Catherine Needham, Catherine Mangan, and Helen Sullivan, 39–54. Singapore: Routledge.

Miller-Fox, Geri-Anne. 2018. "Emotional Labor Training Typology for Basic Peace Officer Training Curricula." *Administrative Theory & Praxis* 40 (4): 357–79.

Newman, Meredith A., and Mary E. Guy. 1998. "Taylor's Triangles, Follett's Web." *Administrative Theory & Praxis* 20 (3): 287–97.

Pearce, Jone L., and Jessica E. Sowa. 2019. *Organizational Behavior: Real Research for Public and Nonprofit Managers*. Irvine, CA: Melvin & Leigh Publishers.

Perkins, Frances. 1934. *People at Work*. New York: John Day Company.

Rubaii, Nadia. 2016. "Bringing the 21st-Century Governance Paradigm to Public Affairs Education: Reimagining How We Teach What We Teach." *Journal of Public Affairs Education* 22 (4): 467–82.

Sawbridge, Yvonne, and Alasdair Hewison. 2012. *Time to Care: Responding to Concerns About Poor Nursing Care*. HSMC Policy Paper. Birmingham, UK: University of Birmingham.

Schon, Donald A. 1983. *The Reflective Practitioner: How Professionals Think in Action.* New York, NY: Basic Books.

Schon, Donald A. 1987. "Changing Patterns of Inquiry in Work and Living." *Journal of the Royal Society of Arts* 135 (5367): 225–37.

Shields, Patricia, ed. 2017. *Jane Addams: Progressive Pioneer of Peace, Philosophy, Sociology, Social Work, and Public Administration.* Cham, Switzerland: Springer International Publishing.

Stivers, Camilla. 2018. *Creativity in the Face of Uncertainty: PA Theory as a Generative Force.* Video retrieved from https://www.youtube.com/watch?v=yJ5oR-FQR6Y.

United Nations Development Programme. 2014. *Civil Services Competency Dictionary.* Material downloaded March 8, 2019. http://persmin.gov.in/otraining/Competency%20Dictionary%20for%20the%20Civil%20Services.pdf.

United States Merit Systems Protection Board. 2015. "Emotional Labor: Often Overlooked, Always Present." *Issues of Merit Newsletter* (Winter), 1 and 7. Accessed at https://www.mspb.gov/MSPBSEARCH/viewdocs.aspx?docnumber=1130380&version=1134867&application=ACROBAT.

United States Merit Systems Protection Board. 2019. "The Price of Masking Our True Emotions at Work." *Issues of Merit Newsletter*, February 7. Accessed at https://www.mspb.gov/MSPBSEARCH/viewdocs.aspx?docnumber=1585933&version=1591693&application=ACROBAT.

Wallbank, Sonya. 2013. "Maintaining Professional Resilience Through Group Restorative Supervision." *Community Practitioner* 86 (8): 26–81.

Wilson, Edward. 1998. *Consilience: The Unity of Knowledge.* New York, NY and Cambridge, UK: Knopf and Cambridge University Press.

24

From Measuring Results to Managing Relationships

Mary E. Guy, Sharon H. Mastracci and Seung-Bum Yang

The line of inquiry reported in these chapters opens the "black box" of interpersonal dynamics in governance processes. As globalization advances, so does the desire to reconcile the gaps in our knowledge about how administrative processes function and how public service professionals go about doing their work. Some nations are in an era of weakened administrative sovereignty and are relying more on flattened hierarchies and networked alignments. Some function with centralized authority. Some function with administrative structures that barely comport with national culture. Regardless of the governmental structure and program delivery system, the human factor is present around the globe. The irony is that the field of public administration focuses on the state and its agencies; international relations focuses on nations as a whole but not agencies; and globalists focus not on states, but on international organizations. At the heart of all these

M. E. Guy (✉)
School of Public Affairs, University of Colorado Denver, Denver, CO, USA
e-mail: mary.guy@ucdenver.edu

S. H. Mastracci
Department of Political Science,
University of Utah, Salt Lake City, UT, USA
e-mail: Sharon.mastracci@poli-sci.utah.edu

S.-B. Yang
Department of Public Administration, Konkuk University, Seoul, South Korea
e-mail: sbyang@konkuk.ac.kr

M. E. Guy et al. (eds.), *The Palgrave Handbook of Global Perspectives on Emotional Labor in Public Service*, https://doi.org/10.1007/978-3-030-24823-9_24

instrumentations are people working with people to accomplish public purposes, and this is the focus of the book.

The information provided in these chapters makes it safe to say that emotional labor is a universal attribute of public service work. Furthermore, its performance and its consequences are subtly shaped by the confluence of culture and political dynamics in each nation. For the public service professional, being good at it, regardless of nation, contributes to feelings of personal fulfillment and usually increases job satisfaction. The downside of emotional labor—emotional exhaustion, burnout, and feeling "used up"—varies more by nation than does its positive effects, job satisfaction, and fulfillment. The answer to why this is the case can be found in the unique constellation of elements that each nation presents. The emotive component in public service in each country is shaped by how history, traditions, and identity uniquely combine to temper the interpretation of feelings and to sculpt the outcome of citizen–state encounters.

Those who work in public service are the connectors between state and citizen. Around the globe, they are the people every nation relies on to bring public policies to fruition and to make public programs work. Public service is a bold and noble profession—whether as teachers, caseworkers, police officers, zoning officials, healthcare workers, disaster response teams, or transit planners—but it is hard work, especially in regard to its emotive demands. Citizens come to government when their needs cannot be met by family, neighbors, or the market, so they arrive in an already heightened emotive state: anxious, fearful, angry, frustrated, vulnerable, and needy. In order to perform their job, public service workers must manage the citizen's emotive state at the same time that they meet the cognitive demands and affective display rules of their job description.

The feeling that citizens have for their government is both the beginning point and end point of the citizen–state relationship. For governing to be effective, citizens must feel good about those who govern. Why does it matter? Because out of rapport comes trust, willingness to comply with laws, identification with the government as being "of them," and a higher likelihood that coproduction strategies will be productive. Emotional labor is instrumental in this new paradigm, and this is why the affective component belongs in the canon of public administration, just as the cognitive component already resides there.

Public service *should* be a field that is aware of its dual load of both cognitive and emotive demands. While benchmarks and outcomes measures have their place, glorification of data dashboards overlooks an essential dimension. The current emphases on governance, collaboration, coproduction, citizen engagement, and relational contracting, all assume, but fail to comprehend and explicate, the foundation upon which they are built: It is the relationship between citizens and between citizen and state. The closest that current theory comes to acknowledging this appears in writings about social capital, a subject of inquiry that addresses the topic from on high, understanding neither its component parts nor how it is nurtured. A paradigmatic shift is in order for public administration theory and inquiry to embrace relationship.

Textbooks written to teach aspiring public managers how to plan, organize, staff, direct, coordinate, report, and budget do just that. But most fail to include an essential element in the citizen–state encounter: the emotive engagement that motivates commitment to public purposes on the part of the worker and that builds trust and rapport on the part of the citizen. As these chapters demonstrate, the emotive component hides in plain sight. Those engaged in public service around the globe employ emotional labor just as they engage in cognitive labor. The resilience and "grit" that international disaster relief workers must have to continue doing what they do, the perseverance of child protective workers who return to work day after day and encounter anguishing dilemmas, the "toughness" of law enforcement officers, the nurturance of effective teachers, the patience and confidence of public information officers, the coolness of emergency responders: All of these jobs come with a large emotive burden. It is a mistake to treat their jobs as if they are accountants, carefully following invariant protocol, assigning numbers to the correct columns. There may be paperwork in their jobs, but there is much more than that.

In the everyday work experience of civil servants, it is evident that emotional labor is a main contributor to job satisfaction, feelings of self-fulfillment, and the feeling that one's work makes a difference. It is also obvious that dynamics within each nation sculpt its administrative processes and affect how services are delivered, how they are received by citizens, and how meaningfulness is achieved. These chapters also demonstrate that broad generalities about cultural differences, collectivism versus individualism, global North versus global South, and East versus West, miss the mark when used to categorize public service practice. Because dynamics differ in each nation, both cultural competence and mindful "rowing" are necessary in order for public service to be responsive.

Observations

Below are six take-aways from the findings reported in these chapters. They range from commentary on the citizen–state encounter, to the difference that national context makes, to issues of social capital and human capital, to the importance of incorporating an appreciation for the emotive dynamic in theory, research, and practice.

Emotional Labor Is an Important Element in the Public Encounter

Administrative processes provide moments for dialogue with the public, whether the goal is to render services or enforce laws. Every encounter carries forward to the next, setting the tone for how government's actions will be received. The practice of public administration is less the quest for calculable results and more a situational, simultaneous interpretation and communication rooted in the entanglement of experience and language (Stivers 2018). In the encounter, thought and action blend, such that the administrative work carries lived experience forward. It affects how citizens feel about government and how government feels about citizens.

The citizen–state encounter occurs with interaction between any resident and a representative of the state. It is an interpersonal process wrapped in the garb of power. In it, there are mutually understood communicative methods that transmit meaning beyond what the spoken word conveys. The communication is characterized by talk and body language, both of which are infused with emotive displays. The encounter is marked by social, interpersonal, and collaborative characteristics (Hand and Catlaw 2019), and it goes far beyond the sterilized description of "coping." It serves to encourage or discourage coproduction, reinforce or extinguish citizen engagement, and increase or diminish collaboration.

Unlike the sales transaction where the encounter is designed to be positive at each occurrence, the public encounter is not always positive. In circumstances where the political dynamics are such that residents see government as the enemy, or where police or regulators are enforcing unpopular laws, there is rancor and even open hostility toward them as they do their jobs. Mistreatment occurs on a continuum from insults and threats to verbal abuse to physical assault. Persistent abuse has the potential to negatively affect worker's sense of themselves as competent professionals doing worthwhile work. As Chapter 7 shows, those who work in settings where they are treated abusively experience lower job satisfaction, have less trust in citizens, and feel less capable of managing the emotive aspects of their jobs. Just managing one's own emotive expressions can be taxing, especially for those who must exhibit confidence and calmness while being spit at, yelled at, and cursed.

Whether librarian or police officer, zoning regulator or social worker, the emotion regulation that is required to suppress one's own anger or fear while displaying calmness takes a toll on the worker. Interpreting the cause for the abuse, such as the trying circumstances in Rwanda as citizens strive to re-establish their lives, can help workers understand the cause of the frustration. But in some cultures, there is simply a distrust and dislike for power that translates into viciousness toward those who work for government (see, e.g., Vickers 2010, 2011). Regardless of the cause, every job has an emotion culture. From the worker's point of view, it may require putting on a "false face," which means displaying a friendly, calm demeanor regardless of how one actually feels.

In half the nations surveyed, emotive pretending makes work doubly laborious and the threat of burnout rises. This is what the data show in Australia, Bolivia, South Korea, Taiwan, the UK, and the USA. Were this finding only in the USA and the UK, it might be explained this way: That those who admit to feeling burned out do so because they have job options elsewhere and can afford to be ultra-sensitive to emotive stress. However, the fact that the same outcome occurs in Bolivia, a poor country, indicates that burnout is not an affliction reserved for affluent nations. Another explanation might focus on the individualist versus collectivist continuum and assume that individualist nations would be more subject to the deleterious effect of emotive pretending, but such an explanation fails to explain the case of Korea, a collectivist culture rooted in Confucian norms.

Clearly, emotion culture varies across nations. If it were the same in countries with equivalent levels of per capita purchasing power, one could draw an economic conclusion that would go like this: In poor countries, where landing a government job is a mark of success, job security, and salary certainty, consequences from work that could lead wealthy Americans to suffer burnout and seek work elsewhere may be experienced differently. The emotional exhaustion that workers endure would be a welcome price to pay for the standard of living that government jobs provide. For example, Moloney and Chu (2016) report that, in the case of Jamaica, a state with a high unemployment rate where eighty percent of babies are raised by single mothers, and the few jobs that exist are far more secure in government than in business, the tradeoff is obvious. Economic security is more important than succumbing to the effects of burnout. Put another way, when the job, along with the burnout that accompanies it, is better than not being employed, workers may interpret their feelings more positively, essentially denying the burnout they experience. But that is not what the data reveal. Instead, burnout is experienced in some wealthy countries and some poor countries. In other words, wealth or the lack of it does not explain how civil servants experience emotive dissonance on the job.

Although burnout is a substantive outcome of emotional labor and has practice implications, the "bright side" of emotion work also is a substantive outcome and has practice implications. Similar to the conclusion reached by Humphrey et al. (2015)—that authentic emotive expression has positive effects in terms of job satisfaction and feelings of personal fulfillment—findings across all the nations surveyed for this book reveal that a similar dynamic prevails, although the deep acting variable produced consistently positive outcomes in only half of the countries surveyed. Humphrey et al. had conducted a meta-analysis of studies done primarily among Anglosphere settings; in this study, the more potent path across all nations, whether east or west, north or south, emerges in the mere act of performing emotional labor, as measured by the emotive capacity variable.

National Context Influences the Performance, Experience, and Consequences of Emotional Labor

Ways of categorizing nations by collectivism versus individualism, masculinism versus feminism, short-term orientation versus long-term orientation, and so forth are conveniences that do not offer much understanding when it comes to how emotion work is performed. As demonstrated throughout the chapters, emotional labor is experienced differently in various countries, but not according to how standard ways of describing culture would predict. For example, war torn countries such as Rwanda produce a public service climate that is very different from a nation that has enjoyed peaceful stability for a long time. Nations that have been colonized by cultures different from their own, such as India, Pakistan, and the Philippines, have blended public service cultures that contain several parts tradition and several parts that persist but fit uncomfortably with the nation's psyche. While emotional pretense is anathema in the USA, because it is interpreted as disingenuous, it is not viewed as negatively in many other countries. In sum, context matters.

Theory building across regions or around the globe must be cognizant of the uniqueness of nations. As Moloney emphasizes, the positivist-empiricist approach of Anglosphere scholars fails to comprehend the inter-subjective nature of the sociocultural milieu in Asian and African nations (Moloney 2018). Although there are pan-cultural elements to emotive expression, there are also culture-specific, or nation-specific, interpretations and assignment of nuances (Russell 1991). As Chen and Hsieh (2017) conclude, theory with wide generalizability cannot be isolated from cultural settings. The emotive component of the work is intertwined with attitudes about government, causing it to vary from country to country.

At the individual level, political dynamics and the presence or absence of trust between public officials and citizens affect every encounter and become an iterative process. During the citizen–state encounter, the public service professional creates feelings that last long after the encounter concludes. These feelings are the foundation for attitudes about government, and attitudes about government affect the emotive content of the next encounter, just as was revealed in Chapter 7 where mistreatment was discussed.

At the organizational level, dynamics are situated within the larger political and cultural context. They determine the extent to which emotional labor is performed and the types of emotion that are thought appropriate. Just as nations have their own emotion culture, each organization has an emotion culture that subtly defines "appropriate" and "inappropriate" emotive expressions. The "right" emotion is inextricably linked to ideas of what constitutes professional service and proper comportment (Wilding et al. 2014). This study did not isolate respondents by their occupation or agency. Whether law enforcement officers, teachers, social workers, or community organizers, their responses were analyzed according to their country, not their particular occupation or agency for whom they worked. To take the next step and do so, however, would reveal the degree to which socialization to professional norms or organizational norms mitigate national and/ or cultural influences. Suffice it to say that police officers in Thailand can be expected to experience their work somewhat similarly and somewhat differently than police officers in Australia.

Emotional Labor Contributes to Social Capital

Trust, rapport, engagement, and collaboration are words used to describe the desired outcome of public encounters. So many public administration questions tumble forward and beg to be addressed: How are coproduction strategies affected by the emotive in the citizen–state encounter? How does emotional labor factor into collaborative strategies? What aspects of emotional labor impel further engagement? Questions such as these require the convergence of emotional labor and social capital variables. Although the dynamics vary from country to country, and although some languages are better equipped to express emotive concepts, the connections exist in one pattern or another everywhere.

Cultures develop language that suits their needs. For this reason, some languages have more words for emotion than others. Incorporating more terms for emotive subtleties provides a means for people to think in layered ways about their feelings. In Chinese, *yuan bei* refers to a sense of complete and perfect accomplishment (Robson 2017b). *Tarab* in Arabic refers to a musically induced state of ecstasy or enchantment. *Gigil* in Tagalog refers to the irresistible urge to hug or squeeze someone because they are loved or cherished. *Dadirri*, an Australian aboriginal term, refers to a deep, spiritual act of reflective, respectful listening. *Nunchi* in Korean refers to the ability to sense the mood of another person and respond accordingly. These are only a few examples that reveal the contrast between the comparatively blunt emotive terms in English compared to the subtler, more nuanced terms available in other languages.

There are emotive messages contained in words, facial expression, body posture and movements, tone of voice, and choice of phrasing. While generic emotive expression is universal, psychologists suggest that there are "dialects" unique to geographic, national, and social boundaries (Elfenbein and Ambady 2002). Just as linguistic dialects define one social group from another, emotive dialects affect how emotional labor is perceived and they reflect the manner in which emotions are expressed and interpreted. The degree to which emotive expression is nuanced matters in the social capital calculus. This is because it shapes how feelings are experienced and expressed regarding collective action and how attitudes toward government and toward the citizenry are reinforced or discouraged.

To complicate inquiry into social capital further, the same words have different meanings in different countries. For example, the word "democracy" is interpreted differently around the globe. In the USA, it is more likely to be interpreted as a focus on individual freedoms, representativeness, and relatively weak government. In China, it is more likely to be interpreted as a collective respect for central authority that acts in the interest of the people. In some cultures, democracy is conflated with economic equality, and in some, it is treated as a separate concept. Similarly, understandings about the degree to which government can and should rightfully exercise power over citizens vary from nation to nation. It is a mistake to overlook these differences and to fail to understand how they affect the public encounter and how public service professionals perceive their role. The integration of cultural competency into public administration practice is only useful when the subtleties of national context are embraced. To do otherwise is to create intuitively pleasing theory that is irrelevant to practice.

Emotional labor is, by definition, a social exercise because it is performed during interpersonal interaction. Some assume that social orientation changes the way people think about events or problems, generalizing that those in collectivist societies focus more on relationships and the context of the situation, while those in individualistic societies focus on separate elements and consider situations as fixed rather than fluid (Robson 2017a). Generalizations such as this are not sufficiently refined to provide accurate predictions for how emotional labor is experienced by public service professionals in collectivist versus individualist cultures. Chapter 21 shows that in a number of cross-national comparisons, there is as much difference between collectivist countries as there are similarities among them. The same is true for individualist nations. Regardless of the direction of findings, they are grounded in the social capital that unites a nation and differentiates it from others.

Another social capital consideration is that of leadership. Authentic emotive expression and authentic leadership go hand in hand (Newman et al. 2009; Miao et al. 2018). Rationality, alone, is not sufficient for enthusing followers and motivating them to pursue collective goals (Damasio 1994). Self-awareness and the ability to manage one's own emotional state as well as to sense the state of others and to respond appropriately are essential qualities. There are moderators that affect the connection between leadership and good emotional labor skills, such as culture and context, but it is nevertheless one that builds social capital.

The social aspect of the public encounter cannot be removed from the personal because the social is never external to people (Smith 2005). This is one more reason that the emotive communication that occurs in the citizen–state exchange lives beyond the moment. It creates lasting impressions and perceptions of the state. People's experience becomes their working knowledge of how the state functions.

Each person's experience has a foot in two worlds: One remembered affectively and one remembered cognitively. The feeling that citizens carry with them from the encounter informs the cognition, which then is expressed in terms of an evaluation about government performance, the degree of compassion with which they were treated, and the positive or negative halo that they then ascribe to government as a whole.

Emotional Labor Is a Foundational Element in Human Capital

That which happens in the public encounter between citizen and state has effects that extend beyond the service in question; outcomes are both tangible and intangible. As tempting as it is to overlook the emotive in favor of cognitive strategies—to cognitize emotion by calling it "coping"—it is more straightforward to call it what it is. Emotional labor is performed in the immediacy of person-to-person interaction. Analogous to comparing how things look at ground level rather than at altitude, coping strategies describe events from a vantage of 10,000 feet, being far enough removed from the immediacy of the situation to deal with the emotion intellectually, rather than emotively. Rather than discounting workers' ability to perform emotional labor, it is better to integrate recognition of it into human resource functions.

Emotional labor is an aspect of human capital: Robots do not perform it; humans do. It should be embraced throughout job analysis and description, recruitment and selection, training and development, performance management and appraisal, and rewarding employees on the quality not just of their cognitive (technical) skills but also on their emotive skills. Discussion speaks first to job analysis and the value of using job descriptions that include both technical and emotive demands.

Job Analysis and Description

Interpersonal skills and emotional labor are required in most public service jobs. Ironically, most job descriptions fail to mention them because job analyses fail to acknowledge them. For example, whether in Australia or the UK, South Korea or Taiwan, emergency call takers must manage not only telecommunications equipment, but also the emotional state of panicked callers. The emotive content of the call sticks with them long after they have removed the headphones and turned away from the dispatch console, but their job descriptions focus only on cognitive requirements of the job.

Job analyses that include the position's emotive component as well as cognitive component provide a more accurate depiction of the work. An accurate job analysis then assures an accurate job description. And an accurate job description makes it easier for prospective applicants to determine whether the job is right for them. It also paves the way for hiring authorities to incorporate consideration of all necessary skills when interviewing applicants.

Job descriptions and selection mechanisms that have a high goodness of fit between job demands and worker characteristics are necessary for prospective candidates to determine whether they have the temperament and skills for the job. Cross-cultural research suggests that this will differ by context, but the case of India and how it has operationalized emotive competence into its human resource policies as described in Chapter 12 provides a starting point.

The next step in the human resource management process is recruitment and selection.

Recruitment and Selection

Explicit job descriptions that alert job applicants to the kind of work that lay before them help to set realistic expectations. A best practice to follow in job advertisements is to include a description of required emotive skills alongside the cognitive skill requirements. For example, an ad that includes "This is a good job for you if you are good at dealing with emotional issues" or, "if you are good at getting people to calm down," provides an indicator that emotion management is part of the job. This language, adopted from the emotive capacity variable, helps prospective applicants learn the emotive demands and decide whether this is work they want to do.

As discussed in Chapter 4, self-awareness and self-regulation are essential skills for workers who must engage in emotionally intense work, both because they are more likely to be able to endure job demands and because they are more likely to be able to manage the emotional state of others. Interview protocols can provide insight into job candidates' emotive resiliency by asking candidates to describe emotionally intense experiences in prior jobs. Their response provides indicators of their self-awareness and emotion regulation skills. Emotionally aware job candidates will be able to articulate incidents that triggered a strong emotive response. Being able to describe the event and their response to it provides indication that they have the capacity to acknowledge and deal with emotion in a constructive fashion.

Expressive flexibility is helpful in jobs that require workers to be responsive to the emotional state of the citizen. Workers with a diverse repertoire of emotion management strategies are better equipped to engage with citizens, be aware of their own emotive state while sensing that of those around them, and make adjustments as appropriate in their own. Making discussion of emotionally intense work experiences a "normal" expectation at regularly scheduled staff meetings contributes to building a healthy emotion culture for workers.

Training and Development

The importance of training and development cannot be overemphasized. These are organizational mechanisms that help public service professionals make sense of their everyday work experiences and feelings and develop resilience. Agencies that do a good job of training are those that treat emotive skills as being as important as cognitive skills and offer training and development opportunities to build their skills.

Working in emotionally intense jobs has a cumulative effect. Sensitizing workers to this helps to ward off burnout, especially for those who work in disaster recovery, or with crime victims, or who encounter residents who live in squalid conditions. As they counsel people in need, they encounter more detail than their imaginations can bear. Although not victims themselves, this takes a toll over time (Remington and Ganapati 2017). Because they encounter vicarious trauma on a daily basis, they benefit from opportunities to discuss their reaction to it and to share their experiences with others who encounter similar events.

Another dimension to training workers who will be in emotionally intense situations is to prepare them for managing their own emotional overload. A firefighter warns that, when approaching a burning building, he has to make sure it is safe to proceed: "It's very easy to get tunnel vision because of the adrenalin that's going on and it's like the moth to the fire and so that does take training to learn to get those parts of your emotions under control—the adrenalin-junkie emotions—because those are the ones that tend to get people seriously hurt" (Mastracci et al. 2012, 50).

National culture combines with organizational culture to dictate which emotions are appropriate to display and which ones are not. This is why training is contextual to the circumstances. Norms influence how public service professionals do their jobs and whether they disguise how they are feeling or whether they display it. Public administration theory has long acknowledged that workers must be well trained in the technical aspects of their jobs. But the evidence presented in these chapters makes it obvious that they must also be trained in the emotive aspects of their work.

Training in regard to emotional labor must be tailored to the nation. As data in Chapter 20 show in regard to US workers and as the comparisons across countries show in Chapter 21, emotive pretending is especially deleterious in the USA. While a positive work environment is a good thing, mandated display rules that require "positivity" are judged in the USA to be an unfair expectation. This is demonstrated by the fact that the US National Labor Relations Board issued a ruling that employers cannot require workers to wear a smile when they do not feel like it (Konnikova 2016, 1). This might not be the case in China, India, Pakistan, Philippines, Rwanda, or Thailand, where data show that emotive pretending does not have a significant positive relationship to burnout. But in the USA, it does, and emotive display rules that require workers to engage in pretense are ruled to be an unacceptable breach of individual rights. Examples such as this demonstrate how context matters in terms of determinations about what is, and what is not, a reasonable work expectation and whose right it is to govern individual emotive expression.

Another way to think about training and supervision in regard to emotional labor is demonstrated by the importance of caring and compassion in healthcare settings. Mastracci and Sawbridge (2019) make the case that in health services, such as in the National Health Service in the UK, reading the emotions of patients and being responsive to them is as important as drawing blood or performing surgeries. It is part of the treatment, so they recommend establishing learning environments to enhance skills necessary for delivering compassionate care. Training is provided by workshops, team learning activities, peer observations and counseling, classroom work, and treatment team discussions. In this context, emotional labor is a requirement of the job and training is focused on developing worker skills.

Whether training and development strategies focus on building self-regulation skills, awareness of others' emotive state, setting healthy boundaries between work and private life, or articulating emotive responses, they must fit the context. Discretion and autonomy help to stave off burnout among American workers (Humphrey et al. 2015), but they will not be as useful in countries with different emotion cultures.

Performance Management and Appraisal

Skillful performance of emotional labor should be rewarded just as skillful performance of cognitive labor is rewarded. But it rarely is. The lack of acknowledgment renders such labor invisible, fails to reward the worker for that aspect of their performance that gives them the greatest satisfaction, and fails to reward those workers who know how to balance the stress of the job such that it does not wear them down.

There are glimmers of light in some nations. For example, India's human resource system purposely operationalizes emotive competency in a way that provides guidance to supervisors as they coach employees and makes it clear as to what emotive behaviors are encouraged. And recently, the National Assembly of South Korea passed Korea's Occupational Safety and Health Act Amendments for 2018. This law, called the "emotional labor employee protection bill," stipulates that employees have a clear right to suspend work and evacuate when they are subjected to verbal harassment. If employers fail to allow employees to do so, they will be fined up to USD 9000 or imprisoned up to one year. Before this law was passed, call center employees, whether working for government or business, did not have the right to terminate the call when the caller became abusive. This law provides the right for call takers to stop the call when they are subjected to verbal harassment, rather than having to wait for the caller to terminate the call.

Properly conducted job analyses that include the emotive component of the work overcome the silence of performance appraisal forms that fail to include it as skill worth rating. Once tasks are identified in the analysis, they can be included in the job description, in training and development initiatives, in performance coaching, and in the performance appraisal. This, then, leads to a more accurate evaluation that includes consideration of the emotive component in the job and rewards skilled performance.

If there is one over-arching lesson from the survey responses from workers around the globe, it is that the emotion culture varies by country. The emotion culture for Rwanda, for example, is quite different from that which exists in the Philippines, Bolivia, or Australia. The fact that human resource techniques must be tailored to the work context cannot be overstated. One size does not fit all.

Rewarding Emotive Skills

Rewarding employees on the quality not just of their cognitive (technical) skills but also on their emotive skills is a holistic approach to encouraging desired performance. Reward systems that provide feedback and compensation for those who are skilled at emotional labor will reinforce it. In such ideal circumstances, the public encounter is enhanced and the citizen–state relationship benefits.

According to the human resource logic model, the implications for emotional labor in public service are as follows: Through selective recruitment of applicants who are technically skilled and emotionally self-aware, the workforce is better equipped to deliver public services. Training that enhances worker knowledge about emotional labor and the feelings that are normal in such work will advance the performance of emotion work and proactively reduce its downside. Supervisors who are knowledgeable about emotive tasks as well as cognitive tasks are better equipped to train, motivate, and provide support to workers. Performance appraisal and reward systems that acknowledge emotional labor skills will reinforce it and encourage proficiency.

Emotional Labor Belongs in the Public Administration Canon

The fifth takeaway is that there is much to be learned about the emotive component in public service in terms of how it is performed, how both citizens and workers are affected by it, and how it affects citizen engagement. The researchers who surveyed workers and contributed chapters to this book have "surfaced" emotional labor. Now we need to situate the subject within administrative theory, the citizen engagement literature, and human resource management policies and procedures.

While emotional labor in business settings is increasingly studied in multiple countries, emotional labor in governmental settings is more complex and less studied. The power of government accompanies the encounter between citizen and state, creating a heightened emotive cauldron, perhaps with fear, or threat, or relief. Whatever the feelings, they affect the interaction, changing it from any other person-to-person exchange to one that is elevated in importance, meaning, implication, and consequences.

The representation of emotional labor in the public administration literature is like a game of whac-a-mole, where the emphasis on rationality is used to downplay and overlook the role of emotion or at least to beat down the affective and keep it "under control" (Schreurs 2002). Nowhere will a reader find doubts expressed about the utility of rationality, all the while the subtext encourages minimization of emotive expression. Enlightenment thinking truncates what public service is, up to and including the assumption that emotion "gets in the way of" reason. Recent research, however, actually shows that emotion aids reason, that embodied knowledge is just a different kind of knowledge, and that humans use both to understand the world. Ignoring this broader understanding of knowledge is to misunderstand the subjective aspect of public service delivery.

Public administration—the art and science of pursuing public purposes—is messy from beginning to end. First, it is not clear which public purposes should be pursued. Second, there will be disagreement over whichever purposes are selected for attention. Third, the enterprise is a human one, accompanied by all the foibles of human nature. The orderly and systematic rule of reason that exists on the pages of textbooks will rarely be found at the street level where practice happens. To counter wicked problems, administrative responses require more than reason. They require an accompanying affect that will engage citizens in the pursuit of elusive goals. This is true even when the emotion is disgust. Whether it is the child protective services worker who takes away parents' custody because they battered their child, or a public works engineer dealing with a backed-up sewer, the most negative of emotions may be a "comes with" of the job and workers must deal with it (Patterson 2001). Disgust is not often considered among the topics of emotional labor, but it is as real as joy and happiness.

The point is that an expanded theory and practice of public administration must embrace both reason and emotion. But this inclusion must go beyond an "add emotions and stir" sort of integration into the canon. Emotive expression is a source of information: a reality in the public encounter, a guide to decision-making and action, an amplifier of motivation and personal fulfillment, and a requirement for meaningful human functioning. Whether positive or negative, it is present in human interaction. Unlike pain, where one person's suffering cannot be felt by the other, one's emotional state can be felt or at least reflected by the other. Indignation and outrage are normal, as is caring and nurturance. The whole repertoire of human emotions belongs in the canon, in administrative practice, in citizen engagement, and in the public encounter. While emotional labor can be taxing, its potential for accelerating job satisfaction and fulfillment must also be embraced (Hsieh et al. 2016).

There is more to program results than only that which can be counted. There is the importance of relationship and the meaningfulness of the encounter. Meaningfulness is a force for good—a personal experience—and not one that can be mandated. It is work that makes a difference in people's lives (Bailey 2018). To the degree that employees experience meaningfulness through their work, the pursuit of public purposes is benefitted at the same time that the worker benefits.

Whether grief or joy, disgust or happiness, emotive responses amplify the public encounter and give it meaning far beyond the passage of the moment (Kristjansson 2000). To the degree that the encounter advances the connection among people, the state's interests and citizen's interests are both served. Sometimes described as empathy, this experience of connection develops out of shared feelings or an appreciation for one another's feelings.

Trust and meaningfulness do not come from spreadsheets; they are different from the "atomistic contrivances" of rationalism (Scott 2001, 236). They come from the emotive component in public service. This is demonstrated by the paths shown in Table 21.1. For example, emotive capacity contributes to job satisfaction in nine out of the twelve nations surveyed. And it contributes to feelings of self-fulfillment in eleven out of twelve countries. Furthermore, authentic emotive expression contributes to feelings of self-fulfillment in seven countries. Just as interesting is the finding that it does not in the other five countries surveyed. Why might this be the case? Another quandary is why emotive pretending contributes to burnout in half of the countries and does not have a significant effect in the other half. These patterns reveal the degree to which the intertwining of culture and political dynamics shape and sculpt how emotional labor is experienced within countries. Awareness of this fact belongs in the theory of public administration so that those studying to be effective practitioners are sensitized to the interaction between a nation's internal characteristics and their everyday work experience.

There Is Much More to Be Learned About Emotional Labor

International comparative research opens the canon to a broader, deeper understanding of public administration as a contextual enterprise. Absent an appreciation for the difference that comes from national culture, political dynamics, and service traditions, researchers are left to surmise that Anglosphere models are generalizable around the world. That is not the case, just as Allen et al. (2014) learned when they attempted to apply a model of emotive pretending in China that they had used in the USA. The Chinese response to pretending was so different that they had to remove two items from their variables. Data challenges are extreme when comparing across countries, but it is worthwhile because it illuminates the fact that there is significant diversity around the globe.

One of the biggest challenges to cross-national empirical work is the issue of measurement invariance. Failing to check for it results in statistical data that gives the illusion of precision, but it is only an illusion. One must not assume that a mean of "5" in China indicates the same level of intensity as a mean of "5" in the USA. This is the "shoe size" problem described in Chapter 8. When statistical analysis is applied without regard to whether invariance is achieved, numbers will result and statistically significant findings may result, but the results are meaningless. Comparative research must start with the presumption that nations differ in ways that are elusive. Rather than applying a "stamp" from elsewhere, it is important to start from the ground up, generating concepts from those who share the culture and understand its subtleties. Thus, tests must be adapted to fit the constraints posed by the fact that measurement may be variant, rather than invariant. Even with this caveat, cross-national comparisons are well worth doing for they are instructive.

The findings reported in these chapters chart the course for future research.[1] Among the myriad that are possible, we offer three: One deals with questions of ethnicity and class, one deals with the analytical model, and one turns the table on the focus of inquiry, from state to citizen. The first question to pursue is whether ethnic and religious divisions, which are described in each nation's narrative, might influence emotional labor in ways not fully articulated by the variables used in this study. This line of inquiry could also investigate social class divisions in countries such as India and Thailand. Such inquiry would reveal the depth to which personal identity affects the experience of emotional labor.

The second question to pursue surrounds paths used in this analysis. As shown in Table 21.1, the effect of emotive capacity on job satisfaction and on feelings of self-fulfillment produced more statistically significant positive relationships than any other paths. Conversely, the effect of pretending on job satisfaction and on feelings of self-fulfillment, and the effect of emotive capacity on burnout, produced only four statistically significant relationships. And the effect of authentic emotive expression on burnout produced statistically significant relationships in half of the countries, but the direction varied, being negative in two and positive in four. This leads to questions about which paths are more durable when making cross-country comparisons, which are more susceptible to differences caused by national context, and how model assumptions about covariance among the independent variables affect results. Across the board, each path could be its own area of further research to identify sensitivity to context.

A third line of inquiry involves turning the table on the public encounter to see how citizens experience the interaction. While the research in this book analyzes emotional labor from the vantage of the public servant to the citizen, there may also be labor from citizen to civil servant. Questions to be pursued include the following: How do citizens receiving services from the government experience the emotive component of the interaction? What are the emotional labor correlates of their interactions when they feel mistreated by the state? What is the relationship between their level of emotive capacity and authentic emotive expression and trust in government? In other words, what would the correlations look like in Table 7.2 if they measured citizen responses, rather than public servants' responses?

These questions matter because they will illuminate lacunae regarding the encounter between citizen and state. In an era when citizen engagement is garnering much attention, when public service motivation is a popular topic in comparative research, and when deep knowledge is sought about cultural nuances and subtleties, they are timely and promise fruitful findings.

Summary

In conclusion, the "grit" and "resilience" necessary to perform emotional labor day in and day out are an important element in public service, whether in Thailand, Rwanda, or the USA. Whether in China or the Philippines, emotive demands are present and their effects are experienced somewhat similarly and somewhat differently. In some ways, the vernacular "street smarts" captures what emotional labor is. During the public encounter, the public service professional "reads" the emotive state of the citizen and accommodates to it in order to effectuate a transaction. The emphasis in bureaucratic theory on cognitive rationality and the de-emphasis on feelings often cause the emotion work aspects of public service to be viewed as irrelevant and "not work." These chapters say loud and clear, however, that emotional labor accompanies public service work around the globe.

The management of one's own feelings and feelings of others is a topic that deserves more study. It is present in the citizen–state encounter. As Chris Argyris (1964) remarked long ago, emotionality and interpersonal competence are as important as the values of rationality and intellectual competence. These chapters re-affirm Argyris' assertion.

There is a lag between theory and practice. As many nations found when impelled to adopt a marketized "customer-orientation" to public service delivery (especially the UK, the USA, Australia, and South Korea), employee well-being is too often sacrificed at the altar of "countable" work, while that aspect of the job that provides the greatest meaning to both citizen and worker is overlooked. If the citizen needs to be calmer, it is up to the worker to achieve that. If the citizen is angry, it is up to the worker to resolve that anger. If the citizen is panicked, it is up to the worker to calm the situation and cause the citizen to gain composure. If citizens are belligerent, it is up to the worker to engage them in such a way that they agree to comply. Emotional labor is by its very commission, spontaneous, and unique to each situation and each citizen's interaction with the state. It is very real, and it is not programmable. In emotion work, the highs are high and the lows can be very low, whether in China or Bolivia, Pakistan or the Philippines. Despite this, in the words of those who perform it, emotional labor gives meaning to their work.

Whether public servants come in contact with citizens over a reception desk, at the tax assessor's office, in the classroom, or in the neighborhood, emotional labor will be required. Even though most workers operate in an atmosphere of policy manuals, conference calls, emails, and long queues of citizens, face-to-face transactions between the state and the citizen are important and will continue to be. And with them comes the emotive component of the job. And this makes obvious the need to expand the canon in order to embrace the emotive component to the public encounter, a simultaneously public and private space wherever it happens around the globe. Mutual understanding is accelerated when the emotive and the cognitive combine (Gilligan 2014). Trust, empathy, and rapport advance cooperation.

The most compelling aspect of the information provided in these chapters is that it is time to remove the blinders that have hidden the presence and the importance of the emotive in public service. It is present, it is meaningful, and it is important.

Note

1. The editors express their gratitude to Kim Moloney for these suggestions on future research avenues. They offer fruitful areas of inquiry that will broaden and deepen the field's understanding of emotional labor.

References

Allen, Joseph A., James M. Diefendorff, and Yufeng Ma. 2014. "Differences in Emotional Labor Across Cultures: A Comparison of Chinese and U.S. Service Workers." *Journal of Business Psychology* 29: 21–35.

Argyris, Chris. 1964. *Integrating the Individual and the Organization*. New York, NY: Wiley.

Bailey, Katie. 2018. "Mismanaged Souls: Why Does Employee Engagement Remain Stubbornly Low?" *Social Sciences For Business, Markets And Enterprises*, April 25. Blog post accessed at https://blogs.lse.ac.uk/business-review/2018/04/25/mismanaged-souls-why-does-employee-engagement-remain-stubbornly-low/.

Chen, Chung-An, and Chih-Wei Hsieh. 2017. "Confucian Values in Public Organizations: Distinctive Effects of Two Interpersonal Norms on Public Employees' Work Morale." *Chinese Public Administration Review* 8 (2): 104–19.

Damasio, Antonio R. 1994. *Descartes' Error: Emotion, Reason, and the Human Brain*. New York, NY: Putnam.

Elfenbein, Hillary Anger, and Nalini Ambady. 2002. "On the Universality and Cultural Specificity of Emotion Recognition: A Meta-Analysis." *Psychological Bulletin* 128 (2): 203–35.

Gilligan, Carol. 2014. "Moral Injury and the Ethic of Care: Reframing the Conversation About Differences." *Journal of Social Philosophy* 45 (1): 89–106.

Hand, Laura C., and Thomas J. Catlaw. 2019. "Accomplishing the Public Encounter: A Case for Ethnomethodology in Public Administration Research." *Perspectives on Public Management & Governance* 2 (2): 125–37. https://doi.org/10.1093/ppmgov/gvz004.

Hsieh, Chih-Wei, Jun-Yi Hsieh, and Irving Yi-Feng Huang. 2016. "Self-Efficacy as a Mediator and Moderator Between Emotional Labor and Job Satisfaction: A Case Study of Public Service Employees in Taiwan. *Public Performance & Management Review* 40 (1): 71–96.

Humphrey, Ronald H., Blake E. Ashforth, and James M. Diefendorff. 2015. "The Bright Side of Emotional Labor." *Journal of Organizational Behavior* 36: 749–69. https://doi.org/10.1002/job.2019.

Konnikova, Maria. 2016. "What Makes People Feel Upbeat at Work." *The New Yorker*, July 30. Accessed at https://www.newyorker.com/science/maria-konnikova/what-makes-people-feel-upbeat-at-work.

Kristjansson, Kristjan. 2000. "Virtue Ethics and Emotional Conflict." *American Philosophical Quarterly* 37 (3): 193–207.

Mastracci, Sharon H., Mary E. Guy, and Meredith A. Newman. 2012. *Emotional Labor and Crisis Response: Working on the Razor's Edge*. Armonk, NY: M.E. Sharpe.

Mastracci, Sharon H., and Yvonne Sawbridge. 2019. "Showing You Care: Emotional Labor and Public Service Work." In *Reimagining the Future Public Service Workforce*, edited by Helen Dickinson, Catherine Needham, Catherine Mangan, and Helen Sullivan, 39–53. Singapore: Springer.

Miao, Chao, Ronald H. Humphrey, and Shanshan Qian. 2018. "Emotional Intelligence and Authentic Leadership: A Meta-Analysis." *Leadership & Organization Development Journal* 39 (5): 679–90.

Moloney, Kim. 2018. "Hurdles to an Asian Century of Public Administration." In *Public Policy in the 'Asian Century'*, edited by Sara Bice, Avery Poole, and Helen Sullivan, 267–92. London: Palgrave Macmillan.

Moloney, Kim, and Hyo-Youn Chu. 2016. "Linking Jamaica's Public Service Motivations and Ethical Climate." *The American Review of Public Administration* 46 (4): 436–58. https://doi.org/10.1177/0275074014557022.

Newman, Meredith A., Mary E. Guy, and Sharon H. Mastracci. 2009 "Beyond Cognition: Affective Leadership and Emotional Labor." *Public Administration Review* 69 (1): 6–20.

Patterson, Patricia M. 2001. "Viscera, Emotion, and Administration: The Lessons of 'Embodied Disgust'." *Administrative Theory & Praxis* 23 (2): 205–30.

Remington, Christa L., and N. Emel Ganapati. 2017. "Recovery Worker Skills in Post-Earthquake Haiti: The Disconnect Between Employer and Employee Perspectives." *Natural Hazards*. https://doi.org/10.1007/s11069-017-2840-4.

Robson, David. 2017a. "How East and West Think in Profoundly Different Ways." *Future*, January 19. Accessed at http://www.bbc.com/future/story/20170118-how-east-and-west-think-in-profoundly-different-ways.

Robson, David. 2017b. "The 'Untranslatable' Emotions You Never Knew You Had." *Future*, January 26. Accessed at http://www.bbc.com/future/story/20170126-the-untranslatable-emotions-you-never-knew-you-had.

Russell, James A. 1991. "Culture and the Categorization of Emotions." *Psychological Bulletin* 110 (3): 426–50.

Schreurs, Petra. 2002. "Symposium: Rationality and Public Administration: Introduction." *Administrative Theory & Praxis* 24 (2): 279–86.

Scott, Frank E. 2001. "Reconsidering a Therapeutic Role for the State: Anti-Modernist Governance and the Reunification of the Self." *Administrative Theory & Praxis* 23 (2): 231–42.

Smith, Dorothy E. 2005. *Institutional Ethnography: A Sociology for People*. New York, NY: Rowman & Littlefield.

Stivers, Camilla. 2018. "Beyond Calculation: Experience and Language in Administrative Situations." *Administrative Theory & Praxis* 40 (3): 200–10.

Vickers, Margaret H. 2010. "Introduction—Bullying, Mobbing, and Violence in Public Service Workplaces." *Administration Theory & Praxis* 32 (1): 7–24.

Vickers, Margaret H. 2011. "Bullying Targets as Social Performers in the Public Administration Workplace." *Administrative Theory & Praxis* 33 (2): 213–34.

Wilding, Mark, Kyungjin Chae, and Jiho Jang. 2014. "Emotional Labor in Korean Local Government." *Public Performance & Management Review* 38: 316–36.

Appendix A: Data Collection Information

Australia

- Sample size is 80
- The survey language is English
- Data collected in Melbourne, Australia

In Fall 2015, managers in public service organizations were solicited by email through the Institute of Public Administration Australia. Those who agreed to distribute the survey to their employees were supplied a link to an online questionnaire through SurveyMonkey. The Australia survey questionnaire does not include a survey item Q212, which is an indicator for the latent variable Deep Acting. Thus, we performed the structural equation modeling analysis without this item.

Bolivia

- Sample size is 201
- The survey language is Spanish
- Data collected in La Paz, Bolivia

Surveys were administered to employees of the Ministry of Social Development for the department of La Paz. Paper surveys were distributed in Spring 2018, at two locations: the Ministry's central office and the Municipal Center for Child Development. A total of 400 questionnaires were delivered and 201 usable responses returned (50.25%). An initial examination of the data detected a possible mistranslation for survey item Q202, which is an indicator for the latent variable Pretending Expression. Thus, we performed the structural equation modeling analysis without this item.

China

- Sample size is 211
- The survey language is Chinese
- Data collected in Shanghai, China

The survey was administrated to full-time community employees working in front-line government departments. Surveys were administered in June 2015 to those who worked in community development/neighborhood services where interpersonal contact with citizens, either face-to-face or voice-to-voice, was required during their daily work. With the assistance of personnel managers, we delivered 218 questionnaires and received 211 valid responses, yielding a percentage of 96.8%.

India

- Sample size is 206
- The survey language is English
- Data collected in the State of Telangana and the State of Uttar Pradesh

The survey in India was conducted in two geographic locales at three different schools: Telangana, India—the questionnaire was administered to teachers in two public schools in the State of Telangana, India, during the summer of 2016. The permission to administer the survey was sought from the school principal of the two schools. After permission was granted, 120 hard copies of the questionnaire were delivered to the administrative officer of one school and 80 hard copies were delivered to the administrative officer of the other school. The purpose of the survey was explained to the school principals and administrative officers. The administrative officer circulated the surveys among the school teachers at the beginning of the week. Regular follow-ups were done for the next two weeks. There were 70 surveys returned out of 120 from one school, yielding a 58% response rate. There were 38 completed surveys returned out of 80 from the other school, yielding a 48% response rate. In total, 108 completed surveys out of

200 distributed surveys were received, which produced an overall response rate of 54%.

Uttar Pradesh, India—a similar procedure for data collection was used in the second administration, which occurred during the month of December 2017 in the State of Uttar Pradesh, India. The permission for survey administration was granted by the school principal. On a specific day, the school teachers met and 135 questionnaires were distributed to them by the administrative officer. Teachers were given one day to return the completed surveys. Of the 135 that had been distributed, 105 completed questionnaires were returned, yielding a 78% response rate.

Of the total of 213 returned surveys from the two phases of administration, 7 responses were deleted due to missing values. The final sample size from India was 206.

South Korea

- Sample size is 208
- The survey language is Korean
- Data collected in Seoul, Korea

In Seoul, Korea, five towns in Seoul City were surveyed: Guro, Jongno, Seocho, Seodaemun, and Yeongdeungpo. There are 25 towns in Seoul City, each with populations ranging from 130,000 to 650,000 people. Between April and June 2015, survey questionnaires were distributed by the researchers in the five towns. A couple of weeks later, researchers returned to the towns to collect the completed questionnaires. A total of 275 survey questionnaires were distributed and 208 usable responses were returned (75.6%). The survey respondents were local government employees working in various departments.

Pakistan

- Sample size is 386
- The survey language is English
- Data collected in Punjab, Pakistan

Respondents were surveyed in 22 public organizations in Lahore and Rawalpindi, both in the province of Punjab. We distributed surveys through moderators who administered the surveys in their presence in public organizations from August through November 2015. The moderators were selected through personal contacts. Almost 30% of the total surveys were filled as a graded course assignment in the course of "Public Organizations and Management" at the University of Central Punjab, where students were instructed to deliver them to public employees and ask that they be completed. Other moderators, selected from public sector employees, were requested to get the questionnaires filled from fellow employees in their organizations. The respondents held positions in educational departments (three government colleges and three public universities), armed and air forces (serving and retired armed officers), technical departments (engineers and technical staff), hospitals (doctors, nurses, and medical officers), and special services organizations including Pakistan Radio, Punjab Information Technology Board (PITB), and National Engineering and Scientific Commission (NESCOM).

Philippines

- Sample size is 209
- The survey language is English
- Data collected in Manila, Philippines

The survey was conducted in Pasay City during August and September 2015. Pasay City is a city in Metropolitan Manila, the National Capital Region of the Philippines. The population of Pasay City was 417,000 in 2015. We contacted the Pasay City government personnel office and distributed 252 survey questionnaires to city employees. Of the total questionnaires distributed, we obtained 209 usable responses (81.7%). The respondents are from various occupations.

Rwanda

- Sample size is 154
- The survey language is English
- Data collected in Gatsibo, Rwanda

The survey was conducted in Gatsibo District, Eastern Province in the Republic of Rwanda. In April 2015, we contacted the Mayor of Gatsibo District to request a survey of government employees. Gatsibo District is one of the 30 districts in Rwanda with a population of approximately 428,000 people. Between May and July 2015, the Mayor distributed questionnaires to government employees working in the District. A total of 200 survey questionnaires were distributed and 154 usable responses were returned (77.0%). The survey respondents were local government employees working in various departments.

Taiwan

- Sample size is 173
- The survey language is Chinese
- Data collected in Taipei, Taiwan

For the Taiwan sample, the survey was administered online using SurveyMonkey in mid-2015. An invitation email was sent to government employees through a listserv to alumni of a Master of Public Administration program. The email not only invited those targeted recipients to participate in the survey but also asked them to spread the news among their co-workers so that there could be a sufficient number of survey completions. When the survey was concluded, there were a total of 173 responses.

Thailand

- Sample size is 220
- The survey language is Thai
- Data collected in Bangkok, Thailand

In Thailand, the survey was distributed during May and June 2018 to Royal Thai Police Officers with the cooperation of a police officer and a Deputy District Chief in the Ministry of Interior. As for the police officers, the questionnaires were randomly sent to 70 officers in Bangkok police stations. Respondents were randomly selected from among the officers who are dealing with the daily operation in enforcing laws and regulations, and those who are interacting with citizens in the rural areas in various provinces in Thailand. The other 150 questionnaires were given to Deputy District Chiefs from all 77 provinces in Thailand who were participating in a six-week training program for Deputy District Chiefs organized by the Ministry of Interior in Bangkok.

UK

- Sample size is 360
- The survey language is English
- Data collected in Birmingham, UK

Data were gathered from March to May 2015. To be eligible, respondents had paid work experience in public service, defined as having worked in government or in charitable, non-governmental organizations. Of all respondents, 201 are employed by government or nonprofit organizations and an additional sample includes 159 who are nurses in the National Health Service. Response rate is unknown because in some of the data collection sites surveys were dropped off and administered by a moderator and the potential number of respondents is unknown.

USA

- Sample size is 254
- The survey language is English
- Data collected primarily in Denver and Salt Lake City but also Kansas City, Washington, DC, Miami, and Atlanta

Data were gathered throughout 2015, with the majority collected in Denver, Colorado, and Salt Lake City, Utah. Respondents were a convenience sample of employees in a variety of public service jobs at all levels of government or in nonprofits, or they had full-time work experience in public service jobs in the past and were now enrolled in graduate MPA classes. Questionnaires were distributed to those willing to complete them. This involved mailing to those at a distance, handing to those nearby or in the classroom, and relying on moderators to distribute them to co-workers in their offices.

Appendix B: Data Comparisons

The following charts compare our data to the ecological dimension indexes calculated in Project GLOBE. Difference in means tests confirms that, in each country, the samples were drawn from the same overall population. None of the t-statistics reached the critical value for statistical significance at the 95% level.

Figure B.1 provides a visual comparison of the ten countries of this study that were also included in the Project GLOBE study. (Pakistan and Rwanda were not included in Project GLOBE.) Figures B.2, B.3, B.4, B.5, B.6, B.7, B.8, B.9, B.10, and B.11 show pairwise comparisons across the dimensions tested in Project GLOBE and in this study.

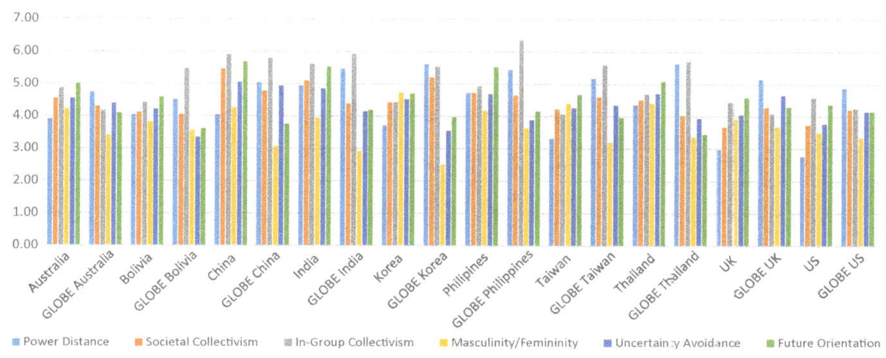

Fig. B.1 All countries and measures

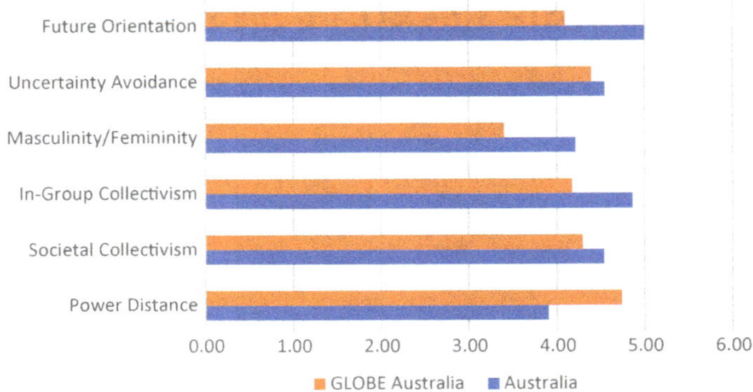

Fig. B.2   Australia

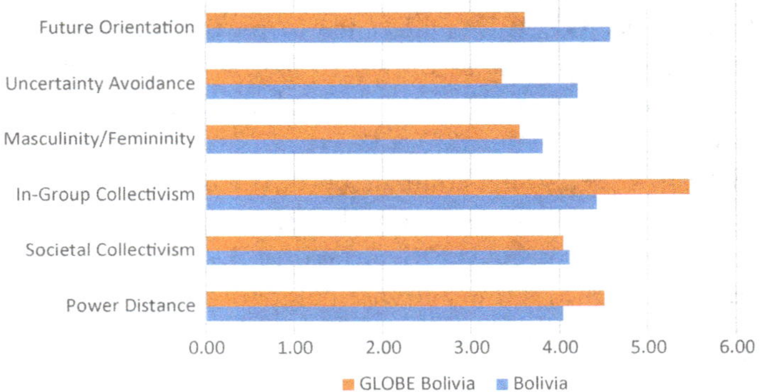

Fig. B.3   Bolivia

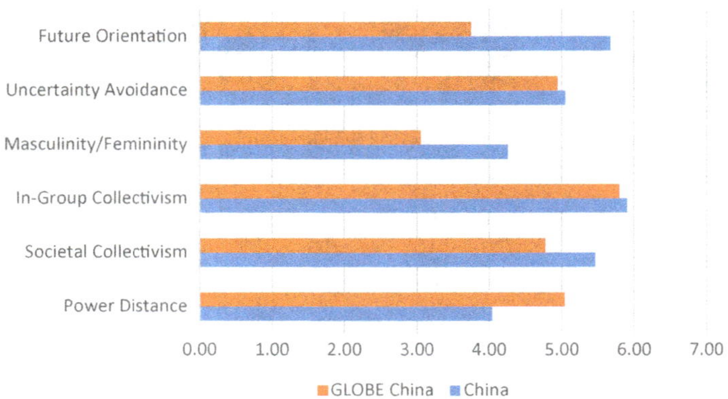

Fig. B.4   China

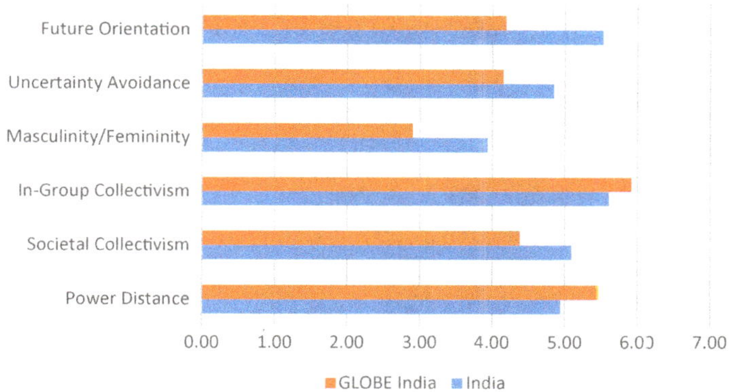

Fig. B.5   India

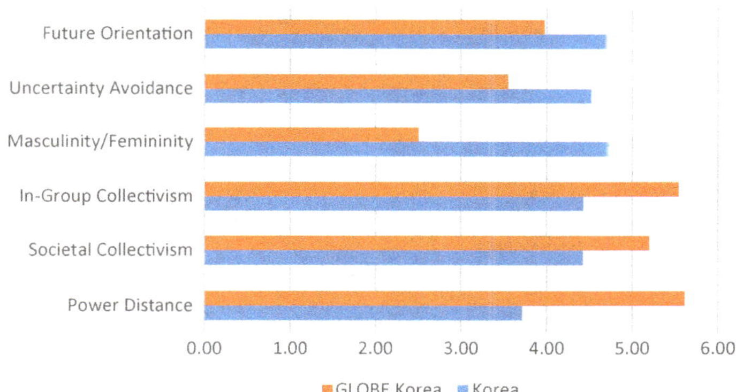

Fig. B.6   Korea, Republic of (South)

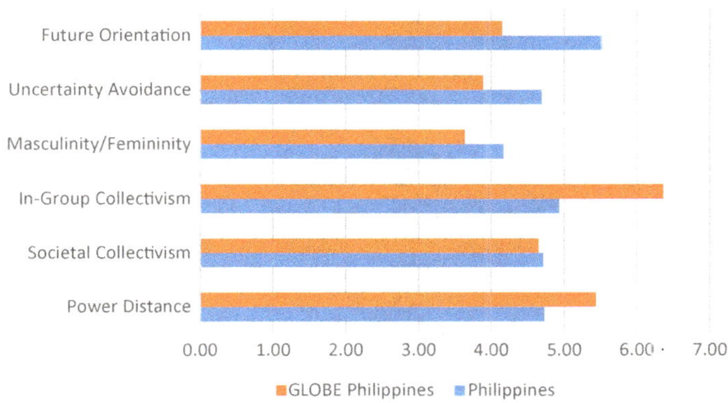

Fig. B.7   Philippines

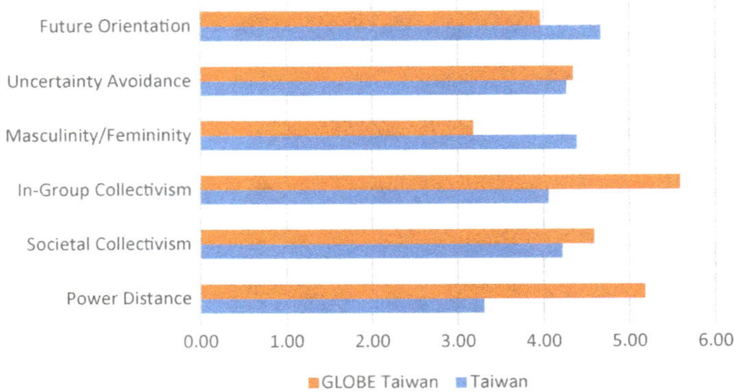

Fig. B.8   Taiwan

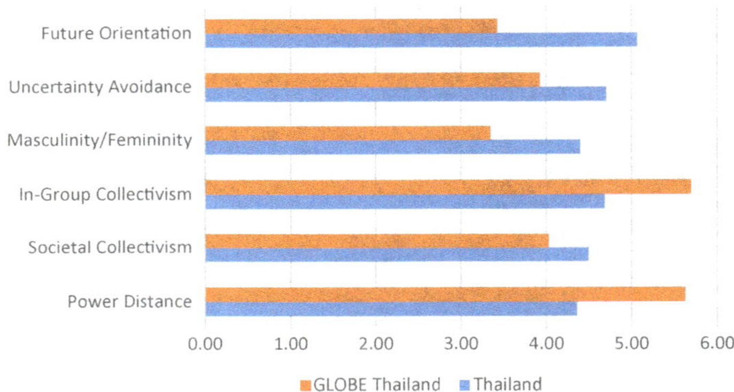

Fig. B.9   Thailand

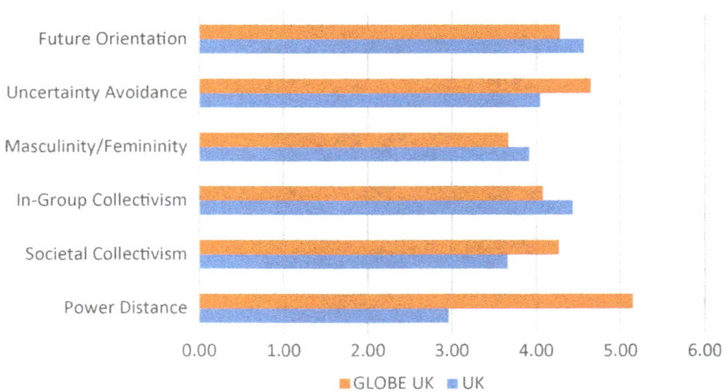

Fig. B.10   United Kingdom

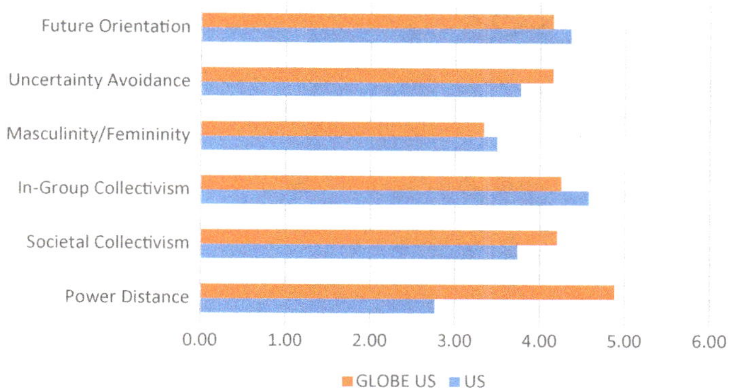

Fig. B.11 United States

Appendix C: Questionnaire (English Version)

GMY Comparative Survey Questionnaire

Thank you for taking the time to complete this survey.

The purpose of this survey is to learn how workplace behaviors vary in different countries. The questionnaire that you are asked to complete will take about fifteen minutes.

Responses from all the questionnaires will be pooled together for a final report and no individual will be identified.

In the following pages, you are asked to respond to a number of statements that reflect your observations of organizational practices, your beliefs, your values, or your perceptions. This is not a test, and there are no right or wrong answers.

The questionnaire is anonymous. The results of the study may be published but your name will not be known. Information obtained during the course of the study will remain confidential, to the extent allowed by law.

If you have any questions concerning the research study, please feel free to contact the following references:

M. E. Guy et al. (eds.), *The Palgrave Handbook of Global Perspectives on Emotional Labor in Public Service*, https://doi.org/10.1007/978-3-030-24823-9

Researcher Name Here
Researcher Title Here
Researcher Institution Here
Researcher Address Here
Email: emailhere@emailhere.edu
Phone: 000-000-0000

Instructions: Each question is rated on a scale of 1 to 7, with 1 being strongly disagree and 7 being strongly agree. For each question please select the answer that best represents your response.

Section 1

			1	2	3	4	5	6	7		
1.01	My employer expects me to express positive emotions to clients/customers as part of my job	Strongly Disagree	○	○	○	○	○	○	○	Strongly Agree	N/A ○
1.02	My employer would say that part of the product for clients/customers is friendly, cheerful service	Strongly Disagree	○	○	○	○	○	○	○	Strongly Agree	N/A ○
1.03	My employer expects me to be enthusiastic in my interactions with clients/customers	Strongly Disagree	○	○	○	○	○	○	○	Strongly Agree	N/A ○
1.04	I am expected to act confident and self-assured	Strongly Disagree	○	○	○	○	○	○	○	Strongly Agree	N/A ○
1.05	I am expected to suppress my bad moods or negative reactions to clients/customers	Strongly Disagree	○	○	○	○	○	○	○	Strongly Agree	N/A ○
1.06	My employer expects me to pretend that I am not upset or distressed, even when I actually am	Strongly Disagree	○	○	○	○	○	○	○	Strongly Agree	N/A ○
1.07	I am expected not to show anger while on the job	Strongly Disagree	○	○	○	○	○	○	○	Strongly Agree	N/A ○

Section 2

		Strongly Disagree	1	2	3	4	5	6	7	Strongly Agree	N/A
2.01	I hide my true feelings so as to appear pleasant at work	Strongly Disagree	○	○	○	○	○	○	○	Strongly Agree	○
2.02	In my job I act confident and self-assured regardless of how I actually feel	Strongly Disagree	○	○	○	○	○	○	○	Strongly Agree	○
2.03	I wear a "mask" in order to deal with clients/customers in an appropriate way	Strongly Disagree	○	○	○	○	○	○	○	Strongly Agree	○
2.04	I let my true feelings show when working with clients/customers	Strongly Disagree	○	○	○	○	○	○	○	Strongly Agree	○
2.05	It is easier for me to show my true feelings than to pretend	Strongly Disagree	○	○	○	○	○	○	○	Strongly Agree	○
2.06	I am good at expressing how I feel	Strongly Disagree	○	○	○	○	○	○	○	Strongly Agree	○
2.07	I am good at getting people to calm down	Strongly Disagree	○	○	○	○	○	○	○	Strongly Agree	○
2.08	Dealing with emotionally charged issues is an important part of my job	Strongly Disagree	○	○	○	○	○	○	○	Strongly Agree	○
2.09	In my job I am good at dealing with emotional issues	Strongly Disagree	○	○	○	○	○	○	○	Strongly Agree	○
2.10	I try to actually experience the emotions that I must show to clients/customers	Strongly Disagree	○	○	○	○	○	○	○	Strongly Agree	○
2.11	I work hard to actually feel the emotions that I need to show to clients/customers	Strongly Disagree	○	○	○	○	○	○	○	Strongly Agree	○
2.12	I work at developing the feelings inside of me that I need to show to clients/customers	Strongly Disagree	○	○	○	○	○	○	○	Strongly Agree	○

Section 3

			1	2	3	4	5	6	7		
3.01	My job provides career development and promotion opportunities	Strongly Disagree	○	○	○	○	○	○	○	Strongly Agree	N/A ○
3.02	I feel I am being paid a fair amount for the work I do	Strongly Disagree	○	○	○	○	○	○	○	Strongly Agree	N/A ○
3.03	I feel satisfied with my supervisor	Strongly Disagree	○	○	○	○	○	○	○	Strongly Agree	N/A ○
3.04	Overall, I am satisfied with my job	Strongly Disagree	○	○	○	○	○	○	○	Strongly Agree	N/A ○
3.05	I am proud to tell people who I work for	Strongly Disagree	○	○	○	○	○	○	○	Strongly Agree	N/A ○
3.06	What this organization stands for is important to me	Strongly Disagree	○	○	○	○	○	○	○	Strongly Agree	N/A ○
3.07	I work for an organization that is competent and able to accomplish its mission	Strongly Disagree	○	○	○	○	○	○	○	Strongly Agree	N/A ○
3.08	I feel a strong sense of belonging to this organization	Strongly Disagree	○	○	○	○	○	○	○	Strongly Agree	N/A ○
3.09	I feel like "part of the family" at this organization	Strongly Disagree	○	○	○	○	○	○	○	Strongly Agree	N/A ○
3.10	The people I work with care about what happens to me	Strongly Disagree	○	○	○	○	○	○	○	Strongly Agree	N/A ○
3.11	This organization appreciates my accomplishments on the job	Strongly Disagree	○	○	○	○	○	○	○	Strongly Agree	N/A ○
3.12	This organization does all it can to recognize employees for good performance	Strongly Disagree	○	○	○	○	○	○	○	Strongly Agree	N/A ○
3.13	My efforts on the job are recognized and appreciated by my employer	Strongly Disagree	○	○	○	○	○	○	○	Strongly Agree	N/A ○

Section 4

			1	2	3	4	5	6	7		
4.01	I often think about quitting this job	Strongly Disagree	○	○	○	○	○	○	○	Strongly Agree	N/A ○
4.02	I will probably look for a job during the next year	Strongly Disagree	○	○	○	○	○	○	○	Strongly Agree	N/A ○
4.03	I think my future is stable	Strongly Disagree	○	○	○	○	○	○	○	Strongly Agree	N/A ○
4.04	I rarely miss a day of work	Strongly Disagree	○	○	○	○	○	○	○	Strongly Agree	N/A ○
4.05	I feel guilty when I miss a day of work	Strongly Disagree	○	○	○	○	○	○	○	Strongly Agree	N/A ○
4.06	Absenteeism is a bad thing	Strongly Disagree	○	○	○	○	○	○	○	Strongly Agree	N/A ○
4.07	I leave work feeling tired and run down	Strongly Disagree	○	○	○	○	○	○	○	Strongly Agree	N/A ○
4.08	I leave work feeling emotionally exhauste	Strongly Disagree	○	○	○	○	○	○	○	Strongly Agree	N/A ○
4.09	I feel "used up" at the end of the workday	Strongly Disagree	○	○	○	○	○	○	○	Strongly Agree	N/A ○
4.10	I help others with work-related issues even when I don't have a personal bond with them	Strongly Disagree	○	○	○	○	○	○	○	Strongly Agree	N/A ○
4.11	I attempt to help people in other departments with their work-related problems	Strongly Disagree	○	○	○	○	○	○	○	Strongly Agree	N/A ○
4.12	I voluntarily help others when they need to know where to go to get what they need	Strongly Disagree	○	○	○	○	○	○	○	Strongly Agree	N/A ○
4.13	I gain a strong sense of personal fulfillment at my job	Strongly Disagree	○	○	○	○	○	○	○	Strongly Agree	N/A ○

			1	2	3	4	5	6	7		
4.14	I feel like my job is something I want to do rather than something I have to do	Strongly Disagree	○	○	○	○	○	○	○	Strongly Agree	N/A ○
4.15	My work is a source of personal meaning in my life	Strongly Disagree	○	○	○	○	○	○	○	Strongly Agree	N/A ○
4.16	I perform my job well	Strongly Disagree	○	○	○	○	○	○	○	Strongly Agree	N/A ○
4.17	I fulfill responsibilities specified in my job description	Strongly Disagree	○	○	○	○	○	○	○	Strongly Agree	N/A ○
4.18	I perform the tasks that are expected of me	Strongly Disagree	○	○	○	○	○	○	○	Strongly Agree	N/A ○

Section 5

			1	2	3	4	5	6	7		
5.01	I have a good sense of why I have certain feelings most of the time	Strongly Disagree	○	○	○	○	○	○	○	Strongly Agree	N/A ○
5.02	I have good understanding of my own emotions	Strongly Disagree	○	○	○	○	○	○	○	Strongly Agree	N/A ○
5.03	I really understand what I feel	Strongly Disagree	○	○	○	○	○	○	○	Strongly Agree	N/A ○
5.04	I always know whether or not I am happy	Strongly Disagree	○	○	○	○	○	○	○	Strongly Agree	N/A ○
5.05	I always know my friends' emotions from their behavior	Strongly Disagree	○	○	○	○	○	○	○	Strongly Agree	N/A ○
5.06	I am a good observer of others' emotions	Strongly Disagree	○	○	○	○	○	○	○	Strongly Agree	N/A ○
5.07	I am sensitive to the feelings of others	Strongly Disagree	○	○	○	○	○	○	○	Strongly Agree	N/A ○
5.08	I have good understanding of the emotions of people around me	Strongly Disagree	○	○	○	○	○	○	○	Strongly Agree	N/A ○
5.09	I am able to control my temper and handle difficulties rationally	Strongly Disagree	○	○	○	○	○	○	○	Strongly Agree	N/A ○
5.10	I am quite capable of controlling my own emotions	Strongly Disagree	○	○	○	○	○	○	○	Strongly Agree	N/A ○
5.11	I can always calm down quickly when I am very angry	Strongly Disagree	○	○	○	○	○	○	○	Strongly Agree	N/A ○
5.12	I have good control of my own emotions	Strongly Disagree	○	○	○	○	○	○	○	Strongly Agree	N/A ○
5.13	I see myself as extraverted, enthusiastic	Strongly Disagree	○	○	○	○	○	○	○	Strongly Agree	N/A ○

			1	2	3	4	5	6	7		
5.14	I see myself as critical, quarrelsome	Strongly Disagree	○	○	○	○	○	○	○	Strongly Agree	N/A ○
5.15	I see myself as dependable, self-disciplined	Strongly Disagree	○	○	○	○	○	○	○	Strongly Agree	N/A ○
5.16	I see myself as anxious, easily upset	Strongly Disagree	○	○	○	○	○	○	○	Strongly Agree	N/A ○
5.17	I see myself as complex and open to new experiences	Strongly Disagree	○	○	○	○	○	○	○	Strongly Agree	N/A ○
5.18	I see myself as reserved, quiet	Strongly Disagree	○	○	○	○	○	○	○	Strongly Agree	N/A ○
5.19	I see myself as sympathetic, warm	Strongly Disagree	○	○	○	○	○	○	○	Strongly Agree	N/A ○
5.20	I see myself as disorganized, careless	Strongly Disagree	○	○	○	○	○	○	○	Strongly Agree	N/A ○
5.21	I see myself as calm, emotionally stable	Strongly Disagree	○	○	○	○	○	○	○	Strongly Agree	N/A ○
5.22	I see myself as conventional, uncreative	Strongly Disagree	○	○	○	○	○	○	○	Strongly Agree	N/A ○

Section 6

			1	2	3	4	5	6	7		
6.01	My employer bases rewards on performance effectiveness	Strongly Disagree	○	○	○	○	○	○	○	Strongly Agree	N/A ○
6.02	My employer rewards innovation	Strongly Disagree	○	○	○	○	○	○	○	Strongly Agree	N/A ○
6.03	In this organization, most employees set challenging goals for themselves	Strongly Disagree	○	○	○	○	○	○	○	Strongly Agree	N/A ○
6.04	My supervisor makes fair and balanced decisions	Strongly Disagree	○	○	○	○	○	○	○	Strongly Agree	N/A ○
6.05	My supervisor can be trusted	Strongly Disagree	○	○	○	○	○	○	○	Strongly Agree	N/A ○
6.06	My supervisor discusses integrity and ethics with employees	Strongly Disagree	○	○	○	○	○	○	○	Strongly Agree	N/A ○
6.07	My supervisor sets an example of how to do things the right way in terms of ethics	Strongly Disagree	○	○	○	○	○	○	○	Strongly Agree	N/A ○

Section 7

			Strongly Disagree	1	2	3	4	5	6	7	Strongly Agree	N/A
7.01	Even when employees feel they deserve a salary increase, it is disrespectful to ask for it		Strongly Disagree	○	○	○	○	○	○	○	Strongly Agree	○
7.02	I believe people are better off not questioning the decisions of those in authority		Strongly Disagree	○	○	○	○	○	○	○	Strongly Agree	○
7.03	I believe communications with superiors should always be done using formally established procedures		Strongly Disagree	○	○	○	○	○	○	○	Strongly Agree	○
7.04	In this organization, managers encourage group loyalty even if individual goals suffer		Strongly Disagree	○	○	○	○	○	○	○	Strongly Agree	○
7.05	The pay and bonus system in this organization is designed to maximize collective interests		Strongly Disagree	○	○	○	○	○	○	○	Strongly Agree	○
7.06	In this organization, group cohesion is more valued than individualism		Strongly Disagree	○	○	○	○	○	○	○	Strongly Agree	○
7.07	In this organization, group managers take pride in the individual accomplishments of group members		Strongly Disagree	○	○	○	○	○	○	○	Strongly Agree	○
7.08	In this organization, employees feel loyalty to the organization.		Strongly Disagree	○	○	○	○	○	○	○	Strongly Agree	○
7.09	I think this organization shows loyalty toward its employees		Strongly Disagree	○	○	○	○	○	○	○	Strongly Agree	○
7.10	In this organization, physically demanding tasks are usually performed by men		Strongly Disagree	○	○	○	○	○	○	○	Strongly Agree	○
7.11	In this organization, tasks that demand nurturance and supportiveness are usually performed by women		Strongly Disagree	○	○	○	○	○	○	○	Strongly Agree	○
7.12	In this organization, most management positions are filled by men		Strongly Disagree	○	○	○	○	○	○	○	Strongly Agree	○

			1	2	3	4	5	6	7		
7.13	In this organization, orderliness and consistency are stressed, even at the expense of experimentation and innovation	Strongly Disagree	○	○	○	○	○	○	○	Strongly Agree	N/A ○
7.14	In this organization, work is highly structured, leading to few unexpected events	Strongly Disagree	○	○	○	○	○	○	○	Strongly Agree	N/A ○
7.15	In this organization, job requirements and instructions are spelled out in detail so employees know what is expected of them	Strongly Disagree	○	○	○	○	○	○	○	Strongly Agree	N/A ○
7.16	The way to be successful in this organization is to plan ahead	Strongly Disagree	○	○	○	○	○	○	○	Strongly Agree	N/A ○
7.17	In this organization, the accepted norm is to plan for the future	Strongly Disagree	○	○	○	○	○	○	○	Strongly Agree	N/A ○
7.18	In this organization, meetings are usually planned well in advance	Strongly Disagree	○	○	○	○	○	○	○	Strongly Agree	N/A ○

Section 8

			1	2	3	4	5	6	7		N/A
8.01	When I have contact with clients/customers in my job, I can rely on them to tell the truth	Strongly Disagree	O	O	O	O	O	O	O	Strongly Agree	O
8.02	Clients/customers make demands that I cannot deliver	Strongly Disagree	O	O	O	O	O	O	O	Strongly Agree	O
8.03	Clients/customers generally raise irrelevant discussion	Strongly Disagree	O	O	O	O	O	O	O	Strongly Agree	O
8.04	Clients/customers generally doubt my ability	Strongly Disagree	O	O	O	O	O	O	O	Strongly Agree	O
8.05	Clients/customers often yell at me	Strongly Disagree	O	O	O	O	O	O	O	Strongly Agree	O
8.06	Clients/customers often use condescending language (e.g., "you are an idiot")	Strongly Disagree	O	O	O	O	O	O	O	Strongly Agree	O
8.07	Clients/customers generally speak aggressively to me	Strongly Disagree	O	O	O	O	O	O	O	Strongly Agree	O

Section 9

			1	2	3	4	5	6	7		
9.01	In my work, I perform meaningful public service	Strongly Disagree	○	○	○	○	○	○	○	Strongly Agree	N/A ○
9.02	Employees should put forth honest effort in the performance of their duties	Strongly Disagree	○	○	○	○	○	○	○	Strongly Agree	N/A ○
9.03	Employees should act impartially and not give preferential treatment to any business or individual	Strongly Disagree	○	○	○	○	○	○	○	Strongly Agree	N/A ○

Section 10

Instructions: The following questions will be used only to develop categories for analysis purposes. Your responses will be kept fully confidential. They will NOT be used to identify any individual, nor will they be shared with anyone else. In order to keep your identity confidential, we do not ask for your name or contact information.

10.01. What is your age? __________

10.02. What is your gender? (check one)   ○ Male   ○ Female

10.03. How many years of full-time work experience have you had? __________ years

10.04. How many years of public sector work experience have you had? __________ years

10.05. What is your educational level? (indicate highest level completed)

__1. Less than high school

__2. High school graduate

__3. Some college

__4. 2-year associate degree

__5. College graduate

__6. Some graduate school

__7. Master's degree

__8. Law degree (J.D., LL.B.)

__9. Doctorate degree (Ph.D., M.D., Ed.D., etc.)

__10. Other (please specify):__________

10.06. What service area do you work in? (check all that apply)

________ 1. Administration

________ 2. Community development/neighborhood services

________ 3. Engineering, manufacturing, or production

________ 4. Education

________ 5. Disaster response

________ 6. Finance or accounting

________ 7. Firefighter

________ 8. Health care

________ 9. Housing

________ 10. Human resource management

________ 11. Information & communication

________ 12. Law enforcement

________ 13. Military

________ 14. Public relations

________ 15. Planning

________ 16. Public works: streets, sanitation, utilities

________ 17. Purchasing

________ 18. Recreation and parks

________ 19. Research and development

________ 20. Social services

________ 21. Transportation

________ 22. Support services (e.g., plant and equipment maintenance)

________ 23. Other (please describe)____

Thank you for completing this survey. The researchers invite you to add any comments here:

Glossary

Authentic emotive expression refers to displaying the emotion that one actually feels. The term is reflective of those moments when there is consonance between how one feels and the feeling being displayed. Its opposite is *pretending expression*

Autonomy refers to the level of independence and discretion the employee is allowed to exercise in managing his/her work content, job procedures, work behavior, and emotive expression

Burnout is a work-related outcome of stress on the job. It is manifested by emotional exhaustion, feeling "used up" or hopeless, and thinking that one's work does not matter. It is often accompanied by depression and it results in reduced productivity

Cheong is a Korean word that represents feelings of relatedness and closeness that develop over a long time, such as after having been married for many years, or having worked for the same employer for many years

Citizen engagement refers to an action orientation on the part of citizens to work toward collective goals. It is an important element of civil society and its purpose is for citizens to have a greater say in public decision-making

Civil servant (similar to public servant) is an employee who works for government

Cognitive heuristics are mental "shortcuts" that allow people to consider and solve problems in the absence of perfect understanding

Cognitive intelligence refers to the ability to think analytically, exercise logic, and exercise literacy and numeracy

Cognitive reframing also known as cognitive restructuring, is an attempt to adopt a new perspective on stressful events and reframe beliefs in a constructive way

Collaboration connotes people or entities working together to achieve common ends

Configural invariance is a quality of statistical measurement and is one of three levels for ascertaining the presence of measurement invariance. The term signifies that the basic model has the same factorial structure across countries. It does not

© The Editor(s) (if applicable) and The Author(s) 2019
M. E. Guy et al. (eds.), *The Palgrave Handbook of Global Perspectives on Emotional Labor in Public Service*, https://doi.org/10.1007/978-3-030-24823-9

guarantee equivalence across countries, but it serves as the baseline for establishing measurement invariance

Conservation of Resources Theory holds that the investment of organizational resources in workers (e.g., supervisor support, recognition, rewards, employee assistance programs, and self-care plans) may mitigate the harmful impact of stressful job demands

Coproduction refers to the generation of public goods via willful participation by citizens working together with government

Cultural response bias refers to the culturally-linked tendency to respond to surveys in a certain way, such as avoiding extreme ends of a scale in some countries or a tendency to avoid the midpoint of a scale in others

Culture is a multifaceted concept. First, it is social: It refers to the customary values, conventions, expectations, norms, language, behavior, art, and artifacts that define that which is considered normal. Second, it involves membership, such that its characteristics are shared among a defined group of people. Third, it is transmitted from one generation to another

Deep acting is a term used to refer to authentically experiencing the emotion being expressed. When emotional labor is thought of as theater performance, this dramaturgical term is used to mean the opposite of pretending. Similar to actors on stage who invoke emotions through trained imagination, workers are experiencing the feelings they display to their clients. Deep acting is authentic emotive expression, such that there is consistency between how the worker feels and the emotion on display. In theater lingo, its antonym is *surface acting*

Display rules are regulations—sometimes explicit, but more often implicit—governing what workers' observed affect, or outward expression, should be

Ecological fallacy is the error of assuming that indices designed for making inferences about the group are equally valid for making inferences about individuals in the group

Ego Depletion Theory posits that decision-making prowess diminishes with extended trials, particularly when having to make decisions that differ from one's preferences. Thus, exerting self-control when confronting challenges will consume individual strength. For instance, remaining calm in the midst of badgering and hostility requires a significant amount of self-control, which, in turn, degrades decision-making over time

Embodied knowledge refers to ways of knowing that emerge from feelings, perceptions, and sensations. Such knowledge is different from that which results from cognition

Emotion management refers to sensing and regulating one's own emotional state as well as sensing the other's state and adjusting one's own response in order to elicit a desired response from the other

Emotion regulation refers to regulating one's emotions by means of suppression or expression, such as using quieting or enhancing strategies to hide or to amplify how one feels

Emotion suppression occurs when one must not display the emotion being felt

Emotion work refers to sensing and managing one's own emotions as well as the emotions of the other. It is synonymous with *emotional labor*

Emotional control refers to the ability to sense how one is feeling and to regulate one's feelings

Emotional dissonance is the conflict between one's own feelings and the feeling that must be displayed

Emotional intelligence refers to the ability to sense and regulate one's own emotions as well as to sense others' emotional state

Emotional labor refers to employees managing their own emotional state as well as managing the emotional state of the other—whether citizen, client, or co-worker—in order to do their job. It involves expressing job-appropriate emotions whether one actually feels them or not, by either pretending or by authentically reflecting their true feelings. For example, it may require calming, energizing, or comforting someone in order to elicit a desired response. It is done for a wage, just as cognitive labor and physical labor are performed for a wage

Emotional other-awareness refers to an individual's ability to perceive and understand the emotions of those around him/her as well as the ability to interpret body language, facial expression, and tone of voice. It is an element of emotional intelligence

Emotional self-awareness refers to the degree to which people are able to identify their own feelings and understand the causes of those feelings. Self-awareness includes attention to one's internal state, as well as to thoughts or feelings about that state. It provides a basis for assessing one's own abilities and knowing how to respond emotively. It is an element of emotional intelligence

Emotive awareness refers to the degree to which one is aware of the emotional state of self and others

Emotive capacity is the extent to which individuals sense emotion and respond to it. As a latent variable in this study, it reflects employees' perception of their ability to deal with emotions in the workplace. This includes sensitivity to their own emotional state as well as responsiveness to that of other people

Emotive competencies are those capabilities that are related to emotive expression and suppression, emotion regulation, self-awareness, and other-awareness. Competence is the level of skill with which someone senses and manages emotion, displays emotion appropriately, and is responsive to the emotional state of others

Emotive display rules refer to the emotion expression norms or standards set and defined by the organization in relation to each job. In most jobs where workers meet the public, they are required to express positive emotions and suppress negative ones

Emotive expression refers to a display by facial expression, tone of voice, or body language that communicates an emotion, whether it is cheeriness, sadness, fear, or confidence

Emotive pretending means hiding true feelings while expressing and displaying other feelings. It occurs when there is dissonance between the felt emotion and the expressed emotion. Under conditions of emotive dissonance, employees hide how they actually feel in order to express an emotion that is job-appropriate, such as the cheery receptionist who actually feels aggravated

Empathy ranges from the ability to understand and vicariously experience the feelings of another, to a way of grasping another's emotive state, to the ability to recognize, understand, and respond to the feelings, thoughts, and experience of another without having to have them communicated in an objectively explicit manner

Enlightenment era also known as the Age of Reason. It is marked by a philosophy that spread primarily in Europe during the late seventeenth and early eighteenth centuries and continues to influence Western thought. It elevates cognitive, rational thought and diminishes other ways of knowing, especially the emotive

Equity refers to justice and fairness for all constituencies, rather than to only those who hold advantaged status

Extraversion is on a continuum between introvert and extravert. Extraverted individuals are characterized as assertive, energetic, and outgoing. Introverts, on the other hand, are shy

False Face refers to emotive pretending, in which the person displays an emotion that is not what is actually felt. As if wearing a mask, the person gives the appearance of an emotion, as if an actor on stage

Familism is a Korean word that refers to the subordination of personal interest and prerogatives to the values, interests, and demands, of the family

Formal organizations are a means of structuring relationships between people. Architectural elements, such as hierarchy, unit groupings, and line versus staff distinctions, structure the way people relate to one another, define who has more or less power than others, and set boundaries around the reach of each person's job duties

Fu-mu-guan is a Taiwanese term meaning father/mother-like officials, in which paternal or maternal behavior is expected and exhibited

Gameface is a form of emotive pretending in which the display is one of a confident swagger or a serious or determined expression. It requires suppressing how one actually feels in order to display a different countenance. It is a form of *false face* acting

Gapjil is a Korean word meaning the abuse of power by someone in power against a person in a lower position. It results from arrogant and authoritarian attitudes and actions of those who hold power over others

Gender egalitarianism is the degree to which gender role differences are minimized and gender equality is promoted

Global administration refers to the implementation and management of policies that transcend political borders

Group affective tone is defined as the shared emotion in a group, further categorized into two dimensions: positive and negative. It is measured using the Positive

Affect/Negative Affect Scale, which contains simple phrases that describe a person's psychological state

Gu is a Korean word for municipal districts, a gu is similar to a borough in the USA

Heterarchy is a system of organization in which each entity has equal power and authority, rather than graded levels as in hierarchies. This flattened, horizontal structure emphasizes collaborations across agencies, levels of government, and stakeholder groups. It is encountered in networks

Hojuje is the Korean system that legally approved men as the head of the family. It was disallowed by law in 2004, but remains a force in the political culture

Homeostasis theory of emotion assumes that the body sends signals to the brain via emotional knowing and the brain moves the body to do what is needed to restore emotive homeostasis. For instance, calming oneself when hyper-excited and energizing oneself when depressed are examples

Humane orientation is the degree to which a culture encourages and rewards individuals for being altruistic, generous, caring, and kind to others

Job demands include all those elements of work that draw upon one's physical, cognitive, and emotive skills, as well as work expectations that place a burden on, or conflict with, the worker's sense of self. Demands become physical or emotional stressors

Job Demands-Resources **(JD-R)** is a theory suggesting that strain is a response to imbalance between demands on workers and the resources they have to deal with those demands. It is a relatively new theory in the field of human resource management, developed to understand occupational satisfaction and job stress

Job resources are the personal, physical, social, and organizational factors that help workers perform their jobs and achieve their goals

Job satisfaction is the degree to which intrinsic and extrinsic work-related factors lead to feelings of contentment, achievement, and accomplishment

Matchers are those who strive to achieve and sustain a balance between giving and taking

Mateship is a term that refers to friends, usually men, providing unconditional support to one another and having shared experiences amid the toughest conditions. It has deep historical roots in Australia, where early settlers needed one another to survive in often adverse environments

Measurement Invariance **(synonymous with measurement equivalence)** refers to a statistical property of measurement in which the same construct is being measured similarly across different groups. It is measured by three hierarchical levels: configural, metric, and scalar

Mediator is a variable that serves as a mechanism to enable a relationship between the independent variable and the dependent variable

Metric invariance signifies that factor loadings of measurement items are equivalent across countries

Mistreatment occurs when citizens treat the targeted worker in discourteous, demeaning, hostile, impolite, or unreasonable ways

Moderator is a variable that affects the magnitude or direction of the relationship between an independent variable and a dependent variable

Neuroticism is on a continuum between being emotionally unstable and stable. Emotionally unstable people are nervous, vulnerable, and insecure

New Public Governance **(NPG)** relies on coproduction, citizen engagement, and flattened hierarchies that invite more, rather than fewer, meaningful encounters between state and citizen. All sectors of the economy are engaged in the pursuit of public purposes

New Public Management **(NPM)** is an approach to public administration that relies on economic rationalism. It assumes that contracting services out to vendors and relying on supply and demand dynamics in the contract bidding process will reduce costs and improve service delivery. Citizens are viewed as customers

New Public Service **(NPS)** is a phrase coined by Janet and Robert Denhardt. It refers to an approach to governing where public officials work with, rather than over, citizens. Collaboration, participation, and consultation are watchwords for the processes by which public actions are designed and delivered. Citizens are seen as partners in public endeavors

Nunchi is a Korean term signifying the subtle art and ability to sense the other person's mood and respond accordingly. The term blends the emotional intelligence skills of other-awareness and self-regulation with the emotional labor requirement to alter one's own emotive response according to what is appropriate to facilitate effective communication

Openness to experience is described as being flexible, open-minded, and creative

Organizational justice is a subjective judgment regarding whether an individual is being treated fairly by an organization's processes and members. It is generally classified into four dimensions—distributive, procedural, interactional, and informational—and it deeply influences individual attitudes, behaviors, and assumptions about the organization

Other-awareness is the ability to perceive and understand the emotions of others, including the ability to hear, sense, and intuit what others are feeling. This awareness derives from tone of voice, body language, facial expression, pace of speech, and comprehending how they describe their feelings. In other words, it involves active listening, sensing the mood of an individual, and "reading between the lines." It is an element of emotional intelligence

Outcome measures focus on the effect of government actions, rather than the actions themselves. It is related to, but different from, output measures

Output measures focus on the "things" government does, rather than the effects of government action. It is related to, but different from, outcome measures

Personality is the complex of characteristics—emotional, intellectual, moral—that distinguishes one individual from another. When combined, the characteristics explain a person's reactions, responses, and behavior

Plural state refers to public service delivery by private- and third-sector organizations, especially in the UK

Political culture is the constellation of widely shared beliefs, feelings, values, traditions, history, expectations, and attitudes that shape how a nation's government is structured, how it performs, and what actions are thought of as normal

Political nous refers to political awareness, knowledge, and savvy

Pretending expression means hiding true feelings while expressing and displaying other feelings. It occurs when there is dissonance between the emotion that the worker feels and the emotion being displayed. Suppression of the undesired emotion is required in order to display the desired emotion. Its opposite is *authentic emotive expression*

Professional demeanor is defined by each discipline and the appearance is accompanied by an emotive presentation. For example, law enforcement officers are expected to appear confident, assertive, and self-assured. Social workers are expected to appear nurturant and caring. Teachers are expected to act with confidence and grace. Doctors are to appear compassionate and confident

Public administration is the art and science of pursuing public purposes. It involves three major elements: politics, management, and law

Public encounter occurs when a citizen and a government official meet person-to-person or voice-to-voice for the purpose of an exchange, communication, or transaction. It may be initiated by the official or the citizen

Public policy is the set of actions (or inactions) taken by government

Public servant refers to those who work for government or public service-minded non-governmental organizations. The term is used interchangeably with *public service professional* and *civil servant*

Public service motivation is a desirable attribute of public service professionals. It is motivation to serve the public and connect one's personal effort to the overall public interest

Public service professional refers to those whose careers are committed to the pursuit of public purposes. While most often employed by government, they also work in non-governmental organizations that pursue humanitarian, educational, health care, public policy, social welfare, human rights, environmental and related goals

Rational instrumentalism refers to adopting suitable means to achieve ends. It is a mechanistic approach to classical public administration and relies solely on cognition, treating decisions as if they are a set of levers to pull in order to achieve specified ends

Relational competencies refer to characteristics and skills that manifest themselves as respect, attentiveness, responsiveness, and concern for others

Relational contract is a set of understandings that are based on a relationship of trust between the parties involved

Representative bureaucracy theory prescribes that all constituencies affected by a public program should be included in the planning, organizing, staffing, directing, co-ordinating, reporting, and budgeting of it. By having their views and voices expressed in the design and maintenance of programs, the outcome is likely to be acceptable to all

Reverse ecological fallacy occurs when comparing cultures on indices created to compare individuals

Rites refer to prescribed norms and procedures that have been established by custom

Scalar invariance indicates that intercepts of measurement items are the same across the countries. In other words, it indicates that values and means are comparable across groups

Secretariats are offices entrusted with administrative duties, maintaining records, and overseeing activities, especially for international organizations

Self-awareness is an element of emotional intelligence. It refers to an individual's ability to sense his/her own emotional state

Self-fulfillment refers to the feeling that one's ambitions and desires are met through one's efforts

Self-regulation refers to the ability to regulate the display of one's emotions so that the intensity is controlled to fit the circumstance. Suppressing, or quieting one's emotions, or hiding them in order to display an opposite countenance, is also a part of self-regulation. It is an aspect of emotional intelligence that involves awareness of which emotion is appropriate to exhibit and the ability to display it

Social Cognitive Theory is a learning theory based on the assumption that knowledge acquisition occurs by observing others in social interactions

Surface acting is a dramaturgical term coined to describe emotive pretending. It means a superficial emotive display that occurs when the worker is merely pretending to feel the emotion being displayed. It is the antonym of *deep acting*

Surgency is an emotive trait in which a person tends toward high levels of cheerfulness, spontaneity, and sociability

Transparency is the requirement that proceedings, documents, and records be available to anyone who wants them. Most governments are expected to practice transparency in their decision-making and actions

Trust is a state of mind in which the person opens him/herself to vulnerability based on the positive expectation of the intention and behavior of the other

Umuganda is a Rwandese word meaning to come together in common purpose. It promotes unity and reconciliation in a society devastated by conflict

Universalism is the notion that the same exists everywhere

Use of emotion is more of a cognitive than an emotive ability because it pertains to a cognitive decision to use emotion as an instrumental means to an end

Verbal judo is the use of words to prevent, de-escalate, or end an assault. It involves tone of voice and choice of words to calm a potentially volatile situation

Vicarious trauma results from indirect exposure to a hurtful event, usually through hearing of the event from the person who experienced it first-hand

Westphalian sovereignty is a term for describing the fundamental principles of the modern sovereign state, particularly the principle that states retain exclusive sovereignty over their territory, which is defined by inviolable borders

Woori is a Korean word that represents a strong collectivist identity and sense of belonging and identity attached to South Korean society

Index

CPSIA information can be obtained
at www.ICGtesting.com
Printed in the USA
LVHW081735170421
684800LV00003B/48